ICSEA 2017

The Twelfth International Conference on Software Engineering Advances

October 8 - 12, 2017

Athens, Greece

ICSEA 2017 Editors

Luigi Lavazza, Università dell'Insubria - Varese, Italy

Roy Oberhauser, Aalen University, Germany

Radek Koci, Brno University of Technology, Czech Republic

Stephen Clyde, Utah State University, USA

Printed from e-media with permission by:

Curran Associates, Inc.
57 Morehouse Lane
Red Hook, NY 12571

Some format issues inherent in the e-media version may also appear in this print version.

Printed by Curran Associates, Inc. (2017)

International Academy, Research, and Industry Association (IARIA)
412 Derby Way
Wilmington, DE 19810

Phone: (408) 893-6407
Fax: (408) 527-6351

petre@iaria.org

Additional copies of this publication are available from:

Curran Associates, Inc.
57 Morehouse Lane
Red Hook, NY 12571 USA
Phone: 845-758-0400
Fax: 845-758-2633
Email: curran@proceedings.com
Web: www.proceedings.com

Table of Contents

ICSEA 2017

Forward

The Twelfth International Conference on Software Engineering Advances (ICSEA 2017), held on October 8 - 12, 2017- Athens, Greece, continued a series of events covering a broad spectrum of software-related topics.

The conference covered fundamentals on designing, implementing, testing, validating and maintaining various kinds of software. The tracks treated the topics from theory to practice, in terms of methodologies, design, implementation, testing, use cases, tools, and lessons learnt. The conference topics covered classical and advanced methodologies, open source, agile software, as well as software deployment and software economics and education.

The conference had the following tracks:

- Advances in fundamentals for software development
- Advanced mechanisms for software development
- Advanced design tools for developing software
- Software engineering for service computing (SOA and Cloud)
- Advanced facilities for accessing software
- Software performance
- Software security, privacy, safeness
- Advances in software testing
- Specialized software advanced applications
- Web Accessibility
- Open source software
- Agile and Lean approaches in software engineering
- Software deployment and maintenance
- Software engineering techniques, metrics, and formalisms
- Software economics, adoption, and education
- Business technology
- Improving productivity in research on software engineering

Similar to the previous edition, this event continued to be very competitive in its selection process and very well perceived by the international software engineering community. As such, it is attracting excellent contributions and active participation from all over the world. We were very pleased to receive a large amount of top quality contributions.

We take here the opportunity to warmly thank all the members of the ICSEA 2017 technical program committee as well as the numerous reviewers. The creation of such a broad and high quality conference program would not have been possible without their involvement. We also kindly thank all the authors that dedicated much of their time and efforts to contribute to the ICSEA 2017. We truly believe that thanks to all these efforts, the final conference program consists of top quality contributions.

This event could also not have been a reality without the support of many individuals, organizations and sponsors. We also gratefully thank the members of the ICSEA 2017 organizing committee for their help in handling the logistics and for their work that is making this professional meeting a success.

We hope the ICSEA 2017 was a successful international forum for the exchange of ideas and results between academia and industry and to promote further progress in software engineering research. We also hope Athens provided a pleasant environment during the conference and everyone saved some time for exploring this beautiful historic city.

ICSEA Steering Committee

Herwig Mannaert, University of Antwerp, Belgium
Mira Kajko-Mattsson, Royal Institute of Technology, Sweden
Luigi Lavazza, Università dell'Insubria - Varese, Italy
Roy Oberhauser, Aalen University, Germany
Elena Troubitsyna, Abo Akademi University, Finland
Radek Koci, Brno University of Technology, Czech Republic
Stephen W. Clyde, Utah State University, USA
Sébastien Salva, University Clermont Auvergne (UCA), Limos, France
Krishna M. Kavi, The University of North Texas, USA
Christian Kop, Universitaet Klagenfurt, Austria
Luis Fernandez-Sanz, Universidad de Alcala, Spain
Bidyut Gupta, Southern Illinois University, USA

ICSEA Industry/Research Advisory Committee

Teemu Kanstrén, VTT Technical Research Centre of Finland - Oulu, Finland
J. Paul Gibson, Telecom Sud Paris, France
Adriana Martin, National University of Austral Patagonia (UNPA), Argentina
Muthu Ramachandran, Leeds Beckett University, UK
Michael Gebhart, iteratec GmbH, Germany

ICSEA 2017

Committee

ICSEA Steering Committee
Herwig Mannaert, University of Antwerp, Belgium
Mira Kajko-Mattsson, Royal Institute of Technology, Sweden
Luigi Lavazza, Università dell'Insubria - Varese, Italy
Roy Oberhauser, Aalen University, Germany
Elena Troubitsyna, Abo Akademi University, Finland
Radek Koci, Brno University of Technology, Czech Republic
Stephen W. Clyde, Utah State University, USA
Sébastien Salva, University Clermont Auvergne (UCA), Limos, France
Krishna M. Kavi, The University of North Texas, USA
Christian Kop, Universitaet Klagenfurt, Austria
Luis Fernandez-Sanz, Universidad de Alcala, Spain
Bidyut Gupta, Southern Illinois University, USA

ICSEA Industry/Research Advisory Committee
Teemu Kanstrén, VTT Technical Research Centre of Finland - Oulu, Finland
J. Paul Gibson, Telecom Sud Paris, France
Adriana Martin, National University of Austral Patagonia (UNPA), Argentina
Muthu Ramachandran, Leeds Beckett University, UK
Michael Gebhart, iteratec GmbH, Germany

ICSEA 2017 Technical Program Committee

Shahliza Abd Halim, Universiti of Technologi Malaysia (UTM), Malaysia
Muhammad Ovais Ahmad, University of Oulu, Finland
Jacky Akoka, CNAM & IMT, France
Mohammad Alshayeb, King Fahd University of Petroleum and Minerals, Saudi Arabia
Zakarya Alzamil, King Saud University, Saudi Arabia
Vincenzo Ambriola, Università di Pisa, Italy
Daniel Andresen, Kansas State University, USA
Gilbert Babin, HEC Montréal, Canada
Doo-Hwan Bae, School of Computing - KAIST, Korea
Aleksander Bai, Norsk Regnesentral, Norway
Jorge Barreiros, ISEC (Instituto Superior de Engenharia de Coimbra) / NOVA-LINCS, Portugal
Bernhard Bauer, University of Augsburg, Germany
Ateet Bhalla, Independent Consultant, India
Kenneth Boness, University of Reading, UK
Mina Boström Nakicenovic, NetEnt, Stockholm, Sweden
Hongyu Pei Breivold, ABB Corporate Research, Sweden
Georg Buchgeher, Software Competence Center Hagenberg GmbH, Austria
Luigi Buglione, Engineering Ingegneria Informatica SpA, Italy

Copyright Information

A Teaching Method for Software Measurement Process based on Gamification

Lennon Sales Furtado, Sandro Ronaldo Bezerra Oliveira
Graduate Program in Computer Science
Federal University of Pará
Belém, Pará, Brazil
e-mail: lennonsfurtado@gmail.com, srbo@ufpa.br

***Abstract*—The value of an effective measurement program lies in the ability to control and predict what can be measured. Thus, the measurement program has the capacity to provide a basis in decision-making to support the interests of an organization. This means it is only possible to run an effective measurement program with a team of software engineers who are well trained in this area. However, as the literature shows, there are few computer science courses that include the teaching of software process measurement in their program. Even these, generally only discuss the basic theoretical concepts of this process with little or no measurement in practice, which discourages the students from's learning the measurement process. In this context, according to some experts in software process improvement, one of the most widely used approaches to maintaining the motivation and commitment to improving the program, is the use of gamification. In light of this, the aim of this paper is to set out a proposal for teaching the gamification measurement process. This seeks to improve student motivation and performance in carrying out tasks related to software measurement, by incorporating elements from games into the measurement process, and thus making it more attractive for learning.**

Keywords-education; gamification; teaching method; software engineering; software process measurement.

I. INTRODUCTION

The purpose of the software measurement process is to collect, store, analyze and report data on developed products and implemented processes within an organization, in order to support organizational goals [1]. Moreover, the importance of an efficient measurement program lies in its ability to control what can be measured [2]. By being able to control the metrics of the measurement program, the organization will be capable of predicting organizational and marketing behavior [3].

Even though the measurement process is of such importance to Software Process Improvement (SPI), the software industry has been reluctant to employ efficient measurement programs [4][5]. This is because many software managers and software engineers, including academics in software engineering and computer science, seem to have little or no practical knowledge of this subject [6].

In general, in every software measurement program, what determines its success is the human factor, because if there is a lack of commitment to this program, it is unlikely to achieve the desired results, i.e., the visibility and control of software metrics to aid in decision-making. In this context, one of the most widely used methods to maintain the motivation and commitment of the people involved in a SPI program is the use of gamification [7].

Gamification by definition is the use of game elements and game design techniques outside their usual context [8]. This process seeks to improve the commitment, motivation and performance of a user when carrying out any task, by incorporating features of games and game mechanics, and thus, make the task more attractive [9].

By means of this educational tool, this paper seeks to address the problem of teaching the measurement process by exploring aspects of gamification. This involves adopting and evaluating an approach for the use of this tool as a motivating factor in the teaching of software process measurement.

In addition to this introductory section, this paper is divided into the following sections: Section II will cover factors that explain and identify the question under study. Section III will outline the problem addressed in this paper and discuss related work and the limitations of its approaches. In Section IV, a number of research questions will be raised that will guide future investigations covered by this research. In Section V the methods used to answer the research questions will be examined in detail, and finally, in Section VI the expected results will be discussed, together with a report on the progress of the research.

II. A GAP IN THE AREA AND SCOPE OF THE RESEARCH

This section describes the gap in the area and the scope of the research discussed in this paper.

A. A Gap in the Area

As pointed out by Jones [6], many software managers and software engineering professionals are unaware of the key aspects of measurement (planning, preparing, collecting data and analyzing them for decision-making). One factor in this problem that must be taken into account is the way the process of measurement and analysis is taught.

This concern is directly related to the fact that the measurement process is generally regarded as difficult and time-consuming [8][10][11][12]. An initial assumption that must be made when seeking to understand this problem, lies in the way this discipline is taught [13], since it has been neglected in the undergraduate curriculum and its importance is not stressed enough to encourage students to learn in practice [14]. In addition, another serious factor is the lack of guidelines on how to implement the practice of measurement [15][16][17].

In other words, the dynamics of expository lectures,

(where students passively construct their knowledge), tend to be very time-consuming and have inherent weaknesses with regard to the difficulties of transferring knowledge to real life situations [18].

Furthermore, the measurement process is only one of several processes taught in the software quality assurance disciplines, and because of this, there is little time to show its practical application. This is the main obstacle to the establishment of knowledge in the measurement process. It means that the students clearly have difficulties in applying software measurement to real-life situations.

In attempting to meet the needs of the students involved in Software Quality Assurance, this research will set out a proposal for the gamification of the software measurement process. This is a way of overcoming the problem of a lack of opportunity to practice this process in the undergraduate curriculum, by introducing the concepts of basic measures, derived measures, indicators, Goal Question Metrics (GQM) [19] and a Practical Software Measurement (PSM) program [20].

B. *Scope of the Research*

This study will investigate the following: the conceptual factors involved in the development of the proposal, and the implementation and evaluation of the gamification tool for teaching the software measurement process. In addition, it should be mentioned that this research has the following objectives:

- To set out a teaching proposal for the software measurement process by the application of gamification,
- To analyze the state-of-the-art in the use of gamification for the teaching of software processes,
- To identify different approaches to the use of gamification, which can provide the user with greater ease when learning the discipline of software measurement,
- To identify the limitations of gamification as a teaching method,
- To examine the concepts of basic and derived units of measurement,
- To define the concept of indicators,
- To set out the GQM and PSM paradigms,
- To predict the expected outcomes and practices contained in the Nationwide Program for Software Processs Improvement in Brazil (MPS.BR-SW) and Capability Maturity Model Integration (CMMI-DEV) programs, which include the measurement processes,
- To describe the most widely used metrics in the market, such as metrics for product maintenance, performance, and reliability,
- To describe the metrics that do not depend on the programming language,
- To define the concepts of the Organizational Measurement Plan, GQM Plan and Measurement Report,
- To evaluate the teaching proposal by comparing it with traditional teaching methods

Apart from these objectives, this research aims to prove or refute the following hypothesis: the gamification research proposal to teach software process measurement is an appropriate way of motivating students to acquire the necessary skills for its practical application.

III. PROBLEM STATEMENT AND RELATED WORKS

The research problems can be categorized into three groups, which are as follows:

- The need to analyze the measurement practices used in the software industry, i.e., to determine which activities are really useful for the training of a software engineering professional,
- The need to analyze the references for a curriculum and the teaching approaches adopted by teachers in the area, to identify which measurement practices are covered,
- To identify the different approaches in the use of gamification, which provide the user with greater ease when learning the software measurement discipline.

A. *The Background of the Teaching of Software Measurement*

According to Bass [21], software measurement can be defined as a quantitative assessment of any aspect of software processes and products. It allows a better understanding of these areas and thus helps in planning, controlling and improving what is produced and how it is produced.

In summary, the measurement program is designed to generate information on products, processes and people. This kind of information serves as a framework for decision-making, which can guide organizations and their projects [22]. That is, it is a very important process for organizations and for programs designed for software process improvement.

However, organizations often make complaints about students who enter the job market, usually on the grounds that they are not prepared to tackle the real problems found in industry [23]. This is due to the difference between the industrial environment and academic programs [24]. For a better understanding of this problem, it is necessary to check how software measurement is being addressed in academic courses of computer science, and if organizations think that students who enter the job market have a sufficient knowledge of software measurement. These questions were raised and explored in a study carried out by [25] and its results are summarized below:

- A survey answered by students and teachers pointed out that the software engineering course is generally mandatory in graduate programs, while software measurement is, in most cases, an optional course,
- All the teachers and students who took part in the survey indicated that the teaching of software measurement is mainly given in expository lectures

and more than 50% through a case study. In addition, in some cases, students learn from another approach, such as applying measurement strategies in real projects,

- Software measurement courses are usually taught in graduate programs, although these courses are mostly optional,
- The level of student learning is usually assessed by written exams (75%) and by projects (58%).

To meet the needs of industry, it is necessary to prepare students for these environments and their real problems. There are many approaches for this, including in-context learning, where the student learns to use knowledge in a context with the same real-world challenges [26]. That is, the student will learn software process measurement by measuring actual software, as well as by designing measurement plans and putting them into effect.

Another approach is the application of teaching by Problem Based Learning (PBL), which follows the principle of learning by solving problems or addressing challenges related to the practice of software measurement.

In addition to these approaches, one of the approaches found in the literature is the use of serious games for teaching a subject [18], where the student plays a game as an educational tool to introduce the theoretical concepts and simulate the practical application of these concepts As a result, it can be seen that an important feature in the teaching of software measurement, is to adopt innovative approaches in the way the education will be conducted [17]. This is because universities have a myriad of student profiles with different levels of interest and motivating factors that will lead them to obtain the desired knowledge from an educational institution.

Among these new approaches is the use of game elements in terms of mechanics and dynamics, which are a motivational factor in teaching or carrying out a task. This approach is known as gamification and seeks to improve the commitment, motivation and performance of a user when learning a subject or carrying out a task [9]. In addition, one of its great advantages is the familiarity of the students of this generation with games, because they have grown up with them and actively play games as both a form of entertainment and learning.

In summary, the objective of this research is the development and validation of an educational tool that uses gamification for the teaching of software measurement.

B. Problem Areas

Despite its importance in industry, in many cases, the measurement process has failed to yield benefits to organizations.

Following a survey conducted in Brazil in 2012 by the American Chamber of Commerce (AMCHAM) [27] with 44 Information Technology (IT) executives, it was found that 86% of the executives interviewed were not satisfied with the way the measurement was conducted in their organizations. Among the main difficulties highlighted were the following: a) obtaining tangible benefits and producing a return on measurement activities (41%), b) establishing performance indicators (30%), c) obtaining information on the impact of IT on other sectors of the company (18%), and d) quantifying the efficiency of the processes and systems (14%).

All the difficulties found arise from the capacity of the professionals responsible for the measurement process, since they fail to conduct a process efficiently that covers all aspects of measurement (measuring, storage, analysis and reporting).

The problems reported by the industry are just a few of the symptoms of an aging education in software measurement. This is corroborated in Jones's paper [28], which found that there were 28 problems that need to be addressed while measuring software, the most serious being the absence of a proper training system for students, to enable them to enter the world of industry with real problem-solving skills.

In addition to the problems pointed out by Jones [28], the literature states that software measurement is a complex and time-consuming task [8][10][11][12]. Apart from these problems, software measurement in education faces other challenges, such as being one issue among the 83 topics covered by software engineering and the fact that in most courses, it is treated as an optional subject [25]. Moreover, there are the problems arising from the dynamics of expository lectures, where students passively construct their knowledge, and thus tend to waste a lot of time. There are also the inherent weaknesses in this methodology with regard to the difficulties in the transfer of knowledge to real-life situations [18]. This makes it difficult for the student to understand the subject in depth, since this is only possible when a student is motivated and engaged with the subject. However, it can be achieved by exposing these students to situations that allow them to participate in problem-solving activities and tasks related to the issue of software measurement. Hence, these difficulties provide opportunities for improvement, and will thus lead to the maturity of the software measurement process. However, this process is still regarded as an "immature" field [23], due to the lack of a consensus on international software standards for measurement [29] and divergences in the implementation and interpretation of software metrics with tools [30]. That is, it is a field of study that needs to undergo several improvements and also be standardized.

C. Limitations of Related Works

With regard to related works, only those will be evaluated that provide mechanisms for teaching software engineering through gamification or serious games.

The closest approach to this research is in the exploratory study conducted by Gresse von Wangenheim [18], which employs a serious game (X-MED) for teaching software measurement. In this work, the student plays the role of a measurement specialist who has to carry out the measurement process in a movie rental company. As the users progress in the game, they must answer some questions and earn points, so that they can produce a result that corresponds to the level of learning of the student.

The most significant contributions made by this system

are:

- It provides a comprehensive study that covers all the stages of creating the proposed game,
- It provides a complex theme that can be measured by a game that simulates a situation which involves a real application of this process,
- It validates the game proposed by applying it in undergraduate classes so that it is able to evaluate the degree of acceptance and benefits of the game in practice by pre and post questionnaires with the users.

However, the game devised by Wangenheim did not show any improvements in teaching measurement when compared with the traditional teaching method based on lectures. This can be attributed to some weaknesses in this work, such as:

- The game makes use of game mechanics and elements that are not very attractive, for example mechanics quizzes. The game mechanics and their related elements are determining factors to motivate and engage the student,
- The aesthetic appeal and sound of the game are not attractive; this is a very important factor in maintaining the user's interest in the game,
- The game is not suitable for mobile devices. This is a weakness, as most students are used to making use of this platform as a means of entertainment. Thus, it is more likely that students will make use of the game in their free time.

The works [31][32][33] were also evaluated, which made use of gamification or serious games for the teaching of software engineering.

In the work conducted by Bartel [31], which includes a gamified course for the teaching of design patterns, the students were encouraged to work as a team. Different tasks were assigned to each of the students in the team and each team had to find solutions to the problems raised in the classroom. On the completion of every task, the students were awarded a score by their classmates and the teacher. In this work, the following difficulties were detected:

- The proposal is very simple and limited since it is basically a quest list,
- Feedback is given by classmates and not by an automated system, which meant it was based on the subjective opinions of the students,
- The evaluation of the results of the game was not compared with the traditional teaching methods to validate its usefulness.

In the course of the paper [32], which employed a gamified classroom for teaching extreme programming, the students who took part, stated in the questionnaires that they thought the learning experience was good when compared with the learning experience that involved conventional lectures.

The participants showed an improvement in learning and coding performance after they had become used to the gamification teaching method. Despite this there were a number of limitations in this paper which are listed below:

- The lack of immediate feedback and transparency in the data collected, as students were only given an assessment of their progress at the end of the cycle,
- The experiment undertaken in the paper needs a special kind of class where students work 8 hours a day and use gamification as a part of the teaching method,
- In the paper, few topics are discussed about the planning of the gamification (e.g. the game elements and mechanics), only the results of the experiment are given.

In addition, the study conducted by Chaves [33] included a serious game, which taught how to design software processes, and made evaluations of the pre and post questionnaires that were employed in undergraduate classes on computer science. The class that took part made a significant contribution to the efficacy of learning and the application of acquired knowledge in its results. Nonetheless, the study had the following drawbacks :

- The constraints imposed by the game can restrict the creativity of the player, because only the traced path can be followed,
- The students only memorize the proposed models rather than learn them,
- There are few levels in the game and hence a considerable increase in difficulty, which distorts it.

IV. Questions, Hypotheses and Discussion

The main goal of our research is to set out a teaching method based on gamification for software measurement, as an educational tool for computer courses, and this approach is based on the results of different kinds of research methods such as: a survey, a systematic review of the literature, a literature review of the the curriculum guidelines and user testing.

In addition, we found many references [6][13][14][21] that support our initiative and point to the need to approach software measurement education in a non-traditional way.

The following research questions should be addressed to understand the needs of students and industry, as well as the accuracy of the gamification system :

- **RQ1.** What is the state-of-the-art on software measurement education when gamification is used as an educational tool?
- **RQ2.** How can educators benefit from gamification in measurement education and learning?
- **RQ3.** What are the metrics and indicators that are most widely used by the software industry?
- **RQ4.** What are the measurement skills required by the software industry and which of them were acquired in the computer courses?
- **RQ5.** What are the metrics (i.e., metrics for product maintenance, performance, reliability, and other features) covered in the computer science course curriculum?
- **RQ6.** What are the measurment topics (collecting,

storage, analysis and reporting) covered in the computer science course curriculum?

- **RQ7.** Can the educational game be considered to be appropriate in terms of content relevance, correctness, sufficiency and degree of difficulty, sequence, teaching methodology and duration in the context for which it is intended? Is the game considered to be "engaging"? What are its strengths and weaknesses?
- **RQ8.** How does the effectiveness of learning measurement through gamification compare with that of using traditional learning, in the pre and post questionnaries?

These research questions were defined in an attempt to refute the following null hypothesis:

- **H0.** *There will be no difference in the pre test and post test scores between the two groups (the experimental and control group will have equal skills) when applying the measurement in pratice.*

If the null hypothesis is refuted, we intend to test our alternative hypothesis:

- **H1:** *There will be a difference in pre and post test scores between the two groups (the experimental and control group will not have equal skills) when the measurement strategy is employed in pratice.*

V. RESEARCH METHOD AND PROGRESS

Since this paper forms a part of a doctoral research, we still do not have sufficient results to effectively answer the research questions; however, all these questions are addressed by discussing the research methods used. The research methods employed to answer the research questions and test the hypothesis will be outlined in this Section.

A. *Identifying the Diferent Approaches and Benefits of Gamification for the Teaching of Software Measurement*

When answering RQ1 and RQ2, a systematic review of the literature will be carried out to analyze the results, methodologies and tools of the works that are aligned with the subject of gamification and applied to the teaching of software measurement. This systematic review will entail adopting a simplified and adjusted approach from the Kitchenham guidelines [34]. Figure 1 shows the systematic review protocol; the following questions were raised during the the systematic review of the literature (SRLQ) with the aim of finding out about other gamification approaches applied in the area of software measurement. This review will also be used to explore the validation methods applied in other gamification systems and their measurement elements. It should be noted that we are currently working on the systematic review of the literature. The research questions in this review are:

- **SRLQ1.** Based on ISO 15939 where the software measurement features were addressed in the gamification systems?
- **SRLQ2.** In what contexts (i.e., education, work, and other areas) were the measurements for gamification software applied?
- **SRLQ3.** What were the limitations reported in the use of gamification for software measurement education?
- **SRLQ4.** What research methods were used to validate the gamification system?
- **SRLQ5.** What game elements were used in gamification for teaching software measurement?
- **SRLQ6.** What game mechanics were used in gamification for teaching software measurement?
- **SRLQ7.** What game dynamics were used in gamification for teaching software measurement?

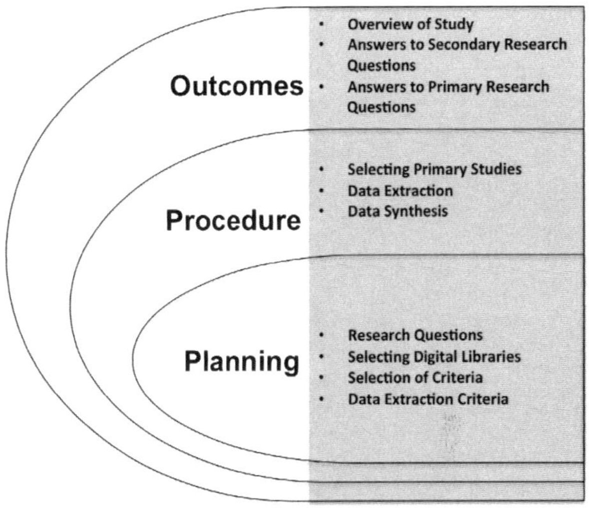

Figure 1. Systematic Review adapted from [34]

B. *Identifying Measurement Strategies included in Computer Courses and Industry*

With regard to the metrics, indicators and strategies employed in industry, these questions will be investigated in papers that cover this area such as Costa's work [35]. In his work, Costa describes the software measurement process using the Goal–Question–Indicator–Metric (GQIM) methodology [40]. This takes the form of a catalog that lists the following: a) the measurement objectives, b) information needs, indicators and measurements that are most widely used in the context of software process development and c) those identified by a Systematic review of the literature. In addition, a survey will be conducted with applied measurement professionals with a view to answering the RQ3, and thus identifying and giving prominence to the need for Brazilian industry tobe involved in the teaching of software measurement process for undergraduate students.

Moreover, another survey will be carried out to answer RQ4, but this will be conducted with students who have already graduated from the Federal University of Pará and are active in industry. In this way, we will be able to determine which measurement strategies were acquired in an academic environment and which are being used in an industrial environment. This will also enable us to fill in any gaps with regard to the measurement process in the teaching environment. Both surveys will follow the guidelines recommended by Kitchenham and Pfleeger [36].

Furthermore, when answering RQ5 and RQ6, a literature review will be carried out on the curriculum guidelines of the ACM / IEEE [37] and the SBC [38] to find out which measurement topics and which metrics they cover. This should provide evidence that the measurement activities suggested by the curriculum guidelines meet the requirements of the software industry.

C. *Defining an Approach for Teaching Measurement by Gamification*

After the first six research questions (RQ), have been answered, they will be assessed in terms of the following results:

- The set of measurement practices used in the software industry,
- The recommendations in the curriculum guidelines,
- The current approaches to gamification in teaching software measurement,
- And, in particular, the gap between industry and the academic world with regard to what instrumenst should be used in software measurement.

These results will serve as a framework in the teaching of software measurement by gamification. In addition to the application of these answers, this research will make use of the teaching framework of software measurement found in Villavicencio's work [17], where it introduces gamification concepts into teaching and learning activities. This framework is based on Bloom's taxonomy on levels of learning outcomes [41] and adopts a constructivist approach. The six thinking/learning levels that are defined in Bloom's taxonomy are as follows: recognizing / remembering, understanding, applying knowledge and techniques, analyzing, evaluating, and forming a synthesis. The constructivist approach is based on the assumption that the learners can construct their own knowledge and reach higher levels of learning through an engagement and active participation with it. For this reason, the framework established by Villavicencio is suited to this work since the involvement and commitment of the students is embodied in the learning process. This can be achieved by incorporating the concepts of game elements and mechanics that can be defined in the area of gamification. The Framework can be seen in Figure 2.

D. *Performing Case Studies to Evaluate the Teaching Method*

After the software measurement process by gamification has been implemented, this research will make a comparison of the results obtained from two groups of students as a means of validating and answering RQ7 and RQ8. The two groups will be divided into a control group and an experimental group and comprise Software Quality at the Federal University of Pará, which has approximately 20 to 30 students per class. The control group will not carry out teaching through gamification, in contrast with the experimental group. Thus, the objective results obtained from each class will be taken note of before RQ8 is answered. These results will be analyzed on the basis of the grades achieved at the end of the course, while the subjective results of the classes will be drawn on to answer RQ7. This will be undertaken by setting a post test questionnaire to evaluate the opinion of each student on gamification as a teaching method. These experiments will be conducted over a period of 2 semesters and will follow the guidelines recommended by Wohlin [39]. The hypotheses will be tested with the aid of the data collected in the experimental phase, which include descriptive statistics to analyze the high, low and average grades of both the control group and experimental group. On the basis of this, it will be possible to determine if there is any significant difference between both groups.

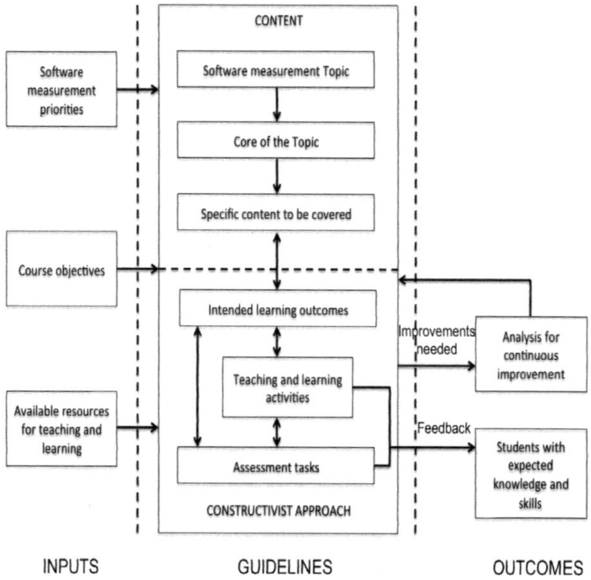

Figure 2. A Framework for software measurement teaching [17]

As the aim of the research is to have an effect on industrial strategies, the survey will have to be conducted in several stages. These will entail the following: a) monitoring the knowledge acquired about the people involved, b) understanding the reality of the students' professional practice, c) undertaking numerous other follow-up research studies, d) taking part in the software development community (SDC) to make use of the improvements in the results and comtribute to them and e) making a practical application of the content in numerous other undergraduate and postgraduate classes.

Finally, it should be emphasized that, to a great extent, this research relies on the quality and quantity of the results obtained from each of the research methods, although the success of each of the methodologies cannot be ensured without first putting them into practice.

VI. Conclusion and Suggestions for Future Work

This paper has underlined the importance of software measurement process, while acknowledging its limitations, especially those aimed at improving teaching practices. In addition, this work forms a part of a doctoral research, which seeks to devise a teaching method of gamification in software measurement and investigate the teaching and learning activities resulting from this.

This involved defining the hypotheses and research questions that will lead to the next stages in this research. In addition, we outlined the research methods that will be used for carrying out this research. These include a systematic review of the literature, surveys, an analysis of curriculum guidelines and the application of a user test conducted at the Federal University of Pará by applying pre and post test questionnaires with students in the subject-area of Software Quality.

In parallel to writing this paper, a systematic review of the literature is being carried out to give an overview of the topic and show the different approaches adopted by the author, while also seeking to answer RQ1 and RQ2. For this reason, the next stage that will be followed will be to conduct a survey to determine the metrics and measurements that are most needed in industry. After this, there will be an analysis of the curriculum guidelines to find out what measurement procedures are needed in the academic world. Thus, as future works, this research will show the state-of-the-art on software measurement education using gamification as an educational tool. It seeks to show the following: i) how educators can benefit from gamification in measurement education and learning, ii) what are the metrics and indicators that are most widely used by the software industry, iii) what are the measurement skills required by the software industry, iv) which of them were acquired in the computer courses, v) what are the metrics (i.e., metrics for product maintenance, performance, reliability, and other factors) covered in the computer science course curriculum, vi) what are the measurement topics (collecting, storage, analysis and reporting) covered in the computer science course curriculum and vii) the most important contribuition - the gamification system to teach software measurement.

This system will be evaluated to determine whether the educational game can be regarded as appropriate in terms of content relevancy, correctness, sufficiency and degree of difficulty, sequence, teaching method and duration, for the purposes to which it is intended. There is also a need to know how the effectiveness of learning measurement with gamification compares with traditional learning methods.

Finally, after all the research questions have been answered, the hypotheses will be tested by the data collected in the experimental phase. This will enable us to determine if there is any significant difference in the learning process of software measurement when the gamification system is applied.

Acknowledgment

The authors would like to thank the Amazon Foundation for Studies and Research Support (FAPESPA) for awarding a doctoral scholarship to PPGCC/UFPA and the Dean of Research and Postgraduate Studies at the Federal University of Pará (PROPESP/UFPA) by the Qualified Publication Support Program (PAPQ), for the financial support.

References

[1] ISO/IEC, "ISO/IEC 15504-1: Information Technology - Process Assessment - Part 1: Concepts and Vocabulary", Geneve, 2004.

[2] T. Demarco, "Controlling software projects", Yourdon Press Prentice-Hall, 1982.

[3] N. Fenton and S. L. Pfleeger, "Software Metrics. A rigorous and practical approach", PWS Pub, 1997.

[4] M. Kasunic, "The state of software measurement practice: results of 2006 survey", Technical report CMU/SEI-2006-TR-009, Carnegie Mellon University/Software Engineering Institute, Pittsburgh, Pennsylvania, 2006.

[5] C. A. Dekkers and P. A. McQuaid, "The dangers of using software metrics to (Mis)Manage", IEEE IT Professional, IEEE Computer Society, 2002.

[6] C. Jones, "Software Metrics: Good, Bad and Missing", Computer, v.27 n.9, p.98-100, 1994.

[7] E. Herranz, R. Colomo-Palacios, A. de Amescua Seco, and M. Yilmaz, "Gamification as a disruptive factor in software process improvement initiatives", Journal of Universal Computer Science, 20(6), pp. 885–906, 2014.

[8] C. G. Von Wangenheim, C. T. Punter, and A. Anacleto, "Software Measurement for Small and Medium Enterprises - A Brazilian-German view on extending the GQM method", in 7th International conference on Empirical Assessment in Software Engineering (EASE), Keele University, Staffordshire, UK, pp. 1-19, 2003.

[9] O. Pedreira, F. Garcia, N. Brisaboa, and M. Piattini, "Gamification in software engineering, a systematic mapping", Information and Software Technology, 57:157–168, 2015.

[10] J. Iversen and O. Ngwenyama, "Problems in measuring effectiveness in software process improvement: A longitudinal study of organizational change at Danske Data", International Journal of Information Management, vol. 26, pp. 30-43, 2006.

[11] A. Gopal, M. S. Krishnan, T. Mukhopadhyay, and D. R. Goldenson, "Measurement programs in software development: determinants of success", IEEE Transactions on Software Engineering, vol. 28, pp. 863-875, 2002.

[12] M. Díaz-Ley, F. García, and M. Piattini, "Implementing a software measurement program in small and medium enterprises: a suitable framework", Software, IET, vol. 2, pp. 417-436, 2008.

[13] S. Löper and M. Zehle, "Evaluation of software metrics in the design phase and their implication on CASE tools", Master Thesis, Blekinge Institute of Technology, Sweden, 2003.

[14] G. T. Hock and G. L. S. Hui, "A study of the problems and challenges of applying software metrics in software development industry", Proceedings of the M2USIC-MMU International Symposium on Information and Communication Technologies, Putrajaya, Malaysia, pp. 8-11, 2004.

[15] M. Díaz-Ley, F. García, and M. Piattini, "MIS-PyME Software Measurement Maturity Model - Supporting the Definition of Software Measurement Programs and Capabilty Determination", Advances in Software Engineering, vol. 41, pp. 1223-1237, 2010.

[16] J. J. M. Trienekens, R. J. Kusters, M. J. I. M. van Genuchten, and H. Aerts, "Targets, drivers and metrics in software process improvement: results of a survey in a multinational organization", Software Quality Journal, vol. 15, pp. 135-153, 2007.

[17] M. Villavicencio and A. Abran, "Towards the Development of a Framework for Education in Software Measurement", Joint Conference of the 23rd International Workshop on Software Measurement and the 8th International Conference on Software Process and Product Measurement, pp. 113-119, 2013.

[18] C. G. Von Wangenheim and M. T. D. Kochanski, "Empirical evaluation of an educational game on software measurement", Empirical Software Engineering, v.14 n.4, p.418-452, 2009.

[19] R. Solingen and E. Berghout, "The Goal/Question/Metric Method: a practical guide for quality improvement of software development. A Practical Guide for Quality Improvement of Software Development", New York, McCraw-Hill Publishers, p. 216, 1999.

[20] J. McGarry et al., "Pratical Software Measurement: Objetive Information for Decision Makers", Addison Wesley, Boston, USA, 2002.

[21] C. Jones, "Software Metrics: Good, Bad and Missing", Computer, v.27 n.9, p.98-100, 1994.

[22] A. R. Rocha, G. Santos, and M. P. Barcellos, "Software Measurement and Statistical Process Control", Publication of the Brazilian Ministry of Science, Technology and Innovation, 2012.

[23] M. Villavicencio and A. Abran, "Educational Issues in the Teaching of Software Measurement in Software Engineering Undergraduate Programs", in Joint Conference of the 21st Int'l Workshop on Software Measurement and the 6th Int'l Conference on Software Process and Product Measurement (IWSM-MENSURA), Nara, Japan, pp. 239-244, 2011.

[24] M. Villavicencio and A. Abran, "Software Measurement in Software Engineering Education: A Comparative Analysis", in International Conferences on Software Measurement IWSM/MetriKon/Mensura 2010, Stuttgart, Germany, pp. 633-644, 2010.

[25] M. Villavicencio and A. Abran, "Facts and Perceptions Regarding Software Measurement in Education and in Practice: Preliminary Results", Journal of Software Engineering and Applications, vol. 4, pp. 227-234, 2011.

[26] L. Lindsey and N. Berger, "Experiential approach to instruction", in Instructional-Design Theories and Models, vol. III, C. Reigeluth and A. Carr-Chellman, Eds., New York: Routledge, Taylor & Francis Group 2009, pp. 117-142. (V1_35), 2009.

[27] AMCHAM, "Only 14% of companies are completely satisfied with the results of IT measurement systems", 2012, Available: http://www.amcham.com.br, retrieved: March 2017.

[28] C. Jones, "Applied Software Measurement: Global Analysis of Productivity and Quality", Third ed.: McGraw-Hill Osborne Media, 2008.

[29] A. Abran, "Software metrics and software metrology", New Jersey: IEEE Computer Society / Wiley Partnership, 2010.

[30] H. Yazbek, "Metrics Support in Industrial CASE Tools", Software Measurement News: Journal of the Software Metrics Community, 40, 2010.

[31] A. Bartel and G. Hagel, "Gamifying the learning of design patterns in software engineering education", 2016 IEEE Global Engineering Education Conference (EDUCON), Abu Dhabi, pp. 74-79, 2016.

[32] B. S. Akpolat and W. Slany, "Enhancing software engineering student team engagement in a high-intensity extreme programming course using gamification", 2014 IEEE 27th Conference on Software Engineering Education and Training (CSEE&T), Klagenfurt, pp. 149-153, 2014.

[33] R. O. Chaves, et al., "Experimental Evaluation of a Serious Game for Teaching Software Process Modeling", in IEEE Transactions on Education, vol. 58, no. 4, pp. 289-296, 2015.

[34] B. Kitchenham, "Procedures for performing systematic reviews", Keele, UK, Keele University, v. 33, n. 2004, pp. 1–26, 2004.

[35] T. S. A. Costa, "A Methodological Approach to the Implementation of a Measurement Process based on a Software Tool and a Measurement Tools Catalogue", Master's Thesis, Federal University of Pará, pp. 74-127, 2016.

[36] B. Kitchenham and S. Pfleeger, "Personal Opinion Surveys", in Guide to Advanced Empirical Software Engineering, Springer, 2008.

[37] ACM/IEEE, "Computer science curricula 2013. Curriculum guidelines for undergraduate degree programs in Computer Science", 2013.

[38] SBC, "Reference curriculum for undergraduate courses in Bachelor in Computer Science and Computer Engineering", 2005.

[39] C. Wohlin et al., "Experimentation in software engineering: an introduction", in Kluwer Academic Publishers, Norwell, MA, 2000.

[40] R. E. Park, W. B. Goethert, and W. A. Florac, "Goal-Driven Software Measurement – A Guidebook", CMU/SEI-96-HB-002 Handbook. Software Engineering Institute, Carnegie Mellon University, Hanscom, MA, pp. 53-59, 1996.

[41] L. Anderson, et al., "A taxonomy for learning, teaching and assessing. A revision of Bloom's taxonomy of Educational Objectives". Addison Wesley Longman Inc, New York, 2001.

A Harmonization with CMMI-SVC Practices for the Implementation of the ITIL Service Design Coordination Process

George Hamilton Barbosa Fernandes Ota, Sandro Ronaldo Bezerra Oliveira
Graduate Program in Computer Science
Federal University of Pará
Belém, Pará, Brazil
e-mail: hamilton.ota@gmail.com, srbo@ufpa.br

Abstract—**This paper proposes a strategy for the harmonization of the Information Technology (IT) service management framework, the Information Technology Infrastructure Library (ITIL) framework, and the process improvement model for service used in the IT industry, called the Capability Maturity Model for Service (CMMI-SVC). The focal point of this harmonization lies in the Design Coordination process included in the ITIL Service Design, which seeks to ensure that the design consists of appropriate services and coordinates all the design features involved in projects, changes, suppliers and support teams. The results of the harmonization were checked step by step (in a procedure that included a peer review) with the assistance of a specialist with a knowledge of the ITIL framework and the CMMI-SVC model. Hence, the aim of this work is to correlate the structures for these standards and thus obtain the benefits of being able to reduce the time and costs through a joint implementation and also to stimulate the implementation of several models designed for IT service management. Thus, the main contribution made by this paper is that it finds a way of implementing ITIL practices through the adoption of the organizational process assets included in CMMI-SVC. This form of implementation was evaluated by specialists with an expert knowledge of both frameworks and adjustments were requested before the final version was completed for this work.**

Keywords-service management; information technology services; IT organization; service management model; ITIL; CMMI-SVC; harmonization.

I. INTRODUCTION

In recent years, both public and private organizations, (regardless of their size), have increased their demand for IT services to achieve their strategic goals. This paradigm has led the IT area to be seen as a strategic partner of businesses by enabling them to act in a competitive way. As a result of this change, there is a need to improve standards when providing these IT services, by employing methodologies to guide their implementation and management. Since they are based on best practices, this has enabled companies to achieve successful results [1].

Several standards of best practice (including proprietary knowledge, norms, models and frameworks designed for IT service quality management) are available in the market, such as the ITIL framework [2], International Organization for Standardization / International Electrotechnical Commission (ISO / IEC) 20000 [3], CMMI-SVC [4] and Control Objectives for Information and Related Technology (COBIT) [5].

According to the Information Technology Service Management Forum (itSMF) UK [1], the ITIL framework offers the following benefits: a) providing value to customers through IT services, b) integrating a strategy for services for business and customer needs, and c) measuring, monitoring, optimizing and reducing the cost of IT services. Companies such as IBM, Microsoft, HP and HSB are success stories in the adoption of the ITIL framework and in the 2011 edition of itSMF. There are 5 stages in the service lifecycle; each stage has a book of its own, together with 26 processes and 4 functions, which assist in achieving the purposes and goals of each stage.

In contrast, the CMMI for Services (CMMI-SVC) [4] is focused on the processes of service companies that are designed to help these companies know and improve their IT service processes. According to the CMMI Institute, until now (2017), their assessment shows that 549 companies have been using this maturity and capability model.

Many organizations see the need to adopt two or more IT best practice models or frameworks to improve efficiency and effectiveness in providing suitable IT services and thus ensure the organization's survival and success in the competitive global market. A set of models or frameworks (rather than just one) is used because when implemented in isolation they may not be able to fully cover all the needs of an organization by improving its IT services. Regardless of differences in concept and structure, IT best practice frameworks and models are not in principle incompatible, which means that they can be combined to improve the organization's IT service management. Hence the challenge of implementing IT service management through more than one standard of best practice, can be overcome by means of harmonization. This task will help to establish the similarities and differences between the models discussed in this paper [6]. The harmonization technique is widely used and accepted by the regulators as a means of enhancing the quality of the products and services provided and managed by the IT organization.

The research question raised in this work is about how ITIL (the IT service quality framework) and CMMI-SVC (the process quality model) can lead to an organizational improvement in an integrated way, by making use of the assets (practices, processes and other features) that these standards have. In this way, this research is driven by the need for materials that can guide the implementation process of the multi-models (ITIL and CMMI-SVC) in companies through the provision of assets to determine their strengths and weaknesses. It is also the purpose of this research to show the relationship between the ITIL framework and the CMMI-SVC quality model, by harmonizing their characteristics to show the level of adherence between their structures and supporting the organizations that wish to implement the framework and model together. Thus, the description of the main goal concerns the application of the practices defined in the quality models for IT service management.

The scope of the business / scientific problem and its challenges is revealed by the number of existing models that are designed to improve the quality of IT services. The harmonization can help to identify the common features of these models by providing the area responsible for the organization's IT service management with an instrument to guide the joint implementation of their practices. In this way, time and costs can be reduced and value delivered to the customers by means of the IT quality services. Thus, the best means to solve this problem is to determine how many of the assets (practices, processes and other factors) that are needed to support the implementation of different standards, can be applied together in the area responsible for the organization's IT service management.

This paper discusses the details of the harmonization of the Design Coordination process included in the ITIL Service Design, together with the process areas of the CMMI-SVC model. In describing the similarities and differences between the models, structures and the coverage criteria, an evaluation has been carried out to validate the correctness of the harmonization between the model and the framework. Thus, the purpose of this work is to design an instrument that can guide the joint implementation of the practices contained in both standards (ITIL Service Design and CMMI-SVC), and explain which CMMI-SVC strategies could be used to implement the ITIL set of practices. This harmonization does not aim to show the mapping between the assets but rather the coverage of ITIL obtained from the implementation of CMMI-SVC.

Several issues need to be addressed in this research, including how the nature and scope of the problem investigated are related to the IT service quality and the improvement of the IT service and process. It also involves attempting to ensure that the service improvement can take place during the IT service lifecycle.

The ITIL Service Design lifecycle consists of 8 processes. The choice of the Design Coordination process for this study, was based on the fact that this process seeks to ensure that the goals and objectives of the stage are met. It also provides and maintains a single point of coordination and control for all the activities and processes at this stage of the lifecycle.

It is hoped that the results of this research will: a) reduce the costs of organizations with joint implementation models, b) overcome the problem of inconsistencies and conflicts between the adopted standards, and c) reduce the costs incurred through this type of multi-model implementation. The difficulty is how to harmonize the ITIL framework with the CMMI-SVC model, as defined by different organizations and decide which practices should be integrated. Finally, this research is constrained by the fact that it is only focused on one process - Design Coordination - which is a part of the ITIL Service Design (although the harmonization of other processes included in the ITIL Service Design are available at the "SPIDER - Software Process Improvement: Development and Research Project SPIDER") and because only one expert has been invited to evaluate this harmonization.

The harmonization of ITIL with CMMI-SVC is significant because both standards include assets for the implementation of the IT process improvement. This means that an organization that is interested in this subject can implement an organizational improvement program with the good practices of different models. For this reason, it is clear that an organization that wishes to achieve this level of improvement, could derive the benefits of being able to reduce the costs and time of an individual implementation of each model, even though it could also carry out a joint implementation. With regard to the Design Coordination process, it is useful for an organization to move from a managed maturity level to a defined maturity level where the processes become standardized, structured and institutionalized.

This paper is structured as follows. Section II examines some related work that harmonize the two standards for IT service management and discusses in detail the fundamental principles of the two standards selected for this research study. Section III describes the harmonization between the Design Coordination process included in the ITIL Service Design and the practices in the CMMI-SVC process areas, as well as examining the evaluation undertaken for this research and the guidelines on how harmonization should be used. Finally, Section IV concludes the paper with some final considerations, including the results obtained and the limitations of this research, followed by some suggestions for possible future work.

II. Related Works and Background

This section provides an overview of the concepts of the CMMI-SVC model and the ITIL framework and some related works.

A. *Related Works*

Bridges and Albuquerque's work [7] set out a hybrid model based on equivalences found between the Service Availability and Continuity Management areas of Information Technology Services Management (ITSM) and the guides for service management, such as CMMI for Services, COBIT, ISO 20000, ITIL and Brazilian Software

Process Improvement (MPS.BR). These are concerned with encouraging the use of a quality improvement model in both areas (harmonically), with a view to consulting the Database of a Supplemental Health Operator in Brazil.

In [8], Ali, Soomro and Brohi mapped some ITIL processes for similar processes in IT standards and best practices in IT services: COBIT, ISO / IEC 27002-2005, Six Sigma, The Open Group Architecture Framework (TOGAF), enhanced Telecom Operations Map (eTOM), CMMI, Payment Card Industry Data Security Standards (PCI DSS) and the Common Security Framework (CSF). This mapping found similarities that enable the simultaneous implementation of ITIL in conjunction with these standards and norms in organizations and thus improve the productivity of business and IT services. Although this work took account of the harmonization between ITIL and CMMI, the CMMI model that was used was CMMI for Development (CMMI-DEV), which is concerned with software development and not IT process management, which is the focal point of the good practices in ITIL and CMMI-SVC used in this paper.

In a study by Pardo *et al.* [9], an integrated model is devised that harmonizes multiple approaches related to IT Governance for the Banking sector, including the Technology Governance Model for Banking (ITGSM). This involved six models and norms, namely Basileia II, COBIT 4.1, RISK IT, VAL IT, ISO 27002 and ITIL V.3, and these were integrated in pairs in an interactive and incremental way to create the ITGSM model. As a result, benefits were obtained for banking organizations, on the basis of a system that harmonized these models and norms.

Espindola and Audy [10] adopt an evolutionary approach to integrate quality models, which define a method that systematically executes a meta-model in Unified Modeling Language (UML). This is based on the features included in the mapping table for a quality framework and several models (CMMI, ISO / IEC 15504, ISO / IEC 20000 and COBIT). As a means of confirming the applicability of the method, the Reference Model of Brazilian Software Process Improvement (MR-MPS) quality model was added to validate if the addition of a model that had not been used in the development of the meta-model, was able to ratify it.

Kusumah, Sutikno and Rosmansyah [11] carried out a case study in an organization called INTRAC, which introduced the Model Design of Information Security Governance Assessment with Collaborative Integration of COBIT 5 and ITIL. This integration was, as far as possible, aimed at eliminating risks and their effects on the organizations, in situations where this had previously been fully ensured through the use of a single standard such as ISO / IEC 27001:2009 and ISO / IEC 27002:2005.

Finally, Garcia, Oliveira and Salviano [12] show the mapping between CERTICS (a national Brazilian model) and CMMI-DEV (an international model), in a situation where the main purpose of harmonization was to improve the area of Information Technology Competence Management of CERTICS. Each stage was evaluated by a specialist in the CERTICS and CMMI-DEV models, 1) to ensure the methodology had been formulated correctly, 2) to ensure the methodology was being employed correctly and 3) to ensure it was appropriate to have this kind of methodology. The main value of this was the reduction of time and costs during the implementation and, in particular, theability to implement several joint projects in the software development.

Organizations can find a wide range of best practices in the frameworks and models available which can lead to improvements in their processes and make their businesses profitable, by attracting companies and customers in very different areas. These frameworks and models have some similarities, strengths and weaknesses. A notable feature of the related work on the harmonization of these practices is that they enhance the organizational processes in business, without the need to employ a large number of quality models, since they are harmonized. As a result of this harmonization, the regulatory agencies of these standards, models and frameworks can find failings in their good practices and correct them in their quality models.

B. The ITIL Framework

ITIL is a public framework owned by AXELOS (a joint venture set up in 2014 by the Government of the United Kingdom and Capita) and based on best practices i.e., "activities or processes that have proven to be successful when used in many organizations" [2], that are widely recognized in the world for IT service management (ITSM). The ITIL Library is made up of a set of 5 books, one for each stage of the service lifecycle, where IT services effectively contribute to the best practices that can be adopted and adapted. It depends on the need and convenience of each organization to obtain business value. "Stages of the lifecycle work together as an integrated system to support the ultimate objective of service management for business value realization" [2].

The ITIL framework and its 5 service lifecycle stages consist of a core publication, which provides a set of best practice guidelines for each stage. This model provides an insight into the service stages from conception to retirement. When each stage is examined, a set of processes and activities can be found for planning each objective in a sequence. The stages of the lifecycle are as follows:

- **ITIL Service Strategy -** this formulates IT strategies and plans that must be appropriately aligned to the business and determine which services the provider must offer to meet the needs of customers or businesses,
- **ITIL Service Design -** at this stage, the design of appropriate and innovative IT services, including their architectures, processes, policies and documentation, to meet current and future agreed business requirements,
- **ITIL Service Transition**, **-** this aims at transferring

a new or changed service to the work environment in a controlled way,

- **ITIL Service Operation** - this is responsible for keeping the service within the work environment in a good operational condition and ensure that users and customers are satisfied with the efficient operation of the service, and
- **ITIL Continual Service** - this provides improvements in services and processes to maintain the value of the service for the customer and business.

Each stage of the ITIL lifecycle has a set of structured processes with activities to achieve a particular goal. The processes start with defined triggers and inputs, which result in defined outputs [2]. The processes of the ITIL Service Design domain are:

- **Design Coordination**, a process that aims at ensuring that the goals and objectives of the stage are properly met and controlled by a single point of coordination and control for all the other processes and activities within this stage of the service lifecycle,
- **Service Catalog Management**, a process responsible for providing and maintaining a consistent flow of information with regard to all the services in operation, as well as the one that is still being carried out to start the operation,
- **Service Level Management**, a process that seeks to ensure that current and planned IT services are delivered in accordance with the goals established in the agreements,
- **Availability Management**, a process that is designed to guarantee the availability levels for IT services and in this way efficiently and effectively meet the requirements for availability and service level goals agreed with the customer or business,
- **Capacity Management**, which is responsible for ensuring that services, service components and the IT infrastructure have the required capacity and performance and can operate in a timely and efficient way, while justifying its costs,
- **IT Service Continuity Management**, a process that manages business risks, which have the potential to cause serious damage to IT services and can draw up contingency plans and / or redundancy to mitigate the possible efects of these risks,
- **Information Security Management**, a process that seeks to align IT security with business security and ensure the confidentiality, integrity and availability of IT assets, information, data and services, as agreed with the IT service provider, and
- **Supplier Management**, a process that must be involved with all stages of the service lifecycle in ITIL, because in this stage the suppliers are required to design new and / or updated services and must comply with their contractual obligations.

Owing to the limited space in scope of this paper, we decided to select the Design Coordination process of ITIL Service Design. This process is structured in two categories [13], each with its respective activities, namely:

- **For the overall service design lifecycle stage:**
  - Define and maintain policies and methods,
  - Plan design resources and capabilities,
  - Coordinate design activities,
  - Manage design risks and issues, and
  - Improve service design.
- **For each design:**
  - Plan individual designs,
  - Coordinate individual designs,
  - Monitor individual designs, and
  - Review designs and ensure handover of service design package.

C. The CMMI-SVC Model

The Capability Maturity Model Integration for Services (CMMI-SVC) is a maturity model for assessing, defining, implementing and improving the quality of an organization's processes and its ability to manage the service. This model was created by the Software Engineering Institute (SEI), and contains 24 Process Areas (PA), 16 of which are core, 1 is shared and 7 are service-specific process areas of CMMI-SVC. This model was designed to meet the need for development and improvement in the maturity of service practices and hence make improvements in the performance of the service provider leading to customer satisfaction [4].

In 2010, the CMMI version 1.3, which brings together three constellations, was published by SEI: CMMI for Development (CMMI-DEV), which deals with development processes, CMMI for Acquisition (CMMI-ACQ), where processes of acquisition are worked out, as well as outsourcing of products and / or services, and CMMI for Services (CMMI-SVC), aimed at improving service processes.

There is a chapter devoted to describing the components in the CMMI-SVC model. Understanding these components is regarded by the model as a critical factor since it seeks to ensure the use of the information is understood. These components are grouped into 3 categories:

- **Required Components** - components considered to be essential to achieve process improvement in a particular process area, and comprising Specific and Generic Goals,
- **Expected Components** - components that describe the activities that are needed to achieve a required component, and are formed of Specific and Generic Practices, and
- **Informative Components** - components that help the model to be understood, and thus have components such as Subpractices, and Examples of Work Products.

The CMMI-SVC consists of process areas (PA) with specific purposes and goals related to each particular process area, as well as generic goals related to all the process areas. Specific goals (SG) are also defined that refer to the unique features of each process area and generic goal (GG) responsible for defining the characteristics that are common to all the process areas. For each specific goal, a set of specific practices (SP) will be outlined, which are activities that need to be completed to ensure that the goal is satisfied in each PA.

The three CMMI-SVC process areas considered in this harmonization are:

- **Organizational Process Definition** - the purpose of this is to establish and maintain a usable set of organizational process assets and work environment standards. This process area includes the following specific practices:
    - SP 1.1 Establish Standard Processes,
    - SP 1.2. Establish Lifecycle Model Descriptions,
    - SP 1.3 Establish Tailoring Criteria and Guidelines,
    - SP 1.4 Establish the Organization's Measurement Repository,
    - SP 1.5 Establish the Organization's Process Asset Library,
    - SP 1.6 Establish Work Environment Standards,
    - SP 1.7 Establish Rules and Guidelines for Teams,
- **Organizational Process Focus** - the purpose of this is to plan, implement, and deploy organizational process improvements based on a thorough understanding of the current strengths and weaknesses of the organization's processes and process assets. This process area includes the following specific practices:
    - SP 1.1 Establish Organizational Process Needs,
    - SP 1.2 Appraise the Organization's Processes,
    - SP 1.3 Identify the Organization's Process Improvements,
    - SP 2.1 Establish Process Action Plans,
    - SP 2.2 Implement Process Action Plans,
    - SP 3.1 Deploy Organizational Process Assets,
    - SP 3.2 Deploy Standard Processes,
    - SP 3.3 Monitor the Implementation,
    - SP 3.4 Incorporate Experiences into Organizational Process Assets,
- **Integrated Work Management** - the purpose of this is to establish and manage the work and involve the stakeholders concerned through an integrated and defined process that is adapted to the organization's set of standard processes. This process area includes the following practices:
    - SP 1.1 Establish the Defined Process,
    - SP 1.2 Use Organizational Process Assets for Planning Work Activities,
    - SP 1.3 Establish the Work Environment,
    - SP 1.4 Integrate Plans,
    - SP 1.5 Manage the Work Using Integrated Plans,
    - SP 1.6 Establish Teams,
    - SP 1.7 Contribute to Organizational Process Assets,
    - SP 2.1 Manage Stakeholder Involvement,
    - SP 2.2 Manage Dependencies,
    - SP 2.3 Resolve Coordination Issues.

The CMMI-SVC model should be consulted for a better understanding of the purpose of each specific practice [4]. This list of specific practices will be used in the section describing the harmonization set out in this paper.

III. The Harmonization between the ITIL Framework and CMMI-SVC Model

Both the ITIL framework and the CMMI-SVC model share the same goal of providing the IT Managers and organizations with a set of best practices to manage information technology services of quality and create value for the organization's business area during the service lifecycle. Although these models have different structures, similarities can be found in the set of specific requirements for the IT service management, as shown in Table I.

TABLE I. Elements that can influence the ITIL framework and CMMI-SVC model

ITIL Elements	CMMI-SVC Elements	
Process	Process Area	
Objectives	Specific Goals (SG)	Generic Goals (GG)
Activity, Methods and Techniques	Specific Practices (SP)	Generic Practices (GP)
Policies, Principles and Basic Concepts	Subpractices	Generic Practice Elaborations
Triggers, Inputs and Outputs	Example of Work Products (WP)	

In each service lifecycle, the ITIL framework has a set of Processes, that are structured by a set of Activities to achieve a certain objective. Similarly, the CMMI-SVC model contains a set of Process Areas (PA), where several Specific and Generic Practices, (component of the PA), are described and must be implemented.

The Objectives element of the ITIL framework is equivalent, in certain respects to the Specific Goals and Generic Goals of CMMI-SVC. This is because they include a set of characteristics that, must be identified in the respective Process of the ITIL by the Objectives element and in the Process Area of CMMI-SVC for the Specific and Generic Goals before they can be certified by the model in the organization. Similarly, the Activities, Methods and Techniques of the ITIL framework include areas that must be defined to achieve a specific result. This can be compared to the Specific Practices and Generic Practices of CMMI-SVC, because this includes the details of how to carry out a practice to meet the goals of the model.

Another similarity that was found refers to the elements that are designed to provide guidelines for the appropriate implementation process of the models. The fact that ITIL framework is present in the Policies, Principles and Basic Concepts and in the CMMI-SVC model, can be observed in the Subpractices and Generic Practice Elaborations.

The Triggers, Inputs and Outputs of the ITIL framework have similar objectives to the Example Work Products of CMMI-SVC, since these elements must be sought during the implementation process in each model to ensure that the requirements have been met correctly.

The integration recommended by this paper refers to the set of concepts in the ITL framework and the CMMI-SVC model elements. It also includes the definition of a set of equivalent technologies that assist in the evaluation and improvement of IT products and services. In this domain, there are tools, techniques, procedures, processes, roles, methodologies, frameworks, languages, standards, patterns, and so on.

It should be emphasized that the mapping between the elements contained in the ITIL and CMMI-SVC were validated through the same correlation in the work [8], which confirms that the results for the relationship between the elements defined in Table I is correct.

A. *A Conformance Analysis of the Design Coordination Process*

The Design Coordination process in the category of **activities relates to the overall service design lifecycle stage**, where the standard service process that needs to be adopted is constructed [13]. It includes the following activities which are mapped in each subsection below.

1) Define and Maintain Policies and Methods

This activity is intended to ensure that a Consistent and Accurate Design(s) for the Service(s) is produced in accordance with the required business outcomes. When made available in the IT Service Operational Environment, it helps (and continues to help) the organization to achieve its goals. To do this, this activity requires a Process Area and Specific Practices (SP) of CMMI-SVC.

In the *Organizational Process Definition (OPD)* area, SP.1.1 defines and maintains a set of standard processes that can be instantiated to address a particular area of the organization's business. SP.1.2 attempts to describe the lifecycle models that are suited to the needs of the workgroup, the organization, the definitions of the service standard and the environment. SP.1.3 is concerned with drawing up the guidelines that will set out the procedure for the conduct and execution of the defined process. These are based on the information contained in the set of standard processes and in the assets of the organizational process. SP.1.4 aims to design and maintain the Organization Measurement Repository which provides the necessary information to understand and interpret the set of common measurements for products and processes related to the set of standard processes of the organization. Finally, SP.1.5 designs and implements the organizational process asset library, where the procedures are specified for the storage, updating and retrieval of items such as policies, process descriptions, procedures, development plans, and other assets, as well as making these items available for use in workgroups.

The coverage in the *Define and Maintain Policies and Methods* activity was complete, because the CMMI-SVC had met the requirements of this activity.

2) Plan Design Resources and Capabilities

The purpose of this activity is to plan the resources and capabilities of the Design Coordination process, based on the information obtained from the Service Portfolio activities (Service Pipeline) and the Change Management process of the ITIL Service Transition stage. This is because this activity requires a Process Area and Specific Practices of CMMI-SVC to achieve its goals.

In the *Organizational Process Definition (OPD)* process area, SP.1.6 aims to establish and maintain a standard work environment, i.e what resources are required for team work. SP.1.7 allocates people to work in the process and defines the assignments of these people.

There was complete coverage for the *Plan Design Resources and Capabilities*, because the CMMI-SVC had met the requirements of this activity.

3) Coordinate Design Activities

This area coordinates all the design activities in projects and changes, management planning, resources, and conflicts with suppliers and support teams when necessary. It thus requires a Process Area and Specific Practices of CMMI-SVC to achieve its goals.

In the *Integrated Work Management (IWM)* process area, the aim of SP.2.2 is to manage the task dependencies between the activities of the process, since these depend on the inputs of other activities for their execution and must be carefully managed to avoid process gaps. Thus, the SP identifies any critical dependencies and plans the work schedule, while taking account of these critical variables in the process.

The coverage of the *Coordinate Design Activities* was complete, because the CMMI-SVC had met its requirements.

4) Manage Design Risks and Issues

This activity is responsible for assessing risks in design, technical management, managing the risks involved in design activities, and tackling the number of problems that might be subsequently traced to poor design. It requires a Process Area and Specific Practices of CMMI-SVC to achieve its goals.

In the *Integrated Work Management (IWM)* process area, in SP.2.3 the task of management entails the identification, follow-up (status) and communication of the person responsible for tackling and solving the problem.

The coverage in the *Manage Design Risks and Issues* activity was complete, because the CMMI-SVC had met the requirements of this activity.

5) Improve Service Design

The purpose of this activity is to ensure that there is a continuous awareness of the goals and objectives of the service design phase to improve the effectiveness and efficiency of service design activities and processes. This activity requires a Process Area and Specific Practices of CMMI-SVC to achieve its goals.

In the *Organizational Process Focus (OPF)* process area, SP.1.1 records the needs and goals of the organizational process in the context of the business to ensure that it is fully understood. SP.1.2 evaluates and delivers the results of the documents needed with regard to methods and evaluation criteria. These include the following: the CMMI process model, the International Organization for Standardization (ISO) or benchmarking. SP.1.3 seeks to discover if there is a need for improvement in the processes and process assets of the organization and involves training for teams, and improvement of the tools used, among other factors. In SP.2.1 the focus is on how to enable the organization to establish and maintain plans for improvement. These are subsequently implemented in accordance with the organizational needs defined in SP.2.2. SP.3.1 plans, records and executes the implementation of the Organizational Process assets and their changes, as well as determining what resources are needed to support this implementation and thus ensure its compliance with the organization's current goals and objectives. The aim of SP.3.2 is to implement the organization's standard processes, and work groups, by periodically updating them, and incorporating the latest changes made to the standardization. This ensures that all the work activities can benefit other work groups in the process. SP.3.4 attempts to bring about improvement in the planning and execution of the organizational process and in particular, the lessons learned, measurements periodically measured, and records of improvements in the organizational process activities.

The coverage in the *Improve Service Design* activity was complete, because the CMMI-SVC had met the requirements of this activity.

With regard to Design Coordination Process in the category of **activities relating to each individual design**, each process must be instantiated to allow a service project to be implemented [13]. This includes the following activities, which are mapped in each subsection below.

1) Plan Individual Designs

This activity involves carefully planning each individual project or change to ensure the required business results are obtained. This activity requires a Process Area and Specific Practices of CMMI-SVC to achieve its goals.

In the *Integrated Work Management (IWM)* process area, SP.1.1 seeks to define and maintain a process in accordance with its contractual obligations, operational needs, opportunities and constraints. SP.1.2 uses the tasks and work products of the process defined for the work as a basis for planning the work activities. SP.1.3 seeks to plan, design and implement a work environment, in terms of its equipment, tools, facilities, operations and manuals. SP.1.4 is concerned with the management of integrated work plans, and ensuring the controlled participation of human resources in integrated projects to avoid labor conflicts. The objective of SP.1.6 is to form the teams that will work in the process.

The coverage in the *Plan Individual Designs* activity was complete, because the CMMI-SVC had met its requirements.

2) Coordinate Individual Designs

This activity is often carried out by a project manager or someone else with direct responsibility for the project. He / she is also responsible for making changes in the coordination of activities and in the instantiation of the standard process in response to the customer's demands. This activity requires a Process Area and Specific Practices of CMMI-SVC to achieve its goals.

In the *Integrated Work Management (IWM)* process area, SP.2.1 undertakes the management and scheduling of the collaborative activities of the stakeholders (the integrated work plan has already been defined in SP.1.4). The coordination of people's dependencies and the negotiation of critical issues (contingencies) is carried out in SP 2.2 in case there is a need to change the agenda and introduce collaborative schedules for the stakeholders. SP.2.3 is designed to tackle issues that are important for the stakeholders. The ability of the appropriate manager to solve these problems depends on their scale.

The coverage in *Coordinate Individual Designs* was complete, because the CMMI-SVC had met the requirements of this activity.

3) Monitor Individual Designs

The purpose of this activity is to monitor all aspects of the project to ensure the following: a) the agreed methods are being adhered to, b) there is no conflict of interest with other ongoing design projects, c) the website design milestones are reached, and d) the development of a design is comprehensive enough to support the required organizational results. This activity requires a Process Area and Specific Practices of CMMI-SVC to achieve its goals.

In the *Integrated Work Management (IWM)* process area, SP.1.5 focuses on monitoring and controlling work activities. It is also concerned with work products from the defined processes, work plans, and other plans that can affect the work.

The coverage in *Monitor Individual Designs* activity was complete, because the CMMI-SVC had met the requirements of this activity.

4) Review Designs and Ensure Handover of SDPs

The final review of the individual designs is carried out to ensure that the standards and conventions are being fully complied with in the service design package (SDP). Problems should be documented and there is a need to determine if alterations are needed in any part of the service design or if they can be viewed as a part of the service transition plan. This activity requires two Process Areas and Specific Practices of CMMI-SVC to achieve its goals.

In the *Integrated Work Management (IWM)* process area, SP.1.7 establishes the following: a) the contributions made by the defined process information to the work, b) organizational process assets and c) proposed improvements. The processes and product measurements are stored in the organization's measurement repository. In the *Organizational Process Focus (OPF)* area, the SP.3.4 is responsible for the improvement of planning and execution of the process in the organizational process assets. Its activities depend on what has been found out about its strengths and weaknesses in the SP.1.7.

The coverage in the *Review Designs and Ensure Handover of SDPs* activity was complete, because the CMMI-SVC had met its requirements.

B. An Evaluation of the Harmonization of Technology Management

The peer review technique was employed to evaluate the harmonization that was obtained between the requirements of the ITIL framework and CMMI-SVC model, as outlined in the last section. This was overseen by an expert, who has over 5 years of experience of implementing quality models in IT (Information Technology) companies. He has a recognized certification in ITIL and CMMI-SVC, as well as being a certified SCAMPI High Maturity lead appraiser. The expert was given the document that contains the harmonization of ITIL and CMMI-SVC. He carried out the review in accordance with a set of criteria, which were defined on the basis of Araújos's work [6], as shown in Table II.

TABLE II. CRITERIA DEFINED FOR THE HARMONIZATION EVALUATION.

Criteria	Definition
TH (Technical High)	Indicates that a problem in a harmonization item was found and, if not changed, would impair the system.
TL (Technical Low)	Indicating that a problem in a harmonization item was found and a change would be appropriate.
E (Editorial)	Indicating that a Portuguese language error was found or the text can be improved.
Q (Questioning)	Indicating that there were doubts about the content.
G (General)	Indicates that in general a comment is needed.

When reviewing the harmonization of Design Coordination process, the expert detected a problem, which was classified as General (G). It was suggested that an analysis should be conducted of all the CMMI-SVC specific and generic practices that have been mapped in the ITIL process with the aim of determining whether they are listed and described at the end of the document. If any mapped practice had not been listed, the expert suggested that it should be included in the document, as a means of enabling the purpose e of these practices to be understood.

The specialist found a problem in the 4 ITIL activities, which was classified as TL. Since in this outcome the Specific Practice was unnamed, the expert suggested that its name should be included in the harmonization document. These problems were caused by the following: a) a lack of a suitable relationship between some good practices of ITIL with CMMI-SVC, b) a lack of detail about what level of coverage was determined after the relationship had been established between the assets of the two frameworks, c) a lack of clarity about what each asset represents (i.e., ITIL and CMMI-SVC), and d) a lack of an explanation for the relationship between the elements of ITIL and CMMI-SVC.

The expert did not find any problem classified as TH, E or Q.

After this first peer review the authors of this paper sent the corrected harmonization to 3 other experts in the field, who are certified and have more than 7 years of experience of implementing the two models used in the work. However, none of these experts suggested any adjustments should be made, although they showed an interest in the use of this harmonization for making improvements to the implementation of the program.

C. How should the Harmonization be used?

The purpose of the harmonization of the ITIL framework and CMMI-SVC model is to help businesses that wishing to obtain certifications through multi-model implementations or even by making evaluations of the two standards. The use of harmonization can optimize cost-effectiveness, time and effort because the standards now have their structures harmonized and interrelated.

It was possible to highlight the differences and similarities included in the requirements of ITIL and CMMI-SVC. Hence, it can be seen that although some requirements of the standards are similar or even complementary, they are not always able to achieve their goals in the same way. According to the Association for Promoting Excellence in Brazilian Software (SOFTEX) [14], this may occur because of the different requirements of some of the practices, outcomes and expected results of the standards.

The harmonization spreadsheets have become an important support tool for the joint evaluation or implementation of the standards, because they provide inputs that allow their frameworks to be adapted / harmonized and predict their expected results, practices and outcomes. This can enable the multi-models to be implemented in companies.

As a result, the company benefits from the implementation of joint standards, because it will not have to spend time on separately analyzing the frameworks for the standards. This means that there is a need to determine in what way one standard can suit another one, because all the structures and requirements, (which are the same for all the standards), have been identified, harmonized and documented in the spreadsheet used for the standards.

A qualitative criterion for the successful harmonization in the design coordination process can be defined as a standard process that is well structured, and is subject to rules for its adaptation and institutionalization, as well as the fact that it can be integrated with different projects.

IV. CONCLUSION AND SUGGESTIONS FOR FUTURE WORK

This research study examined the harmonization of the Design Coordination process with the ITIL framework by carrying out the practices defined in the CMMI-SVC process areas. Its goals were achieved by seeking to determine the similarities and differences between the structures of ITIL and CMMI-SVC, and investigating their degree of harmonization. To avoid misunderstandings and inconsistencies, an expert in these standards evaluated the harmonization by means of the peer review technique. The results of this review were analyzed and changes were suggested to remove any inconsistencies or failure to understand the problems detected by the expert.

The lessons learned from this research stem from the fact that there is both an analytical and comparative domain between the framework and the object model of this research. Thus, it is recommended that more than one person should undertake it so that any conflicts or uncertainties can be discussed and addressed by a peer review.

A limitation of this study is that the harmonization was not evaluated in a public / private company or organization, but only assessed by peer review. However, an assessment of the harmonization of a public company is now being completed in Brazil and its processes are in accordance with the practices of maturity level 3 of CMMI-SVC. As a result, it will be possible to determine if the harmonization had a positive or negative influence on a multi-model implementation. A further limitation is the fact that the peer review was only conducted by a single expert, which means that there can only be a limited view of the results obtained from the research. However, this expert has extensive experience with the implementation of the CMMI-SVC model and the ITIL framework, and this should reduce the risk of bias in the results obtained from the review.

In a future work, we intend to continue to expand this research and apply it to other organizations, so that the positive and negative aspects of the use of harmonization can be quantified through a multi-model implementation (ITIL framework with CMMI-SVC). Another future study could involve defining the complete cycle of harmonization based on the results of Araújo's research [6] and the CMMI guide [4].

So far, it has not been possible to finalize the case study, although it is worth drawing attention to the benefits of multi-model implementation. These include, the reduction of costs and time needed to comply with the expected results and practices of the ITIL framework and the CMMI-SVC, as well as the creation of a unified and standardized system to achieve the two standards. Finally, there is the advantage of being able to standardize the technical language that is used among them to define the process of IT service management.

ACKNOWLEDGMENT

The authors would like to thank the Dean of Research and Postgraduate Studies at the Federal University of Pará (PROPESP/UFPA) by the Qualified Publication Support Program (PAPQ), for the financial support.

REFERENCES

[1] ItSMF UK, "An Introductory Overview of ITIL® 2011", IT Serv. Manag. Forum UK, London, 2011.

[2] OGC, "ITIL Service Strategy", London: The Stationery Office, 2011.

[3] ISO/IEC, "ISO/IEC 20000- 1:2011 Information technology — Service Management — Part 2: Guidance on the application of service management systems", Geneva, 2011.

[4] SEI, "CMMI® for Services", Version 1.3, no. November. 2010.

[5] Isaca, "COBIT 5: A Business Framework for the Governance and Management of Enterprise IT", 2013.

[6] L. L. Araújo, "Mapping between MPS.SW and MPT.BR and CERTICS", Dissertação de Mestrado, COPPE/UFRJ, Brazil, 2014.

[7] L. Pontes and A. Albuquerque, "Managing Database Services: An Approach Based in Information Technology Services Availabilty and Continuity Management", J. Inf. Syst. Eng. Manag., vol. 1, pp. 1–5, 2017.

[8] S. M. Ali, T. R. Soomro, and M. N. Brohi, "Mapping Information Technology Infrastructure Library With Other Information Standards And Best Practices", J. Comput. Sci. 9(9), vol. 9, no. 9, pp. 1190–1196, 2013.

[9] C. Pardo et al., "Integrating Multiple Models for Definition of IT Governance Model for Banking ITGSM", Int. Bus. Manag., vol. 10, pp. 4644–4652, 2016.

[10] R. S. de Espindola and J. L. N. Audy, "An Evolutionary Approach for Quality Models Integration", in Proceedings of the 11th International Conference on Enterprise Information, 2009, pp. 231–236, doi: 10.5220/0002008202310236.

[11] P. Kusumah, S. Sutikno, and Y. Rosmansyah, "Model design of information security governance assessment with collaborative integration of COBIT 5 and ITIL (case study: INTRAC)", Proc. - 2014 Int. Conf. ICT Smart Soc. "Smart Syst. Platf. Dev. City Soc. GoeSmart 2014, ICISS 2014, 2014, pp. 1–6, doi: 10.1109/ICTSS.2014.7013193.

[12] F. W. S. Garcia, S. R. B. Oliveira, and C. F. Salviano, "CERTICS - A Harmonization with CMMI-DEV Practices for Implementation of Technology Management Competence Area", in ICSEA 2016 : The Eleventh International Conference on Software Engineering Advances, , no. c, pp. 10–15, 2016.

[13] OGC, "ITIL Service Design". London: The Stationery Office, 2011.

[14] SOFTEX, "MPS . BR - Brazilian Software Process Improvement Assessment Guide:2016", Brazil, 2016.

Automatic Documentation of the Development of Numerical Models for Scientific Applications using Specific Revision Control

Martin Zinner*, Karsten Rink†, René Jäkel*, Kim Feldhoff*, Richard Grunzke*,
Thomas Fischer†, Rui Song‡, Marc Walther†§, Thomas Jejkal¶, Olaf Kolditz†‖, Wolfgang E. Nagel*

* Center for Information Services and High Performance Computing (ZIH)
Technische Universität Dresden
Dresden, Germany
E-mail: martin.zinner1@mailbox.tu-dresden.de, {rene.jaekel, kim.feldhoff}@tu-dresden.de,
{richard.grunzke, wolfgang.nagel}@tu-dresden.de
† Department of Environmental Informatics
Helmholtz Centre for Environmental Research (UFZ)
Leipzig, Germany
E-mail: {karsten.rink, thomas.fischer, marc.walther, olaf.kolditz}@ufz.de
‡ Technical Information Systems
Technische Universität Dresden
Dresden, Germany
E-mail: rui.song@tu-dresden.de
§ Professorship of Contaminant Hydrology
Technische Universität Dresden
Dresden, Germany
E-mail: marc.walther@tu-dresden.de
¶ Institute for Data Processing and Electronics
Karlsruhe Institute of Technology (KIT)
Karlsruhe, Germany
E-mail: thomas.jejkal@kit.edu
‖ Professorship Applied Environmental System Analysis
Technische Universität Dresden
Dresden, Germany
E-mail: olaf.kolditz@ufz.de

***Abstract*—As software becomes increasingly complex, automatic documentation of the development is becoming ever more important. In this paper, we present a novel, general strategy to build a revision control system of the development of numerical models for scientific applications. We set up a formal methodology of the strategy and show the consistency, correctness, and usefulness of the presented strategy to automatically generate a documentation for the evolution of the model.**

Keywords–Software development; Automatic generation of documentation; Revision control; Backup and Restore; Metadata; Improvement of research environment; Support of research process.

I. Introduction

In scientific applications, dedicated software packages are used to create numerical models for the simulation of physical phenomena, in particular environmental phenomena, such as flooding, groundwater recharge or reactive transport using innovative numerical methods. Such simulations are crucial for solving major challenges in coming years, including the prediction of possible effects of climate change [1] [2], the development of water management schemes for (semi) arid regions [3] [4] or the reduction of groundwater contamination [5] [6].

The modeling process is usually a complete workflow, starting with data acquisition and integration to set up a model, simulate (multiple) processes, and as well as the analysis, and visualization of calculated results. Unfortunately, the modeling process itself in general is not transparent and traceable and often poorly documented. A typical model – conceived as a set of parameter files – is developed over many weeks or months and usually a large number of revisions are necessary for updating and refining the model, such that the simulation represents the natural process as realistically and plausibly as possible.

In this paper, we address this challenge, specifically, we present a revision control system, which in addition to the backup/restore functionality tracks the changes in each modeling step, thus generating an internal documentation of the evolution of the model.

The structure of the paper is as follows: In Section II, we define the environment and set up the terminology; in Section III, we give a short overview over the state of art and detail some differences of our approach, both in concept and realization; in Section IV, we demonstrate our novel strategy, which is used for the revision control system to generate the implicit documentation of the evolution of the model; in Section V, we augment the classical pseudo code presentation of the algorithms to a formal, mathematical description of our selective backup strategy and show the consistency and correctness of the backup and restore functionalities. We present the software implementing the formal description and its application to a use case of the UFZ in Section VI. Finally, we conclude our work and give an outlook for future research and development in Section VII.

II. Main Challenges and Objectives

The basic concept for the simulation is the model. It is developed over several modeling steps, named revisions, compare Figure 1. After each revision, a simulation is performed (see Figure 2). The first setup of the model is often used to get an overview over existing data and to detect potential problems. Further revisions try to solve these problems by adding data, mesh refinements, new parametrizations, etc.

The framework for revision control for scientific applications is being implemented at the Helmholz-Centre for Environmental Research (UFZ) [7] using Karlsruhe Institute of Technology Data Manager (KIT DM) [8] as a software framework for building up repositories for research data.

The Metadata Management for Applied Sciences (MASi) [9] research data management service is currently being prepared for production at the Center for Information Services and High Performance Computing (ZIH) at Technische Universität Dresden. It utilizes the advanced KIT DM framework to enable a service that enables the metadata-driven management of research data from arbitrary communities. This includes automating as many processes as possible including metadata generation and data pre-processing.

The current solution, utilized at UFZ, is fully file based and it is usually stored locally on the laptop of each scientist. The

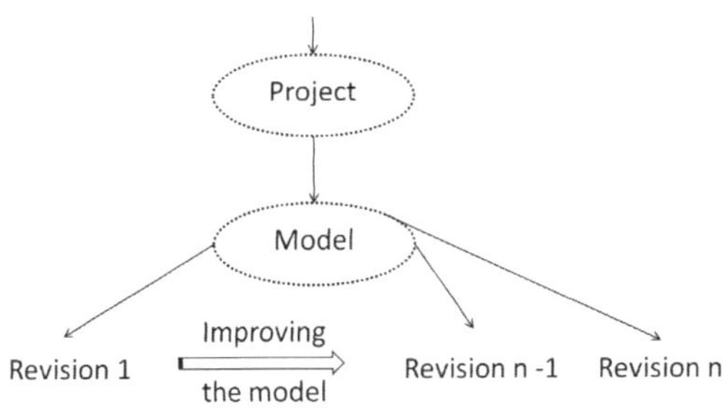

Figure 1. Model development over revisions

number of parameter files is up to several hundreds, with each file up to several megabytes. The changes from one modeling step to the next can be a) minor, e.g., one parameter value

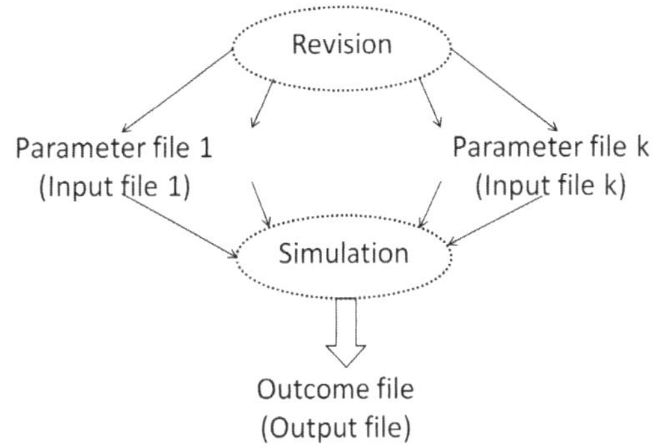

Figure 2. Revision and simulation as part of the model development process

changed in a single input file; b) major, e.g., both geometry and the grid are modified.

The main deficiencies of the current solution at UFZ are:

1) Overview is lost (especially after handling the model for a long time),
2) difficult to trace which parameter has been changed when and why,
3) no implicit or explicit documentation of the changes,
4) each user stores the data on his laptop at his own discretion,
5) data is lost if hard disk crashes and there is no backup,
6) joint working on the same model is laborious.

The benefits of the new framework will include those of a classical revision control system (like Git [10], or Apache Subversion [11]), especially:

1) Uniform, central, and consistent storage of the individual modeling steps a) each scientist will be able to view the simulation data he is entitled to b) backup functionality if the data is lost,
2) possibility to track and analyze / evaluate the changes,
3) data is still available if the PhD student leaves the company,
4) shared access of the latest development of the model.

We define by a revision the state of the components already persisted and accessible by a unique identifier. Thus, the content of the components of a revision cannot be altered any more. The current set of the components, which can be actively changed is called the *working set*.

The main objectives we focus on, to achieve our scope, are:

1) Central persistent storage of the model to include all the modeling steps and the management of the revisions.
2) Design and development of a metadata repository regarding a) revision control and b) the changes of the parameter files between subsequent revisions. Additionally, information regarding parameter values, simulation software, etc. can be persisted.

3) An efficient and disk space saving strategy, such that a specific parameter file is stored only if its content has been modified.

4) Generation of an internal documentation of the model development, such that it can be easily understood and reconstructed.

It is out of scope of this research to persistently store the results of the simulation. If necessary, it can be generated again or a direct storage strategy could be used. Storing the results of the simulation together with the parameter files would leverage our sophisticated storage strategy, since the size of the parameter files is in the range of megabytes, where the size of the simulation files is in the range of gigabytes. The storage of the simulation results is only meaningful if it takes too long to newly generate the results.

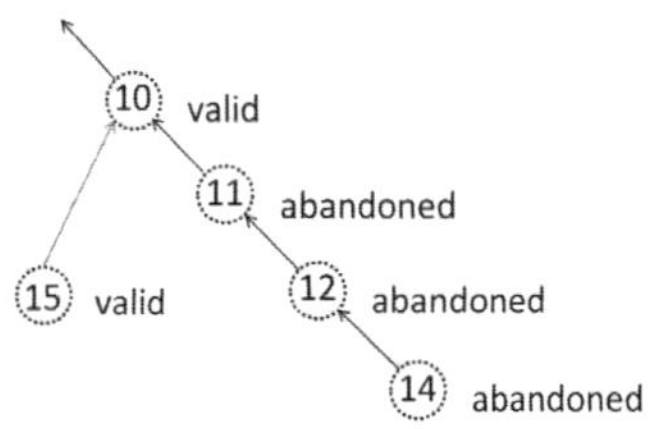

Figure 3. Tree structure of the development of the model

The model development is stored in a tree structure, such that each node (revision) has a unique link to its predecessor, see Figure 3. The tree structure is necessary to be able to identify modeling steps where the results of the simulation are not promising, and thus this revision is not pursued further (termed *abandoned)*. In this case, the development of the model is continued from a previous revision (termed *active*), thus performing a rollback on the evolution of the model and creating a new branch in the version control tree structure.

Usually, metadata is defined as data about data. Metadata files can be generated automatically or they can be set up manually. The *flow configuration file* is the main metadata file and it is generated automatically during the evolution process of the model and contains the basic information regarding the revision control system, which is necessary to generate the internal documentation of the evolution of the model, i.e.,

a) model name;

b) predecessors and the current revision;

c) cryptographic hash value and status of the parameter files;

d) parameter change information in condensed form, etc.

The main metadata file sustains the possibility to automatically capture, track, analyze, and evaluate the changes in each modeling step.

Additionally, users can define their own metadata files, which can be created for the whole case study or for a specific revision and could contain additional information regarding a) name of the project; b) model area; c) modeled process; d) software used, including the version; e) contact person; f) source reference regarding the applied methods and data used; g) utilization rights, etc.

Besides documentation, metadata also allows for easy identification of the uploaded data. Search for specific values (e.g., model name, author, etc.) over all metadata elements can be performed for example by using ElasticSearch [12].

III. Related work

The concept of revision control systems (RCS) is not new (see Tichy [13]). The task of the RCS as defined by Tichy is version control, i.e., keeping software systems consisting of many versions and configurations well organized. The concept of a revision is similar to our approach, an ancestral tree is used for storing revisions. The major difference is that – as set up by Tichy – each object (like a file) has his own revision tree, whereas we follow an overarching concept, such that files may remain unchanged between revisions. Furthermore, the evolvement of the revision is linear, but it can use *side branches*, for example one for the productive version and one for the development [13].

Löh et al. [14] present a formal model to reason about version control, in particular modeling repositories as a multiset of patches. Patches abstract over the data on which they operate, making the framework equally suited for version control from highly-structured XML to blobs of bits. The mathematical definition of patches and repositories enable Löh et al. to reason about complicated issues, such as conflicts and conflicts resolution. The main application field that Löh et al. targets is the distributed (software) development with its challenges regarding the complex operations on the repositories, such as merging branches or resolving conflicts. They introduce a precise, mathematical description of the version control system to accurately predict when conflicts may arise and how they may be resolved.
Our mathematical model is not based on the work of Löh et al., it has been developed from scratch to enable the characterization of the selective backup strategy.
The possibility to use metadata, such as the patch's author, time of creation, or some form of documentation is shortly discussed in [14]. Details are left to the designers of a specific revision control system. Also the concept of reverting changes, i.e., the ability to return to a previous version by undoing a modification that later turns out to be undesired, is discussed from a theoretical point of view.

As stated in [15] there are some basic goals of a versioning system, such that:

1) People are able to work simultaneously, not serially.
2) When people are working at the same time, their changes do not conflict with each other.

These two goals do not apply in our case. Formally, users can work simultaneously, making changes independently, but for a simulation they need all the parameter files. The classical use case, such that a programmer changes the internal specification of a module without changing the external interface is not applicable in our case, each change in a parameter file leads to different simulation results. Unfortunately, the usual versioning systems do not support our advanced requirements regarding usage of metadata and enhanced automatic documentation generation of the evolution of the model.

The automatic generation of documentation has also been the scope of intense academic and industrial research. It has been recognized that the importance of good documentation is critical for user acceptance [16]. Jesus describes in [17] a paradigm for automatic documentation generation based on a set of rules that, applied to the models obtained as result of the analysis and design phases, gives an hypertext network describing those models. On the contrary, our approach has the advantage that the algorithm that is used for the selective backup strategy also delivers the data for the automatic documentation. PLANDoc [18] documents the activity – of planning engineers – by taking as input a trace of the engineer's interaction with a network planning tool. Similarly, in [19] Alida, an approach for fully automatic documentation of data analysis procedures, is presented. During analysis, all operations on data are registered. Subsequently, these data are made explicit in XML graph representation, yielding a suitable base for visual and analytic inspection. The high level approach in Alida – using the information generated during the production process to automatically create the documentation – is similar to ours.

IV. Selective Backup Strategy

The aim of our revision control system is to provide an enhanced backup strategy, termed *selective backup strategy*, such that only the components of the working set that have been modified are considered for backup, see Figure 4. This is an enhancement of the usual incremental backup strategies – such that a particular modification of a file is stored only once – in order to provide the framework to generate the metadata regarding the modifications and accordingly to generate the implicit documentation of the model.

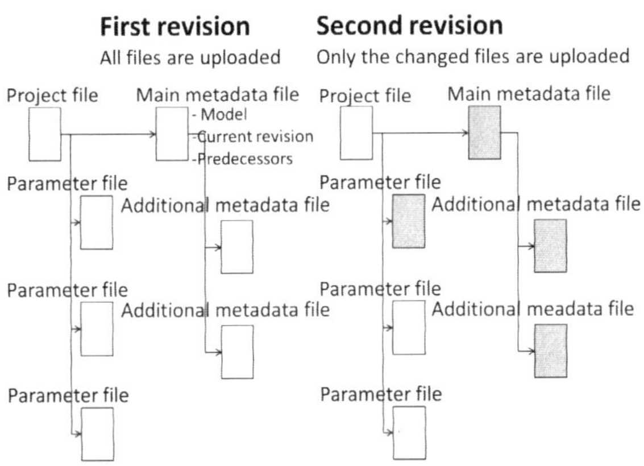

Figure 4. Selective backup strategy. Uploaded files at first and second revision.

A correspondent *selective restore strategy* is used, i.e., the latest versions of all components are downloaded, such that at the end the recent version of the model is assembled out of the historical backups.

A. Backup

Only part of the current working set is uploaded into the data repository, and the uploaded information cannot be altered or removed later. According to our selective backup strategy a) for the first revision: all components are uploaded (see Figure 4 left side); b) for the subsequent revisions: only the components that have been modified are uploaded (see Figure 4 right side).

B. Restore

It will be possible to download all relevant information regarding a specific revision (including parameter files and metadata files). This requires identifying and downloading the full set of components necessary to run a simulation. The required information is stored in the main metadata file during the backup process. Hence, the main metadata file stores information regarding all files that have been uploaded including the unique identification of the uploaded object and the cryptographic hash values of the respective files.

1) Full Restore: The full restore should be applied if files have been lost, or the development of the model is intended to be pursued by other users, etc. The full restore retrieves the whole set of parameter files, such that a simulation can be done on the restored system.

2) Revision Restore: This functionality restores the files corresponding to a (previous) revision and permits to continue the simulation corresponding from that revision. This method enables the tree structure of the revision history. The corresponding information is retrieved from/written to the main metadata file.

C. Flow Configuration

We present now some implementation details. The relevant information for the functioning of the selective backup and the corresponding restore strategy is stored / updated automatically – using XML – in the flow configuration file.

This file stores general information as: a) short name of the model; b) the number of the last revision; c) the object id under which the files belonging to that revision were uploaded; d) additional information in order to identify the project, the revision, etc. A simple example is given in Figure 5. Additionally, general information regarding the revision history

```
<GeneralConfiguration>
   <ModelShortName>cube_1e0_neumann</ModelShortName>
   <LastRevisionNr>25</LastRevisionNr>
   <LastDigitalObjectID>3ccafed6-cf0d-486d-bbe3-
        edff4159f6c5</LastDigitalObjectID>
   <LastNotes>cube_1e0_neumann / Incr. / It.Nr.: 25 /
        Standard Incremental Upload</LastNotes>
</GeneralConfiguration>
```

Figure 5. Excerpt 1 of example configuration file

such as: a) the revision number; b) the object id of the uploaded object; c) the predecessor (parent revision); the total number of files versus the number of files, which have been changed and in consequence uploaded, etc., as given in Figure 6. File and revision specific information are also tracked, such that for each file the revision where the file has been changed and the corresponding cryptographic values are tracked. This way, it is ensured that a specific state of a file is stored only once and that the revision under which this file has been stored can unambiguously be identified, see Figure 7 for an example.

```
<Revision>
<RevisionNr>7</RevisionNr>
<DigitalObjectID>8ce20b42-c15f-427c-ac1a-d575295f5412</
    DigitalObjectID>
<ParentRevisionNr>3</ParentRevisionNr>
<TotalNrFiles>20</TotalNrFiles>
<NrFilesUploaded>1</NrFilesUploaded>
<Notes>cube_1e0_neumann / Incr. / It.Nr.: 2 / For Testing
    Upload and Download</Notes>
</Revision>
```

Figure 6. Excerpt 2 of example configuration file

```
<FileCharacteristics>
   <FileName>cube_1x1x1.gml</FileName>
   <FileLastRevision>43</FileLastRevision>
   <FileHistory>
      <FileRevision>
         <StorageRevisionNr>1</StorageRevisionNr>
         <StorageDigitalObjectID>8aac5970-a366-49ce-a052
            -6c8f82ced85c</Storage\-Digital\-ObjectID>
         <FileSize>1622</FileSize>
         <FileCreationTime>2016-08-18T08:25:33Z</
              FileCreationTime>
         <FileLastAccessTime>2016-08-23T15:59:55Z</
              FileLastAccessTime>
         <FileLastModifiedTime>2016-08-18T08:25:33Z</
              FileLastModifiedTime>
         <FileCryptoIDMD5>66
              a9800e8b02d85001cdd13930b85ea3</
              FileCryptoIDMD5>
         <FileCryptoIDSHA1>5
              c942ba146b41e38262f23ed350e214c757d8803</
              FileCrypto\-IDSHA1>
      </FileRevision>
```

Figure 7. Excerpt 3 of example configuration file

D. Accurate versioning

Based on the architecture of they system, the selective backup strategy corresponds to a centralized revision control system, i.e., there is a central revision number – in our case the modeling step –, such that the version of each file is tied to this central revision number. In contrast, revision control systems like Git [10] are decentralized, i.e., generally, users maintain the versioning of their part, without affecting the overall release number. In our case, this centralized approach is of crucial importance, since small changes in one parameter file can substantially affect the outcome of the simulation. The selective backup strategy enables a paradigm change in the theory and practice of (centralized) revision control systems, it enables an accurate tracking of the changes during each revision on file level including the identification of the effective version of each file. This means especially that in contrast to Git and SVN [11], during revision change, each file is compared to previous versions and either assigned a new version number or – if possible – reassigned a previous one. Such a distinction is not absolutely necessary, for example during software development (main application field for Git and SVN), but it is of crucial importance for pursuing the exact model development.

We illustrate now the selective backup strategy by means of the example as delineated in Table I. Let $\{F_1, F_2, F_3, \ldots, F_n\}$ be files comprising a numerical model and $\{R_1, R_2, R_3, \ldots, R_m\}$ the revisions to adjust the model for a successful simulation of a process. According to the architecture we use, the number of revisions is greater than the number of the files involved, i.e., $n < m$. We number the versions of a specific file continuously in the order they were generated, starting with 1. We notate by an upper index the revision during which the version was generated, i.e., for the file F_1 the version $V_4^{R_6}$ represents the fourth version generated during revision R_6. Not all files are necessarily updated with a revision. For instance, file F_1 is unchanged during revisions R_4, R_5, thus the model keeps using the file version $V_3^{R_3}$. In contrast, file F_2 is modified in each revision. However, during revision R_5, the file is reverted to a previous state such that its version is equal to $V_2^{R_2}$ and, instead of storing a duplicate, the previous copy of the file is used.

	R_1	R_2	R_3	R_4	R_5	R_6	$\ldots$	R_m
F_1	$V_1^{R_1}$	$V_2^{R_2}$	$V_3^{R_3}$	$V_3^{R_3}$	$V_3^{R_3}$	$V_4^{R_6}$	$\ldots$	$V_{m_1}^{R_{m_{k1}}}$
F_2	$V_1^{R_1}$	$V_2^{R_2}$	$V_3^{R_3}$	$V_4^{R_4}$	$V_2^{R_2}$	$V_5^{R_6}$	$\ldots$	$V_{m_2}^{R_{m_{k2}}}$
F_3	$V_1^{R_1}$	$V_1^{R_1}$	$V_2^{R_3}$	$V_3^{R_3}$	$V_1^{R_1}$	$V_4^{R_6}$	$\ldots$	$V_{m_3}^{R_{m_{k3}}}$
$\vdots$	$\vdots$	$\vdots$	$\vdots$	$\vdots$	$\vdots$	$\vdots$		$\vdots$
F_n	$V_1^{R_1}$	$V_1^{R_1}$	$V_1^{R_1}$	$V_1^{R_1}$	$V_2^{R_5}$	$V_2^{R_5}$	$\ldots$	$V_{m_n}^{R_{m_{kn}}}$

Table I. Example for the selective backup strategy.

Using revision systems like Git or SVN, a new version of the file F_2 would be created. Instead, our algorithm, using the selective backup strategy, verifies if a version with new content has been created or the respective content has already been used before.

The use of the selective backup strategy is not restricted to the model development for scientific application, but can be applied everywhere where a centralized revision control system is used. Its intended target are applications, which need to track the effective version of the files, potentially related to revision numbers.

V. The Formal Model

We introduce a mathematical model in order to use the advantages of the rigor of a formal approach over the inaccuracy and the incompleteness of natural languages. We augment the classical pseudo code presentation of the algorithms to a formal, mathematical description and show the consistency and correctness of the backup and restore functionalities.

A. Notations

We use a calligraphic font to denote the index sets. We denote by $\mathscr{C} := \{C_i \mid i \in \mathscr{C}$ and C_i is a component$\}$ the finite set of the components, i.e., the disjunct union of the parameter files and the metadata files. Let S be an arbitrary set. We notate by $\mathscr{P}(S)$ the power set of S, i.e., the set of all subsets of S, including the empty set and S itself. By $card(S)$ we notate the cardinality of S. Let $n \in \mathbb{N}$ and let $f : X \to X$ be a function. Finally, we denote by $f^n : X \to X$ the function obtained by composing f with itself n times, i.e., $f^0 := id_X$ and $f^{n+1} := f^n \circ f$.

B. Introducing Components and Revisions

Some components – at least one, but not necessary all – are modified, then a simulation is performed. We call this state of the components a *revision*. Each revision is backed up to a persistent storage. We have in a natural way a total ordering $<$ on the set of the revisions considering the order they were generated. We denote by $\mathscr{R}$ the ordered set of the revisions, i.e., $\mathscr{R} := \{R_i \mid i \in \mathscr{R}$ and R_i is a revision$\}$. Let $m := card(\mathscr{R})$ be the number of revisions. In order to keep the notations straightforward we set $\mathscr{R} := \{1, 2, 3, ..., m\}$, such that $\forall i \in \mathscr{R} \setminus \{m\} : R_i < R_{i+1}$. We denote by $C_k^{(i)}$ the component C_k having the state at revision R_i, therefore, we denote by $\mathfrak{R}_i := \{C_k^{(i)} \mid k \in \mathscr{C}\}$ the set of the components having the state corresponding to revision R_i.

We denote by $\mathfrak{R}$ the matrix of the evolution of the model, hence $\mathfrak{R} := \{C_k^{(i)} \mid k \in \mathscr{C}$ and $i \in \mathscr{R}\}$. Therefore, $\mathfrak{R}$ contains the history of the content changes of the components during the evolution process of the model.

Let *HASH* be the set of all the hash values. We define the content of a component $C_k \in \mathscr{C}$ corresponding to a revision R_i formally as the function:

Definition V.1 (Content of components) *We set*

$$\begin{aligned} &CONT\colon \mathfrak{R} \to HASH,\\ &C_k^{(i)} \mapsto CONT(C_k^{(i)}) := \text{hash value of } C_k^{(i)}. \end{aligned}$$

Remark V.1 *Let $k \in \mathscr{C}$, let $i, j \in \mathscr{R}$, such that $i \neq j$. In order to track the change process during the evolution process of the model, we are interested only in comparing the content of the same component at different revisions (i.e., the content of $C_k^{(i)}$ versus the content of $C_k^{(j)}$).* ■

Definition V.2 (Origin of a revision) *Let $R, Q \in \mathscr{R}$. We say that Q is the origin of R, notated by $Q = ORIGIN(R)$, if and only if the revision R has been obtained by direct modification of the content of the components having the state at revision Q. For formal reasons we define $ORIGIN(R_1) := R_1$.*

Remark V.2 *Let $R \in \mathscr{R}$ arbitrarily chosen. Then there exists a unique $Q \in \mathscr{R}$, such that $Q = ORIGIN(R)$. This is a direct consequence of the definition above (see Definition V.2).* ■

Let $m = card(\mathscr{R})$, such that $m \geq 1$. We define the predecessor and the successor of a revision formally as:

Definition V.3 (Predecessor of a revision) *We set*

$$\begin{aligned} &PRED\colon \mathscr{R} \to \mathscr{R},\\ &R \mapsto PRED(R) := ORIGIN(R). \end{aligned}$$

Definition V.4 (Successor of a revision) *We set*

$$\begin{aligned} &SUCC\colon \mathscr{R} \to \mathscr{P}(\mathscr{R}),\\ &R \mapsto SUCC(R) := \{Q \in \mathscr{R} \mid R = ORIGIN(Q)\}. \end{aligned}$$

Remark V.3 *$\forall R \in \mathscr{R} \Rightarrow PRED(R)$ is unequivocally determined (see Remark V.2), in contrast, there exists to a revision $R \in \mathscr{R}$ a subset J of $\mathscr{R}$, such that $SUCC(R) = \{R_j \mid j \in J\}$.* ■

Unfortunately, the structure of the evolution of the model is not linear. If for any reason the evolution of the model is in impasse, then the development of the model is not continued from the latest revision, but a previous revision is taken as a starting point. The revision, which led to the impasse is not pursued any more (i.e., it is *abandoned*). On the other side, a revision is *active* if it is part of the successful completion of the model. Formally, we define the status of a revision as follows:

Definition V.5 (Status of a revision) *Let $m := card(\mathscr{R})$ the number of revisions. We set*

$$STATUS\colon \mathscr{R} \to \{active, abandoned\},$$

$$R \mapsto STATUS(R) := \begin{cases} active & \text{if } \exists n \geq 0 : \\ & R = PRED^n(R_m), \\ abandoned & \text{otherwise}. \end{cases}$$

Informally, the predecessor of a component $C_k^{(i)}$ is the component $C_k^{(j)}$, such that R_j was the latest revision where the component C_k has been changed. Formally, we model the successor and predecessor of a component C_k during the revision process as a function.

Let $i \in \mathscr{R}$ and $k \in \mathscr{C}$ arbitrarily chosen. Set $A(i,k) := max\{l \in \mathscr{R} : l < i$ and $CONT(C_k^{(i)}) \neq CONT(C_k^{(l)})\}$ then

Definition V.6 (Predecessor of a component) *We set*

$$PRED\colon \mathfrak{R} \to \mathfrak{R},$$

$$C_k^{(i)} \mapsto PRED(C_k^{(i)}) := \begin{cases} C_k^{(i)} & \text{if } (i = 1), \\ C_k^{(A(i,k))} & \text{if } (i > 1) \\ & \quad \text{and } A(i,k) \text{ exists}, \\ C_k^{(1)} & \text{otherwise}. \end{cases}$$

Definition V.7 (Successor of a component) *We set*

$$\begin{aligned} &SUCC\colon \mathfrak{R} \to \mathscr{P}(\mathfrak{R}),\\ &C_k^{(i)} \mapsto SUCC(C_k^{(i)}) := \{C_k^{(j)} \in \mathfrak{R} \mid C_k^{(i)} = PRED(C_k^{(j)})\}. \end{aligned}$$

Remark V.4 *The predecessor of $C_k^{(i)}$ is uniquely determined. This follows directly from the definition above. In contrast, the successor of $C_k^{(i)}$ is not necessary unique, but there exists a unique $R_j \in \mathscr{R}$, such that $C_k^{(j)} \in SUCC(R_k^{(i)})$ and $STATUS(R_j)$ is active. Similar considerations also hold for revisions.* ■

Proposition V.1 (Existence and uniqueness) *Let $R \in \mathscr{R}$, such that $STATUS(R) = active$. If $SUCC(R) \neq \varnothing$ then there exists a unique $Q \in \mathscr{R}$, such that $Q \in SUCC(R)$ and $STATUS(Q) = active$.*

Hint *The existence and the uniqueness follows directly from the definition of the status of a revision (see Definition V.5) and the uniqueness of the predecessor (see Remark V.3).* ■

We are now able to formulate our strategy to generate the successive revisions.

Lemma V.1 (Linearity) *Let $m = card(\mathscr{R})$. Then there exists a unique subset $\mathscr{R}'$ of $\mathscr{R}$ with $\mathscr{R}' = \{R_1, R_{i_1}, R_{i_2}, R_{i_3}, ..., R_{i_l}, R_m\}$, such that $R_{i_1} \in SUCC(R_1)$ and $\forall i_k : i_1 \leq i_k < i_l \Rightarrow R_{i_{(k+1)}} \in SUCC(R_{i_k})$ and $R_m \in SUCC(R_{i_l})$ and $\forall R \in \mathscr{R}' : STATUS(R) = active$ and $\forall R \in \mathscr{R} \setminus \mathscr{R}' : STATUS(R) = abandoned$.*

Hint *It is a direct consequence of the uniqueness of active successors (see Proposition V.1).* ■

Corollary V.1 *The sequence of the active revisions is linear.* ■

Let $i \in \mathscr{R}$ arbitrarily chosen, a component can have at the revision R_i two statuses *modified* and *preserved*, the value *modified* means that the component has been modified during the revision R_i, in contrast *preserved* means that the component remained unchanged at revision R_i. More formally, we define the function:

Definition V.8 (Status of a component) *We set*

$$STATUS: \mathfrak{R} \rightarrow \{modified,\ preserved\},$$
$$C_k^{(i)} \mapsto STATUS(C_k^{(i)}) := \begin{cases} modified & \text{if } (i=1), \\ modified & \text{if condition 2 holds,} \\ preserved & \text{otherwise.} \end{cases}$$

with condition 2: $\forall j \in \mathscr{R}$ *with* $1 \leq j < i : CONT(C_k^{(i)}) \neq CONT(C_k^{(j)})$.

Remark V.5 *From a formal point of view, all components corresponding to the first revision are considered modified. For the subsequent revisions only the components whose content has been altered are considered modified.* ■

C. Backing up a revision

Based on the values of the *STATUS* function, we define the upload strategy. We are interested to upload only those components, which have been modified since the latest revision and the current state has not been uploaded previously.

Definition V.9 (Upload of a component) *We set*

$$UPLOAD: \mathfrak{R} \rightarrow \{yes,\ no\},$$
$$C_k^{(i)} \mapsto UPLOAD(C_k^{(i)}) := \begin{cases} yes \text{ if condition 1 holds,} \\ no \text{ otherwise.} \end{cases}$$

with condition 1: $STATUS(C_k^{(i)}) = modified.$

Remark V.6 *This means especially that* $C_k^{(i)}$ *will be uploaded if and only if it has been modified and its content is different from the content of all its predecessors.* ■

We will define now a function in order to model the backup process of an entire revision. As we will see, only those components will be backed up at a specific revision R_i, which have been modified at this revision.

Definition V.10 (Backup of a revision) *We set*

$$BACKUP: \mathscr{R} \rightarrow \mathfrak{R},$$
$$R_i \mapsto BACKUP(R_i)$$
$$:= \{C_k^{(i)} \mid k \in \mathscr{C},\ \text{such that } UPLOAD(C_k^{(i)}) = yes\}.$$

Remark V.7 *This means especially that the components that have not been changed at revision* R_i *are not included in the backup of the revision* R_i*, this is the quintessence of the selective backup strategy.* ■

In order to be able to model the download and restore process, we need to do some additional analysis. Those opposite functions cannot be defined straightforwardly as the reverse function of *BACKUP* and *UPLOAD*, since after the restore is fulfilled, all the relevant components must be available, not only those persisted at the corresponding revision.

In order to have all the relevant information for the restore process, we build during the evolution of the model a matrix $(INF_k^{(i)})_{k \in \mathscr{C}, i \in \mathscr{R}}$, such that this matrix contains the information relevant for the download and restore operations. This information contains the content of the components, such that comparisons can be done and relate it to the previous backups.

Hence, the matrix $(INF_k^{(i)})_{k \in \mathscr{C}, i \in \mathscr{R}}$ contains at least the information regarding the revision at which the component was physically stored, such that it can be retrieved from there and additional information regarding the content (hash value) of the components.

Formally, we define $(INF_k^{(i)})_{k \in \mathscr{C}, i \in \mathscr{R}}$ as a function:

Definition V.11 (Component upload meta inf) *We set*

$$INF: \mathscr{R} \times \mathscr{C} \rightarrow \mathscr{R} \times HASH,$$
$$(i,k) \mapsto INF(i,k) := (j,v)$$
$$\text{if } \left(C_k^{(i)} \in BACKUP(R_j) \text{ and } CONT(C_k^{(i)}) = v\right).$$

Remark V.8 *This means especially that a component* $C_k^{(i)}$ *having the hash value = v has been backed up at revision* R_j *and* $j \in \mathscr{R}$ *is the lowest index number, such that* $CONT(C_k^{(i)}) = CONT(C_k^{(j)})$. ■

D. Restoring a revision

We define now the opposite function to *UPLOAD* as follows:

Definition V.12 (Download of a component) *We set*

$$DOWNLOAD: \mathfrak{R} \rightarrow \mathfrak{R},$$
$$C_k^{(i)} \mapsto DOWNLOAD(C_k^{(i)}) := C_k^{(j)}$$
$$\text{if } (UPLOAD(C_k^{(j)}) = yes$$
$$\text{and } CONT(C_k^{(j)}) = CONT(C_k^{(i)})).$$

Remark V.9 $DOWNLOAD(C_k^{(i)}) = C_k^{(j)}$ *means especially that the component* C_k *was uploaded at the revision* R_j. ■

We define the restore function having the opposite functionality to the backup function. The main difference to the usual restore strategy is that restoring the components backed up at revision R_i is not enough, since usually only a subset of the components are backed up at a specific revision. To circumvent this impediment, the revisions at which those components have been physically uploaded are identified and are restored from those locations. When the restore operation is completed, then, the complete set of components necessary for a simulation is available.

Formally as a function:

Definition V.13 (Restore of a revision) *We set*

$$RESTORE: \mathscr{R} \rightarrow \mathscr{P}(\mathfrak{R}),$$
$$R_i \mapsto RESTORE(R_i) :=$$
$$\{C_k^{(j)} \mid k \in \mathscr{C},\ \text{such that } DOWNLOAD(C_k^{(i)}) = C_k^{(j)}\}.$$

Remark V.10 *This means especially that the latest version of the components are restored.* ■

We are now able to formulate the Lemma regarding the uniqueness of the upload, i.e., a new state of a component C_k during the revision process is backed up only once.

Lemma V.2 (Uniqueness of the upload) *Let* $k \in \mathscr{C}$ *and* $v \in HASH$ *be arbitrarily chosen. If* $\exists j \in \mathscr{R} : CONT(C_k^{(j)}) = v$ *then there exists a unique* $i \in \mathscr{R}$*, such that* $UPLOAD(C_k^{(i)}) = yes$ *and* $CONT(C_k^{(i)}) = v$.

Hint *Set* $i := min\{l \in \mathscr{R} \mid CONT(C_k^{(l)}) = v\}$*. Then according to the definition of the status of a component (see Definition V.8)* $STATUS(C_k^{(l)}) = modified$ *holds true. The result follows from the definition of the upload of the components (see Definition V.9).* ■

We can formulate now the main Lemma, which states that we have no spurious downloads.

Lemma V.3 (Accuracy and completeness) *Let* $k \in \mathscr{C}$ *be arbitrarily chosen. We have:*

$$\begin{aligned} &a)\forall i,j \in \mathscr{R} : DOWNLOAD(C_k^{(i)}) = C_k^{(j)} \\ &\quad \Rightarrow \big(UPLOAD(C_k^{(j)}) = yes \\ &\qquad and\ CONT(C_k^{(j)}) = CONT(C_k^{(i)})\big), \\ &b)\forall i \in \mathscr{R}\ \exists j \in \mathscr{R} : (j \leq i), \\ &\qquad such\ that\ C_k^{(j)} \in DOWNLOAD(C_k^{(i)}). \end{aligned}$$

Remark V.11 *The property in a) means that we have no false downloads, i.e., each downloaded component has been uploaded some time ago. It follows from the definition of the download of a component (see Definition V.12). The property in b) means especially that the download is complete, i.e., the latest version of each component is downloaded. It is a direct consequence of the uniqueness of the upload (see Lemma V.2).* ■

Corollary V.2 (Complementarity) *The two functions RESTORE and BACKUP are complementary, i.e.,*

$$\begin{aligned} &\forall k \in \mathscr{C}, \forall i \in \mathscr{R} : \left(C_k^{(i)} \in RESTORE(R_i)\right) \\ &\Leftrightarrow (\exists j \in \mathscr{R} : C_k^{(j)} \in BACKUP(R_j) \\ &\qquad and\ CONT(C_k^{(i)}) = CONT(C_k^{(j)})). \end{aligned}$$

■

VI. Implementation and Application to UFZ

We developed and tested AGEDRE (**A**utomatic **GE**neration of **D**ocumentation using **RE**vision control) as a prototype at UFZ and validated our theoretical concepts. We used a client / server environment at the ZIH of the Technische Universität Dresden, implementing our client in Java from scratch. On the server side, we used KIT DM [8] as the repository.

AGEDRE is a command line utility, offering the basic functionality required for a revision control system and a sophisticated error handling to deal with the complexity of the selective backup strategy on the client side and of KIT DM on the server side. In order to persist the data, AGEDRE offers two primitives, `FullUpload` as a primitive for a complete upload of all data related to a project and `Upload` as a selective backup strategy to store only modified files. Accordingly, the opposite primitives to retrieve the data are `Download`, `DownloadRevision` and `DownloadFile`. The primitive `Download` is only formally the counterpart of `Upload`, it retrieves the latest version of each file, which has been uploaded, i.e., the files of the latest revision. As mentioned, the user needs the latest version of all parameter and metadata files in order to be able to perform the simulation. In contrast, the primitive `DownloadRevision` is used to continue the modeling process from an older revision, it restores the files into the working directory, thus overwriting the latest revision. The latest revision is backed up to the file system, in order to avoid loss of data in case of inadvertent use of this primitive. The primitive `DownloadFile` has been introduced in order to restore the latest backed up version of a file, if it has been accidentally deleted or has been corrupted.

The project file (see Figure 8 for an example) is the leading file regarding the configuration of a simulation. It contains the names of the additional parameter files (namely `cube_1x1x1_hex_1e0.vtu` and `cube_1x1x1.gml`) and the configuration parameters for the simulation. Hence, each project file corresponds to a model

```
<OpenGeoSysProject>
    <mesh>cube_1x1x1_hex_1e0.vtu</mesh>
    <geometry>cube_1x1x1.gml</geometry>

    <processes>
        <process>
            <name>GW23</name>
            <type>GROUNDWATER_FLOW</type>
            <process_variable>pressure</process_variable>
            <hydraulic_conductivity>K</hydraulic_conductivity
            >
            <linear_solver>
                <lis>-i cg -p jacobi -tol 1e-16 -maxiter 10000
                    </lis>
                <eigen>
                    <solver_type>CG</solver_type>
                    <precon_type>jacobi</precon_type>
                    <max_iteration_step>10000</
                        max_iteration_step>
                    <error_tolerance>1e-16</error_tolerance>
```

Figure 8. Excerpt of example project file `cube_1e0_neumann.prj`

```
<points>
    <point id="0" x="0" y="0" z="0"/>
    <point id="1" x="0" y="0" z="1"/>
    <point id="2" x="0" y="1" z="1"/>
    <point id="3" x="0" y="1" z="0"/>
</points>

<surfaces>
    <surface id="0" name="left">
        <element p1="0" p2="1" p3="2"/>
        <element p1="0" p2="3" p3="2"/>
    </surface>
    <surface id="1" name="right">
        <element p1="4" p2="6" p3="5"/>
        <element p1="4" p2="6" p3="7"/>
    </surface>
```

Figure 9. Excerpt of example geometry file `cube_1x1x1.gml`

and accordingly, the development of the model comprises modifications of the project file and the corresponding parameter files.

When the primitive `Upload` is called for a project file for the first time, the corresponding dynamic flow configuration file is initialized. For an example of a flow configuration file, see the excerpts in Figures 5–7. The revision number is set to one and the cryptographic MD5 and SHA-1 hashes of each file are calculated and stored in the dynamic flow configuration file. While SHA-1 is practically collision free and it is also used by Git for integrity purposes [20], alternatively, SHA-512 could be used for enhanced security [21] [22]. For subsequent uses of the `Upload`-primitive, the cryptographic values of the parameter and metadata files are compared to the respective values stored – for previous revisions – in the flow configuration file. If the cryptographic values of file F is different of all the previous cryptographical values of file F, then the content of F is considered modified and it is backed up within the current revision. Otherwise, F is not part of the current revision. A corresponding entry is made in the dynamic flow configuration file regarding the revision under which the file – having the given content – has been backed up. Hence, the file `cube_1x1x1.gml` has the cryptographic values stored at revision 1 (see Figure 7). If the file `cube_1x1x1.gml` has, for example, not been altered at revision 2 then no similar entry is performed in the dynamic flow configuration file.

When starting the primitive `Download` – i.e., downloading the files corresponding to the latest revision – then the relevant information regarding the physical storage place of the latest version of each file – i.e., <StorageDigitalObjectID> – is retrieved from the dynamic flow configuration file, by considering the latest entry for each file (see Figure 7). Hence, all the related files can be accessed on the repository and retrieved accordingly.

The use case at UFZ is not designed for concurrent use, where users are confronted with conflicts and their resolution, as it is the case for the software development environment. In contrast, at UFZ simultaneous work is strictly related to the model development process. The model is developed in steps, small changes in a few parameter files can have tremendous impact on the model. Hence, members of a team can download the latest revision, can work simultaneously improving the next step, can compare the changes of the parameter files and the simulation results, but eventually, the members of the team have to agree on the best outcome for the next step, thus uploading it as the next revision. Alternatively, they can agree on abandoning the current revision by continuing the model development from an older revision. The team members have to download the revision, they agreed upon, and continue developing the model from there.

In addition to the dynamic flow configuration file – upon whose content they do not have direct influence – users can define and set up their own metadata files. These metadata files can contain additional – high-level or aggregated – information regarding the model development and can be used for additional documentation or for identifying model or revision characteristics. The metadata files are also very important to enable the differentiated security policy at UFZ, such that users can access the metadata files – for example by using ElasticSearch [12] – if they have the appropriate rights on the file system. In contrast, users can access simulation data (parameter files) according to their rights on the repository system KIT DM. Thus, metadata for projects is accessible for all members within the UFZ, while sensible data can only be accessed by a small number of researchers related to the project. All files of the examples can be found at [23].

VII. Conclusion and Future Work

Irrespective of the fact that creating documentation is a very challenging task and that writing documentation is considered by most of the developers as an extra-effort rather than a commendation, it is rather impossible providing precise, exact, accurate, uniform and consistent documentation for developers and users requirements. Therefore, formalized automated documentation methods are necessary to develop.

The main advantage of the automatic generation of the documentation of the modeling process is the accuracy of the documentation, since there is no discrepancy between the actual generation of the model (developer's perspective) and the corresponding documentation (user's perspective). This way, we have circumvented the dilemma of writing exact manual documentation and have contributed to the paradigm change towards design and implementation of automatic documentation assuring accuracy and exactness.

Since our formal model is independent of the use case at UFZ, our approach has a generic character and it can be applied to all domains where numerical models are developed.

Currently, there is little comfort for the user who employs the framework. In the current implementation, the executable is started in the command line, also the flow configuration file, which contains the documentation for tracking the evolution of the model is in XML-format. Accordingly, additional research is necessary to define and implement corresponding GUI to assure the expected readability of the document by extracting and visualizing the appropriate information. In order to build meaningful user interfaces, an intense dialog between developers and users is essential [24].

Additionally, further research is necessary to generate a high level form documentation of the changes in the parameter files. For example, when running stochastic simulations (e.g. Monte Carlo approach [25]) if parameters are changed in many places, then appropriate mechanism should be set up assuring the consistency of the changes and the appropriate documentation.

We think that by studying the automatically generated documentation regarding the development of the modeling workflows – especially those steps, which did not lead to a successful completion of the simulation – there is an increased possibility of knowledge extraction (by using machine learning strategies or similar techniques), such that the generation of the modeling workflows can be dramatically improved and the number of modeling steps can be considerably reduced.

Acknowledgment

This work was supported in parts by the German Federal Ministry of Education and Research (BMBF, 01IS14014A-D) by funding the competence center for Big Data "ScaDS Dresden/Leipzig". This work was also supported in parts by the German Research Foundation (DFG) via the MASi project (NA 711/9-1, STO 397/4-1). We are also thankful to Dr. Nico Hoffmann (Technische Universität Dresden) for his valuable advices and comments during the developing and writing process.

REFERENCES

[1] Intergovernmental Panel on Climate Change, Climate Change 2014 – Impacts, Adaptation and Vulnerability: Regional Aspects. Cambridge University Press, 2014.

[2] C. J. Vörösmarty et al., "Global threats to human water security and river biodiversity," Nature, vol. 467, 2010, pp. 555–561.

[3] J. Grundmann, N. Schütze, G. H. Schmitz, and S. Al-Shaqsi, "Towards an integrated arid zone water management using simulation-based optimisation," Environ Earth Sci, vol. 65, no. 5, 2012, pp. 1381–1394.

[4] H. Hötzl, P. Möller, and E. Rosenthal, The Water of the Jordan Valley. Springer, 2009.

[5] M. Walther, J.-O. Delfs, J. Grundmann, O. Kolditz, and R. Liedl, "Saltwater intrusion modeling: Verification and application to an agricultural coastal arid region in Oman," Journal of Computational and Applied Mathematics, vol. 236, no. 18, 2012, pp. 4798–4809, fEMTEC 2011: 3rd International Conference on Computational Methods in Engineering and Science, May 9–13, 2011. [Online]. Available: http://www.sciencedirect.com/science/article/pii/S0377042712000659

[6] C. Liu, Q. Wang, C. Zou, Y. Hayashi, and T. Yasunari, "Recent trends in nitrogen flows with urbanization in the shanghai megacity and the effects on the water environment," Environmental Science and Pollution Research, vol. 22, no. 5, Mar 2015, pp. 3431–3440. [Online]. Available: https://doi.org/10.1007/s11356-014-3825-4

[7] Helmholtz Centre for Environmental Research – UFZ, "Homepage of Helmholtz Centre for Environmental Research," https://www.ufz.de/index.php?en=34216, retrieved: July 2017.

[8] Karlsruhe Institute of Technology – KIT, "KIT Data Manager," http://datamanager.kit.edu/index.php/kit-data-manager, retrieved: July 2017.

[9] R. Grunzke et al., "Towards a metadata-driven multi-community research data management service," PeerJ PrePrints, vol. 5, 2017, p. e2831. [Online]. Available: https://doi.org/10.7287/peerj.preprints.2831v1

[10] S. Chacon and B. Straub, Git and Other Systems. Berkeley, CA: Apress, 2014, pp. 307–356. [Online]. Available: http://dx.doi.org/10.1007/978-1-4842-0076-6_9

[11] C. M. Pilato, B. Collins-Sussman, and B. W. Fitzpatrick, Version control with subversion - the standard in open source version control. O'Reilly, 2008, retrieved: July 2017. [Online]. Available: http://www.oreilly.de/catalog/9780596510336/index.html

[12] C. Gormley and Z. Tong, Elasticsearch: The Definitive Guide, 1st ed. O'Reilly Media, Inc., 2015.

[13] W. F. Tichy, "Rcs – a system for version control," Software: Practice and Experience, vol. 15, no. 7, 1985, pp. 637–654. [Online]. Available: http://dx.doi.org/10.1002/spe.4380150703

[14] A. Löh, W. Swierstra, and D. Leijen, "A Principled Approach to Version Control," http://citeseerx.ist.psu.edu/viewdoc/summary?doi=10.1.1.108.8649, retrieved: July 2017.

[15] E. Sink, Version Control by Example, 1st ed. PYOW Sports Marketing, 2011.

[16] C. L. Paris, Automatic documentation generation: Including examples. Berlin, Heidelberg: Springer Berlin Heidelberg, 1995, pp. 12–25. [Online]. Available: http://dx.doi.org/10.1007/BFb0034794

[17] R. Swan and J. Allan, "Automatic generation of overview timelines," in Proceedings of the 23rd Annual International ACM SIGIR Conference on Research and Development in Information Retrieval, ser. SIGIR '00. New York, NY, USA: ACM, 2000, pp. 49–56. [Online]. Available: http://doi.acm.org/10.1145/345508.345546

[18] K. McKeown, K. Kukich, and J. Shaw, "Practical issues in automatic documentation generation," in Proceedings of the Fourth Conference on Applied Natural Language Processing, ser. ANLC '94. Stroudsburg, PA, USA: Association for Computational Linguistics, 1994, pp. 7–14. [Online]. Available: http://dx.doi.org/10.3115/974358.974361

[19] B. Möller, O. Greß, and S. Posch, "Knowing what happened - automatic documentation of image analysis processes," in Computer Vision Systems - 8th International Conference, ICVS 2011, Sophia Antipolis, France, September 20-22, 2011. Proceedings, 2011, pp. 1–10. [Online]. Available: https://doi.org/10.1007/978-3-642-23968-7_1

[20] M. Stevens, E. Bursztein, P. Karpman, A. Albertini, and Y. Markov, "The first collision for full sha-1," Cryptology ePrint Archive, Report 2017/190, 2017, http://eprint.iacr.org/2017/190.

[21] C. Dobraunig, M. Eichlseder, and F. Mendel, Analysis of SHA-512/224 and SHA-512/256. Berlin, Heidelberg: Springer Berlin Heidelberg, 2015, pp. 612–630. [Online]. Available: https://doi.org/10.1007/978-3-662-48800-3_25

[22] M. Szydlo and Y. L. Yin, Collision-Resistant Usage of MD5 and SHA-1 Via Message Preprocessing. Berlin, Heidelberg: Springer Berlin Heidelberg, 2006, pp. 99–114. [Online]. Available: https://doi.org/10.1007/11605805_7

[23] D. Y. Naumov et al., "ufz/ogs-data: Initial zenodo release," Aug. 2017. [Online]. Available: https://doi.org/10.5281/zenodo.840660

[24] C. Helbig, L. Bilke, H.-S. Bauer, M. Böttinger, and O. Kolditz, "Meva - an interactive visualization application for validation of multifaceted meteorological data with multiple 3d devices," PLOS ONE, vol. 10, no. 4, 04 2015, pp. 1–24. [Online]. Available: https://doi.org/10.1371/journal.pone.0123811

[25] E. Jang et al., "Identifying the influential aquifer heterogeneity factor on nitrate reduction processes by numerical simulation," Advances in Water Resources, vol. 99, no. Complete, 2017, pp. 38–52.

The Blockchain-based Internet of Things Development: Initiatives and Challenges

Sergio F. T. de O. Mendonca[1,2], Joao F. da Silva Junior[1] and Fernanda M. R. de Alencar[1]
[1]Departamento de Eletrônica e Sistemas, Universidade Federal de Pernambuco, Recife, Brazil
[2]Unidade Acadêmica de Garanhuns, Universidade Federal Rural de Pernambuco, Garanhuns, Brazil
e-mail: sergio.mendonca@ufpe.br, joao.fsilva2@ufpe.br, fmra@ufpe.br

Abstract—**The Internet was originally built based on trust. After several leaks of information, new risks and challenges are introduced. In recent years, we have used even more new devices based on the Internet. Among the main concerns reported on the literature, we need some special attention to trust, protection of data and privacy. In this scenario, a new paradigm has emerged, some information security based on transparency instead of current models of information security on closed and obscure approaches. Some initiatives have been emerging with Blockchain methods and technologies. In this paper, we propose to build an initial view of the model, as a result of our preliminary investigations, described in the Methodology as systematic mapping. The initial results allowed the perception of the initial requirements involved and open problems. We report on some frameworks, models, approaches, and other Blockchain-based Internet of Things (IoT) initiatives. We also evaluate the adherence of each paper to ten IoT key requirements. This work contributes to the new and still developing body of knowledge in the areas of security, privacy and trust. Our findings are useful not only for future studies in the Academy but also for companies from various sectors present in the Internet ecosystem. They can benefit from the consolidated knowledge and use it to guide the definition of their development processes geared to the new paradigms of the IoT.**

Keywords—Blockchain; Internet of Things; IoT; Ontology; Privacy; Security.

I. INTRODUCTION

The Internet of Things (IoT) is an application domain that integrates different technological and social fields. Despite the diversity of research on IoT, its definition remains fuzzy [1]. With the increase in demand and production of the new devices based on the IoT paradigms, trust and privacy can be even harder for the engineering field. Security flaws in the IoT might lead, for instance, to malicious attacks on secrecy and authentication, silent attacks on service integrity, or attacks on network availability, such as the Denial of Service (DoS). However, privacy and anonymity, on the other hand, are no less severe issues and must be integrated into the design to give users control over their privacy.

In this respect, a new approach has arisen in the security and transparency of information, which takes the place of current models of information security and is based on closed and obscure approaches. Some initiatives have come up with Blockchain methods and technologies [2].

Among the problems of building devices (or embedded systems) based on the IoT paradigm, we can highlight the absence of formalism, language or modeling architecture that enables the unified development and integration among the various disciplines of the Semantic Web Stack. We are faced with certain difficulties; in addition to complexity and scalability, there are also time latency problems (currently 10 minutes in the Bitcoin network) and the number of confirmations that must be required for transactions, contradicting IoT conceptions regarding real-time processing [1]. The transactions in the Bitcoin network are visible to all nodes. That presents some difficulties (i.e., transactions carried out only for a few nodes of the network), when we need devices for controlled environments [3].

In this context, it is fundamental to comprehend how the traditional software development could be adapted or evolved to support those new Blockchain-based IoT requirements. What consolidated knowledge is, which factors influence on device development are.

To achieve the goal of this study, we are conducting a systematic mapping of critical factors in IoT paradigms-based, embedded systems building. In this research, we are looking for answers to the following questions: i) has Blockchain-based IoT been constructed to stand on development processes? Also, ii) which Blockchain-based IoTs characteristics, principles or requirements have been considered in Blockchain-based IoT development processes? These research questions will be answered in Section IV.

The main objective of this research is to understand Blockchain-based IoT domains as well as best practices in the field, and to present the latest research about the construction of devices (or things). In addition, this effort contributes to the very new and still growing knowledge regarding security, privacy and trust (areas still very undeveloped) of the IoT. This study is useful not only for future studies in academia but also for companies from various sectors operating in the Internet ecosystem. These companies can benefit from the consolidated knowledge and use it to guide the definition of their development processes geared to the new paradigms of the IoT.

The remainder of this paper is organized as follows. In Section II, a briefing about the state of the art is presented. Section III presents the planning, conduction, and reporting of the Systematic Mapping. Section IV presents the preliminary studies results. Section V presents current trends and challenges; and in Section VI, conclusions and future work are discussed.

II. State of the Art

In this section, we present initial concepts for the understanding of this paper. The IoT and the Blockchain and its ontology overviews are briefly presented below.

A. *The Internet of Things overview*

The IoT consists of a global network of billions of uniquely identifiable and addressable objects, embedded with sensors, actuators, and controllers. Those are connected to the Internet in wireless mode [4]. The IoT is a "dynamic global network infrastructure that can self-configure using standards and using interoperability protocols where things (physical and virtual) have identities, attributes, and uniqueness, feature intelligent interfaces, and it can be seamlessly integrated into the network" [2].

The IEEE presents IoT as an application domain that incorporates different technological and social fields. IEEE described the phrase Internet of Thing as a network of items each embedded with sensors which are connected to the Internet [5]. It is a (non-approved) description of the Internet of Things. However, this statement is treating just one of the physical aspects of Internet of Things [6].

B. *The Blockchain overview*

The Blockchain is a universal digital ledger that works at the core of decentralized financial systems, such as Bitcoin and many other decentralized systems. The blockchain keeps a record of all transaction made by each participant. Cryptography is used to verify operations and keep information on the blockchain private. Several participants verify each transaction, providing highly redundant verification and are rewarded for the computational work required.

The Blockchain technology has the ability to make the organizations that use it transparent, democratic, decentralized, secure, and efficient. The Blockchain can be used to access to financial services, it presents the primary advantages of the traditional correspondent banking system: i) consistent process standards; ii) more long-range global reconnaissance.

C. *The Blockchain Ontology*

A first effort to standardize this technology is the BLONDIE (Blockchain Ontology with Dynamic Extensibility) ontology. This OWL ontology can be used to express in RDF different fields of the structures of Ethereum or Bitcoin. It can also be extended to cover other Blockchain technologies. In addition, BLONDIE being OWL has the ability to make explicit knowledge available [3].

Ugarte [3] says that an ideal scenario would be that everyone would use only the original Bitcoin technology, or forks with minimum modifications. The protocol itself is already standardized and well-defined, but since Bitcoin presents many limitations and was not designed for other functionalities besides financial transactions, it is not a realistic scenario.

Currently, the interoperability between Blockchain technologies is one of the most discussed issues in the Blockchain world and this is where we must focus our efforts on. The devices would be able to communicate to each other directly to update software, manage bugs, and monitor energy usage.

III. Methodology

The research methodology was divided into four steps. In this paper, we will present only Step #2 (Systematic Mapping) of this Doctoral research, as shown in Fig. 1, and described in detail as follows.

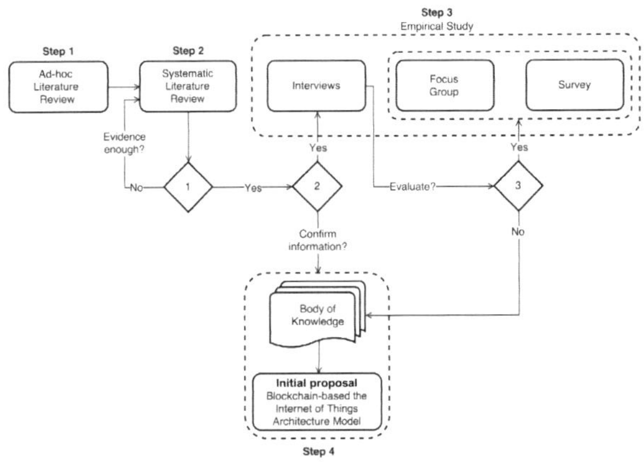

Figure 1. Scientific methodology steps. Adapted from [7].

A. *Step 2—Systematic Mapping*

The systematic mapping study was deemed warranted after an initial foray into the discussed topic. Before starting a systematic mapping, we came across a very broad question. To obtain an overview of this research topic and identify evidence to provide the best positions on the issues of research, we have established a systematic mapping [8],], as shown a summarization in Fig. 2. The authors still saying that the systematic mapping allows:

- Mapping the evidence of a domain at a high level of granularity;
- The identification of clusters and void of evidence to enable future systematic reviews; and
- Discover areas to conduct new primary studies.

B. *Blockchain-based Internet of Things: a Systematic Mapping*

1) Protocol: We have conducted this study based on the conscious guidelines and procedures. This protocol specifies the basis for the study research questions, search strategy, selection criteria, and data extraction and synthesis. The protocol was mainly developed by one of the researchers and reviewed by two of the senior researchers aiming to mitigate any bias [8].

Search string. The standard version of search string was designed to include variations and synonym terms related to

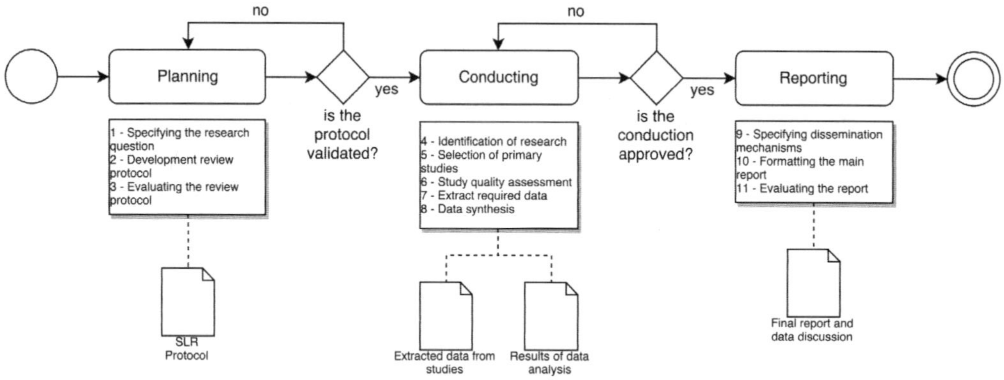

Figure 2. Systematic Literature Mapping. Adapted from [8]

"Internet of Things", "Blockchain" and their "Development Processes".

(((model OR framework OR architecture OR process OR method OR approach OR design OR procedure) AND (development)) AND ((internet of things OR iot OR internet of everything OR web of things OR smarter planet))) AND (blockchain)

Search strategy. We selected the following search engines: ACM Digital Library, IEEE Xplorer, ISI Web of Science Science Direct, Scopus, Engineering Village. We have considered opinion of experts, gray literature, and related works of the included studies.

Inclusion and exclusion criteria. The studies were selected according to the inclusion and exclusion criteria described below. In order to select suitable studies to answer our research questions, we established the following Inclusion (IC) and Exclusion Criteria (EC):

- IC_1. The study discusses Blockchain-based IoT development processes.
- IC_2. The study addresses Blockchain-based IoT characteristics, requirements, problems or activities related to Blockchain-based IoT development processes.
- EC_1. The study is not related to Blockchain-based IoT.
- EC_2. The study does not discuss any Blockchain-based IoT development process.
- EC_3. The complete study is not available.

2) *Conduction of the Research:* Once the protocol had been agreed, the review review itself can be initialized. However, as noted previously, researchers were expected to try each of the steps described in this section when they construct their research protocol [8].

The author [9] recommends the adoption of effective criteria for inclusion and exclusion of relevant studies to answer the research questions. Some of the criteria are essential for the collection of a rigorous and defensible set of data for evaluation.

Therefore, we applied the inclusion and exclusion criteria involved in the analysis of the parameters 1) title and keywords check out, it was applied one 2) summary of the analysis in the work identified in the previous phase, if there are questions, reading the introduction and conclusion; and 3) the complete reading of the paper.

IV. Preliminary Studies Results

The results are reported in the systematic mapping as follows.

Table I shows the selection of studies by database (source studies). The initial search resulted in 25 works. In the first analysis, we excluded 2 items, 23 papers remaining. In the second selection, applying the criteria of inclusion and exclusion in the reading of the summary, the number of articles was reduced to 21. Upon complete reading of each of the other items, two papers, which had the same content or similar (duplicate), were found, resulting in their exclusion, leaving at the end 17 papers with strong and relevant indications to the area of investigation.

TABLE I. PRIMARY STUDIES INCLUEDED FOR SEARCH STRATEGY.

Source Studies	Retrieved	Duplicated	First Phase	Second Phase	Included
ACM Digital Library	6	-	6	5	5
IEEE Xplore	1	1	-	-	-
ISI Web of Science	1	1	-	-	-
Science Direct	3	-	1	-	-
Engineering Village	2	-	2	2	2
Manually	5	-	5	5	4
Snowballing	7	-	7	7	6
Total	25	2	21	19	17

Based on the analysis of the 17 primary studies included, we have addressed the Research Questions (RQ). In this section, we will be addressing these Questions.

RQ_1. Has Blockchain-based IoT been constructed to stand on development processes?

We have identified 17 initiatives of Blockchain-based IoT development as shown the Table I. Three of these initiatives are classified by the authors as Frameworks, four as Models, six as Approaches, and four as Other Initiatives. For the other studies, we created the classification Other Initiatives to Blockchain-based IoT Development, which includes single initiative of methodology, description, [re]engineering, ontology, or simulation platform for Blockchain-based IoT.

TABLE II. LIST OF INCLUDED PRIMARY STUDIES.

Study ID	Included Study	Source
S1	[10]	ACM
S2	[11]	ACM
S3	[12]	ACM
S4	[13]	ACM
S5	[6]	IEEE
S6	[14]	IEEE
S7	[15]	Snowballing
S8	[4]	Manually
S9	[16]	Snowballing
S10	[17]	Manually
S11	[5]	Manually
S12	[18]	Manually
S13	[19]	Manually
S14	[20]	Snowballing
S15	[21]	Snowballing
S16	[22]	Snowballing
S17	[23]	Snowballing

RQ_2. Which Blockchain-based IoT's characteristics, principles or requirements have been considered in Blockchain-based IoT development processes?

We reported on some frameworks, models, approaches, and other Blockchain-based IoT initiatives that reflect adherence to well-known development processes to build an initial Body of Knowledge. We detected key requirements in the IoT and we determined whether they were functional and non-functional requirements. Authors of the primary studies classified their works as follows: four as Frameworks, four as Models, two as Methods, and three as Approaches. We classified four papers as Other Initiatives addressed in initial descriptions or superficial studies.

Uckelmann, Harrison and Michahelles described key requirements (kR) that need to be considered in the IoT, as seen in Table III.

We summarized the domain type: six as generic, eight as specific, and three as non-specific. We then identified essential characteristics, processes, modeling phases, tasks and products. Most of these works (16) emphasized domain analysis, but just seven these presented a domain design, into three discussed architecture design and only two presented a detailed and comprehensive design. These papers addressed the product modeling: ten as a domain model, five as an architectural model, and one as agent model. The community still has no better support for the design, architecture, integration and testing processes to build Blockchain-based IoT.

Considering the IoT key requirements by [19], Table III depicts 100% of all studies addressed the kR1 (meet key societal needs for the IoT including open governance, security, privacy and trustworthiness). This was followed by 70.6% which addressed both kR2 (bridge the gap between B2B, business-to-consumer (B2C) and machine-to-machine (M2M) requirements through a generic and open IoT infrastructure) and kR3 (design an open, scalable, flexible and sustainable infrastructure for the IoT). Requirement kR4 (develop migration paths for disruptive technological developments to the IoT) is covered by 64.7% and kR5 (excite and enable businesses and people to contribute to the IoT) is covered by 58.8%, followed by 52.9% for both kR6 (enable businesses across different industries to develop high added value products and services) and kR8 (provide an open solution for sharing costs, benefits and revenue generation in the IoT). The other IoT key requirements did not achieve at least 50%.

We have also evaluated the adherence of each paper. In this analysis, the papers are evaluated against the ten IoT key requirements described in Table III. We highlight the importance of the studies S1, S8, S14, S15 and S16. They discuss some main activities or artifacts or modeling of design, but they did not explicitly address these activities or artifacts or modeling design in their propositions. However, they did mention some essential IoT characteristics and processes. On the other hand, we considered that studies S2, S3, S4, S5, S6, S7, S9, S10, S11, S12, S13 and S17 covered 50% or less and therefore did not explicitly address all of the IoT fundamental processes.

V. CURRENT TRENDS AND CHALLENGES

The main trends and challenges discussed by the authors of the included papers about Blockchain-based IoT are described in this section.

One author [4] says that security flaws in the IoT may lead, for instance, to malicious attacks on secrecy and authentication, silent attacks on service integrity, or attacks on network availability such as the DoS. Privacy and anonymity, on the other hand, are no less serious issues. IoT devices are natural "collectors and distributors of information", so they represent a unique challenge to individual privacy.

In particular, the challenges include the ubiquitous interaction of users with smart objects and groups of things, as well as the uncontrolled concentration of such data on platforms lacking in transparency, perhaps systematically exposing users to several threats, such as identification, localization, monitoring, tracking, surveillance, manipulation, profiling, targeted advertising, data linkage, and even social engineering.

The authors in [16] investigated which are the main factors affecting the levels of integrity, anonymity, and adaptability of the blockchain. They should further analyze what are the security properties provided by the Proof of Work, which up to now is one of the key factors allowing for the achievement of distributed consensus.

The Ethereum platform supports a feature to encode rules or scripts for processing transactions through smart contracts. The authors in [10] investigated the security of running smart contracts based on Ethereum in an open distributed network. According to the authors [10][11]there are several new security problems. These bugs suggest subtle gaps in the understanding of the distributed semantics of the underlying platform. Those authors propose ways to enhance the operational semantics to make contracts less vulnerable through a symbolic execution tool called Oyente.

Blockchain has recently attracted the interest of stakeholders from the most varied sectors, from finance and health-care to utilities, real estate, and the government sector. That explosion

TABLE III. IoT KEY REQUIREMENTS ADHERENCE OF THE INCLUDED STUDIES.

Key Requirements	Frameworks				Models				Methods		Approaches			Other Initiatives				%
	S2	S14	S15	S16	S1	S5	S6	S11	S4	S7	S3	S9	S10	S17	S8	S12	S13	
1. Meet key societal needs for the Internet of Things including open governance, security, privacy and trustworthiness.	x	x	x	x	x	x	x	x	x	x	x	x	x	x	x	x	x	100,0
2. Bridge the gap between B2B, business-to-consumer (B2C) and machine-to-machine (M2M) requirements through a generic and open Internet of Things infrastructure.	x	x	x	x	x		x	x	x	x			x	x	x			70,6
3. Design an open, scalable, flexible and sustainable infrastructure for the Internet of Things.		x	x	x	x	x		x		x	x	x	x		x		x	70,6
4. Develop migration paths for disruptive technological developments to the Internet of Things.		x	x	x	x		x	x	x	x		x		x			x	64,7
5. Excite and enable businesses and people to contribute to the Internet of Things.	x	x	x	x	x	x					x		x		x		x	58,8
6. Enable businesses across different industries to develop high added value products and services.		x	x	x		x	x	x	x						x	x		52,9
7. Encourage new market entrants, such as third party service and information providers, to enter the Internet of Things.		x	x	x					x			x						29,4
8. Provide an open solution for sharing costs, benefits and revenue generation in the Internet of Things.	x	x			x	x	x			x			x	x	x			52,9
9. Public initiatives to support the usage of the Internet of Things for social relevant topics.		x	x															11,8
10. Enable people to seamlessly identify things to access as well as contribute related information.		x	x	x											x			23,5
Total adherence	40,0	100,0	90,0	80,0	60,0	50,0	50,0	50,0	50,0	50,0	30,0	40,0	50,0	40,0	70,0	20,0	40,0	

of interest in Blockchain-based applications has happened because we need applications that can run only through a trusted intermediary. And, with the adoption of Blockchain strategies, we can operate without the need for a central authority [17].

The authors in [24] also say we can then create some knowledge basis by defining individual instances of these classes, filling in specific slot value information and additional slot restrictions.

A. *Threats to Validity*

We have detected some threats to validity in this Systematic Mapping:

- **The specic group of interest:** This Systematic Mapping used a specic group of search engines considered the most relevant. However, some primary studies may be missing. To mitigate this threat, we adopted the opinion of experts and snowballing.
- **The choice of primary studies:** The classication of the authors was the only evaluation criterion to select each study, restricted to IoT and Blockchain. No other nomenclature was considered.
- **Placebo effects or courtesy bias or inadequate survey instrument:** Anything that seemed to be real research, containing results without errors.
- **Number of reviewers:** SM was conducted by one researcher. We considered adopting the support of experts.
- **Study not available**: Six primary studies were not available.
- **Data extraction doubts:** Some information was not clearly available and it was very difcult to interpret. Discussions with experts were considered.

VI. Concluding Remarks and Future Work

We conducted a Systematic Mapping to investigate which primary development processes have been used in, and which factors have been influencing Blockchain-based IoT building. The ultimate goal of our research is to present the current panorama about best practices outlined in the literature to develop an initial Blockchain-based ontology model for IoT projects. The Blockchain-based IoT research area is so new and most of the papers and publications (such as a book, a technical report and others works) are concentrated in the last ve years (i.e., 17 of the studies that were considered, and seen in Table II).

We reported on some frameworks, models, approaches, and other Blockchain-based IoT initiatives that present adherence to well-known development processes and endeavor to build an initial body of knowledge. We detected key requirements on the IoT and, we sorted them by functional and non-functional requirements. We also evaluated the adherence of each paper. In this analysis, the papers are evaluated against the ten IoT key requirements.

Thus, the main contribution of this paper is the understanding of the realm of Blockchain-based IoT development, and we aim to establish best practices in the construction of devices (or things) that inspire more condence in their use (or transactions). These are the essential requirements for building a Blockchain-based IoT, and we have identified as well as characteristics, processes, former initiatives and current challenges of Blockchain-based IoT.

Our future work will address the main characteristics, models and tasks to integrate existing approaches and scalable blockchains, and in designing an architecture for IoT applications which addresses integrity, trust and security issues. Moreover, we will concentrate on building an initial body of knowledge about Blockchain-based IoT devices. We intend to conduct semistructured interviews with specialists to evaluate the original understanding.

REFERENCES

[1] M. Atzori, "Blockchain Technology and Decentralized Governance: Is the State Still Necessary?" *SSRN Electronic Journal*, pp. 1–37, 2015. [Online]. Available: papers.ssrn.comhttp://www.ssrn.com/abstract=2709713

[2] M. Pilkington, "Blockchain technology: Principles and applications," pp. 1–39, Sep. 2015. [Online]. Available: http://papers.ssrn.com/abstract=2662660

[3] H. Ugarte. (2016, Nov.) Semantic blockchain: Semantic web on/with the blockchain. [Online]. Available: https://semanticblocks.wordpress.com/

[4] M. Atzori, "Blockchain-based architectures for the internet of things: A survey," Oct. 2016. [Online]. Available: https://ssrn.com/abstract=2846810

[5] S. H. Hashemi, F. Faghri, P. Rausch, and R. H. Campbell, "World of empowered iot users," in *2016 IEEE First International Conference on Internet-of-Things Design and Implementation (IoTDI)*, April 2016, pp. 13–24.

[6] Y. Zhang and J. Wen, "The iot electric business model: Using blockchain technology for the internet of things," *Peer-to-Peer Networking and Applications*, vol. 10, no. 4, pp. 983–994, Apr. 2016. [Online]. Available: http://dx.doi.org/10.1007/s12083-016-0456-1

[7] A. C. Dias-Neto, R. O. Spnola, and G. H. Travassos, "Developing software technologies through experimentation: experiences from the battlefield," in *XIII Ibero-American Conference on Software Engineering*. XIII Congreso Iberoamericano en Software Engineering, May 2010.

[8] B. A. Kitchenham and S. Charters, "Guidelines for performing systematic literature reviews in software engineering," Keele University, Keele, Newcastle ST5 5BG, UK, techreport 2.3, Jul. 2007. [Online]. Available: https://pdfs.semanticscholar.org/e62d/bbbbe70cabcde3335765009e94ed2b9883d5.pdf

[9] T. Meline, "Selecting studies for systematic review: Inclusion and exclusion criteria," *Contemporary issues in communication science and disorders*, vol. 33, pp. 21–27, Mar. 2006.

[10] L. Luu, D.-H. Chu, H. Olickel, P. Saxena, and A. Hobor, "Making smart contracts smarter," in *Proceedings of the 2016 ACM SIGSAC Conference on Computer and Communications Security*, ser. CCS '16. New York, NY, USA: ACM, 2016, pp. 254–269. [Online]. Available: http://doi.acm.org/10.1145/2976749.2978309

[11] L. Luu, J. Teutsch, R. Kulkarni, and P. Saxena, "Demystifying incentives in the consensus computer," in *Proceedings of the 22Nd ACM SIGSAC Conference on Computer and Communications Security*, ser. CCS '15. New York, NY, USA: ACM, 2015, pp. 706–719. [Online]. Available: http://doi.acm.org/10.1145/2810103.2813659

[12] P. Vigna and M. J. Casey, *The Age of Cryptocurrency: How Bitcoin and Digital Money Are Challenging the Global Economic Order*. New York, NY, USA: St. Martin's Press, Inc., Jan. 2015.

[13] A. Biryukov, D. Khovratovich, and I. Pustogarov, "Deanonymisation of clients in bitcoin p2p network," in *Proceedings of the 2014 ACM SIGSAC Conference on Computer and Communications Security*, ser. CCS '14. New York, NY, USA: ACM, 2014, pp. 15–29. [Online]. Available: http://doi.acm.org/10.1145/2660267.2660379

[14] Y. Zhang and J. Wen, "An iot electric business model based on the protocol of bitcoin," in *2015 18th International Conference on Intelligence in Next Generation Networks*, Feb 2015, pp. 184–191.

[15] T. Hardjono and N. Smith, "Cloud-based commissioning of constrained devices using permissioned blockchains," in *Proceedings of the 2Nd ACM International Workshop on IoT Privacy, Trust, and Security*, ser. IoTPTS '16. New York, NY, USA: ACM, 2016, pp. 29–36. [Online]. Available: http://doi.acm.org/10.1145/2899007.2899012

[16] M. Conoscenti, A. Vetr, and J. C. D. Martin, "Blockchain for the internet of things: A systematic literature review," in *2016 IEEE/ACS 13th International Conference of Computer Systems and Applications (AICCSA)*, Nov 2016, pp. 1–6.

[17] K. Christidis and M. Devetsikiotis, "Blockchains and smart contracts for the internet of things," *IEEE Access*, vol. 4, pp. 2292–2303, 2016.

[18] S. Huckle, R. Bhattacharya, M. White, and N. Beloff, "Internet of things, blockchain and shared economy applications," *Procedia Computer Science*, vol. 98, no. Supplement C, pp. 461 – 466, 2016, the 7th International Conference on Emerging Ubiquitous Systems and Pervasive Networks (EUSPN 2016)/The 6th International Conference on Current and Future Trends of Information and Communication Technologies in Healthcare (ICTH-2016)/Affiliated Workshops. [Online]. Available: http://www.sciencedirect.com/science/article/pii/S1877050916322190

[19] D. Uckelmann, M. Harrison, and F. Michahelles, *An Architectural Approach Towards the Future Internet of Things*. Berlin, Heidelberg: Springer Berlin Heidelberg, 2011, pp. 1–24. [Online]. Available: https://doi.org/10.1007/978-3-642-19157-2_1

[20] S. Panikkar, S. Nair, P. Brody, and V. Pureswaran, "Adept: An iot practitioner perspective," IBM, techreport, 2015.

[21] A. Norta, *Creation of Smart-Contracting Collaborations for Decentralized Autonomous Organizations*. Cham: Springer International Publishing, 2015, pp. 3–17. [Online]. Available: https://doi.org/10.1007/978-3-319-21915-8_1

[22] G. Zyskind, O. Nathan, and A. Pentland, "Enigma: Decentralized computation platform with guaranteed privacy," *arXiv preprint arXiv:1506.03471*, 2015.

[23] G. Zyskind, O. Nathan, and A. . Pentland, "Decentralizing privacy: Using blockchain to protect personal data," in *2015 IEEE Security and Privacy Workshops*, May 2015, pp. 180–184.

[24] N. F. Noy and D. L. McGuinness. (2001, Feb.) Ontology development 101: A guide to creating your first ontology. [Online]. Available: http://liris.cnrs.fr/amille/enseignements/Ecole_Centrale/What%20is%20an%20ontology%20and%20why%20we%20need%20it.htm

Authentication and the Internet of Things:

A Survey Based on a Systematic Mapping.

Emidio de Oliveira e Silva
CESAR - Recife Center for Advanced Studies and Systems
Recife, Brazil
eos@cesar.org.br

Wallace Thierre Souza de Lima
CESAR - Recife Center for Advanced Studies and Systems
Recife, Brazil
wtsl@cesar.org.br

Felipe Silva Ferraz
CESAR - Recife Center for Advanced Studies and Systems
Recife, Brazil
fsf@cesar.org.br

Francisco Icaro do Nascimento Ribeiro
CESAR - Recife Center for Advanced Studies and Systems
Recife, Brazil
finr@cesar.org.br

Abstract—The term Internet of Things (IoT) is used to describe many objects connected and communicating with each other. In this scenario, where different things share information in distinct environments, some security problems become evident. Among those issues, authentication is an important technique for ensuring a reliable and secure communication between objects in an IoT environment. This paper has mapped the current state of the authentication use in an IoT environment, highlighting the challenges and the main techniques used in authentication solutions.

Keywords- internet of things; authentication; authorization; systematic mapping;

I. INTRODUCTION

Nowadays it is natural to face a scenario in which smart objects are connected to the Internet, exchanging data and information, interacting with users and other devices. It is possible to notice these objects in several different areas, such as, healthcare monitoring, telecommunication, vehicular automation, traffic, elderly and children care, etc. [1]. This group of connected objects is denominated IoT.

According to Gartner institute, it is expected that 8.4 billion smart devices will be connected and in use by the end of 2017. It is also estimated that a number close to 20.4 billion devices will be connected by the end of 2020. This demonstrates a growing investment in the new business niche involving IoT solutions. Still, in the same article, it is presented that companies are expected to invest around US$ 1.7 trillion in IoT applications by the end of 2017 and reach US$ 3 trillion by 2020 [2].

IoT is not just a machine-to-machine network or a network, with smart and physical objects, that contains embedded technology to sense/interact with their internal state or external environment. IoT defines an ecosystem that includes things, communication, applications, data analysis, business opportunity and innovation [3]. In this context, IoT will enable a broad variety of new ways to interact in citizens cotidianum, connecting smart objects, interacting in different environments, using different protocols and combining a natural heterogeneous environment through a set of different approaches [4]. This way, many companies develop platforms to explore and facilitate internet solutions of things like the KNoT, a meta platform that focuses on implementing the integration between existing hardware and software IoT platform [5].

In this complex heterogeneous structure of IoT environments, in which connected solutions are already part of people and companies practices, manipulating and storing information, many security issues can be highlighted. Data privacy, device identification, authentication, authorization and software vulnerability are some of these concerns, that must be addressed while IoT are still in its early stages of development [4][6][7].

In order to provide trust of the information, that the confidentiality, integrity and availability of the information are not violated, security mechanisms must be considered. In terms of information security, authentication is a property of a system that is related to an actor being able to provide a set of information to prove that he is indeed who it claims to be.

In the context of IoT, authentication is related to any claim of an object, from a system, another object or user, and it validates if the claimer is who it affirms it is.

Authentication is important not only to authenticate a user, but also to manage credentials as a whole, ensuring that those who do not have permissions are blocked from accessing. Since IoT is a new and challenging area, this work will focus in a research about what has been studied and built in terms of authentication in IoT.

In order to provide a broad overview about authentication in an IoT environment and also identify opportunities, challenges and other matters on this topic, this paper conducts a systematic mapping. A systematic mapping aims to identify the quantity, type of research and results available within a specific area. It also aims to verify the evolution and state of the art in that area [8]. This work is divided, as follows: in Section 2, the methodology used to perform this research will be described, along with the protocol, methods, and the processes used in this mapping review. Section 3 presents the results and summarizes the main points about the subject addressed. Finally, in the last section, conclusions and future works will be presented.

II. Applied Protocol

Based upon the guidelines for the development of systematic reviews in software engineering described by Kitchenham et al. [8] and the analysis of the review model by Dybå and Dingsøyr [9], a new methodology for revision was created. Our review methodology is composed of six steps: (1) development of the protocol, (2) identification of inclusion and exclusion criteria, (3) search for relevant studies, (4) critical assessment, (5) extraction of data, and (6) synthesis. The steps applied to the study contained herein are presented below:

The objective of this review is to identify primary studies that focus on the use of authentication techniques that aims to solve IoT security problems. The following question helps identifying primary studies.

- How important are authentication techniques on IoT environments and what are the challenges, concerns, and expectations about these techniques?

From this central question and after an internal debate between the authors, other secondary questions were developed to help comprehending the problem:

1. What are the main challenges about authentication in an IoT environment?
2. What are the main authentication methods or techniques used in an internet environment of things?
3. What are the advantages, benefits and challenges in the use of techniques that use RFID as an authentication artifact?

A. Inclusion and Exclusion Criteria

For this review, studies that aim to analyze the use of authentication techniques to improve security in IoT environments were considered. Since this field of research is recent, this review limited the examined studies to the ones published starting from the year of 2015, due to the great emergence of relevant studies as of this year.

The following works were also excluded:

- Studies not published in the English language;
- Studies that were unavailable online;
- Studies not based on research or that are incomplete;
- Call for works, prefaces, conference annals, handouts, summaries, panels, interviews and news reports.

B. Search Strategies

The databases considered in the study were:

- ACM Digital Library;
- IEEE Xplore;
- SpringerLink;

Some terms were defined and combined based on the proposed questions. As a result, a set of five strings were defined and used to conduct the search in the databases.

((IOT or internet of things) and security) and authentication);

(((IOT or internet of things) and authentication) and challenges);

(((IOT or internet of things) and authentication) and techniques);

(((IOT or internet of things) and authentication) and methods);

(((IOT or internet of things) and authentication) and RFID);

In the process of extracting information from the databases, the search strings were used separately on each database. The searches were performed between March 2017 and April 2017. The results of each search were grouped together according to the database and were, later, examined closer in order to identify duplicity. Table 1 shows the amount of studies found on each database.

TABLE I. AMOUNT OF STUDIES FOUND ON EACH DATABASE

Database	Amount of studies
ACM Digital Library	*112*
IEEE Xplore	*417*
SpringerLink	*1366*

C. Studies Selection Process

This section describes the selection process from the beginning: from the initial search using the Search Strategies previously described to the identification of primary studies.

At the first step, an analysis was realized to remove all duplicated articles from the set of studies obtained. After removal, 1208 non-duplicated works remained, they were added to Mendeley's citation management tool.

In a second phase, the titles of all works selected in the previous step were analyzed to determine its relevance in this systematic mapping. At this stage, many works that did not mention using authentication into IoT, authentication techniques or methods were eliminated.

Due to the use of terms related to authentication in IoT environment, many works depicting about cloud authentication, biometric authentication and biological identification were found. In those cases, all works whose titles did not conform to the scope of the review were eliminated. In other cases, when the works titles were vague or unclear, they were put aside to be analyzed in the next step. At the end of this stage, 553 citations were excluded, thus remaining 205 items for further analysis.

In the third step, all abstracts of the filtered works were closely examined, showing an enormous quality variation. Once again, many studies were eliminated due to their non conformity to the scope of authentication being used to solve privacy and security issues in IoT environments. Others had no abstracts or had abstracts that did not clearly presented what the article was about. In the end, a total of 99 papers were selected.

Table 2 presents the amount of studies filtered in each step of selection process.

TABLE II. AMOUNT OF STUDIES FILTERED IN EACH STEP OF SELECTION PROCESS

Engine	Returned Studies	Title	Abstract
ACM	69	34	7
IEEE	298	112	40
Springer Link	391	59	10
Total	758	205	57

D. Quality Assessment

In this assessment stage, the works were submitted to a critical analysis. In this stage, the complete studies were analyzed, instead of only the titles or abstracts. After this, the last studies that were considered uninteresting for the review were eliminated resulting in the final set of works. After the quality assessment, relevance grades were attributed to the remaining works. The relevance grades are going to be useful in the next stage. Six questions, based on Kitchenham et al. [8], were used to guide quality assessment. Those questions determine the credibility, rigor and relevance of the article to be analyzed. Out of the six, the first is the most important due to its capability to determine if the work is addressed to the review subject. The five remaining questions are useful in determining the quality of the work, so they were used to classify the works according to the quality. The questions were:

1. Does the study analyze the benefits of using authentication in an IoT environment?
2. Is the study based on research - not merely on specialists' opinions?
3. Are the objectives of the study clearly stated?
4. Is the context of the study adequately described?
5. Was the research project adequate to reach the research objectives?
6. Were the research results adequately validated?

After a deep analysis at the quality assessment stage, 49 of the remaining 57 studies were selected to the stage of data extraction and synthesis and were, thus, considered as the primary studies. The quality assessment process will be presented in detail in the result section along with the assessment of the 49 remaining studies.

III. RESULTS

In total, 49 primary studies were identified, each one dealing with a wide array of research topics and using a wide set of exploration models for different scenarios.

After evaluating the primary studies, the works revealed patterns related with authentication and identification in IoT environment. Several studies had a theoretical essence centered on the proposal of an authentication mechanism, using it in two or more steps. Many of the solutions analyzed use the authentication scheme applying elliptic curve cryptosystem (ECC), which is a public key cryptography method, that uses points on an elliptic curve to derive a 163-bit public key, equivalent in strength to a 1024-bit RSA key and XOR operations. In further studies, authentication occurs through devices that use Radio-Frequency Identification (RFID). RFID is one of the most important technologies used in IoT area, as it can store sensitive data, communicate with other objects wirelessly and identify/track objects automatically in user identification.

A. Quantitative Analysis

The developed research process resulted in 49 primary studies. They were written by 193 authors linked to institutions based on different countries, distributed on four continents, and were published between 2015 and 2017. In total, the authors identified 225 different keywords in their work. In many works, the authors approach different ways to make authentication, with two or three steps or using RFID. To emphasize this affirmation, Figure 1 presents a word cloud generated with all works titles.

Figure 1. Word cloud from the primary studies.

The most common keywords used in the remaining works with their respective frequency were: authentication (10), Internet of things (8), security (3), privacy (3), wireless sensor networks (3), techniques (1), methods (1), RFID (1). The first three keywords - authentication, internet of things and security - reflect precisely the theme of the research contained herein.

B. Qualitative Analysis

As described in the quality assessment, each one of the primary studies was assessed according to six quality criteria related to rigor and credibility, as well as to relevance. If considered as a whole, these six criteria provide a good measure to the conclusions that a particular study can bring to the mapping. The classification for each criteria used a scale of positives and negatives.

In Table 3, columns 'q1' to 'q6' represent the 6 criteria defined by the questions used on the quality assessment: Focus in Authentication, Research, Clearly, Context, Project, and Validation.

For each criteria, '1' represents the positive answer and '0' the negative one.

TABLE III. QUALITATIVE TABLE

Study	q1	q2	q3	q4	q5	q6	Total
[1]	1	1	1	1	1	1	6
[2]	1	1	1	1	1	0	5
[3]	1	1	1	1	1	0	5
[6]	1	1	1	1	1	0	5
[10]	1	1	1	1	0	0	4
[11]	1	1	1	1	1	0	5
[13]	1	1	1	1	1	1	6
[14]	1	1	1	1	0	0	4
[15]	1	1	1	1	1	0	5
[16]	1	1	1	1	1	0	5
[17]	1	1	1	1	1	0	5
[18]	1	1	1	1	1	1	6
[19]	1	1	1	1	0	0	4
[20]	1	1	1	1	1	0	5
[21]	1	1	1	1	1	1	6
[22]	1	1	1	1	1	1	6
[23]	1	1	1	1	1	0	5
[24]	1	1	1	0	1	1	5
[25]	1	1	1	1	1	1	6
[25]	1	1	1	1	1	0	5
[28]	0	1	1	1	0	0	3
[30]	1	1	1	1	1	0	5
[31]	0	1	1	1	1	1	5
[32]	1	1	1	1	1	1	6
[33]	1	1	1	1	0	0	4
[34]	1	1	1	1	1	1	6
[35]	1	1	1	1	1	0	5
[36]	1	1	1	1	1	0	5
[37]	1	1	1	1	1	0	5
[38]	1	1	1	1	0	0	4
[39]	0	1	1	1	1	0	4
[40]	1	1	1	1	1	0	5
[41]	0	1	1	1	0	0	3
[42]	1	0	1	1	1	0	4
[43]	1	0	1	0	1	1	4
[44]	1	1	1	1	1	0	5
[45]	1	1	1	1	1	1	6
[46]	1	1	1	1	1	1	6
[47]	1	1	1	1	1	0	5
[48]	1	1	1	1	1	0	5
[49]	1	1	1	1	1	0	5
[50]	1	1	1	1	1	0	5
[51]	1	1	1	1	1	0	5
[52]	0	0	1	1	1	1	4
[53]	1	1	1	1	1	1	6
[54]	0	1	1	0	0	0	2
[55]	1	1	1	1	0	0	4
[56]	1	1	1	1	1	1	6
[57]	1	1	1	1	1	0	5

Table 3 presented the quantitative analyses; based on that, it is possible to check that the following works were marked with higher scores: [1], [2], [3], [6], [11], [13], [15], [16], [17], [18], [20], [21], [22], [23], [24], [25], [27], [30], [31], [32], [34], [35], [36], [37], [40], [44], [45], [46], [47], [48], [49], [50], [51], [53], [55], [56] and [57]. These will serve as a base to the following section, in which discussion about the main topics will be conducted.

Some studies were analyzed [28], [31], [39], [41], [52] and [54] did not have positive result in the first question ("Q1"). However, the articles provided information on the context of the work and contributed, in some way, to the research.

IV. Discussion

After analysis and data extraction, steps performed on the primary studies, it was possible to identify some aspects related with authentication in IoT application environments.

First, it is possible to conclude that security in IoT environment is a very recent field of research since the majority studies used in this article have been published after 2015. Secondly, it was possible to conclude that in many applications, different ways are used to make authentication. In some cases, when using two or more authentication steps, it is possible to work with digital and iris recognition or RFID for identification.

In these works, it was possible to identify the importance of creating an efficient mechanism against the most common internet attacks such as MitM, replay, forward secrecy and DoS. Therefore, in order to get this efficiency, many works used elliptic curve cryptosystem (ECC) scheme.

A. What are the main challenges regarding authentication in an IoT environments?

There are challenges that need to be addressed in IoT authentication. The first challenge is to reduce the energy cost on the authentication process; for example, elliptic curve cryptography (ECC) is an authentication protocol, which uses implicit certificate aiming to reduce energy consumption and computation overhead [11] in wireless sensor networks for distributed IoT Applications.

The second challenge [12] introduced is to deploy authentication protocols adapted to the IoT environment. Different network architectures are based on different IoT notions and need to deploy authentication schemes to secure communications [13].

Another challenge is to design an authentication scheme identifying the users in their respective devices without maintaining permanent contact between those parts [14].

The last challenge is to achieve cross network security in machine to machine communications issues like diverse channels, interfaces, and context environments of heterogeneous networks [15] need to be addressed.

B. What are the main authentication methods or techniques used in the internet of things?

Similar to the current internet applications, there are many mechanisms to provide authentication in an IoT platform. In this way, one possible solution is to use three factors for authentication which includes, ID, password and fingerprint [2]. In other words, Mbarek et al. [16] explains three methods used in authentication. The first method consists in a signature-based mechanism, this signature could be an ID or an elliptic curve signature, for example. The advantage of this authentication method is that it provides fast messaging authentication, with sender repudiation [16]. The second method ensures immediate messaging authentication and inherits security of different signatures, such as Winternitz, which is a one-time signature that are proven to be existentially unforgeable under adaptive chosen message attacks. The third method implements a lightweight symmetric primitives, like the ones used in μTESLA context, where the authentication key is secret for a time interval and will be disclosed after a certain period of time [16].

Other technique that can be used in IoT architecture is identification of neighbor nodes and a data aggregation to authenticate group members that uses an authentication scheme in wireless sensor network (WSN) using elliptic curve cryptosystem (ECC) and XOR operation [17].

Another paper cites RFID authentication due to its strong requirements and the ability to ensure secure communication between RFID tags and the server [18]. In the next question this subject will be more discussed.

Other uncommon mechanism used to improve security is presented in the second step of the authentication process. First, the user enters with his/hers username and password. If the verification is completed successfully, the second step of authentication is started by allowing the user to enter a registered and predefined sequence of events, such as menu or mouse activity, on a fake server screen [1].

One of the most secure mechanism of authentication is cited in [19]. It is the One Time Password (OTP) technique developed with elliptic curves cryptography (ECC). It is the most efficient and secure compared to the existing methods like the Key Distribution Center (KDC). This method does not store the device's private and public keys, it only stores their IDs.

Finally, the most popular method used to secure authentication is the two step verification. It sends a verification code to a mobile phone or uses a smart card for generating keys on the devices directly [19].

C. What are the advantage, benefits and challenges in the use of techniques that use RFID as an authentication artifact?

Radio-Frequency IDentification (RFID) is one of the most important technologies used in the IoT, as it can store sensitive data, communicate and identify objects [18]. The RFID system is composed of three components: RFID tag, reader and a trusted back-end server [19].

Zeadally et al. [18] show that the RFID has advantages if compared to the traditional barcode reader. It can be applied to objects with rough surfaces, provide both read/write capabilities, it requires no line-of-sight contact with RFID readers, it is able to read multiple RFID tags simultaneously, and provides strong authentication to the user data [21].

To reduce communication and computation overheads, the RFID reader uses a scheme that enables to resist various common attacks such as the MitM, replay, forward secrecy, and DoS [22]. ECC-based RFID authentication schemes have attracted a lot of attention, Zeadally et al. [18] argue that the PKC-based RFID authentication schemes are necessary for secure communication in RFID systems because many security attributes cannot be implemented. However, elliptic curve cryptosystem (ECC) is more suitable because it can provide similar security level but with a shorter key size and has low computational requirements [18].

V. CONCLUSION

The purpose of this review was to identify primary studies that focus on the use of authentication, with its challenges and opportunities. In the searching phase, 1208 studies were found, out of which 49 were classified as primary studies after the selection and the quality criteria were applied. Many of the studies found in the first steps did not focus on IoT authentication solutions. Such works focused only in cloud computing and techniques that deal just with data privacy were not selected to compose the search.

In the analysis performed on the group of selected articles, theoretical and practical solutions that described techniques and methods of authentication were found. The vast majority of the studies were validated in a more superficial and theoretical way, highlighting their strengths and their advantages.

This systematic review has found different ways to perform authentication in IoT environments and, among them, the use of ECC was present in majority of articles aiming to ensure security with low power consumption.

This work also showed the main challenges of applying authentication in an IoT environment. The low energy storage capacity of connected devices can be highlighted as one of the main concerns. In the process of solving this major challenge, a large number of authentication solutions use elliptic curve cryptography (ECC) that provides security with low processing power, adding more efficiency in authentication algorithms.

Regarding the future work, a comparison between light authentication solutions based on elliptic curve cryptography is proposed. A more detailed analysis about elliptic curve cryptography can be performed in order to validate if the use of the technique satisfies the challenges of security and low power consumption in an IoT environment.

ACKNOWLEDGMENT

This work was developed under the Professional Master of Software Engineer's program of the Educational branch of CESAR, a Brazilian innovation center.

REFERENCES

[1] M. Saadeh, A. Sleit, M. Qatawneh, and W. Almobaideen, C. Conference, "Authentication Techniques for the Internet of Things: A Survey," 2016.

[2] "Gartner,"http://www.gartner.com/newsroom/id/3598917, accessed: 2017-05-02.

[3] K. Gupta, "Internet of Things: Security Challenges for Next Generation Networks," no. Iciccs, pp. 315–318, 2016.

[4] M. Weber, "Security challenges of the Internet of Things," pp. 638–643, 2016.

[5] "Knot: the open source meta platform for iot," https://www.knot.cesar. org.br/, retrieved: August, 2017.

[6] O. O. Bamasag and K. Youcef-toumi, "Towards Continuous Authentication in Internet of Things Based on Secret Sharing Scheme."

[7] O. Bamasag, "Efficient Multicast Authentication in Internet of Things," pp. 429–435, 2016.

[8] B. Kitchenham and S. Charters, "Guidelines for performing systematic literature reviews in software engineering," 2007.

[9] T. Dybå and T. Dingsøyr, "Empirical studies of agile software development: A systematic review," Inf. Softw. Technol., vol. 50, no. 9–10, Aug. 2008, pp. 833–859.

[10] S. Lin and C. Wen, "Energy-Efficient Device-Based Node Authentication Protocol for the Internet of Things," no. 1, pp. 1–2, 2016.

[11] H. Khemissa, D. Tandjaoui, T. Information, T. Houari, and B. Algiers, "A Lightweight Authentication Scheme for E-health applications in the context of Internet of Things," 2015.

[12] H. Khemissa and D. Tandjaoui, "A Novel Lightweight Authentication Scheme for heterogeneous Wireless Sensor Networks in the context of Internet of Things *†," 2016.

[13] N. W. Interfaces, "Continuous Authentication and Authorization for the Internet of Things," 2017.

[14] "ECC Based Self-Certified Key Management Scheme for Mutual Authentication in Internet of Things," pp. 3–8, 2016.

[15] S. Arasteh, S. F. Aghili, and H. Mala, "A New Lightweight Authentication and Key agreement Protocol For Internet of Things," pp. 52–59, 2016.

[16] B. Mbarek, A. Meddeb, W. Ben Jaballah, and M. Mosbah, "A Secure Authentication Mechanism for Resource Constrained Devices," pp. 1–7, 2015.

[17] Y. Park and Y. Park, "A Selective Group Authentication Scheme for IoT-Based Medical Information System," pp. 1–8, 2017.

[18] S. Zeadally, "An Analysis of RFID Authentication Schemes for Internet of Things in Healthcare Environment Using Elliptic Curve Cryptography," vol. 4662, no. c, 2014.

[19] O. Salman, S. Abdallah, I. H. Elhajj, A. Chehab, and A. Kayssi, "Identity-based authentication scheme for the Internet of Things," *Proc. - IEEE Symp. Comput. Commun.*, vol. 2016–Augus, pp. 1109–1111, 2016.

[20] P. Ghosh, "A Privacy Preserving Mutual Authentication Protocol for RFID based Automated Toll Collection System," 2016.

[21] S. M. Sujatha, "Design and Implementation of IoT Testbed with Three Factor Authentication."

[22] Y. Huang and J. Jiang, "Ultralightweight RFID Reader-Tag Mutual Authentication Revisited," 2015.

[23] J. Huang, W. Juang, C. Fan, Y. Tseng, and H. Kikuchi, "Lightweight Authentication Scheme with Dynamic Group Members in IoT Environments," pp. 88–93, 2016.

[24] S. Janbabaei, H. Gharaee, and N. Mohammadzadeh, "Lightweight, Anonymous and Mutual Authentication in IoT Infrastructure," pp. 162–166, 2016.

[25] M. B. Tamboli, "Secure and Efficient CoAP Based Authentication and Access Control for Internet of Things (IoT)," pp. 1245–1250, 2016.

[26] T. Marktscheffel et al., "QR Code Based Mutual Authentication Protocol for Internet of Things," 2016.

[27] L. Feng, X. Yao, and C. Engineering, "RFID System Mutual Authentication Protocols Based on ECC," pp. 1645–1650, 2015.

[28] E. Song, "Enabling RFID technology for healthcare: application,

architecture, and challenges," 2014.

[29] J. Shen, H. Tan, Y. Zhang, X. Sun, and Y. Xiang, "A new lightweight RFID grouping authentication protocol for multiple tags in mobile environment," 2017.

[30] S. Peter, "Multi-level Authentication System for Smart Home-Security Analysis and Implementation."

[31] B. Tank, H. Upadhyay, and H. Patel, "A Survey on IoT Privacy Issues and Mitigation Techniques," pp. 9–12, 2016.

[32] C. Author, "Study of Authentication with IoT Testbed," 2015.

[33] A. H. Moon, I. Technology, U. Iqbal, I. Technology, and G. M. Bhat, "Light Weight Authentication framework for WSN," pp. 3099–3105, 2016.

[34] M. Komar, S. Edelev, and Y. Koucheryavy, "Handheld Wireless Authentication Key and Secure Documents Storage for the Internet of Everything."

[35] Wei-Tsung Su, Wei-Ming Wong and Wei-Cheng Chen, "A survey of performance improvement by group-based authentication in IoT" Applied System Innovation (ICASI), 2016 IEEE International Conference on Applied System Innovation, 2016.

[36] A. Cherkaoui, L. Bossuet, L. Seitz, G. Selander, and R. Borgaonkar, "New Paradigms for Access Control in Constrained Environments."

[37] J. K. Zao, D. A. Ha, and K. T. Nguyen, "Efficient Authentication of Resource-Constrained IoT Devices based on ECQV Implicit Certificates and Datagram Transport Layer Security Protocol," pp. 173–179.

[38] C. Camichel, U. M. R. Cnrs, and A. Thomas, "Evaluation of RAIN RFID authentication schemes," 2016.

[39] H. Zhang and T. Zhang, "Short Paper: 'A Peer to Peer Security Protocol for the Internet of Things,'" pp. 154–156, 2015.

[40] I. Computing, M. Barbareschi, P. Bagnasco, and A. Mazzeo, "Authenticating IoT Devices With Physically Unclonable Functions Models," 2015.

[41] H. Luo, G. Wen, J. Su, and Z. Huang, "SLAP: Succinct and Lightweight Authentication Protocol for low-cost RFID system," *Wirel. Networks*, 2016.

[42] N. Singh, "Improved Authentication Scheme Using Password Enabled Persuasive Cued Click Points," pp. 1394–1398, 2015.

[43] A. V Kamath, K. Kataoka, N. Vijayvergiya, G. B. Reddy, and S. Phatale, "SAFE: Software-defined Authentication FramEwork."

[44] S. Emerson, Y. Choi, D. Hwang, K. Kim, and K. Kim, "An OAuth based Authentication Mechanism for IoT Networks," pp. 1072–1074, 2015.

[45] S. Patel and D. R. Patel, "Energy Efficient Integrated Authentication and Access Control Mechanisms for Internet of Things," pp. 304–309, 2016.

[46] M. A. Crossman and H. Liu, "Two-Factor Authentication through Near Field Communication," 2016.

[47] Y. Sharaf-dabbagh and W. Saad, "On the Authentication of Devices in the Internet of Things," pp. 1–3, 2016.

[48] P. H. Griffin, "Security for Ambient Assisted Living: Multi-factor Authentication in the Internet of Things," 2015.

[49] Y. Essadraoui, "Wireless sensor node's authentication scheme based on Multivariate Quadratic Quasigroups," 2015.

[50] M. P. Pawlowski *et al.*, "Towards a Lightweight Authentication and Authorization Framework for Smart Objects *," vol. 8716, no. c, pp. 1–14, 2015.

[51] W. Xi *et al.*, "Instant and Robust Authentication and Key Agreement among Mobile Devices," pp. 616–627.

[52] S. Kumari, M. Karuppiah, A. K. Das, X. Li, F. Wu, and N. Kumar, "A secure authentication scheme based on elliptic curve cryptography for IoT and cloud servers," *J. Supercomput.*, 2017.

[53] C. Shen, H. Li, G. Sahin, and H. Choi, "Low-Complexity Scalable Authentication Algorithm with Imperfect Shared Keys for Internet of Things," pp. 3–8, 2016.

[54] M. Schukat, "Peer to Peer Authentication for Small Embedded Systems," pp. 68–72, 2014.

[55] I. Technology *et al.*, "Digital Memories Based Mobile User Authentication for IoT," 2015.

[56] O. Bamasag, "Efficient Multicast Authentication in Internet of Things," pp. 429–435, 2016.

[57] T. Markmann, T. C. Schmidt, and M. Wählisch, "Federated End-to-End Authentication for the Constrained Internet of Things Using IBC and ECC," *ACM SIGCOMM Comput. Commun. Rev.*, vol. 45, no. 5, pp. 603–604, 2015.

CLIPS: Customized Levels of IoT Privacy and Security

Rohith Yanambaka Venkata, Krishna Kavi

Computer Systems Research Lab
Dept. of Computer Science and Engineering
University of North Texas
Denton, Texas 76207, USA
Email: RohithYanambakaVenkata@my.unt.edu, Krishna.Kavi@unt.edu

Abstract—**Internet of Things (IoT) refers to systems that can be attached to the Internet and thus can be accessed and controlled remotely. Such devices are essential for creating "smart things" like smart homes, smart grids, etc. IoT has achieved unprecedented success. It offers an interconnected network where devices (in the consumer space) can all communicate with each other. However, many IoT devices only add security features as an afterthought. This has been a contributing factor in many of the recently reported attacks and warnings of potential attacks such as those aimed at gaining control of autonomous cars. Many IoT devices are compact and feature limited computing resources, which often limits their ability to perform complex operations such as encryption or other security and privacy checks. With capabilities of devices in IoT varying greatly, a one-size-fits-all approach to security can prove to be inadequate. We firmly believe that safety and privacy should both be easy to use, present little inconvenience for users of non-critical systems, yet be as strong as possible to minimize breaches in critical systems. In this paper, we propose a novel architecture that caters to device-specific security policies in IoT environments with varying levels of functionalities and criticality of services they offer. This would ensure that the best possible security profiles for IoT are enforced. We use a smart home environment to illustrate the architecture.**

Keywords–Internet of Things (IoT); Software Defined Networking (SDN); IoT Security.

I. INTRODUCTION

Internet of Things (IoT) refers to systems that can be attached to the Internet and thus can be accessed and controlled remotely. Such devices are essential for building "smart things" like smart homes, smart grids, etc. The proliferation of IoT has been undeniably progressive and uninhibited.

The total investment in IoT is predicted to touch the $5 trillion mark in the next five years [1]. More specifically, a recent market study shows that the market with the fastest growing adoption rate is smart homes [2] with the market predicted to generate $ 2.5 billion [2]. Consumers are choosing to invest in IoT for convenient and comfortable lives [3]. Devices such as refrigerators, light bulbs and thermostats can be controlled remotely, which can also result in power savings and reduced operational costs [3].

With an industry as diverse and prevalent as smart homes, security is paramount. Users like to be assured that the devices they invested in are safe and cannot be attacked. Providing this assurance, however, is not an easy task.

Securing network infrastructure often entails shutting services down. For example, a widely accepted response to a denial of service attack (DoS) is to shut down network services. Ideally, securing the devices in a network should go a long way toward ensuring the security of the network itself. Frequently, companies enforce a uniform policy model (specific to a department or section). This compromises flexibility and control. With a traditional networking model, control over the network topology is limited. By leveraging Software Defined Networking (SDN), fine-grained control over the network topology is possible. A diverse network comprised of devices with varied capabilities would be constrained by the device with the least computational or networking abilities. For example, if one of the security requirements is end-to-end network encryption, a non-IP addressable device with minimal computational power may be unable to enfforce such a requirement. We firmly believe that security and privacy should both be easy to use, present little inconvenience to users of non-critical systems, yet be as robust as possible to minimize breaches.

A device-specific and user-selectable approach that caters to the need of all devices in IoT is required. Security policies, tailored to the network and computing capabilities of those devices will result in a good IoT security posture. Otherwise, users will either object to the privacy/security requirements or undermine the security with default or weak security configurations.

We propose a device-specific approach to security using SDN that addresses the needs of individual classes/categories of devices that are trying to access the LAN or WAN network in a smart home. Such an approach to security provides flexibility and control over device and network security.

The main contribution of this paper is an SDN administered security framework that caters to device-specific protection needs in IoT environments with varying levels of functionalities and criticality of the services they offer.

This paper is organized as follows. We present our architecture for enforcing device-specific security policies for IoT devices in Section II. In Section III, we describe the topology detailing the various threat protection and avoidance schemes that are implemented in the architecture. We detail the countermeasures in place against some of the most important attacks targeting IoT in Section IV. Section V contains some related work that is aligned with this research. Section VI describes the configuration and set up of a prototype, followed by conclusions.

II. ARCHITECTURE OVERVIEW

For the purpose of this paper, we use a smart home as an example environment and illustrate how our architecture can implement device-specific security and privacy policies. We will describe individual components in this Section.

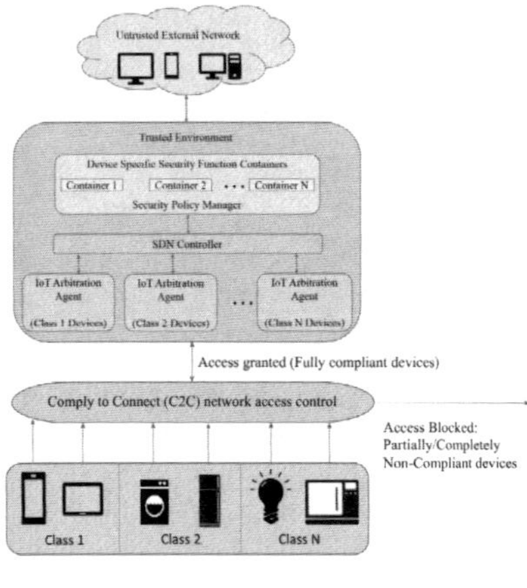

Figure 1. CLIPS architecture.

Figure 1 shows a high-level view of the proposed architecture which consists of a single standalone device that replaces a wireless router. The device hosts a secure trusted environment to which the IoT devices connect to communicate with each other, i.e., Machine to Machine (M2M) or to access the Internet. The functions offered by our device are two-fold:

- Provide networking functionality using SDN.
- Provide a secure environment for device communication (M2M and access to the Internet).

A. *Untrusted external networks*

An untrusted network is one which provides no information regarding data safety, the authenticity/identity of the communicating device, or the communication link itself. This is the most common source for attacks on devices. We need to have mechanisms in place in the smart home network to detect and handle any attacks. The only sensible approach is to monitor and filter traffic at the device itself. This is generally achieved by configuring firewalls and intrusion detection systems to monitor network traffic. Additional protection schemes are discussed in Section III.

B. *Trusted environment*

A trusted environment is one where there is a good degree of confidence in the integrity and confidentiality of the network components (see Figure 2). The first level of defense in the trusted environment is a set of Intrusion Detection Systems (IDS) such as Snort and a firewall service. The final objective is to enforce device (device class) specific security policies. Kerberos provides all the authentication needs for network communication. Additional policies are discussed later in this Section.

1) Security policy manager: Device-specific security policies are stored in Linux containers which are assigned to each category of IoT devices that may be present in a smart home network. Once the device has been identified and grouped, the

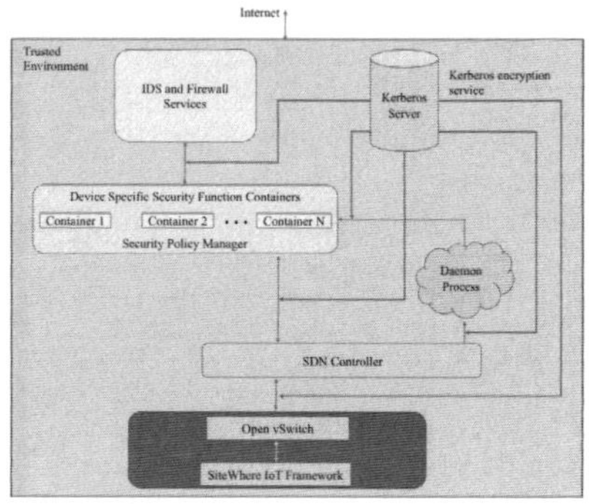

Figure 2. A closer look at the trusted environment.

corresponding container is invoked and the SDN controller initiates a daemon process that runs in the background. This daemon process is then tasked with invoking one of the many device-class specific security function containers that are either suspended or powered down. Powering down containers minimizes the chances of corrupting the code of the container. The container, once invoked, retrieves the required security policies for the identified device. These rules are downloaded onto the SDN controller via the northbound interfaces and the security function container goes back to the suspended state or powers down. The communication link between the container and the SDN controller is encrypted.

The reason for the security policies residing in containers and not configured into the SDN controller is to minimize exposure of the policies to adversaries. When these policies are configured onto the controller, the attackers may find an exploit (in the source code) and gain access to the rules. If, however, they were to reside in a sand-boxed environment, it would make things much harder for them to be accessed, since the policies are exposed to attacks only when the container enforcing these polices is active.

2) IoT arbitrator: An IoT arbitrator resides in the trusted environment and its responsibilities are to host the virtual switch that the SDN controller communicates with (an SDN controller can only communicate with switches and not the devices themselves) and to host an IoT framework for low-powered devices (constrained devices that are not IP accessible) to communicate with each other.

An IoT environment may be an amalgam of devices that communicate using a variety of network protocols, each using different MTUs (Maximum Transmission Unit). Hence, a broker needs to mediate the communication between devices. An example of an IoT framework is SiteWhere [4]. It provides a framework to obtain, store, process and migrate data among IoT devices, which happens through the MQTT (Message Queue Telemetry Transport) protocol.

3) Open vSwitch: Once the policies for a specific class of devices are downloaded onto the SDN controller, they have to be conveyed to the respective switch. The SDN controller maintains flow tables and controls the topology of its assigned network. The controller contacts the OVS switch (Open vSwitch) to which the devices in question are connected.

The appropriate flow table entries are made in the switch and additional security policies are downloaded. Once this is complete, the security policies that were downloaded onto the SDN controller are wiped clean (to prevent attackers from gaining access). The switch uses this newfound information to forward the packets accordingly. Each class of devices will have a designated IoT Arbitrator. In essence, the container that hosts an IoT agent is only invoked when a device first connects to the CLIPS security administrator and goes back to the suspended state or powers off when no device of the designated class is connected.

III. Topology

Securing the Internet of Things is a complex process. A one-size-fits-all approach is impractical given that IoT encompasses a wide variety of devices with varying capabilities. Hence, a device (or device class) specific approach is needed.

A. Comply to Connect (C2C)

Comply to Connect (C2C) is described as a standards-based approach to securing devices that connect to a network [5]. C2C consists of a pre-defined set of standards and security profiles that a device must meet before its is permitted to access the network. For example, an Android device trying to access the network may be required to run OS version 6.0 with the latest security patches before it can connect to the network.

Our implementation of C2C performs a series of checks on the device trying to access the network. Some of the parameters collected include the version of the OS, version of the kernel currently running, security patches installed, ports currently open, etc. Additional checks such as deep packet inspection are performed to ensure that the device is secure and can access the network. Each 'class' of devices has a set of security requirements which can be enforced by C2C. For example, all mobile devices (such as tablets, smart phones, smart watches) are expected to support network encryption and two-factor authentication. Devices are first identified by the certificates issued by an internal certification agent controlled by C2C.

If one or more checks fail, the devices are provided limited access until security definitions are updated. If the devices are deemed unfit to access the network until a major upgrade is performed, they are quarantined in a VLAN.

Most of the vulnerabilities listed by OWASP for IoT devices [6] can be prevented or addressed by C2C. At the top of the list is Insecure Web Interface [6] which includes lack of encryption. Use of plain text for storing passwords could lead to issues such as cross-site scripting to inject malicious code [6].

IoT devices are often targeted for DDoS attacks. A famous example is the attack on Dyn's DNS systems that brought down popular services like Netflix and Facebook [7]. A majority of the vulnerabilities can be prevented by ensuring that the recommended software/firmware and security patches are installed and by ensuring that the encryption and authentication schemes used are sufficiently strong. We intend to achieve this through C2C. A brief description of the protection offered against some other IoT attacks is discussed in Section IV.

B. Leveraging SDN to secure the IoT

SDN is one of the most important advances in networking in recent history. It has accelerated the rate of connected devices [7]. We intend to leverage SDN to ensure network security. Every class of devices has a pre-defined set of security rules that are stored in Linux containers assigned to them. When a device is first granted access to the network by C2C, the appropriate container is started, corresponding security rules present in the container are downloaded onto the SDN controller via the Northbound API and the container is placed in a suspended state to restrict visibility to the external network.

The secondary objective of the containers is to perform arbitration functions between the devices and the SDN controller, which includes hosting an Open vSwitch with which the controller communicates. Not all security policies need to be exposed to the devices themselves. For example, consider a security policy requiring webcams to be placed under a NAT for a secure (encrypted) network segment created specifically for webcams. All the device needs to know is that the network connection must be encrypted. Since the NAT functionality is handled by the controller and does not rely on native support from the device, it need not be advertised. The devices may remain ignorant of the network topology.

With device manufacturers unwilling to offer security configuration options for devices, ensuring security by enforcing protection schemes at the devices themselves can be challenging. In fact, this is listed as number 8 in OWASP's Top 10 Vulnerabilities in the IoT report [6]. We aim to address this issue by employing an arbitration agent that mediates operations between the controller and a device.

C. Integrity measurement using RADIUM

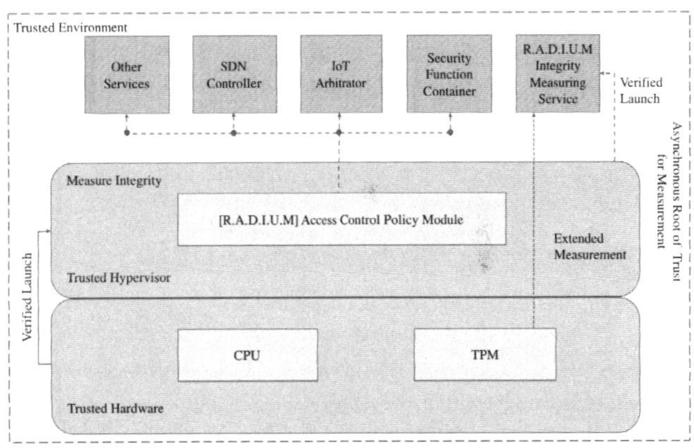

Figure 3. Integrity measurement using RADIUM.

RADIUM (Race-free On-demand Integrity Measurement Architecture) is, as the name suggests, an architecture that measures trustworthiness by providing on demand measurement (of integrity and trustworthiness) of software components. Figure 3 demonstrates this process. To ensure that the measured components are trustworthy, they have to be compared against some the integrity measurement in known "good" state (such as when the component was first developed or a trusted patch was made). This architecture was created using research conducted at the University of North Texas [8].

RADIUM establishes a chain of trust between software and the underlying hardware. This is achieved as follows. The hardware is tasked with measuring the firmware, the firmware is tasked with measuring the system software and the system software measures the application [8]. One way to establish the chain of trust is through Dynamic Root of Trust for Measurement (DRTM). The idea is to create a secure, isolated and measured environment for software to be executed (called measured launch environment MLE) [8].

To initiate a virtualized environment, a hypervisor is the primary component to be invoked. It is done so during the system boot using DRTM. The bootloader is responsible for invoking a DRTM MLE using a set of special instructions to prepare an isolated execution environment [8]. The hypervisor is then measured and compared to a previously known "good" value which is stored in the trusted platform module (TPM). If everything checks out, the hypervisor is deemed trustworthy and executed. The hypervisor then takes control of the platform [8].

For the hypervisor to be mindful of the existence of a measuring service, registration needs to take place. During registration process, it is the responsibility of the measuring service to provide all the ACPM rules for its own functioning to the hypervisor. Also, the hypervisor measures the measuring service itself and saves its "good" value for future comparisons. The measuring service is encrypted and the key is stored in the TPM.

Any virtual machine, that has to run on the hypervisor needs to be registered with the hypervisor before executing. During this registration, a set of policy rules are provided to the hypervisor, which contain the ID of the measuring service that can access the target virtual machine with the appropriate permissions. The hypervisor registers the ID of the target virtual machine and it will be invoked after it's registration.

The simplest method to measure integrity is to store the hash codes of the entire binary (for each software) in a container. RADIUM is configured to compute hash codes at regular intervals. The computed hash code is then compared against the stored hash code. If everything checks out, RADIUM measuring service goes back to a suspended state (or is powered down) and is only invoked when a measurement is again necessary. If there is a mismatch between the measured and stored hashes, however, the application is run on an Intel SGX enclave, which functions as a sandbox. The integrity of the measuring service itself is ensured by the TPM that is present along with the CPU.

All the containers that are invoked in the trusted environment run on a single hypervisor. This makes it a lot easier to ensure their integrity and trustworthiness.

IV. IoT VULNERABILITIES AND ATTACK VECTORS

In this Section, we attempt to identify attack vectors for IoT and describe our approach to addressing them. Nawir et. al do a good job of tabulating and describing the taxonomy of attacks targeting IoT [9].

1) Distributed Denial of Service (DDoS): On 21 October 2016, a large scale DDoS attack on Dyn's DNS systems resulted in popular services such as Netflix, Facebook and Google becoming inaccessible [10]. The attack was perpetrated using Mirai botnet that infected thousands of devices around the world. Some 100,000 devices bombarded Dyn's systems with network traffic at 1.2 Tbps which is a new record [11]. The attackers used a simple brute force attack to infect various DVR players, smart televisions, refrigerators and CCTV cameras using the default passwords that the products were shipped with. The objective in this case was evident; to utilize the popularity of IoT, the lack of sophistication or technical literacy on the part of end users to infiltrate IoT devices to sabotage networks.

We intend to address this issue by protecting devices against brute force attacks by screening them through the C2C architecture discussed in Section III-A. Assuring that they are running the latest software with the appropriate security patches installed will safeguard against a majority of the vulnerabilities.

Ultimately, we intend to create a hierarchical and distributed SDN network segment that shares the network load. This should add an additional layer of security against DDoS attacks.

2) Ransomware attacks: The summer of 2017 saw the emergence of the dreaded WannaCry ransomware which targeted windows machines. The attack used an exploit in the SMB transactions. When it gains access to a machine, the worm encrypts the file system. The attackers then offer to unlock the system in exchange for a ransom. Some 400,000 devices were affected around the world [12]. What is interesting to note is that almost 98% of the devices affected by this attack were running an outdated version of Windows 7.

An attack such as this would be catastrophic for IoT, especially for business-critical systems or devices in the health care domain, as evident from the ransomware attack on a children's hospital in Boston [13] where some personally identifying patient records were deleted.

Our architecture has several safeguards in place to prevent such attacks:

- C2C ensures that devices are running the latest software and have the latest security patches installed. Most ransomware attacks use an open port to inject the encryption program. Oftentimes, the vulnerability is already patched by the manufacturer of the product. Hence, safeguarding against such attacks is a simple matter of updating the software and security patches on the devices.
- The RADIUM architecture ensures integrity of the application.
- Anomaly detection ensures that suspicious activity on the network will either invoke shutdown or containment protocols.

3) Man-in-the-Middle Attacks: Man-in-the-Middle attacks involve an adversary impersonating a legitimate communication node in a network. A successful impersonation will result in sensitive/confidential data being shared with the adversary which leads to a breach or gaining access to a device. Li et. al describe an approach using fog nodes that mediate between servers and clients [14]. One of the countermeasures they proposed was to modify package types in OpenFlow [14].

We intend to use RADIUM to establish a chain of trust between software applications and the underlying hardware. This ensures that a device is properly identified, authenticated and monitored at all times in a network. Applications are run in secure containers called Enclaves, which an illegitimate user would be unable to access because each process would have its own trusted environment with integrity being measured by RADIUM.

4) Spoofing Attacks: An adversary may be able to masquerade as a legitimate user/entity in a network by spoofing IP addresses, ARP entries or MAC addresses. Preventing such attacks is easier than detecting them. Xiao et. al proposed a method of identifying spoofing using reinforcement learning in wireless networks [15]. The spoofing detection algorithm aims to identify spoofing attacks using Q learning [15].

We intend to prevent spoofing attacks by employing a few protection schemes:

- We aim to prevent IP spoofing by employing packet filtering that is usually achieved by configuring a firewall and IDPS (Intrusion Detection and Prevention System). We use the signature matching algorithm proposed by Meng et. al [16], but we replace the pre-filtering of packets with access control through the C2C architecture. The challenge is to ensure that these systems are properly configured, so we follow Cisco's guide to best firewall configuration practices [17].
- We employ encryption during device authentication and communication to overcome vulnerabilities arising as a result of the design of the TCP suite.
- We are exploring the advantages offered by IPv6 in securing network communication.
- Preventing MAC spoofing may be somewhat challenging in a Smart home because most embedded devices with limited capabilities are not IP addressable and do not possess a MAC address. Consequently, the arbitration agent has to spoof MAC addresses for such devices. Our approach to preventing malicious spoofing does not rely on authenticating by MAC addresses. Rather, device certificates that are validated by an internal certification authority are used by the C2C architecture to control and moderate access to the network.

We have focused on some of the most important vulnerabilities in IoT for a Smart home setting to highlight the capabilities of our proposed architecture. We have not considered physical side channel attacks because we have assumed that the users have suitable measures in place to ensure that no unauthorized person may gain physical access to devices in such a setting.

V. Related work

Flaunzac et al. proposed a distributed SDN architecture aimed at preventing DDoS attacks [18]. The objective is to authenticate network devices and ensure that only services that the authenticated user is permitted to access are allowed. A distributed SDN architecture contains border controllers that negotiate security policies with neighboring domains [18]. Our proposed architecture can help counter some of the shortcomings of Flaunzac's approach.

- The definition of security policies is optimized to the network domain in which the devices reside and not to the devices themselves. This may not be the ideal approach to securing a diverse set of devices with varying capabilities. This is not an ideal approach because this architecture can be subject to TOCTOU (Time of Check to Time of Use) attacks. We intend to prevent these using RADIUM.
- Integrity measurement is not implemented in the architecture which exposes it to man-in-the-middle attacks. We have a robust integrity measurement architecture in place to address this.
- It may be unsafe to expose security policies by defining them at the border controller. Instead, we package them into Linux containers that are always in a suspended state and are only started when required.
- There is no pre-screening of devices before they connect to the network. A major portion of the vulnerabilities that exist are a result of outdated software and security patches which, when updated, will mitigate those risks.

Agarwal et. al proposed an architecture using edge computing [19] that is very similar to the one proposed by Flaunzac et al [18]. The idea is to compartmentalize networks into zones with each zone being controlled by a gateway controller. Security is enforced by authenticating a device and collecting TCP (Transmission Control Protocol) dumps to perform Deep Packet Inspection [19]. An analysis of the packets determines if a device is safe to be granted permission to proceed to the next hop in the flow entry [19]. The process continues at every hop. Our proposed architecture employs a C2C architecture that performs pre-screening of devices and recommends fixes which should address a majority of the vulnerabilities. Deep packet inspection and authentication of devices is a subset of all security policies we enforce through our proposed architecture.

Most of the solutions we reviewed focus on enforcing network security by controlling the flow table in SDN. The solution proposed by Bull et al. is also a similar approach [20]. The idea is for a controller to detect malicious activity by constantly monitoring network flow in an SDN network. If a suspicious activity is detected, the data is forwarded to a quarantine zone where further processing of the packet occurs [20]. This is somewhat similar to other anomaly detection schemes employed by Brocade and Rackspace [20].

VI. Prototype

A proof of concept prototype of CLIPS was developed in the Computer Systems Research Lab (CSRL) at the University of North Texas. The test environment contains the following components.

- A Netgear W3800 running OpenWRT functions as a data plane. The control plane (routing brains) of the router has been disabled by creating a virtual bridge using Open vSwitch which renders the device incapable of performing routing operations.
- The Open vSwitch is connected to a Floodlight SDN controller running on a Linux machine. The controller interfaces with the virtual switch using OpenFlow. All networking operations are performed by the controller and communicated to the switch.

The router, functioning as a wireless access point, helps deploy a local network to host the CLIPS architecture. The wireless SDN network is set up using the WiFISDN project [21].

Ideally, from a security standpoint, direct communication between devices (bypassing the SDN controller) should not be permitted, but the only way to achieve this is by disabling machine to machine M2M communication. This can prove to be counter-productive because the objective of this research is to secure the network without placing heavy restrictions on normal use of services.

To work around this issue, we enabled wireless isolation, which prevents devices on the same network from communicating with each other [21]. This forces additional processing of network packets. Additional OpenFlow rules are required to permit communication. Hence, security policies can be designed around wireless isolation. For example, eliminate communication between a refrigerator and a light bulb to keep non-essential communication to a minimum. This reduces the attack vector for DDoS attacks and enables simpler network analysis and anomaly detection.

Before a device connects to the CLIPS network, the user is expected to register it and install the required certificates. In this prototype, we have designed security policies for a microwave oven and a refrigerator using SiteWhere [4]. For a refrigerator to first connect to a network, the user is expected to authenticate it using a password. The bandwidth of the communication channel for a refrigerator is limited using the QoS parameters of Floodlight and no communication is permitted with a microwave oven. On the other hand, when a microwave oven first connects to the network, an authentication code is sent to a registered phone number. This code, in addition to a password, will serve as the authentication token. A microwave is permitted to communicate with a refrigerator and it is offered the lowest bandwidth in the network due to potential ramifications from its exploit.

The prototype demonstrated that this approach to security offers flexibility and control over the entire network topology. In addition, the architecture does not place unreasonable requirements on a novice user and has proved to be fairly user friendly. We are currently working on identifying, designing and deploying appropriate security policies in similar IoT environments.

VII. Conclusion

In this paper, we have outlined the issues of a generic approach to IoT security. As more devices with unique features and capabilities become increasingly popular, tailored security policies must be adopted.

We have argued for a more meticulous, fine-grained approach to securing IoT devices by leveraging SDN. We have proposed a novel architecture where devices are evaluated to certify that they are competent to access the network, classified into categories based on security policy requirements, and continuously monitored for suspicious behavior. We are currently in the process of evaluating the performance and feasability of the proposed architecture in a real world setting by deploying it in various IoT environments.

We have demonstrated and validated the idea using a Netgear W3800 running OpenWRT and OpenVSwitch connected to an SDN network hosted by a Floodlight controller. We found that such an approach greatly enhances the security of a home network and ensures that such devices cannot be exploited by DDoS attacks. The focus of our approach has been a balanced one in regards to convenience and security. As illustrated, an overly aggressive approach could prove to be detrimental and a highly accommodating one could leave devices open to attacks. The challenge is to find the right balance and we would like to believe that we have found such an approach for IoT security.

Acknowledgment

The authors would like to acknowledge the editorial contributions of Mr. David Struble, former Senior Software Technologist at Raytheon's Net-Centric Systems Division. This work is supported in part by the NSF Net-Centric and Cloud Software and Sytems Industry/University Cooperative Research Center and its industrial members, including Lockheed Martin Missile and Fire Control and Ashum Corp.

References

[1] "The Internet of Things 2017 Report: How the IoT is Improving Lives to Transform the World," 2017, URL: http://www.businessinsider.com/the-internet-of-things-2017-report-2017-1 [accessed: 2017-05-04].

[2] "The 10 Most Popular Internet of Things Applications Right Now," 2015, URL: https://iot-analytics.com/10-internet-of-things-applications/ [accessed: 2017-06-23].

[3] "How IoT & Smart Home Automation Will Change the Way We Live," 2016, URL: http://www.businessinsider.com/internet-of-things-smart-home-automation-2016-8 [accessed: 2017-05-21].

[4] "Sitewhere IoT Framework," 2017, URL: http://www.sitewhere.org/ [accessed:2017-06-16].

[5] "Comply to Connect Solution Overview," 2012, URL : https://trustedcomputinggroup.org/comply-connect-solution-overview/ [accessed:2017-06-10].

[6] "The Open Web Application Security Project," 2017, URL: https://www.owasp.org/index.php/ [accessed: 2017-03-20].

[7] "DDoS attack that disrupted internet was largest of its kind in history, experts say," 2016, URL: https://www.theguardian.com/technology/2016/oct/26/ddos-attack-dyn-mirai-botnet [accessed: 2017-03-26].

[8] S. Kotikela, M. Gomathisankaran, T. Shah and G. Taban, "Race free on demand integrity measurement architecture," International Conference on Privacy Security Risks and Trust (PASSAT) ASE., 2014.

[9] M. Nawir and A. Amir and N. Yaakob and O. B. Lynn, "Internet of Things (IoT): Taxonomy of security attacks,," in 3rd International Conference on Electronic Design (ICED), August 2016, pp. 321–326.

[10] "Dyn Analysis Summary Of Friday October 21 Attack," 2016, URL: https://dyn.com/blog/dyn-analysis-summary-of-friday-october-21-attack/ [accessed: 2017-05-13].

[11] "Lessons From the Dyn DDoS Attack," 2016, URL: https://securityintelligence.com/lessons-from-the-dyn-ddos-attack/ [accessed: 2017-06-2].

[12] "WannaCry Ransomware Statistics: The Numbers Behind the Outbreak," 2017, URL: https://blog.barkly.com/wannacry-ransomware-statistics-2017 [accessed: 2017-05-06].

[13] "Children's Clinic Hit by Ransomware," 2016, URL: http://www.healthcareitnews.com/news/childrens-clinic-hit-ransomware [accessed: 2017-03-22].

[14] C. Li, Z. Qin, E. Novak and Q. Li, "Securing sdn infrastructure of iot-fog network from mitm attacks," IEEE Internet of Things Journal, vol. PP, no. 99, 2017, pp. 1–1.

[15] L. Xiao and Y. Li and G. Han and G. Liu and W. Zhuang, "Phy-layer spoofing detection with reinforcement learning in wireless networks," IEEE Transactions on Vehicular Technology, vol. 65, no. 12, December 2016, pp. 10037–10047.

[16] W. Meng, W. Li and L. F. Kwok, "Towards effective trust-based packet filtering in collaborative network environments," IEEE Transactions on Network and Service Management, vol. 14, no. 1, March 2017, pp. 233–245.

[17] "Cisco Firewall Best Practices Guide," 2017, URL: http://www.cisco.com/c/en/us/about/security-center/firewall-best-practices.html [accessed: 2017-06-13].

[18] O. Flauzac and C. Gonzlez and A. Hachani and F. Nolot, "SDN Based Architecture for IoT and Improvement of the Security," in 2015 IEEE 29th International Conference on Advanced Information Networking and Applications Workshops, March 2015, pp. 688–693.

[19] C. Aggarwal and K. Srivastava, "Securing IOT devices using SDN and edge computing," in 2nd International Conference on Next Generation Computing Technologies (NGCT), October 2016, pp. 877–882.

[20] P. Bull, R. Austin, E. Popov, M. Sharma and R. Watson, "Flow Based Security for IoT Devices Using an SDN Gateway," in IEEE 4th International Conference on Future Internet of Things and Cloud (FiCloud), August 2016, pp. 157–163.

[21] "Software-Defined Wi-Fi Networks with Wireless Isolation," 2017, URL: https://wiki.helsinki.fi/display/WiFiSDN/Software-Defined+Wi-Fi+Networks+with+Wireless+Isolation [accessed: 2017-04-12].

Sustainability and Diversity of Open Source Software Communities:

Analysis of the Android Open Source Project

Remo Eckert, Andreas Mueller
University of Bern
Institute of Information Systems
Bern, Switzerland
e-mail: remo.eckert@iwi.unibe.ch, andreas.mueller@students.unibe.ch

***Abstract* — Open Source Software (OSS) projects rely on the efforts of thousands of software developers. The sustainability and diversity of these communities are two important factors for the long-term viability of OSS communities. This paper reviews the research on OSS sustainability and diversity. Drawing on the findings of measures on sustainability and diversity, we applied a number of the established metrics to the Android Open Source Project and found that over a third of all contributions originate from Google. Surprisingly, in 2015 we saw a decrease in the total number of contributors within the Android project. Findings from our analysis highlight the importance of sustainability and diversity for the development of OSS.**

Keywords-Open Source Software; Sustainability; Diversity; Android.

I. INTRODUCTION

Companies need to preserve their systems and digital assets for a considerable time. In such scenarios, problems would arise if the commercial vendor of adopted proprietary software were to leave the market or stop its development [1]. Popular OSS projects attract thousands of individuals and firms who collectively contribute to the software. OSS has seen a considerable increase in attention over the last few years. The success of various OSS projects such as Linux and Apache is now widely recognized. OSS has become a strategic asset for various firms who even choose to dedicate development resources to OSS projects [2]. Similarly, in the context of OSS development, if a dominant player leaves or stops its contributions to the project, this may influence the success of the OSS. Therefore, both for companies and for the individuals contributing to OSS projects, the stability and long-term success of the projects are key.

In many ICT sectors, OSS has been found to be relevant when it comes to sustainability [1]. According to Gamalielsson and Lundell [3], a primary factor for the success of any OSS project lies in the sustainability of the community. There are many aspects of OSS projects that can affect community sustainability, such as project management, incentives for contributors or the license of the project [4].

Building on diversity literature, Daniel et al. [5] show that diversity influences two critical outcomes of OSS projects - the community engagement and market success. Another recent study on social diversity by Aué et al. [6] investigated the relationship between project growth and the social diversity of OSS projects on GitHub. They found a statistically significant link between project rating and gender and geographical diversity. Drawing on measurements found in the literature on sustainability and diversity, this paper analyzes the sustainability and diversity of the Android Open Source Project (AOSP).

Section II presents our research questions. In Section III, previous research on OSS sustainability and diversity is shown. An overview of the AOSP and the OSS sustainability and diversity measures applied to the AOSP are outlined in Section IV. The discussion follows in Section V.

II. RESEARCH QUESTIONS

According to Chengalur-Smith et al. [7], sustainability is defined as *"the ability of an organism or an ecosystem to maintain its activity and productivity over time."* However, this definition of sustainability is a vague concept. Our aim is to find measurements on OSS community sustainability. RQ1 deals with the sustainability of OSS communities and is as following:

- **RQ1: How can sustainability of OSS communities be measured?**

In their study, Daniel et al. [5] investigated whether different types of diversity influence the success of OSS. They found that projects in later stages benefit more from diversity than projects in earlier stages. RQ2 deals with the diversity of OSS communities and is as follows:

- **RQ2: How can diversity of OSS communities be measured?**

The goal of this paper is to show measurements of OSS community sustainability and diversity found in the literature, then apply and discuss them in the context of a well-known OSS project. This is why we chose the AOSP community.

III. Literature Review

This section analyzes existing work in the context of OSS sustainability and OSS diversity.

A. *OSS Sustainabiliy*

Gamalielsson and Lundell [3] underline how the sustainability of communities is one of the most important factors for the long-term sustainability of OSS itself. They highlight the significance of governance for sustainability, which is also identified by O'Mahony and Becky [8].

Ghapanchi [9] provides an overview of prior research on OSS development sustainability and summarizes the various drivers of OSS projects, such as: developer and user attraction, development base, project age, having developers with higher levels of different skills, project status & activity, having a nonmarket sponsor and having a copyleft license. He investigated the impact of a project's capabilities on its development sustainability and found that OSS projects are more likely to succeed if they are able to: process a higher percentage of suggested features, quickly remove identified defects and release the software them at a faster rate.

Chengalur-Smith et al. [7] tested software projects empirically in terms of their activity and contribution patterns. They used a model of project sustainability based on organizational ecology, termed Structural Equation Modelling. As a contribution to research, they provide a table of measurements, comprising indicators and descriptions. They derive the following statement as a conclusion: *"Sustainability requires certain levels of activity to be maintained over a long period of time"* [7].

Farmer and Norman [10] made a case study review on OSS sustainability in which they describe and analyze seven successful OSS projects. They define sustainability of OSS at two levels: Sustainability I with a more innovative early product stage and Sustainability II which is product and service oriented.

It is Wilson [11] and Gonzalez-Barahona [12] who provide a framework for how to measure OSS sustainability. Both have published their approaches on OSS sustainability measures on the Internet; neither has been published in a journal to date. Wilson [11] provides five key indicators as informal criteria for evaluating the sustainability of an OSS community. The key indicators are code contribution activity, release history, user community, longevity and ecosystems. Beginning with code contribution activity, contributions can be tracked and the community activity visualized through tables and charts. In combination with a release history, interesting insights about governance issues can be found. The user community is the core of the software project. Wilson [11] brings out its essence *"Software isn't sustainable without users"*. When it comes to longevity, projects pass through different phases: From creation through intense activity into a stable productive stage and then, finally, dying or becoming forked or replaced by a new project. The last key indicators shift the focus of the ecosystem onto developers and users of a project. Companies will engage or initialize an OSS project and provide their own software engineers, financial resources and other services to the project [11].Furthermore, Kilamo et al. [13] show the increasing trend for companies to release their proprietary software as OSS.

Finally, Gonzalez-Barahona [12] provides a group classification on OSS starting with the fundamental question for empirical research on OSS communities - which metrics should be used. His article classifies five metrics for sustainable OSS: activity, size, performance, demographics and diversity.

B. *OSS Diversity*

In their study, Daniel et al. [5] investigated whether different types of diversity influence OSS success in terms of community engagement and market success. They understand separation diversity to be the differences in position or opinion within the community. Variety diversity captures the range of information that members bring into the community. Disparity diversity specifies the power and resource differences within the communities. To measure community engagement, they calculate the contributions to the project, and to determine market success they evaluate the attention the project receives from users. In general, their empirical results show that diversity has both positive and negative effects on OSS project success. They found that projects in later stages benefit more from disparity and separation diversity than projects in earlier stages. If a project reaches later stages of development, it increases in size and complexity and attracts more users with more varied needs. If the project is dealing with more external stakeholders, it benefits from having more disparity and separation diversity within its own developers. Other findings are the positive effect of cultural separation diversity on market success where cultural separation has a negative effect on community engagement.

Vasilescu et al. [14] applied a regression analysis to GitHub data to study how gender and tenure diversity relates to team productivity and turnover. They explain why diversity attributes may be different in online groups (e.g., OSS communities) than for offline groups and identify four factors. Firstly, geographic and cultural dispersion is common in OSS and contributors rarely meet face-to-face. Secondly, OSS teams are fluid and rather task-focused. Thirdly, OSS teams are comprised mainly of volunteers and have a high turnover. Fourthly, often a small group of developers in OSS develop the majority of the software. They found that gender and tenure diversity are significant and positive predictors of productivity.

Vasilescu et al. [15] performed a user survey of software teams working on GitHub. They analyzed how teamwork and individual attributes were perceived by developers. One of their findings is that developers have embraced the inherent diversity from GitHub teams and, for the most part, benefit from it. Another positive effect is at the team level, where diversity can provide new ideas, perspectives, skills, and approaches to problem-solving.

In another study, Vasilescu et al. [16] gathered information on alias resolution, location data and gender inference techniques from a large dataset of GitHub projects. For the gender inference techniques, they applied an approach including heuristics (e.g., Russian surnames ending in -ova are female) and female/male frequency name lists for different countries.

Another recent study on social diversity from Aué et al. [6] investigated the relationship between project growth and social diversity of OSS projects on GitHub. They found a statistically significant correlation between project rating and gender and geographical diversity.

Alfaro [17] focuses on nationality diversity in global software development. Despite not including OSS, his research involves aspects relevant to OSS diversity. He states that global teams are diverse by nature since individuals come from different countries and cultural backgrounds, which is a general characteristic of many OSS projects. One of his findings is the positive effect between nationality diversity on team performance. In addition, he explains how teams with low temporal dispersion have performed better compared to teams with high temporal dispersion, independent of their degree of nationality diversity.

Diamant and Daniel [18] investigated developer's learning and the culture context in OSS projects. Their results show that diversity exposes developers to different work styles, problem-solving approaches and development techniques which offer opportunities for learning.

IV. THE CASE OF THE ANDROID OPEN SOURCE PROJECT

Android dominates the market for Mobile Operating Systems [19]. Google, under the holding Alphabet Inc. enjoys increasing economic supremacy and influence on Android. However, there are numerous other companies, non-profit organizations (NPO) and individuals who contribute to the project. The AOSP consists of an ecosystem of sub-projects and activities with numerous protagonists. There is a whole industry behind it: NPOs like, for instance, the Linux Foundation; several original equipment manufacturers such as Garmin and Huawei; as well as service companies such as eBay and Accenture [20].

Data gathering: To answer the two research questions, we cloned the AOSP repositories and extracted the commit history from the AOSP as described by Shihab et al. [21]. The commit history was cloned and converted to 1,144 XML files and consists of 14,150,546 data entries. The 1,144 XML files were merged into one large dataset which comprises the following information: author date, author e-mail, author name, committer e-mail, committer name, committer date, project, subject and commit hash codes. The author is the person who originally wrote the patch, whereas the committer is the person who applied the patch.

Data cleansing: Some entries were invalid due to data errors, missing content or unreasonable dates: for example, commits with a timestamp before the launch of the Android project, such as 1st January 1970 or, alternatively, dating from 25th April 2037. By choosing a start date of 2005-01.01, 132,527 (0.94%) observations were excluded from the dataset. The Android repositories were cloned on 2016-12-21. As the data for the full month December 2016 was not complete, choosing 2016-11-30 as the end date for the dataset meant that 9,639 (0.07%) observations were not included in the dataset. Finally, seven repositories are outside the chosen period. The final dataset consists of 14,008,380 observations from 1,135 repositories.

Single Commit Hash: An analysis of the dataset indicated how several commit entries contained exactly the same XML tags, such as alias, e-mail, date for authors and committers, subject and hash codes. The only difference was in the sub-project name. An investigation of the commit hash code's purpose and how it is generated, confirms that it is a unique identifier. The commit hash code is generated by an algorithm based on the commits content. If a change is part of several sub-projects, relevant titles and their commits will be cloned several times. In conclusion, it is questionable whether the overall number of commits for the whole AOSP is an appropriate community activity measure when an indefinite number of commits are cloned several times.

If the whole dataset of 14,008,380 observations is adjusted for the single commit hashes, the adjusted dataset retains 3,085,901 observations. This leads to the question: Which dataset is the correct one? This depends on what one wants to measure. If the overall activity of the AOSP is to be measured, then the 3,085,901 observations are more appropriate because work conducted on the code base is not overestimated through cloning the commit several times. On the contrary: if questions relating to individual committers' involvement in different sub-projects and activity in sub-projects is to be answered, then the 14,008,380 observations are appropriate.

A. *Android Community Sustainability*

To answer the first research question, this paper applies approaches and metrics from literature relating to OSS community sustainability.

Firstly, Gonzalez-Barahona [12] used five metrics to track an OSS community: activity, size, performance, demographics and diversity. Secondly, Wilson [11] suggested key indicators such as code activity, releases, user community, longevity and ecosystem to evaluate OSS community sustainability. To merge both approaches into a common basis and to start the investigation on the AOSP community development, this paper uses elements of community activity, size and demographics to answer RQ1.

Activity: Starting with activity, Gonzalez-Barahona [12] proposes this measure as a first view of how active a community is and recommends tracking the number of commits over time. As Wilson [11] describes, for a project to be sustainable, it must have contributors, and its codebase needs to be evolving.

Similar to Wilson [11], Figure 1 shows the time stamp of each commit over all Android sub-projects clustered into quarterly periods. As discussed, to relate the issue to cloned commits, the data in Figure 1 is adjusted to contain only one single commit hash.

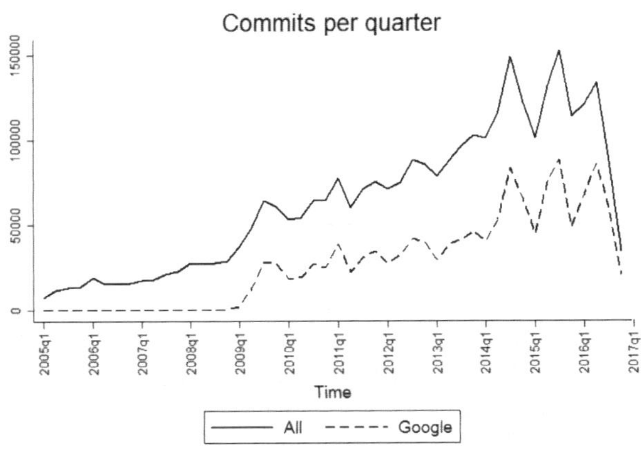

Figure 1. Commits per quarter (author perspective).

In general, Figure 1 indicates an increasing pattern of commits over time. To identify Google's share in overall commit activity, a second time series for commits originating from Google is included, using the e-mail domain part. As Figure 1 shows, Google's share of the AOSP is significant. A surprising finding is the commencement of Google's activity in early 2009, despite Google having already acquired Android Inc. in 2005. One possible explanation for this is that Android Inc. core developers may have switched to Google e-mail domains in early 2009.

Disregarding the drop in activity from summer 2016, the data curve for the AOSP indicates steadily increasing activity. This is the intuitive expectation of a successful project since, according to Wilson [11], it is "*...a good sign as it indicates that the project is picking up developers...*".
A possible explanation for the decrease after summer 2016 could be that there is a time delay from the author code commit Git push until it is applied in the master branch. The following two explanations are proposed: A first possible reason for the delay could lie in the Android development process. The Gerrit process flow chart for the AOSP illustrates the different steps necessary for a change to be applied, a process that could result in a delay. It takes a certain amount of time until a proposed code change from an author, via his commit, is processed, tested, reviewed, potentially modified and finally submitted to the public depot for future synchronizations [22]. Secondly, the most compelling evidence comes from the AOSP web page which suggests that a reason for the delay could come from the next generation of Android, which would first be developed privately and then released to the public domain at a later stage [23].

Size: According to Gonzalez-Barahona [12], project size includes aspects of the number of people participating and the number of contributors in an OSS project. He specifically highlights the importance of active contributors because they lead the community and often deliver a major portion of the source code. Table I shows the 10 most active Android sub-projects, including their number of commits, authors and committers. As Table I shows, the AOSP attracts thousands of different authors.

TABLE I. 10 MOST ACTIVE ANDROID SUB-PROJECTS.

#	Sub-Project	#Commits	#Authors	#Committers
1	platform_external_linux-kselftest	616,038	15,731	581
2	kernel_hikey-linaro	567,369	15,001	576
3	platform_hardware_bsp_kernel_common_v4.4	564,251	14,814	546
4	kernel_msm	563,484	14,777	571
5	platform_hardware_bsp_kernel_common_v4.1	521,866	13,910	524
6	platform_hardware_bsp_kernel_imagination_v4.1	521,401	13,858	551
7	kernel_common	483,913	13,026	541
8	kernel_goldfish	483,913	13,026	541
9	kernel_mediatek	483,913	13,026	541
10	platform_hardware_bsp_kernel_freescale_picoimx	440,446	12,196	527

To understand the calculated figures and to compare them with the size of other OSS projects, we referred to the highest ranking projects on OpenHub.net which provides descriptive information about OSS projects, including the number of commits and different authors. Only Chromium with 578,455 commits and 5,406 authors almost reaches this level, but is in fact a Google-driven project too. Of the non-Google OSS, Mozilla Firefox with 343,841 commits and 4,813 authors reaches a comparable scale in the top-ranked AOSP sub-projects.

Demographics: Gamalielsson and Lundell [3] accentuated how important it is for an OSS project with long life-cycles to recruit new and retain current contributors to its community. An instrument to visualize this attribute on an OSS project is the aging chart proposed by Gonzalez-Barahona [12].

The main components of the aging chart are two graphical bar categories, which indicate the attracted and retained developers over time. Figure 2 shows the aging chart for the AOSP community. The attracted bar (red color) summarizes the new developers who contributed for the first time in that particular year. Unlike the aging chart proposed by Gonzalez-Barahona, a third bar is included to summarize the lost developers (blue color). This additional bar makes the representation more intuitive, as the retained developers (green color) can be estimated visually. In the Aging Chart shown in Figure 2, a developer is still considered as active even if the developer made a break in some following years after the first contribution and then contributed again.

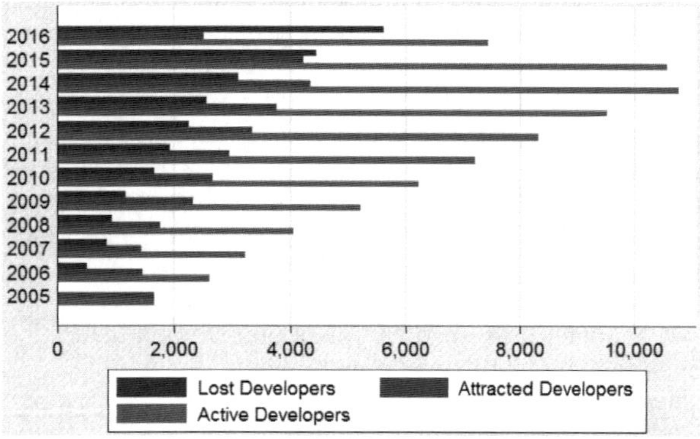

Figure 2. Aging chart of the AOSP.

The AOSP from 2005 onwards indicates a rapidly increasing trend in attracting new developers, which peaks in 2014, which is in general a good sign for the AOSP. Nevertheless, the number of developers leaving the project is also increasing and exceeds the number of new attracted developers in 2015. As indicated through the retained bars, the absolute peak of the AOSP developers is reached in 2014 and then starts to decline. 2016 is not representative, since the data set does not include the entire year. Furthermore, another fuzziness which influences 2016 data is the delay on reported commits from announcement until release on the Android repositories, as discussed. It seems that the AOSP reached its peak in 2014. It would be interesting to investigate for the coming years whether the AOSP manages to retain a stable amount of developers.

B. *Android Community Diversity*

To answer the second research question, this paper applies approaches and metrics from literature relating to OSS community diversity.

Wilson [11] described the importance of the ecosystem, taking into consideration the diversity between the companies that engage with a project. Likewise, Gonzalez-Barahona [12] questions what will happen if a major contributor leaves the project. Considering the composition of the AOSP in which a major firm such as Google takes on a significant role in the dispersion and enhancement of OSS, major contributors shall be identified.

To determine whether a contributor had a commercial, independent or educational background, an approach comparable to Heppler et al. [24] working with the domain-part of the e-mail address was used. The entries were manually selected and classified based on the number of contributions. If the domain-part included ".edu", for example, we labelled the entity as Education; ".org" specified an organization. Companies were manually identified through their company domain, such as "google.", "Samsung." or "ibm.". Overall, 197 entities were manually selected.

A total of 300,142 (9.8%) observations remain unidentified and will not be further disentangled, because the effort increases disproportionately for every fraction additionally identified. The search field controls the accuracy of the identified entities. More specific terms increase the accuracy but lower the possibility of identified entities. For instance, by choosing "intel" instead of "intel." more entries can be identified. It was decided on a case to case basis whether more specific or open terms were used to identify an entity.

Tables II and III list the top 15 entities and the number of commits from an author and committer perspective.

TABLE II. TOP 15 IDENTIFIED AUTHORS.

#	Entity	Branch	#Commits	%
1	Google	Firm	1,189,998	38.6
2	Individual Gmail	Individual	200,155	6.49
3	Jet Brains	Firm	145,140	4.7
4	Android	Firm	122,551	3.97
5	Intel	Firm	94,278	3.06
6	Linux Foundation	Organization	87,274	2.83
7	RedHat	Firm	74,110	2.4
8	Apple	Firm	73,855	2.39
9	Chromium	Organization	52,933	1.72
10	not provided	Individual	31,804	1.03
11	Gentoo	Organization	29,079	0.94
12	Suse	Firm	24,930	0.81
13	Samsung	Firm	24,621	0.8
14	IBM	Firm	23,415	0.76
15	Linaro	Organization	22,279	0.72

TABLE III. TOP 15 IDENTIFIED COMMITTERS.

#	Entity	Branch	#Commits	%
1	Google	Firm	833,857	27.02
2	Android	Firm	546,935	17.72
3	Linux Foundation	Organization	267,127	8.66
4	Jet Brains	Firm	145,381	4.71
5	Individual Gmail	Individual	140,068	4.54
6	RedHat	Firm	81,361	2.64
7	Intel	Firm	78,278	2.54
8	Apple	Firm	70,496	2.28
9	Suse	Firm	49,317	1.6
10	Chromium	Organization	42,110	1.36
11	not provided	Individual	32,499	1.05
12	Gentoo	Organization	28,792	0.93
13	Linaro	Organization	25,718	0.83
14	Go Lang	Individual	25,539	0.83
15	Kitware	Firm	23,706	0.77

The results demonstrate Google's dominant position with 38.6% of all identified commits. Other major contributors came from companies such as Intel, Apple, Samsung and IBM. Top ranked firms such as Suse and RedHat sell OSS services and distribute their own Linux distribution. Other top contributors are Jet Brains, Gentoo and Linaro. An interesting observation was that the Linux Foundation made a contribution to the AOSP that, at 8.66% was higher on the committer side than on the author side (2.83%). In other words, the Linux Foundation was more focused on reviewing and applying changes than in bringing in new ones.

Gini coefficient: The Gini coefficient is a measure to determine inequality. The Gini coefficient is often used to express a status criterion because it describes heterogeneity and is the most frequently used measure of inequality [25]. In our case, the Gini coefficient is used to portray the inequality in the distribution of contributions by authors. The Gini coefficient indicates how unequal contributions are distributed among the authors. A Gini coefficient of zero expresses equality, whereas a coefficient of one expresses inequality. Using the Gini coefficient for the AOSP allows comparison to other OSS or, in an extended perspective, to other applications in general. Figure 3 shows the Lorenz curve of the AOSP.

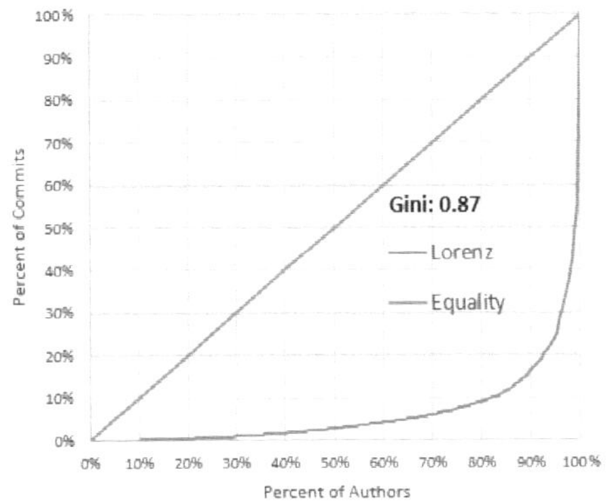

Figure 3. Lorenz curve for the AOSP.

The Gini coefficient of 0.87 for the AOSP is close to one, which describes a strongly unequal distribution. The main reason for this is Google's relative large share (38.6%) in the overall number of commits. However, an unequal distribution of commit activity in OSS projects is not uncommon [26].

V. DISCUSSION

This paper contributes to the literature on OSS community sustainability and diversity in two ways: First, it provides a broad literature review on OSS measurements of diversity and sustainability; and, second, it applies a number of these measures to the AOSP. Both the literature on OSS community sustainability and on diversity highlight the importance of the OSS ecosystem for the development of OSS.

According to Gamalielsson and Lundell [3], a primary factor for the success of any OSS projects is the sustainability of their community. Sustainability of OSS communities can be measured in various different ways, as our literature review shows. When it comes to diversity, there are effects on the long-term viability on OSS, since diversity influences the OSS success in terms of community engagement and market success, as Daniel et al. [5] show.

In our paper, we examine these two concepts with special regard to the AOSP project. As we have demonstrated, the AOSP ecosystem has grown steadily since 2005. The AOSP has been able to maintain a high level of activity over a prolonged period of time. As the aging chart indicates, the AOSP attracted new developers and kept them within the project between 2005 and 2014. However, in 2015, there is a surprising result: the number of lost developers is higher than the number of new developers attracted. Because the dataset for 2016 is incomplete, we are unable to determine whether this is the same for 2016. If Google is not able to attract and retain developers for the AOSP, the sustainability of the project may be decreasing. A project's ability to attract developers and active user resources was found to have a positive effect on project sustainability [7].

Google's dominant position within the AOSP cannot be overlooked. The overall size of the AOSP is vast and is separated into several sub-projects, each of which is comparable in size and activity to other complete OSS projects, such as Mozilla Firefox.

Although hundreds of different firms, organizations and individuals were identified, at 38.6% of all commits, Google's share is tremendous. Moreover, the Gini coefficient of 0.87 for the AOSP shows that the distribution is highly unequal. Google's dominant role poses risks for the AOSP if Google were to leave the project or decrease its investments in it.

Communities with a small number of major contributors are more dependent on those contributors than are communities with several major contributors. Diversity is therefore important for the resilience of an OSS community. The more diverse a community in terms of the different individuals and organizations contributing to the project, the less dependent it is on a single contributor and the more resilient it will be. However, having a major contributor for an OSS project can boost its development.

It would be beneficial for future research to analyze the implications on the project success when core contributors leave the project. The relationship between core contributors and project success could bring some interesting insights on the sustainability and diversity of OSS communities.

ACKNOLEDGEMENTS

The authors thank Michael Single for his constructive suggestions and comments on this research.

REFERENCES

[1] B. Lundell, B. Lings, and A. Syberfeldt, "Practitioner perceptions of Open Source software in the embedded systems area," *Journal of Systems and Software*, vol. 84, no. 9, pp. 1540–1549, Sep. 2011.

[2] G. von Krogh and S. Spaeth, "The open source software phenomenon: Characteristics that promote research," *The Journal of Strategic Information Systems*, vol. 16, no. 3, pp. 236–253, 2007.

[3] J. Gamalielsson and B. Lundell, "Sustainability of Open Source software communities beyond a fork: How and why has the LibreOffice project evolved?," *Journal of Systems and Software*, vol. 89, pp. 128–145, 2014.

[4] A. Bonaccorsi and C. Rossi, "Comparing motivations of individual programmers and firms to take part in the open source movement: From community to business," *Knowledge, Technology & Policy*, vol. 18, no. 4, pp. 40–64, 2006.
[5] S. Daniel, R. Agarwal, and K. J. Stewart, "The Effects of Diversity in Global, Distributed Collectives: A Study of Open Source Project Success," *Information Systems Research*, vol. 24, no. 2, pp. 312–333, Jun. 2013.
[6] J. Aué, M. Haisma, K. F. Tómasdóttir, and A. Bacchelli, "Social Diversity and Growth Levels of Open Source Software Projects on GitHub," in *Proceedings of the 10th ACM/IEEE International Symposium on Empirical Software Engineering and Measurement*, 2016, p. 41.
[7] I. Chengalur-Smith, A. Sidorova, and S. Daniel, "Sustainability of free/libre open source projects: A longitudinal study," *Journal of the Association for Information Systems*, vol. 11, no. 11, p. 657, 2010.
[8] S. O'Mahony and B. A. Bechky, "Boundary organizations: Enabling collaboration among unexpected allies," *Administrative Science Quarterly*, vol. 53, no. 3, pp. 422–459, 2008.
[9] A. H. Ghapanchi, "Predicting software future sustainability: A longitudinal perspective," *Information Systems*, vol. 49, pp. 40–51, 2015.
[10] J. Farmer and J. Norman, "A case study review of open source sustainability models." JISC University of Oxford, 2007.
[11] S. Wilson, "How to evaluate the sustainability of an open source project," 11-Dec-2013. [Online]. Available: http://oss-watch.ac.uk/resources/evaluatingsustainability. [Retrieved: August 2017].
[12] G.-B. Jesus M., "Top 5 open source community metrics to track," 2015. [Online]. Available: https://opensource.com/business/15/12/top-5-open-source-community-metrics-track. [Retrieved: August 2017].
[13] T. Kilamo, I. Hammouda, T. Mikkonen, and T. Aaltonen, "From proprietary to open source—Growing an open source ecosystem," *Journal of Systems and Software*, vol. 85, no. 7, pp. 1467–1478, 2012.
[14] B. Vasilescu *et al.*, "Gender and Tenure Diversity in GitHub Teams," in *Proceedings of the 33rd Annual ACM Conference on Human Factors in Computing Systems*, 2015, pp. 3789–3798.
[15] B. Vasilescu, V. Filkov, and A. Serebrenik, "Perceptions of Diversity on Git Hub: A User Survey," in *Cooperative and Human Aspects of Software Engineering (CHASE)*, 2015, pp. 50–56.
[16] B. Vasilescu, A. Serebrenik, and V. Filkov, "A data set for social diversity studies of GitHub teams," in *Proceedings of the 12th Working Conference on Mining Software Repositories*, 2015, pp. 514–517.
[17] I. Alfaro, "Nationality diversity and performance in global software development teams: The role of temporal dispersion and leadership," in *International Conference on Information Systems (ICIS)*, 2010, pp. 116–134.
[18] E. I. Diamant and S. L. Daniel, "Learning in Open-Source Software (OSS) Development: How Organizational and National Culture Impact Developers' Learning.," in *International Conference on Information Systems (ICIS)*, 2010, pp. 66–76.
[19] International Data Corporation (IDC), "Smartphone OS Market Share 2016 Q3," 2016. [Online]. Available: http://www.idc.com/promo/smartphone-market-share/os. [Retrieved: August 2017].
[20] Open Handset Alliance, 2017. [Online]. Available: http://www.openhandsetalliance.com. [Retrieved: August 2017].
[21] E. Shihab, Y. Kamei, and P. Bhattacharya, "Mining challenge 2012: The android platform," in *Proceedings of the 9th IEEE Working Conference on Mining Software Repositories*, 2012, pp. 112–115.
[22] A. Hoog, *Android Forensics: Investigation, Analysis, and Mobile Security for Google Android*. Elsevier, 2011.
[23] Android Source, "Codelines, Branches, and Releases | Android Open Source Project," 2017. [Online]. Available: https://source.android.com/source/code-lines.html. [Retrieved: August 2017].
[24] L. Heppler, R. Eckert, and M. Stuermer, "Who cares about my feature request?," in *IFIP International Conference on Open Source Systems*, 2016, pp. 85–96.
[25] P. M. Blau, "A macrosociological theory of social structure," *American journal of sociology*, vol. 83, no. 1, pp. 26–54, 1977.
[26] M. Goeminne and T. Mens, "Evidence for the pareto principle in open source software activity," in *the Joint Porceedings of the 1st International workshop on Model Driven Software Maintenance and 5th International Workshop on Software Quality and Maintainability*, 2011, pp. 74–82.

Extracting Executable Architecture From Legacy Code Using Static Reverse Engineering

Rehman Arshad,Kung-Kiu-Lau
School of Computer Science, University of Manchester
Kilburn Building, Oxford Road, Manchester, United Kingdom
e-mail: rehman.arshad, kung-kiu.lau @manchester.ac.uk

***Abstract*—Static reverse engineering techniques are based on structural information of the code. They work by building a model of abstraction that considers control structures in the code in order to extract some high-level notation. So far, most of these techniques produce abstraction models or feature locations but not the executable architecture that can transform the legacy code into modern paradigm of programming. Few approaches that extract architectural notation either require the code to be in component based orientation or lack automation. This paper presents an ongoing research that can extract executable architecture as X-MAN (component model) components from legacy code. An executable architecture contains structural and behavioural aspects of the system in an analysed manner. The extracted components can be integrated with other systems due to re-usability of the X-MAN component model. This approach neither requires the source code to be in component based orientation nor it lacks automation.**

***Keywords*—Reverse Engineering; Static Analysis; Component Based Development; Abstract Syntax Tree.**

I. INTRODUCTION

Reverse Engineering techniques are classified into *Static*, *Textual*, *Dynamic* and *Hybrid* [1]. Static techniques are based on structural information of the code. They work by building a model of states of the program and then determine all possible routes of the program at each step. Such model is called static abstraction model and it requires a fair consideration between preciseness and granularity [2]. As these techniques consider all control flows, they provide the maximum recall; this recall comes at the price of false positive results.

Reverse engineering is mostly used to extract high level abstraction models or semantics from the source code [1]. Such extraction is useful for documentation, variability management, etc., but it cannot provide an executable architecture after extraction. "An executable architecture is a dynamic simulation of an architecture model. It captures both structural and behavioural aspects of the architecture in a form that can be visualised and analysed in a time dependent manner" [3]. A reverse engineering approach that can provide executable architecture can transform the source code into a specific notation that can be used in further implementation. In order to get an executable architecture from the source code, a technique has to consider every line of code by following the abstraction model of analysis. Textual techniques are mostly used for bug localisation or finding feature locations in the source code [4] and dynamic techniques can only produce results based on the execution trace [5]. Extracting an architecture is different form extracting high level abstraction models because an architecture has to show that every functionality exists in the original source code. Therefore, due to some important characteristics like maximum recall and minimum loss of information, static reverse engineering is the best analysis technique to consider for extracting an executable architecture from the legacy systems [2].

This paper presents an ongoing research on the extraction of executable architecture from legacy systems. The proposed technique is called Reverse Engineering X-MAN *(RX-MAN)*. RX-MAN uses static reverse engineering to extract X-MAN components [6] from the legacy code.

The remainder of this paper is organised as follows: Section II includes related work in the domain of static reverse engineering. Section III includes the basics of X-MAN component model. Section IV explains the proposed research methodology. Section V shows a simple evaluation and Section VI includes conclusion and future work.

II. RELATED WORK

Static reverse engineering techniques can be classified by several parameters and [1] [7] [8] are some of the detailed surveys in the domain of static reverse engineering. Most of the static approaches are used for finding feature locations in the legacy systems. Some of the most well-known techniques are RecoVar [9], FLPV [10], Dependency Graph [11], Concern Graph [12], Automatic Generation [13], Language Independent Approach [14], Concern Identification [15] and Semi-Automatic Approach [16]. Out of the above-mentioned techniques, RecoVar [9] produces variability model from the source code. FLPV [10] generates code as set of optional and mandatory. Dependency Graph [11], Concern Graph [12] and Concern Identification [15] produce high level abstraction of code as graphs. Language Independent Approach [14] produces feature model from the source code. Automatic Generation [13] and Semi-Automatic Approach [16] generate a tool based view that helps in understanding the source code. All these techniques produce results in the form of high level abstraction that can help in understanding the legacy systems. Such outputs can help in analysing the system but cannot reuse the legacy code to transform it into executable architecture. Such architecture can be reused to build modern systems or can be extended to existing systems, e.g., X-MAN components can be re-composed to form family of systems and same components can be used across many systems due to modularity and separation of concerns in X-MAN component model. Such architectural output can also help against system erosion with time [17].

There are few approaches with aim to extract architecture from the source code. One of them is JAVACompExt [17] by Anquetil et al. It is a heuristic based approach that extracts Architecture Description Language (ADL) components along with the communication and services among them. This approach however requires the source code to be written with "componentization" in mind. Componentization is the process of atomizing resources into separate reusable packages that can be easily recombined [18]. Another approach by Antoun et al. [19] re-engineers the JAVA code into Arch JAVA [20], though the process lacks automation. The approach by Chouambe et al. [21] produces composite components but the source system has to be implemented in component based notation. The presented approach in this paper is different from the above approaches because:

- It is automated.
- It does not require the source code to be in component notation.
- Unlike those approaches that are focused on architecture retrieval, our approach aims for component creation by source code transformation.

III. X-MAN Component Model

A component is defined by its unit of composition and composition mechanism, [22] e.g., in ADL, composition takes place via ports and unit of composition is an architectural unit defined as a class with provided and required services. X-MAN is different from other well-known component models because it separates control and computation unlike ADL based component models in which control and data cannot be separated and transmitted via ports together, e.g., Koala [23].

X-MAN components are defined by computation units (unit of composition) and connectors (composition mechanism). There are two types of components in X-MAN: atomic and composite. Atomic components have a computation unit and an invocation connector (composition mechanism) that acts as an interface of that component. Composite components can consist of set of atomic or composite components that are connected by composition connectors (composition mechanism). Composition connector of a composite component can be: (i) Sequencer, or (ii) Selector. A sequencer provides sequencing of atomic/composite components in a composite component and a selector provides conditional branching. All X-MAN components preserve encapsulation. Atomic components do this by encapsulate computation unit and composite do so by encapsulate computation units and composition connectors. It means composite components also preserve encapsulation of their nested components, which provides a hierarchy of encapsulated components. That is why X-MAN component model is hierarchical in nature. Further details of X-MAN component model have been discussed in [22]. Basic semantics of X-MAN component model are presented in Figure 1. Each component can have a set of services. A service is exposed functionality of a component that is used to send and receive data elements, needed for execution, e.g., A *Bank* component can have *Deposit*, *Withdraw* and *CheckBalance* services with *BalanceInformation* and *AccountNumber* as send/receive data elements.

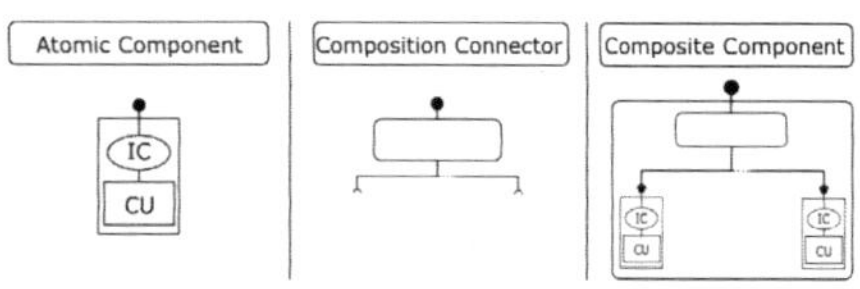

Fig. 1. X-MAN Component Model.

IV. RX-MAN: A static reverse engineering approach

Figure 2 shows the methodology of RX-MAN. Java has been selected as the language of source code to be analysed. The source code to be reverse engineered can be: (i) A single application system (ii) Just a set of classes, e.g., any library or SDK that cannot be executed on its own.

In case of single application system, output will be a one big X-MAN system that will show the whole functionality of the source code with the benefits of modularity and hierarchy of X-MAN component model. Control structures in the source code will be transformed as composition connectors. In case of the source code which is just a SDK or a set of classes, the output will be X-MAN atomic components. These components can be deposited to X-MAN repository and can be recomposed for further implementation. The brief overview of the whole process is as follows:

1) AST Tree Generation: Abstract Syntax Tree (AST) is a powerful parser in JAVA. In this step, the source code is transformed into AST nodes. Each node is mapped to its respective sub nodes, e.g., each package node is mapped to its class nodes, each class node is mapped to its method nodes and each method node is mapped to its parameters, return node, function type node etc. Detailed algorithm is not given due to its voluminous details.

2) Parsing the Nodes: AST allows the code re-writing in order to implement small changes in the code. However, AST re-writing is not powerful and convenient enough to transform the system into some other complex notation. Therefore, an intermediate data structure has been used to extract information from the nodes to preserve it in a meaningful notation. In this step, invocations of all methods are indexed and mapped against each other.

Algorithm 1 METHOD ALLOCATION

```
Require: PackageClassList, MethodClassList, utilityComponentList
  while i < MethodClassList do
    if Mi.Visited ← False then
      Get Invocations of Mi
      if Mi.invocations is NULL then
        Mi.getPackageName
        if Mi.PackageName already exists then
          AddU(PackageName,Mi)
          Mi.visited ← TRUE
        else
          Create U(PackageName)
          AddU(U,Mi)
          Mi.visited ← TRUE
        end if
      else
        ExtractEachInvocation(Mi)
      end if
    end if
  end while
```

Fig. 3. Component-Method Allocation.

3) Static Abstract Model of Abstraction: This step shows the first cycle of reverse engineering. This step maps the rules to create X-MAN atomic components and then assign methods to components based on the rules of allocation. One important parameter that has to be defined is size of the component. Size of the components should be realistic. If an approach extracts 10 components from the source code with only 7 classes then it does not justify the use of components. Similarly, one big component that represents 50 classes is not ideal either. There are two ways in which the component size can be defined in our tool: (i) Package Based Restriction (ii) Number of methods in each computation unit. Depending on the source code, a reasonable restriction can be applied to limit the number of methods in each computation unit. The package based restriction is compatible with JAVA because packages are usually created and designed to differentiate specific set of tasks. Package based restriction does not mean that a method M1 in class C1 of package P1 always belongs to the component of P1. It means that the maximum number of extracted components cannot exceed the total number of packages in the code, where the minimum number of components that can be extracted is 1. Method M1 can belong to any component depending on the rules of algorithm of allocation.

Algorithm 1 shows the start of allocation. *MethodClassList* has all the methods we have extracted from AST nodes and stored in our data structures. Similarly, *PackageClassList* has all the classes against their packages. Additional information like method parameters, return types and method invocation list can also be retrieved by using a *HashMap* against each index of these lists. Invocation list of each method will be matched and the methods with zero invocations will be considered as utility components. Such methods are not invoking any other method, it means they are mostly conducting simple tasks for other methods but do not require anything from any other method in the source code. Such methods will be placed

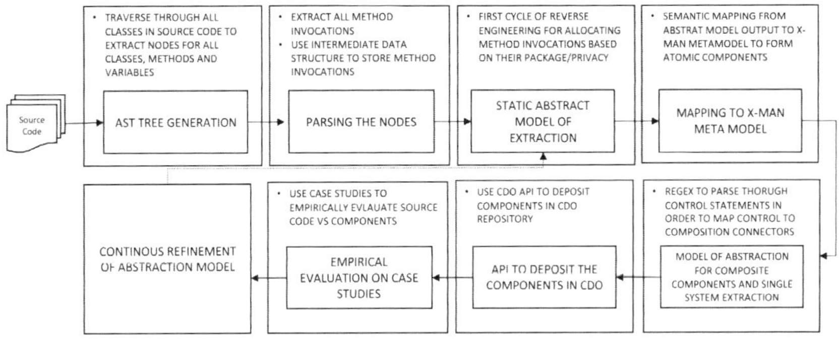

Fig. 2. RX-MAN Methodology.

Algorithm 2 Extract Each Invocation

Require: Mi,index
while $Mi.invocationList! = Empty$ **do**
  if $Mi.PackageName == Mi.invocationList(index).packageName$ **then**
    if $C.PackageName \leftarrow FALSE$ **then**
      CreateComponent(PackageName)
    end if
    CheckDuplication(Mi,Mi.invocationList(index),PackageName)
    if $Duplication == FALSE$ **then**
      ADD (Mi,Mi.invocationList(index),PackageName)
    end if
    ExtractEachInvocation(Mi.invocationList(index),index)
  else
    if $Mi.invocationList(index).package \leftarrow FALSE$ **then**
      CreateComponent(PackageName)
    end if
    CheckDuplication(Mi,Mi.invocationList(index),PackageName)
    if $Duplication == FALSE$ **then**
      CheckPrivateMemberAccess(Mi.invocationList(index))
      if $CheckPrivateMemberAccess \leftarrow FASLE$ **then**
        ADD (Mi,Mi.invocationList(index),PackageName)
      else
        SetAllocation(Mi.invocationList(index).PackageName)
      end if
      ExtractEachInvocation(Mi.invocationList(index),index)
    end if
  end if
end while

Fig. 4. Methods Invocations Extraction.

in utility components. Each X-MAN component will have its own utility component in which all such methods will be placed. This approach will help in reducing the coupling in the original source code. Method *createU* creates a utility component if a utility function belongs to a X-MAN component and method *AddU* adds a utility function in a utility component if it already exists. All other methods will be considered to place in X-MAN atomic components and their invocations will be extracted for further allocations.

In algorithm 2, for each method, its invocation list is extracted and compared with it. If the method Mi and its invoked method belongs to same package, then a component with that package name is created and both methods will be placed in computation unit along with their imports and class variables they use. If both belong to different packages, then a privacy check will be conducted by function *CheckPrivateMemberAccess*. If the method being invoked accesses the private variables or calls private functions in that package in its invocation list, then that method cannot be placed with method Mi. In that case, the invoked method will be placed in a newly created component (if does not already exist) along with the private methods it is accessing (*SetAllocation()* in Algorithm 2). Same process will be applied to all the invoked methods in the invocation list of Mi. Several factors have to be considered before placing a method at appropriate location, e.g., its access to global variables, usage of its local variables in other private methods etc. Function *Duplication* checks whether the method being invoked is already part of the component. At the end of this cycle, each method will be placed in appropriate component in a notation which will be mapped to X-MAN meta model. A user can select any combination of the public methods in a computation unit as a service for that component. For *Number of methods in each computation unit* approach, rules will be applied based on the number of methods in each computation unit and not on the package based allocation.

4) Mapping to X-MAN MetaModel: Extracted results are mapped to X-MAN meta-model. This step also involves the X-MAN validation to make sure only valid X-MAN components can be deposited. Validation involves the semantic checks against X-MAN meta-model in order to check that there is no violation against the semantics of X-MAN component model. X-MAN meta-model is presented here [24].

5) Single System Extraction: For single application systems, second cycle of reverse engineering is needed in order to extract composite components and composition mechanism among them. So far, we have considered *if-else*, *While*, *For* and *Switch* statements as candidates of composition connectors. They can appear in any combination hence each possible scenario should be mapped to X-MAN semantics. Few examples of such mapping are shown in Figure 5. This part of research is theoretically completed but still under development in our tool.

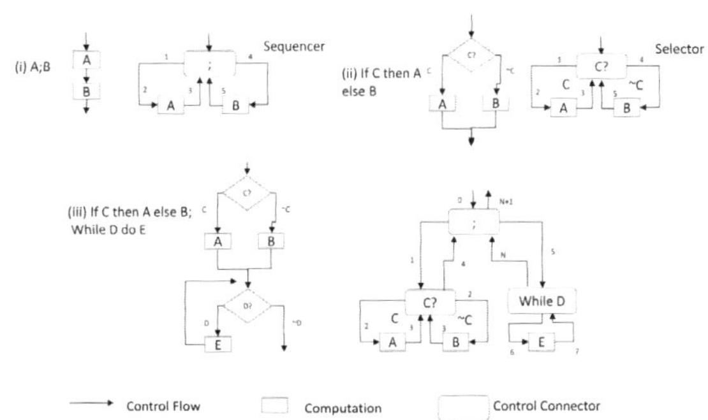

Fig. 5. Control Structures VS X-MAN Equivalent.

6) CDO Repository: CDO is a framework with development time model repository. It is implemented along with EMF (Eclipse Modelling Framework) in implementation of X-MAN tool. Every extracted component can be deposited, retrieved and recomposed according to needs.

TABLE I. RX-MAN INITIAL RESULTS

Application	Classes	X-MAN Components	Component To Class Size %
JabRef	35	8	4.3%
TeamMates	51	4	12.7%
EverNote	27	4	6.75%

V. EVALUATION

So far, we have applied our approach to extract atomic X-MAN components on the variety of JAVA based projects. These results are output of the first cycle of reverse engineering, whereas second cycle implementation is in development. Three most notable application we have used are Jabref [25], Evernote-sdk and Teammates. Jabref is a well-known database management tool and widely used by researchers along with latex. TeamMates is a free online tool for managing peer evaluations and Evernote is a famous cross platform app. All are open source JAVA based projects.

Table I shows the results of R-XMAN. The result is quite diverse and depends on the nature of the code. In case of Jabref, we got 8 components out of 35 classes (it means each component has average size equal to 4.3 classes of the original source code) and in case of Team-mates, we got 4 components out of 51 classes. We have only used that part of the code which is related to model and middle layer of the applications. In case of Evernote-sdk, we got 4 components out of 27 classes. Figure 6 shows R-XMAN tool with extracted components of JabRef. The main panel shows two

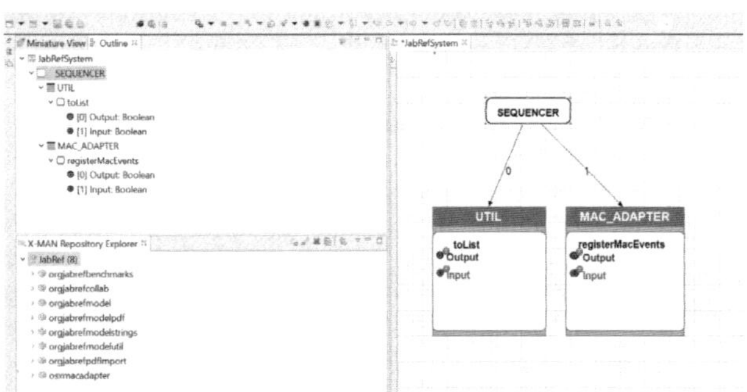

Fig. 6. RX-MAN Tool.

of the extracted components composed by sequencer. Sequencer will execute Route 0 before the route 1 hence *UTIL* component will be executed before *ADAPTER* component. *registerMacEvents* and *toList* are services of these components.

An important point to consider here is that the X-MAN is a model for computation, not a model for resource allocation. Of course, we can study resource and memory problems for X-MAN systems but major thing to consider here is that the components will be stored only once, but reused many times. Therefore, we need less memory overall.

VI. CONCLUSION AND FUTURE WORK

RX-MAN is a static reverse engineering approach that can extract executable architecture from source code as X-MAN components. So far, we have implemented the first cycle of reverse engineering. Comprehensive evaluation of the methodology demands the completion of second cycle of reverse engineering in order to compare the extracted system with original source code. The approach has been applied on several small examples, but significant case studies are needed for further evaluation. We have picked *Qualitus Corpus* [26] for evaluation. *Qualitus Corpus* is a well-known collection of JAVA systems for empirical studies and three systems will be selected for evaluation. Further future work includes the integration of reverse engineering with software product lines in order to achieve product line architecture from legacy systems.

Overall, there are the following benefits for selecting X-MAN over other component models as an output notation of reverse engineering:

- Separation of control (composition connectors) and computation (computation unit).
- Ability to compose in both design and deployment phase of component life cycle. One can deposit, retrieve, re-compose and tailor X-MAN components according to needs where it is not possible with ADL based component models.
- No required services like ADL based component models due to exogenous composition.

REFERENCES

[1] K.-K. Lau and R. Arshad, *A Concise Classification of Reverse Engineering Approaches for Software Product Lines*. 4 2016.

[2] M. D. Ernst, "Static and dynamic analysis: Synergy and duality," in *WODA 2003: ICSE Workshop on Dynamic Analysis*, pp. 24–27, Citeseer, 2003.

[3] P. Helle and P. Levier, "From integrated architecture to integrated executable architecture," in *Enabling Technologies: Infrastructures for Collaborative Enterprises (WETICE), 2010 19th IEEE International Workshop on*, pp. 148–153, IEEE, 2010.

[4] D. Poshyvanyk and A. Marcus, "Combining formal concept analysis with information retrieval for concept location in source code," in *Program Comprehension, 2007. ICPC'07. 15th IEEE International Conference on*, pp. 37–48, IEEE, 2007.

[5] A. D. Eisenberg and K. De Volder, "Dynamic feature traces: Finding features in unfamiliar code," in *Software Maintenance, 2005. ICSM'05. Proceedings of the 21st IEEE International Conference on*, pp. 337–346, IEEE, 2005.

[6] K.-K. Lau, L. Safie, P. Stepan, and C. Tran, "A component model that is both control-driven and data-driven," in *Proceedings of the 14th international ACM Sigsoft symposium on Component based software engineering*, pp. 41–50, ACM, 2011.

[7] B. Dit, M. Revelle, M. Gethers, and D. Poshyvanyk, "Feature location in source code: a taxonomy and survey," *Journal of Software: Evolution and Process*, vol. 25, no. 1, pp. 53–95, 2013.

[8] M. L. Nelson, "A survey of reverse engineering and program comprehension," *arXiv preprint cs/0503068*, 2005.

[9] B. Zhang and M. Becker, "Recovar: A solution framework towards reverse engineering variability," in *Product Line Approaches in Software Engineering (PLEASE), 2013 4th International Workshop on*, pp. 45–48, IEEE, 2013.

[10] Y. Xue, Z. Xing, and S. Jarzabek, "Feature location in a collection of product variants," in *Reverse Engineering (WCRE), 2012 19th Working Conference on*, pp. 145–154, IEEE, 2012.

[11] K. Chen and V. Rajlich, "Case study of feature location using dependence graph.," in *IWPC*, pp. 241–247, Citeseer, 2000.

[12] M. P. Robillard and G. C. Murphy, "Concern graphs: finding and describing concerns using structural program dependencies," in *Proceedings of the 24th international conference on Software engineering*, pp. 406–416, ACM, 2002.

[13] M. P. Robillard, "Automatic generation of suggestions for program investigation," in *ACM SIGSOFT Software Engineering Notes*, vol. 30, pp. 11–20, ACM, 2005.

[14] T. Ziadi, C. Henard, M. Papadakis, M. Ziane, and Y. Le Traon, "Towards a language-independent approach for reverse-engineering of software product lines," in *Proceedings of the 29th Annual ACM Symposium on Applied Computing*, pp. 1064–1071, ACM, 2014.

[15] M. Trifu, "Improving the dataflow-based concern identification approach," in *Software Maintenance and Reengineering, 2009. CSMR'09. 13th European Conference on*, pp. 109–118, IEEE, 2009.

[16] M. T. Valente, V. Borges, and L. Passos, "A semi-automatic approach for extracting software product lines," *Software Engineering, IEEE Transactions on*, vol. 38, no. 4, pp. 737–754, 2012.

[17] N. Anquetil, J.-C. Royer, P. Andre, G. Ardourel, P. Hnetynka, T. Poch, D. Petrascu, and V. Petrascu, "Javacompext: Extracting architectural elements from java source code," in *Reverse Engineering, 2009. WCRE'09. 16th Working Conference on*, pp. 317–318, IEEE, 2009.

[18] "What do we mean by componentization (for knowledge)? – open knowledge international blog," April 2007. (Accessed on 07/31/2017).

[19] M. Abi-Antoun, J. Aldrich, and W. Coelho, "A case study in re-engineering to enforce architectural control flow and data sharing," *Journal of Systems and Software*, vol. 80, no. 2, pp. 240–264, 2007.

[20] J. Aldrich, C. Chambers, and D. Notkin, "Archjava: connecting software architecture to implementation," in *Proceedings of the 24th international conference on Software engineering*, pp. 187–197, ACM, 2002.

[21] L. Chouambe, B. Klatt, and K. Krogmann, "Reverse engineering software-models of component-based systems," in *Software Maintenance and Reengineering, 2008. CSMR 2008. 12th European Conference on*, pp. 93–102, IEEE, 2008.

[22] K.-K. Lau, L. Safie, P. ˇ Stˇ epán, and C. Tran, "A component model that is both control-driven and data-driven," in *Proc. 14th Int. ACM SIGSOFT Symp. on Component-based Software Engineering, LNCS 6092*, pp. 41–50, ACM, 2011.

[23] T. Asikainen, T. Soininen, and T. Männistö, "A Koala-Based Approach for Modelling and Deploying Configurable Software Product Families," in *Software Product-Family Engineering*, pp. 225–249, Springer, 2004.

[24] K.-K. Lau and C. M. Tran, "X-man: An mde tool for component-based system development," in *Software Engineering and Advanced Applications (SEAA), 2012 38th EUROMICRO Conference on*, pp. 158–165, IEEE, 2012.

[25] M. Alver, N. Batada, M. Baylac, K. Brix, G. Gardey, C. D'Haese, R. Nagel, C. Oezbeck, E. Reitmayr, A. Rudert, *et al.*, "Jabref reference manager," 2003.

[26] E. Tempero, C. Anslow, J. Dietrich, T. Han, J. Li, M. Lumpe, H. Melton, and J. Noble, "The qualitas corpus: A curated collection of java code for empirical studies," in *Software Engineering Conference (APSEC), 2010 17th Asia Pacific*, pp. 336–345, IEEE, 2010.

Analyse Agile Software Development Teamwork Productivity using Qualitative System Dynamics Approach

Israt Fatema
Institute of Information Technology
University of Dhaka
Dhaka, Bangladesh
email: mph001@iit.du.ac.bd

Kazi Muheymin Us Sakib
Institute of Information Technology
University of Dhaka
Dhaka, Bangladesh
email: sakib@iit.du.ac.bd

Abstract—**A highly productive team throughout an agile software development process is very instrumental in achieving project success. This research presents a system dynamics (SD) based approach to model agile software development teamwork productivity by analyzing productivity influence factors. Identification of main factors influencing productivity and how they impact agile teamwork are carried out through interviews, survey and literature review. A study has been conducted on seventeen software companies in Bangladesh. From the perspective of agile team members, the four most perceived factors impacting on their productivity are team effectiveness, team management, motivation and customer satisfaction. Lack of management support is found to be the most mentioned reason for failed agile project. The findings from these sources are compiled into a Causal Loop Diagram (CLD) for qualitative analysis of the teamwork productivity influencing factors. The resulting qualitative model is expected to provide more insight into the agile teamwork dynamics and establish a basis for a further quantitative modelling. Using the proposed model, the project manager may find the origin of a decrease in productivity, evaluate management strategies along with their effects on teamwork productivity. The future step will be the dynamic simulation of the teamwork productivity model based on the qualitative model in this paper.**

Keywords-agile teamwork productivity; influence factors; qualitative system dynamics; team effectiveness.

I. INTRODUCTION

The objective of any software company is to be efficient and achieve maximum team productivity by being cost effective and reducing development time. A highly productive team is the most important factor in achieving project success at different stages of an agile software development. For efficient management and a better control over the agile project team, it is important to understand the team dynamics and effects related to agile practices that influence the development team's productivity.

Research has been largely carried out to identify factors that contribute and influence productivity in traditional software development. There are four main factors generally discussed [1]: the product being developed (characterization of the specific software), people (team members, capabilities, experience, motivation), project (management and resourcing) and processes (tools and software methods). However, agile teamwork productivity is a function of various controllable and uncontrollable factors [2]. The relationships between some of these factors and productivity may change under new software engineering practice and culture [3]. The factors change over time as expectations change. The software industry is also different from country to country as are the resource availability, the laws which govern it and the developer's cost [4]. In addition, actual productivity measurement becomes more difficult when agile software developers perform knowledge-related tasks (e.g., creating, storing, sorting, retrieving, applying and acquiring knowledge) where the product is usually intangible, rarely has single way of doing it, and it is difficult to quantify [2]. Since knowledge is complex and hard to evaluate, it is difficult to interpret the productivity of the agile team member's simply by source line of code (SLOC) or function points produced per unit of time/cost [3].

Despite the increasing acceptance of the agile methods, insufficient research has been empirical on the effect of software development productivity [5]. A better knowledge of the factors and the mediators that influence agile teamwork productivity could help determine where management efforts would be focused to improve productivity. Agile team members also should learn to interpret and manage productivity factors regularly as they are self-managed. The researchers have highlighted the value of team learning to help organization achieving team effectiveness, better ways to solve problem and increased productivity.

Since the agile project team is the most dynamic element in the software development sector, improving team productivity has become a target for software companies in everywhere. The aim of this study is to analyse and understand the complex interdependences and underlying structures at the team's perception level, which influence agile teamwork productivity over time. This paper determines the major factors impacting teamwork productivity in Bangladeshi software companies through a survey and interviews that have been conducted with agile teams to rank the most influential ones among them. The major factors are to be modelled using a qualitative SD approach. This conceptual model will be used to examine the internal dynamics existed within the team and the organizational resources that are used to support them. The future contribution of this research shall provide a strategic (quantitative) model that tells the project manager in advance about the degree of impact these factors will have on teamwork and may identify the origin of a decrease in productivity. Therefore, the agile teamwork productivity may be improved by implementation of management strategies. The scope of this empirical findings considers the Bangladeshi software companies as a case study, which can in turn make the research results beneficial to these companies. However, it is thought that other countries will follow a similar affect to those identified here and its results could be generalized by following the proposed model.

The remainder of this paper is organized as follows. Section II includes a literature review, section III presents the research method and design. Section IV describes the survey results and Section V explores the structure of the qualitative SD model. Section VI describes some limitations of this work. Finally, Section VII describes the conclusion and future work.

II. LITERATURE REVIEW

There are several studies that attempted to assess the impact of some of the influencing factors on agile teamwork productivity. Only Melo et.al [2] analysed the major factors influencing agile teamwork productivity using the team's perception as one potential dimension to understand their overall productivity. Through perceptions, they found that team management is the most influencing factor on agile team productivity. SD technique has been applied in software engineering fields for modelling purposes, which is important for the organization and the project. There are few researches [6][7][8] that attempted to evaluate the impact of some of the influencing factors on productivity separately using SD. However, the complex inter-related structure of all the major factors effecting the teamwork productivity was not considered by the previous works. Abdel-Ahmed [7] investigated the effect of various management policies on development cycle time, quality and effort. His works however adopt the waterfall method which limits their applicability in recent software project and more importantly, does not focus on the agile principles.

In addition, evaluation of individual productivity may not affect the productivity of other team members [9]. These ideas provide a motivation to study teams' productivity, not individuals. A number of studies exist on teamwork in agile software development on a range of topics relevant to composition of team [10], task-effective norms in teams [11], team member's motivation [12], and the importance of a team vision. Yet others have focused on team's communication [10], decision making [13] and self-management [10].

Another stream of research has focused on team performance in agile software development to analyse the teamwork. Team performance refers to evaluation of the results of the teamwork. Moe et al. used two team performance models to explain teamwork in a project adopting Scrum: The Salas et al. model [14] and the Dickenson McIntyre model [15]. Melo et al. used the 'Input Process Output' model to identify team productivity factors in a multiple case studies. Dingsoyr et al. [16] described agile software development as a sociotechnical system comprised of human (socio) and technical entities. Technological interventions do not increase sociotechnical system effectiveness if they are not supported by social (self-managing team and group) components of the system. Such team interactions are one of the important parts in software development. Thus, recent focus on agile software development has increased interest in analysing self-managing agile teams and how to effectively make team productive [16]. Boehm [17] reported in his productivity estimation model, Constructive Cost Model (COCOMO), that productivity of a software development project is mostly affected by the development team and their team management. Scacchi [18] also identified that poorly managed or organized project's productivity was mostly lower than those projects which were well managed. Throughout the literature review, it has been observed that there is a lack of well-established dynamic theory about agile teamwork. This study seeks to fill this gap by developing an integrated model, which represents the inter-related structure of productivity influence factors and how they impact (positively or negatively) agile teamwork's productivity. In order to do so, this study applies a system dynamics approach, which can study complex system by exploring underlying relationships and connections between the components of a system that normally are not discovered by the input-output-process type of models used in organizational studies.

III. RESEARCH METHODOLOGY

The methodological approach of this research is based on the system dynamics (SD), as a modelling and simulation methodology enables to model complex system considering all the influencing factors [19]. There are many modelling techniques developed and used so far, according to the modelling goal and perspective. However, system dynamics modelling chosen for this research because it provides a systematic method for description, exploration and analysis about the dynamic behavior of complex systems [18]. SD methodology has been applied by many researchers [19][20] [24][25] for studying and managing complex feedback system, where feedback is understood as a closed sequence of causal relationships. The concept of a feedback loop reveals that any actor in a system will eventually be affected by its own action.

A number of diagramming tools are used in SD to capture the structure of systems, including causal scale/influence diagrams, stock and flows. Each causal link is assigned a polarity, either positive or negative to represent a causal relationship between two factors. It indicates how the dependent variable changes when the independent variable changes. The important loops are highlighted by a loop identifier, which shows whether the loop is a '+' (reinforcing) or '-' (balancing) feedback [18].

A. *Identification of different factors affecting agile teamwork productivity*

Data collection: The model developed for this work is based on data collected from the software companies in Bangladesh. There are three important objectives of collecting information; to determine what factors affected productivity of agile team members, to determine how these factors impacting project productivity in the team's perception and to determine the significance of the factors. Identification of the factors was initially carried out through an intensive literature review. A set of semi-structured interviews and face-to-face discussions were also conducted with twelve key project members from four software companies including project managers, scrum masters, developers, project owners, and considering also different experience profiles.

Using the factors identified in this first step, a questionnaire [26] was developed. In an attempt to identify the perceived influencing factors and their impact on agile team members, the survey questionnaire was distributed to a total of seventeen software companies in Bangladesh. The company selection criteria for this preliminary study were: companies using agile methods for at least 1 year, developing software for both offshore and local market, and top listed companies in Bangladesh.

Data were collected throughout a period of three months in 2017 (January-March). In order to ensure the quality of data, team members were all self-selected by their organization based on their work roles as members of existing agile teams. Therefore, participants responded to survey questionnaires were already aware of agile team environment and mostly experienced. The filled-in questionnaires were then analysed to identify factors, which have major influences on agile teamwork productivity. Currently, more software companies are being requested to participate in this survey, as the plan is to collect more than 100 responses from different agile teams.

B. *Selection of factors for inclusion in the model*

Data analysis: Factors affecting agile teamwork productivity are rarely independent of the others, but a set of factors interacting with each other to build the final result [7]. The important factors identified in literature and interviews were taken as a starting point for the system approach in this research. In total, 38 factors were chosen for analysis even though not all of them are presented in this paper. In order to create a system model to analyse the teamwork productivity, it is required to determine the importance of the individual factors, their correlation with one another and their effects on productivity itself. The agile team members were asked to fill in the questionnaire to indicate the strength (high, medium or low) of the factors that they perceived influenced their productivity [25].

The procedure followed to extract the agile team member's perception of the influence factors affecting their productivity can be summarized in the following steps:

1. Convert the qualitative scale to a quantitative one. The qualitative scale of high, medium or low was converted to a number scale of 3, 2, and 1, respectively.

TABLE I. ARITHMETIC MEAN OF QUESTIONNAIRE RESULTS FROM FREQUENCY ANALYSIS

SL	Factor	Me-an	SL	Factor	Me-an
1	Culture	**2.23**	20	What is the staff turnover rate in the project	**1.82**
2	Staffing	**2.76**	21	Reuse	**2.17**
3	Size of team	**2.29**	22	What is the software reuse level in the project	**2.00**
4	Project complexity	**2.23**	23	Goals	**2.29**
5	Team Leadership	**2.52**	24	Intra group wage inequality	**1.94**
6	Mutual performance monitoring	**2.41**	25	Team measurement	**2.17**
7	Backup Behaviour	**2.41**	26	Self-management	**2.17**
8	Team orientation	**2.52**	27	Task variety and Innovation	**2.41**
9	Adaptability	**2.35**	28	External Dependencies	**2.17**
10	Feedback	**2.70**	29	Tools usage	**2.29**
11	Mutual trust	**2.76**	30	Programming language	**2.05**
12	Coordination	**2.70**	31	Schedule pressure	**2.29**
13	Communication	**2.82**	32	Impact of Pair programming on productivity	**2.11**
14	Staff are appreciated for working long hours	**1.76**	33	Resource constraints	**2.41**
15	Staff are rewarded (then or later) for working long hours	**2.11**	34	Project Management	**2.58**
16	Adequate technical training for team	**2.41**	35	Motivation	**2.58**
17	Adequate team skills training for team	**2.35**	36	External project factors	**2.41**
18	Team member turnover	**1.64**	37	Dealing with cultural differences among offshore organizations	**2.17**
19	Key personnel stayed throughout the project	**2.23**	38	Working environment	**2.35**

2. Find the total score of each factor for frequency analysis. Then, the arithmetic mean of the total counts was calculated to eliminate the factors below the average (Table. 1) mean.

IV. SURVEY RESULTS

Characteristics of the sample software companies can be found in Table II. Fig. 1 presents the agile practices adopted by the participating software companies and it shows daily stand up meeting mostly used by all of them. Fig. 2 shows that lack of management support (e.g., resource constraint, team design choice and motivation) is the main reason for failure in agile projects.

In most of the interviews, the team members could not define productivity as their performance measurement. Most of them mentioned that team management has their own ways of measuring productivity. Although at the end of the project, the management assessed their productivity on the basis of timeliness and quantity. At the same time, ten interviewees and survey respondents (Fig. 3) also mentioned customer satisfaction as a criterion for measuring or perceiving productivity. Customer satisfaction is very important to software development companies in Bangladesh as a rising market for outsourced software destination. According the product owner interview, dealing with cultural differences among offshore organisation influences teamwork productivity. Two main reasons behind this are time and culture differences.

TABLE II. CHARACTERISTICS OF PARTICIPATING SOFTWARE COMPANIES

Characteristic	Category	Number	%
Main team assignment	Development project	10	58.82
	Maintenance project	7	41.17
Team role	Project manager	4	23.52
	Developer	6	35.29
	Software engineer	3	17.65
	Team lead	2	11.77
	Quality assurance engineer	2	11.77
Experience in agile practice	1-2 years	8	47.8
	2-5 years	7	41.2
	More than 5 years	2	11.8
Development method	Scrum	17	100
Size of the company (person)	30-50	2	12
	50-100	1	6
	100-150	5	29
	150-200	6	35
	200-250	1	6
	250-300	1	6
	More than 300	1	6

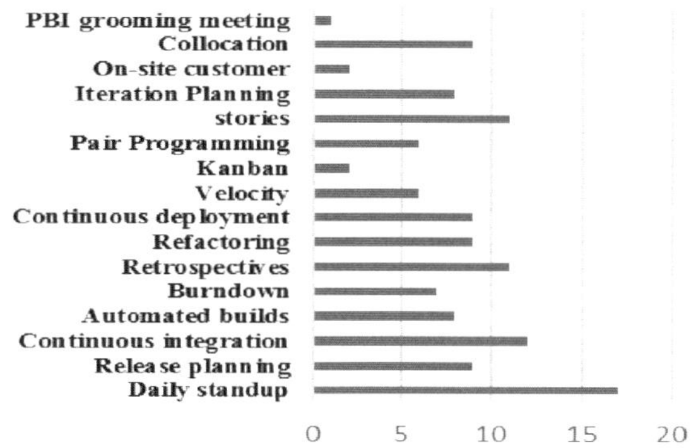

Figure 1. Agile practices adopted in software companies

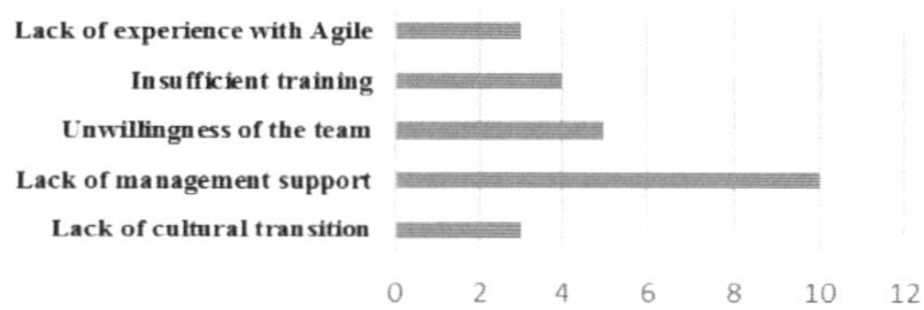

Figure 2. Main reasons for failure in agile projects

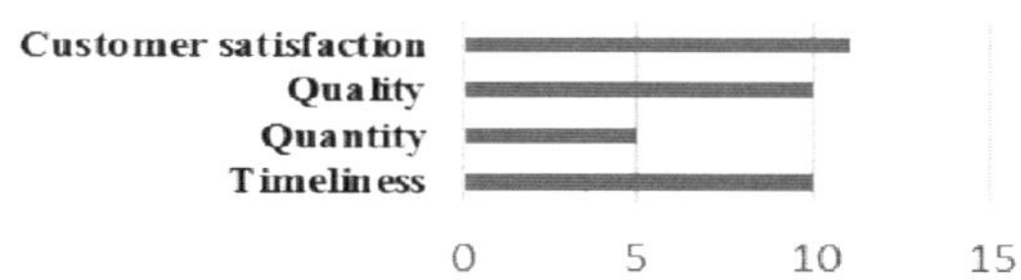

Figure 3. Criterion for measuring or perceiving productivity

Figure 4. Agile team perceived productivity influence factors

Sometimes it becomes difficult to keep contact with the offshore client on urgent issues due to time difference between places. Moreover, offshore client's expectations are different, both in terms of their general culture and their views on life and work. Project developed within western cultures are different from eastern cultures. For example, daily traffic condition consumes most of the working time in Bangladesh, which makes the developers less motivated. Since, staff are not rewarded enough for working long hours. However, schedule pressure can be easily dealt with overtime working because it costs less in Bangladesh.

Five interviewees (project leads and managers) also mentioned that culture is a big barrier for working in an agile team. This factor affects communication between team members. In addition, sometimes language barrier hinders communication. Transitioning from individual work to self-management team requires a reorientation not only by developers but also by management. This changeover takes time and resources. For this reason, these project managers prefer freshers as a team member. Their software companies like to groom up with training than changing mind set up of the team members. Besides that, self-management and adaptability are considered key for agile development. But these two factors have less influence (Table. 1) on agile teamwork productivity and mostly depends on competent project management.

Fig. 4 provides highlights of the most influencing productivity factors that are perceived by the agile team members. This study results show that agile teamwork is highly dependent on team effectiveness. Project manager is usually a technical lead and many management decisions are made by the top management since the majority of the projects are outsourced projects. Their offshore clients' satisfaction (external factors dependency) is very important to them. Team leadership and team orientation are very important for teamwork motivation. The factors impacting on agile teamwork productivity mentioned by the team members suggested that feedback, team orientation, communication, coordination and mutual trust improve team effectiveness. Eventually, this will enable team to learn how to effectively manage relation within team in order to become more productive.

V. QUALITATIVE MODELLING OF AGILE SOFTWARE DEVELOPMENT TEAMWORK PRODUCTIVITY

Each factor that affects agile teamwork productivity is itself affected by other factors [9]. Some factors may be the result of the same cause [19]. Fig. 5 presents the overall conceptual model of agile teamwork productivity. It shows all the influence factor's affect found in this study. It can be seen in Fig. 5 that the arrows between every two variables differ in sign (positive or negative) to express direct or indirect cause-effect relationships between the two variables they connect.

Distinct from previous studies [7][24] this model represents the team dynamics which is a collection of "soft factors" [23] and effects related to agile methods that influence the teamwork's productivity. The soft factors that can affect the software development teamwork productivity include motivation, team management efficiency, customer satisfaction, skillfulness and team effectiveness (communication, coordination, adaptability, feedback, leadership, team orientation, mutual trust, monitoring, backup-behavior, self-management). Teams require a complex mixture of factors that include organizational support, individual skills and also teamwork skills [10] to work effectively. This study also found these are the most influential productivity factors from the agile team's perspective. Within the model (see Fig. 5), it is shown that team effectiveness is influenced by team management, motivation, team design, skillfulness, resource constraint, communication and coordination. Team effectiveness can be improved by team learning processes which include activities such as feedback, mutual performance monitoring and back-up behavior. These learning activities are likely to create a positive change and to influence the productivity. On the other hand, motivation influenced by team management, reward, goal, salary, working environment, morale and external factor (customer satisfaction).

Fig. 5 illustrates that motivation is positively related to team effectiveness. A motivated team is much more likely to be involved with the learning oriented activities to develop better interpersonal relations and that eventually will increase the team effectiveness. On the other hand, lack of team management skill negatively influences teamwork productivity. It mainly refers to team design choice and resource constraint. Another factor that influences skillfulness is pair programming; however, this factor is not encouraged in Bangladeshi software companies. Management does not want to engage two resources for single work due to increase in expenses. It is mostly practiced by the developers when they need assistance to complete a difficult work.

Getting the right person with suitable skills and knowledge for an agile team is a difficult job for the software companies in Bangladesh. Staffing (right person selected) happened to be as one of the most important factors impacting teamwork productivity, as Table I and Fig. 4 show. Consequently, team design choice became a significant influencing factor for agile teamwork productivity (Fig. 5). It affects the amount of knowledge that team members must apply to improve the team effectiveness (Fig. 5).

VI. LIMITATIONS OF THE STUDY

There are a number of limitations to this study. First, this study was limited to 17 respondents and 12 interviewees from 17 software companies only. It was challenging to get access to more software companies due to time constraint. Respondents were carefully chosen from different roles within the agile team in order to get different perspectives of productivity in the context of Bangladesh software Industry.

Another limitation of this study is the agile team members' perceptions used as a response. However, with survey, this study relies on what the respondents provided to the researcher. It is possible that the respondents' perception

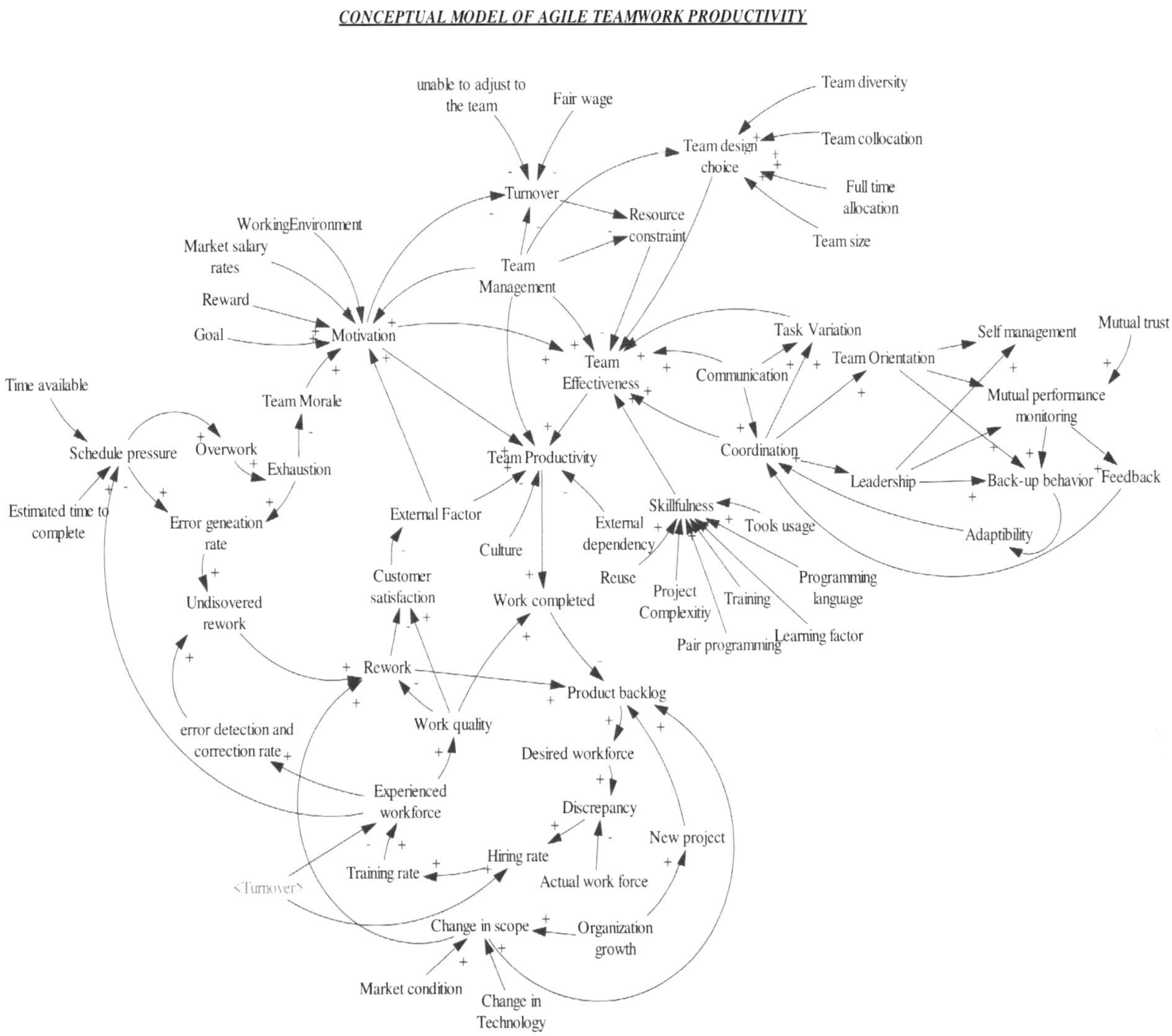

Figure 5. Overall conceptual model of Agile teamwork productivity

may change and be different after the end of the project. To minimise the impact of this effect, the survey and interviewees' responses were compared for factors selection to include in the model. The questionnaire used for this study had been used successfully in other research [9][22] and was developed after a detailed literature review. Some of the questions were included in the survey after getting knowledge about the working conditions of software companies in Bangladesh from the interview sessions.

Finally, this conceptual model certainly has its limitations and is not complete because it only focuses on the influence factors. The multiple feedback processes and delays are not incorporated in this model.

VII. CONCLUSION AND FUTURE WORK

Teamwork productivity determines the overall project performance in an agile software development process. Therefore, researchers have gained increasing interest in studying agile teams' productivity. Agile team members should be taught to interpret and manage productivity factors regularly as they are self-managed.

The researchers concluded that productivity improvement programs would become effective only if all the variables are simultaneously controlled and monitored. One effective solution to improve productivity is to look into the factors influencing productivity and also have a dynamic strategical model that tells the project manager in advance the degree of impact that these factors will have on team productivity. In order to achieve that, the main factors that affect teamwork productivity were determined. The findings of this stage are the main influencing factors which are team effectiveness, team management, motivation and customer satisfaction. Lack of agile team management support was found to be the most mentioned reason for failed agile project. Most followed agile method was SCRUM for all the respondents. Among agile practices, daily stand-up meeting and continuous integration were the most cited practices impacting teamwork productivity. Customer satisfaction was found as main criterion for measuring or perceiving productivity by the interviewees and survey respondents.

As a future work, the soft factors are to be quantified to incorporate in system dynamics model. The proposed system dynamics model will provide more strategic insights and understanding about the effectiveness of different managerial policies based on non-straight forward cause-effect relationships hidden in the system. Furthermore, this qualitative CLD will be used as a basis for a stock and flow model development of the quantitative SD method. Further research need to be conducted to validate the conceptual model against a real-world agile software development project.

REFERENCES

[1] A. Trendowicz and J. Münch, "Factors Influencing Software Development Productivity—State-of-the-Art and Industrial Experiences," Advances in computers, vol. 77, pp. 185-241, Dec. 2009.

[2] C. D. O. Melo, D. S. Cruzes, F. Kon, and R. Conradi, "Interpretative case studies on agile team productivity and management," Information and Software Technology, vol. 55, pp.412-427, Feb.2013.

[3] K. Petersen, "Measuring and predicting software productivity: A systematic map and review," Information and Software Technology, vol. 53, pp.317-343, Apr.2011.

[4] Y. Ramírez and D. Nembhard, "Measuring knowledge worker productivity: A taxonomy," Journal of Intellectual Capital, vol. 5, no. 4, Dec. 2004, pp. 602–628.

[5] C. D. O. Melo, D. S. Cruzes, F. Kon, and R. Conradi, "Agile team perceptions of productivity factors," In Agile Conference (AGILE), IEEE, 2011, pp. 57-66.

[6] X. Kong, L. Liu, and D. Lowe, "Modeling an agile web maintenance process using system dynamics," In 11th ANZSYS/Managing the Complex V conference, ISCE Publishing, Christchurch, NZ. Dec. 2005.

[7] T.K. Abdel-Hamid and S. Madnick, "Software productivity: potential, actual, and perceived,". System Dynamics Review, 5(2), pp. 93-113, June. 1989.

[8] J. M. Lyneis and D. N. Ford, "System dynamics applied to project management: a survey, assessment, and directions for future research," System Dynamics Review, vol. 23, no. 2-3, pp. 157-189, Jun. 2007.

[9] C.O. Melo, "Productivity of agile teams: an empirical evaluation of factors and monitoring processes," Ph.D. dissertation, Universidade de São Paulo, 2015.

[10] T. Dingsøyr and Y. Lindsjørn, "Team performance in agile development teams: findings from 18 focus groups," International Conference on Agile Software Development, Springer Berlin Heidelberg, June. 2013, pp. 46-60.

[11] A. Teh, E. Baniassad, D. V. Rooy, and C. Boughton, "Social Psychology and Software Teams: Establishing Task-Effective Group Norms," IEEE Software, vol. 29, no.4, pp.53–58, Jul. 2012.

[12] B. Tessem and F. Maurer, "Job Satisfaction and Motivation in a Large Agile Team," In International Conference on Extreme Programming and Agile Processes in Software Engineering, Springer Heidelberg, vol. 4536, pp. 54–61., 2007.

[13] N. B. Moe, A. Aurum, and T. Dybå, "Challenges of shared decision making: A multiple case study of agile software development," Information and Software Technology, vol. 54, pp.853–865, Aug. 2012.

[14] N. B. Moe and T. Dingsøyr, "Scrum and team effectiveness: Theory and practice," International Conference on Agile Processes and Extreme Programming in Software Engineering, Springer Berlin Heidelberg, Jun. 2008, pp. 11-20.

[15] N. B. Moe, T. Dingsøyr, and T. Dybå, "A teamwork model for understanding an agile team: A case study of a Scrum project," Information and Software Technology, vol. 52, pp. 480-491, May. 2010.

[16] T. Dingsøyr and T. Dybå, "Team effectiveness in software development: Human and cooperative aspects in team effectiveness models and priorities for future studies," Proceedings of the 5th International Workshop on Co-operative and Human Aspects of Software Engineering. IEEE Press, 2012, pp. 27-29.

[17] B. Barry, "Software Engineering Economics," New York, vol. 197, NY: Prentice-Hall, 1981.

[18] W. Scacchi, "Understanding and improving Software Productivity," Advances in Software engineering and Knowledge engineering, 2005.

[19] F. Nasirzadeh and P. Nojedehi, "Dynamic modelling of labour productivity in construction projects," International Journal of Project Management, vol. 31, no. 6, Aug. 2013, pp. 903-911.

[20] A. Rodrigues and J. Bowers, "The role of system dynamics in project management," International Journal of Project Management, vol. 14, no. 4, Aug. 1996, pp. 213-220.

[21] B. Barry, "Centre for Systems and Software Engineering," Oct. 2012. [Online] Available http://sunset.usc.edu/csse/research/COCOMOII/cocomo_main.html. [retrieved: August, 2017].

[22] J. M. Verner, M. A. Babar, N. Cerpa, T. Hall, and S. Beecham, "Factors that motivate software engineering teams: A four country empirical study,". Journal of Systems and Software, vol. 92, June. 2014, pp. 115-127.

[23] V. Lalsing, S. Kishnah, and P. Sameerchand, "People factors in agile software development and project management," International Journal of Software Engineering & Applications, vol. 3, pp. 117, Jan.2012.

[24] L. L. R. Rodrigues, N. Dharmaraj, and B. R. Shrinivasa Rao, "System dynamics approach for change management in new product development," Management Research News, vol. 29, no. 6, Aug. 2006, pp. 512-523.

[25] M. J. Mawdesley and S. Al-Jibouri, "Modelling construction project productivity using systems dynamics approach," International Journal of Productivity and Performance Management, vol. 59, no.1, Dec. 2009, pp. 18-36.

[26] I. Fatema, "Agile teamwork productivity influence factors," Jan. 2017. [Online] Available https://goo.gl/forms/I5xGdQGqFMk9he5f2. [retrieved: August, 2017].

Accuracy Evaluation of Model-based COSMIC Functional Size Estimation

Luigi Lavazza

Dipartimento di Scienze Teoriche e Applicate
Università degli Studi dell'Insubria
Varese (Italy)
Email: luigi.lavazza@uninsubria.it

***Abstract*—Functional Size Measurement is widely used, especially to quantify the size of applications in the early stages of development, when effort estimates are needed. However, the measurement process is often too long or too expensive, or it requires more knowledge than available when development effort estimates are due. To overcome these problems, early size estimation methods have been proposed, to get approximate estimates of functional measures. In general, early estimation methods adopt measurement processes that are simplified with respect to the standard process, in that one or more phases are skipped. So, the idea is that you get estimates affected by some estimation error, instead of accurate measures performed following the standard measurement process, but at a fraction of the cost and time required for standard measurement. In this paper, we consider some methods that have been proposed for estimating the COSMIC (Common Software Measurement International Consortium) size of software during the modeling stage. We apply the most recent methodologies for estimation accuracy, to evaluate whether early model-based estimation is accurate enough for practical usage.**

Keywords–Functional size measurement; COSMIC Function Points; Measurement process; Functional size estimation; Accuracy estimation.

I. Introduction

Functional Size Measurement (FSM) is widely used. Among the reasons for the success of FSM is that it can provide measures of size in the early stages of software development, when they are most needed for cost estimation. However, FSM requires that the functional requirements of the application to be measured are available in a complete and quite detailed form. Often, this is not possible in the very early stages of development. Therefore, to get measures even when requirements are still incomplete or still defined at a coarse level of detail, estimation models have been proposed. There are different types of FSM and many estimation methods. Here, we concentrate on the COSMIC FSM [1] –one of the most widely used methods– and on model-based COSMIC size estimation [2].

When applying a size estimation method, we expect that the method –being applied to incomplete or not thoroughly detailed software specifications– requires less time and effort than the standard measurement process. However, we also expect that the size estimates so obtained contain some estimation error. In general, we are ready to accept a relatively small estimation error in exchange of being able to get size estimates without having to apply the standard measurement process. On the contrary, an excessively large estimation error would defeat the very reason for measuring. Hence, we are interested in knowing the likely accuracy of measure estimates. To this end, we need reliable methods to evaluate the accuracy of estimates.

Unfortunately, it has been shown that the most popular estimate accuracy statistic, the Mean Magnitude of Relative Errors (MMRE) is flawed, in that it is a biased estimator of central tendency of the residuals of a prediction system because it is an asymmetric measure [3][4][5]. So, MMRE and similar indicators are not suitable for providing practitioners who are potentially interested in applying estimate methods with reliable information upon which they can base informed decisions.

Luckily, sound estimate evaluation methods have been proposed recently (as described in Section III). It is thus possible to apply such new methods to size estimation methods.

The main purpose of this paper is the evaluation of the actual accuracy of model-based COSMIC size estimation method: to this end, we use the new sound evaluation methods (described in Section III), together with more traditional statistical tools.

It should be noted that the paper does not aim at introducing new COSMIC size estimation methods, rather the goal of the paper is (re)evaluating the accuracy of the formerly [2] proposed ones. However, by applying these new evaluation methods, as a side effect we also get some indications on their expressiveness.

The paper is structured as follows. Section II briefly illustrates the COSMIC FSM, and the model-based simplified COSMIC measurement method. Section III illustrates the methods used for evaluating the accuracy of estimates. Section IV describes the application of the accuracy evaluation methods to model-based simplified COSMIC measurement, while Section V illustrates and discusses the results of the analysis. Section VI accounts for related work. Finally, Section VII draws conclusions and briefly sketches future work.

II. COSMIC Functional Size Measurement and Model-Based COSMIC Estimation

COSMIC measurement is based on the analysis of the specification of functional user requirements (FUR). The FUR can be described in various ways, including the Unified Modeling Language (UML): functional size measurement of UML models was widely studied [6][7][8], also when FUR concern real-time applications [9]. During the initial stage of development, UML models are built, progressively incorporating more knowledge concerning the software to be developed: this results in progressively more complete and detailed specifications. More specifically, the UML modeling process can be seen as organized in the phases described in Figure 1. The more complete and detailed the UML model, the more elements needed for COSMIC measurement become available. Figure 1 shows the relationship between the UML diagrams that are made available by each modeling phase and the COSMIC measurement elements. During the initial UML modeling phases –i.e., before the complete and detailed FUR specifications are available– it is often the case that size measures are needed anyway. In such cases –not being possible to measure the COSMIC size of the application– we can think of *estimating* the COSMIC size, based on the information that is present in the available UML diagrams.

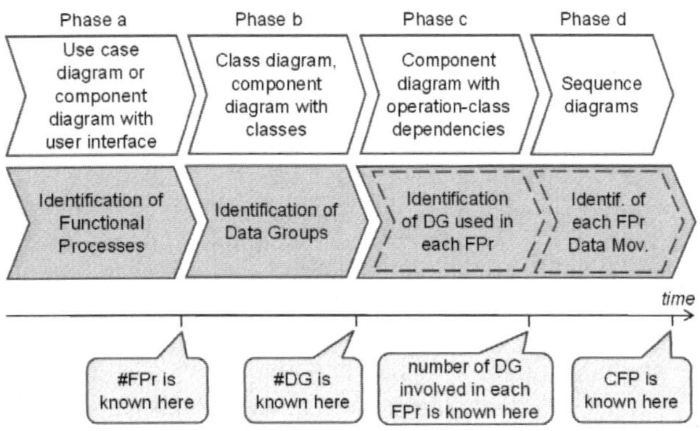

Figure 1. UML modeling process and COSMIC measurement process phases.

Specifically, del Bianco et al. proposed a few families of statistical models that can be used to estimate COSMIC size based on information derived from UML diagrams [2]. These models are described in Table I.

A first family of COSMIC size estimation models requires only the knowledge of the number of functional processes (FPr's). These models have form ECFP = f(#FPr) where ECFP is the estimated size in CFP (COSMIC Function Points), and #FPr is the number of functional processes. As shown in Figure 1, the statistical model can be built after the completion of phase a), when class or component diagrams properly specifying the user interfaces are delivered.

Another family of COSMIC size estimation models requires also that the number of Data Groups (#DG) is known. These models can be built after phase b), when UML diagrams fully describing the involved classes are delivered. The models found by del Bianco et al. involve the parameter AvDGperFPr, namely the average number of data groups per functional process, which requires that both the functional process and the data groups (i.e., classes in UML diagrams) are known.

Figure 1 shows that potentially one could use also the knowledge of the number of data groups involved in each functional process, which is available after phase c). However, no statistically significant models of this type were found.

Finally, we observe that after phase d), i.e., when the complete UML models of FUR are available, the standard COSMIC measurement process is applicable, and proper COSMIC measures –instead of estimates– can be achieved.

It is expected that models based on more information are more accurate than models based on less information.

TABLE I. COSMIC SIZE ESTIMATION MODELS.

Name	*Formula*
avg1	$ECFP = 7.3\ \#FPr$
reg1	$ECFP = -16.5 + 6.698\ \#FPr$
avg2	$ECFP = AvDGperFPr\ 1.8\ \#FPr$
reg2	$ECFP = -64.6 + 7.63\ \#FPr + 9.71\ AvDGperFPr$
log2	$ECFP = 1.588\ \#FPr^{1.00357}\ AvDGperFPr^{1.0312}$

In [2], the accuracy of the models given in Table I was evaluated based on the traditional indicators MMRE –the Mean Magnitude of Relative Errors– and Pred(25) –the fraction of applications for which the absolute relative estimation error is less than 0.25. The evaluation of accuracy performed in [2] indicated that models using both #FPr and AvDGperFPr (that is, models avg2, reg2 and log2) are more accurate than models based only on #FPr (that is, models avg1 and reg1). However, it has been shown that indicators based on the magnitude of relative errors are biased [10]. Hence, we repeat here (in Section IV) the analysis of accuracy using more reliable methods (described in Section III).

III. A METHOD FOR EVALUATING THE ACCURACY OF ESTIMATES

The method we use for evaluating the accuracy of a given model's estimates involves two activities: 1) comparing the model's estimates with "baseline" estimates, and 2) evaluating the size effect. The former activity –described in Section III-A– is aimed at verifying that the given model's estimates are "good enough:" if they are less accurate than the estimates provided by the baseline, the given models does not yield any improvement, at least as far as accuracy is concerned, and can be rejected. The second activity –described in Section III-B– verifies whether the given model provides an increase in accuracy that is large enough to make the given model a desirable alternative with respect to the baseline.

A. Baselines

Let us suppose that in n previous projects we measured the value of interest (in our case, the size of applications, measured in CFP). Accordingly, we have a set $Y = \{y_i\}$ (with $i \in [1, n]$) of observations (where y_i is the actual size of the ith project, expressed in CFP).

A new estimation method P is proposed: for the n known projects, method P yields n estimates $\hat{y}_i$ with $i \in [1, n]$, and we need to evaluate the accuracy of these estimates.

The most popular way of evaluating estimation accuracy is the MMRE, the mean of the magnitude of absolute errors, which is defined as

$$MMRE = \frac{1}{n} \sum_{i=1..n} \frac{|y_i - \hat{y}_i|}{y_i} \qquad (1)$$

MMRE has been shown to be a biased estimator of central tendency of the residuals of a prediction system, because it is an asymmetric measure [3], [4], [5]. In practice, MMRE is biased towards prediction systems that under-estimate [10].

Shepperd and MacDonell [10] proposed that the accuracy of a given estimation method P is compared to the accuracy of a reference estimation method $P0$. The indicator to be used is the Mean Absolute Residual (MAR), which, unlike MMRE, is not biased:

$$MAR = \frac{1}{n} \sum_{i=1..n} |y_i - \hat{y}_i|) \quad (2)$$

So we have MAR_P (the MAR of the proposed method) and MAR_{P0} (the MAR of the reference method). Based on the MAR values, Shepperd and MacDonell propose to compute a Standardized Accuracy measure (SA) for estimation method P:

$$SA = 1 - \frac{MAR_P}{MAR_{P0}} \quad (3)$$

Values of SA close to 1 indicate that P outperforms $P0$, values close to zero indicate that P's accuracy is similar to $P0$'s accuracy, negative values indicate that P is worse than $P0$, hence it should be rejected.

As a referenced model, Shepperd and MacDonell suggest to use random estimation, based on the known (actual) values of previously measured projects. A random estimation $\hat{y}_i$ is obtained by picking at random y_j, with $j \neq i$. Of course, in this way there are $n-1$ possible estimates for y_i, so to compute the MAR of rnd we need to average all these possible values. Shepperd and MacDonell suggest to make a large number of random estimates (typically, 1000), and then take the mean $\overline{MAR_{rnd}}$. Langdon et al. showed that it is not necessary to make 1000 guesses, since the average of the random estimates can be computed exactly [11].

So, a first evaluation consists in computing

$$SA = 1 - \frac{MAR_P}{\overline{MAR_{rnd}}}. \quad (4)$$

Achieving a value substantially greater than zero is clearly a sort of necessary condition that the estimation method P must satisfy, otherwise we could simply guess (instead of estimating using P) and get similarly accurate estimates.

Lavazza and Morasca [12] observed that the comparison with random estimation is not very effective in supporting the evidence that P is a good estimation model. Instead, they proposed to use a "constant model" (*CM*), where the estimate of the size of the ith project is given by the average of the sizes of the other projects, that is

$$\hat{y}_i = \frac{1}{n-1} \sum_{j \in Y - \{y_i\}} y_j \quad (5)$$

So, we can compute the MAR_{CM} of these estimates, and then compute SA, but this time comparing P with CM:

$$SA = 1 - \frac{MAR_P}{MAR_{CM}}. \quad (6)$$

Again, we require that SA is substantially greater than zero, to deem P acceptable.

Finally, note that SA can be used to compare a method P against any other model $P1$ used as a reference method, simply by computing

$$SA = 1 - \frac{MAR_P}{MAR_{P1}}. \quad (7)$$

B. Size Effect

Suppose that we have two estimation methods $P1$ and $P2$, and $MAR_{P2} < MAR_{P1}$ (hence, $SA = 1 - \frac{MAR_{P2}}{MAR_{P1}} > 0$). We can conclude that $P2$ is more accurate than $P1$. Anyway, suppose that we are using $P1$ and we are considering the possibility of switching to using $P2$, which involves some effort, because $P2$ requires some activity or data or programs that $P1$ does not require. We would like to know if the improvement that $P2$ offers in terms of accuracy is possibly so inconsequential as to not be worth the effort.

To judge the effect size, Shepperd and MacDonell suggest using Glass's Δ [13] or Hedges's g, which might be preferred when the sample size is small [14]. The effect size –which is scale-free– can be interpreted in terms of the categories proposed by Cohen [15] of small (≈ 0.2), medium (≈ 0.5) and large (≈ 0.8).

IV. Experimental Evaluation

The five size estimation models given in Table I were applied to the projects in the dataset that was used to derive the models [2]. The MAR for each model was then computed. Similarly, the data from the same dataset were used to compute $\overline{MAR_{rnd}}$ and MAR_{CM}, as described in Section III. The values of the methods' MAR are given in Table II.

Note that here we do not explicitly compute SA. Instead, we give the values of MAR needed for the computation. The reason is that with 7 methods there are 21 possible comparison among methods, hence 21 values of SA. Listing all these SA values could create confusion, while to compare two methods' accuracies, we just need to compare their SA's: the model featuring the smaller SA is likely the best.

TABLE II. Mean absolute residuals of models.

Name	*Formula*	*MAR*
rnd	–	146
CM	–	114
avg1	$ECFP = 7.3 \#FPr$	56
reg1	$ECFP = -16.5 + 6.698 \#FPr$	48
avg2	$ECFP = AvDGperFPr1.8 \#FPr$	28
reg2	$ECFP = -64.6 + 7.63 \#FPr + 9.71\ AvDGperFPr$	40
log2	$ECFP = 1.588 \#FPr^{1.00357}\ AvDGperFPr^{1.0312}$	25

Table II provides a first piece of evidence: model-based COSMIC size estimation are definitely more accurate than both the random and constant models.

Table II also confirms that the constant model is always more accurate than the random model, as demonstrated by Lavazza and Morasca [12]. For this reason, in the remainder of the paper the random model is no longer used.

To establish if the estimations of one method were significantly better than the estimations provided by another method, we tested the statistical significance of the absolute errors achieved with the two estimation methods [3]. Namely, we compared the absolute residuals provided by every pair of methods via Wilcoxon Sign Rank Test. To check for statistical significance we used the Wilcoxon Signed Rank Test [16] because it is a safe test to apply to both non-normally distributed (as are often MAR distributions) and normally distributed populations.

The results are given in Table III, where in each cell the sign ">" (respectively, "<", "=") indicates that the absolute residuals of the model on the cell's row are larger (resp., smaller, equal) than the absolute residuals of the model on the cell's column.

TABLE III. COMPARISON OF ABSOLUTE RESIDUALS USING WILCOXON SIGN RANK TEST.

	CM	avg1	reg1	avg2	reg2	log2
CM		>	>	>	>	>
avg1	<		>	>	>	>
reg1	<	<		=	>	>
avg2	<	<	=		=	>
reg2	<	<	<	=		=
log2	<	<	<	<	=	

The results provided by Wilcoxon Sign Rank Test confirm the indications provided by MAR and SA in that the constant model is outperformed by all other models and that avg1 is outperformed by all other model-based size estimation methods. However, Wilcoxon Sign Rank Test provides further insights with respect to MAR and SA:

- There is no sufficient evidence to conclude that log2 is better than reg2 (this fact could be guessed, based on the fact that MAR_{log2} and MAR_{reg2} are quite close).
- Similarly, there is no evidence that reg2 (which has $MAR_{reg2} = 40$) is actually more accurate than reg1 (which has $MAR_{reg1} = 48$).
- Somewhat surprisingly, there is no evidence that avg2 (which has $MAR_{avg2} = 28$) is actually more accurate than reg2 (which has $MAR_{reg2} = 40$).

The latter result is especially interesting, in that by just looking at the MAR values we could have concluded that avg2 is more accurate than reg2, while –according to Wilcoxon Sign Rank Test– there is no statistically significant evidence of this fact. The explanation of why MAR can be somewhat misleading in this case is given in Figure 2, where the boxplots of the absolute residuals of models avg2 and reg2 are given: it is easy to see that the distributions are similar, but reg2 has a greater MAR because of three applications, whose size estimation error is quite large.

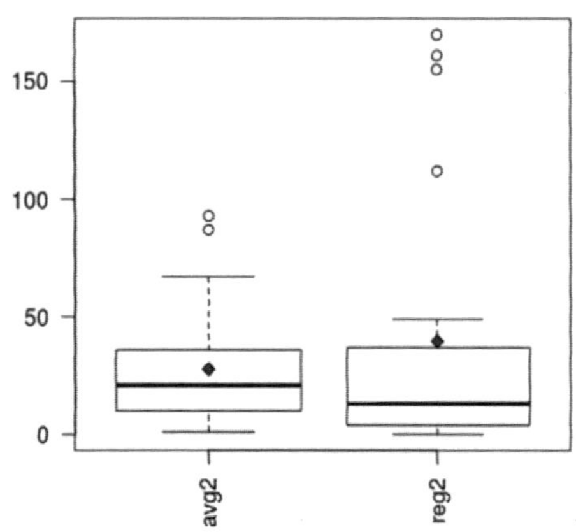

Figure 2. Absolute residuals of models avg2 and reg2.

Now, as recommended by Shepperd and MacDonell (see Section III-B) we evaluate the size effect. To this end, we computed Hedges's g for all model pairs. The results are given in Table IV.

TABLE IV. EFFECT SIZE (HEDGES'S g).

	CM	avg1	reg1	avg2	reg2	log2
CM	–	0.75	0.82	1.30	0.98	1.36
avg1	-0.75	–	0.12	0.58	0.27	0.66
reg1	-0.82	-0.12	–	0.38	0.13	0.44
avg2	-1.30	-0.58	-0.38	–	-0.26	0.12
reg2	-0.98	-0.27	-0.13	0.26	–	0.33
log2	-1.36	-0.66	-0.44	-0.12	-0.33	–

It is easy to see that all model-based size estimation methods appear definitely preferable with respect to the constant model. Models avg2 and log2 appear preferable to the other model-based estimation methods, with log2 only marginally better than avg2.

The indications provided by Hedges's g are also consistent with the indications obtained from Wilcoxon Sign Rank Test, e.g., according to Hedges's g avg2 is only marginally better than reg2.

V. DISCUSSION OF RESULTS

With reference to Figure 1, at the end of phase a), we know the number of Functional Processes (#FPr), thus models avg1 and reg1 are applicable. At the end of phase b), the other models are also applicable.

According to the analysis of experimental data, we have that the models that are applicable at the end of phase b) are –to different extents– more accurate than the models that are applicable at the end of phase a). This was expected, since by progressing from phase a) to phase b), more information concerning the application is made available through UML models, thus we can exploit this information to achieve more accurate size estimates. However, having reliable empirical evidence that progressing trough application modeling phases enable the construction of progressively more accurate models of the functional size is quite important. It also indicates that collecting measures of COSMIC elements (especially #FPr and #DG, hence AvDGperFPr) and building several statistical models of COSMIC size is useful to get a progressively more accurate notion of the size of the application being built. Actually, the size effect indicators (see Table IV) suggest that the models available at the end of phase b) allow only for a medium-small improvement over the best model available at the end of phase a), especially as far as reg1 is concerned. However, to achieve this moderate improvement, all you have to do is counting the data group (i.e., classes in UML models): since this counting is very easy (it can even be automated) building more accurate models at the end of phase b) is not only possible, but most probably always convenient.

Like in any empirical study, we have to deal with some threats to the validity of our analysis.

We see no construction issues with our analysis, since all the used techniques are statistically sound; in fact, they have been proposed to correct the problems with previous indicators, such as MMRE.

The main problem we face is probably the generalizability of results. In fact, our results derive from the analysis of a dataset that collects data from only 21 projects. It is possible that other datasets could support somewhat different conclusions. However, the fact that our dataset includes several industrial projects, and that the size of the dataset is not excessively small (especially in the context of empirical software engineering studies) supports the hypothesis the results presented here are sufficiently representative in general. Also, the logical coherence of the results –namely the fact that the more information is available from UML models, the more accurate is size estimation– supports the hypothesis the results presented here are valid.

VI. RELATED WORK

The accuracy evaluation techniques used in this paper are being increasingly used by researchers that need to evaluate the accuracy of new effort estimation proposals. For instance, Sarro et al. used the Mean Absolute Error and the Standardized Accuracy to assess the accuracy of a bi-objective effort estimation algorithm that combines confidence interval analysis and assessment of mean absolute error [17]. To establish if the estimations of one method were significantly better than the estimations provided by another method, they tested the statistical significance of the absolute errors achieved with different estimation methods via the Wilcoxon Signed Rank Test, as we did in Section IV.

The techniques used here are becoming quite popular, but there are also several alternative proposal, actually too many to be mentioned here. As an example of an alternative to SA, Tofallis proposed to use the logarithm of the accuracy ratio: $log\frac{prediction}{actual}$ [18]. As an example of an alternative to Hedges's g, Vargha and Delaney proposed the A12 statistic, a non-parametric effect size measure: given a performance measure M, A12 indicates the probability that running algorithm A yields higher M values than running another algorithm B [19]. Finally, a quite different but interesting proposal is StatREC, a Graphical User Interface statistical toolkit designed to provide a variety of graphical tools and statistical hypothesis tests to facilitate strategies for an intelligent decision-making [20].

Concerning the assessment of accuracy of functional size estimation methods, to the best of the author's knowledge, very little work has been done. In general, some evaluation is done when a method is proposed, as in [21], where the NESMA estimated method is proposed and its accuracy is evaluated on the training set. A noticeable exception is [22], where several early estimation methods for Function Point measures are evaluated via an empirical study.

VII. CONCLUSION

In this paper, the accuracy of a set of model-based methods to estimate the COSMIC size of software applications has been evaluated. The relevance of the paper is based on two factors:

- For practitioners (as well as for researchers) knowing the accuracy that can be achieved via size estimation methods is very important. Consider for instance that the application of the considered size estimation methods could provide the most important piece of information upon which the cost of software is estimated.
- To evaluate the accuracy of estimates, you need reliable indicators. Traditional indicators like MMRE have been proved to be biased. So, finding and testing more reliable indicators is necessary. Consider for instance a new estimation technique proposed by some researchers: how can they confidently claim that their new technique is good, and possibly even better than existing techniques? They need reliable accuracy evaluation techniques and indicators.

According to our empirical study, we can recommend that the accuracy of estimates be evaluated by

- Computing the mean of absolute residuals (MAR) of all the models to be tested.
- For any estimation method, doing better than the baseline models (the constant model and the random model) is a must. Hence, one should always test models against the constant model. In addition, one should also evaluate new estimation methods against the currently used estimation technique, to see it the change is worthwhile.
- Using Wilcoxon Sign Rank Test is advisable, since it can give statistically significant indications that are particularly informative when two methods' MAR values are close.
- Also looking at the boxplots of absolute residuals can help, especially when a few outliers affect the MAR at a great extent (as in Figure 2).
- Finally, assessing the effect size using Hedges's g (or similar indicators) is useful to assess the extent of the improvement that a new technique can guarantee over another one.

When evaluating the accuracy of model-based COSMIC size estimation methods, we got easily quite representative indications via the MAR, as shown in Table II. By means of more sophisticated statistical tools –such as the Wilcoxon Sign Rank Test and Hedges's g– we achieved indications that are slightly more informative, e.g., that there is no statistically significant evidence that the log 2 model is more accurate than the reg2 model.

As a final observation, we note that the analyses reported in this paper were carried out quite easily via simple R [23] programs. So, practitioner and researchers that need to evaluate estimation accuracy can invest a small amount of effort to program a few hundred lines of R code that will make the analysis reported here totally automatic.

Future work includes:

- Further evaluating model-based COSMIC size estimation methods via additional evaluation methods and against additional datasets.
- Experimenting the accuracy evaluation methods used in this paper with other estimation techniques and using other datasets.

ACKNOWLEDGMENT

The work presented here has been partly supported by the "Fondo di Ricerca d'Ateneo" of the Università degli Studi dell'Insubria.

REFERENCES

[1] The COSMIC consortium, Functional Size Measurement Method Version 4.0.1 Measurement Manual (The COSMIC Implementation Guide for ISO/IEC 19761:2011), 2015.

[2] V. Del Bianco, L. Lavazza, G. Liu, S. Morasca, and A. Z. Abualkishik, "Model-based early and rapid estimation of cosmic functional size– an experimental evaluation," Information and Software Technology, vol. 56, no. 10, 2014, pp. 1253–1267.

[3] B. A. Kitchenham, L. M. Pickard, S. G. MacDonell, and M. J. Shepperd, "What accuracy statistics really measure," IEE Proceedings-Software, vol. 148, no. 3, 2001, pp. 81–85.

[4] T. Foss, E. Stensrud, B. Kitchenham, and I. Myrtveit, "A simulation study of the model evaluation criterion MMRE," IEEE Transactions on Software Engineering, vol. 29, no. 11, 2003, pp. 985–995.

[5] I. Myrtveit, E. Stensrud, and M. Shepperd, "Reliability and validity in comparative studies of software prediction models," IEEE Transactions on Software Engineering, vol. 31, no. 5, 2005, pp. 380–391.

[6] K. Berg, T. Dekkers, and R. Oudshoorn, "Functional size measurement applied to UML-based user requirements," 2005, pp. 69–80.

[7] L. A. Lavazza, V. Del Bianco, and C. Garavaglia, "Model-based functional size measurement," in Proceedings of the Second ACM-IEEE international symposium on Empirical software engineering and measurement. ACM, 2008, pp. 100–109.

[8] A. Živkovič, I. Rozman, and M. Heričko, "Automated software size estimation based on function points using UML models," Information and Software Technology, vol. 47, no. 13, 2005, pp. 881–890.

[9] L. Lavazza and V. Del Bianco, "A case study in COSMIC functional size measurement: The rice cooker revisited," Software Process and Product Measurement, 2009, pp. 101–121.

[10] M. Shepperd and S. MacDonell, "Evaluating prediction systems in software project estimation," Information and Software Technology, vol. 54, no. 8, 2012, pp. 820–827.

[11] W. B. Langdon, J. Dolado, F. Sarro, and M. Harman, "Exact mean absolute error of baseline predictor, MARP0," Information and Software Technology, vol. 73, 2016, pp. 16–18.

[12] L. Lavazza and S. Morasca, "On the evaluation of effort estimation models," in Proceedings of the 21st International Conference on Evaluation and Assessment in Software Engineering. ACM, 2017, pp. 41–50.

[13] R. Rosenthal, H. Cooper, and L. Hedges, "Parametric measures of effect size," The handbook of research synthesis, 1994, pp. 231–244.

[14] P. D. Ellis, The essential guide to effect sizes: Statistical power, meta-analysis, and the interpretation of research results. Cambridge University Press, 2010.

[15] J. Cohen, "A power primer." Psychological bulletin, vol. 112, no. 1, 1992, pp. 155–159.

[16] ——, Statistical power analysis for the behavioral sciences. Hillsdale, NJ: Lawrence Earlbaum Associates, 1988.

[17] F. Sarro, A. Petrozziello, and M. Harman, "Multi-objective software effort estimation," in Proceedings of the 38th International Conference on Software Engineering. ACM, 2016, pp. 619–630.

[18] C. Tofallis, "A better measure of relative prediction accuracy for model selection and model estimation," Journal of the Operational Research Society, vol. 66, no. 8, 2015, pp. 1352–1362.

[19] A. Vargha and H. D. Delaney, "A critique and improvement of the cl common language effect size statistics of mcgraw and wong," Journal of Educational and Behavioral Statistics, vol. 25, no. 2, 2000, pp. 101–132.

[20] N. Mittas, I. Mamalikidis, and L. Angelis, "A framework for comparing multiple cost estimation methods using an automated visualization toolkit," Information and Software Technology, vol. 57, 2015, pp. 310–328.

[21] H. van Heeringen, E. van Gorp, and T. Prins, "Functional size measurement-accuracy versus costs-is it really worth it?" in Software Measurement European Forum (SMEF), 2009.

[22] L. Lavazza and G. Liu, "An empirical evaluation of simplified function point measurement processes," International Journal on Advances in Software, vol. 6, no. 1 & 2, 2013, pp. 1–13.

[23] R Core Team, R: A language and environment for statistical computing. R Foundation for Statistical Computing, 2014.

Measuring Differences To Compare Sets Of Models And Improve Diversity In MDE

Adel Ferdjoukh*, Florian Galinier‡, Eric Bourreau†, Annie Chateau† and Clémentine Nebut†

*Atlanmod, University of Nantes, Inria and LS2N, France
email: adel.ferdjoukh@univ-nantes.fr

†Lirmm, CNRS and University of Montpellier, France

‡IRIT, University Paul Sabatier, Toulouse. France

Abstract—**Owning sets of models is crucial in many fields, so as to validate concepts or to test algorithms that handle models, model transformations. Since such models are not always available, generators can be used to automatically generate sets of models. Unfortunately, the generated models are very close to each others in term of graph structure and element naming is poorly diverse. Usually, they cover very badly the solutions' space. In this paper, we propose novel measures to estimate differences between two models and we provide solutions to handle a whole set of models and perform several operations on its models: comparing them, selecting the most diverse and representative and graphically view the diversity. Implementations presented in this paper are gathered in a tool named COMODI. We applied these model comparison measures in order to improve diversity in MDE using a genetic algorithm.**

Keywords–Model Driven Engineering; Comparing sets of models; Diversity of Models.

I. Introduction & Motivations

The increasing use of programs handling models, such as model transformations makes the need for model benchmarks more and more important. Elements of the benchmarks are models which need to be, at the same time, as representative as possible of their domain-specific modelling language, and as diverse as possible in order to chase the potentially rare but annoying cases where programs show a bad behaviour. The difficulty of finding real test data that fulfil both requirements, and in sufficient quantity to ensure statistical representativeness, leads to consider automated generation of sets of diverse models. Many approaches and tools can be used in this purpose: *ferdjoukh et al.* [1], *Sen et al.* [2], *Cabot et al.* [3], *Gogolla et al.* [4].

One of the main issues when attempting to produce different and diverse models, is to state in what extent, and according to which criteria, the models are actually "different" and "diverse". The most natural way to formalize this notion is to define and use metrics comparing models and measuring their differences.

Determining model differences is an important task in Model Driven Engineering. It is used for instance in repositories for model versioning. Identifying differences between models is also crucial for software evolution and maintainability. However, comparing models is a difficult task since it relies on model matching. This latter can be reduced to graph isomorphism that is an NP-hard problem [5]. Kolovos et al. [5] draw up an overview of this issue and give some well-known algorithms and tools for model comparison. Most of these approaches compare only two models between them and find their common elements. This is insufficient for the problem of diversity improving because differences have to be measured and a whole set of models has to be considered.

In this work, we propose a distance-based approach to measure model differences and we provide solutions to handle sets of models in order to compare them and to extract the most representative models. A human readable-graphical viewing is also given to estimate the diversity of a set of models.

In this paper, we consider models which are conform to meta-models, according to the Ecore/EMF formalization [6]. Model generation is performed using $\mathcal{G}$RIMM [1] [7], which is based on the Constraint Programming paradigm [8]. Basically, $\mathcal{G}$RIMM reads a meta-model and translates all elements of the meta-model into a Constraint Satisfaction Problem (CSP). A CSP solver is then used to solve the obtained constraint network, leading to one or more models which are conform to this meta-model, and meeting a given set of additional parameters describing the characteristic of desired models. The relevancy of the produced models is managed through the use of domain-specific probability distributions, given by the user, and extend the $\mathcal{G}$RIMM tool to $\mathcal{GA}$RIMM tool [9]. Schema on Figure 1 shows the steps for model generation using $\mathcal{GA}$RIMM tool. Constraint Programming provides a deterministic behavior for the generation, it is then difficult to encode diversity directly in the heart of the tool. Other model generation tools can be coupled with our approach. For example, during our experiment we also used models that have been generated using PRAMANA tool (Sen et al. [2]).

Our contributions are: (1) novel metrics measuring model differences using distances coming from different fields (data mining, code correction algorithms and graph) and adapted to Model Driven Engineering (MDE) (2) solutions to handle a whole set of models in order to compare them, to extract the most representative models inside it and to give a graphical viewing for the concept of diversity in MDE (3) A tool implementing these two previous contributions (4) an application of these distance metrics in improving diversity in MDE using a

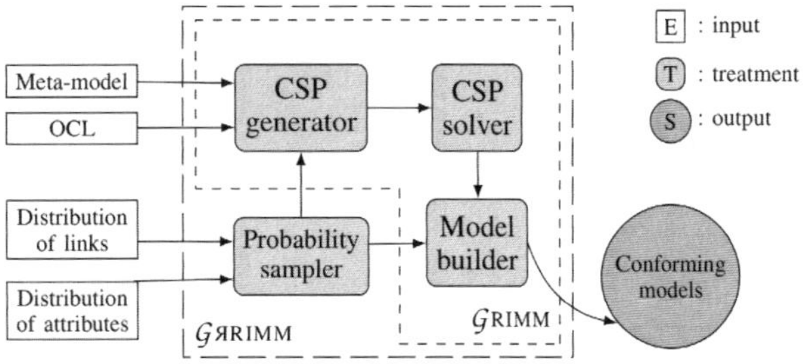

Figure 1. Steps for model generation using GRIMM/GRIMM tool.

genetic algorithm.

The rest of the paper is structured as follows. Section II details the considered model comparison metrics. Section III details the solutions for handling a set of models (comparison, selection of representative model and graphical viewing). The tool implementing these contributions is described in section IV. An application of our method to the problem of improving diversity in MDE is shown in Section V. Section VI relates about previous work. Section VII concludes the paper.

II. Measuring model differences

Brun and Pierantonio state in [10] that the complex problem of determining model differences can be separated into three steps: *calculation* (finding an algorithm to compare two models), *representation* (result of the computation being represented in manipulable form) and *visualization* (result of the computation being human-viewable).

Our comparison method aims to provide solutions to compare not only two models between them but a whole set of models or sets of models. The rest of this section describes in details the calculation algorithms we choose to measure model differences. Since our method aims to compare sets of models, we took care to find the quickest algorithms. Because chosen comparison algorithms are called hundreds of time to manipulate one set containing dozens of models.

As a proof of concept, we consider here four different distances to express the pairwise dissimilarity between models. As stated in [11], there is intrinsically a difficulty for model metrics to capture the semantics of models. However, formalizing metrics over the graph structure of models is easy, and they propose ten metrics using a multidimensional graph, where the multidimensionality intends to partially take care of semantics on references. They explore the ability of those metrics to characterize different domains using models. In our work, we focus on the ability of distances to seclude models inside a set of models. Thus, we have selected very various distances, essentially of 2 different area: distances on words (from data mining and natural language processing) and distances on graphs (from semantic web and graph theory). Word distances have the very advantage of a quick computation, whereas graph distances are closer to the graph structure of models. As already said, an interesting feature is the fact that all those distances are, in purpose, not domain-specific, not especially coming from MDE, but adapted to the latter.

A. Words distances for models

We define two distances for models based on distances on words: the hamming distance and the cosine distance. The first one is really close to syntax and count the number of difference between two vectors. The second one is normalized and intends to capture the multidimensional divergence between two vectors representing geometrical positions.

1) From models to words: We define the vectorial representation of a model as the vector collecting links and attributes' values of each class instance, as illustrated on the model of Figure 2. At the left-hand-side of the figure is an example of meta-model. At the right-hand-side of the figure are two models conform to this meta-model, and their vectorial representation. The obtained vector from a model m is composed of successive sections of data on each instance of m, when data is available. Each section of data is organized as follows: first data on links, then data on attributes. When there is no such data for a given instance, it is not represented. In the example of Figure 2, instances of B, which have no references and no attributes, as imposed by the meta-model, are not directly represented in the vectors. However, they appear through the links attached to instances of A. An attribute is represented by its value. A link from an instance i to an instance j is represented by the number of the referenced instance j. Each instance of a given meta-class mc, are represented by sections of identical size. Indeed, all the instances of mc have the same number of attributes. The number of links may vary from an instance to another, but a size corresponding to maximal cardinality is systematically attributed. This cardinality is either found in the meta-model or given in the generation parameters. When the actual number of links is smaller than the maximal number of links, 0 values are inserted.

2) Hamming distance for models: Hamming distance compares two vectors. It was introduced by *Richard Hamming* in 1952 [12] and was originally used for fault detection and code correction. Hamming distance counts the number of differing coefficients between two vectors.

The models to compare are transformed into vectors, then we compare the coefficients of vectors to find the distance between both models:

$$\begin{array}{rcllllllll} \text{a} & = & (5, & 4, & 0, & 2, & 4, & 3, & 6, & 1) \\ \text{b} & = & (6, & 5, & 3, & 3, & 4, & 7, & 0, & 1) \\ \hline \text{d(a,b)} & = & 1+ & 1+ & 1+ & 1+ & 0+ & 1+ & 1+ & 0 \\ & = & \frac{6}{8} \end{array}$$

Richard Hamming's original distance formula is not able to detect permutations of links, which leads to artificially higher values than expected. In our version, we sort the vectors such as to check if each link exists in the other vector. In the previous example, the final distance then equals to $\frac{5}{8}$. The complexity is linear in the size of models, due to the vectorization step. Notice also that this distance implies that vectors have equal sizes. This is guaranteed by the way we build those vectors.

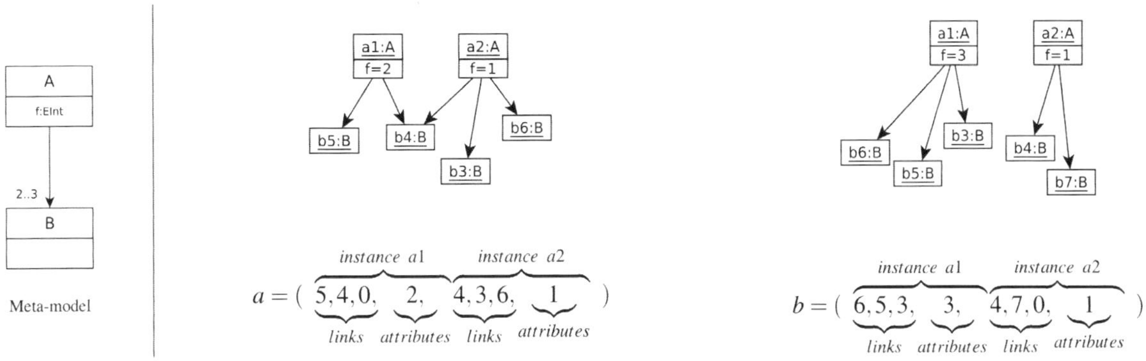

Figure 2. Two small models and their vectorial representation.

3) Cosine distance: Cosine similarity is a geometric measure of similarity between two vectors, ranging from -1 to 1: two similar vectors have a similarity that equals 1 and two diametrically opposite vectors have a cosine similarity of -1. Cosine similarity of two vectors a and b is given by the following formula:

$$C_S(a,b) = \frac{a.b}{||a||.||b||} = \frac{\sum_{i=1}^{n} a_i.b_i}{\sqrt{\sum_{i=1}^{n} a_i^2}.\sqrt{\sum_{i=1}^{n} b_i^2}}$$

After a vectorization of models, cosine similarity is then used to compute a normalized cosine distance over two vectors [13]:

$$C_D(a,b) = \frac{1 - C_S(a,b)}{2}$$

Again, the time complexity of the computation is linear in the size of models.

4) Levenshtein distance for models: Levenshtein distance [14] (*named after Vladimir Levenshtein*) is a string metric used to compare two sequences of characters. To summarise the original idea, a comparison algorithm counts the minimal number of single-character edits needed to jump from a first string to a second one. There exist three character edit operations: addition, deletion and substitution.

Our customized Levenshtein distance is based on the vectorial representation of a model. Each character in original distance is replaced by a class instance of the model. So, we count the minimal cost of class instance edit operations (addition, deletion or substitution) to jump from the first model to the second one.

First, a vectorial representation of a model is created according to the class diagram given in Figure 3. Then, we determine the cost of each one of the three edit operations over instanceOfClass objects. `instanceCost` method gives the cost to add or to delete an instanceOfClass. It counts the number of edges and the number of attributes of this instance. `substituCost` method gives the cost to substitute an instance by another one. To determine the substitution cost, we count the number of common links and attributes. Thus, two `instanceOfClass` are exactly equal if they have the same

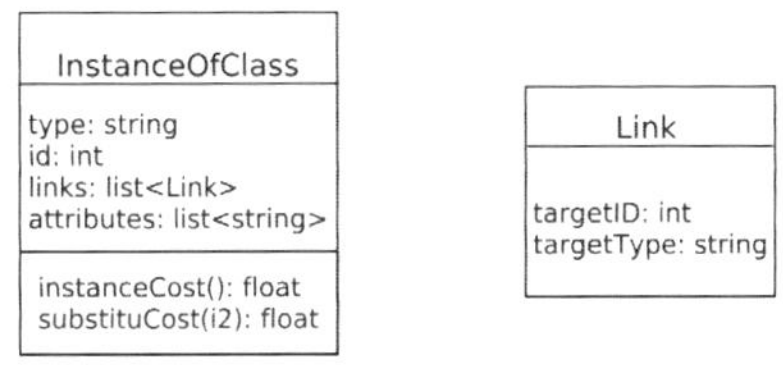

Figure 3. Class diagram for instanceOfClass and Link to build a vectorial representation of a model.

type, their links have the same type and all their attributes have the same values.

Finally, Levenshtein algorithm [14] is applied and a metric of comparison is computed. Our comparison metric gives the percentage of common elements between two models.

B. Centrality distance for models

Centrality is a real function that associates a value to each node of a graph [15]. This value indicates how much a node is *central* in this graph, according to a chosen criterion. For example, in a tree, the highest value of centrality is given to the root of the tree, whereas the smallest values are associated to the leaves. A centrality function C is defined by:

$$C: \begin{array}{l} E \rightarrow \mathbb{R}^+ \\ v \mapsto C(v) \end{array}$$

Many usual centrality functions exist. The simplest one, the *degree centrality*, associates to each node its degree. Among the well-known centrality functions, we can cite: betweenness centrality, closeness centrality, harmonic centrality, etc.

In this paper, we propose a novel centrality function adapted for MDE and based on *eigenvector* centrality. This centrality was also used in the first published version of `PageRank` algorithm of the `Google` search engine [16]. In `PageRank`, eigenvector centrality is used to rank the web pages taken as nodes of the same graph.

1) From models to graphs: Centrality functions are defined on graphs, and models could be considered as labelled and typed graphs. Our graph representation of models is obtained as follows:

TABLE I. NODES TRANSFORMATION RULES.

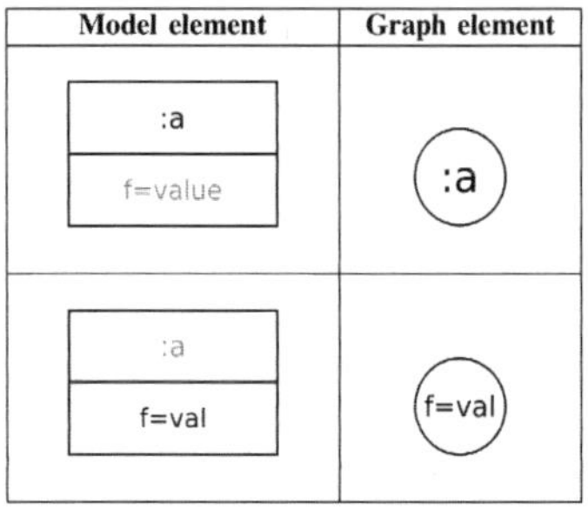

TABLE II. EDGES TRANSFORMATION RULES.

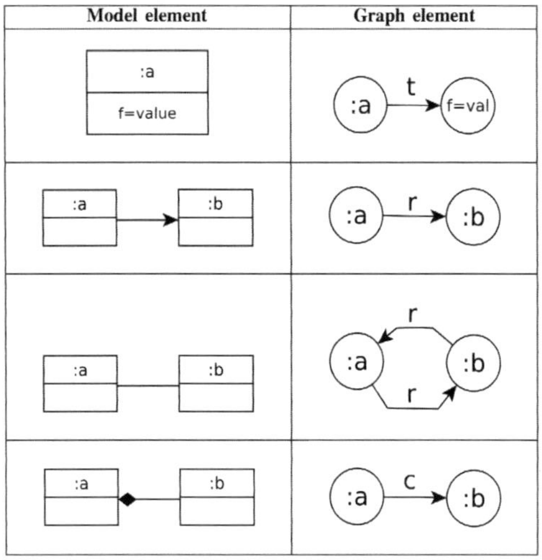

- Create a node for each class instance (central nodes).
- Create a node for each attribute (leaf nodes).
- Create an edge from each class instance to its attributes.
- Create an edge for each simple reference between two class instances.
- Create two edges if two class instances are related by two opposite references.
- Create an edge for each composition link.

Tables I and II summarize and illustrate these transformations rules. Real numbers c, r and t represent the weights assigned to composition links, reference links and attributes.

2) Centrality measure: Our centrality is inspired from `pagerank` centrality and adapted to models, taking into account class instances and their attributes, links between classes (input and output) and types of link between two classes (simple references, two opposite references or compositions). For a given node v of the graph, we denote by $N(v)$ the set of its neighbors. The following function gives the centrality of each node v:

$$C(v) = \sum_{u \in N^+(v)} \frac{C(u)}{deg(u)} \times w(v,u).$$

$w(v,u)$ gives the weight of the link between node v and u, determined by the kind of link between them (attribute, reference or composition). The weight of a link can be given by the user or deduced from domain-based quality metrics. For instance, *Kollmann and Gogolla* [17] described a method for creating weighted graphs for UML diagrams using object-oriented metrics.

3) Centrality vector: The centrality vector C contains the values of centrality for each node. The previous centrality function induces the creation of a system of n variables equations: $C(v_i) = c_1C(v_1) + c_2C(v_2) + \ldots + c_iC(v_i) + \ldots + c_nC(v_n)$.

To compute the centrality vector C we must find the eigenvector of a matrix A whose values are the coefficients of the previous equations: $C = AC$, where A is built as follows:

$$A_{ij} = \begin{cases} 0 \text{ if } (v_i, v_j) \notin \text{ Graph}, \\ \dfrac{w(v_i, v_j)}{N(v_i)} \text{ otherwise.} \end{cases}$$

After building matrix A, we use the classical algorithm of power iteration (also known as Richard Von Mises method [18]) to compute the centrality vector C.

The result centrality vector has a high dimension (see example on Figure 4). To reduce this dimension therefore improve the computation's efficiency, we group its coefficients according to the classes of the meta-model. Then the dimension equals to the number of classes in the meta-model.

4) Centrality distance: Roy et al. proved in [19] that a centrality measure can be used to create a graph distance. Here, the centrality vectors C_A and C_B of two models A and B are compared using any mathematical norm: $d(A,B) = ||C_A - C_B||$.

C. Discussion

We use in previous paragraphs representations of models which could be discussed. Indeed, there are potentially many ways to vectorize models, and we choose one highly compatible with our tool. Since CSP generation already provides a list of classes attributes and links, we simply used this representation as entry for the metrics. Again, transforming models into graphs and trees may be done through several ways. We arbitrarily choose one way that seemed to capture the graph structure. Our goal here, was to test different and diversified manners to represent a model and proposed some distance between them, not to make an exhaustive comparison study between quality of representation versus metrics. This study will be done in future works.

III. HANDLING SETS OF MODELS

In this section, we propose an automated process for handling model sets. The purpose is to provide solutions for comparing models belonging to a set, selecting the most representative models in a set and bringing a graphical view of the concept of diversity in a model set.

This process helps a user in choosing a reasonable amount of models to perform his experiments (e.g., testing a model transformation). Moreover, using our approach, the chosen

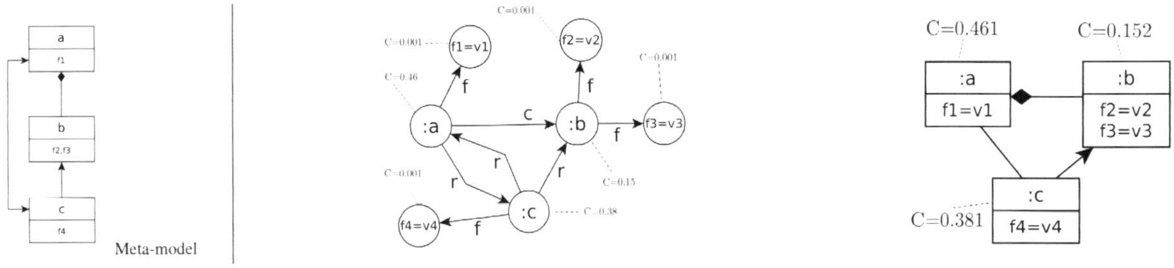

Figure 4. Centrality vector computed for an example model and its equivalent graph.

model set aims to achieve a good coverage of the meta-model's solutions space.

If there are no available models, a first set of models is generated using $\mathcal{G}$ЯRIMM tool [9]. These generated models are conform to an input meta-model and respect its OCL constraints. When probability distributions related to domain-specific metrics are added to the process, intra-model diversity is improved. Our goal is to check the coverage of the meta-model's solutions space. In other words, we want to help a user to answer these questions: (1) how to quantify the inter-model diversity ? (2) Are all these models useful and representative ? (3) Which one of my model sets is the most diverse ?

A. *Comparison of model sets*

Distance metrics proposed in Section II compare two models. To compare a set of models, we have to compute pair-wise distances between models inside the set. A symmetrical distance matrix is then created and used to quantify the inter-model diversity. It is noticeable that, thanks to the modularity of the approach, this step can be replaced by any kind of dataset production. For instance, if the user already has a set of models, it is possible to use it instead of the generated one. Moreover, another distance metric can be used instead of the metrics we propose.

B. *Selecting most representative models*

Our idea is that when a user owns a certain number of models (real ones or generated ones), there are some of them which are representative. Only these models should be used in some kind of tests (e.g., robustness or performance). Most of other models are close to these representative models.

We use *Hierarchical Matrix clustering* techniques to select the most representative models among a set of models. The distance matrix is clustered and our tool chooses a certain number of models. In our tool, we use the hierarchical clustering algorithm [20], implemented in the R software (*hclust, stats package, version 3.4.0*) [21]. This algorithm starts by finding a tree of clusters for the selected distance matrix as shown in Figure 5. Then, the user has to give a threshold value in order to find the appropriate value. This value depends on the diversity the user wants. For example, if the user wants models sharing only 10% of common elements, then 90% is the appropriate threshold value. This value depends also on the used metric. Thus, Levenshtein distance compares the names of elements and the values of attributes, leading to choose a smaller threshold value (for the same model set) than for centrality distance which compares only the graph structure of the models.

Using the clusters tree and the threshold value, it is easy to derive the clusters, by cutting the tree at the appropriate height (Figure 5). The most representative models are chosen by arbitrarily picking up one model per cluster. For instance, 3 different clusters are found using the tree of clusters in Figure 5. Clone detection can also be performed using our approach by choosing the appropriate threshold value. Indeed, if threshold equals to 0, clusters will contain only clones.

TABLE III. AN EXAMPLE OF DISTANCE MATRIX (HAMMING) FOR 10 MODELS.

	m_1	m_2	m_3	m_4	m_5	m_6	m_7	m_8	m_9	m_{10}
m_1	0	12	27	27	27	26	46	44	45	39
m_2	12	0	27	26	27	27	45	45	43	40
m_3	27	27	0	18	17	16	46	45	46	39
m_4	27	26	18	0	18	18	45	44	45	40
m_5	27	27	17	18	0	18	45	43	44	38
m_6	26	27	16	18	18	0	45	44	46	40
m_7	46	45	46	45	45	45	0	36	36	41
m_8	44	45	45	44	43	44	36	0	34	37
m_9	45	43	46	45	44	46	36	34	0	39
m_{10}	39	40	39	40	38	40	41	37	39	0

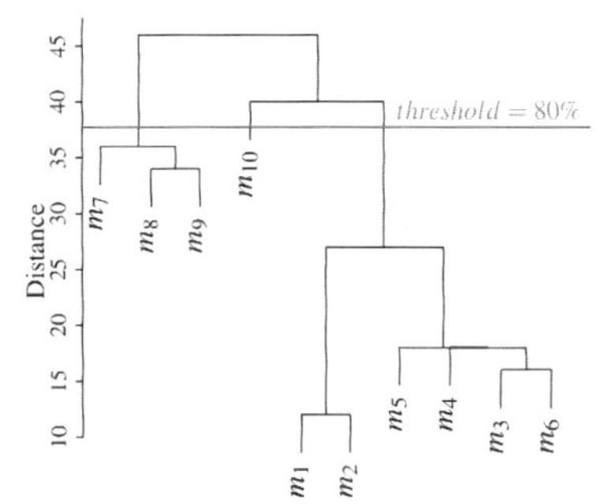

Figure 5. Clustering tree computed form matrix in Table III.

C. *Graphical view of diversity*

Estimating diversity of model sets is interesting for model users. It may give an estimation on the number of models needed for their tests or experiments and they can use this diversity measure to compare between two sets of models.

When the number of models in a set is small, diversity can be done manually by checking the distance matrix. Unfortunately, it becomes infeasible when the set contains more than an handful of models. We propose a human-readable graphical representation of diversity and solutions' space coverage for a set of models.

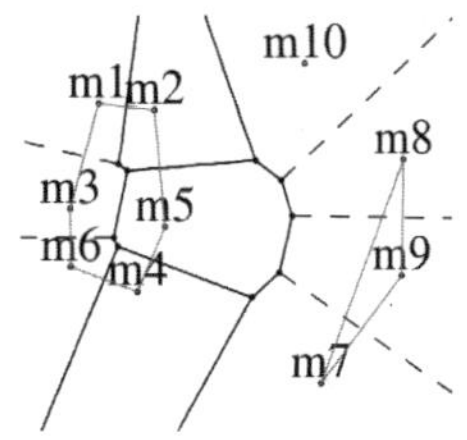

Figure 6. Voronoi diagram for 10 models compared using Hamming distance.

Our tool creates *Voronoi tessellations* [22] of the distance matrix in order to assist users in estimating the diversity or in comparing two model sets. A *Voronoi* diagram is a 2D representation of elements according to a comparison criterion, here distances metrics between models. It faithfully reproduces the coverage of meta-model's solutions space by the set of models. Figure 6 shows the Voronoi diagram created for the matrix in Table III. The three clusters found in the previous step are highlighted by red lines. We use the Voronoi functions of R software (available in package *tripack, v1.3-8*).

IV. TOOLING

This section details the tooling implementing our contributions. All the algorithms and tools are in free access and available on our web pages: http://adel-ferdjoukh.ovh/index.php/research/.

Our tool for comparing models and handling model sets is called COunting MOdel DIfferences (COMODI). It consists in two different parts. The first one, written in *java*, is used to measure differences between two models using the above 4 metrics. The second part, written in *bash* and *R*, provides algorithms for handling model sets (comparison, diversity estimation and clustering).

A. Comparing two models

It is possible to measure the differences between two models using COMODI. For that you just need to give as input two models and their *ecore* meta-model. Out tool supports two different formats: *dot* model files produced by GRIMM and *xmi* model files. COMODI supports all xmi files produced by EMF of generated by GRIMM, *EMF2CSP* or PRAMANA tools.

The first step is to parse the input models into the appropriate representation (graph or vector). Then, the above distance algorithms are applied. COMODI outputs different model comparison metrics in command line mode. Process of COMODI is described in Figure 7.

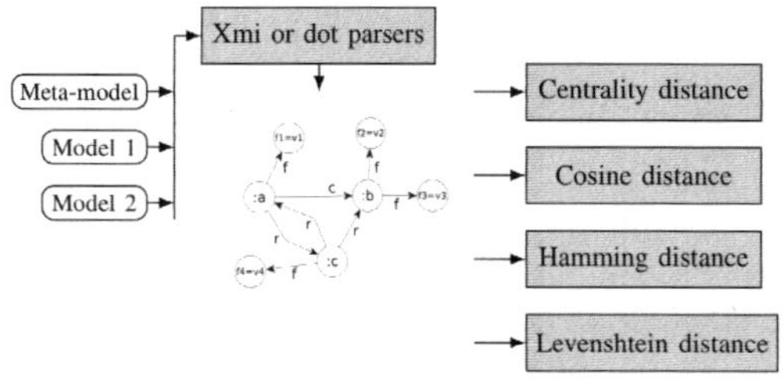

Figure 7. Comparing two models using COMODI tool.

B. Handling a set of models

Our tool is also able to handle sets of models and produce distance matrices, perform clustering and plot diagrams and give some statistics. The input of the tool is a folder containing the models to compare and their *ecore* meta-model. The supported formats for models are the same as described above (xmi and dot).

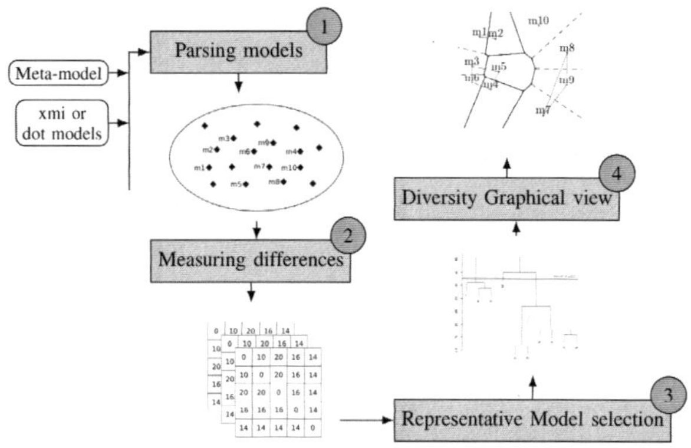

Figure 8. Handling a set of models using COMODI tool.

After parsing all the models into the appropriate representation for each metric, distance matrices are produced by pairwise comparison of models. *R* scripts are called to perform hierarchical clustering on these matrices. This allows us to select the most representative models of that folder. Voronoi diagrams are plotted and can be used to estimate the coverage of the folder and to compare the diversity of two folders. COMODI prints also some simple statistics on models: closest models, most different models, etc. These steps are shown in figure 8.

V. APPLICATION: IMPROVING DIVERSITY

The main contributions of this paper - distances between models, representative model selection to improve diversity - were used in a work in bioinformatics (named scaffolding). A genetic approach is paired with GƎRIMM model generation tool to improve the diversity of a set of automatically generated models. Figure 9 shows how we start from a GRIMM model set (left) with few difference between them, to GƎRIMM (center) with a better distribution due to the probability sampler, to something very relevant by using a genetic approach (right) based on these model distances in order to improve diversity.

We want to address the following question: do proposed distances and process of automated models selection help to

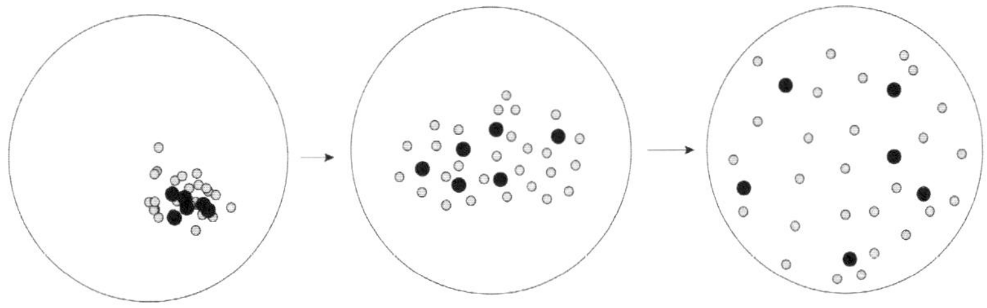

Figure 9. Diversity improving process. Black circles are the most representative models of the set.

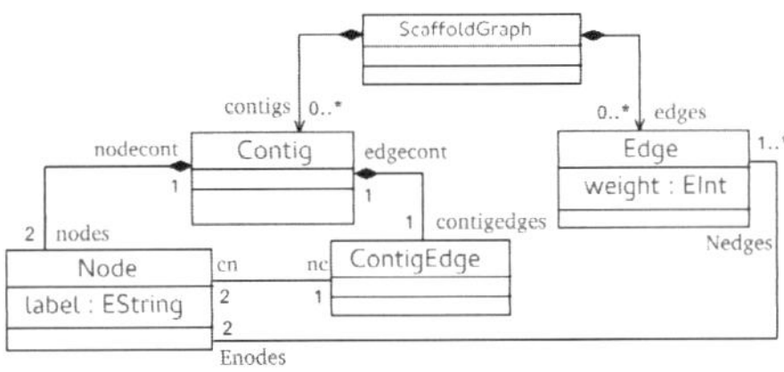

Figure 10. The meta-model of Scaffold graphs.

improve the diversity and the coverage of generated models. We chose one meta-model (Figure 10) modeling a type of graphs involved in the production of whole genomes from new-generation sequencing data [23]. Hereinafter we give the experimental protocol:

- Generate 100 initial models conforming to the scaffold graph meta-model using $\mathcal{G}$ЯRIMM tool [9].
- Model the problem of improving diversity using genetic algorithms (GA). Our modeling in GA can be found in [24].
- Run 500 times the genetic algorithm. At each step, use model distances and automatic model selection to choose only the best models for the next step.
- View final results in terms of model distances and meta-model coverage using Voronoi diagrams.

The whole process induces the creation of up to 50,000 different models. Each following figures required about 3h CP to be computed.

The curves on Figure 11 show the evolution of hamming and cosine distance while the genetic algorithm is running (minimum, maximum and mean distance over the population at each generation). We can observe that both cosine distance and hamming distance help to improve diversity of generated models. The quick convergence of both curves (around 100 iterations of GA) is a good way to check the efficiency of both models distances. We observe that the worst case in the final population is better than the best case in the initial population, thus we reached a diversity level that we did not obtained in the initial population obtained with $\mathcal{G}$ЯRIMM.

We introduce several improvements to describe the fitness function used in genetic selection [24] and improve median value for final population from 0.7 up to 0.9 for Hamming and from 0.11 to 0.15 for maximum with Cosinus distance. Figure 12 compares the models produced by the different distances. Red (resp. blue) dotplots represent the distribution of distances on the final population computed using Hamming distance (resp. Cosine distance). On the left, models are compared using Hamming distance, on the right, they are compared using Cosine distance. We remark that different distances do not produce the same final models. We can observe that the best selected models for Hamming distance obtain lower scores when compared using Cosine distance, and vice versa. Other experimental results show that our four model distances can be used in a multi-objective genetic algorithm since they treat different constructions of the meta-model. Results are better on the final model set in terms of diversity and coverage, than when only one kind of distance is used.

Figure 13 shows two Voronoi diagrams of 100 models. The first one is computed on the initial set of models, the second on the set of models generated after the 500th iteration of the genetic algorithm. We kept the same scale to visualize the introduced seclusion. Here we can see the insufficient solutions' space coverage of the first Voronoi diagram. After running the multi-objective genetic algorithm, we observe a better coverage of the space. At the end of the process, we obtain 100 very distinct models.

VI. Related Work

This section draws a state of the art of the topics related to the work we presented in our paper. So, we give the most important techniques for the comparison of models and the approaches that select models to measure and improve the diversity in MDE.

A. Model comparison

The challenging problem of model comparison was widely studied, many techniques and algorithms were proposed for it. Two literature studies are proposed in [5] and [25]. Among all the techniques, we describe here the techniques that are close to the model distance algorithms we propose, in both comparison and objective.

Falleri et al. [26] propose a meta-model matching approach based on *similarity flooding* algorithm [27]. The goal of this approach is to detect mappings between very close meta-models to turn compatible models which are conform to these meta-models. The comparison algorithm detects two close meta-models. A transformation is then generated to make the models of the first meta-model conform to the second one. However, in such kind of work, the similarity between models cannot be detected without using the names of elements:

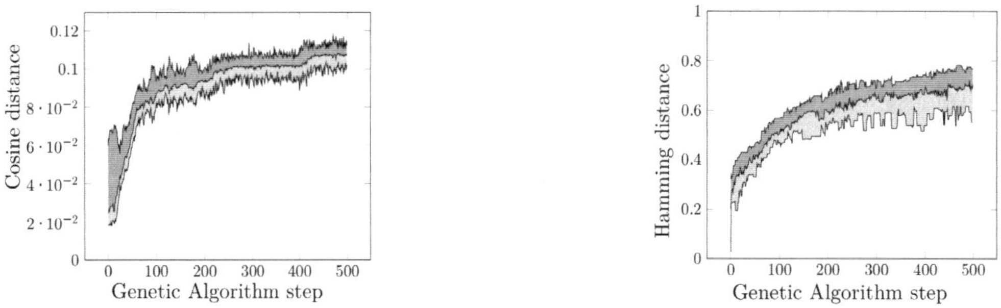

Figure 11. Minimum, average and maximum hamming and cosine distance while running the genetic algorithm.

Figure 12. Comparison of best selected models pairwise distances distributions.

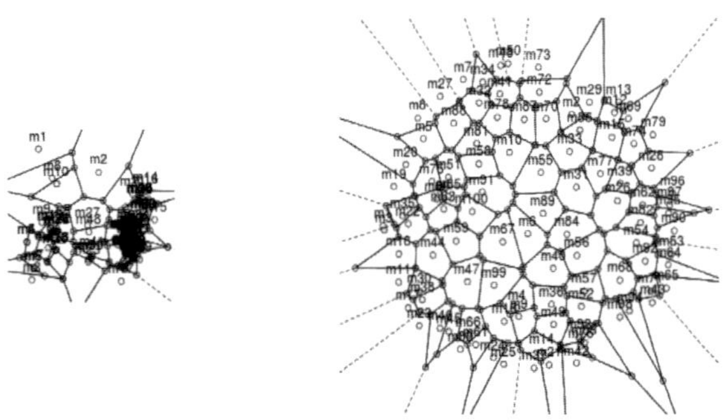

Figure 13. Solutions' space coverage of the initial set of models (left) compared to the last iteration (500th) of the genetic algorithm (right).

lexical similarities are propagated through the structure to detect matchings. Our approach is more structural.

Voigt and Heinze present in [28] a meta-model matching approach. The objective is very close to the previous approach. However, the authors propose a comparison algorithm that is based on graph edit distance. They claim that it is a way to compare the structure of the models and not only their semantics as most of techniques do.

B. Model selection

Cadavid et al. [29] present a technique for searching the boundaries of the modeling space, using a meta-heuristic method, *simulated annealing*. They try to maximize coverage of the domain structure by generated models, while maintaining diversity (dissimilarity of models). In this work, the dissimilarity is based on the over-coverage of modeling space, counting the number of fragments of models which are covered more than once by the generated models in the set. In our work, the objective is not to search the boundaries of the search space but to select representative and diverse elements in the whole search space. More recently, Batot et al. [30] proposed a generic framework based on a multi-objective genetic algorithm (NSGA-II) to select models sets. The objectives are given in terms of coverage and minimality of the set. The framework can be specialized adding coverage criterion, or modifying the minimality criterion. This work of Batot et al confirms the efficiency of genetic algorithms for model generation purposes. Our work is in the same vein but focuses on diversity.

Hao Wu [31] proposes an approach based on *SMT (Satisfiability Modulo Theory)* to generate diverse sets of models. It relies on two techniques for coverage oriented meta-model instance generation. The first one realizes the coverage criteria defined for UML class diagrams, while the second generates instances satisfying graph-based criteria.

Previous approaches guarantee the diversity relying only on the generation process. No post-process checking is performed on generated model sets to eliminate possible redundancies or to provide a human-readable graphical view of the set.

VII. Conclusion

Counting model differences is a recurrent problem in Model Driven Engineering, mainly when sets of models have to be compared. This paper tackles the issue of comparing two models using several kinds of distance metrics inspired from distances on words and distances on graphs. An approach and a tool are proposed to handle sets of models. Distance metrics are applied to those sets. Pair of models are compared and a matrix is produced. We use hierarchical clustering algorithms to gather the closest models and put them in subsets. Our tool, COMODI, is also able to choose the most representative models of a set and give some statistics on a set of models. Human readable graphical views are also generated to help users in doing that selection manually.

The first application of our contributions is improving diversity when generating models. Sets of non-diverse models are automatically generated. COMODI is coupled to a genetic algorithm to improve the diversity of this first set of models.

The problematic of handling sets of models and the notion of distance is also involved in many other works related to testing model transformations. All these issues are interesting applications to the contributions of this paper. For example, *Mottu et al.* in [32] describe a method for discovering model transformations pre-conditions by generating test models. A first set of test models is automatically generated and used to execute a model transformation. Excerpts of models that make the model transformation failing are extracted. An expert then tries manually and iteratively to discover pre-conditions using these excerpts. Our common work aims to help the expert by reducing the number of models excerpts and the number of iterations to discover most of pre-conditions. A set of models excerpts is handled using COMODI and clusters of close models are generated. Using our method, the expert can find many pre-conditions in one iteration and using less model excerpts.

Future work will consist in performing large experiments involving and comparing other kinds of distances, and to measure to what extend the way models are encoded into other structures (e.g., words or trees) affects the results. We remark that metrics and distances have also very different effects on the evolution of the models set, and intend to further investigate and characterize this phenomenon.

REFERENCES

[1] A. Ferdjoukh, A.-E. Baert, A. Chateau, R. Coletta, and C. Nebut, "A CSP Approach for Metamodel Instantiation," in IEEE ICTAI, 2013, pp. 1044–1051.

[2] S. Sen, B. Baudry, and J.-M. Mottu, "Automatic Model Generation Strategies for Model Transformation Testing," in ICMT, International Conference on Model Transformation, 2009, pp. 148–164.

[3] C. A. González Pérez, F. Buettner, R. Clarisó, and J. Cabot, "EMFtoCSP: A Tool for the Lightweight Verification of EMF Models," in FormSERA, Formal Methods in Software Engineering, 2012, pp. 44–50.

[4] F. Hilken, M. Gogolla, L. Burgueño, and A. Vallecillo, "Testing models and model transformations using classifying terms," Software & Systems Modeling, 2016, pp. 1–28.

[5] D. S. Kolovos, D. Di Ruscio, A. Pierantonio, and R. F. Paige, "Different models for model matching: An analysis of approaches to support model differencing," in CVSM@ICSE, 2009, pp. 1–6.

[6] D. Steinberg, F. Budinsky, M. Paternostro, and E. Merks, EMF: Eclipse Modeling Framework 2.0. Addison-Wesley Professional, 2009.

[7] A. Ferdjoukh, A.-E. Baert, E. Bourreau, A. Chateau, and C. Nebut, "Instantiation of Meta-models Constrained with OCL: a CSP Approach," in MODELSWARD, 2015, pp. 213–222.

[8] F. Rossi, P. Van Beek, and T. Walsh, Eds., Handbook of Constraint Programming. Elsevier Science Publishers, 2006.

[9] A. Ferdjoukh, E. Bourreau, A. Chateau, and C. Nebut, "A Model-Driven Approach to Generate Relevant and Realistic Datasets," in SEKE, 2016, pp. 105–109.

[10] C. Brun and A. Pierantonio, "Model differences in the eclipse modeling framework," UPGRADE, The European Journal for the Informatics Professional, vol. 9, no. 2, 2008, pp. 29–34.

[11] G. Szárnyas, Z. Kovári, Á. Salánki, and D. Varró, "Towards the characterization of realistic models: evaluation of multidisciplinary graph metrics," in MODELS, 2016, pp. 87–94.

[12] R. W. Hamming, "Error detecting and error correcting codes," Bell System technical journal, vol. 29, no. 2, 1950, pp. 147–160.

[13] A. Singhal, "Modern information retrieval: A brief overview," IEEE Data Engineering Bulletin, vol. 24, no. 4, 2001, pp. 35–43.

[14] V. Levenshtein, "Binary codes capable of correcting deletions, insertions, and reversals," in Soviet physics doklady, vol. 10, no. 8, 1966, pp. 707–710.

[15] G. Kishi, "On centrality functions of a graph," in Graph Theory and Algorithms. Springer, 1981, pp. 45–52.

[16] L. Page, S. Brin, R. Motwani, and T. Winograd, "The PageRank citation ranking: bringing order to the web," Stanford InfoLab, Tech. Rep., 1999.

[17] R. Kollmann and M. Gogolla, "Metric-based selective representation of uml diagrams," in CSMR. IEEE, 2002, pp. 89–98.

[18] R. von Mises and H. Pollaczek-Geiringer, "Praktische verfahren der gleichungsauflösung," ZAMM-Journal of Applied Mathematics and Mechanics, vol. 9, no. 2, 1929, pp. 152–164.

[19] M. Roy, S. Schmid, and G. Trédan, "Modeling and measuring Graph Similarity: the Case for Centrality Distance," in FOMC, 2014, pp. 47–52.

[20] F. Murtagh, "Multidimensional clustering algorithms," Compstat Lectures, Vienna: Physika Verlag, 1985, 1985.

[21] R Development Core Team, R: A Language and Environment for Statistical Computing, R Foundation for Statistical Computing, 2008.

[22] F. Aurenhammer, "Voronoi diagrams a survey of a fundamental geometric data structure," CSUR, ACM Computing Surveys, vol. 23, no. 3, 1991, pp. 345–405.

[23] M. Weller, A. Chateau, and R. Giroudeau, "Exact approaches for scaffolding," BMC Bioinformatics, vol. 16, no. 14, 2015, pp. 1471–2105.

[24] F. Galinier, E. Bourreau, A. Chateau, A. Ferdjoukh, and C. Nebut, "Genetic Algorithm to Improve Diversity in MDE," in META, 2016, pp. 170–173.

[25] Voigt, Konrad, "Structural Graph-based Metamodel Matching," Ph.D. dissertation, Dresden University, 2011.

[26] J.-R. Falleri, M. Huchard, M. Lafourcade, and C. Nebut, "Metamodel matching for automatic model transformation generation," in MODELS, 2008, pp. 326–340.

[27] S. Melnik, H. Garcia-Molina, and E. Rahm, "Similarity flooding: A versatile graph matching algorithm and its application to schema matching," in ICDE, 2002, pp. 117–128.

[28] K. Voigt and T. Heinze, "Metamodel matching based on planar graph edit distance," in Theory and Practice of Model Transformations, 2010, pp. 245–259.

[29] J. Cadavid, B. Baudry, and H. Sahraoui, "Searching the Boundaries of a Modeling Space to Test Metamodels," in IEEE ICST, 2012, pp. 131–140.

[30] E. Batot and H. Sahraoui, "A Generic Framework for Model-set Selection for the Unification of Testing and Learning MDE Tasks," in MODELS, 2016, pp. 374–384.

[31] H. Wu, "An SMT-based Approach for Generating Coverage Oriented Metamodel Instances," IJISMD, International Journal of Information System Modeling and Design, vol. 7, no. 3, 2016, pp. 23–50.

[32] J.-M. Mottu, S. Sen, J. Cadavid, and B. Baudry, "Discovering model transformation pre-conditions using automatically generated test models," in ISSRE, 2015, pp. 88–99.

Proposal of a Computer Supported Collaborative Work Model for E-Commerce Web Sites Based on a Quality Guiding Framework

Hédia Jegham
ISITCom University of Sousse
Sousse Tunisia
e-mail: jegham_hedia@yahoo.fr

Sonia Ghannouchi
ISG Sousse University of Sousse
Sousse Tunisia
e-mail: sonia.ayachi@isgs.rnu.tn

Abstract—**The exponential growth of e-commerce practices around the world is about to transform drastically traditional commerce by its infrastructure potential, the measurement of its intensity and its effects on the emergence of an information society. The study of the quality of e-commerce web sites is then prevalent; it is based on a review of literature in several fields: management, web-marketing, software engineering and Computer Supported Collaborative Work. The paper has a dual purpose, to propose at first a framework to guide the quality of e-commerce web sites and then to validate it by designing and developing a Computer Supported Collaborative Work. The framework was based on e-commerce web site's life cycle and Deming's wheel in addition to a quality measurement scale named e-ComDecaQual as it is in ten areas: ergonomics, features, content structure and information richness, compatibility, security, accessibility, referencing-positioning and e-reputation, adherence to regulations, compliance with standards, and sustainable development.**

Keywords-e-commerce; quality; dimension; measurement scale; CSCW.

I. INTRODUCTION

The World Wide Web, being a giant of information and communication technology, allows millions of Internet users to engage in business transactions that literally transcribe reality and even surpass it by imposing new practices and by building creative horizons towards new uses and new business models. The United Nations Economic and Social Council [42] considers that Information and Communication Technologies (ICTs), characterized as universal technologies, have a great capacity to enhance development by increasing:

- Efficiency of economic and social processes;
- Efficiency of cooperation between different stakeholders;
- The volume and range of information available to individuals, businesses and governments.

In the e-commerce domain in particular, we are indeed witnessing a frenetic development of applications constantly enriched with new services, new forms of navigation, and new features of interfaces ranging from flash animations that apply quick-views, various zooms on product store, specialized research, price comparisons, virtual visits and virtual fitting by augmented reality. On certain sites, the user becomes "prosumer". "Prosumer" is a new marketing concept; it is a diminutive, shortcut and concatenation of two words producer and consumer [15]. Consumer becomes "prosumer" by participating in the design of his own product or service as it is possible on "freeyourshirt" site [69]; the examples are multiple. The "prosumer" chooses his location, product, then the colour, the size, the picture or design or text to be printed on thus he becomes producer of his individualized product.

There is much material for the study of the quality of e-commerce web sites (E-CWS), which can play a major role in improving the turnover of e-commerce by increasing traffic. The quality of merchant sites can play a key role in attracting customers, gaining their trust and increasing their satisfaction, in retaining them and generating competitive success. We will therefore base the foundation of a framework using a measuring scale that emphasizes the quality of an E-CWS. This quality guidance framework would constitute an infrastructure of a Computer Supported for Cooperative Work (CSCW).

This paper is structured into six sections. In Section 2, the subject is framed in its context and explained by a set of questions. In Section 3, a review of the literature is exposed and dispatched on the specialties that gave serious consideration to the subject, namely management, software engineering, web-marketing scholars and practitioners. Section 4 gives a synthesis of literature and classifies quality domains to prepare Section 5, which is reserved for the design of quality guidance framework for e-commerce web sites. In Section 6, a validation aspect of quality guidance Framework is offered by Computer Supported Cooperative Work.

II. GENERAL CONTEXT AND RESEARCH QUESTIONS

Several factors come into play to boost or to slow down the flowering rate of e-commerce and consequently economy. Among these factors we can cite the degree of adherence to technological progress, comprehensive requirement engineering for a project as E-CWS, legislation in force in a country, rigorous compliance with standards. Adopting a framework for enhancing E-CWS' quality must be considered as part of a quality strategy. During the resolution of this issue the study sought to respond these questions:

- How do companies that practice e-commerce guarantee their evolution and their sustainability despite their competitors?
- Are there precedent means for improving E-CWS' quality? What are the main guidelines or quality domains for E-CWS? How these domains are refined and how can they be measured?
- How do quality dimensions of E-CWS help satisfy the customer?

- How to prove and verify such a framework for E-CWS' quality?

As the study seeks to formalize a framework of quality for E-CWS, several examinations of theoretical foundations about quality were made as a review of literature in different domains such as in general management, in merchant web practices, in software engineering and in web technologies. The objective guided by a firm desire for a continuous improvement of quality is firstly to identify relevant dimensions and items of E-CWS' quality, in order to propose them a set of control tools. In a second step, by dispatching the quality control tools on the various jobs profiles, which intervene throughout the life cycle of E-CWS, we end up formalizing a quality framework for E-CWS. In a third step, because of an intensive collaborative work between team members, CSCW was checked to learn how it is possible to concretize the framework in it.

III. LITERATURE REVIEW

According to John Ruskin, "*Quality is never an accident; it is always the result of an intelligent effort*" [70]. Considering that we are dealing with e-commerce quality we need to come back to former disciplines' contributions as management, web-marketing and software engineering. These ones will be introduced in following sub-sections.

A. *Quality in management*

The quality has blossomed in the United States through the works of Shewart and Deming, but it has also flourished in Japan, and its pioneers are Ishikawa et al. [23][47]. Quality is a constantly evolving and predictive foundation closely linked to developments in the industrial sectors. It is marked by economic movements and the history of companies, in particular globalization and the gathering of international markets. It focuses on an ultimate goal of **customer satisfaction**, delivering quality products and services. The company must deploy a continuous quest to identify and define customer needs and expectations in order to improve itself, and improve the quality of its products and services. Giordano [25] defines quality as "the set of sensory and sensorial impressions, as well as clues that appeal and attract attention from the first glance, interpreted by the consumer as a promise of quality that gives him trust, and satisfies him during the use". Yu and his collaborators propose that perceived quality is a subjective judgment constructed in the mind of the user and it is him who determines its value [67].

According to the quality management researcher Ishikawa [47], it can only be defined in terms of whoever does it; for the worker: quality means "being proud of his work". For the manager of the company: quality means "the realization of the requested production". For the manager of the methods: "the quality is the respect of the specifications". For the marketing director: "quality is the best fit of the product to the expectations of the public". As maintained by Chikli [5], "Quality is not the only goal to hold a diploma or a certification, the aim is to improve the company continuously so that it is more in step with the demands of the market". Literature detects the addition of other terms, which are embedded to quality in order to imply various meanings: Quality inspection, quality control, quality insurance and total quality management. All the tools and means used to achieve a quality level must be replicated on all internal and external processes that contribute to the manufacturing of the product or the design of the service. In this way, if quality is the act of satisfying the customer, total quality concerns the whole company, with its environment relations.

This induces that quality has different views and it is oriented to satisfy customer. It concerns every worker and it must be replicated all over a firm's functions and aspects.

B. *Quality in software engineering*

From a computer science perspective, according to Burdet [63], the quality of software raises the problem of confusion due to the overuse of the reference framework for a given specialty. This fact runs counter the achievement of satisfaction, which is the first quality challenge. Indeed, the programmer will be interested in the possibility of code reuse; the system engineer will be interested in the performance and the optimized use of resources; the maintenance specialist will more aim at the predisposition of the software to modification, improvement and evolution. "The ability of a set of intrinsic characteristics to meet requirements" is the definition that was adopted by ISO 9000 for quality software. It dismisses all subjective and personal vision; it reveals its strong link to demands or requirements engineering. Kano distinguishes between explicit and implicit or latent requirements [71]. The satisfaction levels of the clients are combined in the Kano diagram and are analysed in this way: The quality of software is therefore its ability to satisfy expressed but also tacit demands. The Kano diagram presented on an orthonormal frame includes a diagonal line that goes through the origin and represents the expressed functionalities; they are formulated by the client who feels more satisfied as they are more controlled. On the other hand, if the functionalities include any defect, they lead to a fall in proportional satisfaction. The Kano diagram [71] also includes two hyperbolas: the one at the bottom of the diagonal represents the obvious and basic functionality to talk first about product and neutral satisfaction. The smallest defect in these functions is disastrous (personal data security, payment security and product delivered not conforming to the representation on the site). The hyperbola at the top is that of the attractive and unpredictable features that are part of the provocation of the client's latent needs and the creation of expectations. With a minimum of these functions, the customer can be exalted. These are value-adding functions and an opportunity for innovation. This can be noticed in virtual testing interfaces on some E-CWS or in the interfaces completing the design of customizable products. Keeping up with a highly competitive conjecture, which includes taking possession of ICT implies that it is no longer worth to conform to the quality of the explicit requirements or the basic ones for software. One should rather look for attractive features to be distinguished.

Consistent with software engineering, it should also be pointed out that quality is governed by two model families, the models of certification and those of maturity and improvement [52]. As examples of the first family of models, we can quote the ISO 9000 certification, the France Telecom TQE and the DOD 2167A certification. In the second family whose purpose is to measure the ability of engineering company to develop and maintain quality software, we can enumerate the Software-Capability Maturity Model (SW-CMM), Trillium (from Bell Canada for Telecommunications) and the Software Process Improvement and Capability Determination (SPICE) project launched in 1993 with the objective of establishing a normative model for the evaluation of software development processes in the organizations concerned [52]. Without pretending to reach the scale of such projects that require great human and material investments, it is in the second family that we place our attempt to propose a framework and a CSCW to enhance E-CWS' quality.

C. *Quality according to Web-marketing scholars and practitioners*

Several studies have been carried out to find domains that greatly influence the perceived quality of E-CWS. Parts of them have confirmed the importance of certain domains without constructing scales. Some other contributions have resulted in formal scales for measuring e-commerce service quality. Practically all the studies are based on the same research methodology: considering client satisfaction by making assumptions, formulating each hypothesis with a set of questions that can have qualitative and measurable answers according to Lickert scale. The hypothesis is used to verify the importance of an aspect of perceived quality. This would insinuate a quality dimension. The different questions that define a hypothesis transcribe some detail that corresponds to a quality item. Results of the questionnaires administered to a public of respondents lead to various statistical models confirming or invalidating hypotheses. They also yield indicators for the degree of correlation of quality items. The scale's coherence is high if the responses to the elements are correlated with each other and with the total score of the scale. The scale's coherence is doubtful if the scores of several elements are in contradiction with the total score. Researchers resort to calculate the Cronbach alpha as a method to estimate the internal coherence of their scales [17].

Among the recurring fixed hypotheses that led to quality dimensions and that can be named, we can mention the quality of design or ergonomics, information richness, reliability, ease of use, responsiveness, security, service, efficiency, privacy. Domains found in literature are organized separately based on whether they emanate from simple studies or from famous scales or further more if they are introduced by practitioners. In the following passages we list them in descending order of number of authors who cited them.

In studies that did not officialise scales, most quoted domain was quality of design, number of researchers included it in their surveys [1][13][27][31][33]-[36][39][43][48][49][50][54][55][57].

Second, scholars dealt with variety and quality of information in their studies such as[1][12][13][27][29]-[31][34][36][43][48][49][54][55][57]. Security domain is in third place as well as reliability and reactivity. These scholars took security into account [12] [13][27][31][34][39][43][48][49][54][57][64]. Then ease of use was quoted by [13][35]-[36][43][48][50][54][55][64][65]. A quality criterion called customization was evoked by [33][34][39][43][48][50][55]. Performance (or quoted by some ones efficiency) was cited by [13][31][39][46][54][56]. Privacy was quoted by [13][46][49][56]. We found also reputation quoted by [39][46][57][64][65]. Feeling quoted by [12][31][39][46][50][55].

Despite the fact that Paschaloudis's study [46] does not fall directly within the domain of e-commerce and even if it does not bring a new scale, we consider it for several reasons: It is a solid exploratory study based on the seven dimensions of the most famous scales. The study resulted in 487 valid responses on a volume of 800 questionnaires, a factor and correlation analysis followed by a series of regression analysis. Its interest lies in the fact of bringing back a double proof, one first proof confirming the reliability and consistency of the two scales mentioned above. One second proof confirms the strong and positive correlation between them and the perception of the quality of the banking sites and thus follows the possibility of their applicability and reusability in other fields.

To be complete, other to lesser degrees of citations were found in literature are quality of service, access, ease of contact, customer loyalty, interactivity, structure, trust, incitement, ease of ordering, ease of terms, ease of responding, speed of delivery, customer support, community for e-reputation, storage capacity, maintainability and web store policies.

As came first, the study was also extensively interested in proper quality scales. The scale **Webqual™** proposed by Loiacono [37][38] is in 12 domains : (1) accommodation of information to the task, (2) trust, (3) response time, (4) attractiveness of design, (5) intuitiveness, (6) visual attraction, (7) creativity, (8) empathy, (9) integrated communication, (10) interactivity, (11) business process and (12) availability. **SiteQual** accredited by Yoo [66], has 4 domains (1) ease of use of the site, (2) site design, (3) speed of the order process and (4) security. **WebQual** scale belongs to Barnes [7] and contains 3 quality domains (1) quality of interactivity and service (trust, empathy), (2) site usability (design), (3) quality of the information presented on the site.

PIRQUAL of Francis [24] encloses 6 quality domains (1) online store features, (2) design of the product sheet, (3) conditions of sale, (4) conformity of delivered products, (5) customer service, (6) security.

e-ServQual the most famous and former scale coined by Zeithaml [68]and Parasuraman [44] as cited by Buttle [11] is based on 11 domains : (1) reliability, (2) liability, (3) access, (4) flexibility, (5) navigational facility, (6) efficiency, (7) insurance / trust, (8) security, (9) knowledge of prices, (10) aesthetics, (11) customization. **eTailQscale** is the work of Wolfinbarger [62] based on 4 domains (1) reliability and compliance with commitments, (2) site design, (3) security / privacy, (4) services provided to consumers. **E-S-QUAL and E-RES-QUAL** is a double scale considered as the most famous scale set up by Parasuraman [45], **E-S-QUAL** contains (1) efficiency of the site, (2) compliance with commitments, (3) system availability, (4) respect for the privacy of users and **E-RES-QUAL** contains (1) reactivity, (2) compensation and (3) contact.

NetQu@l conceived by Bressolles in 2006 [10], is composed by (1) quality and quantity of the information presented on the site, (2) ease of use of the site, (3) design or the graphic style of the site, (4) reliability and compliance, (5) security and privacy of personal data, (6) offer proposed on the site, (7) interactivity and customization. **eTransQual** formalized by Bauer and co-authors [8] who recognize that a quality scale should integrate functional elements and hedonic ones. Their scale accommodates (1) features and design, (2) enjoyment (Pleasure), (3) business process, (4) reliability and (5) reactivity (responsiveness). **PeSQ** is the measurement tool of Cristobal [16] who analysed seriously what leads to user satisfaction levels? And what leads to loyalty? It is based on (1) website design, (2) customer service, (3) insurance and order management. The scale **E-SELFQUAL** proposed by Ding [18] was refined in 4 domains so thus: (1) Perceived control: you know what to expect in following steps, you know how long it takes to complete the transaction, and you know information will be provided in each page. (2) Service convenience: convenience for registration, convenience for changing items in the basket, convenience to update your order. (3) Customer service: customer service is easy to access, customer service is responsive, and customer service shows a sincere interest in solving problems. (4) Service fulfilment: you get what you ordered, the order is delivered as promised, the final price reflects the true value, and the product was presented accurately on the site.

D. *Quality according to practitioners*

Some other quality criteria were gathered from practitioners' experience. According to Malassingne [40], web quality is the best way to produce content and web services. This encompasses the end result, but also the way to do it. It is determined on the basis of identified objectives, which make it possible to orient the choices and to measure the continuous improvement with regard to these objectives. The web quality is managed using all the disciplines of the web pages' design and realization. The set is to ensure the best possible user experience while optimizing the realization processes [40]. The same reference quoted Lafon who started from the definition of the web's god-father Tim Berners Lee: "Put the Web and its services at the disposal of all individuals, whatever their hardware or software, their network infrastructure, their native tongue, their culture, their geographical location, or their physical or mental abilities". Lafon quickly realized that what comes out of the Tim Berners Lee's definition is the importance of practicing web quality. In its approach, it fits perfectly with the precursors, those of the management field: To deploy quality measures on all the professions of the web useful during the process of any website's design and construction. Lafon bases his method on seven quality domains: (1) compliance with standards, (2) accessibility, (3) performance, (4) security, (5) functionalities (or features), (6) ergonomics and (7) referencing [40].

Sloïm, a purely quality control manager defines web quality as "The ability of an online service to meet implicit or explicit requirements". He emphasizes the difference between Web Quality and Web Quality Management. The latter is a "Set of coordinated activities whose objective is to evaluate, improve and guarantee web quality" [40].

The same reference talked about Taillandier who dealt with W3C standards and accessibility in the digital world to achieve quality. He gives this definition: "Quality is pre-eminently an ideal to be achieved and not an end in itself" [40]. The challenge is to arrive at taking into account and to cohabit for the best all disciplines supposed to intervene in a modern web production chain – (1) user experience, (2) information architecture, (3) ergonomics, accessibility, (4) web design, (5) performance, (6) mobility, and (7) security – all of them according to the project specific constraints. In conformity with Google's guidelines, there are seven high-quality criteria [4]: (1) the site must have good content, (2) no technical error, (3) positive reputation, (4) website must reveal reliability, high level of expertise in addition to some authority, (5) site must rotate design around its features, (6) the site must provide useful information about the site, and (7) the site must offer sufficient quantities of relevant and satisfactory information.

IV. SYNTHESIS OF LITERATURE AND CLASSIFICATION OF QUALITY DOMAINS

As outcomes of literature review, many apprenticeships are won: Quality is a continuing occupation and labour. Quality Management is a set of coordinated activities whose objective is to evaluate, improve and guarantee web quality. Quality must be considered according to the job profile. Quality must be deployed in minute details of domains. E-CWS must rotate design around its features. Great control of programming technologies allows offering expressed and attractive features. Nearly thirty domains have been identified, a great part of them are dealing with customer relationship and customer satisfaction that should be transposed on web sites by features.

Every domain contains a set of items. In an effort to draw up an almost exhaustive list of quality domains, terminology has been first brought closer and unified. Table 1 shows a decreasing classification of quality domains in terms of citation in the literature and according to practitioners' recommendations.

TABLE I. QUALITY DOMAINS' RATE ACCORDING TO SCHOLARS AND PRACTITIONERS

Quality Domain and its rank	Rate	Quality Domain and its rank	Rate	Quality Domain and its rank	Rate
1- Design /Ergonomics	26	**11**-Privacy	7	**21**-Maintainability	2.5
2- Information variety	22	**12**-Access	6.5	**22**-Customer support	2
3- Reliability	17	**13**-Insurance	5.33	**23**-Customer loyalty/Fidelity	2
4-Security	17	**14**-Feeling	4.5	**24**-Incitement	2
5- Ease of use	16	**15**-Trust	4.16	**25**-Ease of terms	1
6- Reactivity	14.33	**16**- Ease of ordering	4	26-Ease of responding	1
7- Service quality	12.33	**17**-Structure	3.5	**27**-Speed of delivery	1
8- Performance/Efficiency	11.5	**18**-Interactivity	3	**28**-Community for e-reputation	1
9- Reputation	10.33	**19**-Web store policies	3	**29**-Storage capacity	1
10- Customization	9	**20**- Ease of contact	2.5	**30**-Low prices	0

V. DESIGN OF QUALITY GUIDANCE FRAMEWORK FOR E-COMMERCE WEB SITES

In the development of a quality framework for E-CWS, steps that were followed are described in these sub-sections.

A. *Research methodology*

The quality of a diagnosis depends on the model's quality; the model describes the organization's vital aspects [19]. In order to design a model for quality guidance framework, an ad-hoc approach was adopted. It is described as follows:

1) *Step 1 Gathering domains and items*

- Collect the maximum of E-CWS' quality domains cited by scholars and some practitioners.
- Collect items for each domain.
- Move certain domains closer and unify them as they have common sense, 30 domains were retained. Prepare a matrix: with authors on lines and quality domains on columns.
- Add a mark at the crossing if the author talks about the quality domain in his study.
- Sum marks for each quality domain to calculate relevance degree for a given quality domain according to literature.
- Sort totals by domains as shows Table 1

Three separate matrixes have been produced, depending on whether the work proceeds from exploratory studies by researchers (Researchers' domains) or whether they are quality measurement instruments formalized on formal scales (Researchers' formal scales) or from the recommendations of practitioners (Practitioner domains). The overall frequency of each of the thirty domains was calculated, sorted and combined in Table 1.

2) *Step 2 Structuring domains in a scale*

- Highlight the best domains that meet certain conditions: those that occupy the best ranks, those that correspond to the criteria of software quality according to software engineering, those for which we are able to find control tools and those that are easily placed on E-CWS' life cycle. Indeed, what we are interested in, are domains that are currently possible to control by tools and those completely under the control of the team members (designers, developers, salesmen and web-marketers).
- Structure domains with low rates as sub-domains or domain items of high domains as depicted in Figure 1.
- As a first outcome we selected the seven first domains as follows: Ergonomics, i.e., Design, Features, Content structure and Information Richness, Security, Compatibility, Accessibility and Referencing SEO e-reputation.

3) *Step 3 Enriching the scale*

- As a contribution, three domains were added. They were not sufficiently dealt with until then, but they were actually with imminent importance in e-commerce field according to a number of scholars:

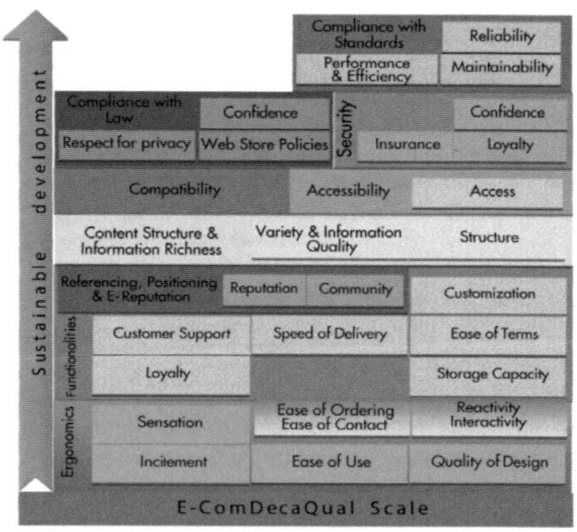

Figure 1. E-ComDecaQual Scale Composition.

E-commerce regulation [6][32][53], Respect of standards [3][26][60] and Sustainable development[9][14][20].

- Establishing a new quality scale based on ten domains hence the name E-ComDecaQual Figure 1.

4) Step 4 Associating control tools to job profiles

- Search for tools and test them to control the quality of domains' items.
- Assign one or more quality domain to one or more job profiles.
- Locate quality domains on E-CWS life cycle as a first view of the framework, see Figure2.

E-CWS's quality is quality perceived by the customer. Thus, it mainly revolves around the customer's satisfaction. To reach customer's satisfaction, we concentrate on all job profiles that intervene and operate during E-CWS's life cycle from its birth as a project until its decline. The process of designing, developing and exploiting an E-CWS is no more than conducting its life cycle while arranging, combining and calculating sequential and parallel steps with various profiles of jobs. In the schematic representation of this point of view, we distribute the quality domains of e-ComDecaQual scale on different stages. The role of this framework view is to highlight job profiles and to ensure staff satisfaction according to quality's predecessors; the managers.

5) Step 5 Integration in PDCA wheel

- Distribute quality domains on Deming's PDCA wheel as another view of the framework and to emphasize the continuous and evolving quality undertaking as shows Figure 3.

Being aware that improvement must be continuous to strengthen the efficiency of any project [63], the quality guidance framework was built around the PDCA model of Deming and then map the E-CWS life cycle on it. Deming distinguishes three types of quality [2]:

The quality of the design / redesign: it begins from the expression of consumer needs and prototyping. That's what we planned in the Act of the first round of the wheel Figure 3. The company must adopt the predictive attitude and have a long-term vision of the needs and behaviours of consumers. It also must continuously operate adaptations of production and the commercial apparatus, that's what we planned for further rounds of the wheel.

Compliance quality is measured by the company's ability to conform to and then to exceed the basic product specifications. It is based on a managerial and organizational willpower that leads all processes involved in delivering the product / service to do so with a zero-defect goal. These are possible due to regular turns of the wheel and aiming for attractive features, see Figure3.

Quality of performance: it observes, through sales analysis, how the product is perceived on the market and perceives the use that the customer makes. It is through use that his consciously expressed and unconscious expectations are revealed. The quality of performance will influence the quality of re-design to spin the wheel of continuous improvement [2]. That's what we expressed by the e-commerce life cycle and implication of all actors.

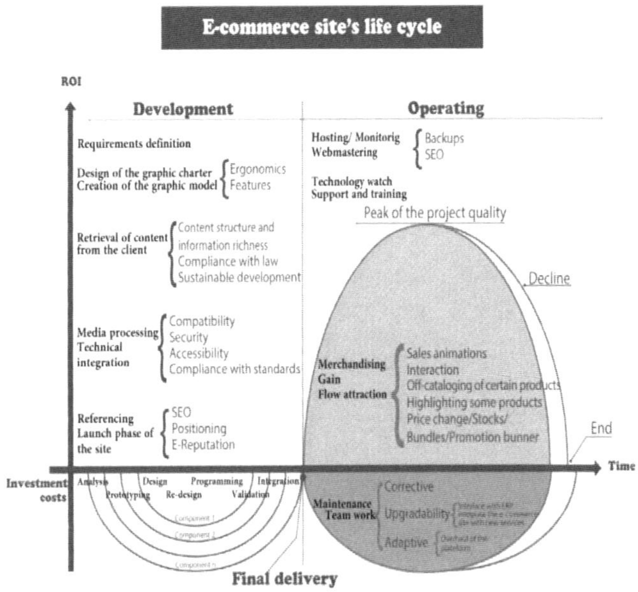

Figure 2. E-commerce Site's Life Cycle and Quality Domains.

B. A model abstraction for e-ComDecaQual

An overview of the semantics described throughout this study is now possible by an object data model. UML allows practicing an abstraction of the static vision for the quality guidance framework and its e-ComDecaQual scale by means of a class diagram, see Figure 4. The domains class is at the moment instantiated to the **ten domains** identified in the **e-ComDecaQual** scale, but it is scalable and dynamic to accommodate other domains with their possible structuring items and tools since the E-CWS are in perpetual relationship with technological progress. The tracking of including a quality domain is taken into account by monitoring the publications, dates and authors who brought back the proof and the demonstration in the manner of the present study. The domains class is in full aggregation with itself to present the possibility that a domain could be divided into sub-domains for a better dispatching of items and their measurement tools like ergonomics, which allow studying behavioural and structural sub-domains. The functional domain is also subdivided into common or standard functionalities, e-commerce functionalities and collaborative or community functionalities [59].

Sub-domains can have a different meaning, which is rather a technical structuring such as user tests, statistical analysis and eye-traking [59]. Each domain or sub-domain is a collection of items. The model even allows multi domain patterns (structuration or imbrication). Most items are measurable by tools. Tools are known to be specialised in one domain. E-commerce compliance with law and sustainability do not have classic control tools at present, they are related to datamining tools. As dealt with in the Deming's wheel, in Figure 3, E-CWS are inventoried and

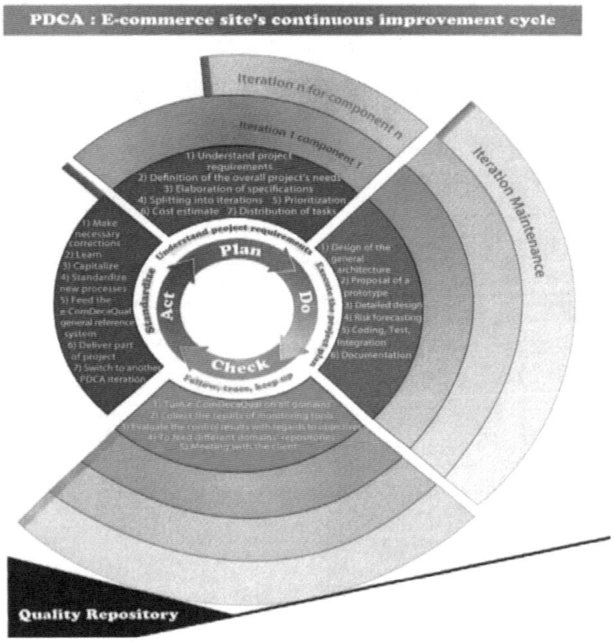

Figure 3. PDCA Cycle of Continuous Improvement of an e-Commerce Web Site.

they are subject to periodic quality control by a tool that measures the quality of items' set, therefore of a particular domain or sub-domain. The control is requested by a member of the team specialized in a domain, it could be a content editor, a developer or integrator, a web designer or computer graphics designer. The quality project manager or the administrator coordinates their jobs. A tool naturally returns a comprehensible report deciphered for a domain specialist. The report is taken into account for the Check and the Act. The report is recorded and archived in the domain quality repository.

The inheritance between the team member and the quality administrator designates that the population concerned is entirely either team members or quality administrator and that a member could combine two different roles, which is in general the case of the project manager who may have another specialty. Quality tools are selected and proposed by the specialists of a domain. A team member chooses to control E-CWS domain quality from this validated set of tools. The quality reports are ordered and dated; the PDCA wheel runs continuously.

VI. VALIDATION OF QUALITY GUIDANCE FRAMEWORK BY A COMPUTER SUPPORTED COLLABORATIVEWORK

As a guidance framework named e-ComDecaQual to foster the quality of E-CWS based on two axes and a measurement scale was specified in a first part of the present study, it made it possible to ascertain that it is closely related to domains specialities, but with great regard, it was also recognized that quality implicates a high collaboration, cooperation, coordination and communication between group of actors working together around an e-commerce project, e.g., various reports monitoring tools often address several domains for instance ergonomic tools, features, content structure and information richness – Thus the second part of the study is to validate the earlier specified quality guidance framework by adapting a CSCW.

In the following section, conceptual specification based on computer-based technologies is presented from two points of view, from 3C specification (Collaboration, Cooperation, and Communication) and then from functional specification to give finally an overall view.

A. *Preliminary*

At present it is a clear fact that among most visited websites, we find social networks as Facebook and Google Hangout, collaborative document editors as Google docs, online games, which are part of collaborative applications. According to Teruel et al. [58], there is a collaborative trend for modern software nevertheless, despite the possibility to adopt exhaustive methodologies to design them, these methodologies have a great deficiency, and they do not seriously treat Requirement Engineering stage. This lack comes from the complexity of dispatching user requirements on CSCW's conventional tasks (3C: Collaborating, Cooperating, and Communicating), which in turn is subject to the degree of users' awareness [58]. Consequently, to avoid these weaknesses, a special consideration will be taken while designing e-ComDecaQual's CSCW. Before that, there is a need to clarify the ambiguity between groupware and CSCW.

By focusing on how computer networking technologies can support collaborative control quality activities, great polemic was felt to firmly settle on a similar or a distinguished definition for CSCW and groupware. According to Whitaker [61], it is in 1984 that Greif and Cashman coined the label Computer-Supported Cooperative Work (CSCW) as a marketing tag for a vision of integrated office IT support. He also presents the first definition introduced by Bannon and Schmidt in 1989 [61]: "*...A shorthand way of referring to a set of concerns about supporting multiple individuals working together with computer systems*". But the definition of Eseryel et al. [22] seems to be more close to context of quality: "*CSCW systems are collaborative environments that support dispersed working groups so as to improve quality and productivity*".

CSCW is also known as a multi-disciplinary research field bearing upon tools, techniques, task orientation and workflows that are networked and/or distributed. It is belonging to an emergent phenomenon that deals with Technological Support for Work Group Collaboration, Collaborative Systems, Workgroup Computing, Group Decision Support Systems (GDSS), Interpersonal Computing, Augmented Knowledge Workshops, Coordination Technology, Computer-Assisted Communications (CAC), Computer-Mediated Communication (CMC) and Flexible Interactive Technolo-

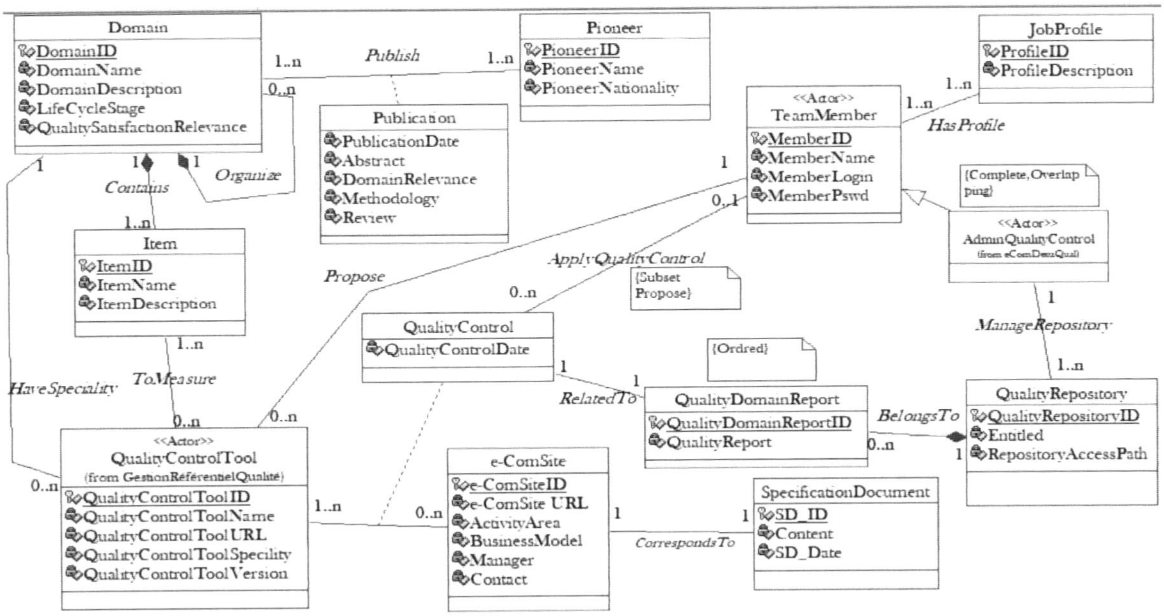

Figure 4. e-ComDecaQual Framework Abstraction by a Class Diagram.

gies for Multi-Person Tasks. According to Whitaker too [61], in 1978 the word Groupware was conceived by Johnson-Lenz and Johnson-Lenz to mean:" *Intentional **GROUP** processes and procedures to achieve specific purposes plus soft**WARE** tools designed to support and facilitate the group's work*".

"*A groupware makes the user aware that he is part of a group, while most other software seeks to hide and protect users from each other ... Groupware ... is software that accentuates the multiple user environment, coordinating and orchestrating things so that users can "see" each other, yet do not conflict with each other*", a definition of Kevin J. Lynch brought back by Griffiths [51].

At the end, we are perfectly at ease with claiming that groupware refers to computer-based systems to assist interacting groups whereas Computer Supported Cooperative Work (CSCW) focuses on the study of how groups work and how implement technology to boost their interaction and collaboration in addition to studying their psychological, social, and organizational effects [21][41].

B. Collaboration, Cooperation, and Communication (3C) specification of e-ComDecaQual's CSCW

Dealing with CSCW implies several kinds of interactions: Collaboration, Cooperation, Coordination, Contribution, and Communication. For each one, there is a battery of supporting tools and techniques such as e-mails, discussion forums, chat-rooms, videoconferences, and posts announcements for communication. Distributed learning environment besides web-based tool kit, facilitate the sharing, and organization of ideas for collaboration. Control access to different documents, granting rights and prioritization for coordination and control is also made possible.

The collaborative and cooperative approaches can be considered as two poles rather than two distinct apprehensions; one evolves from cooperation to collaboration. In order to grasp their differences, it is necessary to observe the nuances relating to the autonomy and the degree of control as well as the means used to achieve the goal and to carry out the task and to clearly differentiate the level of interdependency between the participants.

Cooperative and collaborative groups work towards a common or shared goal. It is in the way of sharing work that difference is most visible. Indeed, the way to achieve the goal through cooperation is based on the distribution of tasks and responsibilities within the group to achieve the goal cooperatively. This corresponds to the nature of work to lead an e-commerce website project in its entirety and in full respect of its life cycle.

On the other hand collaboration requires individual responsibility to achieve the goal, which corresponds to the intrinsic responsibility of a specialist member of one domain of the e-ComDecaQual scale: Member or team of graphic designer, member or group of developers, member or group of marketers etc. In the way of carrying out common task, there are other dependencies: The maturity of groups, interactions between members and the way every one considers the goal [28].

Collaboration implies a shared vision of a very high level with a derisory importance for the division of tasks. On the other hand, coordination requires a high control level of the subdivisions of the tasks with moderate look for a shared vision. Cooperation is between the two.

The ability to collaborate involves a gradual prior appropriation of other abilities, such as cooperation, coordination, contribution and communication.

The model of the e-ComDecaQual scale with the PDCA axis has clearly emphasized the involvement of a member specialized in a domain. This detail is made explicit in Figure 5 and its legend in Table 2.

C. Functional specification of e-ComDecaQual's CSCW

The proposal for quality guiding framework of E-CWS' is being concretized and validates by developing a CSCW structured around ten domains scale named e-ComDecaQual and which offers a range of tools broken down according to the items of each domain. Some tools can be measuring instruments for several domains. Domains as well as their tools are specific to the various job profiles of the team around the E-CWS. The CSCW allows creation of domains, their possible structuring in sub-domains and the arrangement of items in various domains / sub-domains. It allows assignment of tools to check items. CSCW allows registration of team members and their association to job profiles.

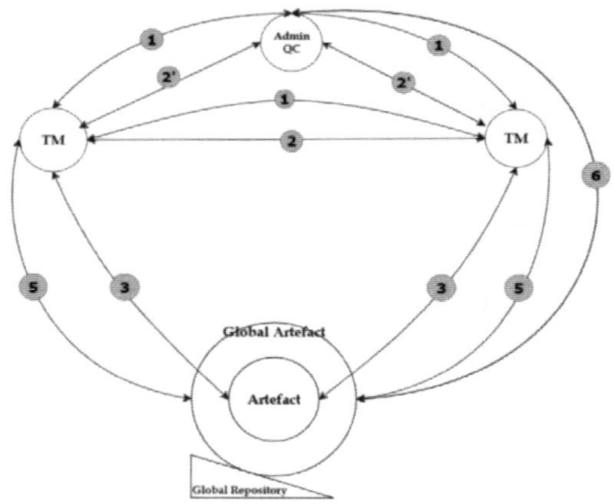

Figure 5. 3C Network of e-ComDecaQual's CSCW

TABLE II. 3C SPECIFICATION OF E-COMDECAQUAL'S CSCW

Legend			
Admin QC	Quality Control Administrator /Project Manager	**2**	2- Direct communication between team member with the same profile: Computer-Mediated communication (CMC)
TM	A Team Member : can have different or same speciality with another TM	**2'**	2'- Coordinate
Art	Art: Artefact of work of domain and its items	**3**	3- Collaboration: Working using platforms, APIs, languages, design tools, frameworks etc…
GA	Global Artefact	**4**	4- Control quality with dedicated tools, retrieving control report and feedback with shared work objects (versioning Domain quality report) (feedback mistakes weaknesses and warnings)
QDR	QDR: Quality Domain Repository. To be verified	**5**	5- Cooperate
GR	GR: Global Repository: to be verified and to feed through for communication of awareness.	**6**	6- Knowledge management by gathering and collecting final quality control reports to constitute the Global Repository
1	1- Understanding: meeting and decision support systems for common understanding		

It allows collaborative work between them supervised by a Quality Control Administrator who could have the function of project manager. Team members exchange messages with the administrator and receive notifications.

The E-CWS either under construction, or operating, are registered by their URLs and their specifications or user requirements (Plan) in order to ensure their quality control by rotating (Do) each time a quality domain controlling tool and by getting back a report (Check). As an e-commerce web site advances his life cycle, a domain or sub-domain is monitored. E-ComDecaQual groupware centralizes the reports in a repository by allowing their versioning (Act). The repository is a capitalization of know-how in the various quality domains and an experience accumulation of all domains.

The CSCW functional aspects are represented according to the formalism of UML's Use Case Diagram (UCD).Figure 6(a) shows the overall functionality supported by the groupware and offered to the main actor: The Quality Control Manager or Administrator. Figure 6(b) shows the functional aspects permitted for any job profile carried out by any team member. It is naturally allowed for the administrator. Figure 6(c) details the features related to quality reports management and related to the global repository for e-commerce web site, which leads to the accumulation of domains know-how. Figure 6(d) shows what is involved in managing the e-ComDecaQual quality repository framework.

An overall view of the work is conjugated in Figure7; it shows the goals of the research, it recalls the quality guidance framework stand on two axes (life cycle and PDCA cycle) and a scale, it summarizes the details of the measurement tool e-ComDecaQual based on ten quality domains, and it evokes the most important kind of interactions between actors.

VII. CONCLUSION

Although e-commerce web sites' quality is progressively attracting researchers' attention, existing scientific literature is mainly focused on identifying quality dimensions from Internet users' viewpoint. This has not been taken in a comprehensive approach taking into account the work force around it. It pays no deep attention to total quality management for an E-CWS. It therefore did not focus on quality domain constituents' census and their structuring, no longer on the identification of instruments and tools for quality measurement and control. Almost all studies are based on working hypotheses and surveys to produce mathematical and statistical models without proposing any quality approach. This work attempted to fill the gap by proposing a quality guiding framework based on a model and axes. One axis was to dispatch quality domains on E-CWS's life cycle, another axis for continuous quality by Deming's wheel in addition to a measurement scale named e-ComDecaQual. The quality guidance framework was after that, validated by conceiving a CSCW. Immediate work requires the development of a detailed CSCW architecture, but the research has established the basis for a number of other future works, such as proving the scale e-ComDecaQual by an exploratory study on a representative sample. Managing the quality repository leads first to an aspect of knowledge management that can enrich the functionality of the CSCW. The repository requires a serious work on formatting, unifying and aggregating quality tool reports. The study also opens the opportunity for further refinements such as proposing quality Frameworks and CSCW for other e-commerce business models such as B2B, e-Gov and intermediation models.

(a) Use Case Diagram e-ComDecaQual Groupware System Overview.

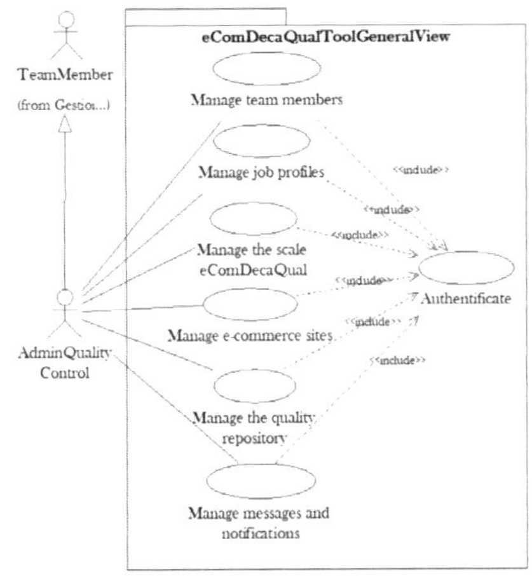

(b) Use Case Diagram Work of a Member with a Job Profile

(c) Use Case Diagram Management of e-ComDecaQual scale.

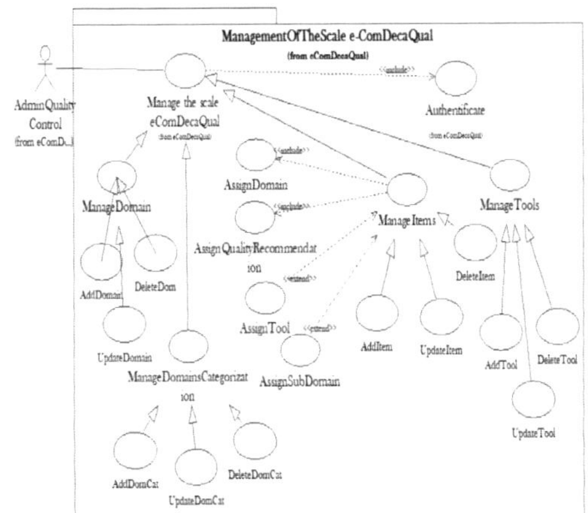

(d) Use Case Diagram Management of the Quality Repository

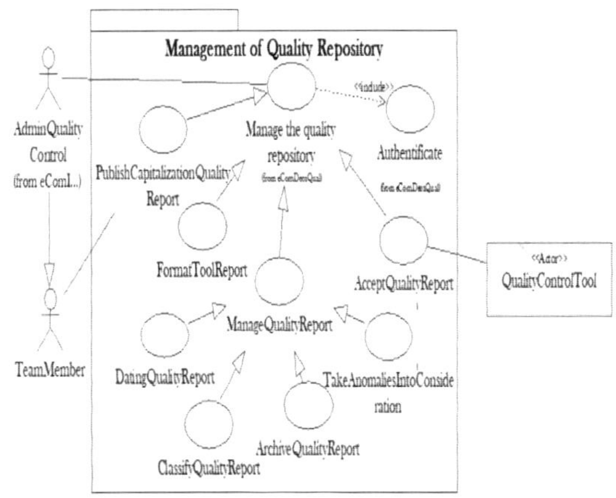

Figure 6. Functional Specification of e-ComDecaQual's CSCW.

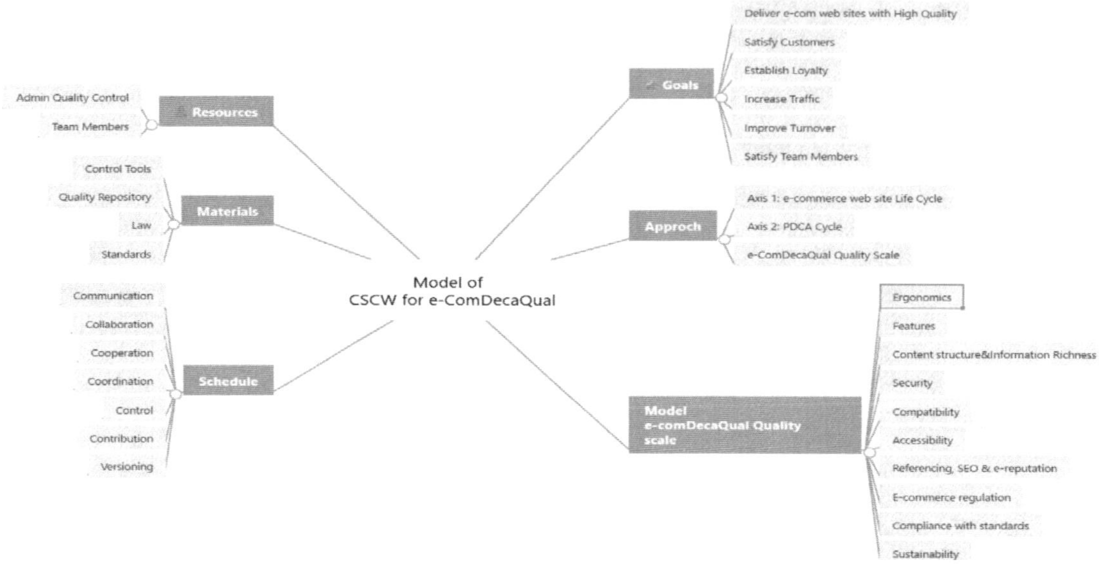

Figure 7. CSCW Model for E-Commerce Web Sites Based on Quality Guiding Framework

REFERENCES

[1] M. Aladwani and P. C. Palvia, "Developing and validating an instrument for measuring user-perceived web quality". Information & management, vol. 39, no. 6, pp. 467-476, 2002.

[2] A. Jouandeau, "Contribution to the modeling of customer satisfaction by the fuzzy logic". Available from:http://theses.insa-lyon.fr/publication/2004ISAL0063/these.pdf 8 octobre 2004. Retrieved: August, 2017.

[3] M. Alshamari, "Accessibility Evaluation of Arabic E-Commerce Web Sites Using Automated Tools". Journal of Software Engineering and Applications, vol. 9, no 09, pp. 439, 2016.

[4] A. Voget, "Official: Google's definition of a high quality website". Available from: http://newsletter.seoprofiler.com/newsletter709.htm 24 novembre 2015. Retrieved: June, 2017.

[5] B. Chikli, "Memory: The process of continuous improvement within an IT services company". Available from: http://fr.slideshare.net/baptistechikli/la-dmarche-damlioration-continue-au-sein-dune-ssii?qid=0b3c0151-326f-49a8-8695 fb96d319306b&v=default&b=&from_search=205 juillet 2012. Retrieved: May, 2017.

[6] C. E. Barnat, "Computer Law Course 2014/2015".University of Manouba Higher School of Digital Economy. Available from:http://chemsjuris-dr-e-com.blogspot.com/2012/11/cours-de-droit-du-commerce-electronique.html. Retrieved: May, 2017.

[7] S. J. Barnes and R. T. Vidgen, (2001,) "Assessing the Quality of Auction Web Sites". System Sciences. Proceedings of the 34th Annual Hawaii International Conference on. IEEE, 2001, pp. 10.

[8] H. H. Bauer, T. Falk, and M. Hammerschmidt, "eTransQual: A Transaction Process-based Approach for Capturing Service Quality in Online Shopping". Journal of Business Research, vol. 59, no. 7, pp. 866-875, 2006.

[9] L. B. Chevalier, F. De Coninck, and B. Motte-Baumvol (2014). "The peri-urban sustainability of the automotive sector in relation to online purchasing practices of households". 51st colloquium of the Association of Regional Science of French Language: Metropolisation, cohesion and performance: what future for our territories?, In ASRDLF 2014.

[10] G. Bressolles, "Electronic Quality of Service: NetQu @ 1 Proposal of a Measurement Scale Applied to Merchant Sites and Moderator Effects". Research and Applications in Marketing (French Edition),vol. 21, no. 3, pp. 19–45, 2006. Available from :www.jstor.org/stable/40572002.

[11] F. Buttle, "SERVQUAL: Review, Critique, Research Agenda". European Journal of Marketing, Vol. 30 No. 1, pp. 8-32, 1996.

[12] M. Cao, Q. Zhang, and J. Seydel, (2005), "B2C e-Commerce Web Site Quality: an Empirical Examination". Industrial Management & Data Systems, vol. 105, no 5, p. 645-661, 2005.

[13] C. Hamadi, "The perceived quality of Internet banking and its impact on customer satisfaction and commitment". Doctoral dissertation, Toulouse 1, 2007.

[14] C. Larre and C. Magdelaine, "The Internet consumes more and more energy: how to avoid saturation?". Available from: http://www.notre-planete.info/actualites/4328-consommation-energie-web-saturation 27 août 2015. Retrieved: May, 2017.

[15] B. Cova and P. Ezan. "The consumer-collaborator: activities, expectations and impacts. The case of Warhammer passionate". Acts JRMB 2008.

[16] E. Cristobal, C. Flavián, and M. Guinalíu, "Perceived e-service quality (PeSQ) Measurement validation and effects on consumer satisfaction and web site loyalty". Managing service quality: An international journal, vol. 17, no 3, p. 317-340, 2007.

[17] L.J. Cronbach, "Coefficient alpha and the internal structure of tests". Psychometrika 1951, vol. 16, no 3, p. 297-334, doi: 10.1007/BF02310555.

[18] D. X. Ding, P. J. H. Hu, and O. R. L. Sheng, "e-SELFQUAL A scale for measuring online self-service quality". Journal of Business Research, May 2011, vol. 64, no 5, pp. 508-515.

[19] D. Proulx, "Management of public organizations". 2nd edition reviewed and corrected. Theory and applications Press edition of University of Quebec, 2010.

[20] D. Desbois, C. Gossart, N. Jullien, and J. B. Zimmermann, "Sustainable development in the face of ICT". No. hal-00609295, 2011.

[21] C. Ellis and J. Wainer, "10 Groupware and Computer Supported Cooperative Work". Multiagent Systems: a modern approach to distributed artificial intelligence, pp. 425, 1999.

[22] D. Eseryel, R. Ganesan, and G. S. Edmonds, (2002). "Review of computer-supported collaborative work systems". Educational Technology &Society, vol. 5, no 2, pp. 130-136, 2002.

[23] F. Elgamouz, M. Firni, and A. Ismaili, "Management de la qualité dans les entreprises marocaines". Université Moulay Ismail de Meknès - Licence en sciences économiques et gestion. Available from:http://www.memoireonline.com/11/12/6506/m_Management-de-la-qualite-dans-les-entreprises-marocaines1.html#fn1, 2009. Retrieved: May, 2017.

[24] J. E. Francis and L. White, "PIRQUAL: A scale for measuring customer expectations and perceptions of quality in Internet retailing". K. Evans & L. Scheer (Eds.), pp. 263-270, 2002.

[25] J.L. Giordano, The perceived quality approach. Groupe Eyrolles 2006, ISBN : 2-7081-3493-0. 380 p.

[26] G. Davis, G. Olsen, and J. Zeldman,"Working together for standards The Web Standards Project". Available from: http://www.webstandards.org/learn/faq/#p2. Retrieved: July, 2017.

[27] H. Djajadikerta and T. Trireksani, "Measuring University Web Site Quality: A Development of a User Perceived Instrument and its Initial Implementation to Web sites of Accounting Departments in New Zealand's Universities". School of Accounting, Finance and Economics & FIMARC Working Paper Series, September 2006, pp. 1-23.

[28] F. Henri and K. Lundgren-Cayrol, "Cooperative Learning vs. Collaborative Learning". Available from:http://www.ticeduforum.ci/henri-lundgren-cayrol-apprentissage-cooperatif-vs-apprentissage-collaboratif/. Retrieved: August, 2017.

[29] D. L. Hoffman and T. P. Novak, "Marketing in hypermedia computer-mediated environments: Conceptual foundations". The Journal of Marketing 1996, pp. 50-68.

[30] D. L. Hoffman, W. D. Kalsbeek, and T. P. Novak, "Internet and Web use in the US". Communications of the ACM, vol. 39, no 12, pp. 36-46, 1996.

[31] S. Janda, P. J. Trocchia, and K. P. Gwinner, "Consumer perceptions of Internet retail service quality". International Journal of Service Industry Management, vol. 13, no 5, p.p. 412-431, 2002.

[32] Official Journal of Republic of Tunisia, no 64, 11 August 2000.

[33] G. G. Lee and H. F. Lin, "Customer perceptions of e-service quality in online shopping". International Journal of Retail & Distribution Management, vol. 33, no 2, p.p. 161-176, 2005.

[34] H. Li and R. Suomi, "A proposed scale for measuring e-service quality". International Journal of u-and e-Service, Science and Technology, vol. 2, no 1, p.p. 1-10, 2009.

[35] C. Liu and K. P. Arnett, (2000). "Exploring the factors associated with Web site success in the context of electronic commerce". Information & management, vol. 38, no 1, p.p. 23-33, 2000.

[36] C. Liu, K. P. Arnett, and C. Litecky, "Design Quality of Websites for Electronic Commerce: Fortune 1000 Webmasters' Evaluations". Electronic Markets, vol. 10, no 2, p.p. 120-129, 2000.

[37] E.T. Loiacono, "WebQual: A Website Quality Instrument". Doctoral Dissertation: University of Georgia, 2000, ISBN: 0-599-90483-6.

[38] E. T. Loiacono, R. T. Watson, and D. L. Goodhue, "WebQual: An instrument for consumer evaluation of web sites". International Journal of Electronic Commerce, vol. 11, no 3, p.p. 51-87, 2007.

[39] C. N. Madu, and A. A. Madu, "Dimensions of e-quality". International Journal of Quality & reliability management, vol. 19, no 3, p. 246-258, 2002.

[40] D. Malassingne, "What is the web quality?". Available from:http://w3qualite.net/metier/qu-est-ce-que-la-qualite-web 11 octobre 2011. Retrieved: July, 2017.

[41] M. -G. Park and M. H. Kim,"Chapter XI.6 Knowledge Workforce Development for Computer-Supported Collaborative Work Environments. From the book "International Handbook of Education for the Changing World of Work: bridging academic and vocational learning". By Rupert Maclean; David N Wilson. Springer ; Bonn : UNESCO UNEVOC, International Centre for Technical and Vocational Education and Training, cop. 2009 Available from: https://link.springer.com/chapter/10.1007/978-1-4020-5281-1_129. Retrieved: July, 2017.

[42] United Nations, Economic and Social Council. Information and communication technologies for equitable economic and social development, Geneva, 2014, p.p.4.

[43] J. Ojasalo, "E-service quality: a conceptual model". International Journal of Arts and Sciences, vol. 3, no 7, p.p. 127-143, 2010.

[44] A. Parasuraman, V. A.Zeithaml, and L. L. Berry, "Alternative scales for measuring service quality: a comparative assessment based on psychometric and diagnostic criteria". Handbuch Dienstleistungsmanagement, Gabler Verlag, pp.449-482, 1998.

[45] A. Parasuraman, V. A. Zeithaml, and A. Malhotra, "ES-QUAL a multiple-item scale for assessing electronic service quality". Journal of service research, vol. 7, no 3, p.p. 213-233, 2005.

[46] D. Paschaloudis and M. Tsourela, (2015). Using ES-QUAL to Measure Internet Service Quality of EBanking Web Sites in Greece. The Journal of Internet Banking and Commerce, vol. 19, no 2, p.p. 1-17, 2015.

[47] R. Abdelkader, "Le management de la qualité totale. La qualité totale : les outils du développement de la performance des entreprises". Available from : http://www.iefpedia.com/france/wp-content/uploads/2011/07/Le-management-de-la-qualit%C3%A9-totale-La-qualit%C3%A9-totale-les-outils-du-d%C3%A9veloppement-de-la-performance-des-entreprises-RACHEDI-ABDELKADER1.pdf. Retrieved: May, 2017.

[48] M. K. Mphil, "Information Technology in Malaysia: E-service quality and Uptake of Internet banking". Journal of Internet Banking and Commerce, vol. 13, no 2, p.p. 1, 2008.

[49] C. Ranganathan, and S. Ganapathy, (2002). "Key dimensions of business-to-consumer web sites". Information & Management, vol. 39, no6, p. 457-465, 2002.

[50] D. Ribbink, A. C. Van Riel, V. Liljander, and S. Streukens, "Comfort your online customer: quality, trust and loyalty on the internet". Managing Service Quality: An International Journal, vol. 14, no 6, p.p. 446-456.

[51] R. Griffiths, "Computer Supported Co-operative Work (CSCW) and Groupware". Available from:http://www.it.bton.ac.uk/staff/rng/teaching/notes/CSCWgroupware.html. Retrieved: August, 2017.

[52] E. Ringenbach and A. Ajraou, "Presentation: Quality Assurance - Software Engineering". January 2000 Available from:http://users.polytech.unice.fr/~hugues/GL/SPICE/index.htm. Retrieved: August, 2017.

[53] R. V. Gola, E-commerce law Practical guide to e-commerce. Gualino Editor, fev 2013; Collection : Guides Pro, ISBN : 978-2-297-02478-5

[54] J. Santos, "E-service quality: a model of virtual service quality dimensions". Managing Service Quality: An International Journal, vol. 13, no 3, p.p. 233-246,2003.

[55] S. S. Srinivasan, R. Anderson, and K. Ponnavolu, "Customer loyalty in e-commerce: an exploration of its antecedents and consequence"s. Journal of retailing, vol. 78, no 1, p. 41-50, 2002.

[56] Q. Sun, C. Wang, and H. Cao, "Applying ES-QUAL scale to analysis the factors affecting consumers to use internet banking services". In Services Science, Management and Engineering, 2009. SSME'09. IITA International Conference on (pp. 242-245). IEEE, 2009.

[57] S. I. Swaid, and R. T. Wigand, "Measuring the quality of e-service: scale development and initial validation". Journal of Electronic Commerce Research, vol. 10, no 1, p.p. 13, 2009.

[58] M. A. Teruel, E. Navarro, V. López-Jaquero, F. Montero, and P. González, "A comprehensive framework for modeling requirements of CSCW systems". Journal of Software: Evolution and Process, vol. 29, no 5, 2017.

[59] V. Hiard, Website Auditing, ENI Edition, June 2016.

[60] W3C, Web Accessibility Evaluation Tools List. Available from: http://www.w3.org/WAI/ER/tools/. Retrieved: January 2016.

[61] R. Whitaker, "Computer Supported Cooperative Work (CSCW) and Groupware Overview, Definitions, and Distinctions". Available from: http://www.enolagaia.com/UMUArchive/CSCW.html#I. Retrieved:August 2017.

[62] M.F. Wolfinbarger and M.C. Gilly, "ETAILQ: Dimensionalizing, measuring and predicting e- tailing quality". Journal of Retailing, vol. 79, no 3, p.p. 183-198, 2003.

[63] X. Burdet under the leadership of Ph. Duguedil, Impact of computer decisions Introduction to informatics for the non-computerized decision-maker, Chapter 11, PPUR Polytechnic and Academic Romandy Press, 2005.

[64] Z. Yang, M. Jun, and R. T. Peterson, "Measuring customer perceived online service quality: scale development and managerial implications". International Journal of Operations & Production Management, vol. 24, no 11, p.p. 1149-1174, 2004.

[65] Z. Yang, S. Cai, Z. Zhou, and N. Zhou, "Development and validation of an instrument to measure user perceived service quality of information presenting web portals". Information & Management, vol.42, no 4, p.p. 575-589, 2005.

[66] B. Yoo and N. Donthu, "Developing a Scale to Measure the Perceived Quality of an Internet Shopping Site (SITEQUAL)", Quarterly Journal of Electronic Commerce, vol. 2, no 1, p.p. 31-45, 2001.

[67] S. Yu, L. Al-Jadir, and S. Spaccapietra, "Matching user's Semantics with Data Semantics in Location-Based Services". In: 1st Workshop on Semantics in Mobile Environments (SME 05), 2005.

[68] V. A. Zeithaml, L. L.Berry, and A. Parasuraman, "The behavioral consequences of service quality". The Journal of Marketing, p.p. 31-46, 1996.

[69] http://www.freeyourshirt.com/. Retrieved: August, 2017.

[70] http://evene.lefigaro.fr/citations/john-ruskin. Retrieved: August, 2017.

[71] http://people.ucalgary.ca/~design/engg251/First%20Year%20Files/kano.pdf . Retrieved: August, 2017.

Developing Architecture in Volatile Environments

Lessons Learned from a Biobank IT Infrastructure Project

Jarkko Hyysalo, Gavin Harper, Jaakko Sauvola, Anja Keskinarkaus, Ilkka Juuso, Miikka Salminen, Juha Partala
Faculty of Information Technology and Electrical Engineering
University of Oulu
Oulu, Finland
e-mail: jarkko.hyysalo@oulu.fi, gavin.harper@oulu.fi, jaakko.sauvola@oulu.fi, anjakes@ee.oulu.fi, ilkka.juuso@ee.oulu.fi, miikka.salminen@ee.oulu.fi, juha.partala@ee.oulu.fi

***Abstract*—The architecture specifies how the system should be designed and built. Several architecture frameworks exist for implementing the architectural design process. However, shortcomings are identified in current architectural design processes, especially concerning volatile domains like healthcare. We claim that an iterative architectural design process is required, where the technical concerns are separated from the non-technical ones. Furthermore, a strong guiding vision is required. Based on our experiences from a biobank IT infrastructure process, we present a Continuous Renewability architectural design process that is modular, interoperable, controlled and abstracted, thus being capable of handling complex systems with severe uncertainties.**

***Keywords-** Architecture; design; lessons learned; post-mortem; process.*

I. INTRODUCTION

Software systems are becoming ever more complex. Consequently, software and systems development has become increasingly challenging and intellectually demanding [1][2]. Therefore, it has been proposed that coherent and comprehensive modelling approaches be applied. Subsequently many approaches are developed in the field of systems architecture modelling [3].

Defining the architecture is an activity that specifies how a system is to be designed and implemented. Several architectural frameworks are available providing guidance on how to enact the architectural design process. However, in domains that are not established or stable, there exist variables that may cause changes and unexpected events that require non-routine solutions. The wider the scope of the project and the more stakeholders that are involved, the more difficult the architecture definition is [3].

Moreover, if the development problem is not well structured, it becomes increasingly more challenging to address and communicate [4]. Healthcare is one such domain that is constantly evolving. There exist several stakeholders from different domains, various laws and regulations are in effect, some of which are still emerging, e.g., General Data Protection Regulation [5], services and service models are still being refined. It is then easy to see the inherent volatility within this particular domain. Hence, we claim that an incremental and iterative process is necessary, where the outcome is built gradually. These facilitates observations of the evolution of the design and implementation over time, and to better understand its requirements and potential– gradually gathering feedback and incorporating it into the development. However, not only design and implementation, but also system use and renewability has to be acknowledged in the architecture.

Furthermore, there is a need to have a strong guiding vision towards which the architecture development efforts can be compared to. In order to define such a process, we propose the following research question: *What form of architectural design process is suitable for volatile environments?* To address our research question, we used a post-mortem analysis to study the process of building a biobank IT infrastructure. As a result, we propose a Continuous Renewability approach to architectural design process.

The remainder of the paper is organised as follows. Section II studies the background. Section III presents the research approach. Section IV presents the architectural design process and the empirical experiences from healthcare domain. Section V evaluates our approach. Section VI discusses the results and implications. Section VII summarises this work.

This paper is an extended version of [6] including, e.g., more detailed literature study, extended description of the proposed approach, and evaluation of the approach.

II. BACKGROUND AND RELATED WORK

The healthcare domain is one example of domains that are constantly evolving by means of new technological innovations, new requirements for efficiency and cost and new regulations being introduced. There also exists the continued interaction and dependency on legacy systems and data formats. The design reality of healthcare IT architecture is sketched in Figure 1.

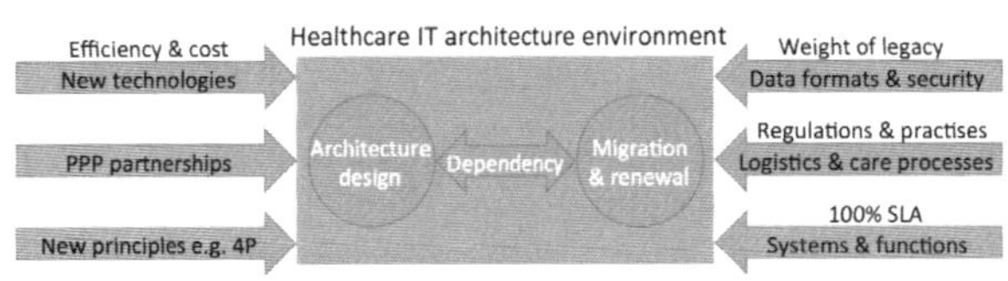

Figure 1. Design reality of healthcare IT architecture.

Legacy systems and data formats that are widely utilised in the medical domain create challenges by means of potentially isolated and non-interoperable systems. In particular, legacy issues arising from the use of existing data formats, processes, applications and service-level agreements (SLA) increase the level of complexity involved in designing a unified technical solution. Thus, there exists a need for migration and renewal strategies in addition to strategies that enable complying with the legacy systems.

Architectural design is heavily guided by requirements regarding efficiency and cost. Emerging technologies may provide better and more efficient solutions to current challenges, public-private partnerships (PPP) funded by a partnership of government and a number of private sector companies and new principles like 4P medicine, referring to preventive, predictive, personalised, and participatory medicine [7]. 4P medicine is also sometimes referred to as personalised or precision medicine. It can be seen as the tailoring of medical treatment to the individual characteristics, needs, and preferences of a patient during all stages of care, including prevention, diagnosis, treatment, and follow-up. It will also include enhancing the awareness about lifestyles and preventive lifestyle changes. The goal is to enhance the health outcomes with integration of evidence-based medicine and precision diagnostics into clinical practice.

Through this holistic approach, in combination with several divergent stakeholders and new technologies, it is easy to see that the design environment may become fragmented and volatile. Furthermore, the healthcare sector is examining new strategies and business models, such as PPP, where the strategic and business drivers are diverse. The gradual evolution of legacy systems towards new solutions must enable the continuing use of existing systems integrated into the current environment. This may potentially result in a complex environment with combination of both legacy systems and applications with brand new solutions [8]. The ongoing evolution through changing legislation, regulations and improvements in medical practices creates an environment that is constantly changing.

Various architectural frameworks have been proposed to address the different design realities, including standards, such as ISO/IEC/IEEE 42010. In addition a general model for architectural design is presented in [9]. Architectural frameworks have been analysed extensively [1][10][11], and a recurring theme across the frameworks is that each describes the role of the architecture in the product development process as a "*systematic analysis and design of related information to provide model for guiding the actual development of information systems*" [10]. The architectural design process is a one that guides the definition of a given system architecture, however, there is no general solution for the representation of a system's architecture [10]. Many architecture frameworks discuss the architecture creation process yet few focus on the process [11]. The value of the processes is shown in the literature and it has been suggested that processes ensure that activities in an organisation are performed consistently and reliably [12]. The architectural design process should provide a structured approach to architecture activities in the product development process [10]. Furthermore, it is also important to acknowledge the phases of system in use and renewability. Thus, architecture should cover: 1) design, 2) implementation, 3) deployment, 4) usage, and 5) renewability. The lack of proper planning for items usage and renewability can often lead to problems for customers, because evolution and renewability is expensive or impossible, system use may be restricted, and new processes are not supported. Maintenance can also suffer if developers only do design, implementation, and deployment.

Several frameworks exist for modelling architecture. While different frameworks have different content and target a different audience [11], they aim to provide structure and systematic processes for systems design [10]. Examples of well known and established architecture frameworks are the Zachman Framework for Enterprise Architecture [13], 4+1 View Model of Architecture [14], Federal Enterprise Architecture Framework (FEAF) [15], Reference Model for Open Distributed Computing (RM-ODP) [16], The Open Group Architectural Framework (TOGAF) [17], DoD Architecture Framework by the US Department of Defense (DoDAF) [18], and a general model of software architectural design by Hofmeister et al [9].

While each architecture framework is suitable for different environments, they may result in similar outcomes based on their architecture goals and viewpoints. Viewpoints are an important feature of architecture frameworks as they represent the goals and focal points that the architecture framework emphasises like business, information, software and technical architectures. The analysis revealed that only three of the frameworks, FEAF, TOGAF and DoDAF, provided explicit support for the architectural design process, RM-ODP provided partial support, ZF and 4+1 View provided no support. ZF and TOGAF have a focus on enterprise architecture, 4+1 View and RM-ODP on software systems (typically distributed), FEAF is primarily a framework for architecture planning and DoDAF focuses on enterprise architecture related to defence operations and business operations and processes. It is thus typically quite domain specific. The general model by Hofmeister et al. is based on synthesis of several existing approaches. [3][9][10][11]

Evaluations of architecture frameworks are presented, e.g., in [3][9][11]. While there are pros and cons for each method, common deficiencies in the architecture frameworks can be identified [10]: 1) The level of details required in models is not specified enough, 2) Rationales are not considered in models, thus no verification is possible, 3) Non-functional requirements are not considered in all frameworks, 4) Software configuration is not considered in all frameworks.

There are also more recent approaches to systems design that aim at tackling the challenges of modern development environments. Palladio Component Model (PCM) is one such approach; among other benefits it enables the analysis of different architectural design alternatives (i.e., optimisation) and aims to address the challenges during the early development stages, thus avoiding costly redesigns

[19]. Software architecture optimisation has also been studied to help the search for optimal architectural design, e.g., Aleti et al. [20] performed an extensive systematic literature review focusing on software architecture optimisation.

Even with software architecture optimisation efforts, architectural design still involves complex trade-off analyses that may require expertise in several domains or the environment may be more variable and dynamic than current process can support. It is even possible that not all stakeholders are known or they may not already know what the intent for the product to accomplish. Thus, such uncertainty may exist that the guiding vision for the product is impossible to be fully defined during the early stages of development. Instead, it is suggested that it is built incrementally.

In conclusion, there is a need for an architectural design process that addresses the identified shortcomings, including: volatile environments, the availability of specific details, design rationales, non-functional requirements, and software configurations.

III. Research Approach

The results are based on experiences gathered during a biobank IT infrastructure development project. The research consisted of studying several organisations related to biobank activities. The purpose of this was to define architecture for a biobank and implement a functional infrastructure. Managing the large number of stakeholders and constantly changing environment requires carefully considered architecture approach, thus creating the need and basis for this work.

During the project several challenges were identified. A post-mortem analysis was conducted to analyse these findings and to identify the shortcomings and improvements for the architectural design process. A post-mortem analysis is a study method that may be used to gather empirical knowledge. The benefits of a post-mortem analysis include revealing findings more frequently than other methods, such as project completion reports. It is beneficial to conduct post-mortem analyses after important milestones and events in addition to the end of a project. Post-mortem analysis can be used as a project-based learning technique [21][22]. In addition to finding the impediments of the development process, post-mortem analyses may be used to improve methods and practises [23]. During this research project, a post-mortem analysis was used to study our development process to facilitate identifying potential sources for improvement or optimisation.

Our post-mortem analysis follows the general iterative post-mortem analysis proposed by Birk et al. [21], as shown in Figure 2.

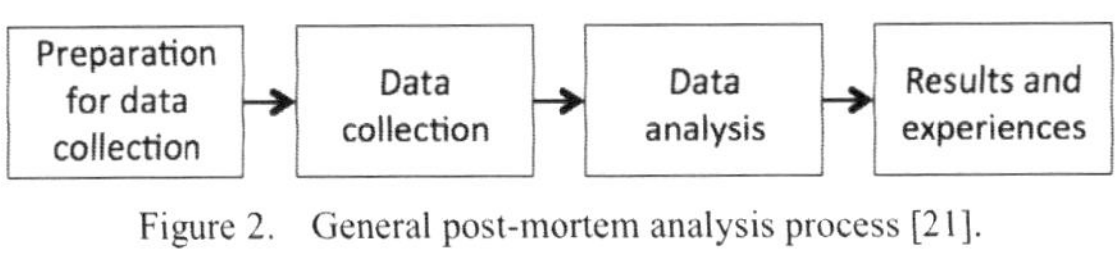

Figure 2. General post-mortem analysis process [21].

TABLE I. Various Stakeholders in Biobank Domain

Stakeholder	Input
Valvira (National Supervisory Authority for Welfare and Health)	- Biobank permission - Supervision
Sample donor, person	- Consent - Samples
KELA (The Social Insurance Institution of Finland)	- Information systems service
THL (National Institute for Health and Welfare in Finland)	- Architecture - BBMRI-ERIC: Obligations
BBMRI (Biobanking and BioMolecular resources Research Infrastructure)	- Common methods
Registry	- Source data
Service provider	- Service
Health care units	- Sample and data - Support services
Research	- Sample and data
National ethical board (TUKIJA)	- Reports
STM (The Ministry of Health and Social Affairs)	- National biobank overall architecture

Our research started with an initial preparation stage where we carefully identified the key participants involved with our effort and selected viable methods and procedures.

Project history was examined with the key participants involved in the project (primarily project managers and system architects) and project documents were studied. Then our goal for the post-mortem analysis was determined–to understand the needs for the architectural design process as well as identify potential sources for improvement and optimisation.

Data collection involved gathering relevant project experiences from team members and key stakeholders (Table I). Participants of our data collection as well as data analysis session were project managers (1), system architects (2) and developers (2). A decision was made to conduct a lightweight post-mortem analysis. KJ sessions [24] with thematic analysis [25][26] were utilised to gather and organise ideas and data.

In the analysis phase, findings and ideas were organised into groups based on their relationships. Post-It notes were used to record the ideas and findings and related notes were then grouped together. Based on our results, we present Continuous Renewability architectural design process. Table I presents the key stakeholders that participated in the definition of the biobank. The organisations were chosen as they could each provide potential data related to the research question. Experts and managers from different organisational levels were involved. Examples of input by the sources are also presented.

IV. Examining the Architectural Design Process

A. Preparation

In the planning phase, project results were studied. These results included meeting memorandums, requirements, company materials and the results produced. The focus of the post-mortem analysis was decided to be to understand and improve the current processes, to find out what challenges regarding to architectural design process exist and where we succeeded. Post-mortem analysis participants were informed of the procedures and schedules were agreed upon and the goal of the post-mortem analysis was determined. A lightweight post-mortem analysis was selected as it fits the project size best [27].

B. *Data Collection and Data Analysis*

In this step, a summary of project history was explored with key members of the project to better understand the history of the project. Then we gathered the relevant project experience, and participants were asked to provide their views on the development process and practises. The views were documented using KJ sessions.

Participants were given a set of Post-It notes and they were asked to write down one issue on each note including both challenges and successes. Each note was then attached to a whiteboard and the person was asked to explain why the issue is important. When all the notes were on the whiteboard, they were discussed thoroughly and then they were organised into thematic groups and each group was named, see Table II. Grouping the findings revealed nine themes. These groups indicate the main challenges or needs that were encountered in the development of the biobank IT-infrastructure. These challenges are issues that may often be met in the architecture development in volatile environments.

Data analysis was done in the same session as data collection.

TABLE II. SUMMARY OF THE MOST IMPORTANT FINDINGS

Theme	Finding
Abstraction	+ Abstracting the system design is useful
Change and uncertainty	- Changing requirements, components and environment - Unclear responsibilities - Ongoing efforts that affect the work disruptively
Communication	- Understanding stakeholders from other domains is challenging - Various general communication issues are met - Unclear stakeholders complicates the communication - Critical information not available + Constant communication within the development team was useful + Common vision and shared understanding within the development team was helpful + Building trust between the stakeholders enabled the communication channels to be build
Controlled	+ Planning and decision-making built within the process
Guiding vision	+ First architecture draft providing a guideline + Defining the basic data flows before trying to integrate with the hospital systems
Interoperability	- Numerous interfaces to existing systems - Vast number of systems and applications, including legacy systems
Iterative approach	+ Iterative process builds the outcome gradually
Modularity	+ Following system architecture principles allowing for modular system
Separation of concerns	- Non-technological issues complicating technological issues (politics, rigid processes, etc.) - Complex operational environment requires examination of the system from different views + Identifying new separation opportunities in existing architecture enabled development of isolated domains

After the views and ideas were recorded, they were discussed in detail. A root-cause analysis was conducted to find out why those items occurred. Identifying root causes of the identified issues included consideration of how general these issues are and whom they concern.

Analysis suggests that the most important issue affecting the architectural design was change and uncertainty in addition to communication issues and complexity in the system and environment. Together these hindered development efforts and may potentially affect quite severely the quality of the product. However, we also found ways to tackle these issues. For example, applying good communication practices, iterative development and having a guiding vision are all suggested.

In summary, our architectural design process was iterative in nature. This allowed us to build a shared understanding of the work to be done, to shape the goals, and to react to numerous changes and uncertainties as well as the knowledge gaps between different stakeholders. The work started with a stakeholder analysis to find the relevant stakeholders and their viewpoints regarding biobank IT infrastructure. The key problem in gathering stakeholder views was their wide array of potential wishes and then implementing them on a technical level. Several stakeholders were not technically oriented in their background, thus they did not know the technical restrictions that may exist in such an environment.

Similarly from both a legal perspective and a technological perspective, the various stakeholders had difficulty grasping adequately other domains than their own. Especially challenging were the legal issues regarding sensitive and personally identifiable information. Getting the stakeholder views and mapping them to a technical level in addition to ensuring compliance with laws and regulations is time consuming since there needs to be a consensus amongst the stakeholders. Multiple requirements were identified ranging from very abstract to very concrete. Based on this analysis we were able to come up with an architectural design process for volatile environments.

C. *Experiences*

Here we summarise our experiences from the architectural design process conducted in order to build a biobank IT infrastructure. The aim is to provide hands-on experience on architectural design process and to provide guidance on how to define architectures for systems that exist in volatile environments, and as with many other frameworks to control the complexity of development by abstracting the system design and modelling the intended system at different abstraction levels.

We suggest an iterative approach in the form of Continuous Renewability, where the work is done iteratively and incrementally with feedback loops throughout the process improving communication. At each level, there are discussions about what is required, and what is already available. Frequently, comparisons to previous levels are done. As the process progresses, the need for changes and their associated effects grows smaller.

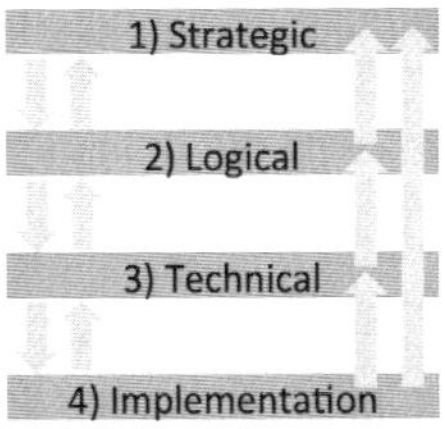

Figure 3. Four levels of abstraction for describing software architectures.

Different approaches can be used, as there are different needs, requirements, environments, etc. In our case, Continuous Renewability approach was required. Biobank data does not become old or obsolete. Instead, the amount of data grows over time. Similarly, the architectural design must be continuous to account for changes and new events and to have scalability and potential for upgrade while still keeping the whole system interoperable.

In the Continuous Renewability model, four levels of abstraction are identified each representing a distinctive view of the architecture from enterprise level to technical details of the system/software architecture, see Figure 3. Each level implements the level above with more detailed technologies and descriptions. Each level is also a phase in our architectural design process. Moreover, each level corresponds to a set of stakeholders, and together the different views form the complete architecture specification.

1) Strategic architecture is the starting point providing the overall description of the development problem, defining business views, business processes and rules, and performance goals. It also defines the conceptual architecture that connects the architecture effort with the visions, organisational strategies, business drivers and goals in addition to processes and functional perspectives.

One of the main contributions is to communicate the vision and define the rationale–why things are required. External input can come from multiple sources including but not limited to various communities, laws and regulations.

At this level, a strategic architecture is defined with the following output: A semantic model defining the relationships of business entities and business processes. Most of the external requirements and customer feedback come through this level as this level is typically closest to the customer interface of an organisation. It must have a solid understanding of customer requirements and it should communicate these requirements in addition to their rationale to internal stakeholders. A strategic architecture is also influenced by the business strategies and other high-level visions. Furthermore, it also receives feedback in an iterative manner from the whole architecture development cycle. It was noted that frequently this strategy consumes a disproportionate amount of time and effort, as it must be strictly representative of reality in order to provide a good basis for further actions.

2) Logical architecture defines the functions and various resources or components of the system including their relations and how information flows throughout the system. Furthermore, this level defines the qualities of the system, i.e., gives the measurements on how to achieve the business goals specified at the strategic level. External input is the inventories of available building blocks for the system.

The results from level 1 are further examined and developed in level 2, where the logical architecture is defined. The output of level 2 provides a logical data model that defines the relationships of data entities.

3) Technical architecture implements the logical level and provides a foundation by defining the technical architecture including technology platforms, information system environments, hardware, software, network components, interfaces, platforms, etc. External input comes from sources including standards, non-functional requirements (NFR) (like redundancy, security, availability, scalability and interoperability). The output of level 3 is to provide a technical architecture that defines the physical data model and a technological architecture.

4) Implementation architecture focuses on details, such as hardware and software, operating systems and middleware in addition to interoperability and data definitions. External input comes from sources including configuration documents, technical constraints and application requirements. The output of level 4 is an implementation architecture that defines the implementation details, such as components, applications and software and hardware configurations. This implementation architecture takes into account all the technical constraints. Furthermore, it also has to communicate back to level 1, e.g., the weight of legacy (like data formats and applications), which will affect planning, system interoperability, business decisions, etc. The weight of legacy is a critical factor in system design in the healthcare domain where there may not exist alternatives that are readily available to replace existing systems.

If changes are made at any level, it may have an effect on any other level. The Master Architecture is defined to guide the development effort, structure and scope of the process. This is illustrated in Figure 4.

The Master Architecture maintains the up-to-date specification in addition to a specification document produced for each level. Defining the Master Architecture can start from the current architecture or current standards and infrastructures.

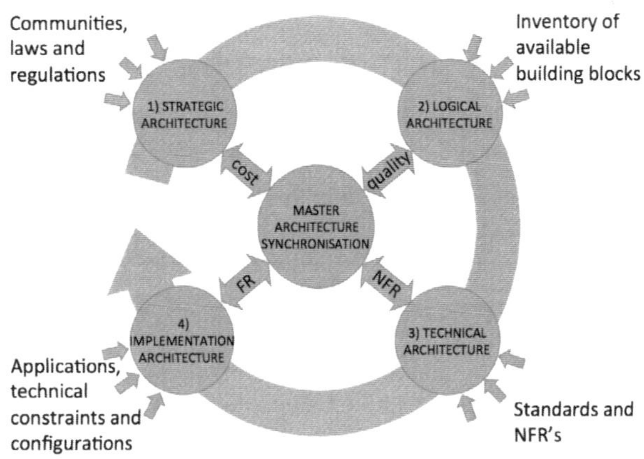

Figure 4. Continuous Renewability architectural design process.

First, a high level architecture is used which will then be further specified as the architectural design process progresses. The Master Architecture may also illustrate a set of use-case scenarios that can be referred to at each level to understand requirements of the system to be designed.

The model has to account for 1) reality, 2) methodologies, 3) design models, and 4) design functionalities.

Each phase has to correspond to the Master Architecture to verify the feasibility and progress of the development towards the set criteria. For example, phase 1 relates to synchronisation of costs and trade-offs, phase 2 to quality aspects, phase 3 to NFR's and phase 4 to Functional Requirements (FR). Similarly, the produced documents and items are verified against the Master Architecture.

The resulting architecture from this process is available at [28].

V. EVALUATION

Our Continuous Renewability approach is an amalgamation of several best practices found in other approaches and design methods. Table III presents a comparison of several commonly used approaches with our approach, and consider how they address the challenges and needs encountered in the architecture development in volatile environments. The themes captured in post-mortem analysis provide a good starting point for identifying requirements for architecture development in volatile environments. These themes are also recognised in the literature. The approaches are evaluated towards the identified requirements. The evaluation is literature based. Each approach is checked if they fulfil the requirement fully, partially or not at all. The Continuous Renewability approach (CR in the Table III) is built to address the identified requirements fully.

It should be noted, however, that DoDAF is limited in scope and it does not address the relevant views for implementing the system as a software architecture as well as the other approaches [29].

Abstraction is one of the requirements for architecture description languages [30], furthermore, abstraction is necessary to enable the examination of architecture from different perspectives. Zachman, FEAF and DoDAF address the abstraction requirement, while TOGAF has very limited views [31]. Abstraction is addressed in 4+1 at least partially with different views.

Changes and uncertainty. In real life, work has many variables, changes and unexpected events are met, vast amounts of data must be handled, and innovative solutions are needed [12][32][33]. Readiness for changes is necessary to adapt to future situations [9], furthermore, uncertainty and changes are also often met during the development work. Flexibility minimise the impact of changes. Change and uncertainty is addressed in Zachman, DoDAF and Hofmeister. FEAF accommodates changes at least partially through flexibility of methods, work products and tools [30]. TOGAF has a flexible process and accommodates changes and promotes change management [10][34]. RM-ODP does not consider the future needs or evolution of the architecture [10]. 4+1 does not address system evolution [10].

Communication is a mediating factor in coordinating and controlling the collaborative work. Software development requires a vast amount of communication, especially when dealing with complex infrastructures. These issues have been reported to decrease both the frequency and quality of communication, and ultimately, productivity. To mitigate these issues, tools, processes, and methodologies are required. [35][36]

Communication is addressed in Zachman (through abstraction, simplification and common vocabulary) and Hofmeister, but not explicitly. FEAF provides a common language and facilitates communication [34]. DoDAF address communication at least partially through extensive documentation [10]. 4+1 address communication requirement fully. RM-ODP provides a framework for defining the languages for the viewpoints to be used as a dictionary for architecture description [29].

Controlled refers to rigid processes and best practices that the architectural design process is based on. It also overlaps with the guiding vision, as control also comes from the ability to evaluate constantly the results towards set targets, ensuring the correct architectural decisions [9].

FEAF (partially) and TOGAF (fully) provides process support [10][31][34]. FEAF measures success [34], while TOGAF lacks the continuous evaluation or validation. 4+1 provides partial support through the validation of the architectural design, while DoDAF defines the process and evaluation [10][31][34] and Hofmeister provide full support for controllability. RM-ODP does not describe the architectural design process [10].

Guiding vision provides a common goal to guide the development and harmonise the practices. Guiding vision also acts as a baseline towards which the development can be verified.

TABLE III. COMPARISON OF APPROACHES (0=NO SUPPORT, 1=PARTIAL SUPPORT, 2=FULL SUPPORT)

Requirement	Zachman	FEAF	RM-ODP	TOGAF	DoDAF	4+1	Hofmeister	CR
Abstraction	2	2	1	2	2	1	1	2
Change & Uncertainty	2	1	0	2	2	0	2	2
Communication	1	2	1	0	1	2	1	2
Controlled	0	1	0	1	2	1	2	2
Guiding vision	0	1	0	2	2	2	2	2
Interoperable	0	2	2	2	2	0	0	2
Iterative	0	1	0	1	2	2	2	2
Modular	0	1	1	0	0	2	0	2
Separation of concerns	1	2	1	0	1	1	2	2

Evaluation is ensuring that the architectural decisions are the correct ones [9]. DoDAF provides description of the intended product, with guidance and rules for consistency [18]. TOGAF and 4+1 guides the organisation with an architectural vision. In FEAF each segment has a guiding vision [34].

Interoperability is one of the drivers that contribute to the success of the product and it is necessary to address interoperability already in the architectural design [39].

FEAF, RM-ODP, TOGAF and DoDAF explicitly promote interoperability [10].

Iterative development is emphasised in [9], it was also revealed as one of the success factors in our post-mortem analysis. FEAF, TOGAF and 4+1 are iterative, however, FEAF and TOGAF do not explicitly propose iterations after each phase, but only after the whole process [9][34]. DoDAF is iterative [18].

Modularity is recognised as a crucial attribute in software architecture [40][41]. FEAF uses autonomous partitions to manage complexity [34]. 4+1 supports modularity to promote ease of development, software management and reuse as well as addressing environmental constraints [10].

Separation of concerns provides several benefits, such as reduced complexity, improved reusability and simpler evolution [37][38]. Zachman, RM-ODP, DoDAF and 4+1 partially address this requirement through views. Hofmeister address the complexity and separation of concerns. FEAF address this, as it is built on segments and enterprise services, which can be seen as views to development [34].

VI. DISCUSSION

Volatile environments present many non-trivial challenges for architectural design and specification. A post-mortem analysis was conducted on a biobank IT infrastructure project to understand the architecture based on real problems and attempted solutions. A post-mortem analysis is a tool that can be used to learn from the experiences of previous iterations or completed projects. It can also be used to improve and adapt current software development processes [22]. Here, our aim was to learn from our experiences and then suggest improvements for architectural design processes, especially for volatile environments.

Our Continuous Renewability approach to architecture is a) modular, b) interoperable, c) controlled and d) abstracted. This way we can handle complex systems with significant inherent uncertainties. The design philosophy is that when designing the architecture, the requirements were separated into technical and non-technical requirements whereby the non-technical requirements included requirements specialised to the biobank domain, like sample management and identification and table structures. These are requirements that do not affect the design of data flow, as we only need to know that the data exists and will be in some form that can be trivially read from, written to and transmitted securely over an encrypted socket-based connection directly to the next stage. The specific content of the data is largely irrelevant in most cases.

Incremental and iterative development is suggested as it allows observing the outcome and improving it as new information becomes available. Our proposal is a Continuous Renewability architecture model, which is intended to be general, such that it does not mandate how each level should be modelled. This allows several architectural styles and notations to be utilised. More important is that all the necessary views to a development are addressed. Furthermore, our architecture is modular to allow flexibility and extendibility. Modularity allows the reconstruction of any part of the system, such that an area-of-effect can potentially be localised to just those components directly connected to the modified region. In the case of the biobank, the system has been designed such that successive system component regions typically form a directional data flow through standardised and well-defined interfaces. Interoperability is similarly achieved through the specification of interfaces defining various domains with utilisation of open-standard communication protocols. Controllability comes from the rigorous process and from the Master Architecture that guides the development and verifies the outputs against the set targets. Architecture should also be highly abstracted. For example, there exist requirements that are irrelevant when designing a data flow because we only require knowledge that a given data exists and will be in some form that we can work with. The specific content of the data is largely irrelevant in most cases. This is highly beneficial in an evolving healthcare environment whereby the specific content of a data set in addition may frequently be in a state of flux while the laws and regulations surrounding the data set are interpreted. Increasing or decreasing the level of abstraction as required allows the examination of the system from different perspectives. The separation of technical concerns from non-technical concerns allows us to adapt to future needs, as the design is not relying on specific technologies or solutions.

In volatile environments, constant comparison to the Master Architecture is required. It allows for the verification of compliance for all the relevant inputs and design choices, even if those vary during development. The Master Architecture provides the goals towards which the effort is pushed as well as the guidelines that determine how those goals should be reached. Structure for the process is also provided. Design rationales guide the overall work and are kept up-to-date by continuous communication with the stakeholders who see the system being defined incrementally. Continuous communication also helps building trust between the stakeholders. This allows them to understand the rationale for design and implementation decisions better throughout the process as a consequence of context being more localised. Input is verified at each level and every iteration. Additionally, the Master architecture is updated accordingly. Comparing the results to the Master Architecture enables a constant feasibility analysis, and enables corrective actions if necessary.

We suggest an approach to architecture whereby domains are the fundamental units and the communication pathways between the domains indicate connectivity between domains. The internal structure of a given domain remains unspecified in the highest level of abstraction. It is only specialised once the requirements for that domain are exhibiting some form of stability. For example, we can consider the anonymising encoding service of the biobank not as a part of the architecture, but as a specialisation of a domain for a specific task. Thus, if for example, the law changes or it turns out it was misinterpreted, the specialised components of the domain may be updated or replaced with minimal impact to the architecture assuming the new specialisation utilises the existing connection path and communicates using compatible data storage and communication formats. It then follows that any connected domains from which it receives from or transmits to must be able to accept that communication readily.

This is accomplished by initially designing the system at a high of abstraction, modelling the transformations that occur in a domain as a function with an argument type T that maps to some other type U where T, U may have some structure or may represent a collection of different data types. It is also important to note that type identifiers, such as T or U are arbitrarily chosen and the label communicates only the preservation, or lack thereof, of the structure of the input data. The labelling of an input and output type is defined such that if the input and output types of a domain are identical as is the case in a mapping from T to T then the transformation that occurs is said to be structure preserving such that the output contains an identical structure to the input type. An example of this could be structured tabular data with given column headings. If the transformation does not modify this table structure, instead only reading the contents or modifying the table contents then it is said to be structure preserving. It is then possible once a directed graph of each transformation is obtained to perform algebra upon this graph. Such operations may include the simplification of the structure through composing transformations or identifying potential incompatibilities between domains through type mismatches. Each domain in the architecture is constructed from many transformations composed in such a manner that the functionality of a domain may be mapped as the composition of many functions.

In practise, many concepts may not map naturally to this model. Examples include data storage on disc and databases. In such cases, it is possible to map these as either state machines or simply as entities in the data flow that label a particular complex process. As requirements stabilise and become readily available, the intent is for an architecture defined in this abstract manner to reduce down to a traditional architecture specification.

Designing the system this way allows us to largely disregard the shifting external environment and design a system around the modelled data flow rather than the specific form of the transformations until such time that information exhibits stability. It is only required that information regarding what transformations are required exists. This way, the architecture is largely resilient against variation in both non-functional and many non-technical requirements as each domain is intended to be entirely self-contained with all state being local to that domain and any information that enters the domain is passed directly to it and the given output from a domain depends only upon information contained within that domain.

We propose that architecture specifies the interfaces to the various domains and utilise open standard protocols for communication. It is specified that all data be retained so any variation in requirements downstream can be trivially propagated through the signal chain or the entire data set can be rebuilt at any time if a failure occurs somewhere. Similarly, by defining the interfaces between domains, it is possible to enforce properties, such as strong and guaranteed cryptography on communications and storage in addition to simple topology modifications due to a standardised interface between domains. While this requires additional work in the implementation stage, by communicating through a unified routing system, it ensures that future software replacing legacy or unsuitable components may develop against a known, open communication protocol removing the possibility that proprietary vendor communication methods hamper third-party inclusion into the architecture. There are many benefits of this approach, as shown in Table IV.

With this in mind, we believe that this approach is not limited to a single field (pathology, genetics or similar) and does not depend on a single company. This is a general model that can apply to any domain of any size.

TABLE IV. BENEFITS

- Since the creation of abstract domains is largely trivial and the communication between those domains follows open standards, each domain is fully knowable and may be audited. The system may then easily adapt by localising changes to only the affected domains.
- Adapting to future needs is made viable using this architecture, as it doesn't matter whether the software used to power a particular domain is open source or proprietary as long as it conforms to the open standard data storage formats and communication protocols, it can be replaced or upgraded.
- There is much less chance of a given software company creating a monopoly in the business domain by providing a large monolithic system that is proprietary and does not allow (or limits) the ability for third-parties to build upon or interface with it.
- There is opportunity for innovation because anyone can develop candidate solutions for domain specialisation without needing to invest effort in satisfying criteria regarding licensing other vendor APIs. It also allows for larger scale international collaboration.
- The organisation is free to choose any software, open source or proprietary to specialise each domain. We specify in our prototype biobank implementation architecture open source software because for our purposes existing solutions exist for many of the domain specialisations and it is possible to implement new functionality upon the existing code bases with relative ease. However, the client remains free to choose the software solutions they deem adequate. The only requirement is that the communication between domains follows open protocols with implementations provided either by an existing library or directly as part of the core infrastructure.
- It has a potential to be cheaper to maintain. For example, if there is a decision to go for an entirely open source system, not only does there not typically exist a license cost, there may exist multiple potential options regarding which organisation to hire for supporting and maintaining the system. That way they can receive quotes and optimise expenditure based on the value each quote offers.
- Since rigid software design processes may stagnate and impede innovation. By having a modular system, any organisation may be required to innovate whether it is by feature set or cost as there may not exist a possibility to implant a system at the project's inception and rely on the difficulty of switching to a competing product as a source of longevity in the deployed infrastructure.

This is where the novelty and innovativeness of this approach lies. We suggest a system design method that is resilient to changing requirements and constraints and is dependent only upon technological requirements, one that can adapt and grow to any scale and is both modular and knowable.

There do, however exist limitations to this approach. In this case, there is limited access to end-users as only a limited number of healthcare professionals were directly participating in the process.

We had to rely on application and service providers, who served as an intermediary between the researchers and the end-users. However, the application and service providers are established and well known in their domain and have a strong knowledge of the needs and requirements. We can thus rely on their experience for making informed decisions.

The results should interest both academics and practitioners as they provide an experience report on a generalised architectural design process for volatile environments. This is a method for designing a system in such a way that it bypasses many non-technical issues by separating the technical concerns from the non-technical concerns through modular design. The study also lays the groundwork for further scholarly inquiry, including validating the findings in practice.

VII. Conclusion and Future Work

This paper presented lessons learned from a biobank IT infrastructure project. A post-mortem analysis was conducted for biobank IT infrastructure process, where several challenges are encountered. Further challenges were presented by the strict requirements for privacy and anonymity as well as rigid processes involved with the patient data. We have identified several challenges and solution proposals.

Table V shows the overview of proposed solutions and summarises how the challenges may be addressed.

By following these proposals the resulting architecture will be a) modular, b) interoperable, c) controlled and d) abstracted. It is also suitable for volatile environments, thus addressing our research question.

Continuous Renewability approach is general by definition and should be easily adapted to other domains. However, the practical generalisability of our results is limited until the process is used in other domains. It is important to note that the viability of this approach will need to be verified through controlled experiment and observation. Though, the generalisability is one of our main design philosophies guiding the development, hence we believe that generalisability issues are likely to be negligible. This model should be refined as feedback from applications is received.

TABLE V. Overview of Proposed Solutions

- Changing requirements, components and environments are tackled with iterative process that builds shared understanding, shape the goals and allow reacting to changes. Furthermore, Continuous Renewability approach enables constant feedback and mitigates the effects of changes as the process progresses.
- Several communications related issues are tackled with iterative process, as it allow stakeholders to see the system grow, and their understanding improves along with the system. Improved communication practices also are necessary, starting from the planning to create a common vision on what to build and continuing through the whole development cycle. Constant communication also builds trust between the stakeholders.
- The Master Architecture provides the scope and guidance for the development work. First architecture draft is defined to provide a guideline for development. Then the basic data flows are defined. Master Architecture provides a checkpoint towards which the design can be verified, while designing the system around data flows mitigates the complexity as well as the effects of changing external environment.
- An iterative approach was adopted to build the outcome gradually. With the modular system architecture and abstracted systems design it allows for updating the design with minimal effort and minimal impact to other parts of the system. Abstraction and separation of concerns allows for adaptable design that accommodates the future needs and is scalable. It also is not reliant on certain technologies or solutions.
- Separation of non-technological issues from technological issues simplifies the design, as it isolates, e.g., the effects of politics and rigid processes from the technological concerns.
- The separation of the architecture into isolated domains connected through a common interface can serve to restrict the propagation of errors through the system in the event of component failure or modification. This in turn has the potential to offer greater flexibility and expansion of the system to meet future needs.
- Interfaces between the domains and to existing systems utilise the open-standard communication protocols. This ensures interoperability, as the components can be changed according to future needs.

References

[1] P. Robillard, "The Role of Knowledge in Software Development," *Communications of the ACM 42(1)*, pp. 87-92, 1999.

[2] F. O. Bjørnson and T. Dingsøyr, "Knowledge Management in Software Engineering: a Systematic Review of Studied Concepts, Findings, and Research Methods Used," *Information and Software Technology, vol. 50*, pp. 1055-1068, 2008.

[3] S. Leist and G. Zellner, "Evaluation of current architecture frameworks." In *Proceedings of the 2006 ACM symposium on applied computing*, pp. 1546-1553, 2006.

[4] J. C. Brancheau, L Schuster, and S. T. March, "Building and implementing an information architecture," *ACM SIGMIS Database 20(2)*, pp. 9-17, 1989.

[5] European Union, "General Data Protection Regulation 2016/679." 2016 URL http://eur-lex.europa.eu/eli/reg/2016/679/oj, 2017.07.19

[6] J. Hyysalo et al., "Defining an Architecture for Evolving Environments." In *Proceedings of SAC 2017*. In Press.

[7] C. Auffray, D. Charron, and L. Hood, "Predictive, preventive, personalized and participatory medicine: back to the future," *Genome Med 2(8)*, p. 57, 2010.

[8] F. M. Ferrara, "The standard 'healthcare information systems architecture and the DHE middleware," *International Journal of Medical Informatics 52(1)*, pp. 39-51, 1998.

[9] C. Hofmeister et al., "A general model of software architecture design derived from five industrial approaches" *Journal of Systems and Software*, *80*(1), pp. 106-126, 2007.

[10] A. Tang, J. Han, and P. Chen, "A comparative analysis of architecture frameworks." In *11th Asia-Pacific Software Engineering Conference, 2004*, pp. 640-647, 2004.

[11] U. Franke et al., "EAF2-a framework for categorizing enterprise architecture frameworks." In *10th ACIS International Conference on Software Engineering, Artificial Intelligences, Networking and Parallel/Distributed Computing*, 2009, pp. 327-332, 2009.

[12] P. Mangan and S. Sadiq, "On Building Workflow Models for Flexible Processes." In *Proceedings of the 13th Australasian Database Conference*, pp. 103-109, 2002.

[13] J. Zachman, "A framework for Information Architecture," *IBM Systems Journal 38(2&3)*, pp. 454-470, 1987.

[14] P. Kruchten, "The 4+1 View Model of Architecture," *IEEE Software 12(6)*, pp. 42-50, 1995.

[15] FEA, "Federal Enterprise Architecture Framework version 2." 2013 URL https://obamawhitehouse.archives.gov/sites/default/files/omb/assets/egov_docs/fea_v2.pdf, 2017.05.04

[16] J. Putman, "*Architecting with RM-ODP*," Prentice Hall, NJ, 2001.

[17] The Open Group, "The Open Group Architecture Framework (Version 9.1 "Enterprise Edition")." 2003 URL http://www.opengroup.org/architecture/togaf/#download, 2017.05.04

[18] Department of Defense, "Department of Defense Architecture Framework Version 2.02 - Vol 1 Definition & Guideline and Vol 2 Product Descriptions." 2010 URL http://dodcio.defense.gov/Portals/0/Documents/DODAF/DoDAF_v2-02_web.pdf, 2017.05.04

[19] R. Reussner et al., *The Palladio component model*. Technical report, Karlsruhe Institute of Technology, 2007

[20] A. Aleti, B. Buhnova, L. Grunske, A. Koziolek, and I. Meedeniya, "Software architecture optimization methods: A systematic literature review," *IEEE Transactions on Software Engineering*, *39*(5), pp. 658-683, 2013.

[21] A. Birk, T. Dingsoyr, and T. Stalhane, "Postmortem: Never leave a project without it," *IEEE Software 19(3)*, pp. 43-45, 2002.

[22] M. Myllyaho, O. Salo, J. Kääriäinen, J. Hyysalo, and J. Koskela, "A review of small and large post-mortem analysis methods." In *Proceedings of the ICSSEA*, pp. 1-8, 2004.

[23] B. Collier, T. DeMarco, and P. Fearey, "A defined process for project postmortem review," *IEEE Software 13(4)*, pp. 65-72, 1996.

[24] R. Scupin, "The KJ Method: a technique for analyzing data derived from Japanese ethnology," *Human Organization, vol. 56*, pp. 233-237, 1997.

[25] V. Braun and V. Clarke, "Using thematic analysis in psychology," *Qualitative research in psychology 3(2)*, pp. 77-101, 2006.

[26] D. S. Cruzes and T. Dyba, "Recommended steps for thematic synthesis in software engineering." In *International Symposium on Empirical Software Engineering and Measurement*, 2011, pp. 275-284, 2011.

[27] T. Dingsøyr and N. B. Moe, "Augmenting experience reports with lightweight postmortem reviews." In *Product Focused Software Process Improvement*, pp. 167-181, 2001.

[28] J. Hyysalo, A. Keskinarkaus, G. Harper, and J. Sauvola, "Architecture Enabling Service-oriented Digital Biobanks." In *Proceedings of the 50th Hawaii International Conference on System Sciences (HICSS-50)*, January 4-7, 2017, Hawaii, pp. 3469-3478, 2017.

[29] N. May, "A survey of software architecture viewpoint models." In *Proceedings of the Sixth Australasian Workshop on Software and System Architectures*, pp. 13-24, 2005.

[30] N. Medvidovic and R. N. Taylor, "A classification and comparison framework for software architecture description languages," *IEEE Transactions on software engineering*, *26*(1), pp, 70-93, 2000.

[31] L. Urbaczewski and S. Mrdalj, "A comparison of enterprise architecture frameworks," *Issues in Information Systems*, *7*(2), pp. 18-23, 2006.

[32] M. M. Kwan and P. R. Balasubramanian, "Dynamic Workflow Management: A Framework for Modeling Workflows." In *Proceedings of the 30th Hawaii International Conference on System Sciences (HICSS-30)*, pp. 367-376, 1997.

[33] M. Klein and C. Dellarocas, "A Knowledge-Based Approach to Handling Exceptions in Workflow Systems," *Computer Supported Cooperative Work 9*, pp. 399-412, 2000.

[34] R. Sessions, "Comparison of the top four enterprise architecture methodologies." 2007 URL https://msdn.microsoft.com/en-us/library/bb466232.aspx, 2017.05.04.

[35] M. Jiménez, M. Piattini, and A. Vizcaíno, "Challenges and improvements in distributed software development: A systematic review," *Advances in Software Engineering*, 2009 (3), pp 1-16, 2009.

[36] E. Carmel and R. Agarwal, "Tactical approaches for alleviating distance in global software development," *IEEE Software 18*(2), pp. 22–29, 2001.

[37] D. Soni, R. L. Nord, and C. Hofmeister, "Software architecture in industrial applications." In *Proceedings of the 17th International Conference on Software Engineering (ICSE 1995)*, pp. 196-196, 1995.

[38] P. Tarr, H. Ossher, W. Harrison, and S. M. Sutton Jr, "N degrees of separation: multi-dimensional separation of concerns." In *Proceedings of the 21st international conference on Software engineering*, pp. 107-119, 1999.

[39] D. Garlan and D. E. Perry, "Introduction to the special issue on software architecture," *IEEE Transactions on Software Engineering 21*(4), pp. 269-274, 1995.

[40] K. J. Sullivan, W. G. Griswold, Y. Cai, and B. Hallen, "The structure and value of modularity in software design." In *ACM SIGSOFT Software Engineering Notes 26*(5), pp. 99-108, 2001.

[41] K. Sethi, Y. Cai, S. Wong, A. Garcia, and C. Sant'Anna, "From retrospect to prospect: Assessing modularity and stability from software architecture." In *Proceedings of the Joint Working Conference on Software Architecture & European Conference on Software Architecture (WICSA/ECSA 2009)*, pp. 269-272, 2009.

Unifying Definitions for Modularity, Abstraction, and Encapsulation as a Step Toward Foundational Multi-Paradigm Software Engineering Principles

Stephen W. Clyde
Computer Science Department
Utah State University
Logan, Utah, USA
email: stephen.clyde@usu.edu

Jorge Edison Lascano
Departamento de Ciencias de la Computación
Universidad de las Fuerzas Armadas ESPE
Sangolquí, Ecuador
email: edison_lascano@yahoo.com

Abstract—**The concepts of modularity, abstraction, and encapsulation have been an integral part of software engineering for over four decades. However, their definitions and application vary between software development paradigms. In some cases, conflicting definitions exist for a single paradigm. This paper first defines the concept of a principle for software-engineering, in general, and then provides a template for documenting principles so they can be easily referenced and taught. Next, it proposes initial unified definitions for modularity, abstraction, and encapsulation that are applicable to multiple programming paradigms. It then shows that these unified definitions for modularity, abstraction, and encapsulation are non-redundant but complimentary of each other. Finally, it discusses future work for refining and validating these unified definitions through a series of empirical studies.**

Keywords-software engineering principles; modularity; encapsulation; abstraction.

I. INTRODUCTION

Ideally, software engineers aim to build quality products on time and within budget [1, p. 8], where a quality product is one that supports the required functionality and has appropriate levels of understandability, testability, maintainability, efficiency, reliability, security, extensibility, openness, interoperability, reusability, and other desirable characteristics. On the surface, different programming paradigms appear to embrace different principles for helping developers achieve these characteristics. However, there are more commonalities than dissimilarities among these principles and developers would benefit from more general, unified definitions, especially as mixed-paradigm software development becomes more prevalent.

Object orientation (OO), which is currently the most common paradigm, places considerable importance on encapsulation and abstraction [2][3], but it also advocates modularity with low coupling and high cohesion [2][4]. Structural programming emphasizes modularization, but can be make use of control abstraction, certain kinds of data abstraction, and encapsulation. Functional programming (FP) emphasizes modularity and encapsulation using pure functions that have no side-effects [5][6], but also benefits from control abstraction. Logic programming (LP) emphasizes behavior (rule) and data (predicate) abstraction, but can leverage modularity and encapsulation. LP also takes advantage of control abstraction by hiding nearly all the underlying inference algorithm.

The *modularity*, *abstraction*, and *encapsulation* (MAE) principles are beneficial to virtually every programming paradigm. Unfortunately, there are no generally accepted definitions for the MAE principles or agreement on their application and potential benefits.

One problem is that software-engineering publications typically focus on a single paradigm, and if they define principles, do so using concepts and terms specific to that paradigm. Also, pressure to push the state-of-art forward and publish innovations encourages authors to reinvent or recast principles instead of adapting or generalizing existing work.

A lack of general, unifying definitions has led to overlapping and sometimes conflicting ideas about design principles. Consider for example, the SOLID principles [7]-[10], which are five design principles popular in object orientation (OO). Their definitions, which are specific to OO, have significant similarities with early work on the MAE principles, but differ in some subtle ways. Specifically, the first SOLID principle, called the *Single Responsibility Principle* (SRP), overlaps with the original notation of modularity for high cohesion but only deals with it at a class level [2, p. 54][11]. Similarly, the *Open/Closed Principle* overlaps with modularity for minimal coupling [2, p. 54], at least at a class-level. The five SOLID principles also overlap with themselves. For example, the *Interface Segregation Principle* can be re-cast as an application of SRP in the context of interface abstractions.

Literature about design principles is sparser for some paradigms than others. For example, there is relatively little written about design principles for FP and LP compared to OO and SP. This does not mean, that design principles are less important in these paradigms, but that developers are expected to carry them over from more mainstream paradigms, like OO and SP.

Problems caused by the lack of unified definitions for design principles is becoming more serious as new paradigms continue to emerge and programming languages evolve to support multiple paradigms. Java, C#, JavaScript, and C++, for example, now support mixed-paradigm approaches, where developers can use constructs from OO, FP, Aspect Orientation (AO), and Generic Programming (GP), and more, together within the same system [5][12].

This paper makes three initial contributions towards addressing this problem. First, Section II clarifies the purpose of software-engineering principles, in general, and distinguishes them from "best practices", idioms, and patterns. Section II also purposes a template for documenting principles that allows a principle's definition to go beyond just communicating the underlying concepts. Specifically, it provides a basis for assessing of adherence to the principle and a foundation for teaching the principle to programmers. Next, using this template, Sections III-V propose drafts of paradigm-independent definitions for the MAE principles. There are undoubtedly other paradigm-independent design principles besides the MAE, but these three are a good starting point because of their non-redundant yet complimentary relationships with each other. An explanation of these two relationships is given in Section VI and as another contribution of this paper.

The work presented here is not about inventing or reinventing the concepts of modularity, abstraction, or encapsulation. Instead, it aims to synthesize existing knowledge into a simple, accessible form for software developers and software-engineering education. Although this paper presents three contributions towards meeting this objective, it is just the first step that provides 1) a starting point for formulating research questions related to software quality across multiple paradigms, 2) a foundation for designing and conducting empirical studies, and 3) a basis for eventually defining metrics for systematically assessing quality in mixed-paradigm software systems. Section VII discusses these follow-on efforts in more detail, in addition to providing a summary of the contributions of this paper.

II. Design Principles

Before considering the MAE principles in detail and presenting unified definitions for them, it is necessary to first establish the meaning and purpose of software design principles and distinguish them from desirable characteristics, metrics, processes, best practices, patterns, idioms, and artifacts. This is important to reduce potential confusion, because existing literature uses a term, like "abstraction" to represent more than one of these ideas. For example, some authors define abstraction as the process or practice of isolating and distinguishing common features among objects [13]-[15]. Others define abstraction as software artifacts that specify conceptual boundaries between objects or types of objects [2, p. 38][16]. In this paper, we will define abstraction as a principle, and not as a process or artifact.

The Merriam-Webster and Oxford dictionaries define a *principle* as 1) a truth or proposition that supports reasoning, 2) a rule or code of conduct, or 3) an ingredient that imparts a characteristic quality (e.g., desirable characteristic) [17][18]. We specialize these definitions for software as follows: a *software design principle* is 1) a truth or proposition that supports reasoning about the desirable characteristics of a software system, 2) a rule for creating software with certain desirable characteristics, or 3) an aspect of software design that imparts certain desirable characteristics. In other words, a principle is a foundational concept (truth, proposition, rule, etc.) that leads to and supports reasoning about desirable characteristics, such as maintainability, efficiency, openness, reusability, etc.

If some concept, P, is a good principle for achieving a set of desirable characteristics Q, then the degree to which a software engineer adheres to P should predicate the degree to which Q is present in the software artifacts. In other words, the presence of Q is the goal or purpose of P. Ideally, the presence of Q in artifacts should be detectable or measurable through metrics based on the P [19][20]. However, creating valid and reliable metrics for measuring desirable qualities has proven to be challenging. We believe that one reason for this is that the principles upon which they are supposed to be based are not yet sufficiently defined and details about their relationships to desirable characteristics are still lacking.

Best practices are procedures or techniques that help developers adhere to principles without having to consider the details of a situation at a theoretical level. For example, consider the practices of "prefer aggregation over inheritance" and "program to an interface or abstract" [21][22]. By knowing and using these practices, a developer can improve modularity, abstraction, and encapsulation, without having to analyze in detail all the alternatives in terms of their resultant desirable characteristics. Unfortunately, best practices like these two tend to be specific to a programming paradigm or language.

Patterns also help developers achieve desirable characteristics; they exemplify principles by providing proven solutions to reoccurring problems in specific contexts [23]. Similarly, an idiom can help developers adhere to a principle by providing a solution for expressing a certain algorithm or data structure in a specific programming language [24].

Although software design principles are themselves not desirable characteristics, practices, patterns, idioms, or artifacts, they are at the heart of software engineering and their definitions should give developers the means to 1) reason about design decisions, 2) assess whether or how well a design either conforms to a principle, and 3) balance choices between conflicting objectives and design alternatives. The latter is important because software engineers must often make choices that weaken one desirable characteristic in favor of strengthening another. For example, a developer may have to sacrifice some extensibility in favor of efficiency.

Table I shows a template for capturing the definition of a software design principle in a way that accomplishes the three objectives listed above. As with practices, patterns, and idioms, a principle's *name* must accurately express the nature of the concept, because that name will become part of a vocabulary. The *essence* of a principle's definition is a short statement that aims to covey the fundamental concept at level that is understandable for most programmers and can be taught to beginning programmers. The essence should highlight the principles relationship to hoped-for desirable characteristics.

The next element of the template is a section that describes practices for following the principle and criteria that can be used to determine if a software system or component adheres to the principles. Like the essence, the practices and criteria need to be paradigm-agnostic and written a level that is understandable for most programmers.

TABLE I. PRINCIPLE-DEFINITION TEMPLATE

Name	*The name of the principle*
Essence	*A statement of the truth, proposition, or rule embodied in the principle and its relationship to hoped-for desirable characteristics*
Practices and Criteria	*Processes or criteria that, if followed, should help the developer adhere to the principle and lead to the hoped-for desirable characteristics*
Tradeoffs	*Factors that can help a developer decision when to go against a principle, in lieu of a conflicting objective. These factors may include the consequences of not meeting the criteria or common tradeoffs*
Paradigm Notes	*Notes about applying the principle in various paradigms*
Examples	*Good and poor examples in different paradigms*

The next element is a section that describes costs or other factors associated with following the principle that can help developers decide when to violate a principle, in lieu of some other conflicting objective. It may also include notes about the consequences of not meeting following the suggested practices or meeting the adherence criteria.

The last two elements of the template are optional, but serve to help developers apply a principle for a specific paradigm and to teach the principle to new programmers. Naturally, the knowledge captured in these two elements will be paradigm specific and could refer to a wide range of artifacts, like source code, build scripts, hyper-text, style sheets, and configuration files.

III. MODULARITY

Over the last 50 years, many respected authors have addressed the topic of modularity or modularization, which is the process of trying to achieve good modularity. One of the first was David Parnas, who, in 1972, outlined criteria for decomposing software into modules such that individual design decisions could be hidden in specific components [25]. His landmark paper set the stage for other research on using modularization to manage complexity [26]-[28].

These early works illuminated an important facet of good modularity, namely that a decision design, particularly one that is likely to change, should be isolated in one software component. We call this rule for modularity "localization of design decisions". By itself, this rule does not prescribe where the implementation of design decision should be placed, just that it should not be replicated or spread across multiple components. Failure to follow this rule leads to the "Duplicate Code" smell [29], which in turn can reduce maintainability.

Two other propositions or rules that are frequently associated with modularity are low coupling and high cohesion [4][30]-[32]. Low coupling exists when each component of a system is free of unnecessary dependencies (explicit or implied) on other components. Although coupling was first defined for SP, other definitions have been created for OO and AO [30][33]. It has even been applied to LP [34]. Cohesion is the degree to which the elements of one component relate to each other or the component's primary responsibility [31]. Ideally, each component should have a single responsibility, as advocated by SRP [7]. Like coupling, definitions for cohesion have been proposed in multiple paradigms [35]-[37].

Grady Booch said that the objective of modularization is "to build modules that are cohesive (by grouping logically related abstractions) and loosely coupled (by minimizing the dependencies among modules)" [2, p. 54]. It is widely believed that achieving low coupling and high cohesion results in software programs that are more understandable, testable, maintainable, reliable, secure, extensible, and reusable. It is also believed that they will avoid common code smells, like *Long Method*, *Large Class*, *Long Parameter List*, *Feature Envy*, and *Inappropriate Intimacy* [29][38].

Another facet of modularity deals with how far away from some component, *C*, a developer must look to reason about the functionality of *C*, particularly in preparation for making corrections or extensions. The component *C* has *modular reasoning* if a developer only needs to examine its implementation, public abstraction (e.g., its interface), and the public abstractions of referenced components [39]. *Extended modular reasoning* is a looser form of modularity, where developers also need to examine the internal details of referenced components [39]. *Global reasoning* is the loosest form of modularity, where developers may need to examine some other component in the system to reason about *C* [39]. A system comprised primarily of components with modular reasoning or extended modular reasoning is considered better than those with lots of components that require *global reasoning*. Some paradigms try to minimize global reasoning by introducing constructs that encourage the localization of certain design decisions, e.g., interfaces for responsibilities in OO and aspects for crosscutting concerns in AO.

Below is a definition for modularity, following the template given in Section II. This definition addresses the issues discussed above and is applicable to multiple programming paradigms. Due to the space limitations of this paper, the paradigm notes are limited and detailed examples are not show.

A. Essence

Modularity exists in a software system when it is comprised of loosely coupled and cohesive components that isolate each significant or changeable design decision in one component and ensure that related ideas are as close as possible. Modularity can improve understandability, testability maintainability, reliability, security, extensibility, and reuse. It can also help with collaboration during the software development process by outlining loosely coupled work units [2, p. 54].

B. Practices and Criteria

1) Localization of design decisions: Design decisions are identified and prioritized by significance and likelihood for future change. In a system with localization of design decisions, every significant or changeable decision is implemented in one component.

2) High cohesion: When making design decisions, a developer considers all the responsibilities of a given component and tries to ensure that there is just one or that responsibilities are all closely related. In a system with high cohesion, every component has one primary responsibility or reason to change. Component's primary responsibility may be a high level, when the component is an aggregate or when it directs behaviors in other components.

3) Low coupling: When making design decisions, a developer aims to minimize the degree and number of dependencies (explicit or hidden) between components. In a system with low coupling, the components are free of hidden dependent and unnecessary explicit dependencies. Also, explicit dependencies are directly visible in the code, e.g., data-type references and function calls.

4) Modular reasoning: Developers should give preference to decompositions with modular reasoning over extended modular reasoning, and to extended modular reasoning over global reasoning. A system has modular reasoning if developers can understand the details of a component by examining only its implementation, public abstraction, and the public abstractions of referenced components.

C. *Tradeoffs*

Localization of design decisions and high cohesion can lead to many fine grain components. Although these help with testability, extensibility, and reuse, it can sometimes hinder readability. One common solution is to package small, related components into aggregation components.

Although modularity by itself will not guarantee understandability, testability maintainability, reliability, security, extensibility, and reuse, the lack modularity will compromise these desirable characteristics. Adherence or violation of the modularity principles typically affects multiple components. For example, if a design decision is not localized, then it can comprise the maintainability of every component that deals with that design decision.

D. *Paradigm Notes*

Only snippets of the paradigm notes from the full principle definition are shown here.

For OO, packages, classes, and methods are the primary types of components that developers need to work with when modularizing, but they may also consider other types of artifacts like build scripts, configuration files, and style sheets. Composite components, like packages, often have multiple responsibilities, but those responsibilities should be cohesive as described above in practices and criteria section.

For FP, the components are primarily functions, but could also include other artifacts like build scripts. By definition, a pure function in FP only depends on values that are passed in as input parameters, so developers can minimize coupling by ensuring that a function's parameters represent nothing than exactly what the function needs.

For LP, the components are primarily predicates, rules, and facts. Modularity is achieved by doing three things. First, developers must ensure every predicate represents a single idea or responsibility. In other words, every predicate should be highly cohesive. Second, every interesting or potentially changeable decision decisions need to be localized. This is done by defining a predicate and set of rules for each design decision.

IV. Abstraction

From a process perspective, abstraction is the act of bringing certain details to the forefront while suppressing all others. John Guttag said that "the essence of abstractions is preserving information that is relevant in a given context, and forgetting information that is irrelevant in that context" [40]. This is something that most humans learn naturally as part of their cognitive and social development, in conjunction with learning to think conceptually and symbolically [41].

Nevertheless, it is interesting that a significant percentage of computer science students, and by extension software engineers, struggle with creating good software abstractions [15]. Perhaps, this is because creating good software abstractions are much harder to create than everyday abstractions. Software abstraction requires developers to sift through large and diverse collections of details about legacy systems, current and future requirements, existing and emerging technologies, tool-stack idiosyncrasies, work allocation nuances, and more, and then determine the most salient and distinguishing concepts. Fittingly, Abbott et al. described an abstraction as the "reification and conceptualization of a distinction" [13].

From an artifact perspective, every software component has an abstraction, independent of whether the developer thought about or declared it explicitly. A component's abstraction is everything about the component that is visible externally. Examples of common elements that contribute to component abstractions include descriptive or identifying labels like function names, class names, predicate names, and CSS style names; the public data members and methods of classes; the parameters of a function or method; meta-data annotations; and much more. None of these elements alone can represent a complete abstraction for the component to which they belong. A component's full abstraction consists of everything that other components might explicitly or implicitly depend on. Ideally, a full abstraction should be programmatically declared or documented, so it is readily accessible to developers and other components. However, this is rarely the case. Instead, components typically end up with leaky abstractions [42]. One reason for this is that developers often do not take the time to document all external discernable characteristics, like performance properties and side effects. Other sources of leaky abstractions are incomplete thinking, design errors, and implementation bugs that do not immediately contradict required functionality or exhibit damaging characteristics. Overtime, other components can come to depend on those erroneous characteristics. Then, when the original problems are corrected, all the components that depended on the erroneous characteristics fail.

Another potential problem is too much abstraction. This occurs when a component's abstraction does not expose all elements that others need to use or the abstraction does not provide sufficient parameterization for the elements that need to be customizable. These kinds of problem lead to lack of flexibility, which in turn leads to sloppy hacks that can compromise the overall quality of a system.

Below is a simple definition for the abstraction principle that can help developers capture and communicate meaningful abstractions without leakage or over abstraction. The definition is sufficiently broad to cover control, function, behavior, and data abstraction. Note that the abstraction principle by itself does not address the placement or organization of design decisions, i.e., the decomposition of a system into components. The modularity principle guides decomposition and refactoring. Instead, the abstraction principle focuses on exposing and communicating the right aspects of a component, namely those that others will need to depend on.

A. Essence

For each component, there is an explicit and clear declaration of the component's accessible features or functionality. Depending on the paradigm and programming language, this declaration may be part of the source code, meta data, or documentation. The exposed features and functionality should be no more and no less than what other components may need or depend on.

Adherence to the abstraction principle can improve understandability, testability, maintainability, and reusability. It can also allow developers to follow modularity more effectively, because it will bring to light weakness with localization of design decisions, unnecessary coupling, and low cohesion.

B. Practices and Criteria

1) Meaningful labels and identifiers: A system has meaningful labels and identifiers, when each one expresses the essence and distinguishing aspect(s) of its associated component or element.

2) Context-aware labels and identifiers: This exists when the label or identifier for a component does not contain redundant information that can be inferred from the component's context or scope. For example, a method called *GetFirstName* in a Person class makes for better abstraction than *GetPersonFirstName*, because the context of person can be derived from the class name.

3) Abstraction completeness: Whenever possible, all externally visible characteristics for a component are explicitly declared as part of the component's definition, implementation, or meta data. When that is not possible, documentation must explain these characteristics clearly and concisely, and the closer document is to the component's implementation, the better.

4) Abstraction sufficiency: This exists when all the elements of a component that should be visible to outside components are exposed through the component's abstraction.

C. Tradeoffs

Not following the practices and criteria listed above can result in the loss of the hoped-for desirable characteristics in portion to the degree and amount of non-adherence.

D. Paradigm Notes

Only snippets from the notes for LP are shown here to give the reader a sense of what this part of the full definition contains.) As mentioned, the primary components in LP are predicates, rules, and facts. The abstractions for these components expose the "logic" of system while hiding most of its control aspects, namely the process for drawing conclusions or deductions. Predicates represent relations from the problem domain or design decision. Given a predicate, all the rules with the predicate in their heads and facts stated with that predicate form another kind of higher level abstraction in LP. One of these abstractions exposes all that is known about a relation or decision.

The abstraction for a predicate is comprised of a name and some number of parameters. A developer should choose a name that expresses the predicate's essence clearly, concisely, and accurately. Doing so not only improves understandability from an abstraction perspective, it helps with modular reasoning, which in turn contributes to better modularity. Facts and rules are typically given labels in LP, but can be grouped together into higher level packages to form higher level abstractions.

V. ENCAPSULATION

Encapsulation is typically equated with OO, but it is not unique to OO nor did it originate with OO. In fact, many old devices, like mechanical clocks from the middle ages, are good examples of encapsulation. All their implementation details, e.g., the time keeping mechanisms, are hidden behind a clock face in a sealed container.

In English, encapsulation means to enclose something inside a capsule or container [43]. In other words, it involves two things: the thing is being enclosed and the enclosure. In physical systems, like a train station that needs a clock, the choices for enclosures are relatively limited compared to those available in software systems, where developers have total control over the system's decomposition. As described in Section III, modularity can guide a developer in making good choices for the components, i.e., enclosures, such that each has a cohesive purpose and is loosely coupled to others. Abstraction, as discussed in Section IV, can help developers communicate the essence of component and expose only external characteristics. The principle of encapsulation can then help developers isolate or hide the internal characteristics of a component so others do not accidently become dependent on them.

Unfortunately, the close relationship among encapsulation, abstraction, and modularity has led to some ambiguity in use of these terms. This is particularly true for encapsulation. The various definitions for encapsulation in software engineering literature can be grouped into three categories. The first category includes definition that equate encapsulation to the bundling of data with operations on that data to create *Abstract Data Types* [44][45]. These definitions take either a process or artifact perspective, but typically lack a proposition, rule, or practice that qualify them as principle definitions. Also, these definitions sometimes overshadow or ignore modularity and its associated criteria like localization of design decisions, low coupling, high cohesion, and modular reasoning.

The second category includes definitions that represent encapsulation as a process or technique for hiding decisions behind logical barriers, preventing outsiders from modifying or even viewing the implementation details of components. This category of encapsulation definitions stems from work on information hiding, which is the dual of abstraction. It has given rise to access-restricting language constructs, such as the *private* and *protected* modifiers in class-based languages. Although definitions of this category are valuable by themselves, they do not capture encapsulation's full potential.

In the third category, definitions explain encapsulation as a process for organizing components so the implementation details of one component can be modified without causing a ripple effect to other components [46]. These definitions focus on the minimization of inter-component dependencies, i.e., coupling. By themselves, these definitions miss other important aspects of encapsulation and blur it with modularization.

There are many documented "best practices" that experts believe can help programmers achieve good encapsulations. For example, in C#, experts believe that the use of auto-implemented properties is much better than public data members because they provide for stronger barrier between the abstraction and implementation details [47]. Unfortunately, such "best practices" tend to be language or paradigm specific.

As mentioned earlier, a design principle must be a truth, proposition, rule, or practice that yields desirable qualities. Below is a definition for encapsulation that aims to comply with this requirement for principles and can guide a developer achieve good encapsulation, independent developer's adherence to the principles of modularity and abstraction.

A. Essence

Ensure that the private implementation details (i.e., the internal characteristics) of a component are insulated so they cannot be accessed or modified by other components. Doing so will lead to better testability, maintainability, and reliability. It will also help with a clear separation of concerns and avoid accidental coupling.

B. Practices and Criteria

1) Conceptual barriers: For each component, a developer should identify the internal structures, behaviors, procedures, and definitions of that component and ensure that they are protected behind conceptual barriers. More specifically, developers should try to identify the minimum required scope for each internal element. For example, in OO, if a data member is only used within the scope invocations for a single method, then that data member should be refactored to a local variable of the method.

2) Programmatic barriers: Developers should ensure that the modifiability and visibility of every internal element is programmatically restricted to the desired scope. Developers should leverage the available features of the chosen programming language, whenever possible.

3) Usage barriers: If there are internal elements that cannot be isolated programmatically, then document appropriate rules for correct usage of the component, so developers can avoid accidental violations of the intended encapsulation.

C. Tradeoffs

Failure to protect a component's internal characteristics from other components opens the doors for abstraction leakage and hidden dependencies, which can damage testability, maintainability, and reliability in surreptitious ways. In cases where programmers are tempted to weaken the encapsulation of some element in a component, like make a data member in a class definition public, they could at least document the intended usage to minimize the formation of accidental hidden dependencies.

D. Paradigm Notes

Only a few snippets of the full paradigm notes are shown here. The mechanisms for achieving encapsulation vary greatly among paradigms and programming languages. For FP in compiled languages, functions can be strongly encapsulated behind their declarations. This is true even for anonymous function. But, for interpretative languages that support FP, functions are just other forms of data and the decisions they encapsulate may be externally visible and modifiable. In those cases, developers need to document what others may and may not access or change.

For OO and typed languages, developers can restrict the scope for each element to the smallest scope within which the element is used. Data members, for example, are typically private and made accessible only through methods. Some languages provide convenience short hands for getter and setter methods to help programming adhere to this best practice. Only methods that need to be used by other components should be public. Also, developers can use package-level scoping to restrict access to public classes or method that are only needed within a package.

VI. The Non-Redundancy and Complimentary Nature of the MAE Principles

To be effective for multiple paradigms and for the long-term advancement of software engineering, it is important for general principles to be non-redundant with each other in two ways: 1) no general principle can be a special case of or subsumed by another principle or combination of principles and 2) developers should be able to choose to follow one principle but not the others.

The case for MAE principles meeting the first is condition is relatively straight forward. The essence of modularity deals with the decomposition of a system into components. Neither of the other two principles prescribe guidelines for organizing a system into modules. So, modularity cannot be subsumed by abstraction or encapsulation, and conversely. Abstraction and encapsulation both apply to individual components, which from an artifact perspective, can be thought of as "abstractions" and "encapsulations." However, abstraction and encapsulation from a principle perspective are fundamentally different from each other. In fact, from a principle perspective, they are approximate duals of each other. Abstraction guides a developer in exposing just the right elements of a component so it is easy to understand and use. Encapsulation guides a developer in hiding internal design decisions so other components cannot intentionally or accidentally depend on them. Abstraction cannot be recast or explained as a special type, variation, or subpart of encapsulation. Similarly, encapsulation cannot be fully explained in terms of just abstraction.

The satisfaction of the second condition for non-redundancy can be shown using a simple example plus three variations, where each one illustrates adherence to one principle but not the others. The example, shown in Figure 1, consists of two classes: *Line* and *Point*, where the *Point* class represents movable points in a 2D coordinate space and the *Line* class represents lines comprised of two points and that know how to compute their own lengths. Fig. 1 shows an implementation that of this simple system that has good modularity, abstraction, and encapsulation according to the definition given in Sections III-V.

```
public class Line {
  private Point point1;
  private Point point2;

  public Line(Point point1, Point point2) {
      this.point1 = point1;
      this.point2 = point2;
  }

  public double ComputeLength() { /* .. */ }
}

public class Point {
  private double x, y;

  public Point(double x, double y) {
    this.x = x; this.y = y; }

  public double getX() { return x; }
  public void moveX(double deltaX) { x += deltaX;}
  public double getY() { return y; }
  public void moveY(double deltaY) { y += deltaY;}
}
```

Figure 1. A simple example implementation with good modularity, abstraction, and encapsulation.

In the first variation (see Fig. 2), the designs decisions are still localized, the classes still have low coupling and high cohesion, and they support modular reasoning. In other words, the system's decomposition has good modularity. However, the system has poor abstraction or encapsulation, caused unnecessary exposure of the internal design decisions and by poor identifiers, which are either do not communicate the true essence of the elements. Of course, there could be other ways that the abstraction and encapsulation could be degraded, but

```
public class Line {
  public XY point1;
  public XY point2;
  public Line(XY point1, XY point2) { /* … / }
  public double Calc() { /* Compute length … */ }
}

public class XY {
  public double x, y;
  public XY(double x, double y) { /* … / }
}
```

Figure 2. A simple example implement with good modularity, but poor abstraction and encapsulation.

the purpose of this example is to simply show that modularity can exist without abstraction and encapsulation.

In the second variation (see Fig. 3), the *Line* and *Point* classes have good abstractions, but lack modularity and encapsulation. Specifically, the class definition expose the functionality that other components need to use, with sufficient flexibility. However, the decision for calculating the distance between two points is not localized, which goes against the modularity principle, and the data members in both classes are public, which violates the intended encapsulation.

```
public class Line {
  public Point point1;
  public Point point2;

  public Line(Point point1, Point point2) {/* … */}

  public double ComputeLength()
  {
    return Math.sqrt(Math.pow(point2.getX() -
                         point1.getX(), 2) +
                    Math.pow(point2.getY() -
                         point1.getY(), 2));
  }
}

public class Point {
  public double x, y;

  public Point(double x, double y) { /* … *. }

  public double getX() { return x; }
  public void moveX(double deltaX) { x += deltaX;}
  public double getY() { return y; }
  public void moveY(double deltaY) { y += deltaY;}

  public double ComputeDistance(Point otherPoint)
  {
    return Math.sqrt(Math.pow(otherPoint.x - x, 2) +
                    Math.pow(otherPoint.x - y, 2));
  }
}
```

Figure 3. A simple example implementation with good abstraction, but poor modularity and encapsulation.

A third variation with good encapsulation but poor modularity and abstraction would be an implementation that had the poor names, i.e., poor abstraction, from the first variation plus the lack of localization of decision designs, i.e., poor modularity, from the second variation.

These three variations show that it is possible for a developer to apply each of the three MAE principles, independently of each other. In fact, there may be some special circumstances where this is exactly what a developer needs to do to meet external requirements or adjust for limitations of a programming language or framework. However, such cases should be rare.

Although the MAE principles are non-redundant, they complement each other nicely. In other words, adherence to one encourages, but does not require, adherence to the others. Specifically, adhering to modularity will set the stage for adherence both abstraction and encapsulation, because modularity brings to light what the components need to know about each other and which the design decisions need to be encapsulated. Likewise, abstraction can lead to better understanding of the inter-component couplings and therefore better modularization. Also, elements that are not part of a component's abstraction are candidates for encapsulation. Finally, doing encapsulation will act as a double check and balance for both modularization and abstraction.

VII. SUMMARY AND FUTURE WORK

This paper has explained the purpose of design principles, in general, and provided a template for establishing working definitions that can help with teaching the principles to software developers, assessing adherence, and pursuing research questions. This paper then provided an overview of existing ideas related to modularity, abstraction, and encapsulation and unifying them into initial paradigm-independent definitions. Finally, it showed that these principles are non-redundant and complimentary, in the sense that no combination of two could replace the third and that adherence to one encourage adherence to the others.

The work reported in this paper is just one step forward in a larger effort. Our next step is to formulate research questions related the application of MAE principles in mixed-paradigm environments and then setup concrete empirical studies to explore those questions. Below is a sampling of the research questions that we hope to pursue soon:

- When using OO together with LP, what kinds of functionality or responsibility are best handled using LP?
- When using OO with LP, FP, or GP, is it best to design the overall architecture using an OO approach and encapsulate specific responsibilities in LP-based, FP-based, or GP-based components? If so, why and what kinds of components are best suited for LP, FP, and GP?
- What kinds of responsibilities are best encapsulated in aspects when using AO with OO?
- When using FP with OO, how can developer know if high-order functions are following the MAE principles?

After exploring these and other research questions, we believe that another important step would be to explore metrics for systematically assessing quality in mixed-paradigm software systems. The details of any given metric may end up being platform dependent. However, if there were a suite of metrics based on a unified principle definition, then the metrics might yield measurements that are comparable across software components, even when those components are implemented with different languages or paradigms.

Finally, our plans for future work include investigations into other design principles beyond MAE. For example, we hope to unify definitions for classification and generalization/ specialization. Although these principles are heavily used in OO, they can apply to other paradigms as well.

Overall, the effort to unify principle definitions is important as programming languages continue to expand to support multi-paradigm software development. This effort will require input from many different sources and involve a wide range of subfields within software engineering. To this end, we welcome and encourage collaboration from all who are interested in creating a stronger foundation for software methods, teaching software engineering, improving development tools, or assessing software quality.

REFERENCES

[1] I. Sommerville, Software Engineering, 10 edition. Boston: Pearson, 2015.

[2] G. Booch, R. A. Maksimchuk, M. W. Engle, B. J. Young, J. Conallen, and K. A. Houston, Object-Oriented Analysis and Design with Applications, 3 edition. Upper Saddle River, NJ: Addison-Wesley Professional, 2007.

[3] "Abstraction (software engineering)," Wikipedia. 06-Jun-2017.

[4] I. Candela, G. Bavota, B. Russo, and R. Oliveto, "Using Cohesion and Coupling for Software Remodularization: Is It Enough?," ACM Trans Softw Eng Methodol, vol. 25, no. 3, pp. 24:1–24:28, Jun. 2016.

[5] "Functional programming," Wikipedia. 03-Jun-2017.

[6] "Purely functional programming," Wikipedia. 10-Apr-2017.

[7] R. C. Martin, "The Principles of OOD," PrinciplesOfOod, 2005. [Online]. Available: http://butunclebob.com/ArticleS.UncleBob.PrinciplesOfOod. [Accessed: 07-Jun-2017].

[8] R. C. Martin, "Getting a SOLID start. - Clean Coder," 2009. [Online]. Available: https://sites.google.com/site/unclebobconsultingllc/getting-a-solid-start. [Accessed: 07-Jun-2017].

[9] S. Metz, "SOLID Object-Oriented Design - GORUCO 2009." [Online]. Available: http://confreaks.tv/videos/goruco2009-solid-object-oriented-design. [Accessed: 07-Jun-2017].

[10] R. C. Martin, Agile Software Development, Principles, Patterns, and Practices, International ed edition. Harlow: Pearson Education Limited, 2013.

[11] T. DeMarco and P. J. Plauger, Structured Analysis and System Specification, 1 edition. Englewood Cliffs, N.J: Prentice Hall, 1979.

[12] "Comparison of multi-paradigm programming languages," Wikipedia. 22-Mar-2017.

[13] R. Abbott and C. Sun, "Abstraction Abstracted," in Proceedings of the 2Nd International Workshop on The Role of Abstraction in Software Engineering, New York, NY, USA, 2008, pp. 23–30.

[14] "abstraction | cognitive process," Encyclopedia Britannica. [Online]. Available: https://www.britannica.com/topic/abstraction. [Accessed: 06-Sep-2017].

[15] J. Kramer, "Is Abstraction the Key to Computing?," Commun ACM, vol. 50, no. 4, pp. 36–42, Apr. 2007.

[16] W. R. Cook, "On Understanding Data Abstraction, Revisited," in Proceedings of the 24th ACM SIGPLAN Conference on Object Oriented Programming Systems Languages and Applications, New York, NY, USA, 2009, pp. 557–572.

[17] "Definition of PRINCIPLE." [Online]. Available: https://www.merriam-webster.com/dictionary/principle. [Accessed: 07-Jun-2017].

[18] "principle - definition of principle in English | Oxford Dictionaries," Oxford Dictionaries | English. [Online]. Available: https://en.oxforddictionaries.com/definition/principle. [Accessed: 07-Jun-2017].

[19] V. R. Basili, G. Calderia, and H. D. Rombach, "The Goal Question Metric Approach," in Encyclopedia of Software Engineering, vol. 2, John Wiley & Sons Ltd, 1994, pp. 528–532.
[20] C. N. Sant'Anna, A. F. Garcia, C. von F. G. Chavez, C. J. de L. Lucena, and A. von Staa, "On the reuse and maintenance of aspect-oriented software: An assessment framework," in Proc. 17th Brazilian Symposium on Software Engineering, Manaus, Brazil, 2003.
[21] "GOF Advice: Favor Aggregation over Inheritance | Net Objectives." [Online]. Available: http://www.netobjectives.com/competencies/favor-aggregation-over-inheritance. [Accessed: 06-Sep-2017].
[22] E. Freeman, B. Bates, K. Sierra, and E. Robson, Head First Design Patterns: A Brain-Friendly Guide, 1st edition. Sebastopol, CA: O'Reilly Media, 2004.
[23] E. Gamma, R. Helm, R. Johnson, J. Vlissides, and G. Booch, Design Patterns: Elements of Reusable Object-Oriented Software, 1 edition. Reading, Mass: Addison-Wesley Professional, 1994.
[24] A. J. Perlis and S. Rugaber, "Programming with Idioms in APL," in Proceedings of the International Conference on APL: Part 1, New York, NY, USA, 1979, pp. 232–235.
[25] D. L. Parnas, "On the Criteria to Be Used in Decomposing Systems into Modules," Commun ACM, vol. 15, no. 12, pp. 1053–1058, Dec. 1972.
[26] G. J. Myers, Composite/Structured Design. New York: Van Nostrand Reinhold, 1978.
[27] B. H. Liskov, "A Design Methodology for Reliable Software Systems," in Proceedings of the December 5-7, 1972, Fall Joint Computer Conference, Part I, New York, NY, USA, 1972, pp. 191–199.
[28] D. L. Parnas, P. C. Clements, and D. M. Weiss, "The Modular Structure of Complex Systems," IEEE Trans. Softw. Eng., vol. SE-11, no. 3, pp. 259–266, Mar. 1985.
[29] M. Fowler, K. Beck, J. Brant, W. Opdyke, D. Roberts, and E. Gamma, Refactoring: Improving the Design of Existing Code, 1 edition. Reading, MA: Addison-Wesley Professional, 1999.
[30] Y. Press and L. L. Constantine, Structured Design: Fundamentals of a Discipline of Computer Program and Systems Design, 1 edition. Englewood Cliffs, N.J: Prentice Hall, 1979.
[31] W. P. Stevens, G. J. Myers, and L. L. Constantine, "Structured Design," IBM Syst J, vol. 13, no. 2, pp. 115–139, Jun. 1974.
[32] S. R. Chidamber and C. F. Kemerer, "A Metrics Suite for Object Oriented Design," IEEE Trans Softw Eng, vol. 20, no. 6, pp. 476–493, Jun. 1994.
[33] M. H. Samadzadeh and S. J. Khan, "Stability, Coupling, and Cohesion of Object-oriented Software Systems," in Proceedings of the 22Nd Annual ACM Computer Science Conference on Scaling Up : Meeting the Challenge of Complexity in Real-world Computing Applications: Meeting the Challenge of Complexity in Real-world Computing Applications, New York, NY, USA, 1994, pp. 312–319.
[34] S. Kramer and H. Kaindl, "Coupling and Cohesion Metrics for Knowledge-based Systems Using Frames and Rules," ACM Trans Softw Eng Methodol, vol. 13, no. 3, pp. 332–358, Jul. 2004.
[35] G. Gui and P. D. Scott, "Coupling and Cohesion Measures for Evaluation of Component Reusability," in Proceedings of the 2006 International Workshop on Mining Software Repositories, New York, NY, USA, 2006, pp. 18–21.
[36] A. Kumar, R. Kumar, and P. S. Grover, "Towards a Unified Framework for Cohesion Measurement in Aspect-Oriented Systems," in Proceedings of 19th Australian Conference on Software Engineering, Australia, 2008, pp. 57–65.
[37] B. C. da Silva, C. Sant'Anna, and C. Chavez, "Concern-based Cohesion As Change Proneness Indicator: An Initial Empirical Study," in Proceedings of the 2Nd International Workshop on Emerging Trends in Software Metrics, New York, NY, USA, 2011, pp. 52–58.
[38] "Code Smells," Code Smells. [Online]. Available: https://sourcemaking.com/smells. [Accessed: 08-Jun-2017].
[39] G. Kiczales and M. Mezini, "Aspect-oriented Programming and Modular Reasoning," in Proceedings of the 27th International Conference on Software Engineering, New York, NY, USA, 2005, pp. 49–58.
[40] J. Guttag, Introduction to Computation and Programming Using Python. The MIT Press, 2013.
[41] J. Piaget and B. Inhelder, The Psychology Of The Child, 2 edition. New York: Basic Books, 1969.
[42] "The Law of Leaky Abstractions," Joel on Software, 11-Nov-2002. [Online]. Available: https://www.joelonsoftware.com/2002/11/11/the-law-of-leaky-abstractions/. [Accessed: 18-May-2017].
[43] "Definition of ENCAPSULATE." [Online]. Available: https://www.merriam-webster.com/dictionary/encapsulate. [Accessed: 10-Jun-2017].
[44] "Encapsulation (computer programming)," Wikipedia. 08-Jun-2017.
[45] "Abstract data type," Wikipedia. 10-Jun-2017.
[46] "Encapsulation & Modularity." [Online]. Available: https://atomicobject.com/resources/oo-programming/encapsulation-modularity. [Accessed: 10-Jun-2017].
[47] B. Wagner, "Auto-Implemented Properties (C# Programming Guide)." [Online]. Available: https://docs.microsoft.com/en-us/dotnet/csharp/programming-guide/classes-and-structs/auto-implemented-properties. [Accessed: 10-Jun-2017].

iMobile: A Framework to Implement Software Agents for the iOS Platform

Pedro Augusto da Silva e Souza Miranda, Andrew Diniz da Costa, Carlos José Pereira de Lucena
Laboratório de Engenharia de Software – LES
Pontifícia Universidade Católica do Rio de Janeiro
Rio de Janeiro, Brazil
email: pedro.augusto@les.inf.puc-rio.br, email: andrew@les.inf.puc-rio.br, email: lucena@inf.puc-rio.br

***Abstract*—Appropriate implementation of software agents for the iOS platform able to represent their main features, such as distribution, autonomy and pro-activity, is still an open issue. Therefore, this paper proposes the iMobile Framework that allows the creation of software agents for applications (apps) made for iPhone and iPad devices. A developed scenario demonstrates the applicability of the proposed framework, where an app allows registration of issues identified in some company. The main goal of the software agents is to speed up the process of contacting people, as quickly as possible, to solve critical issues.**

Keywords-mobile computing; software agent; framework; iOS platform.

I. INTRODUCTION

Currently, the development of complex apps for mobile platforms (e.g., iOS and Android), which have autonomous, pro-active and distributed entities, is common. Taking this scenario into consideration, the use of software agents [2][3][4][16][39][40] is expected.

In the literature, there are several proposals [1][5][6][15][17][18][29][30] that help the development of software agents. However, few solutions are directed to mobile environments, such as agents being executed in smartphones and tablets. Even with the exponential evolution of hardware used for manufacturing, mobile device memory, processing and disk drive space are still concerns. In most cases, an important reason is that a mobile operating system (OS) has very restricted policies regarding what an application may or may not do with its memory, processor and disk drive. This situation is different from desktop applications, where services may run in the background until the user stops the application, or when the OS is shut down.

One of the best-known mobile-oriented frameworks is JADE-Leap [5]. It is an extension of the Java Agent Development Framework (JADE) framework [6], but with a limited feature set. JADE already offers support to the implementation of autonomous and pro-active agents. Such limitation of features by JADE-Leap was defined to avoid performance issues when ran on tablets or smartphones. Furthermore, JADE-Leap was developed in Java [9] and it may not be used on the iOS platform.

In 2014, Apple presented a new programming language for the iOS platform, called Swift. It came to replace the Objective-C, the language used for many years to develop the iOS apps. Thereafter, in 2015, a library called GameplayKit [35] was presented to offer the collection of foundational tools and technologies for building games. One of the facilities provided was to simulate characters of a game to react based on high-level goals and to react to their surroundings. GameplayKit used the agent term to represent these characters, however, it did not reproduce all characteristics that represent software agents [2][3][4], such as sociability.

According to [31], Swift is a programming language that quickly became one of the fastest growing languages in history. Swift has been an open source since 2015. It was widely adopted by developers and now is one of the top 10 most-searched languages on the internet [32].

Considering the growth of this language and the complexity of developing iOS apps, approaches that help to improve software agents for the iOS platform are expected. Then, based on this context, this paper presents the iMobile, a practical development framework. It allows the creation of software agents for the iOS platform using native resources, such as the Bonjour API [20], which helps the discovery of devices and services published on networks. Consequently, the agents' development for the iOS environment will be easier and faster with iMobile.

This paper is organized as follows: Section II describes the related works that helped to identify which information could and should be represented in an agent framework for the iOS platform. In Section III, the proposed iMobile framework is explained in detail. In Section IV, a use case scenario that extends the iMobile framework and uses agents to speed up the process of contacting people, as quickly as possible, in order to solve critical issues in a company, is presented. Finally, in Section V, the conclusions and future works are presented.

II. RELATED WORKS

In order to propose a framework that could help to create software agents to the iOS platform, several frameworks offered in the literature, that allow the agents' development, were studied. The main works that greatly influenced our proposal are presented below.

As mentioned in Section I, JADE-Leap [5] is an extension of the JADE Framework [6]. It allows the use of software agents in a variety of mobile platforms, such as Android and MIDP (Mobile Information Device Profile) [12]. In the JADE framework, agents inhabit containers and every JADE agent application must have a main container, in which all secondary agents on the system are registered. Containers are Java processes that provide the JADE run-time and all the necessary services for hosting and executing agents [13].

From the JADE framework, you may create software agents that are able to trade messages with each other, change behaviors and migrate to another container. JADE agents are

Foundation for Intelligent Physical Agents (FIPA) compliant [14], which means that they obey certain structures when they are trading messages. These messages, called Agent Communication Language (ACL), meet FIPA's ACL standards. The ACL message standard considers a protocol that allows message exchanges between agents, even if they are in different systems. Each ACL message has, at least, one receiver, one language and one ontology, which are the message context and the message content itself. More details about that standard can be seen at [28].

JADE LEAP extends all these JADE features for a mobile environment using the same concept of containers. In other words, JADE LEAP, just as JADE, forces the user to have a fixed IP server in order to make its agents communicate with each other. Then, for years, JADE and JADE LEAP were useful and mature agents' frameworks, besides being excellent standards to begin understanding how to work with software agents. However, they were created from the Java language and cannot be used for the iOS platform.

Another known solution analyzed was the Jadex framework [15]. The JADE framework was developed from the Java language and it implements the Belief, Desire and Intent (BDI) concept [16] for the software agents. BDI stands for:(i) Belief, (ii) Desire and (iii) Intention. Belief represents the group of information that an agent has concerning its environment and itself. Desire represents the agent's wishes and directly influences its actions to achieve its goals. Intention represents the selected desire to be achieved by the agent. Therefore, the intention is the momentary state of the agent until the plan has been executed and its results analyzed.

It was very important to learn about JADE, Jadex and implementing examples of both frameworks (for instance, examples with until 30 agents simultaneously executing) to better understand how a multi-agent software works and how agents communicate between themselves.

BDI4JADE [18] is another framework that, as the name implies, extends the JADE framework. BDI4JADE allows JADE developers to design multi-agents systems with agents that implement BDI architecture. The main motivation for the BDI4JADE creation is because the JADE framework is not Domain Specific Language (DSL), in other words, it is not dependent like JADEX and JACK [17] on another agent framework. The work in [18] informs that BDI4JADE, even though based on general purpose programming languages, limits the integration with up-to-date, available technologies and the use of advanced features of the underlying programming language. Therefore, BDI4JADE agents are called BDI agents. These agents have a reasoning cycle. The algorithm used for the implementation of BDI4JADE reasoning cycle is presented by the work in [18]. The reasoning cycle contains six main procedures, that involve revising agent's beliefs and desire management and generation, removing agent's undesired desires and agents' intentions generation (selected desires within all desires and the unselected ones are still desires, but not intentions) and updating intentions status (working, finished, fail, etc.). For more details of the framework, please see [16] and [18].

All the proposals mentioned are known frameworks in the community and they allow the development of software agents. However, none of these approaches allow the creation of agents for the iOS platform. Moreover, considering such a platform, to have a framework that could use native resources would bring a set of advantages that have not been properly exploited, such as better performance, easier understanding to develop from the language used, in order to create new iOS apps, and the reuse of known libraries that help to represent agents' concepts (e.g., communication among agents, distribution, etc.).

In Table I, the main features of the iMobile Framework, in comparison with other known software agent frameworks, are presented. It is important to notice that iMobile was created to offer support to the iOS platform and, in addition, the framework followed recommendations offered by FIPA, such as providing services of yellow pages to meet agents. It is also relevant to mention that since the iMobile framework uses Bonjour Networking services to solve network communication between agents, there is no need for a main container like the JADE framework. Agent services are published in the same DNS-Zone [42]. For local network communication, a DNS-Zone is not necessary.

TABLE I. COMPARISON OF IMOBILE WITH OTHER AGENT FRAMEWORKS

Features	**Agent Frameworks**		
	iMob ile	***JADE/JA DE Leap***	***JA DEX***
Offering multiple agent's behaviors	Yes	Yes	Ye s
Offering distributed agents	Yes	Yes	Ye s
Allowing the communication between one or more agents	Yes	Yes	Ye s
Representing the BDI concept	No	No	Ye s
Offering iOS support	Yes	No	No
Offering services of yellow pages	Yes	Yes	Ye s

III. IMOBILE FRAMEWORK

This section presents the iMobile Framework that allows the development of software agents for the iOS platform. The iMobile agents are able to manage the gathering and to exchange and display information from a given iOS app. Furthermore, the framework helps to discover agents that are on the same network to identify rendered services and to exchange messages.

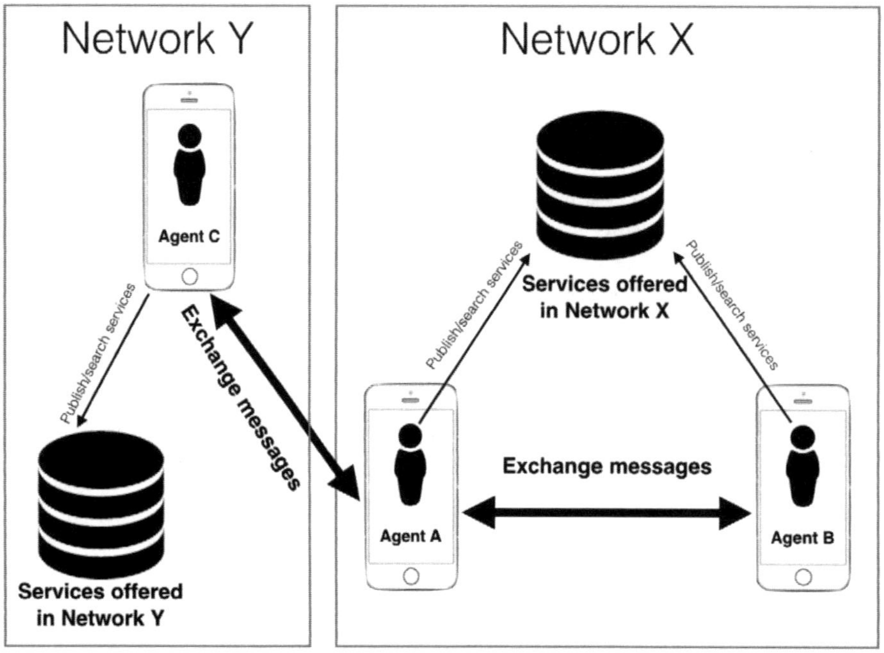

Figure 1. Use case scenario to apply the iMobile framework.

Figure 1 shows an example that illustrates the main idea behind how iMobile may be used. In this image, there are three iPhones connected to some network (Network X or Y). Each iPhone has an iMobile agent that may exchange messages with agents on the same or a different network. For each network, there is a database with all services offered for agents connected on the same network. Then, to discover such available services, it is not necessary to directly exchange messages with other agents. To discover and publish services and exchange messages among agents, iMobile uses an API [21] offered by Apple and which is explained in detail on the next subsection. Therefore, the overall communication is performed and it is not necessary to create containers and platforms as it is to other frameworks, such as JADE, JADE-Leap and JADEX.

In order to present how the iMobile framework was created, an overview of the architecture is demonstrated in subsection A. Then, in subsection B, the hot-spots and frozen-spots [36] are explained in detail. In subsection C, a guiding step to instantiate the framework is described.

A. Architecture Overview

Figure 2 presents the framework's class diagram. It is possible to realize that a software agent (*Agent* class) may execute a set of behaviors (*Behavior* class). Two different types of behaviors are offered by the framework: Cyclic Behavior (*CyclicBehavior* class) and One-Shot Behavior (*OneShotBehavior* class). The first one is a type of action that executes in loop. On the other hand, the second executes an action only once.

At any time, an agent may send or receive some message (*AgentMessage* class) from some agent. *AgentMessage* implements the *NSCoding* protocol [24], which is already offered by Apple, to allow the serialization of messages to be sent to other agents.

iMobile allows that agents, on the same network, may exchange messages among themselves faster, aiming to offer a polite communication solution. The technology that helps this improved communication is the Bonjour API. It is a solution created by Apple for the iOS platform and which is a zero-configuration network solution [21], that has a very important role on the design of this framework. Zero-configuration means that you may publish services on a network without the need of any network troubleshooting.

In order to use the Bonjour API, iMobile offers the *BonjourServer* class, which is used by the agent to look for services offered by agents (from the *NSNetServiceBrowser* class) to publish its services (from the *NSNetService* class) and to send and receive messages to/from other agents (from the *NSNetService* class). *BonjourServer* applies the Façade design pattern [37][40] to offer all the necessary methods to agents to perform these actions. In addition, iMobile offers a protection against object substitution attacks, because *AgentMessage* class implement the *NSSecureCoding* protocol [42]. If developers desire to provide some additional treatment of the data (e.g., performing cryptography), they may use some native library that is available at [43].

B. *Hot-spots and Frozen-spots*

Below, the hot-spots defined by iMobile and registered by using the stereotype <<hot-spot>>, in Figure 2, are explained in detail.

Representing a software agent (*Agent* Class): There are two ways of developing an agent: (i) creating an instance of the *Agent* class, and (ii) defining a new class that extends the *Agent* class to represent the desired agent. Each agent has a name, may offer a set of services and may execute a set of behaviors.

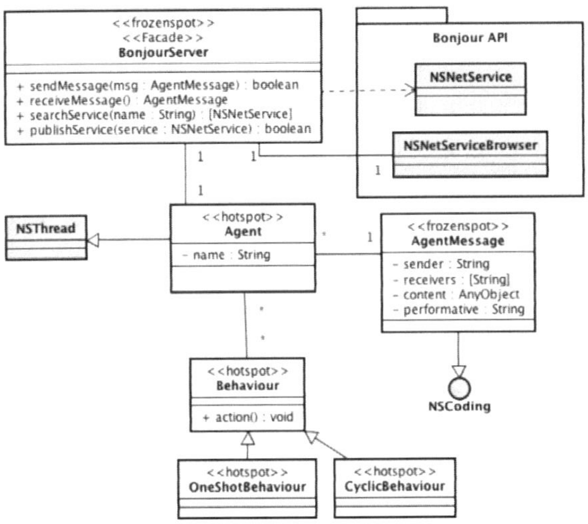

Figure 2. Class diagram of the iMobile framework.

Behaviors executed by agents (*Behavior* Class): Such class represents the behavior of an agent. Behaviors are actions that agents may execute on an application. This class has a method called *action* that, when executed, initiates the agent's behavior. Their subclasses should have it implemented.

Behavior executed once (*OneShotBehavior* Class): It represents a generic behavior offered by the framework that is executed only once. When its execution is finished, such behavior is removed from the agent's behaviors list.

Behavior executed in cycle (*CyclicBehavior* Class): Another generic behavior offered by the framework. This behavior is executed in a loop with a predetermined timer to wait between the loops.

Next, iMobile's frozen-spots are explained below.

Manager to use the Bonjour API (*BonjourServer* Class): This class was created to access a set of features offered by Bonjour API: (i) publication of services provided by agents, (ii) search of services offered by other agents, (iii) message sending and receiving to/from agents. *BonjourServer* uses BSD Sockets [23] to create a listening socket for the agent, which allows the agent to receive messages from other agents and filter out unwanted messages.

Messages that are sent and received by agents (*AgentMessage* Class): Such class represents the communication protocol between agents. Most properties of the *AgentMessage* class are basic agent information as name, current service, service type, sender, receiver, data and content. The content property accepts any type of object to be sent to another agent. These objects, that are stored in luggage, should be instances of classes that implement the *NSCoding* protocol in order to send it through the network.

C. *Using iMobile*

These are the main steps that should be performed to use the iMobile framework:

1. Defining which agents will be used in the solution to be developed. Agents may be either created from instantiated objects using the *Agent* class, or from other classes that extend such class;
2. Creating behaviors that will be executed by the agent. For instance, such behaviors may request services and send messages to other agents;
3. Defining which services each agent will be able to offer;
4. Defining which type of service the agent will search. It is necessary for the creation of each agent to inform these service types.

IV. USE SCENARIO: ISSUE TRACK

Daily, it is common for companies to raise issues and some of them have high priority. When such issues are quickly solved, a lot of damage may be avoided, such as losing money. According to [33][34], one of the top reasons for closing companies is the bad management of how issues are handled.

Taking this context into consideration, we implemented an iOS app with software agents that help speed up the process of contacting people, as quickly as possible, to solve critical issues. First, we explain the main solution idea. Secondly, we present in detail how the proposed app extended the iMobile framework.

A. *Main Idea*

The implemented multi-agent app allows users to register issues that occur within a company. When a registered issue is critical and the deadline is short (e.g., maximum of two more days), a software agent verifies if another user connected on the same network may solve it. Considering that all employees use the app (iPhone was the device used) and each one informs his/her data (e.g., name and services that perform), a software agent is created for them.

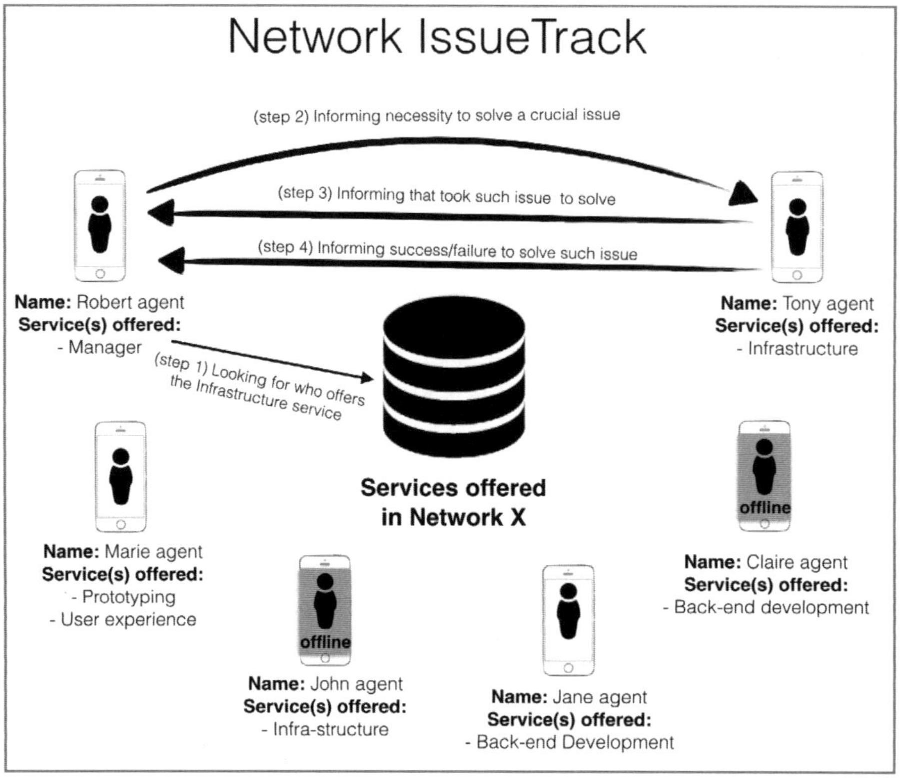

Figure 3. Issue track scenario.

The afore mentioned scenario is illustrated in Figure 3. Notice that six agents are registered. At a given time, two agents are not connected to the company network. Probably, the reason is that these registered employees are not in the company.

As the iMobile framework was extended to create this app, Bonjour API was inherited. Therefore, it is possible to verify which services are registered and which agents offer them. For instance, it considers that a Robert agent (see Figure 3) needs someone to solve a critical issue related to infrastructure with deadline for tomorrow. Hence, it is important to locate a person that may solve it as soon as possible.

In order to identify an infrastructure employee, the Robert agent uses Bonjour to look for such employee (step 1 illustrated in Figure 3). Thereafter, Robert sends a message to the Tony agent, which offers infrastructure services and is connected to the same network (step 2). When Tony receives that message, a notification is created on his smartphone for the employee (user app) confirm that he/she will take it. Upon performing such confirmation, Tony sends a message to Robert (step 3). When Robert receives this message, a notification is presented to Robert's user. Subsequently, when the issue is solved, Tony informs Robert about its resolution (step 4).

When no agent is found (from the step 1), an email is sent to those that could solve the registered issue (considering that they are not in the company). In addition, to allow the messages receiving from agents, at any time, when a person arrives at the company, he/she receives a notification requesting them to open the app. Then, even if the app is not in use, at a given time, but has been opened in the background, the agent will be able to receive messages and perform some executions.

B. Extending the iMobile Framework

In Figure 4, a class diagram, with the main classes made to extend the iMobile framework and to create the issue track app, is presented. The yellow classes are the new developed entities, while the others are offered from iMobile. Below, these new classes are explained in detail.

App User (*User* class): When an employee of the company uses the app for the first time, a set of data should be informed to him/her: name, date of birth, email and cellphone. Part of these data is taken to create a software agent that will represent the employee.

Agent app (*IssueAgent* class): This class represents the responsible agent for executing the following activities: (i) publishing which services are offered in its creation, based on the data informed by app user, (ii) requesting the resolution of critical issues to other agents, and (iii) taking or not taking it to solve these issues. Each iPhone has one *IssueAgent* created to represent the app user.

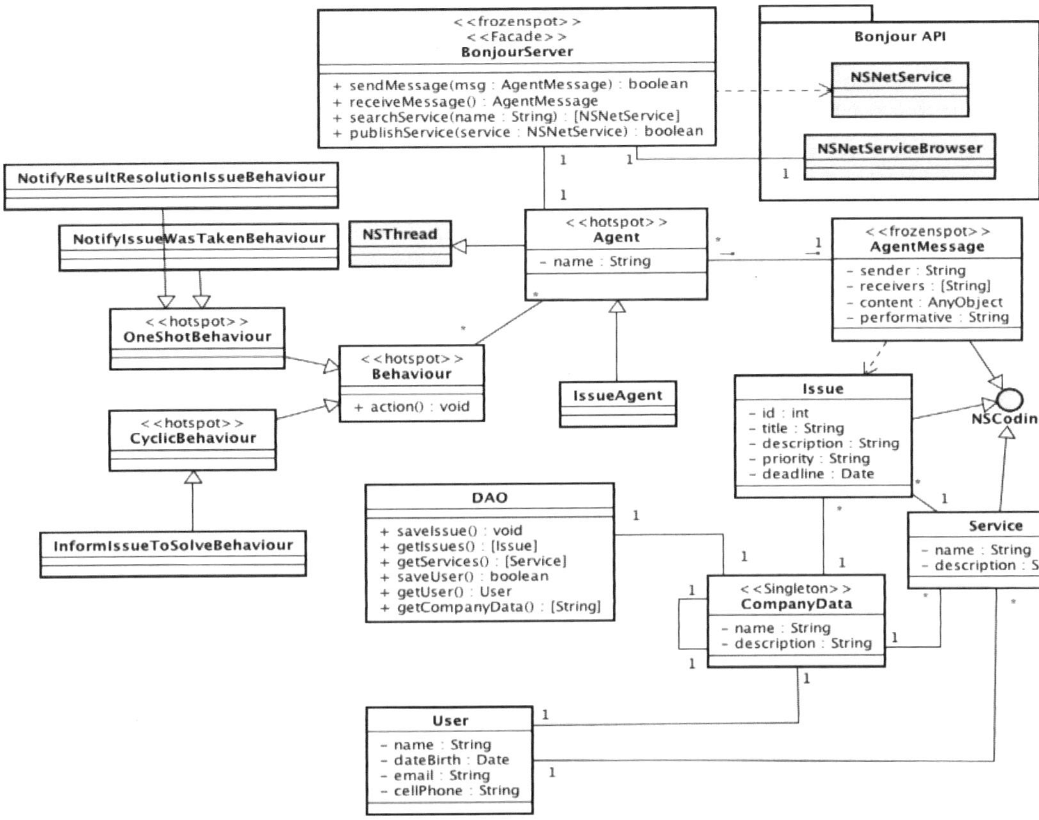

Figure 4. Class diagram of the Issue track scenario.

Registered issue (*Issue* class): It represents a registered issue that needs to be solved. An issue has the following data: an identification represented by an integer number, title, its description, priority (critical, high, medium, low), deadline that such issue needs to be solved and the service type related to the problem.

Service offered in the company (*Service* class): This class represents all the service types performed in the considered company. Some examples of services are the following: infrastructure, back-end development, front-end development, prototyping and user experience. Then, each instance of *Service* has a name and a description giving an overview of its goal.

Management to persist data (*DAO* class): This class is responsible for taking and saving data in a database used by the app. In Figure 4, the main methods offered by class are presented.

Company information (*Company* class): It applies the Singleton pattern [37] and takes into consideration all of the company's data. Thus, it is possible to access the company name and description, besides its issues, app user and registered services.

Behavior which informs that an issue needs to be solved (*InformIssueToSolveBehavior* class): This class represents the behavior executed by an *IssueAgent,* that requests the treatment of some issue by other agents. In order to decide if such a request will be sent, the agent verifies the priority of the registered issue and its deadline. The criteria adopted by the agent to send a request is when an issue has: (i) critical priority, or (ii) high priority with deadline of two more days. Hence, according to the company, critical scenarios were taken into consideration to include an additional way to contact employees that may solve these issues.

Behavior to inform that an agent took an issue to be solved (*NotifyIssueWasTakenBehavior* class): This behavior is executed by agents that received a request to solve a given issue. Such agent informs the requester if it could or could not take that issue. The reasons why an agent may or may not accept to solve a problem are presented below.

Reasons to accept an issue:

- Employee is free to take an issue;
- Employee is working to solve an issue with medium or low priority.

Reasons to not accept an issue:

- Employee is solving an issue with critical or high priority and a short deadline (maximum of two more days);
- Employee is not connected to the company network.

When no agent accepts the requested issue, an email is sent to all employees that offer the necessary service to solve it.

Behavior that informs the result of an issue resolution (*NotifyResultResolutionIssueBehavior* class): Behavior executed by an agent that accepted to solve a given issue. From this behavior, the agent notifies the result of its resolution to the requester: solved or not with additional information reported by the employee.

V. CONCLUSION

This paper presents the iMobile framework created from the Swift language for the iOS platform. With iMobile, developers will be able to speed up the creation of software agents for the iOS. This framework used the Bonjour API in order to help identifying which agents are or are not on the same network and to allow the communication between them. Bonjour is a solution that does not require the creation of containers to enable agents to exchange messages, as do JADE and JADEX. Before proposing iMobile, known frameworks, that help in the development of software agents, were studied to identify how a mobile framework for the iOS platform could be created and offered.

In order to demonstrate the use of the proposed framework, we have used it to help solving issues that occur in companies. Agents are responsible for identifying these issues' priorities and deadlines, in order to contact employees that are in the company, and to quickly solve them. This scenario illustrates the use of iMobile agents exchanging messages from Bonjour and executing a set of defined behaviors.

Nowadays, we have two master students of Informatics at PUC-Rio who used the proposed framework. Moreover, a set of ten people, with previous experience developing multi-agent systems, watched a presentation of the iMobile related to its idea, architecture and examples of case studies. From this, we have decided to organize an interview with such people to receive feedbacks of the framework. One of them was that the framework was easy to be extended to create iOS apps. In addition, they gave a set of information that allowed us to achieve the version presented in this paper, such as (i) offering better names for some created classes and methods, and (ii) continuing to offer a short number of classes to create a multi-agent system to the iOS platform.

Currently, we are in the process of analyzing how we may include other important concepts related to the multi-agent paradigm in the framework, such as: offering ways to develop self-adaptive agents, including the concept of Belief-Desire-Intention (BDI) in the framework, bringing more cognition to the agents and providing ways to test the created agents. These three ideas are known research lines investigated in other works. However, considering the mobile scenario, several issues are open and deserve more attention.

REFERENCES

[1] G. Butler, Object-Oriented Frameworks, Available at: http://users.encs.concordia.ca/~gregb/home/PDF/ecoop-tutorial.pdf, [retrieved: June, 2017].

[2] N. R. Jennings and M. Wooldridge, "A Methodology for Agent-Oriented Analysis and Design", In Proc. Of the third annual conference on Autonomous Agents (AAMAS 1999), Seattle, WA, USA, pp. 69-76, 1999.

[3] M. Wooldridge and N. R. Jennings and D. Kinny "The Gaia Methodology for Agent-Oriented Analysis and Design", Autonomous Agents and Multi-Agent Systems, vol. 3, issue 3, Sep. 2000, pp. 285-312, doi: 10.1023/A:1010071910869.

[4] G. Boella, L. Sauro, and L. van der Torre. "Power and Dependence Relations In Groups of Agents", In Proceedings of the conference on intelligent agent technology, (IAT 2004), Beijing, China, China, Sep. 2004, doi: 10.1109/IAT.2004.1342951.

[5] JADE Leap. Available at: http://jade.tilab.com//, [retrieved: June, 2017].

[6] JADE Framework. Available at: http://jade.tilab.com//, [retrieved: June, 2017].

[7] Android. Available at: www.android.com/, [retrieved: June, 2017].

[8] IOS, Available at: https://www.apple.com/ios/, [retrieved: June, 2017].

[9] Java. Available at: http://www.java.com/pt_BR/, [retrieved: June, 2017].

[10] Mobile Application Lifecycle. Available at: https://developer.apple.com/library/content/documentation/iPhone/Conceptual/iPhoneOSProgrammingGuide/TheAppLifeCycle/TheAppLifeCycle.html, [retrieved: June, 2017].

[11] I. Podnar, M. Hauswirth, and M. Jazayeri. Mobile Push: "Delivering content to mobile users", In Proceedings of International Conference on Distributed Computing Systems Workshops, (ICDCS 2002), IEEE, Nov. 2002, pp. 563-568, doi: 10.1109/ICDCSW.2002.1030826.

[12] G. Eric. What is Java 2 Micro Edition, Available at: http://www.developer.com/ws/j2me/article.php/1378921/What-is-Java-2-Micro-Edition.htm, [retrieved: July, 2017].

[13] Y. Weihong and Y. Chen, "The Development of Jade Agent for the Android Mobile Phones", Proceedings of the 2012 International Conference on Information Technology and Software Engineering, (ICITSE 2012), Springer Press, Nov. 2012, pp. 215-222, doi: 10.1007/978-3-642-34531-9_23.

[14] FIPA. Available at: www.fipa.org/, [retrieved: June, 2017].

[15] JADEX. Available at: https://www.activecomponents.org/, [retrieved: June, 2017].

[16] M. Wooldridge and N. R. Jennings, "Intelligent agents: theory and practice", The Knowledge Engineering Review (KER 1995), Cambridge Press, July 2009, pp. 115–152, doi: 10.1017/S0269888900008122.

[17] JACK. Available at: http://aosgrp.com/products/jack/, [retrieved: June, 2017].

[18] I. Nunes, C. J. P. Lucena, and M. Luck, "BDI4JADE: a BDI layer on top of JADE, Monografias em Ciência da Computação", PUC-Rio, No. 15/10, Nov. 2010.

[19] R. P. Bonasso, R. J. Firby, E. Gat and et. al, "Experiences with an architecture for intelligent reactive agents", Journal of Experimental & Theoretical Artificial Intelligence (TAI 1997), Taylor&Francis, Nov. 2010, vol. 9, issue 2-3, pp. 237-256, doi: 10.1080/095281397147103.

[20] Bonjour API. Available at: https://www.apple.com/support/bonjour/, [retrieved: June, 2017].

[21] D. H. Steinberg and S. Cheshire. Zero Configuration Networking: The Definitive Guide, O'Reilly Media, p. 53, 2005.

[22] NSThread. Available at: https://developer.apple.com/reference/foundation/thread, [retrieved: June, 2017].

[23] GCD. Available at: https://developer.apple.com/reference/dispatch, [retrieved: June, 2017].

[23] J. Frost. BSD Sockets: A Quick And Dirty Primer, 1991.

[25] NSCoding. Available at: https://developer.apple.com/reference/foundation/nscoding, [retrieved: June, 2017].

[26] NSObject. Available at: https://developer.apple.com/reference/objectivec/nsobject, [retrieved: June, 2017].

[27] UIApplication. Available at: https://developer.apple.com/reference/uikit/uiapplication, [retrieved: June, 2017].

[28] UIDevice. Available at: https://developer.apple.com/reference/uikit/uidevice, [retrieved: June, 2017].

[29] ACL Message. Available at: http://www.fipa.org/specs/fipa00061/, [retrieved: June, 2017].

[30] A. S. Tanenbaum and V. S. Maarten, Distributed systems: principles and paradigms. New Jersey: Pearson Education. Inc, 2007. p.669

[31] B. A. De Maria, V. T. Silva, C. J. P. Lucena, and R. Choren, "VisualAgent: A Software Development Environment for Multi-Agent Systems", In Proc. of the 19th Brazilian Symposium on Software Engineering (SBES 2005), Tool Track, Uberlândia, MG, Brazil, 2005.

[32] Swift Language. Svailable at: https://swift.org, [retrieved: June, 2017].

[33] PYPL PopularitY of Programming Language. Available at: https://pypl.github.io/PYPL.html, [retrieved: June, 2017].

[34] Top Reasons Businesses Close Down. Available at: http://smallbusiness.chron.com/top-reasons-businesses-close-down-20466.html, [retrieved: June, 2017].

[35] Common Reasons for Closing a Company. Available at: http://www.closeaeuropeancompany.com/common-reasons-for-closing-a-company.html, [retrieved: June, 2017].

[36] GameplayKit. Available at: https://developer.apple.com/library/content/documentation/General/Conceptual/GameplayKit_Guide/, [retrieved: June, 2017].

[37] M. E. Fayad, D. C. Schmidt and R. E. Johnson, Building Application Frameworks: Object-Oriented Foundations of Framework Design (Hardcover),Wiley publisher, first edition ISBN-10: 0471248754, 1999.

[38] Gamma, E., Helm, R., Johnson, R., and Vlissides, J., Design Patterns: Elements of Reusable Object-Oriented Software, 1994.

[39] M. Ivanovic and Z. Budimac, "Software Agents: state-of-the-art and possible applications", In Proceedigns of the 13th International Conference on Computer Systems and Technologies, (CompSysTech 2012), ACM Digital Library, June 2012, pp. 11-22, doi: 10.1145/2383276.2383279.

[40] M. Żytniewski and A. Sołtysik, A., Sołtysik-Piorunkiewicz and B. Kopka, "Modelling of Software Agents in Knowledge-Based Organisations. Analysis of Proposed Research Tools", Springer, Sep. 2015, pp. 91-108, 2015.

[41] J. T. C. Tan and T. Inamura, "Extending chatterbot system into multimodal interaction framework with embodied contextual understanding", In International Conference on Human-Robot Interaction (HRI) (ACM/IEEE 2012), IEEE Press, Mar. 2012, pp. 251-252, doi: 10.1145/2157689.2157780.

[42] DNS Zone, Available at: http://www.dns-sd.org/, [retrieved: July 2017].

[42] NSSecureCoding, Available at: https://developer.apple.com/documentation/foundation/nssecurecoding, [retrieved: July 2017].

[43] Crypto Swift, Available at: http://cocoadocs.org/docsets/CryptoSwift/0.5.2, [retrieved: July 2017].

Software Architecture Modeling for Legacy Health Information Systems Using Polyglot Persistence and Archetypes

André Magno Costa de Araújo[1,*], Valéria Cesário Times[1] and Marcus Urbano da Silva[1]
[1] Center for Informatics, Federal University of Pernambuco, Recife, Brazil
e-mail:{amca,vct,mus}@cin.ufpe.br

Carlos Andrew Costa Bezerra[2]
[2] Software Engineering Department, Recife Center for Advanced Studies and Systems, CESAR
Recife, Brazil
e-mail: andrew@r2asistemas.com.br

Abstract— **Electronic Health Record (EHR) data management in a Health Information System (HIS) has traditionally been done using a single database model. Due to the heterogeneity of such data, this practice increases the complexity in HIS development. This article presents a software architecture for a legacy HIS, which improves data management by using polyglot persistence to decentralize data storage into heterogeneous databases (i.e., relational and NoSQL). In addition, we have developed a tool to dynamically create NoSQL data schemas and Graphical User Interfaces (GUI) using a health informatics standard called archetype. The tool aims to build new functionalities in a legacy HIS using archetype-based EHR specifications imported and customized by the health professionals, thus reducing their dependence on a software team. We validated the proposed solution in a local institution, modeling a new software architecture, creating a NoSQL data schema for heterogeneous data storage and GUIs using archetypes.**

Keywords-Archetypes; Database related software; Software Architecture; E-health related software.

I. Introduction

Health information systems (HIS) are normally built using a single data model to store the various data types (i.e., structured and unstructured data) that make up the Electronic Health Record (EHR) [1]. The variety of data types is justified by the large number of subsystems in the HIS, such as the text from a medical prescription, hierarchical data of a laboratory exam or images used in diagnostic.

Because data heterogeneity often requires the development of solutions that go beyond the capability of a given database model [2], the use of a single data model is limiting at best. For example, representing hierarchical data structures in a relational database requires complex data retrieval sentences that can compromise the performance of an application. In addition, the creation of programming routines to ensure data referential integrity in NoSQL models increases the complexity in HIS development.

Another recurring problem in HIS development is the lack of uniformity in data modeling for attributes that define the EHR and terminologies that give a semantic meaning to clinical data [3][4]. In this context, it is common for software companies to use their own standards when modeling EHR requirements, which in turn hinders data exchange between health applications [5].

To address the issues posed by the use of a single data model and the heterogeneity of EHR data, the concepts of polyglot persistence and archetypes are used in this paper. Polyglot persistence is the use of different data models to deal with different storage needs [6], such as the use of a relational database to store structured data and NoSQL for unstructured and frequently changing data. An archetype is a health informatics standard proposed by the openEHR foundation to standardize EHR data attributes, terminologies and constraints [7]. Among other advantages, it allows health professionals to specify EHR requirements and seamlessly share data with other health sectors and organizations [8].

This paper specifies a software architecture for a legacy HIS applying the concept of polyglot persistence to improve data management in the healthcare sector. In addition, we have developed a tool to dynamically create NoSQL data schemas and Graphical User Interfaces (GUI) using archetypes. The tool aims to build new functionalities in a legacy HIS using archetype-based EHR specifications made by health professionals, thus reducing their dependence on a software team. To validate the solution proposed herein, we modeled a new software architecture for a legacy HIS and evaluated its dynamic generation of NoSQL data schemas and GUIs.

The sections of this article are organized as follows: Section II contextualizes the basic concepts used in this work, while Section III presents and discusses the proposed software architecture for health applications. Section IV demonstrates the generation of data schemas and GUI using the proposed tool, while the final considerations and future work are found in Section V.

II. Basic Concepts and Related Works

This section contextualizes the basic concepts used in the development of this work and provides an analysis of main related works.

A. Archetypes

The openEHR software architecture for HIS aims to develop an open and interoperable computational platform for the healthcare sector [9]. It separates generic EHR structural information and patients' demographics from the constraints and standards associated with clinical data. An archetype consists of a computational expression based on a reference model and is represented by domain constraints and terminologies [9] (e.g., data attributes of a blood test).

Templates are structures used to group archetypes and allow their use in a particular context of application. They are often associated with a graphical user interface.

Dual modeling is the separation of information and knowledge in HIS architecture. In the proposed approach, the components responsible for modeling EHR clinical and demographic data are specified through data structures composed of data types, constraints and terminologies.

In an archetype, the specification of data attributes is achieved through data entry builders named generic data structures. Such structures allow the representation of EHR heterogeneous data through the following types: ITEM_SINGLE, ITEM_LIST, ITEM_TREE and ITEM_TABLE.

ITEM_SINGLE models a single data attribute, such as a patient's weight, height and age. ITEM_LIST groups a set of attributes in a list, such as a patient's address. ITEM_TREE specifies a hierarchical data structure that is logically represented as a tree. It can be used, for instance, to model a patient's physical or neurological evaluations. Finally, ITEM_TABLE models data elements by using columns for field definition and rows for field value, respectively. Each attribute of a structure is characterized by a type of data and can have a related set of associated domain restrictions and terminologies. The terminologies give semantic meaning to clinical data and can be represented as a set of health terms defined by a professional.

B. *Polyglot Persistence*

Polyglot Persistence is the use of different data storage approaches to deal with different storage types and needs [6]. The core idea is to store structured data through a relational approach, while semi-structured or unstructured data is stored in NoSQL data models. Figure 1 shows how the different types of healthcare data can be stored using polyglot persistence.

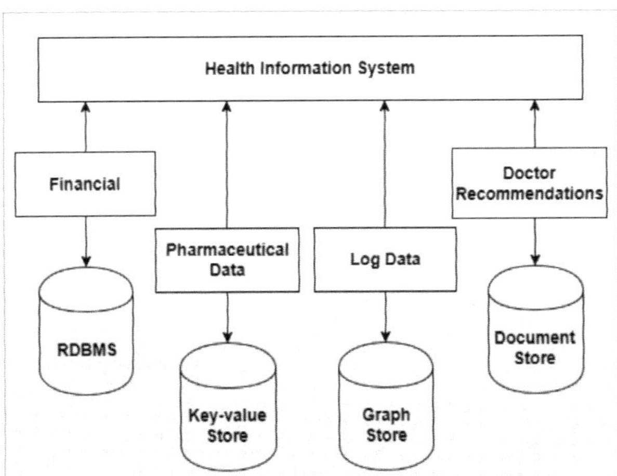

Figure 1. Example of multi-model storage in the healthcare sector.

As shown in Figure 1, polyglot persistence offers different data models such as Relational, Key-value store, Document store and Graph Store, among others.

A relational database is a set of tables containing data arranged in predefined categories. Each table contains one or more data categories in columns. Each row contains a unique instance of data for the categories defined by the columns [10].

NoSQL data models differ from more traditional approaches and offer better support for non-conventional data storage and flexibility when creating or altering a data schema [11]. The key-value store saves information in a table with rows, keys for description and a value field. The document store creates document sets which are collections of fields to be displayed as a single element, a list or nested documents. A graph store uses nodes, relationships and properties to store information. The node represents the vertices in a graph, the relationships, its edges and the properties, the attributes.

C. *Related Works and Motivation*

Polyglot persistence has been applied in a variety of applications, such as IBM's auto scaling PaaS architecture [12], source-code-based data schema identification tools [13] and the re-engineering of legacy systems for heterogeneous databases [6]. To minimize the rigidity caused by relational data schema and provide support to the continuous data requirement changes which commonly occur in legacy HIS, Prasad and Sha [14] specify an architecture and a HIS prototype that allows polyglot persistence and improves health data management in a legacy application. Similarly, Kaur and Rani [6] specify a polyglot storage architecture to store structured data in a relational database (PostgreSQL), while two NoSQL databases (MongoDB and Neo4j) store semi-structured data such as laboratorial exams and medicine prescriptions. Nevertheless, neither solutions use archetypes to standardize EHR data attributes and terminologies.

Recent studies based on openEHR specifications include EHR construction using and customizing archetypes [15], Computer-Aided Software Engineering (CASE) development tools for data schema creation [16] and a study on development patterns for healthcare computing [17]. However, the use openEHR archetypes to build heterogeneous data schema, store and standardize EHR data is an open issue found in the state-of-art.

III. PROPOSED SOLUTION

This section discusses the main problems found in legacy HIS management, describes the proposed software architecture using polyglot persistence and how GUIs and data schemas are dynamically generated using archetypes.

A. *Legagy Health Information System*

Before implementing the proposed solution, we carried out field observation in a local health institution located in northeastern Brazil, where patient care activities are registered in a HIS, including hospitalization, prescription records and laboratory exams. To maintain and develop new HIS functionalities, the institution has a team of eight programmers.

Analyzing HIS implementations carried out in the last 12 months, we found that most requests were related to patient care functions such as prescription, medical history, test results, reports, etc. Meanwhile, structured data such as supply requests, financial and management requirements had suffered few alterations in the same period.

As shown in Figure 2, the legacy HIS architecture is known as Three-Tier. The client layer is responsible for designing the GUI of each feature, while the business logic layer groups and organizes all the application source code. The database access layer contains the classes that perform data persistence in the DBMS. For application development and maintenance, the following technologies are used: Oracle 11g relational database for data storage and Microsoft Asp.Net C# for GUI generation and source code implementation.

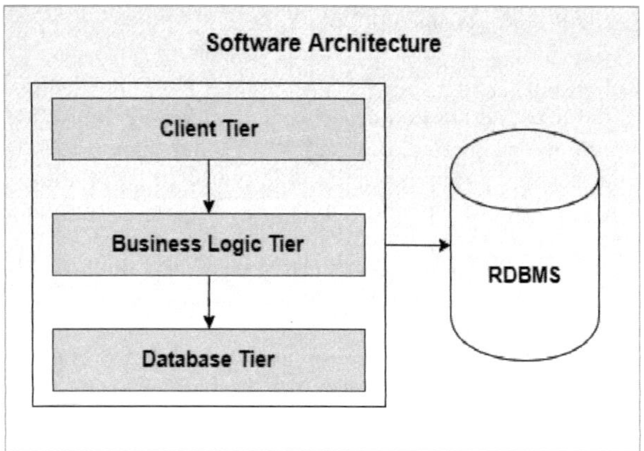

Figure 2. Legacy software architecture

The software architecture illustrated in Figure 2 represents the reality of several HISs in Brazil. In this scenario, two important problems arise: EHR data heterogeneity is represented in single data model and the reliance on a team of programmers for development and maintenance.

B. Modeling a New Software Architecture

The main motivation for the proposed solution is to improve data management by providing a software architecture which uses polyglot persistence to store EHR data in heterogeneous databases and openEHR archetypes to dynamically build HIS features.

Considering the scenario described in Section III-A, we used the following approach in designing the proposed software architecture; structured data which is rarely altered is stored in a relational database, while constantly changing data which requires a flexible data schema is stored in a NoSQL database (Figure 3). We developed a tool capable of reading archetypes to generate new functionalities because their very purpose is to enable health professionals to specify EHR requirements, thus minimizing their dependence on programmers.

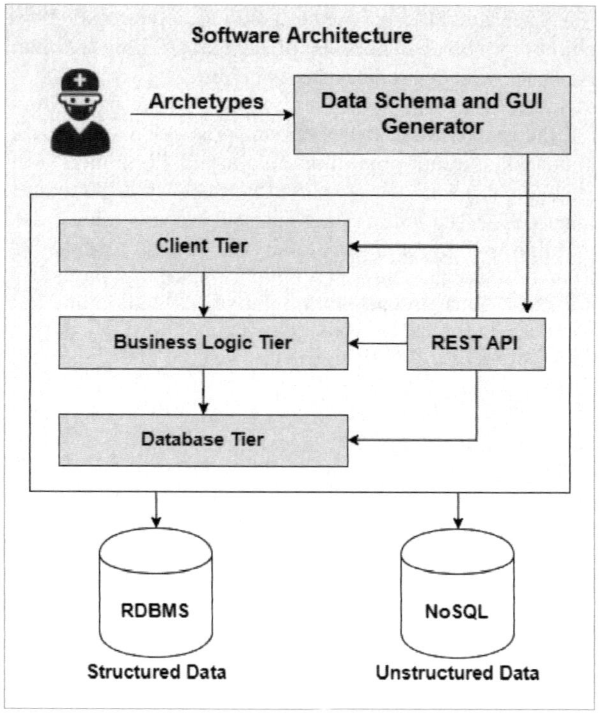

Figure 3. A new software architecture using polyglot Ppersistence and archetypes

As shown in Figure 3, we maintained the three-tier architecture (client, business logic and database) but decentralized EHR storage using two database models (relational and NoSQL). Through a REST API, we extracted data attributes, terminologies and constraints from archetypes and generated GUIs and data schemas at runtime. Because the GUIs generated by our tool use the same web-based technology as the legacy HIS, we inserted the GUIs into the HIS using frames.

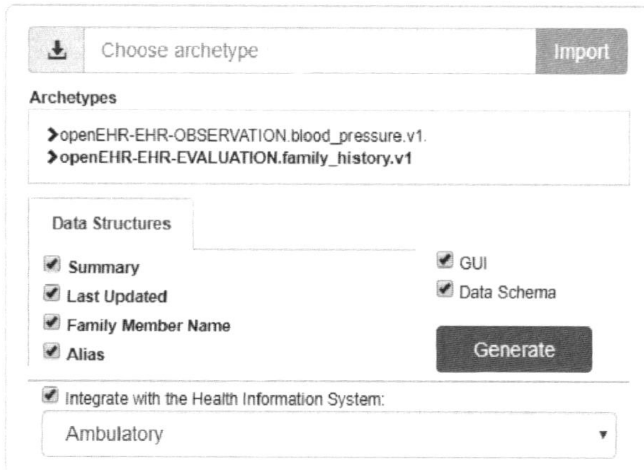

Figure 4. Main features of the developed tool

Figure 4 shows the main functionalities of the tool proposed in this article, while Figure 5 depicts a use case with the following features: i) archetype reading, ii) archetype element selection for GUI and data schema generation, and iii) GUI integration into the legacy application.

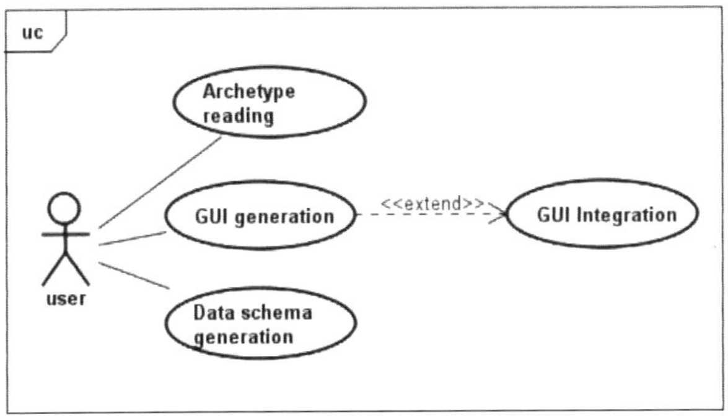

Figure 5. Use case of the developed tool

The developed tool allows one to import and map the archetypes that will be used to generate GUI and data schema. When importing an archetype, the tool enable the user to choose which elements will be part of the data schema and manage the GUI elements by adding, removing or disabling fields. Such elements can be modified at a later time. In this case, the tool will automatically extend the database schema created.

C. Graphical User Interface and Data Schema Generation

The *Generator* component shown in Figure 3 extracts from the imported archetype the attributes that define the EHR, the health care terminologies and vocabulary that give a semantic meaning to the clinical data, as well as constraints specified in the attributes.


```
Code ▾
{
  "Archetype": {
    "DataAttributes": [
      {
        "ArchetypeID": 2,
        "Code": "at0026",
        "Label": "Last Updated",
        "Description": "The date this
        Family History Summary was last updated.",
        "DataType": "DV_DATE_TIME"
      }
    ],
    "Terminologies": [
      {
        "ArchetypeID": 2,
        "Code": "at0002",
        "Label": "Summary"
      }
    ],
    "Constraints": [
      {
        "ArchetypeID": 2,
        "Code": "at0026",
        "Type": "DateTime"
      }
    ]
  }
}
```


Figure 6. A REST API Example

With the extracted elements, the *REST API* executes the following tasks: i) transform data attributes (i.e., text, ordinal, boolean, count, quantity, date and time) into data entry fields in the GUI, ii) use constraints extracted from archetypes as data entry validation mechanisms (e.g., range of values, data type constraints), and iii) provide the terminologies extracted from archetypes to give a semantic meaning to their respective GUI fields. As the Slot type does not represent a data entry attribute in an archetype, the tool did not consider this data type to generate GUI. Figure 6 shows in JSON format the elements extracted from archetypes in the REST API.

Using the extracted elements from archetypes, the NoSQL data schema generation is performed as follows: A routine creates a document database and a set of collections to separately store the data attributes, terminologies and constraints. It then inserts archetype elements in their respective collections.

A loop scans the list of archetype elements and adds the code, description and data type in the attribute collection. To maintain the relationship between elements, attribute reference and constraint description codes are stored in the constraint collection. Finally, in case the data attribute has one or more terminologies, the attribute reference code is stored in its collection along with the list of terminologies found.

IV. RESULTS

In this section, we show GUI and data schema generation using archetypes. The tool was installed on Microsoft's Azure cloud solution and an ArangoDB database was used to generate the data schema exemplified in this evaluation. Both archetypes used in this example are shown in Figure 7 and are available in the openEHR repository [18].

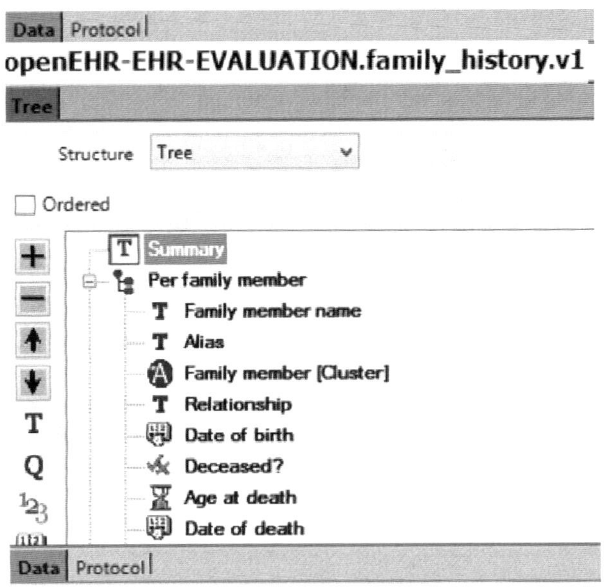

Figure 7. Family history Archetype

The family history archetype models information about significant health-related problems in genetic and non-genetic family members, both alive and deceased. The blood pressure archetype describes systemic arterial blood pressure from any measurement method or physical location.

In order to generate the GUIs and data schema, we import the two archetypes. The GUI generated from the family history archetype can be seen in Figure 8.

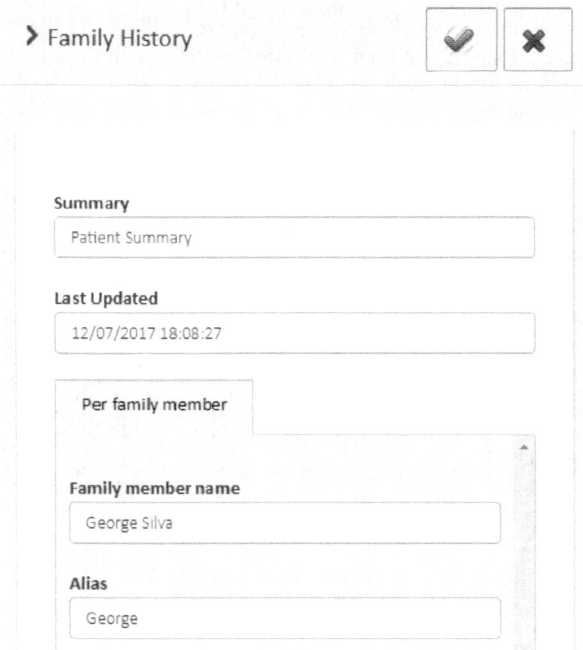

Figure 8. GUI generated from the family history archetype

The tool uses the same elements extracted from the archetype (i.e., data attributes, terminologies, and constraints) to generate both the NoSQL data schema and the GUI. In addition, each generated GUI provides resources for the end user to insert, update, delete, and query data.

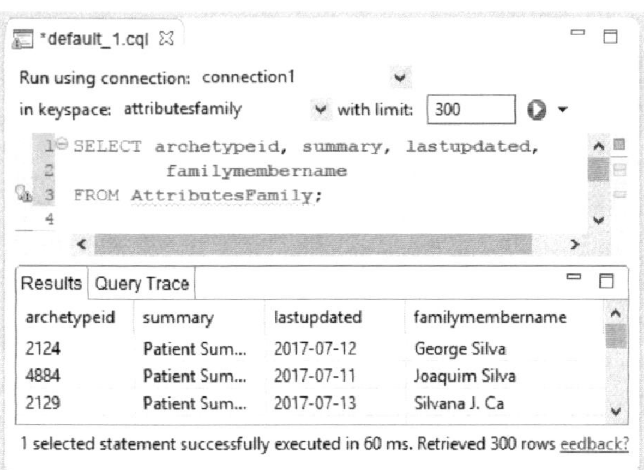

Figure 9. Data schema generated using the family history archetype

Figure 9 shows a data set stored in the database created by the tool. The data entered in the GUI is stored into the database by a REST API. GUI components can be enabled or disabled even when the GUI is in use in the HIS, triggering the data schema to dynamically change.

V. Conclusion and Future Works

In this paper, we presented a software architecture to improve Electronic Health Record data management in a legacy Health Information System using polyglot persistence to decentralize its data storage into two database models (i.e., relational and NoSQL). Using a developed tool, we extract attributes, terminologies and constraints from archetypes and use them to generate a Graphical User Interface and data schemas at runtime. The use of archetypes allows users to create new HIS functionalities without the need of a software development team.

In this paper, we limited the scope of research to data schema and GUIs generation. A forthcoming work will address privacy, performance and security issues by presenting an algorithm to encrypt EHR data on a cloud service or local storage. In addition, we intend to implement a Health Level 7 (HL7) messages system to exchange data between health applications.

Acknowledgment

This work was partially supported by Fundação de Amparo à Ciência e Tecnologia do Estado de Pernambuco (FACEPE), under the grants APQ-0173-1.03/15 and IBPG-0809-1.03/13.

References

[1] V. Dinu and P. Nadkarni, "Guidelines for the Effective Use of Entity-Attribute-Value Modeling for Biomedical Databases," International Journal of Medical Informatics, pp. 769-779, 2007.

[2] C. C. Martínez, T. M. Menárguez, B. J. T. Fernández, and J. A. Maldonado, "A model-driven approach for representing clinical archetypes for Semantic Web environments," Journal of Biomedical Informatics, pp.150–164, 2009.

[3] S. Garde, E. Hovenga, J. Buck, and P. Knaup, "Expressing clinical data sets with openEHR archetypes: A solid basis for ubiquitous computing," International Journal of Medical Informatics, pp. 334–341, 2007.

[4] B. Bernd, "Advances and Secure Architectural EHR Approaches," International Journal of Medical informatics, pp. 185-190, 2006.

[5] K. Bernstein , R. M. Bruun, S. Vingtoft, S. K. Andersen, and C. Nøhr, " Modelling and implementing electronic health records in Denmark," International Journal of Medical Informatic, pp. 213-220, 2005.

[6] K. Kaur and R. Rani, "Managing Data in Healthcare Information Systems: Many Models, One Solution," IEEE Computer Society, pp. 52-59, 2015.

[7] J. Buck, S. Garde, C. D. Kohl, and G. P. Knaup, "Towards a comprehensive electronic patient record to support an innovative individual care concept for premature infants using the openEHR approach," International Journal of Medical Informatics, pp. 521-531, 2009.

[8] L. Lezcano, A. S. Miguel, and S. C. Rodríguez, " Integrating reasoning and clinical archetypes using OWL ontologies and

SWRL rules," Journal of Biomedical Informatics, pp.1-11, 2010.

[9] T. Beale, "Archetypes: Constraint-based domain models for future-proof information systems, " Eleventh OOPSLA Workshop on Behavioral Semantics: Serving the Customer, pp. 16-32, 2002

[10] R. Elmasri and S.B. Navathe, Fundamentals of Database Systems, Addison-Wesley, 6 ed., 1994.

[11] K. k. Lee, W. Tangb, and K. Choia, "Alternatives to relational database: Comparison of NoSQL and XML approaches for clinical data storage," Computer Methods and Programs in Biomedicine, pp. 99-109, 2013.

[12] S. R. Seelam, P. Dettori, P. Westerink, and B. B. Yang, "Polyglot Application Auto Scaling Service for Platform As A Service Cloud," IEEE International Conference on Cloud Engineering, pp. 84-91, 2015.

[13] M. Ellison, R. Calinescu, and R. Paige, "Re-engineering the Database Layer of Legacy Applications for Scalable Cloud Deployment," IEEE/ACM 7th International Conference on Utility and Cloud Computing, pp. 976-979, 2014.

[14] S. Prasad and N. Sha, "NextGen Data Persistence Pattern in Healthcare: Polyglot Persistence," Fourth International Conference on Computing, Communications and Networking Technologies, pp. 1-8, 2013.

[15] M. B. Späth and J. Grimson, "Applying the archetype approach to the database of a biobank information management system," International Journal of Medical Informatics, pp. 1-22, 2010.

[16] D. Georg, C. Judith, and R. Christoph, "Towards plug-and-play integration of archetypes into legacy electronic health record systems: the ArchiMed experience," BMC Medical Informatics and Decision Making, pp. 1-12, 2013.

[17] E. Marco, A.Thomas, R. Jorg, D. Asuman, and L. Gokce, "A Survey and Analysis of Electronic Healthcare Record Standards," ACM Computing Surveys, pp. 277–315, 2005.

[18] Clinical Knowledge Manager. Available from: http://openehr.org/ckm/ 2017.08.10.

Evaluating Enterprise Resource Planning Analysis Patterns using Normalized Systems Theory

Ornchanok Chongsombut and Jan Verelst
Department of Management Information Systems
University of Antwerp
Antwerp, Belgium
e-mail: ornchanok.chongsombut, jan.verelst@uantwerp.be

Abstract— **A dramatically increasing competition in business environment has brought a new characteristic of enterprise information systems called "evolvability". Its on-going changes significantly impact the way information systems are being analysed and designed in practice. Based on Normalized Systems theory, information systems should be designed in 1-1 modular structure to be free from so-called combinatorial effects. Combinatorial effects are one of the biggest obstacles to implementing evolvability of information systems. Combinatorial effects actually occur when a change has a ripple effect on the information system size. Hence, information systems should be designed to minimize combinatorial effects in order to enhance the evolvability of software. Moreover, Normalized Systems theory provides an important practical way of developing evolvable information systems, even huge application systems for organizations. The purpose of the paper is to present an analysis of the analysis patterns of the well-known Microsoft Dynamics CRM 2016 adhering to the design patterns of Normalized Systems theory. Additionally, the paper shows the evaluation of the Enterprise Resource Planning (ERP) analysis patterns from an evolvability point of view and demonstrate both conformance with Normalized Systems theory and violations against it.**

Keywords- Normalized Systems; Evolvability; ERP; Analysis Patterns; Microsoft Dynamics CRM

I. INTRODUCTION

At present, one of the most challenging aspects of designing enterprise information systems is evolvability. Currently, organizations are faced with rapid changes in business environments such as markets, stakeholders, technologies, and so on. Consequently, a high level of evolvability is becoming a highly important issue for software engineering [1][2].

In order to sustain its growth, an organization must deal effectively with all stake-holders. Moreover, the organization should have an information system that collects as much data as possible related to the organization and provides accurate and valuable information about these stakeholders. The information system should be designed to retrieve information in a timely manner for effective decision making and to enhance the overall performance of business operations. Accordingly, ERP systems have become the most important part of enterprises' information systems. Thus, the ERP is generally considered as an integrated business process package [3][4]. However, ERP systems are costly and time-consuming to develop. Moreover, ERP systems have extremely complicated structures, and therefore, they are not easy to implement. Due to both the complexity of ERP systems and organizations' requirement for customized solutions to serve their business objectives, ERP systems should be evolvable. Furthermore, organizations need to be able to respond effectively to their business environment changes in order to maintain a competitive advantage [2][5].

There are a number of products in the ERP market available as both open source and commercial packages. In fact, businesses usually choose standard ERP solutions such as Microsoft Dynamics, SAP, Oracle, Siebel, and PeopleSoft [3]. However, the functionalities of all ERP packages can be changed to meet changing business processes. Therefore, the evolvability of ERP customized solutions has been becoming important in developing ERP systems in order to reduce the cost of maintenance. Here, evolvability means software should be easy to change over time [2][5]-[9].

Based on the stability concept from system theory, a bounded input function should result in bounded output functions, even as $T \rightarrow \infty$. Stability has been applied to Normalized Systems theory, which clarifies how to develop information systems to maximize evolvability [2][5]-[7][9]-[11]. Certainly, information systems should be designed to be able to cope with a set of anticipated changes to increase the level of evolvability. According to the Law of Increasing proposed by Lehman [12], information systems change as time goes by and their structure becomes increasingly complex. It implies that information systems are also faced with the ever increasing size and complexity of their structure and functionality [2][7]. To approach these issues, modularity has been suggested dividing a complicated system into subsystems and coping with the evolvability requirement by allowing the modules to change independently [2][7][13]. However, coupling between modules is the biggest obstacle to evolvable information systems. Coupling relates to the possibility of a change in one module affecting another module. Regarding Normalized Systems theory, a practical guideline for devising evolvable modularity has been provided [2][7][11][13]. Indeed, Normalized Systems theory aims to facilitate the development of highly evolvable information systems [2][5][6][9]-[11][13][14]. To ensure the evolvability of information systems that adhere to Normalized Systems theory, it has been argued that information systems should be developed without combinatorial effects. Combinatorial effects occur when the impact of a change depends on the size of the information system; in other words, they have a ripple effect on the entire information systems. To increase the evolvability of information systems, these combinatorial effects should be minimized. To simplify the way to eliminate combinatorial effects, four theorems and five elements have been established in Normalized Systems theory (this will be discussed fully in Section 2). To date, a number of studies have already been done on Normalized Systems theory and implemented in several software projects [2][5][6][8][9][11][13]-[17]. Nevertheless, the analysis pattern of ERP packages applying Normalized Systems theory has a number of limitations applying Normalized Systems theory.

In the paper, we analysed the partial analysis patterns of the well-known Microsoft Dynamics CRM 2016 adhering to the design patterns of Normalized Systems theory. Additionally, the paper evaluates the ERP analysis patterns from an evolvability point of view and demonstrates conformance with Normalized Systems theory and violations against it.

The remainder of the paper is structured as follows. We start in Section 2 with some works related to our study. In Section 3, the Normalized Systems theory is discussed, emphasizing the design patterns of Normalized Systems theory. In Section 4, the partial analysis patterns of ERP package are analysed, by focusing on conformance and possible violations with respect to Normalized Systems theory. Finally, we provide the final conclusions, limitations and suggestions for future research.

II. RELATED WORK

In this section, some related works on creating evolvable IT artefacts based on Normalized Systems theory and the evaluation of ERPs' reference model will be discussed briefly.

A. *Creating Evolvable IT Artefacts Adhering to Normalized Systems Theory*

Normalized Systems theory has recently proposed a framework for developing evolvable modularity [18]. To create the evolvability of information systems, they should not only support current requirements, but also future requirements [9]. Normalized Systems theory suggested that evolvable information systems should be free from combinatorial effects [2][11]. Oorts et al., showed how the Normalized Systems theory could be applied to develop evolvable software and presented the practical advantages of Normalized Systems theory using a case study [16][19]. Additionally, Op't Land et al., conducted the research to evaluate the possibilities of developing information systems based on Normalized Systems theory. This consequence was consistent with previous findings [2][16][19][20]. They argued that the total development and maintenance time were significantly reduced from other application developments by using NS expander [2][16][19][20].

The conformance and violations to Normalized Systems principles of IT artefacts such as source code, business processes workflow and so on have been investigated [18]. Similarly, Vanhoof et al., analysed GAAP Reporting in Accounting area to list both conformance with Normalized Systems theory and violations against its principle [8]. Furthermore, Normalized Systems theory has suggested that its theorems and elements lead to high evolvability of information systems [2][5][6][8][9][14][16][18]-[20].

B. *The Evaluation of ERP Packages*

The well-known SAP Reference Model was analysed adhering to Normalized Systems theory principles. Some indications were found that seem to reflect Normalized Systems theorems. Moreover, there were some processes of the SAP Reference Model seem to be unrelated to the Normalized Systems theory principles [6]. Mendling et al., stated that there are some error probabilities in enterprise models [21][23]. Additionally, they are usually concealed. Therefore, they evaluated the SAP Reference Model using a verification tool based on Petri net to explore the errors in SAP [21]. The 600 processes of SAP Reference Model were analysed. Consequently, several errors in SAP Reference Model were found [21][23].

III. NORMALIZED SYSTEMS THEORY

Normalized Systems theory provides a practical way of developing evolvable information systems through the so-called pattern expansion of software elements [19].

A. *Normalized Systems Theorems*

To guarantee high evolvability of information systems, Normalized Systems theory proposes four theorems [10]. Furthermore, how the four Normalized Systems theorems are manifested in a practical way is shown in Table I.

TABLE I. NORMALIZED SYSTEMS FOUR THEOREMS IN PRACTICE [18]

Normalized Systems Theorems	The practical way of developing information systems
Separation of Concerns	• Multi-tier architectures separating presentation logic, application or business logic, database logic, etcetera
Data Version Transparency	• Polymorphism in object-orientation • Wrapper functions
Action Version Transparency	• XML-based technology (e.g., for web services) • Information hiding in object-orientation
Separation of States	• Asynchronous communication systems • Stateful workflow systems

B. *Normalized Systems Elements*

Five expandable elements were proposed to ensure the evolvability of Normalized Systems applications. The internal structure of these five elements is described by Normalized Systems design patterns such as data elements, action elements, work-flow elements, connector elements, trigger elements [6][19][16].

IV. Analysing the Partial Analysis Patterns of the ERP Package

In this section, we examine the Microsoft Dynamics CRM 2016 from an evolvability point of view and demonstrate both conformance with Normalized Systems theory and violations against it.

A. Indications towards of conformance with Normalized Systems principles

Here, our aim is to examine conformance between the model of Microsoft Dynamics CRM and Normalized Systems principles.

Based on the Normalized Systems theorems, most of the model of Microsoft Dynamics CRM seem to be related to the Normalized Systems principles. Firstly, the Microsoft Dynamics CRM architecture has a Multitier architecture. Moreover, the Microsoft Dynamics CRM implements cross-cutting concerns, for example, Reporting (Dashboards, Charts, Excel and SRS), Security model that focuses on access rights to the entities in the system [6]-[8]. For first and second points straightforwardly follow from the Separation of Concerns theorem.

According to the Data version transparency theorem, data entities can be modified (insert, delete, update) without affecting the calling actions [9]. In Microsoft Dynamics CRM, the information hiding has been applied to develop the software. Properties cannot be directly accessed, but can be read or written by using provided method. Additionally, Microsoft Dynamics CRM has been implemented using XML based technology that leads to conformance with the Data Version Transparency theorem.

Following the Action Version Transparency theorem, this theorem implies an action can be modified without affecting the calling actions. First, Microsoft Dynamics CRM is usually implemented through wrapper functions through the use of polymorphism in C#.NET or VB.NET. Second, the Microsoft Dynamics CRM implements cross-cutting concerns as explained above. Therefore, the developing of Microsoft Dynamics CRM relates the Action version transparency theorem.

The Microsoft Dynamics CRM relies on asynchronous service to improve overall system performance and scalability [10]. Combinatorial effects can be avoided through asynchronous processing.

B. Indications towards violation of Normalized Systems principles

When analysing the analysis patterns of Microsoft Dynamics CRM, some indications towards violation of the Normalized Systems principles might be noticed. Microsoft Dynamics CRM addresses challenge of customer management, therefore, this module was analysed in point of evolvability. The entities are used to model and manage business data in this module. In programing, an entity is represented by a class, such as the Account class generated from the Account entity.

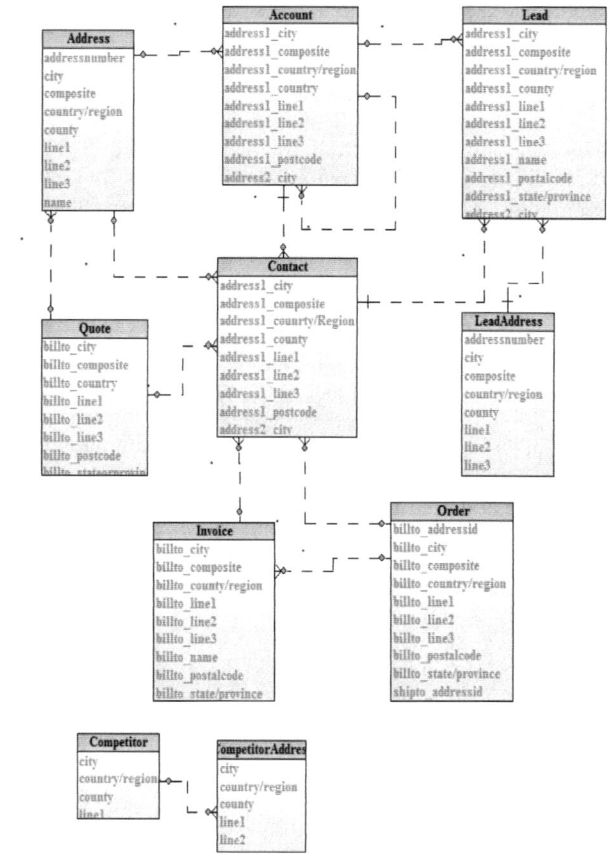

Figure 1. The partial ER diagram of Microsoft Dynamics CRM

Fig. 1 illustrates an ER diagram consisting of ten entities. We have noticed the attribute duplication of address details in many Classes such as Account, Contact, Address, Lead, LeadAddress, Quote, Invoice, and Order. Attribute duplication seems contradictory to Normalized Systems theorem, Separation of Concern. According to the assumption of unlimited systems evolution, software can be changed over time. Therefore, the eventual impact might become related to the overall system size and lead to a combinatorial effect.

V. Conclusion

In this paper, we analyse the analysis patterns of ERP package, Microsoft Dynamics CRM, to explore conformance with Normalized Systems theory and violations against it. While the interpretation of the analysis patterns of ERP package shows some conformance towards Normalized Systems theory, it also presents some analysis patterns towards violations of Normalized Systems principles. The finding is found the developing well-known commercial ERP package seem to relate Normalized Systems theory both four theorems and five elements [2][18]. On the other hand, a few points seem to contradict Normalized Systems principles. Similarly, the finding of Mendling et al., there are some error probabilities in enterprise models. Moreover, they are usually concealed [21]-[23]. This paper makes first contribution towards presenting the possibility of ERP evaluation adhering to Normalized Systems theory in the context of evolvability. Second, the paper contributes to the ERP development applying Normalized Systems theory to achieve the evolvability.

The limitations of our study need to be acknowledged. First, we only analysed partial analysis patterns of one ERP package. We could not perform reverse-engineering and explore more source code of commercial ERP software packages to look at combinatorial effects. As part of future research, we will redesign and rebuild the existing data model of existing ERP software packages based on NS theory. In practice, we will rebuild existing ERP packages using the Normalized Systems expander to obtain high evolvability [2][16][19].

REFERENCES

[1] S. Kelly and C. Holland, "The ERP Systems Development Approach to Achieving an Adaptive Enterprise: The Impact of Enterprise Process Model-ling Tools," in Systems engineering for business process change: new directions. Springer London, pp. 241-252, 2002.

[2] H. Mannaert, J. Verelst, and K. Ven, "Towards evolvable software architectures based on systems theoretic stability," Software: Practice and Experience, vol 42, no. 1, pp. 89-116, 2012.

[3] K. Ganesh et al., "Enterprise Resource Planning: Fundamentals of Design and Implementation," Springer, 2014.

[4] E. Shehab, M. Thomassin, and M. Badawy, "Towards a Cost Modelling Framework for Outsourcing ERP Systems," in Improving Complex Systems Today: Proceedings of the 18th ISPE International Conference on Concur-rent Engineering, D.D. Frey, S. Fukuda, and G. Rock, Editors, Springer London: London, pp. 401-408, 2011.

[5] P. Huysmans and J. Verelst, "Towards an Engineering-Based Research Approach for Enterprise Architecture: Lessons Learned from Normalized Systems theory," in Advanced Information Systems Engineering Workshops: CAiSE 2013 International Workshops, Valencia, Spain, June 17-21, 2013. Proceedings, X. Franch and P. Soffer, Editors, Springer Berlin Heidel-berg: Berlin, Heidelberg, pp. 58-72, 2013.

[6] P. De Bruyn et al., "Towards Applying Normalized Systems theory Implications to Enterprise Process Reference Models," in Advances in Enterprise Engineering VI: Second Enterprise Engineering Working Conference, EEWC 2012, Delft, The Netherlands, May 7-8, 2012. Proceedings, A. Albani, D. Aveiro, and J. Barjis, Editors, Springer Berlin Heidelberg: Berlin, Heidelberg, pp. 31-45, 2012.

[7] P. Huysmans et al., "Positioning the Normalized Systems theory in a Design Theory Framework," in Business Modeling and Software Design: Second International Symposium, BMSD 2012, Geneva, Switzerland, July 4-6, 2012, Revised Selected Papers, B. Shishkov, Editor, Springer Berlin Heidel-berg: Berlin, Heidelberg, pp. 43-63, 2013.

[8] E. Vanhoof et al., "Building an Evolvable Prototype for a Multiple GAAP Accounting Information System," in Advances in Enterprise Engineering X: 6th Enterprise Engineering Working Conference, EEWC 2016, Funchal, Madeira Island, Portugal, May 30-June 3 2016, Proceedings, D. Aveiro, R. Pergl, and D. Gouveia, Editors, Springer International Publishing: Cham, pp. 71-85, 2016.

[9] J. Verelst et al., "Identifying Combinatorial Effects in Requirements Engineering," in Advances in Enterprise Engineering VII: Third Enterprise Engineering Working Conference, EEWC 2013, Luxembourg, May 13-14, 2013. Proceedings, H.A. Proper, D. Aveiro, and K. Gaaloul, Editors, Springer Berlin Heidelberg: Berlin, Heidelberg, pp. 88-102, 2013.

[10] P. De Bruyn, "Towards Designing Enterprises for Evolvability Based on Fundamental Engineering Concepts," in On the Move to Meaningful Internet Systems: OTM 2011 Workshops: Confederated International Workshops and Posters: EI2N+NSF ICE, ICSP+INBAST, ISDE, ORM, OTMA, SWWS+MONET+SeDeS, and VADER 2011, Hersonissos, Crete, Greece, October 17-21, 2011. Proceedings, R. Meersman, T. Dillon, and P. Herrero, Ed-itors, Springer Berlin Heidelberg: Berlin, Heidelberg, pp. 11-20, 2011.

[11] H. Mannaert, J. Verelst, and K. Ven, "The transformation of requirements into software primitives: Studying evolvability based on systems theoretic stability," Science of Computer Programming, vol. 76, no. 12, pp. 1210-1222, 2011.

[12] MM. Lehman, "Laws of software evolution revisited," in European Workshop on Software Process Technology, Springer, 1996.

[13] D. Van Nuffel, "Towards designing modular and evolvable business processes," Universiteit Antwerpen, 2011.

[14] P. Huysmans et al., "Aligning the Normalized Systems theory Constructs of Enterprise Ontology and Normalized Systems," in Advances in Enterprise Engineering IV: 6th International Workshop, CIAO! 2010, held at DESRIST 2010, St. Gallen, Switzerland, June 4-5, 2010. Proceedings, A. Albani and J.L.G. Dietz, Editors, Springer Berlin Heidelberg: Berlin, Heidelberg, pp. 1-15, 2010.

[15] M.R. Krouwel and M. Op't Land, "Combining DEMO and Normalized Systems for developing agile enterprise information systems," in Enterprise Engineering Working Conference, Springer, 2011.

[16] G. Oorts et al., "Easily evolving software using normalized system theory-a case study," Proceedings of ICSEA, pp. 322-327, 2014.

[17] K. Ven et al., "Experiences with the automatic discovery of violations to the normalized systems design theorems," International Journal on Advances in Software, vol. 4, no 1 & 2, 2011, 2011.

[18] P. De Bruyn, D. Geert, and H. Mannaert, "Aligning the Normalized Systems Theorems with Existing Heuristic Software Engineering Knowledge," The Seventh International Conference on Software Engineering Advances, pp. 84-89, 2012.

[19] G. Oorts et al., "Building evolvable software using Normalized Systems theory: A case study. in System Sciences (HICSS)," 2014 47th Hawaii International Conference, IEEE, 2014.

[20] Op't Land et al., "Exploring normalized systems potential for dutch mod's agility," in Working Conference on Practice-Driven Research on Enterprise Transformation, Springer, 2011.

[21] J Mendling et al., "Faulty EPCs in the SAP reference model," in International Conference on Business Process Management, Springer, 2006.

[22] J Mendling et al., "Errors in the SAP reference model," BPTrends, vol. 4, no. 6, pp. 1-5, 2006.

[23] J Mendling et al., "Detection and prediction of errors in EPCs of the SAP reference model," Data & Knowledge Engineering, vol. 64, no. 1, pp. 312-329, 2008.

A Survey and Analysis of Reference Architectures for the Internet-of-things

Hongyu Pei Breivold
Industrial Internet-of-things
ABB Corporate Research
Västerås, Sweden
hongyu.pei-breivold@se.abb.com

***Abstract*—Increased connectivity and emerging autonomous cloud and Internet-of-things (IoT) technologies are motivating the transformation of the traditional product-focused development to cloud-based solutions and service-oriented business model in many companies. In line with this, several reference architectures for the Internet-of-things have been developed. Although some of these reference architectures have continued their development tracks in parallel and have different focus, they also have similarities in many perspectives, which may result in confusion in understanding and applying appropriate reference architectures for specific use cases. The aim of this study is therefore to survey these existing Internet-of-things reference architectures, clarify their characteristics, and analyze them from a variety of perspectives, including technology, process, quality and key system concerns, business and people. We also present several other relevant activities and initiatives related to the Internet-of-things.**

Keywords-reference architecture; industrial internet-of-things; smart industry; industrial automation

I. INTRODUCTION

The German Federal Ministry of Education and Research defines Industrie4.0 [1] as the flexibility to enable machines and plants to adapt their behavior to changing orders and operating conditions through self-optimization and reconfiguration. Consequently, future smart factories require systems to have the ability to perceive information, derive findings and change their behavior accordingly, and store knowledge gained from experiences. Many organizations start to see the potential opportunities of the Internet-of-things and its impacts on providing solutions that could offer operational advantages [2]. In line with this, there are several research initiatives and EU-funded research activities on Internet-of-things, covering various aspects, such as communication, hardware technology, identification and network discovery, security, interoperability, standardization, etc. Some examples are IERC – European Research Cluster on the Internet of Things [3], Industrial Internet Consortium [4], Industri4.0 [5], and the creation of the Alliance for Internet of Things Innovation (AIOTI) [6] by the European Commission [7], which initiates the development and future deployment of the Internet-of-things technology in Europe. There has also been a number of EU-funded research activities in Internet-of-things implementation and adoption, addressing various domains and use cases in smart cities, smart energy and smart grid, healthcare, food and water tracking, logistics and retail, and transportation [8].

Successful adoption of cloud computing and Internet-of-things requires guidance around planning and integrating relevant technologies into the existing services and applications. Both industry and academia that want to implement cloud-based solutions seek for more information about best practices for migrating and adopting cloud computing and Internet-of-things concepts. According to [9], "Defining a cloud reference architecture is an essential step towards achieving higher levels of cloud maturity. Cloud reference architecture addresses the concerns of the key stakeholders by defining the architecture capabilities and roadmap aligned with the business goals and architecture vision". Study [10] holds similar viewpoints. According to [10], in order to effectively build cloud-based enterprise solutions, there is a need for the definition of a systematic architecture that provides templates and guidelines and can be used as a reference for the architects or software engineers within the software development lifecycle. Therefore, several reference architectures have been developed and evolved. According to [11], a reference architecture incorporates the vision and strategy for the future. With high level of abstraction, a reference architecture provides a common structure and guidance for dealing with core aspects of developing, using and analyzing systems and solutions that can be tailored to different use cases and specific needs from multiple organizations.

Although some of the reference architectures in this survey have continued their development tracks in parallel and have different focus, they also have similarities in many perspectives, which may result in confusion in understanding and applying appropriate reference architectures for specific use cases. In this paper, we present a survey of the existing reference architectures for the Internet-of-things, clarify the characteristics of these reference architectures, and analyze them from a variety of perspectives, including technology, process, quality and key system concerns, business and people.

The remainder of the paper is structured as follows. Section II presents an overview of the existing reference architectures for the Internet-of-things. Section III describes some relevant organized Internet-of-things initiatives and activities. Section IV gives a comparison of the surveyed reference architectures from different perspectives, including technology, process, quality and key system concerns, business and people, and discusses the findings from this study, and Section V concludes the paper.

II. REFERENCE ARCHITECTURES FOR THE INTERNET OF THINGS

This section presents some well-known reference architectures for the Internet-of-things.

A. *Reference Architecture Model for Industrie 4.0 (RAMI4.0)*

RAMI 4.0 [12] is a reference architecture for smart factories. It was initiated in Germany, and is driven by major companies in industry sectors. RAMI 4.0 addresses the Industrie4.0 [5] problem space from three dimensions, i.e., it is hierarchically structured to manage both vertical integration within the factory, as well as horizontal integration extending beyond individual factory locations, in combination with lifecycle and value streams of manufacturing applications for all the factories and all the parties involved, from engineering through component suppliers to the customers. This reference architecture aims to address four aspects, including horizontal integration through value networks, vertical integration within a factory, lifecycle management and end-to-end engineering, and human beings orchestrating the value stream. In RAMI4.0, the term Industrie4.0 is used to stand for the fourth industrial revolution in the organization and control of the entire value stream along the life cycle of a product. All relevant information is available in real-time through the networking of all instances, e.g., people, objects and systems involved in value creation. By connecting these instances, the value stream are derived from data at all times to create dynamic, self-organized, cross-organizational, real-time optimized value networks based on a range of criteria, such as costs, availability and consumption of resources.

B. *Industrial Internet Reference Architecture (IIRA)*

IIRA [13] is a standard-based reference architecture developed by the Industrial Internet Consortium [4] for industrial internet systems, which are large end-to-end systems integrating industrial control systems with enterprise systems, business processes and analytics solutions. In this context, the term industrial internet is used to represent Internet-of-things, machines, computers and people, enabling intelligent industrial operations using advanced data analytics for transformational business outcomes. It embodies the convergence of the global industrial ecosystem, advanced computing and manufacturing, pervasive sensing and ubiquitous network connectivity.

This reference architecture is based on ISO/IEC/IEEE 42010:2011 [14] and adopts the general concepts in the specification, such as concern, stakeholder, and viewpoint. The term concern refers to any topic of interest pertaining to the system. The various concerns of an industrial internet system are classified as four viewpoints, i.e., business, usage, functional and implementation. The business viewpoint addresses the concerns of the identification of stakeholders and their business vision, values and objectives. The usage viewpoint addresses the concerns of expected system usage and capabilities. The functional viewpoint focuses on the functional components in an industrial internet system, their interrelation and structure, the interfaces and interactions between them and with external environment. The implementation viewpoint focuses on the technologies needed to implement functional components, communication schemes and lifecycle procedures. Some key system characteristics addressed in IIRA to ensure the core functions of industrial systems over time include safety, security and resilience.

C. *IoT Architectural Reference Model (IoT-ARM)*

IoT-ARM [15], developed within the European project IoT-A, is an architectural reference model that aims to connect vertically closed systems, architectures and application areas for creating open systems and integrated environments and platforms. In this model, Internet-of-things is treated as an umbrella term for interconnected technologies, devices, objects and services. This reference model consists of several sub-models, of which a primary and mandatory model is the IoT domain model, describing all the concepts and their relations that are relevant in the Internet-of-things, such as devices, IoT services, and virtual entities. All the other models, such as the IoT information model, functional model, communication model, IoT trust, security and privacy model, together with the IoT reference architecture are based on the concepts introduced in the domain model. The IoT reference architecture adopts the definition of architectural views and perspectives from [16], though excludes use case specific views to ensure IoT-specific needs and application-independence in the reference architecture. The key architectural views of the Internet-of-things reference architecture include IoT functional view, IoT information view, IoT deployment and operational view. The architectural perspectives of the Internet-of-things reference architecture tackle non-functional requirements, including evolution and interoperability, availability and resilience, trust, security and privacy, and performance and scalability.

D. *IEEE Standard for an Architectural Framework for Internet of Things (P2413)*

The P2413 standard [17] provides an architectural framework that aims to capture the commonalities, interactions and relationships across multiple domains and common architecture elements. It includes descriptions of various Internet-of-things domains, definitions of IoT domain abstractions, and identification of commonalities between different IoT domains. It also provides a blueprint for data abstraction and trust that includes protection, security, privacy, and safety. Similar to the Industrial Internet Reference Architecture, P2413 leverages existing applicable standards and follows the recommendations for architecture descriptions defined in ISO/IEC/IEEE 42010 [14]. According to [17], this standard provides a reference architecture that builds upon the reference model. The reference architecture covers the definition of basic architectural building blocks and their ability to be integrated into multi-tiered systems. The reference architecture also addresses how to document and mitigate architecture divergence. In this standard, things, apps and services can be integrated into what would be abstracted as a "thing". Information exchange could be horizontal or vertical, or both.

E. *Arrowhead Framework*

The Arrowhead framework [18] was developed within an European research project in automation, which aims to facilitate collaborative automation by networked devices for five business domains, i.e., production (manufacturing, process, and energy), smart buildings and infrastructures, electro-mobility, energy production and virtual markets of energy. This framework is based on service-oriented architecture to enable the Industrial Internet-of-things. The loosely coupled and discovery properties of service-oriented architecture improve the interoperability between devices and the integration of services provided by these devices. The concept of local clouds with well-defined isolation from the open Internet is used to support some key requirements of automation systems, such as real-time, security and safety, scalability and engineering simplicity. The dynamic characteristic of Internet of things is key in this framework. On the one hand, things come and go, and they may have limited bandwidth or energy supply. On the other hand, the integration of IoT systems needs to be dynamic based on the demand and availability. There are three core components in the local cloud services, i.e., service registry, authorization, and orchestration. In order to be Arrowhead compliant, the applications within the network should register the services they provide within the service registry component. The authorization component manages the access rules for specific services, and the orchestration component manages connection rules for specific services to allow dynamic reconfiguration of the service consumer and service provider endpoints [19].

F. *WSO2 IoT Reference Architecture*

Based on the projects deployed with customers to support Internet-of-things capabilities, the company WSO2 has proposed a reference architecture [20] that aims to support integration between systems and devices. Their definition of the Internet-of-things is the set of devices and systems that interconnect real-world sensors and actuators to the Internet. The WSO2 reference architecture consists of five layers, i.e., (i) device layer, in which each device has a unique identifier and is directly or indirectly attached to the Internet; (ii) communication layer, which supports the connectivity of the devices with multiple protocols for communication between the devices and the cloud; (iii) aggregation/bus layer, which aggregates communications from multiple devices, brokers communications to a specific device, and transform between various protocols; (iv) event processing and analytics layer; which processes and acts upon the events from the bus, and perform data storage; and (v) client/external communication layer, which enables users to communicate and interact with devices and obtain views into analytics and event processing. Besides these vertical layers, there are also two cross-cutting layers: (i) device manager, which communicates with and remotely manages devices, and maintain the list of device identities; and (ii) identity and access management for access control.

G. *Microsoft Azure IoT Reference Architecture*

The Azure Internet-of-things reference architecture [21] is built upon Microsoft Azure platform to connect, store, analyze and operationalize device data to provide deep business insights. This architecture consists of core platforms services and application-level components to facilitate processing needs across three main areas of IoT solutions, i.e., (1) device connectivity; (2) data processing, analytics and management; and (3) presentation and business connectivity. The guiding principles for the architecture include software and hardware heterogeneity to manage diverse scenarios, devices and standards, security and privacy, as well as hyper-scale deployments. The goal of the reference architecture is to connect sensors, devices, and intelligent operations using Microsoft Azure services. The key architecture components to reach this goal include (1) device connectivity, which manages different device connectivity options for IoT solutions; (2) device identity store, which manages all device identity information and allows for device authentication and management; (3) device registry store, which handles discovery and reference metadata related to provisioned devices; (4) device provisioning, which allows the system to be aware of the device capabilities and conditions; (5) device state store, which handles operational data related to the devices; (6) data flow and stream processing; (7) solution UX for graphical visualization of device data and analysis results; (8) App backend, which implements required business logic of an IoT solution; (9) business systems integration; and (10) at-rest data analytics.

H. *Internet-of-everything Reference Model*

The Internet-of-everything reference model [22] is developed by the Architecture Committee of the IoT World Forum hosted by Cisco. This model defines standard terminology and functionality for understanding and developing Internet-of-things solutions, which connect people, process, data and things to enable intelligent interactions between them to achieve relevant and valuable business opportunities. This reference model is composed of seven levels, including (1) physical devices and controllers that control multiple devices; (2) connectivity for reliable and timely information transmission between devices and the network, across networks, and between the network and low-level information processing level; (3) edge/fog computing that bridges information technology and operational technology, i.e., performing high-volume data analysis and transformation of network data flows into information suitable for storage and higher level processing; (4) data accumulation that converts event-based data generated by the devices to query-based data consumption for applications to access data when necessary; (5) data abstraction that renders data and its storage to enable developing simple and performance-enhanced applications; (6) applications that vary from control application to mobile application or business intelligence and analytics; and (7) collaboration and processes that involve people and business processes to empower smooth communication and collaboration between people.

I. *Intel IoT Platform Reference Architecture*

Intel has defined a system architecture specification (SAS), which is a reference architecture for Internet-of-things, i.e., for connecting products and services so that they can be aware of each other and surrounding systems in their ecosystems [23]. There are two versions of reference architectures: version 1.0 for connecting the unconnected, using an IoT gateway to securely connect and manage legacy devices that are lack of intelligence and Internet connectivity; version 2.0 for smart and connected things, addressing security and integration capabilities that are essential for real-time and closed-loop control of the data shared between smart things and the cloud. Similar to the Internet-of-things reference architecture proposed by IoT World Forum Architecture Committee, version 2.0 also facilitates the integration of operational technology and information technology. The Intel Internet-of-things reference architecture is a layered architectural framework, comprising of (1) communications and connectivity layer, which enables multi-protocol data communication between devices at the edge and between endpoint devices/gateways, the network, and the data center; (2) data layer with analytics distributed across the cloud, gateways, and smart endpoint devices for optimized time-critical or computation-intensive applications; (3) management layer for realizing automated discovery and provisioning of endpoint devices; (4) control layer; (5) application layer; and (6) business layer utilizing the application layer to access other layers in the solution. There is a vertical security layer as well which handles protection and security management across all layers, spanning endpoint devices, the network, and the cloud.

III. OTHER INTERNET OF THINGS ACTIVITIES

In addition to the reference architectures presented in the previous section, there are also several other projects, activities and initiatives dedicated in the architecture context for the Internet-of-things.

A. *IoT European Research Cluster (IERC)*

The objective of IERC initiative [3] is to define a common vision of Internet-of-things technology and address IoT technology research challenges with respect to connected objects, the Web of Things, and the future of the Internet capabilities at the European level, and facilitate knowledge sharing in the view of global development. According to IERC, Internet-of-things is a dynamic global network infrastructure with self-configuring capabilities based on standard and interoperable communication protocols where physical and virtual things have identities, physical attributes, and virtual personalities and use intelligent interfaces, and are seamlessly integrated into the information network. To facilitate the vision of Internet-of-things business ecosystems implementing smart technologies to drive innovation, a wide range of research and application projects have been set up within the IERC initiative, investigating aspects related to (i) devising disruptive business models, transforming traditional business model to data-driven models where all actors in the value chain are closely interconnected; (ii) trust evaluation and management in Internet-of-things, concerning provision of reliable information and maximizing security, privacy and safety; (iii) the impact and consequences of the fast-paced technology development enabling connected things, services, data and people on society with respect to legal considerations, regulations and policies, such as personal data protection, data ownership; (iv) standards and IoT platforms that support open and dynamic interaction across both dimensions of horizontal IoT domains and vertical application domains, and overcome the fragmentation of closed systems, architectures, and applications. A tightly related Internet-of-things activity to IERC is the Alliance for Internet of Things Innovation (AIOTI) [6], which was initiated by the European Commission to address the challenges of Internet-of-things technology and application deployment, including standardization, interoperability and policy issues that are of common interest among various IoT players.

B. *Smart Applicances (SMART)*

SMART is an EU-funded study [24] with focus on semantic assets for smart appliance (i.e., devices used in households capable of communicating with each other and being controlled via Internet) interoperability. It provides a standardized framework for the smart appliances reference ontology, of which recurring concepts can be used and extended in several domains in addition to residential environments.

C. *Architecture and Interfaces for Web-oriented Automation System (WOAS)*

The project WOAS [25] is funded by the German Federal Ministry of Economics and Technology as an industrial joint research project with ten German automation companies involved. The aim of this project is to research a new architecture for automation systems based on cloud-based web technologies. The proposed architecture is referred to as a Web-Oriented Automation System (WOAS). A WOAS comprises a system kernel and a configurable number of automation services that implement and realize the required automation functions. The automation service is realized according to the concept of I40 component [12]. The connection of the automation service with distributed automation devices in the network is implemented via standard industrial interfaces and is also based on the concept of I40 component.

D. *Reference Architecture for IoT-based Smart Factory*

A research study [26] presents a reference architecture for smart factories and defines the main characteristics of such factories with a focus on sustainable energy management perspective. According to this study, Internet of things relies on both smart objects and smart networks. It is a system in which the physical items are enriched with embedded electronics, such as RFID tags and sensors, and are connected to the Internet. This reference architecture builds upon the interactive relations between smart factories and customers, which allow smart factories to collect and analyze data from products and processes for improved perception of customers' needs and behaviors, as well as better products and services. There are several sets of technologies and perspectives in this reference architecture, including smart machines, smart devices, smart manufacturing processes, smart engineering, manufacturing IT, smart logistics, big data and cloud computing, smart suppliers (i.e., building sustainable relations with suppliers), smart customers' behavior, and smart grid infrastructure for energy management.

IV. ANALYSIS AND DISCUSSIONS

The reference architectures described in section II have similarity in technical concepts and architectural principles, but there are also differences in their respective technology approaches and implementations. Therefore, we group particular characteristics that have similar concerns to describe the same or related aspects of these reference architectures. The aspects in the comparison that we are going to address include (i) technology perspective, addressing key concepts and principles used; (ii) process perspective, addressing the coverage of guidelines and process steps involved when using the reference architecture to generate concrete architectures or migrate existing solutions using the reference architecture; (iii) quality and key system concerns perspective, addressing main quality attributes and system characteristics that a specific reference architecture focuses on; and (iv) business and people perspective, addressing the coverage of value stream aspect and users-centered perspective in a specific reference architecture. Table I summarizes a comparison of the surveyed reference architectures

The inclusion of the reference architectures in this survey is based on a mapping study [27] and various research initiatives and activities within the Internet-of-things area, and covers therefore a collection of the existing reference architectures available, which is much more complete than the analysis provided in [28], which analyzes only the IoT architectural reference model and the architecture proposed by WSO2.

From surveying the existing reference architectures for Internet-of-things, we have found out several driving forces of the development of these reference architectures, such as (i) increasing complexity and size of the systems due to the tremendous amount of connected heterogeneous devices both within and across domains; (ii) increased need for shorter time-to-market and rapid development; (iii) new collaborative solutions that require integrated and coordinated information management to ensure improved effectiveness and optimized production processes or process chains in a single plant or across plants; (iv) increasing need to achieve interoperability and compliance between different devices and systems; (v) increased focus on optimizing the assets in a single physical plant, as well as optimizing operations across asset types, fleets, customers and partners involved in the Internet-of-things value chain for value co-creation. Many of these driving forces are also in line with the identified objectives of reference architectures as described in [11].

According to [11], reference architectures should address technical architecture, business architecture and customer context. From surveying the reference architectures, we have found that business architecture and customer context are often missing. Most of the architectures provide technical solutions, design patterns and tactics. For instance, some commonly used architecture patterns among these surveyed reference architectures include multitier architecture pattern using edge tier, platform tier and enterprise tier, edge-to-cloud architecture pattern, multi-tier data storage architecture pattern, distributed analytics architecture pattern, gateway or edge connectivity and management architecture pattern. However, the business models and lifecycle considerations in the business architecture are often missing. In the surveyed architectures, RAMI4.0 and IIRA are two reference architectures that explicitly include business architectures. A main characteristics of RAMI4.0 is the combination of lifecycle and value stream with a hierarchically structured approach. IIRA explicitly defines business viewpoint to address business vision, value proposition and objectives. Similar to business architectures, the customer context that addresses the processes and user considerations in the customer enterprises are often missing as well.

Another important aspect of a reference architecture is to provide practices and guidance for generating new concrete architectures [11]. Some reference architectures explicitly address this issue. For instance, in IIRA, the implementation viewpoint explicitly addresses the technical representation, the technologies and system components required to implement the activities and functions required when generating concrete architectures. Another example is IoT-ARM, which provides best practices and guidance for generating concrete architectures from IoT-ARM. It can also be used to devise system roadmaps that lead to minimum changes between two product generations while guaranteeing system capability and features. Another use of the reference architecture is benchmarking during functional components review process. One example is P2413, which supports system benchmarking, safety and security assessment.

For practitioners in industry, coping with typical characteristics of legacy systems [29] and addressing legacy issues is one important aspect in a reference architecture. Among the surveyed reference architectures, Arrowhead is one example that addresses explicitly the migration of ISA-95 systems to service-based collaborative automation systems in the cloud.

V. CONCLUSIONS

In this paper, we have surveyed well-known existing reference architectures, activities and initiatives for the Internet-of-things. To better understand and apply appropriate reference architectures for specific use cases, we have made a comparison of these reference architectures from different perspectives, including technology, process, quality and key system concerns, business and people. We also discuss the driving forces of these reference architectures, how they address technical, business and customer context, and how they address the generation of concrete architectures, as well as the legacy migration perspective. Although it is difficult to find information on examples of solutions or concrete products implementing each architecture described, we believe that our analysis and discussions would assist practitioners in their choice of reference architectures, and in the meanwhile provide input to further improvement of these reference architectures.

ACKNOWLEDGMENT

Special acknowledgement to the Swedish Foundation for Strategic Research through the project "Internet-of-things and Cloud for Intelligent Manufacturing" (SM16-0025).

REFERENCES

[1] The Economist Intelligence Unit, "The Internet of Things Business Index: A Quiet Revolution Gathers Pace," 2013.

[2] Industrial Internet Insights Report for 2015, Accenture .

[3] European Research Cluster on the Internet of Things, http://www.internet-of-things-research.eu/, retrieved in August 2017.

[4] Industrial Internet Consortium, http://www.industrialinternetconsortium.org/

[5] Industri 4.0, http://www.plattform-i40.de/, retrieved in August 2017.

[6] https://www.aioti.eu/, retrieved in August 2017.

[7] European Commission Internet-of-things, http://ec.europa.eu/digital-agenda/en/internet-things, retrieved in August 2017.

[8] E. Borgia, "The Internet of things vision: key features, applications and open issues", Journal of Computer Communications, 2014.

[9] An Oracle White Paper, "Cloud reference architecture", Oracle Enterprise Transformation Solutions Series, 2012.

[10] J. Liu, L.J. Zhang, B. Hu, and K. He, "CCRA: Cloud computing reference architecture", IEEE International Conference on Services Computing (SCC), 2012.

[11] R. Cloutler, G. Muller, D. Verma, R. Nilchiani, E. Hole, and M. Bone, "The concept of reference architectures", Systems Engineering, vol.13, 2010.

[12] RAMI 4.0, https://www.zvei.org/en/subjects/industry-4-0/the-reference-architectural-model-rami-40-and-the-industrie-40-component/, retrieved in August 2017.

[13] IIRA, http://www.iiconsortium.org/, retrieved in August 2017.

[14] ISO/IEC/IEEE 42010:2011 Systems and software engineering – architecture description, https://www.iso.org/standard/50508.html

[15] A. Bassi et al, Enabling things to talk – designing IoT solutions with the IoT architectural reference model, ISBN 978-3-642-40402-3, Springer, 2013.

[16] E. Woods, and R. Nick, "The system context architectural viewpoint", Joint Working IEEE/IFIP Conference on Software Architecture and European Conference on Software Architecture, WICSA/ECSA, 2009.

[17] IEEE P2413, http://grouper.ieee.org/groups/2413/, IEEE Standards Association

[18] Arrowhead Framework, http://www.arrowhead.eu/, retrieved in August 2017.

[19] H. Derhamy, J. Eliasson, J. Delsing, and P. Priller, "A survey of commercial frameworks for the Internet of things", IEEE Conference on Emerging Technologies and Factory Automation, 2015.

[20] P. Fremantle, "A reference architecture for the Internet of things", WSO2 White Paper, version 0.9.0, 2015.

[21] https://azure.microsoft.com/en-au/updates/microsoft-azure-iot-reference-architecture-available/, retrieved in August 2017.

[22] https://www.iotwf.com/resources, retrieved in August 2017.

[23] http://www.intel.com/content/www/us/en/internet-of-things/white-papers/iot-platform-reference-architecture-paper.html, retrieved in August 2017.

[24] https://sites.google.com/site/smartappliancesproject/home, retrieved in August 2017.

[25] R. Langmann, and L. Meyer, "Automation services from the cloud", IEEE International Conference on Remote Engineering and Virtual Instrumentation, 2014.

[26] F. Shrouf, J. Ordieres, and G. Miragliotta, "Smart factories in Industry 4.0: a review of the concept and of energy management approached in production based on the Internet of things paradigm", IEEE International Conference on Industrial Engineering and Engineering Management, 2014.

[27] H. Pei-Breivold, "Internet-of-things and Cloud computing for smart industry: a systematic mapping study", to be published at the International Conference on Enterprise Systems, 2017.

[28] E. Cavalcante, M.P. Alves, and T. Batista, "An analysis of reference architectures for the Internet of things", International Workshop on Exploring Component-based Techniques for Constructing Reference Architectures, 2015.

[29] S. Demeyer, S. Ducasse, and O. M. Nierstrasz, Object-Oriented Reengineering Patterns, ISBN 978-3-9523341-2-6, Morgan Kaufmann, 2003.

TABLE I. A COMPARISON OF REFERENCE ARCHITECTURES FOR INTERNET OF THINGS

Reference Architectures	Technology	Process	Quality and Key System Concerns	Business and People
RAMI4.0	A key concept is I4.0 component. Service-oriented and layered architecture. Follow and extend IEC62264 and IEC61512 standards. Permit encapsulation of functionalities. Standards compliant.	Address product lifecycle management dimension, horizontal integration across factories and vertical integration within factory. Allow step by step migration to I4.0 components.	Address security for functionality and data, functional safety and safety measures. The I4.0 component possesses the quality of service properties necessary for specific applications.	Address people orchestrating the value stream, and value stream dimension throughout product lifecycle and across factories.
IIRA	Key concepts include concern, stakeholder, and viewpoint. Based on ISO/IEC/IEEE 42010:2011. Standard-based open architecture.	Integration of information technologies and operational technologies.	Address safety, security, trust and privacy, resilience, integrability, interoperability and composability, connectivity.	Business viewpoint to address business vision, value proposition and objectives.
IoT-ARM	Key concepts include aspect-oriented programming, model-driven engineering, views and perspectives. Evolution and interoperability are the main drivers for the reference model and architecture.	Provide guidelines and process steps on how to generate concrete architectures, perform IoT threat analysis, and derive design choices and tactics based on qualitative requirements.	Address evolution and interoperability, performance and scalability, trust, security, privacy, availability and resilience.	Business goals, cost and benefit analysis are used in the architecture generation process. Specification of an IoT business process model to make use cases IoT-ARM compliant.
P2413	Key concepts include concern, stakeholder, and viewpoint. Based on ISO/IEC/IEEE 42010:2011 standard.	Provide guidelines for cross-domain interaction, documenting and migrating architecture divergence.	Address system interoperability, functional compatibility, protection, security, privacy and safety.	People perspective is reflected in the process of identifying stakeholders and their concerns.
Arrowhead	Key concepts include local cloud, global cloud. Automation cloud integration based on service-oriented architecture. Information centric.	Provide maturity levels of legacy system migration to cloud, engineering tools for development, and test support of cloud automation systems.	Address service interoperability and integrability, security, latency, scalability, dynamic/continuous engineering.	Not explicit
WSO2	Influenced by open-source projects and technologies	Not explicit	Address connectivity and communications, device management, data collection, analysis and actuation, scalability, security, and integration.	Not explicit
Azure IoT	Key principles include heterogeneity, security, hyper-scale deployments, and flexibility. Data concepts include device and data model, data streams, and device interaction.	A vendor-specific solution architecture	Not explicit	Business systems integration layer and solution UX are two architecture components relevant to business and people.
Internet-of-everything	A key concept is edge-ware. Multilevel model for IoT;	Integration of information technologies and operational technologies; enablement of legacy applications.	Address interoperability, security, and legacy compatibility.	Application layer covering business intelligence and analytics. Collaboration and processes layer explicitly involves people and processes.
Intel IoT	Building blocks include things, networks, and cloud.	Integration of information technologies and operational technologies.	Address data and device connectivity, security, and interoperability.	Value proposition by smart decision making based on data analytics.

Improving Run-Time Memory Utilization of Component-based Embedded Systems with Non-Critical Functionality

Gabriel Campeanu and Saad Mubeen
Mälardalen Real-Time Research Center
Mälardalen University, Västerås, Sweden
Email: {gabriel.campeanu, saad.mubeen}@mdh.se

Abstract—**Many contemporary embedded systems have to deal with huge amount of data, coming from the interaction with the environment, due to their data-intensive applications. However, due to some inherent properties of these systems, such as limited energy and resources (compute and storage), it is important that the resources should be used in an efficient way. For example, camera sensors of a robot may provide low-resolution frames for positioning itself in an open environment, and high-resolution frames to analyze detected objects. Component-based software development techniques and models have proven to be efficient for the development of these systems. Many component models used in the industry (e.g., Rubus, IEC 61131) allocate, at the system initialization, enough resources to satisfy the demands of the system's critical functionality. These resources are retained by the critical functionality even when they are not fully utilized. In this paper, we introduce a method that, when possible, distributes the unused memory of the critical functionality to the non-critical functionality in order to improve its performance. The method uses a monitoring solution that checks the memory utilization, and triggers the memory distribution whenever possible. As a proof of concept, we realize the proposed method in an industrial component model. As an evaluation, we use an underwater robot case study to evaluate the feasibility of the proposed solution.**

Keywords–embedded system; component-based software development; model-based development; resource utilization; monitor.

I. Introduction

Embedded systems are found in almost all electronic products that are available today. These systems find their applications in a vast range of systems, i.e., from small-sized devices, such as watches and telephones to large-sized systems, such as cars and airplanes. Many modern embedded systems process huge amount of data that is originated from their interaction with the environment. One example is the Google autonomous car that processes around 750 MB data per second [1]. The reduced computation power and sequential execution of software that characterize many embedded systems can represent a challenge to deliver the performance level required by the systems when processing huge amount of data.

Graphics Processing Units (GPUs) represent a solution to deliver the required performance level when the system deals with processing huge amount of data. Characterized by a parallel execution model, the GPU can process multiple data in parallel. An aspect of the GPU is that it cannot function without a CPU; considered as the brain of the system, the CPU triggers all GPU-related activities (e.g., parallel execution of functions). The latest technological developments allow the combination of CPUs and GPUs on the same embedded boards, resulting in various heterogeneous platforms, such as NVIDIA Jetson [2] and AMD R-464L [3].

Due to the specifics of embedded systems, such as limited compute and memory resources, the amount of data captured from the environment can significantly impact the management of the system resources while delivering the required performance. One way to optimize the resource usage is to collect variable stream-size of data from the sensors depending upon different environment situations. For example, camera sensors (e.g., ProcImage500-Eagle [4]) with configurable resolutions may provide: *i)* frames with high resolution, and *ii)* frames with low resolution. While the high resolution frames require larger memory footprints and more computation power (and energy) to be processed (on GPUs), the low resolution frames are delivered with faster frame rate, occupy less memory and require lower computation power for GPU processing. Depending on the environment circumstances, cameras may provide high or low quality frames. For example, a robot fitted with such a camera may use low resolution data frames to examine its position. On the other hand, the robot may use high resolution frames to inspect the target objects in a detailed manner.

The system resources (e.g., memory and computation power) in many embedded systems are shared between the critical (with real-time requirements) and non-critical functionality. The goal in the case of the critical functionality is to meet all the timing requirements. Whereas, the best-effort service is targeted in the case of the non-critical functionality. Hence, the system needs to ensure that all the required resources are always available to the critical part of the application. For example, a vision system of a robot represents critical functionality. This system is designed in such a way that it is always guaranteed enough resources to process the high-resolution frames. Even when the cameras provide lower-resolution frames, the system still occupies the same amount of resources as if it were processing the high-resolution frames. As a result, the system resources are wasted when the critical functionality does not need them. In our point of view, the non-critical functionality can benefit from these resources in the intervals where they are not used by the critical functionality. For example, when the robot utilizes lower resolution frames, a logger system (non-critical functionality) would benefit from extra memory (not being used by the vision system) to save more information about the system activities.

In order to deal with the complexity, among other challenges, the software for embedded systems is developed using the principles of Component-Based Software Engineering (CBSE) and Model-Based Engineering [5] [6]. Using these principles, models are used throughout the development process and the software is constructed by connecting reusable software units, called the software components. CBSE and MBD have been successfully adopted by the industry through component models, such as AUTOSAR [7], Rubus Component Model (RCM) [8] and IEC 61131 [9]. The existing component models that can be used to build stream-of-event applications (e.g., RCM, AUTOSAR, IEC 61131 and ProCom[10]), face a challenge to deal with (streaming) data that can change its memory footprint on-the-fly. For example, RCM defines that its components use the same fixed memory footprint throughout the execution of the application. In order to ensure the required resources to the critical functionality, resources are assigned to each RCM software component, with respect to its worst-case resource demand for the entire system execution. Therefore, RCM and similar component models (discussed above) do not support any mechanism to release the resources when they are not required (by the critical part of the system).

This paper provides an automatic method to compute the unused resources of the critical part of the system, and distribute them to the (non-critical) parts of the system. This is achieved by using a monitoring solution that monitors the critical part of the system and detects when it changes its resource requirements. After detection, the monitoring solution triggers our proposed method that calculates the unused memory, based on the actual resource usage of the critical system. This information is passed to the (non-critical) part of the system that can benefit from utilizing the freed resources.

The rest of the paper is organized as follows. Section II describes the background and related work. Section III formulates the problem and describes it with the help of a case study. The overview of our solution is described in Section IV and its realization is presented in Section V. Section VI discusses the implementation of the solution. The evaluation of our method applied to the case study is discussed in Section VII. Finally, Section VIII concludes the paper.

II. Background and Related Work

GPUs were developed in 90s and were employed only in graphic-based applications. By time, due to the increase in their computation power and ease of use, GPUs have been utilized in different type of applications, becoming the general-purpose processing units referred to as GPGPUs [11]. For example, cryptography applications [12] and Monte Carlo simulations [13] have GPU-based solutions. Equipped with a parallel architecture, the GPU may employ thousands of computation threads at a time through its multiple cores. Compared to the traditional CPU, the GPU delivers an improved performance with respect to processing multiple data in parallel. For example, simulation of bio-molecular systems have achieved 20 times speed-up on GPU [14].

One of the GPU characteristics is that it cannot function without the help of a CPU. The CPU is considered as the brain of the system that triggers all the activities related to GPU, such as the execution of functionality onto GPU. The latest technological developments allow various vendors, such as NVIDIA, Intel, AMD and Samsung to combine CPUs and GPUs on the same embedded board. For example, there are boards known as System-on-Chips (SoCs) that merge together CPUs and GPUs onto the same physical chip, such as NVIDIA Jetson TK1 [2] and Samsung Exynos 8 [15].

Regarding embedded systems that contain GPUs, there are model- and component-based software engineering extensions to facilitate the development of CPU-GPU applications [16] [17]. Component models follow various interaction styles that are suitable for different types of applications [18]. We mention the *request-response* and *sender-receiver* interaction styles that are utilized in AUTOSAR component model when developing automotive applications. Another style utilized by e.g., Rubus and IEC 61131 component models, is the *pipe-and-filter* interaction style. This particular style is characteristic to streaming of event-type of applications and allows an easy mapping between the flow of system actions and control specifications, characteristic to real-time and safety-critical applications.

There exist different methods to increase the memory utilization, which are presented in various surveys [19]. We mention a solution to reduce the actual allocated space for temporary arrays by using a mapping of different array parts into the same physical memory [20]. Another method proposes scratch pad memories to reduce the power consumption and improve performance [21]. These solutions are applicable at a very low level of abstraction and are not suitable to be merged with our approach, which is applicable at the implementation abstraction level where the software architecture of the application is modeled.

Regarding monitors, many works utilize them for different purposes, such as data-flow monitoring solutions to simulate large CPU-GPU systems [22], and GPU monitors for balancing the bandwidth usage [23]. An interesting work conducted by Haban et al. [24] introduced software monitors to help scheduling activities. The authors described the low overhead of the monitoring solutions, which degrade the CPU performance with less than 0.1%. In our work, we use the same type of monitors analyzed by Haban (i.e., software monitors) that have a low impact over the system performance.

III. Problem

One way to reduce resource and energy usage of embedded systems is to decrease the data produced by sensors with respect to e.g., environment conditions. For example, a robot may require low-resolution frames to process open-space environments but may utilize high-resolution frames when analyzing close ups of detected objects. Therefore, the robot cameras may be set to provide, on-the-fly, frames with different resolutions based on e.g., distance to tracked objects.

Due to the rules that existing component models apply for the construction of software components, the size of a component's input data is fixed during the execution of the system. One way to ensure the guaranteed execution of the system is to allocate the system resources to software components, at the design time, to deal with the maximum footprint of data produced by sensors. For example, if a camera produces frames with 1280 x 1024 pixels, the software components that process the camera feedback utilize memory corresponding to the camera's frames. Even when the camera produces lower quality frames (e.g., 640 x 480 pixels) with a lower memory footprint, the software components are set to utilize the memory footprint characteristic to 1280 x 1024 pixel frames, resulting in under-utilization of the system memory.

We use a case study as a running example to discuss the problem in detail. The case study is centered around an underwater robot that autonomously navigates under water, fulfilling various missions (e.g., tracking red buoys) [25]. The robot contains a CPU-GPU embedded board that is connected to various sensors (e.g., cameras) and actuators (e.g., thrusters).

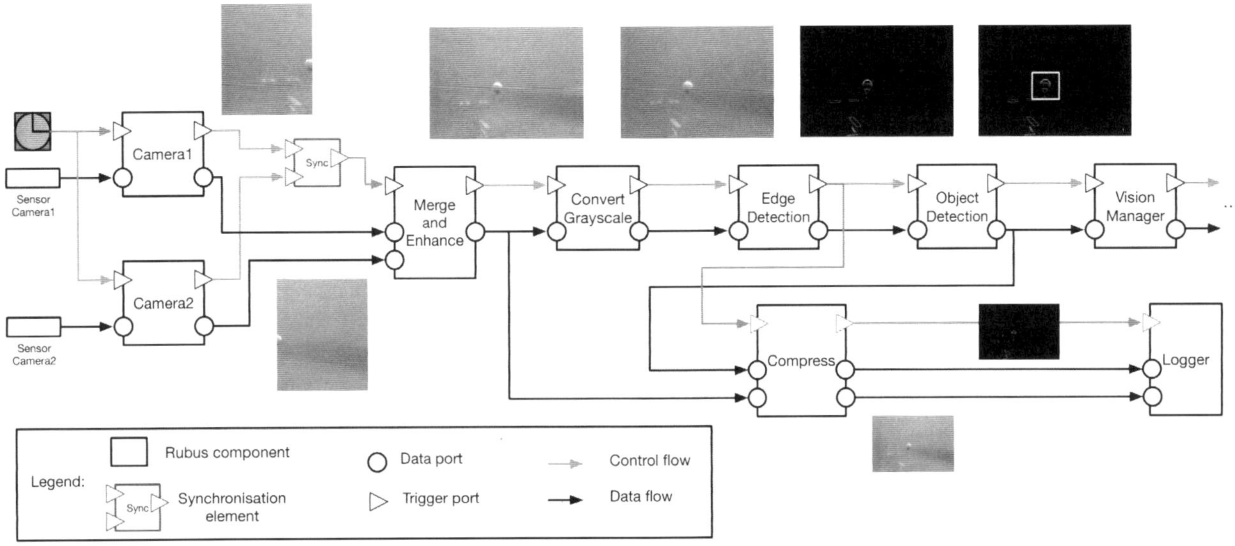

Figure 1. Component-based Rubus vision system of the underwater robot.

Sensors provide a continuous flow of environment data that is processed by the GPU on-the-fly.

A simplified component-based software architecture of the robot's vision system is depicted in Figure 1. The software architecture, realized using RCM, contains nine software components. The *Camera1* and *Camera2* software components are connected to the physical sensors and convert the received data into readable frames. The *MergeAndEnhance* software component reduces the noise and merges the two frames using the GPU. The resulted frame is converted into a gray-scale frame by *ConvertGrayscale* software component (on the GPU), which is forwarded to *EdgeDetection* software component that produces a black-and-white frame with detected edges. The *ObjectDetection* software component identifies the target object from the received frame and forwards the result to the system manager that takes appropriate actions, such as grabbing the detected objects.

When the robot navigates underwater, the cameras are set to produce 640 x 480 pixel frames to track points for positioning itself. Due to the particularities of the water, sometime being muddy or the underwater vision being influenced by the weather conditions (e.g., cloudy, sunny), there is no need for high-resolution frames as the visibility is reduced. Figure 1 presents 640 x 480 pixel frames that contain several objects. While one of the missions is to track and touch buoys, the robot navigates to the detected objects. When the robot is close (e.g., 1 meter away) to the detected object, it requires high-resolution frames to observe and refine the details needed for the distinction between similar type of objects. In this case, cameras produce 1280 x 960 pixel frames.

Following the specifications of RCM, each software component is equipped with a constructor and a destructor. The constructor is executed once, before the system execution, while the destructor is executed when the system is properly switched off or reset. The constructor has the role to allocate resources needed by the component, such as memory required by the internal behavior and output data ports. As it is executed only once, the constructor allocates a fixed memory size for the duration of entire execution life of the component. For the presented vision system, the constructor of each component reserves memory to handle e.g., input data of maximum size. In our running case system, the constructor of *Camera1* allocates memory space that holds 1280 x 960 pixel frames. When sensors provide frames with lower resolution and memory footprint, *Camera1* has reserved the same amount of memory (corresponding to 1280 x 960 pixel frames) from which it uses only a part, resulting in under utilization of the memory.

Another part of the underwater robot is the logger system that is composed of two software components, i.e., *Compress* and *Logger*. This part of the software architecture has a non-critical functionality. The purpose of this non-critical part is to compress and record various information of the robot during the underwater journey. Due to the limited memory (RAM), *Compress* and *Logger* software components save the resulted frames (onto RAM) from *ObjectDetector* software component. These frames are copied from the RAM to a flash memory by a specific service of the operating system. If more memory was available to the logger system, it would have also saved the unaltered (original) frames from the *MergeAndEnhance* software component. This would improve various system activities e.g., checking the (correct) functionality of the vision system by comparing the original and processed frames. Moreover, the logger system may benefit from extra memory by delivering other system information (e.g., energy usage and temperature) that improves the debugging activity of the robot.

IV. Generic Solution

In order to improve the resource utilization of non-critical parts of the embedded systems, we introduce an automatic method that, during run-time, provides information on the additional available resources that can be used by the non-critical parts. Figure 2 presents the overview design of our proposed method and its interactions with the critical and non-critical parts of embedded system.

Our method uses a monitoring solution that periodically checks (e.g., every execution) the memory usage of the critical system. Step (arrow) 1 from Figure 2 expresses the examina-

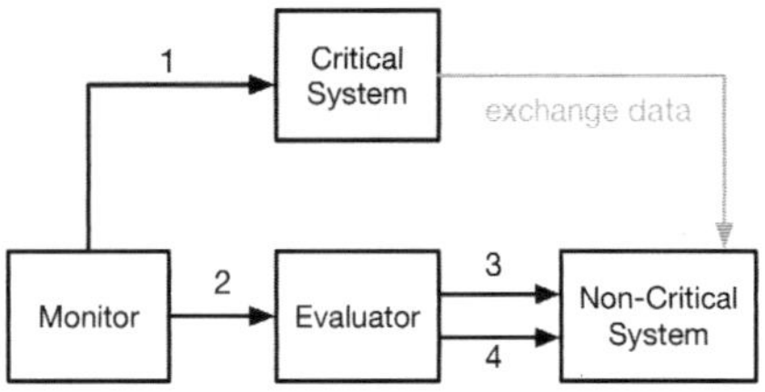

Figure 2. Overview design of the proposed method.

tion of the critical system by the monitoring solution. During step 2, the monitor sends the actual memory usage to the evaluator. Based on the the received information, the evaluator has two following two options.

- If the critical system uses as much memory as its maximum (worst case) requirement, the evaluator informs the non-critical system to use its default memory allocated memory (step 3).
- If the critical system uses less memory than its maximum requirement, the evaluator computes the size of the unused memory and distributes it to the non-critical system (step 4).

V. REALIZATION

This section describes the realization details of our method using the vision system case study. The first part of the section introduces groundwork details on the functionality of the component model, while the second part presents the overall realization of our method.

A. Component Model Functionality

Each component is characterized by a constructor and a destructor. The constructor is executed once, at the initialization of the system, and allocates as much memory as the component requires. The destructor, executing once when the system is properly switched off, has the purpose to deallocate the memory. Figure 3 shows two connected software component from the vision system. In order to simplify the figure, we remove some of the (triggering) connections to the component. Camera1 sends a frame to MergeAndEnhance component. Initially, the constructor of Camera1 allocates memory space to accommodate frames of maximum size (i.e., 1280 x 960 pixels). When the robot changes its mode (e.g., for saving its energy) and its physical cameras send lower size frame (i.e., 640 x 480 pixels), Camera1 uses only a part of the memory, which was allocated by its constructor.

To send large data (i.e., larger than a scalar), components need to use pointers, as follows. The output port of Camera1 is basically a *struct* that contains a pointer variable and two scalars, characteristics to 2D images. The port may cover other types of data, such as 3D images by including additional information, such as a third scalar. The pointer indicates to the memory address that it is at the beginning of the data to be transferred, and the two scalars (i.e., height and width) describe the size of the frame. In this way, Camera1 passes the information (of the pointer and scalars) about the data (from RAM) to be transferred to the MergeAndEnhance component. We can see in the figure that the transferred data is a frame of 640 x 480 pixels, which means that there is some unused memory. Using this information (i.e., size), the Evaluator

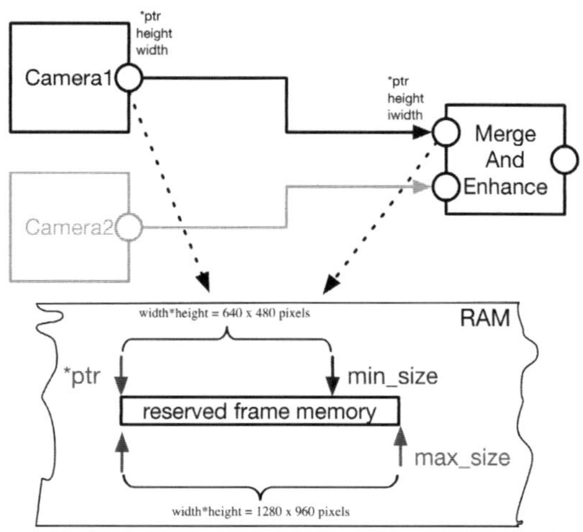

Figure 3. Data transferring between two components.

component calculates the total unused memory of the vision system and inform the Logger system to use it.

B. Vision System Realization

The vision system is composed of four parts and realized as follows.

a) The Critical System. The critical system contains the functionality that has the highest priority in the system. In our case, it produces and processes the frames, and takes decisions based on the findings. There are seven software components included in this part of the system as illustrated in Figure 4.

b) The Monitor. We realize the monitor as a service that is regularly performed by the operating system. The service checks the settings of the camera sensors and produces a value that corresponds to the frame sizes produced by the cameras, i.e., 1024 or 640.

c) The Evaluator. The evaluator is realized as a regular software component that receives its input information from the monitoring service. Because it decides the distribution of the resource memory utilized by the critical system, the priority of the *Evaluator* component is set to the highest level. Based on this value, the Evaluator component decides if the non-critical system can use more resources and produces the data that reflects this decision. For simplicity, the output result is a boolean variable; the output value 1 means that the non-critical system may use more resources than initially allocated, and 0 the opposite. The *Evaluator* component (i.e., its constructor, behavior function and destructor) is entirely automatically generated through our solution.

d) The non-critical system. The part of the system that handles the logging functionality represents the non-critical system. It has a lower priority than the critical system and evaluator software component. It contains two software components, i.e., *Compress* and *Logger* that communicate with the *Evaluator* through an additional port. Based on the (boolean) data received via the additional port, the two non-critical components use one or two frames in their computations.

VI. IMPLEMENTATION

The solution presented in this paper does not interfere with the development and execution of the critical system. It is con-

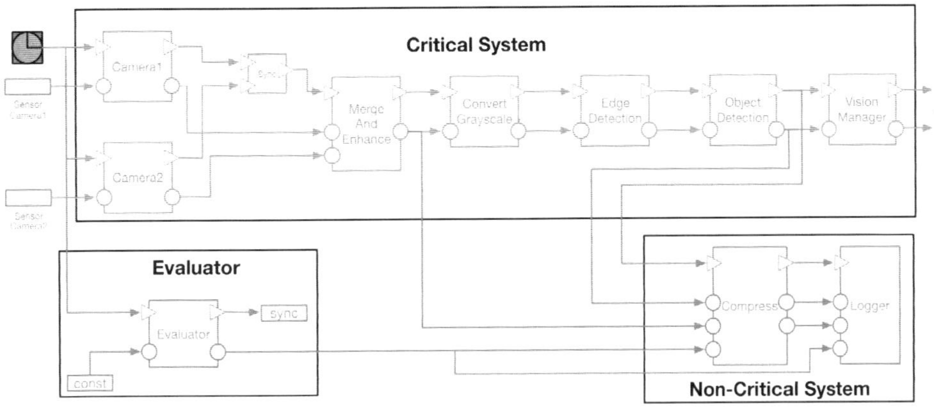

Figure 4. Realization of the proposed method applied on the vision system.

structed by the developer. For the monitoring solution, we use a service provided by the OS. The evaluator is implemented as a regular component with an input and output data port. Through the input port, it receives data from the monitoring solution, while the output port provides a boolean data. At this stage of our solution, the functionality is simple and decides, based on the input value, if the non-critical system can have access to more resources or not. Although the functionality is simple and can be easily merged to the non-critical system, we opt for the separation-of-concerns principle, which is essential in the model- and component-based software development. Moreover, the evaluator functionality can be increased to adapt for more complex systems.

```
1  if(<InPort3.Name>==1)
2  {
3    cl_mem frame2_out = clCreateBuffer(context, CL_MEM_READ_WRITE,
         3*(<OutPort2.Name>->width)*(<OutPort2.Name>->height) *
         sizeof(unsigned char), NULL, NULL);
4
5  /* initialize parameters */
6    clSetKernelArg(kernel, 0, sizeof(cl_mem), (void *)&
         <InPort2.Name>->ptr);
7    clSetKernelArg(kernel, 1, sizeof(int), (void *)&<InPort2.Name>->
         width);
8    clSetKernelArg(kernel, 2, sizeof(int),(void *)&<InPort2.Name>->
         height);
9    clSetKernelArg(kernel, 4, sizeof(cl_mem), (void *)&frame2_out);
10
11 /* execute functionality on the second frame */
12   clEnqueueNDRangeKernel(command_queue, kernel, 2, NULL,
         global_size, local_size, 0, NULL, NULL);
13 }
```

Figure 5. Generated part of the behavior function.

The non-critical system is mostly constructed by the developer, where our approach introduces some elements that are automatically generated. Initially, the non-critical system uses resources to process one frame; the constructors of *Compress* and *Logger* components allocate memory for one frame to be used in their functionality. In order to enforce a larger memory usage, the two components need to allocate more memory to hold the result from processing the second frame. As the constructor is executed once at the system initialization stage, we automatically allocate memory inside the components' behavior function.

Figure 5 illustrates the code generated inside the behavior function of each software component from the non-critical system. We assume that each port has a name. For simplicity, all the components from the non-critical system have an input port with a boolean value (i.e., 1 and 0) that is connected to the *Evaluator* component. Line 1 checks the value sent from the Evaluator, where 1 means that the component can use additional memory to process the second frame. In line 3, memory is allocated to hold the result from processing the second frame. Specific to the GPU functionality implemented using the OpenCL syntax, parameters that correspond to the second frame specifications, are set in lines 6-9. Finally, the same functionality that processes the first frame is applied to the second frame, in line 12.

VII. EVALUATION

As our approach introduces additional elements to the system, this section focuses on the evaluation of overhead incurred due to the proposed solution. There are two parts that influence the overall overhead, i.e., the memory footprint and the execution time.

The memory footprint refers to the generated *Evaluator* component and the generated part of each behavior function of the non-critical system (see Figure 5). The Evaluator component consists of a constructor, behavior function, and a destructor. Moreover, it has specification of its interface (i.e., ports) in a separate header file. The memory footprint of all of its code takes approximately 14 KB. We need to also add the memory size occupied by the generated parts of the *Compress* and *Logger* components, which result in a total of 15 KB. We consider that the memory footprint overhead resulted from our approach is manageable for an embedded systems with GPUs, compared to traditional (CPU-based) embedded systems. The CPU-GPU embedded systems are characterized by a reasonable high amount of memory (i.e., order of tens of Megabyte) due to the computation power that requires high memory specifications.

Regarding the execution time, the generated *Evaluator* component may negatively affect the execution time of the critical system. In this regard, we conducted an experiment to compare the performance with and without our approach. The system on which we executed the experiments contains an embedded board AMD Accelerated Processing Unit with a Kabini architecture (i.e., CPU-GPU SoC). We used two input images, i.e., one with $640 * 480$ pixels and the other with $1280 * 960$ pixels. For each set of images, we executed two cases, one with and the other without our solution. Each case was executed 100 times and we calculated its average execution time.

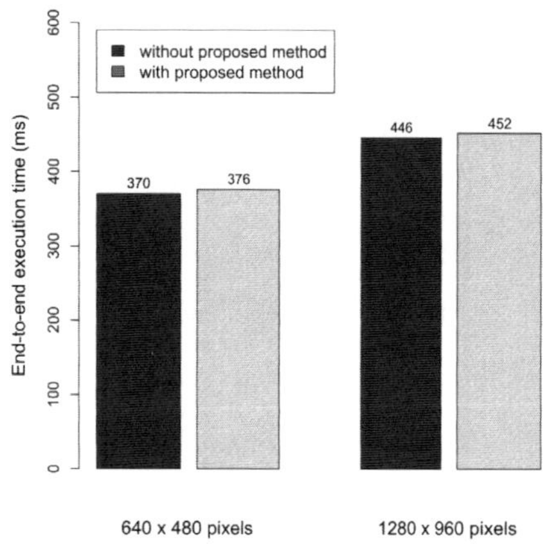

Figure 6. Usage of the proposed method in the vision system execution.

The results of the experiments are shown in Figure 6. A slight increase (1.3 to 1.6%) in the execution time can be observed when our solution is applied. The results indicate that the performance of the non-critical part of these systems can be significantly improved with our method at the very small execution time overhead.

VIII. Conclusion

Modern embedded systems deal with huge amount of data that is originated from their interaction with the environment. GPUs have emerged as a feasible option, from the performance perspective, for processing the huge data inputs. However, with GPU-based solutions the resource utilization remains high, which is an important aspect when dealing with resource-constrained embedded systems. In this paper, we have presented a method that improves the resource utilization for non-critical parts of CPU-GPU-based embedded systems. Whenever the critical part of the system does not fully utilize its required memory due to various reasons, such as reducing energy consumption, our method distributes the unused memory to the non-critical part of the system that can use the resources to improve its performance. As a proof of concept, we have realized the method in a state-of-the-practice model, namely the Rubus Component Model. We have also demonstrated the usability of the method using the underwater robot case study. The evaluation results indicate that the performance of the non-critical part of CPU-GPU-based embedded systems can be significantly improved with our method at the very small execution time overhead of approximately 1.5%.

Acknowledgments

The work in this paper has been supported by the RALF3 project - (IIS11-0060) through the Swedish Foundation for Strategic Research (SSF).

References

[1] Google. Waymo - Google Self-Driving Car Project. https://waymo.com/. Retrieved: July, 2016.

[2] NVIDIA, "NVIDIA Jetson TK1," http://www.nvidia.com/object/jetson-tk1-embedded-dev-kit.html, retrieved: July, 2017.

[3] AMD, "Embedded R-Series Family of Processors," http://www.amd.com/en-us/products/embedded/processors/r-series, retrieved: July, 2017.

[4] See Fast Technologies. High Speed Camera ProcImage500-Eagle. http://www.seefastechnologies.com/procimage-eng1-pi500-eagle.html. Retrieved: July, 2016.

[5] I. Crnkovic and M. P. H. Larsson, Building reliable component-based software systems. Artech House, 2002.

[6] T. A. Henzinger and J. Sifakis, "The embedded systems design challenge," in International Symposium on Formal Methods. Springer, 2006, pp. 1–15.

[7] "AUTOSAR - Technical Overview," http://www.autosar.org, retrieved: July, 2017.

[8] K. Hanninen, J. Maki-Turja, M. Nolin, M. Lindberg, J. Lundback, and K.-L. Lundback, "The rubus component model for resource constrained real-time systems," in Industrial Embedded Systems, 2008. SIES 2008. International Symposium on. IEEE, 2008, pp. 177–183.

[9] I. Application, "Implementation of IEC 61131-3," Geneva: IEC, 1995.

[10] S. Sentilles, A. Vulgarakis, T. Bures, J. Carlson, and I. Crnkovic, "A Component Model for Control-Intensive Distributed Embedded Systems," in 11th International Symposium on Component Based Software Engineering (CBSE), vol. 8. Springer, October 2008, pp. 310–317.

[11] J. D. Owens, M. Houston, D. Luebke, S. Green, J. E. Stone, and J. C. Phillips, "GPU computing," Proceedings of the IEEE, vol. 96, no. 5, 2008, pp. 879–899.

[12] S. A. Manavski, "CUDA compatible GPU as an efficient hardware accelerator for AES cryptography," in IEEE International Conference on Signal Processing and Communications. ICSPC 2007.

[13] T. Preis, P. Virnau, W. Paul, and J. J. Schneider, "GPU accelerated Monte Carlo simulation of the 2D and 3D Ising model," Journal of Computational Physics, vol. 228, no. 12, 2009, pp. 4468 – 4477.

[14] J. E. Stone, J. C. Phillips, P. L. Freddolino, D. J. Hardy, and L. G. Trabuco, "Accelerating molecular modeling applications with graphics processors," Journal of computational chemistry, 2007.

[15] Samsung, "Exynos 8 Octa," http://www.samsung.com/semiconductor/minisite/Exynos/w/solution/mod_ap/8890/, retrieved: July, 2017.

[16] G. Campeanu, J. Carlson, and S. Sentilles, "Component allocation optimization for heterogeneous cpu-gpu embedded systems," in Software Engineering and Advanced Applications (SEAA), 2014 40th EUROMICRO Conference on. IEEE, 2014, pp. 229–236.

[17] G. Campeanu, J. Carlson, S. Sentilles, and S. Mubeen, "Extending the Rubus component model with GPU-aware components," in Component-Based Software Engineering (CBSE), 2016 19th International ACM SIGSOFT Symposium on. IEEE, 2016, pp. 59–68.

[18] I. Crnkovic, S. Sentilles, A. Vulgarakis, and M. R. Chaudron, "A classification framework for software component models," IEEE Transactions on Software Engineering, vol. 37, no. 5, 2011, pp. 593–615.

[19] P. R. Panda, F. Catthoor, N. D. Dutt, K. Danckaert, E. Brockmeyer, C. Kulkarni, A. Vandercappelle, and P. G. Kjeldsberg, "Data and memory optimization techniques for embedded systems," ACM Transactions on Design Automation of Electronic Systems (TODAES), vol. 6, no. 2, 2001, pp. 149–206.

[20] M. A. Miranda, F. V. Catthoor, M. Janssen, and H. J. De Man, "High-level address optimization and synthesis techniques for data-transfer-intensive applications," IEEE Transactions on Very Large Scale Integration (VLSI) Systems, vol. 6, no. 4, 1998, pp. 677–686.

[21] R. Banakar, S. Steinke, B.-S. Lee, M. Balakrishnan, and P. Marwedel, "Scratchpad memory: design alternative for cache on-chip memory in embedded systems," in Proceedings of the tenth international symposium on Hardware/software codesign. ACM, 2002, pp. 73–78.

[22] B. R. Bilel, N. Navid, and M. S. M. Bouksiaa, "Hybrid CPU-GPU distributed framework for large scale mobile networks simulation," in Proceedings of the 2012 IEEE/ACM 16th International Symposium on Distributed Simulation and Real Time Applications. IEEE Computer Society, 2012, pp. 44–53.

[23] M. K. Jeong, M. Erez, C. Sudanthi, and N. Paver, "A QoS-aware memory controller for dynamically balancing GPU and CPU bandwidth use in an MPSoC," in Proceedings of the 49th Annual Design Automation Conference. ACM, 2012, pp. 850–855.

[24] D. Haban and K. G. Shin, "Application of real-time monitoring to scheduling tasks with random execution times," IEEE Transactions on software engineering, vol. 16, no. 12, 1990, pp. 1374–1389.

[25] C. Ahlberg, L. Asplund, G. Campeanu, F. Ciccozzi, F. Ekstrand, M. Ekstrom, J. Feljan, A. Gustavsson, S. Sentilles, I. Svogor et al., "The Black Pearl: An autonomous underwater vehicle," 2013.

From Language-Independent Requirements to Code Based on a Semantic Analysis

Mariem Mefteh
IT department, Mir@cl Laboratory
ENIS, Sfax University
Sfax, Tunisia.
Email: Mariem.Mefteh.Ch@gmail.com

Nadia Bouassida
IT department, Mir@cl Laboratory
ISIMS, Sfax University
Sfax, Tunisia.
Email: Nadia.Bouassida@isimsf.rnu.tn

Hanêne Ben-Abdallah
Faculty of computing and Information Technology, King Abdulaziz University,
Jeddah, KSA
Email: HBenAbdallah@kau.edu.sa

Abstract—**This paper presents a new approach, which allows building Java codes from language-independent requirements. In other terms, it does not require any manual transformation of the requirements into the syntax of a specific programming language. To handle these challenges, our approach relies on a set of English-based mapping rules to generate a semantic representation of the input requirements. This semantic representation is used to produce the source code via existing code generators, such as Pegasus_f. Indeed, our approach extracts the Pegasus code from the semantic representation. This code is refined by eliminating the redundancy among the code elements' names thanks to the Term Frequency/Inverse Document Frequency (TF/IDF) method and the Density-based spatial clustering of applications with noise (DBSCAN) algorithm. Finally, Pegasus_f transforms automatically the resulting Pegasus code to Java. The proposed approach is implemented through the Code Recovery tool (CodeRec-tool), which accepts the English and the French languages in its actual version. The simplicity and the usefulness of our approach have been evaluated using measurements and based on experts' feedback.**

Keywords–Natural Language Processing; Semantics; Requirements; Naturalistic programming; Syntactic/Semantic grammar.

I. INTRODUCTION

All programming languages are progressing. Programmers, working within a company, are forced to update always their knowledge to recover this progress and to be able to use them. This leads to a significant waste of time in acquiring the programming languages' instructions and syntax. However, if programmers were able to express their program ideas in natural language, they would not have to transform them into programming language structures anymore. Programmers are obliged to transform their thoughts into the existing programming languages. Thus, it would be useful if we resort to the development of new ones, which are completely different from what exist. In fact, ideas are almost the same if we express them in several languages. It would be valid as long as the language, in which they are expressed, exists and is understood by people.

Referring to Knöll et al. [1], current programming techniques suffer from four main problems, namely: (i) the mental problem, which reflects the obligation of program ideas' adjustment to the conditions of a specific programming language (like restructuring them in the form of classes, methods and attributes in the object-oriented languages); (ii) the programming language problem, which reflects the mandatory implementation of the same program ideas and algorithms but in many ways depending on each programming language conditions; (iii) the natural language problem, i.e. the fact that people from different countries and working together are obliged to document and comment developed software in a well-known language, especially in English, which is less productive than using their mother tongue (they can make errors when using a non-native language if they could not use it correctly); (iv) the technical problem causing the waste of developers' time, spent for implementing and debugging the programs although ideas are unique. In fact, they still have to deal with minor issues like choosing the right character set and doing number conversions, instead of facing the really challenging tasks of programming: describing, modeling and enhancing the actual idea of a program [2]. These problems incur time loss and productivity decrease for software development companies.

To leverage the aforementioned problems, the project Pegasus [3] was elaborated as a new, naturalistic programming language. Naturalistic Programming means writing computer programs with the help of a natural language [1]. Pegasus accepts instructions written in a semi-natural language, and it produces the respective program accordingly. Besides Pegasus, several works were proposed to generate code from instructions written in a natural language, *cf.* [4]–[7]. The majority of these works is either semi-automated, or accepts inputs that are not written in a purely natural language. Similar to Pegasus, most of them require that the input instructions are in a particularly structured English format.

In this paper, we aim to address the gap between how we think and how we shall resort to operational details to explain the same ideas in several natural languages. To do so, we take advantage of the high stage of advancement achieved in Pegasus and the version Pegasus_f of code generator [8]. We extend this project with a new approach that lets Pegasus_f accept instructions written in any and purely natural language. This approach transforms the language-independent input requirements into a formal, semantic representation within the semantic model. This latter is based on a set of mappings, called mapping rules, that maintain the semantics among the input sentences. The semantic model was initially proposed in [9] [10]. In this paper, we enhance it with new features, useful for treating language-independent requirements. In addition, we apply the enhanced semantic model to different languages, like English and French, in order to show the applicability of our program generation approach, independently of the language used for the requirements specification.

To implement our approach, we created the CodeRec-tool, which automates all its steps. More specifically, we used the linguistic development environment NOOJ [11]. Indeed, we transformed the mapping rules into a NOOJ syntactic/semantic grammar for each supported natural language (English and French for the actual version of CodeRec-tool). The application of this grammar on input requirements generates their representation in the semantic model. This representation is then transformed into a Pegasus code that is finally converted automatically to a Java code using the Pegasus_f generator.

The remainder of this paper is organized as follows: In Section II, we overview existing approaches for information extraction from texts and source code generation from requirements. In Section III, we present our approach for synthesizing source code (in Java) from requirements written in different languages. Our approach is illustrated through the Library management case study [3]. Section IV overviews the implementation of our approach. In Section V, we present and discuss the results of an experimental evaluation of our approach. Finally, Section VI summarizes the paper and presents an overview of our future works.

II. RELATED WORK

This section deals with the state of the art on (i) information extraction from texts, and (ii) source code generation from textual requirements.

A. *Works for Information Extraction from Texts*

There is a large body of the literature that treats the problem of information extraction from texts. For instance, Glavas et al. [12] proposed the event graphs for structuring event based information from text; their system performs anchor (i.e., a word that conveys the core meaning of an event, e.g., "killed" or "bombing") extraction, argument (i.e., protagonists and circumstances of events, e.g., "agent", "time", "location") extraction, and relation extraction (i.e., temporal relation extraction and event coreference resolution). This system treats only the events, i.e., the situations that happen. Thus, we cannot rely on this work because extracting source code from natural language requirements necessitates exploiting various naturalistic entities, not only events; naturalistic types are types for programming, which are inspired by natural-language notions [3].

On the other hand, many works focused on the Frame Semantics and the FrameNet project [13]–[17]. The Framework Semantics is based on lexicons. A lexicon contains entries, which are composed of: (a) some conventional dictionary-type data, mainly for the sake of human readers, (b) FORMULAS that capture the morphosyntactic ways in which elements of the semantic frame can be realized within the phrases or sentences built up around the word, (c) links to semantically ANNOTATED EXAMPLE SENTENCES, which illustrate each of the potential realization patterns identified in the formula, and (d) links to the FRAME DATABASE and to other machine-readable resources such as WordNet and COMLEX [17]. The Framework Semantics assumes that the lexicon is made of a background knowledge, whose structure is represented by "frames"; The definition of a frame implies: (i) the discovery of participants, i.e., the frame elements and are defined as their unique semantic roles to the situation, (ii) the mandatory participants of a frame called core frame elements, and (iii) the optional participants, called peripheral frame elements [13] [15]. The model of frame semantics has attracted the attention of a number of linguists interested in the lexicon of a specialty field [18]. Besides, it was applied to the field of football (e.g., [19]), biomedicine (e.g., [20]), law (e.g., [21]) and environment (e.g., [18]).

Nobody can deny the importance of these works, in general, and the frame semantics approach, in particular. However, they are relevant for specific domains and frames, namely those which are already defined by them, unlike our approach, which is applicable regardless of the studied domain. Besides, the information of the type of a sentence (e.g., a definition, a statement, an assignment, etc.) cannot be determined by the frame semantics approach, although this fact is required for a relevant code extraction method. In this context, the semantic model is one of the best solutions for us while it gives adequate and precise information, relevant for the code derivation task thanks to the naturalistic entities that it relies on (see Section III-A).

B. *Works for Source Code Generation from Textual Requirements*

Several works propose to generate source codes from requirements. For example, Franců et al. [6] propose a framework including a generator that produces an implementation in the form of methods. The major limitation of this work is the necessity of a manual processing to build a domain model, required by the generator. On the other hand, Smialek et al. [22] [7], Nowakowski et al. [23] and Kalnins et al. [24] propose approaches that transform the requirements, in particular behavior scenarios written in a semi-natural language, into UML models and the final Java code. These approaches are based on a special Requirements Specification Language (RSL) to express the use case scenarios of a system. The major limit of these approaches is that the use case scenarios must be pre-processed and written in a semi-natural language, according to the SVO grammar (i.e., in Subject+Verb+Object); this means that there is no use of "naturalistic" types like links, references, etc. For instance, a conditional sentence in RSL must be preceded by "=> cond:" in order to be treated.

On the other hand, Liu et al. [4] developed a tool, called Metaphor, that accepts program ideas written in English with the form of a story, and that generates the corresponding program template in Python; Metaphor mines nouns to program objects, verbs to functions and adjectives to properties. In their work, Cozzie et al. [25] proposed the Macho system; this uses a natural language parser that parses descriptions written in natural language into a simple program, by asking the programmer to provide one or more examples of correct input and output as unit tests. Özcan et al. [26] developed an intelligent natural language interface based on the Turkish language to create Java class skeleton and listing the class and its members; Turkish sentences are converted into instances of schemata representing classes and their members. These above works use simple mapping models that map nouns to objects and arguments, verbs to methods and adjectives to attributes. However, the semantics of a natural language sentence should not be exploited using only these types of mapping models. There are other facts that should be taken into account.

On the other hand, Gvero et al. [5] proposed a system that accepts free-form queries containing a mixture of English and Java, and it produces Java code expressions that take the query into account and respect syntax, types, and scoping rules of Java, as well as statistical usage patterns. This system focuses only on API-related queries, and not any type of instructions.

Overall, the majority of the existing approaches treat only requirements written in one single language (English in most cases). In contrast, ours accepts requirements written, theoretically, in any natural language. Moreover, it does not require a manual transformation of the requirements into the syntax of a specific language. These two merits rely on the concept of semantic model, which we introduce in Section III-A. Moreover, our approach relies on this model as a solution to hold (almost) all the semantics of the input requirements written in a purely natural language.

III. OUR APPROACH FOR SOURCE CODE EXTRACTION FROM REQUIREMENTS

In this section, we describe our approach, which is composed of three main tasks: (i) extraction of the semantic model representation from input requirements written, theoretically, in any and in purely natural language, (ii) conversion of the resulting representation into a Pegasus code, and (iii) refinement and transformation of the Pegasus code to Java. Figure 1 shows the functional structure of our approach.

As illustrated in Figure 1, the proposed approach first applies the semantic model on the input language-independent requirements in order to extract their semantic representation as English-mapping rules (step 1 in Figure 1). Then, our approach applies some transformation rules to extract the Pegasus code corresponding to the extracted mapping rules (step 2 in Figure 1). Afterward, our approach refines the Pegasus code by eliminating the redundancy among the code elements' names (step 3 in Figure 1). The resulting Pegasus code is finally used as an input to the Pegasus_f generator to get the target Java code (step 4 in Figure 1). Note that our approach does not extract directly the Pegasus code from the input texts for two reasons: (i) Pegasus_f accepts Pegasus codes written only in the English language; our approach treats multilingual texts and extracts the corresponding Pegasus codes in English; (ii) Pegasus codes contain instructions written in a controlled natural language (i.e., following a specific syntax); our approach treats quite complex and ambiguous texts, from which it extracts relevant information useful for building the target Pegasus codes. These challenges are handled thanks to the semantic model, which can be considered as a transition model between the language-independent requirements and the Pegasus_f inputs (i.e., Pegasus codes).

In the remainder of this section, we detail the process followed by our approach, which we illustrate through the library management case study [3]. We choose this example because it contains ambiguous sentences' structures, proving the potential of our approach in extracting relevant information leading to good Java codes. The following texts (1 and 2) belong to our case study, where the first is written in the English language, and the second is in French.

1- "A library consists of several rooms containing shelves, on which stand books. A book has a three-letter key, which corresponds to the three initial letters of the surname of its first author. The books are ordered in the library by this key. If a visitor lends a book, then a new loan card is created. Besides, it is added to the card index box. Moreover, the book, as well as the name, the address and the telephone number of the visitor, are noted on the loan card. In addition, the actual date is put down; now the book is not lendable anymore. If a visitant returns a book, then the loan card belonging to the book and the visitor is thrown away; now the book is lendable again.".

2- "Une bibliothèque se compose de plusieurs salles, contenant des étagères, sur lesquelles les livres se positionnent. Un livre a une clé de trois lettres, qui correspond aux trois lettres initiales du nom de famille de son premier auteur. Les livres sont ordonnés dans la bibliothèque par cette clé. Si un visiteur prête un livre, alors une nouvelle carte de prêt est créée. En outre, elle est ajoutée à la boîte d'index de la carte. De plus, le livre, ainsi que le nom, l'adresse et le numéro de téléphone du visiteur, sont notés sur la carte de prêt. Outre, la date actuelle est déposée; maintenant, le livre n'est plus prêtable. Si un visiteur retourne un livre, la carte de prêt appartenant au livre et au visiteur est rejetée; maintenant, le livre devient prêtable."

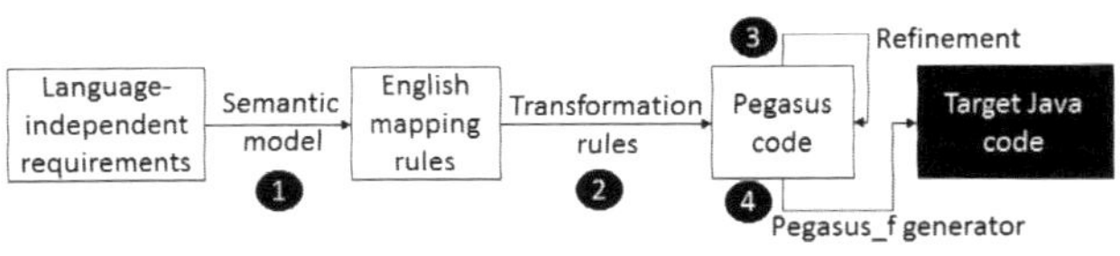

Figure 1. Functional structure of our approach

A. *Requirements Representation within the Semantic Model*

In this section, we present the semantic model, which treats, in particular, the semantic nature of a sentence, as well as its constituents. In this context, Mitch Kapor states that "the critical thing in developing software is not the program, it's the design. It is translating understanding of user needs into something that can be realized as a computer program" [27]. In this sight, we proposed the semantic model as a first step towards representing formally raw ideas (i.e., following the way in which we think) independently of the used natural language and without resorting to operational details (like creating variables, defining their types, methods signatures, etc.). In fact, an idea would be represented always in the same notational way, no matter in which language it was originally expressed. For instance, the following sentences "A loan card is a card" (in English), "Une carte de prêt est une carte" (in French), "Eine Darlehenskarte ist eine Karte" (in German) and "Una carta di prestito è una carta" (in Italian) have equivalent meanings: the hierarchy (i.e., generalization/specialization) relationship between the objects "loan card" and "card". In this context, the semantic model analyzes the semantics among these sentences and represents them by one common representation. Originally [9] [10], the semantic model didn't handle all the characteristics of the natural language, so as to treat any type of sentences. In this paper, we explain in details this model's features. Furthermore, we accomplish it by new entities in order to be more useful for treating language-independent requirements.

The semantic model is based on many naturalistic entities, whose notation is inspired from [8], namely concepts, properties, actions, statements, sentences, references, compression, quantities and ordinalities. In addition, it supports the different types of loops, which are frequently used in natural language. Figure 2 shows the semantic model metamodel; it presents the semantic information that should be extracted from a language-independent instruction. More specifically, our approach relies on this metamodel to build the mapping rules; they represent a text, written in any natural language, in a formal and unique way. They are relevant to all natural languages. In other words, a sentence written in different languages will have the same representation as a mapping rule in English. In this section, we will present each mapping rule by using the EBNF notation [28] as follows: unquoted words denote a non-terminal symbol;

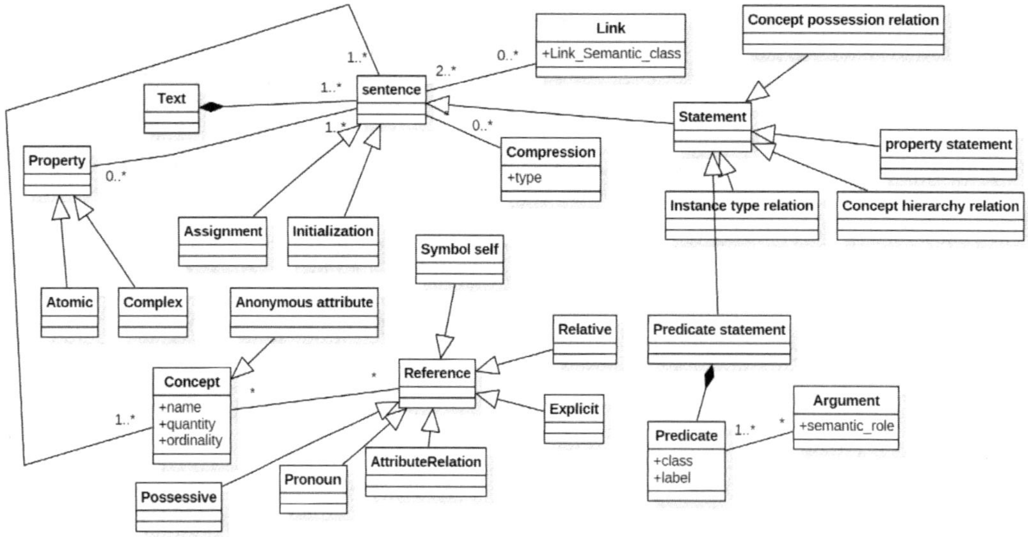

Figure 2. The semantic model metamodel

quoted words denote a terminal symbol, i.e., a symbol, which should be mentioned obligatory; the content of [] is optional; the content of {} denote symbols repeated zero or more times; the content of {}- denote symbols repeated one or more times; the character "=" denotes a definition; the semicolon denotes a rule terminator; the character "|" allows getting a choice from multiple options. In addition, some mapping rules contain the words "type" and "something". A "type" denotes the naturalistic entity. It can be a concept, a property, a quantity, statements preceded by a possessive pronoun, or a combination of these constituent [8]; and "something" stands for the most general type (it corresponds to the class "Object" in Java).

1) Quantification and Ordinality: Natural languages offer an elaborated system of quantification (e.g., "two books", "several books", etc.) over instances. Besides, ordinal numbers are used for counting, e.g., "first", "second", "third", etc. These two concepts are represented by the following mapping rule:

```
Quantity/Ordinality =
 "(quantity/ordinality," value ")";
```

2) Naturalistic References: Referencing is an integral part of natural languages. For example, we say "A book has a three-letter key, which corresponds to the three initial letters of the surname of its first author"; the words "which" and "its" are references, respectively, to "three-letter key" and "book". The semantic model accepts several references' types, such as:

- *Explicit reference:* it allows retrieving a subset of instances from a broader set of instances using the keyword "the" in English, e.g., "the card". It is represented in the semantic model by the following mapping rule:

```
Explicit reference =
 "(reference, explicit," type ")";
```

- *Symbol self reference:* it represents a symbol, which refers to a concept, e.g., "the button 'Loan'"; in this example "Loan" is a symbol that describes the concept "button". This reference is represented in the semantic model by the following mapping rule:

```
Symbol self reference =
 "(reference, symbol self," type, symbol ")";
```

- *Possessive pronoun reference:* it represents possessive pronouns in combination with a type, e.g., "its author". It is represented in the semantic model by the following mapping rule:

```
Possessive pronoun reference =
 "(reference, possessive pronoun," type ")";
```

- *Relative reference:* it is characterized by the use of relative pronouns like "which", "who", "whose", "with", etc. It is represented in the semantic model by the following mapping rule:

```
Relative reference = "(reference,
     relative," ["possessive," type] ")";
```

- *Attribute/relation reference:* it resolves expressions like "the type of the message". In fact, this type of expressions contains two other references. The first one placed before the word "of" is called a "filter reference". The second one, which is placed after the word "of", is called a "collection reference" [8]. The collection reference can be any reference; however the filter reference can be either an explicit or an ordinal reference. It can also consist simply of a concept. The attribute/relation reference is represented in the semantic model by the following mapping rule:

```
Attribute/relation reference = "(reference,
  attribute/relation," collection reference,
                       filter reference ")";
```

For example, considering the sentence "The books have a three-letter key, which corresponds to the three initial letters of the surname of its first author" from our case study; it is represented in the semantic model with the following mapping rule:

```
[...] (reference, attribute/relation,
 (reference, possessive pronoun,
  (author, (quantity/ordinality, first)),
 (reference, attribute/relation,
  (reference, explicit, surname), (letter,
   (quantity/ordinality, three), initial))))
```

3) Concepts: A concept is any "thing" from the real world, being abstract or concrete, e.g., "Book", "Student", "Amount", etc. It is the homologue of an object in object-oriented programming languages. Concepts can contain or be contained in other concepts. This fact corresponds to the "concept possession relation". Likewise, concepts can be sub-concepts of other ones. This fact represents the "concept hierarchy relation". When we use a natural language, we do not create new instances explicitly like in existing programming languages. This process is done implicitly using some words like "take", or by talking about non-existing things like "There are some books on the shelves". The semantic model proposes the following mapping rule to represent the concept initialization (with its eventual properties) formally:

```
Concept initialization =
  "(initialization," concept ")";
```

In some cases, we may find a quoted string, which is not related to any concept. Thus, the semantic model treats it as a symbol with the following mapping rule:

```
Symbol definition= "(symbol," the_string ")";
```

Another type of concepts is the "anonymous concept"; it must be always contained into a concept and it describes different situations of this latter, using properties. For instance, let us consider the sentence "the type of a book can be science fiction, drama, action, romance, mystery or horror"; we note that the concept "type" is anonymous, belonging to the concept "book", and supporting the values "science fiction", "drama", "action", "romance", "mystery" and "horror", which serve to describe the concept "book". We also note that an anonymous concept should contain neither other concepts, nor actions. Otherwise, it would be a simple concept. The anonymous concept is represented by the following mapping rule within the semantic model:

```
Anonymous concept definition = "(anonymous
  concept," concept "," {value}- ")";
```

For instance, considering the above example, it is represented in the semantic model with the following mapping rule:

```
(anonymous concept,
 (reference, attribute/relation,
  (book, (quantity/ordinality, abstract)),
  (reference, explicit, type)),
  (adjunctive, science fiction, drama, action,
   romance, mystery, horror))
```

where "adjunctive" is a type of compression (see section III-A6).

4) Properties: Properties describe concepts. There are several types of properties among which the type "simple" is the most used in the requirements. A simple property can be either the case or not, e.g., "short", "lendable", etc. It can be expressed by an adjective like "The shelve is empty". A simple property is defined by assignment. It can be assigned in two ways: (i) directly, using the predicate "to be", "can be", "equal", etc., which implies that there is a relationship between a concept and possibly several properties; or (ii) by initialization of a new instance. The semantic model represents these two mechanisms by the following mapping rules:

```
Property assignment = "(property assignment,"
 concept "," {property}- ")";
Property concept relation definition =
 "(property concept relation," concept ","
 {property}- ")";
```

For example, considering the sentences "Let the book be borrowable" (in English) and "Lassen Sie das Buch sein ausleihbar" (in German); they are represented by the same mapping rule, as follows:

```
(property assignment,
 (reference explicit, book), borrowable)
```

5) Statements: A statement is a declarative clause that is either true or false. We often use statements to express a relationship between different instances. The semantic model defines five types of statements, namely: Concept hierarchy relation and Concept possession relation statements, Predicate statement, Property statement and Instance type relation statement.

a) Concept hierarchy and possession relation statements:: The two types of concept relations, "concept possession relation" and "concept hierarchy relation", may appear both in concept definitions and in statements. These statements are respectively represented in the semantic model as the following mapping rules:

```
Concept possession relation = "(definition/
 statement, concept possession relation,
  (possessor," possessor_concept "),
  (possessed," possessed concept "))";
Concept hierarchy relation =
 "(definition/statement, concept hierarchy
  relation, (super-concept,"
  general_concept "), (sub-concept,"
  specialized_concept "))";
```

Note that the word "negation" is put when the statement (whatever is its type) is in the negative form. For instance, the clauses "A book has a three-letter key" (in English) and "Un livre a une clé de trois lettres" (in French) from our case study convey to one common representation within the semantic model, as follows:

```
(statement, concept possession relation,
 (possessor,
  (book, (quantity/ordinality, abstract))),
 (possessed, (key, (quantity/ordinality,
  abstract), three-letter)))
```

b) Predicate statement:: This type of statements deals with predicates. A predicate refers to a verb. It belongs to a class (state or action). The difference between a state and a property is that this latter is unchangeable, whereas the state can change depending on the time, the location, etc. A predicate requires a number of arguments, which correspond to specific "semantic roles". The semantic model treats, in particular, the following semantic roles (where some of them are introduced by the semantic model): (i) Agent: the entity that performs the action; (ii) Object: the entity that undergoes the action; (iii) Comparassant: designates the compared element as a part of a comparison; (iv) Comparator: designates the comparing element as a part of a comparison; (v) Possessor: something that has or contains someone/something; (vi) Possessed: something that is owned or in the disposal of someone/something; (vii) Sub-concept: a specialized concept in a hierarchical relationship; (viii) Super-concept: the generalized concept in a hierarchical relationship; (ix) Origin: the place from where an action is done; (x) Destination: the place towards which the action is directed; (xi) Location: the place or space of a predicate expressed by an action or a state; (xii) Time: indicates the date or the period when an action or a state is done; (xiii) Manner: describes the way of doing something. The predicate statements are represented in the semantic model with the following mapping rule:

```
Predicate statement = "(statement,
  (" predicate_class "," predicate "),"
  {"(" semantic_role "," parameter ")"}- ")";
```

For instance, considering the sentence: "Les livres sont ordonnés dans la bibliothèque par cette clé" (in French) from our case study; our approach generates the following English-mapping rule:

```
(statement, (action, order), (object,
  (reference, explicit, (book, multiple))),
 (location, (reference, explicit, library)),
 (manner, (reference, explicit, key)))
```

c) Property statement: : This type of statements focuses on properties. It is represented by the following mapping rule:

```
Property statement =
 "(statement, property," ["negation,"]
  ["comparative"|"superlative",] property_name
  ","{"(" semantic_role "," instance ")"}- ")";
```

For example, considering the sentences "A book has a three-letter key, which corresponds to the three initial letters of the surname of its first author" (in English) and "Un livre a une clé de trois lettres, qui correspond aux trois lettres initiales du nom de famille de son premier auteur" (in French) from our case study; our approach generates the same mapping rule for them:

```
[...]
(statement, property, (reference, relative),
 (reference, attribute/relation,
  (reference, possessive pronoun,
   (author, (quantity/ordinality, first)),
  (reference, attribute/relation,
   (reference, explicit, surname),
   (letter, (quantity/ordinality, three),
     initial)))))
```

d) Instance type relation statement:: This type of statements takes interest in relationships between instances and their properties. It is represented in the semantic model with the following rule:

```
Instance type relation statement =
    "(statement, instance type relation,"
    ["negation,"] something "," type ")";
```

For example, considering the sentence: "If the type of the book is not drama..."; our approach generates the following mapping rule:

```
(condition, (statement, instance type,
 negation, (reference, attribute/relation,
 (reference, explicit, book),
 (reference, explicit, type)), drama)
```

6) Compression: Compression means grouping different syntactic structures together by some special words like "and", "or", etc. We distinguish four types of compression: copulative (using conjunctions like "and", "added to", "as well as"...), adjunctive (using conjunctions like "or"), contravalent (using conjunctions like "either.. or..", "whether.. or..") and exclusion (using conjunctions like "neither.. nor.."). The compression is represented in the semantic model following this rule:

```
Sentence = "(" ("copulative"|"adjunctive"|
          "contravalent"|"exclusion") ","
                               {something}- ")";
```

We will present an example of the compression in the following section.

7) Sentences: A sentence is composed of clauses linked by conjunctions (assembling links). A link belongs to a semantic class among the following ones: (i) Temporal: links two expressions in time; (ii) Condition: uses conditional conjunctions like "if", "in case of"; (iii) Contrary: the opposite of condition using conjunctions like "if not", "otherwise", "else"; (iv) Final: expresses something happening as a result; (v) Cause: refers to a situation which is the cause of another situation; (vi) Illative: expresses something inferred from another statement or fact; (vii) Loop: represents five types of loops, namely: "for", "while", "do...while", "foreach" and "switch". The following mapping rule represents the link relation (excluding loops) within the semantic model:

```
Sentence =
  "(" link_semantic_class "," something ")";
```

For instance, the mapping rule corresponding to the sentence "If a visitant returns a book, then the loan card belonging to the book and the visitor is thrown away" is the following:

```
(condition, (statement, (action, return),
 (agent,
  (visitant, (quantity/ordinality, abstract))),
 (object,
  (book, (quantity/ordinality, abstract)))),
 (statement, (action, throw away),
  (object, (reference, explicit,
   (loan card,
    (statement, possession concept relation,
    (possessor, (copulative,
     (reference, explicit, book),
     (reference, explicit, visitor))),
    (possessed, (reference, relative))))))))
```

Concerning the loops links, the following mapping rules represent them:

```
Loop-do/while = "(loop," ("do"|"while") ","
  statement "," {something_result}- ")";

Loop-for = "(loop, for," counter_start_value
  "," counter_end_value "," step ","
  {something_result}- ")";

Loop-foreach = "(loop, foreach," concept ","
  statement "," {something_result}- ")";

Loop-switch = "(loop, switch," variable_name ","
  { value "," {something_result}- }- ")";
```

In summary, our approach works on requirements written in different languages, even the Asiatic ones, thanks to the semantic model. We refer the reader to our reference [29] for an example of our approach application on requirements, which are written in English, French, Spanish and Chinese languages.

B. Converting the Semantic Model Representation to a Pegasus Code

The resulting mapping rules can be transformed into the input of existing code generators, such as Pegasus_f. This latter accepts requirements written in the Pegasus naturalistic programming language syntax, in English. Besides, it produces the corresponding Java code automatically. In this context, our approach transforms the mapping rules into the corresponding Pegasus code, based on some transformation rules. Due to space limitation, we will present only some of them (we suppose that the resulting Pegasus code is stored in the file "pegasus_code.peg"):

Rule 1: For each concept, $Conc$, involved within a mapping rule, a declaration of $Conc$ as a Pegasus concept is added to the file "pegasus_code.peg" following this syntax:

```
"concept: " Conc "{}"
```

We have to mention that our approach recognizes some keywords within the concepts' names (as well as the properties' and the actions' names). Therefore, it does not create the corresponding objects. For instance, our approach admits that each concept name, which contains at least one of the following words {"text", "string", "word", "letter", "paragraph", "line", "verse", "number", "integer", "float", "sum", "fraction", "numeral", "amount", "period", "menu", "menu-item", "button", "form", "option", etc.} do not correspond to a Pegasus concept. Indeed, Pegasus_f can recognize, automatically, the predefined Java types and GUI components, and thus, it does not require the creation of the corresponding Pegasus concepts.

Rule 2: For each property, $Prop$, in relation with a concept, $Conc$, a declaration of $Prop$ is added to the Pegasus concept $Conc$ in the file "pegasus_code.peg" according to the following syntax:

```
"concept: " Conc "{ property:" Prop "; }"
```

In fact, a Pegasus property declaration does not require the declaration of its type; this latter is deduced automatically by Pegasus_f.

Rule 3: Every concept possession relation within a mapping rule, involving a possessor concept, $c_{possessor}$, and a possessed concept, $c_{possessed}$, leads to the declaration of a Pegasus property $c_{possessed}$ within the concept $c_{possessor}$ following this syntax:

```
"concept:" c_possessor "{
  property:" c_possessed ";}"
```

Rule 4: Every concept hierarchy relation within a mapping rule, involving a sub concept, c_{sub}, and a super concept, c_{super}, leads to the declaration of the two Pegasus concepts c_{sub} and c_{super}, where the first extends the second, by following this syntax:

```
"concept: " c_sub "extends" c_super "{}"
```

Rule 5: Each concept initialization within a mapping rule, involving a concept, $Conc$, and a property, $Prop$, is transformed to a Pegasus instruction according to the following syntax:

```
"let" Conc "be" Prop ";"
```

Rule 6: A copulative compression is transformed into a Pegasus syntax as follows:

- For each type, typ, involved within the compression, create a copy of the current mapping rule, in which the copulative compression clause is replaced by typ.
- Replace the current mapping rule by the new copies of mapping rules and treat them by applying the transformation rules adequate for them.

Rule 7: For each symbol self reference within a mapping rule, which involves a type corresponding to a concept, $Conc$, a Pegasus property called "label" is created within $Conc$. In fact, the involved symbol serves as a label to this concept.

We have to note that the concepts and the properties names convey to the standard notations, i.e., the units composing a noun are separated by putting the first letter of each term capitalized. After applying the transformation rules, we obtain the Pegasus code corresponding to the mapping rules of the input text. For example, our approach generates the following Pegasus code for our case study by applying the guidelines of the above rules on the extracted mapping rules:

```
concept: Library{ property:rooms;}
concept: Room{ property: shelves;}
concept: Shelve{}
concept: Book{
    property: key;
    property: author;
    property: isLendable;
    property: loanCard;
    action: to stand in (shelve){}
    (key) is ((three initial letters)
     of ((surname) of (first author)));}
concept: Author{
    property: isFirst;
    property: surname;}
concept: LoanCard{}
concept: Visitor{
    property: name;
    property: address;
    property: telephoneNumber;
    property: loanCard;
    action: to lend (book){}
    action: to return (book){}}
concept: Visitant{ action: to return (book){}}
[...]
(three-letter key) is ((three initial letters)
 of ((surname) of (first author)));
order (books) in (library) by (key)!
statement:{
    take (loan card)!
    add (loan card) to (card index box)!
    note (book) in (loan card)!
    note ((name) of (visitor)) in (loan card)!
    note ((address) of (visitor)) in
     (loan card)!
    note ((telephone number) of (visitor)) in
     (loan card)!
    put down (actual date);
    NOT((book) is lendable now);
 } : if (visitor) lend (book);
statement:{
    throw away (loan card)!
    (book) is lendable now;
 } : if (visitor) return (book);
```

Hence, this example shows that our approach is capable of generating a structured Pegasus code from quite complex and ambiguous input texts (containing sentences in the passive form with too much references), which are written in different languages.

C. Pegasus Code Refinement

The input textual requirements may use synonymous words to describe the same concept. For instance, in our case study, the input text uses the words "visitor" and "visitant", which are semantically synonyms. They are however represented in the Pegasus code by two concepts, "Visitant" and "Visitor", even though they are equivalent (see the generated Pegasus code in the previous section). To avoid such code redundancy and unify the names of Pegasus concepts, properties and actions belonging to the same concept, our approach uses an unsupervised classification of the names within the group of concepts names; this classification starts by getting the grammatical units from these names, by splitting these latter according to the capitalized letters used in them.

We choose the TF/IDF method [30], which relies on the calculation of the cosine similarity measure. This method is composed of queries and documents; our approach considers that a query consists of the units composing a Pegasus concept name, and a document is made up of the association of these latter, added to their synonyms extracted from WordNet [31]; WordNet is used only for the classification task, independently from the mapping rules synthesis process. TF/IDF begins by computing the weight of each grammatical unit, which composes a query q_j and belongs to a document d_i. The weight of each unit is calculated thanks to the following equation:

$$w_{ij} = tf_{i,j} \times idf_{i,j} = tf_{i,j} \times \log(\frac{m}{D(i)}) \quad (1)$$

where: w_{ij} is the weight of the grammatical unit i in the document j; $tf_{i,j}$ is the frequency of the unit i in the document j; m is the total number of documents in the collection (i.e., the selected group of concepts, in this step); and $D(i)$ is the number of documents where the unit i occurs. After that, our approach computes the cosine similarity, $Sim(d_i, q)$, between a document d_i and a query q, using the following equation:

$$Sim(d_i, q) \approx \cos(\overrightarrow{d_i}, \overrightarrow{q}) = \frac{\sum_{t_j \in U} w_{ij} \times w_{qj}}{\sqrt{\sum_{t_j \in U} w_{qj}^2 \times \sum_{t_j \in U} w_{ij}^2}} \quad (2)$$

where: w_{ij} is the weight of the grammatical unit in d_i; w_{qj} is the weight of the unit u_j in q; and U is the set of grammatical units composing all the documents. Thus, our approach computes the cosine matrix (where the rows are the documents and the columns are the queries) according to equation 2. After performing this calculation, our approach applies the DBSCAN algorithm [32] on the cosine matrix, in order to group the concepts names into semantic classes. Then, it selects a name for each class. After that, it refines the generated Pegasus code by replacing the existing concepts' names by the selected semantic class names and merging the content of the initial similar concepts into the resulting concept names. These same steps are then applied for each group of actions and of properties that belong to the same Pegasus concept. To conclude, our approach generates a refined Pegasus code, which is then transformed automatically to Java using the Pegasus_f generator.

In the following section, we will present an implementation of our approach with the CodeRec-tool.

IV. IMPLEMENTATION OF OUR APPROACH

To implement our approach, we developed a tool, named CodeRec-tool (Code Recovery tool), which allows generating a Pegasus code, as an input to the Pegasus_f generator, by starting from requirements written in different and in purely natural languages. Actually, this tool accepts the French and the English languages. However, it can be extended by integrating other languages.

This tool is composed of three modules: (i) the first module treats an input text and generates the corresponding mapping rules, which are then stored in a TXT file; (ii) the second module converts the mapping rules from the TXT file into a Pegasus code, which is stored in a PEG file, (iii) the third module refines the PEG file's content and uses it as an input to the Pegasus_f generator, which executes automatically the Pegasus code and generates the corresponding JAVA code.

Concerning the implementation of the mapping rules, we used the NOOJ environment [11] (our results are not completely dependent from the use of NOOJ; in fact, relying on this environment in the implementation of CodeRec-tool is just a choice.). NOOJ is a linguistic development environment that includes tools to create and maintain dictionaries, morphological and syntactic grammars. Dictionaries and grammars are applied to texts in order to locate morphological, lexical and syntactic patterns and tag simple and compound words [11]. Our main goal is to synthesize the different mapping rules that match each instruction of the input text to its formal representation within the semantic model in the English language. To this end, our tool does not follow a specific algorithm for the synthesis task, in contrast, it relies on grammars. Indeed, the mapping rules synthesis task is performed by developing a "syntactic/semantic grammar" that treats one specific language. In other words, in practice, we have to build a syntactic/semantic grammar for each natural language to be treated by our tool in order to generate the mapping rules of an input text written in that language.

Taking into account a text written in a language, L, different from English, our tool starts by exploiting this text by using the corresponding developed grammar, as well as the predefined NOOJ dictionary (available in [11]) appropriate to L. Then, our tool generates the corresponding mapping rules. However, these latter contain terms belonging to the language L. To solve the problem of the mapping rules translation to the English language, CodeRec-tool uses the Google Translate API [33] in order to transform the components of the generated mapping rules (i.e., the names of concepts, properties, states, actions, etc.) into English.

CodeRec-tool accepts the English and the French languages. To this end, we developed a NOOJ syntactic/semantic grammar for each language, including the syntactic and the semantic information of each language; these grammars allow to synthesize mapping rules in English, in cooperation with the predefined NOOJ dictionaries for the English and the French languages, as well as the Google Translate API. We refer the reader to our previous work [10] for a detailed example on the application of our NOOJ syntactic/semantic grammar on an input sentence.

Considering our case study, CodeRec-tool generates the corresponding mapping rules, which it stores in the file "Library_management_MRs.txt". After that, it treats this file content, in order to extract the corresponding Pegasus code, which is stored in the file "Library_management_Pegasus.peg". Indeed, CodeRec-tool implements the transformation rules from the semantic model representation to the pegasus syntax (see Section III-B).

The "Library_management_Pegasus.peg" file is then refined and used as an input to the Pegasus_f generator, which produces the corresponding Java code; it generates, in particular, the following extract of Java code:

```
public class Book{
 /*** Attributes declaration ***/
 private Key key;
 private Author author;
 private boolean isLendable;
 private LoanCard loanCard;
 /*** Constructors ***/
 public Book(){
  this.key=new Key();
  this.author=new Author();
  this.isLendable=false;
  this.loanCard=new LoanCard(); }
 public Book(Author author,
   boolean isLendable, LoanCard loanCard){
  this.author=author;
  this.key=this.author.surname.substring(0,3);
  this.isLendable=isLendable;
  this.loanCard=loanCard; }
 /*** Methods declaration ***/
 public void stand(Shelve shelve){}
 /*** Getters and setters ***/
 public Key getKey(){return this.key;}
 public void setKey(Key key){
  this.key=key;} [...] }
[...] }
```

We have to mention that our approach, and thus our tool, are able to generate, automatically, Java packages, as well. For example, let us consider the following sentence "The visitor selects the button 'Lend'"; CodeRec-tool generates the following mapping rule and the corresponding Pegasus code:

```
Mapping rule
------------
(statement, (action, select),
 (agent, (reference, explicit, visitor)),
 (object, (reference, symbol self, button,
   "Lend")))
Pegasus code
------------
[...] (visitor) select (button "Lend");
```

Using this latter Pegasus code as an input to the Pegasus_f generator, CodeRec-tool generates, namely, the following Java code:

```
import java.awt.*;
import java.swing.*;
[...]
public class BookLending extends JFrame
               implements ActionListener{
 JButton button1=new JButton("Lend");
 button1.addActionListener(new ActionListener()
  { public void actionPerformed(ActionEvent e)
    {[...]}});
[...] }
```

V. EVALUATION

To evaluate our approach and our tool, we adopted the process proposed by Wohlin et al. [34], which decomposes the evaluation into different parts, like goal, task, subjects, preparation, conduction and evaluation.

Goal: The overall objectives of our evaluation is to show the ability of our approach, and thus tool, in deriving useful Pegasus codes (implicitly good Java codes) from input requirements, written in purely and in several natural languages (English and French for its current version), and to examine the conformity degree between our Pegasus codes and those built by Pegasus experts. We rely on Pegasus experts in our evaluation, instead of Java programmers because the main outputs of our approach are Pegasus codes. Indeed, producing good Pegasus code leads, implicitly, to the generation of good Java codes.

Subject and Preparation: While a use case scenario contains useful description of a system behavior, from which we can deduce an important amount of source code, we decide to rely of the use case scenarios belonging to five different domains, and which are given to two Pegasus experts (two natural language processing PhD students from our laboratory, who are familiar to Pegasus programs), as follows:

- 16 use case scenarios belonging to a Health complaint application [35]; this latter allows citizens to report complaints (food, animal and special complaints) via internet.
- A well developed scenario of the use case "Withdraw cash" belonging to a banking system [36].
- 28 use case scenarios belonging to the Go-phone system [37]; this latter is based on a hypothetical context of the mobile phone company "Go-Phone" Inc and it has clone based Go-phone products, such as "S", "L", "Elegance", "Com"...
- 9 use case scenarios belonging to a crisis management system [38]; this latter treats crisis, which can range from major to catastrophic affecting many segments of society.
- Use case scenario of the game of war cards [39], which involves two players where the one who has no more cards at the end of the game is the looser.
- 5 use case scenarios belonging to Emptio [40], which is a mobile phone application for selfservice shopping.

Task: We asked the Pegasus experts to give us the correct Pegasus codes corresponding to the adopted subjects.

Conduction: We compare the experts' Pegasus codes to the corresponding ones generated by our tool by using the precision and recall metrics in terms of Pegasus concepts (pC, rC), properties (pP, rP) and actions (pA, rA). For example these measures are calculated as follows for the concepts:

$$pC = \frac{number\ of\ true\ concepts}{number\ of\ found\ concepts} \times 100 \quad (3)$$

$$rC = \frac{number\ of\ true\ concepts}{number\ of\ real\ concepts} \times 100 \quad (4)$$

Moreover, we decide to use two other metrics taken from the standard ISO 25020, in order to measure:

- The completeness (Com) degree of our results according to the input requirements, which are also treated by the Pegasus experts; for example, it is measured, in terms of concepts, as follows:

$$Com_c = 1 - \frac{number\ of\ unfound\ pertinent\ concepts}{number\ of\ pertinent\ concepts} \times 100 \quad (5)$$

- The correctness (Cor) of our results according to the input requirements, which are also treated by the Pegasus experts; for instance, it is computed, in terms of concepts, as follows:

$$Cor_c = \frac{number\ concepts\ adequately\ implemented}{number\ of\ pertinent\ concepts} \times 100 \quad (6)$$

We have to mention that the correctness measure is only computed for the Pegasus concepts and the actions because it deals with their internal implementation. Besides, the number of concepts/actions adequately implemented means that the

TABLE I. EVALUATION

Average	Precision	Recall	Complet.	Correct.
Concepts	73,78%	91,60%	90,43%	80,13%
Properties	81,59%	82,66%	78,41%	-
Actions	70,22%	82,41%	76,78%	83,02%

majority of their implementations are pertinent according to the experts' implementations.

Table I shows the resulting averages of the adopted measurements in terms of Pegasus concepts, properties and actions.

Evaluation: Table I shows the high average values of the adopted metrics, which exceed 73,78% in all cases. More specifically, the precision (respectively recall) values in terms of concepts range from 67,86% to 80% (respectively from 84,62% to 96%). Similarly, we note high average values of completeness and correctness, reaching respectively 90,43% and 83,02%. For example, in the case of the Go-phone system, we obtained the highest values of precision in terms of concepts (80%), with a completeness rate 91,67% and correctness of 87,5%. This fact means that our tool generates a good number of true positives (TP, i.e., the number of pertinent concepts generated by our tool), which equals 24, vs. a low number of false positives (FP, i.e., the number of none-pertinent concepts, not found by the experts and which are generated by our tool), which equals 6. Moreover, the recall value in terms of concepts for the Go-phone system equals 92,31%, reflecting that our tool generates the majority of pertinent concepts. The high values of completeness (91,67%) and correctness (87,5%) confirm this fact. Consequently, we deduce that the code generated by our tool is of a high quality and helps the developers in the programming task by saving their time, and thus money for the companies.

We have to mention that the false positives generated by our tool and decreasing the precision values in some cases (like the case of the Withdraw cash scenario, which equals 67,86% with 38 TPs and 18 FPs) are caused by the fact that our tool generates a Pegasus concept for each met concept within a mapping rule, except for some concepts whose names can be recognized by our tool and for which this latter does not produce a corresponding Pegasus concept (see Rule 1 in Section III-B). For instance, concerning the Emptio application, our tool generates, in particular, the concept "URL". In contrast, the Pegasus experts realize that this concept corresponds to a simple string and puts it as a Pegasus property within the Pegasus concept "Application". This fact is due to the full automation of our approach. However, we believe that the extra-generated concepts do not really matter because they will be removed by the developer, later. Indeed, the completeness (82,81%) and the correctness (81,82%) in terms of concepts for the Emptio application confirm the utility of the Pegasus concepts generated by our tool.

On the other hand, the precision values in terms of properties range from 75% to 96%. For example, in the case of the Health complaint system, our tool generates 42 TPs, vs. 12 FPs; in fact, the use case scenarios of this system treat each "type" of a "query" on its own. Thus, our tool generates four properties corresponding to four queries' types: "onSpecialities", "onHealthUnits", "onDiseases" and "onComplaint" within the concept "Query". In fact, the input scenarios do not contain any information allowing our tool to recognize, automatically, the nature of the property "type". However, the expert realizes that these properties correspond to only one property "type", which corresponds to an anonymous concept with four possible values: "onSpecialities", "onHealthUnits", "onDiseases" and "onComplaint" within the Pegasus concept "Query". In contrary, the important value of recall (80,77%) and completeness (76,19%) confirm that our tool generated a good number of pertinent properties, regardless of some exceptions caused by the full automation of our approach.

Finally, the precision in terms of actions are relatively low in comparison with the concepts and the properties ones. More specifically, the precision in terms of actions for the Game of war equals 66,66%. This result is justified by the fact that our tool generates an action definition for each met action predicate within a mapping rule, especially for the human manual actions, which should not be implemented. For example, our tool generates the Pegasus actions "show(cards)", "select(card,pile)" and "select(menu-item)", although they correspond to simple mouse clicks on buttons or items done by a human actor. However, the experts do not create Pegasus actions for them because they know that they will be treated automatically by Pegasus_f, which will implement the corresponding treatment within their methods "addActionListener". We believe that this fact does not really matter while we get a good correctness value for the Game of war (83,33%) and which implies the good quality of the generated actions' implementations.

Threats to validity. One external threat of our approach consists of the Pegsaus project, in particular the version Pegasus_f of code generator; it has not yet been finished totally; there are still some small improvements to integrate in this project, such as treating the ellipses. However, the current version of Pegasus_f is powerful and it generates good results, shown in our evaluation. Besides, although our approach is original and treats an original topic thanks to its ability to work on any natural language, it is rather theoretic. In fact, on the practical level, we have to possess a huge number of rich dictionaries in order to parse an input instruction and deduce the corresponding mapping rule. However, the NOOJ project is always processing and many dictionaries for many languages are integrated each year. On the other hand, our tool presents an internal threat: a grammar should be created for each integrated language in order to synthesize the mapping rules. However, we believe that this is not a problem while the creation of this grammar is done only one time, then it becomes ready to treat the input instructions in that language. Another internal concern consists of the generation of an important number of concepts and actions (and thus Java classes and methods). However, we believe that this concern does not really matter because the unnecessary classes and methods generated by our approach will be latter removed by the programmer when revising the generated version of source codes. Another threat against our approach is its dependance from the input requirements. More specifically, the more complete input requirements are, the better results we get. In fact, the evaluation of our approach showed interesting results in terms of the adopted measurement values (i.e. precision, recall, F-measure...) because we have got good inputs in terms of use case scenarios. However, these values would decrease in case of a lack of information within the input requirements.

VI. CONCLUSION AND FUTURE WORK

This paper presented a new, original approach for extracting source code from requirements written, theoretically, in any and purely natural language. Firstly, the proposed approach takes the textual descriptions (requirements) and translates them into the semantic model by extracting the corresponding mapping rules. This model gives our approach the advantage of using semantic information to explore and interpret the syntax and the semantics of the requirements. Moreover, our approach allows the translation of the mapping rules to English in case where their contents are in a language different from English. Secondly, our approach deduces a refined Pegasus code corresponding to the mapping rules based on some transformation rules. Finally, Pegasus_f translates this code into Java. Thus, the developers will save time because they are not obliged to create the initial classes of the system (including the constructors, the attributes, the getters and the setters, as well as at least the methods signatures) or to import the required packages. Our approach is implemented by the CodeRec-tool, which automates its steps.

In contrast to the existing approaches, our approach is very simple; it does not necessitate any pre-study on a particular language to be used. In fact, it accepts language-independent descriptions, understandable even by a non-IT person. In addition, another power of our approach is its ability to be used with many code generators, not necessarily Pegasus_f.

We think that the future programming techniques will follow the same direction in which a human thinks. It is our belief that the naturalistic programming will have a prominent place in the future of programming languages. The research that we presented in this paper constitutes a contribution in programming using any and purely natural language thanks to the semantic model.

In our future works, we aim to conduct an evaluation on a larger set of products to confirm the presented results. Another practical extension of the herein presented work is the application of our approach on other code generators, such as the ReDSeeDS tool, which extracts a Java code, following a Model/View/Controller architecture, from use case scenarios written in the RSL language.

REFERENCES

[1] R. Knöll and M. Mezini, "Pegasus: First steps toward a naturalistic programming language," in Companion to the 21st ACM SIGPLAN Symposium on Object-oriented Programming Systems, Languages, and Applications. New York, NY, USA: ACM, 2006, pp. 542–559.

[2] L. Khaylov, "Implementation of the naturalistic programming language pegasus," Master's thesis, Darmstadt University of Technology, Germany, 2009.

[3] R. Knöll. Pegasus project. [Online]. Available: http://www.pegasus-project.org/en/Welcome.html [retrieved: August, 2017] (2006)

[4] H. Liu and H. Lieberman, "Metafor: Visualizing stories as code," in Proceedings of International Conference on Intelligent User Interfaces. New York, NY, USA: ACM, 2005, pp. 305–307.

[5] T. Gvero and V. Kuncak, "Synthesizing java expressions from free-form queries," in Proceedings of ACM SIGPLAN International Conference on Object-Oriented Programming, Systems, Languages, and Applications. New York, NY, USA: ACM, 2015, pp. 416–432.

[6] J. Francû and P. Hnětynka, Automated generation of implementation from textual system requirements. Berlin, Heidelberg: Springer Berlin Heidelberg, 2011, pp. 34–47.

[7] M. Smialek and W. Nowakowski, Introducing requirements-driven modelling. Switzerland: Springer International Publishing, 2015, ch. From Requirements to Java in a Snap, pp. 1–30.

[8] R. Knöll, V. Gasiunas, and M. Mezini, "Naturalistic types," in Proceedings of SIGPLAN Symposium on New Ideas, New Paradigms, and Reflections on Programming and Software. New York, NY, USA: ACM, 2011, pp. 33–48.

[9] M. Mefteh, N. Bouassida, and H. Ben-Abdallah, "Feature model extraction from documented uml use case diagrams," Ada User Journal, vol. 35, no. 2, 2014, pp. 108–117.

[10] ——, "Mining feature models from functional requirements," Computer journal, vol. 59, no. 7, 2016, pp. 1–21.

[11] M. Silberztein, Formalizing natural languages: The NooJ approach. John Wiley Sons, Inc., 2016.

[12] G. Glavas and J. Snajder, "Construction and evaluation of event graphs," Natural Language Engineering, vol. 21, no. 4, 2015, pp. 607–652.

[13] C. J. Fillmore, "Frame semantics and the nature of language," in Origins and evolution of language and speech, S. Harnad, Ed. Academy of Sciences, 1976, pp. 155–202.

[14] C. J. Fillmore and B. T. Atkins, Towards a frame-based lexicon: The semantics of RISK and its neighbors. Hillsdale: Lawrence Erlbaum Associates, 1992, pp. 75–102.

[15] C. J. Fillmore and B. Collin, A frames approach to semantic analysis. Oxford: Oxford University Press, 2010, pp. 313–339.

[16] J. Ruppenhofer, M. Ellsworth, M. R. L. Petruck, C. R. Johnson, and J. Scheffczyk. Framenet II: Extended theory and practice. [Online]. Available: http://framenet.icsi.berkeley.edu [retrieved: July, 2017] (2010)

[17] C. F. Baker, C. J. Fillmore, and J. B. Lowe, "The Berkeley FrameNet project," in Proceedings of the 36th Annual Meeting of the Association for Computational Linguistics and 17th International Conference on Computational Linguistics - Volume 1, ser. ACL '98. Stroudsburg, PA, USA: Association for Computational Linguistics, 1998, pp. 86–90. [Online]. Available: http://dx.doi.org/10.3115/980845.980860

[18] Marie-Claude L'Homme, "Terminologie de l'environnement et sémantique des cadres," Congrès Mondial de Linguistique Franaise, SHS Web of Conferences, vol. 27, 2016, pp. 1–14.

[19] T. Schmidt, "The kicktionary a multilingual lexical resource of football language," in Multilingual FrameNets in computational lexicography : methods and applications, H. C. Boas, Ed., 2009.

[20] A. Dolbey, M. Ellsworth, and J. Scheffczyk, "Bioframenet: A domain-specific framenet extension with links to biomedical ontologies," in In Proceedings of the Biomedical Ontology in Action Workshop at KR-MED, 2006, pp. 87–94.

[21] J. Pimentel, "Description de verbes juridiques au moyen de la sémantique des cadres," in Terminologie and Ontologie : Théories et applications, 2010, pp. 26–27.

[22] M. Smialek, W. Nowakowski, N. Jarzebowski, and A. Ambroziewicz, "From use cases and their relationships to code," in International Workshop on Model-Driven Requirements Engineering, Chicago, IL, USA, September 24, 2012, pp. 9–18.

[23] W. Nowakowski, M. Smialek, A. Ambroziewicz, and T. Straszak, "Requirements-level language and tools for capturing software system essence," Comput. Sci. Inf. Syst., vol. 10, no. 4, 2013, pp. 1499–1524.

[24] A. Kalnins, et al., Handbook of research on innovations in systems and software engineering. IGI Global, 2014, ch. Developing Software with Domain-Driven Model Reuse.

[25] A. Cozzie and S. T. King, "Macho: Writing programs with natural language and examples," University of Illinois at Urbana-Champaign, Tech. Rep., 2012.

[26] E. Özcan, S. E. Seker, and Z. I. Karadeniz, "Generating java class skeleton using a natural language interface," in Natural Language Understanding and Cognitive Science, Porto, Portugal, April 2004, 2004, pp. 126–134.

[27] M. Kapor. Brainy quote. [Online]. Available: http://www.brainyquote.com/quotes/quotes/m/mitchkapor690403.html [retrieved: August, 2017] (1950)

[28] R. S. Scowen, "Extended BNF - A generic base standard," in Proceedings of the 1993 Software Engineering Standards Symposium (SESS'93), Aug. 1993.

[29] M. Mefteh. Requirements analysis with the semantic model. [On-

line]. Available: http://spl-nlp-with-semanticmodel.com/translation.html [retrieved: August, 2017] (2017)

[30] J. Ramos, "Using TF-IDF to determine word relevance in document queries," Department of Computer Science, Rutgers University, 23515 BPO Way, Piscataway, NJ, 08855e, Tech. Rep., 2003.

[31] G. A. Miller. Wordnet. [Online]. Available: https://wordnet.princeton.edu/ [retrieved: August, 2017] (2015)

[32] M. Ester, H. peter Kriegel, J. Sander, and X. Xu, "A density-based algorithm for discovering clusters in large spatial databases with noise," in Proceedings of the International Conference on Knowledge Discovery and Data Mining. AAAI Press, 1996, pp. 226–231.

[33] J. Trimble. et al., Google translate API. [Online]. Available: https://www.programmableweb.com/api/google-translate [retrieved: August, 2017] (2011)

[34] C. Wohlin, M. Höst, and K. Henningsson, Empirical research methods in web and software engineering. Berlin, Heidelberg: Springer Berlin Heidelberg, 2006, pp. 409–430.

[35] L. P. Tizzei, C. M. F. Rubira, J. Lee, A. Garcia, and M. Barros. Health complaint system. [Online]. Available: http://www.ic.unicamp.br/ tizzei/phc/jss2013/ [retrieved: August, 2017] (2013)

[36] K. Bittner and I. Spence, Use case modeling. Pearson Education Inc., 2002, pp. 301–330.

[37] D. Muthig, I. John, M. Anastasopoulos, T. Forster, J. Dörr, and K. Schmid, "Gophone - a software product line in the mobile phone domain," No. 025.04/E, Version 1.0, Fraunhofer IESE, Tech. Rep., 2004.

[38] J. Kienzle, N. Guelfi, and S. Mustafiz, Crisis management systems: A case study for aspect-oriented modeling. Berlin, Heidelberg: Springer Berlin Heidelberg, 2010, pp. 1–22.

[39] G. Blank. Game of war. [Online]. Available: http://www.cse.lehigh.edu/ glennb/csc10/WarDesign.htm [retrieved: June, 2017] (2010)

[40] C. R. van der Burg, T. Kirke, and A. Rokic, "Emptio - a mobile phone application for selfservice," Master's thesis, Aalborg University, Germany, 2011.

GMAP: A Generic Methodology for Agile Product Line Engineering

Farima Farmahini Farahani, Raman Ramsin
Department of Computer Engineering
Sharif University of Technology
Tehran, Iran
e-mail: farimafarahani@ce.sharif.edu, ramsin@sharif.edu

Abstract—**Agile Product Line Engineering (APLE) is a relatively novel approach that has emerged as the result of the combination of two successful software development approaches: Software Product Line Engineering and Agile Software Development. The main goal of this combined approach is to cover the weaknesses of each of these two approaches while maximizing the advantages of both. We propose the Generic Methodology for Agile Product Line Engineering (GMAP), which can be instantiated to produce a bespoke, concrete methodology for any specific project situation. GMAP is generic in that its process covers the main activities of existing APLE methodologies, while refraining from enforcing any specific and concrete method or technique for performing the activities. GMAP has been produced by studying existing APLE methodologies, identifying their strengths and weaknesses, abstracting them into a high-level framework, and finally instantiating this abstract framework so as to address the shortcomings of existing methodologies.**

Keywords—Software Development Methodology; Software Product Line; Agile Method; Agile Product Line Engineering.

I. INTRODUCTION

Product Line Engineering (PLE) and *Agile Software Development* are two successful approaches in the software industry. Both approaches focus on developing high-quality software systems, reducing development costs, managing changes in requirements, and reducing time to market. These common goals have motivated researchers to investigate ways for merging them. This new combined approach, called *Agile Product Line Engineering (APLE)* [1], would help us use the positive features of the individual approaches while maximizing their benefits. Another potential advantage is synergy: each approach can cover the other's weaknesses.

Several methods have so far been introduced in the APLE context. From among these methods, those that have proposed a distinct *process* for this combined approach can be referred to as APLE *methodologies*. We have previously studied and analyzed existing APLE methodologies by using a criteria-based approach [2]. The results of this evaluation showed that despite the benefits that they provide, they are all afflicted with certain problems; for instance, none of them has prescribed a full-lifecycle approach that explains the details of the activities, work-products, and roles. Hence, developing a new APLE methodology that addresses the deficiencies of existing methodologies, while preserving their positive features, is of great potential value. We therefore propose the Generic Methodology for Agile PLE (GMAP) as a high-level full-lifecycle APLE methodology that provides these features and can be instantiated to yield concrete APLE methodologies for different project situations. To this aim, we first evaluated existing methodologies using a criteria-based approach to identify their positive and negative traits. The evaluation criteria and the results of evaluation have been extensively discussed in [2]. We have used the criteria defined in [2] as the requirements for constructing GMAP; this ensures that GMAP possesses the main characteristics of PLE and Agile Development, makes use of the positive features of previous APLE methodologies, and addresses their weaknesses.

GMAP was developed in two steps: We first produced a high-level APLE process framework through applying abstraction to existing methodologies; GMAP was then defined by instantiating this abstract framework and improving the resulting instance to satisfy the requirements of the target methodology. GMAP satisfies the high-level requirements, but is kept independent of specific techniques and practices so that it can be instantiated based on the finer-grained requirements of a specific project. GMAP was evaluated in two ways: 1) by instantiation to a concrete methodology in order to demonstrate that it has the potential to be instantiated into a concrete and applicable methodology, and 2) by applying a subset of the criteria presented in [2] in order to show that GMAP can indeed be considered an improvement to the status quo; the reason for using a subset of the criteria is that some of the criteria are not applicable due to the abstractness of GMAP. The evaluation results show that GMAP does indeed address the weaknesses of existing methodologies; for example, the need for a full-lifecycle APLE process, providing specifications for activities, work-products, and roles, has been adequately addressed in GMAP.

The rest of this paper is structured as follows: Section II discusses the related research; Section III presents the proposed abstract framework for APLE methods; Section IV describes GMAP; Section V presents the evaluation results; and Section VI discusses the conclusions and suggests ways for furthering this research.

II. RELATED RESEARCH

Prominent APLE methodologies and their important features are depicted in Table I; this table has been adapted from our previous research, reported in [2], which presents an extensive review of these methodologies.

TABLE I. PROMINENT APLE METHODOLOGIES (ADAPTED FROM [2])

Feature / Methodology	Brief introduction	Year	Basis (Agile or PLE)	Reuse approach	PLE process coverage (DE, AE)
CDD [4]	Uses FDD [5] to combine PLE and agility.	2005	Agile	N/A	DE (Partially)
de Souza & Vilain [6]	Merging the generic PLE process with the Framework of Agile Practices.	2013	PLE	Proactive, Reactive	DE (Partially), AE
RiPLE-SC [7]	An agile process for PL Scoping in RiPLE methodology.	2011	PLE	N/A	DE (Partially)
Diaz et al. [3]	Utilizes Scrum [5] to define an APLE method.	2011	Agile	Reflexive	DE (Partially), AE
EPLSP [8]	A full-lifecycle methodology that utilizes AUP [9] for product development; thus, agility is limited to this particular activity.	2011	PLE	Reactive	DE, AE
A-Pro-PD [10]	A generic agile framework for product derivation.	2012	PLE	Proactive, Reactive	AE
Ghanam & Maurer 2008 [11]	Aims at agile organizations building several similar systems in a domain. Core assets are derived from the products in a bottom-up fashion.	2008	Agile	Reactive	DE (Partially), AE (Partially)
Ghanam et al. [12]	An agile approach for variability management in which variability analysis is only performed when a new requirement arises.	2010	Agile	Reactive	DE (Partially)
Ghanam & Maurer 2009 [13]	An acceptance-test-based approach for product derivation in PLE; core assets are retrieved (from a repository) based on acceptance tests.	2009	Agile	Reactive	AE
da Silva [14]	An agile process for PL scoping.	2012	PLE	N/A	DE (Partially)
Carbon et al. [15]	The result of incorporating agile practices into PULSE's product-instantiation.	2006	PLE	Reactive	AE
Noor et al. [16]	An agile method for PL scoping that utilizes Collaboration Engineering patterns to promote collaboration among stakeholders.	2008	PLE	N/A	DE (Partially)
SPLICE [17]	Incorporates Scrum [5] practices with core activities of PLE.	2014	PLE	Reactive	DE, AE (Partially)

The review reported in [2] shows that none of the methodologies possess all the features expected in an APLE methodology, including: full coverage of the PLE lifecycle, definition of work-units, roles, and work-products, attention to umbrella activities, management of expected/unexpected changes, configurability, support for learning, active user involvement, and team management. Three reuse approaches have been observed in these methodologies: Proactive (predicting and building the core assets at the beginning of the development process), Reactive (extracting the core assets from previously built products), and Reflexive (predicting the core assets at the beginning of each iteration) [3].

III. PROPOSED ABSTRACT FRAMEWORK FOR APLE METHODOLOGIES

The first step in building the target methodology is to produce an abstract framework for APLE methodologies, which is the result of applying abstraction to the activities prescribed in the methodologies reviewed (listed in Table I); this framework will be introduced in this section.

A. Description

Figure 1 shows the proposed framework. As it covers the activities of the reviewed methodologies in an abstract manner, these methodologies can be regarded as its instances. The white block arrows between DE and AE indicate that any transition between the internal stages of these sub-processes is possible; however, the transitions allowed in existing methodologies are shown with ordinary black arrows. The liberal attitude of the framework towards transitions promotes abstractness and allows the framework to be instantiated into any desired APLE methodology. The white arrow from DE to AE denotes the Proactive approach of reuse, the white arrow from AE to DE denotes the Reactive approach, and the combination of these arrows denotes the Reflexive approach. The activities that belong to some (but not all) of the reviewed methodologies will be referred to as "non-common".

1) Domain Engineering (DE) Sub-process

DE consists of *Scoping* and *Core Assets Development*.

a) Scoping

The PL's scope is determined in the following stages:

- Pre-Scoping: Business goals are identified; non-common activities are: understanding the operational and organizational context of the organization, analyzing stakeholders and target markets, and building a business case.
- Domains Selection: PL domains are selected from among the candidate domains.
- Products and Requirements Selection: The domains' requirements and products are identified.
- Prioritization: Requirements and products are prioritized and selected.

b) Core Assets Development (CAD)

Core assets are built through the following stages:

- Requirements Analysis: The requirements of the PL products are defined in a more fine-grained form, with the commonalities and variabilities specified.
- Core Assets Design: Components and PL architecture are designed. Non-common activities are: Detailed design, and documentation of design decisions.
- Planning: Implementation units are prioritized and assigned to iterations.
- Core Assets Implementation: Implementation units are built, and the required tests are developed.
- Core Assets Validation and Incorporation in the Repository: Implemented units are integrated with other parts, and are incorporated in the repository.

2) Application Engineering (AE) Sub-process

PL products are built and deployed in two phases: *Product Development* and *Transition.*

a) Product Development

This phase is the pivotal part of AE. Its stages are:

- Requirements Definition: The product requirements document is produced, and the core assets are elicited.
- Planning: Implementation units are assigned to iterations.
- Design and Implementation: The PL architecture is instantiated and the product architecture is developed; detailed design is then performed for the product-specific parts (as a non-common activity). Next, product-specific parts are developed and integrated with instantiated core assets to form the final product.
- Increment Validation: The implemented increment is validated against the iteration requirements.

b) Transition

System Validation and Installation is performed. As a non-common activity, training material is produced and a short document of the system is developed for the user.

3) Maintenance Sub-process

In the *Support* phase, bug fixes and new requirements are supplied to the AE team (and to the DE team, if necessary).

B. Realization of the framework in APLE methodologies

Table II shows how the framework's constituent activities correspond to the activities of existing APLE methodologies, thus validating the proposed framework as to its coverage of existing APLE methodologies.

IV. Proposed Generic APLE Methodology (GMAP)

As discussed in [17], the criteria for evaluating methodologies in a given context can serve as the requirements for constructing a target methodology in that context; we have therefore used the criteria defined in [2] as the requirements for constructing GMAP. GMAP is an instance of the proposed APLE framework, and its activities and tasks are abstractions of the activities and tasks prescribed in existing APLE methodologies, composed so that the requirements of the target APLE methodology are satisfied; also, certain activities have been added from existing Agile and PLE methodologies. As GMAP is generic and abstract, it only provides general guidelines and does not enforce any concrete methods or techniques. Thus, it has a high degree of configurability and should be instantiated prior to application; typically, the instantiation process includes the following activities: Decision as to optional activities; addition of project-specific tasks; removing, merging, or decomposing the tasks; determination of concrete methods, practices, and guidelines for performing the tasks; selection from among the methods available for performing the tasks; and changing the roles involved in an activity or task. The process of GMAP and its roles are presented throughout the rest of this section.

A. Roles

GMAP roles have been determined through integrating the roles typically found in agile methodologies with the generic PLE roles defined in [18] and the roles observed in the APLE methodologies reviewed in [2]. The roles are explained below:

- *Senior Manager:* Responsibilities include managing the APLE project, and providing expertise on organizational/business goals and the market.
- *Product Manager:* Responsibilities are: managing PL products and planning for the development of current and future systems, providing expertise on business goals and the PL's target market, and maintaining the PL Scope Document [18].
- *Core Assets Manager:* Duties include performing maintenance and configuration management on the core assets, and helping with their extraction [18].
- *Senior Developer:* This role is performed by experienced developers familiar with the organization's products. Responsibilities include conducting project management, leading teams, and carrying out analysis and design activities during CAD and AE; scoping and code development will also be included if necessary. Responsibilities are equivalent to the collective responsibilities of Domain/Application (D/A) Requirements Engineer, D/A Architect, and D/A Developer roles of [18].
- *Developer:* Responsibilities are working in CAD and AE teams, and performing analysis, design, implementation, and test under the supervision of Senior Developers. Responsibilities are equivalent to the combined responsibilities of D/A Requirements Engineer, D/A Architect, D/A Developer, and D/A Tester of [18]. We recommend that the people in charge of this role be moved between CAD and AE so that their knowledge is shared (akin to the "Move People Around" practice of XP [5]). A number of Developers are also involved in Scoping.
- *Customer:* This role is performed by representatives of the customer organizations who know the system's requirements and act as domain experts.
- *Support Team Member:* This role performs support and maintenance activities on instances of the PL.

B. Process

The process of GMAP is shown in Figure 2. It consists of three sub-processes: DE (consisting of Scoping and CAD), AE, and Maintenance. AE and the two internal phases of DE are run in an iterative-incremental manner. This methodology is applicable under two scenarios: Scenario-1 aims at organizations that have previously developed a number of similar systems. In this case, Scoping is first performed, followed by CAD and AE; after the first run of the CAD phase (so that the CAD team is formed and the reference architecture is built), CAD and AE can be run in tandem. Scenario-2 is aimed at organizations that have not built any similar systems, but are planning to build a PL while the products are being developed. In this case, the organization first develops a predefined number of systems (at least two [11]) using the AE sub-process of GMAP; Scoping is then performed for these systems, followed by CAD and AE. The two scenarios show that the methodology can cover the proactive approach of reuse as well as the reactive approach based on the target organization's needs. In both scenarios, if a new product is to be built in an available domain, core assets are retrieved from the product by requesting for PL extension, and the PL Scope is updated accordingly. If a new product in a new domain is to be built, scoping should precede CAD.

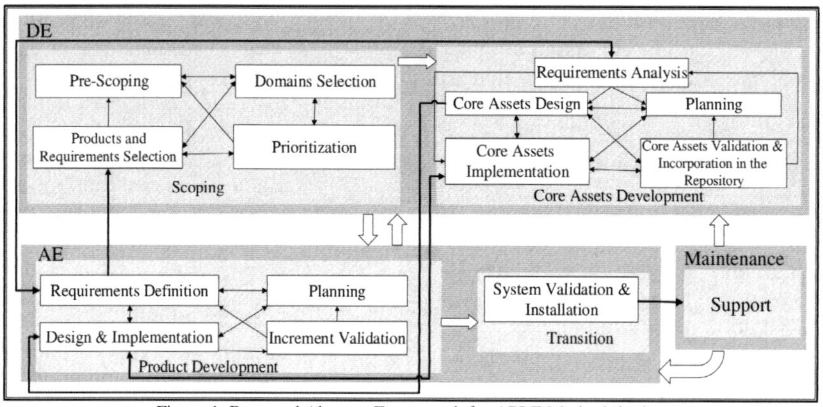

Figure 1. Proposed Abstract Framework for APLE Methodologies

TABLE II. REALIZATION OF PROPOSED FRAMEWORK IN REVIEWED APLE METHODOLOGIES

Stage in Framework			**Corresponding phases in APLE methodologies**
Domain Engineering	*Scoping*	Pre-Scoping	*Pre-scoping* in RiPLE-SC [7]; *Define pre-scoping* (Partially) in da Silva [14], *Select business goals and marketing strategies* in SPLICE [17].
		Domains Selection	*Identify and agree on relevant domains* in Noor et al. [16]; *Define pre-scoping* (Partially) in da Silva [14]; *Domain scoping* in RiPLE-SC [7].
		Products & Requirements Selection	*Define features for each domain, Discuss, analyze, and agree on products, Define products in terms of features* in Noor et al. [16]; *Product scoping* in RiPLE-SC [7]; *Define features, Define pre-scoping* (partially) in da Silva [14], *Identify products, Identify major features, Build initial product map* in SPLICE [17].
		Prioritization	*Release scope* in da Silva [14]; *Prioritize product map* in Noor et al. [16]; *Assets scoping* in RiPLE-SC [7], *Prioritize major features* in SPLICE [17].
	Core Assets Development	Requirements Analysis	*Develop an overall model* (Partially), *Build a features list* in CDD [4]; *Domain analysis* in de Souza & Vilain [6]; *Pregame* (Partially) in Diaz et al. [3]; *Evaluation and extraction* (Partially) in Ghanam & Maurer 2008 [11]; *Eliciting new requirements* (Partially), *Variability analysis, Updating the variability profile* in Ghanam et al [12]; *Analyze commonality and variability* in da Silva [14]; *Core assets development* (Partially) in EPLSP [8], *Sub-features definition, Commonality and variability analysis* in SPLICE [17].
		Core Assets Design	*Develop an overall model* (Partially), *Design SPL architecture, Build a components list, Design by components* in CDD [4]; *Domain design, Develop system increment* (DE) (Partially) in de Souza & Vilain [6]; *Architecture evolution* in Ghanam & Maurer 2008 [11]; *Sprint-domain engineering* (Partially) in Diaz et al. [3]; *Refactoring the architecture* in Ghanam et al [12]; *Core assets development* (Partially) in EPLSP [8].
		Planning	*Plan by components* in CDD [4]; *Iteration definition* in de Souza & Vilain [6]; *SPL release definition* (Partially); *Sprint planning* (Partially) in Diaz et al. [3]; *Select features for implementation* (Partially) in da Silva [14]; *Eliciting new requirements* (Partially) in Ghanam et al [12], *Release planning, Sprint planning* in SPLICE [17].
		Core Assets Implementation	*Build by components* (Partially) in CDD [4]; *Develop system increment* (DE) (Partially) in de Souza & Vilain [6]; *Refactoring* in Ghanam & Maurer 2008 [11]; *Select features for implementation* (Partially) in da Silva [14]; *Sprint-domain engineering* (Partially) in Diaz et al. [3]; *Realizing the new requirements* in Ghanam et al [12]; *Core assets development* (Partially) in EPLSP [8], *Sub-features implementation, Sub-features testing* (Partially) in SPLICE [17].
		Core Assets Validation & Incorporation in the Repository	*Running the tests* in Ghanam et al [12]; *Build by components* (Partially) in CDD [4]; *Develop system increment* (DE) (Partially), *Validate increment* in de Souza & Vilain [6]; *Managing core assets* in Ghanam & Maurer 2008 [11]; *Review and retrospective* (Partially) in Diaz et al. [3]; *Core assets development* (Partially) in EPLSP [8], *Sub-features testing* (Partially), *Sprint review and retrospective* in SPLICE [17].
Application Engineering	*Product Development*	Requirements Definition	*Definition of requirements* in de Souza & Vilain [6]; *Preparing for derivation* (Partially) in A-Pro-PD [10]; *Select acceptance tests, Execute acceptance tests, Extract code* (Partially) in Ghanam & Maurer 2009 [13]; *Plan for a product line instance, Instantiate and validate product line model* in Carbon et al. [15]; *Pregame* (Partially), *SPL release definition* (Partially) in Diaz et al. [3]; *Evaluation and extraction* (Partially) in Ghanam & Maurer 2008 [11]; *Product Development* (Partially) in EPLSP [8].
		Planning	*Assign requirements to iterations* in de Souza & Vilain [6]; *Preparing for derivation* (Partially) in A-Pro-PD [10]; *SPL release definition* (Partially), *Sprint planning* (Partially) in Diaz et al. [3].
		Design and Implementation	*Instantiate & validate reference architecture, Construct product* in Carbon et al. [15]; *Develop system increment* (AE) in de Souza & Vilain [6]; *Product configuration, Product development & testing* (Partially) in A-Pro-PD [10]; *Core asset incorporation* in Ghanam & Maurer 2008 [11]; *Extract code* (Partially), *Verify & build* (Partially) in Ghanam & Maurer 2009 [13]; *Sprint-application engineering* in Diaz et al. [3]; *Product Development* (Partially) in EPLSP [8], *Products derivation* (Partially) in SPLICE [17].
		Increment Validation	*Validate increment, Integrate increment* in de Souza & Vilain [6]; *Review and retrospective* (Partially) in Diaz et al. [3]; *Verify and build* (Partially) in Ghanam & Maurer 2009 [13]; *Product development and testing* (Partially) in A-Pro-PD [10].
	Transition	System Validation & Installation	*Validate system* in de Souza & Vilain [6]; *Product development and testing* (Partially) in A-Pro-PD [10]; *Deliver system* in Carbon et al. [15].
Maintenance		***Support***	*Product release* in EPLSP [8].

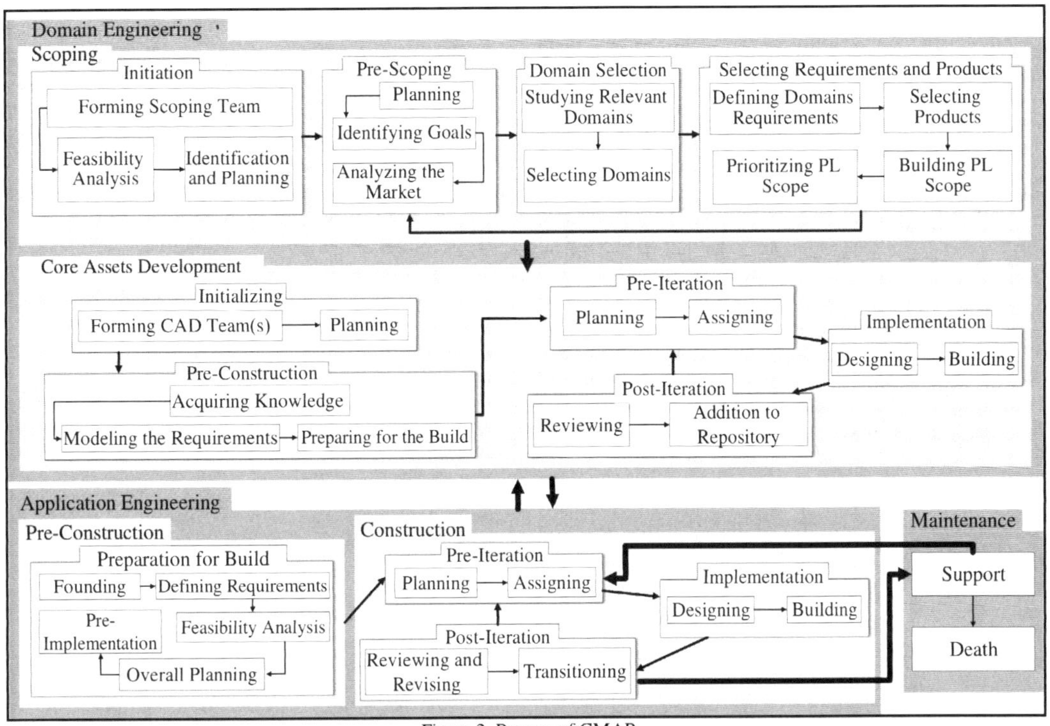

Figure 2. Process of GMAP

GMAP is described throughout the rest of this section by using a *process-centered* approach [5]: the focus is on describing the high-level *phases*, intermediate-level *stages*, and bottom-level *tasks* of the methodology; the roles involved and the work-products produced are seen as secondary to these process constituents.

1) Domain Engineering (DE) Sub-process

DE aims at building the PL infrastructure. AE team members are the main customers of DE, as they use the core assets developed in DE.

a) Scoping

The PL scope is defined in this phase. It continues in an iterative-incremental manner until the PL scope becomes stable enough for the core assets to be built based on it. The PL scope is then completed while new PL products are being developed. The constituent stages are explained below.

1) Initiation

The preliminary activities for identifying the PL scope are performed in three sub-stages:

Forming Scoping Team: The Scoping Team is formed by analyzing the experiences and skills required; team members include the product manager, a number of senior developers and developers, and selected customer representatives [7].

Feasibility Analysis: This stage is performed by the senior manager, product manager and senior developers of the scoping team. The results of analyzing the risks and constraints and estimating the required resources are recorded in the PL Vision. Finally, feasibility study is performed based on the PL Vision, and a Go/No-Go decision is made.

Identification and Planning: Organizational factors are identified by the senior manager, product manager, and senior developers of the scoping team; the organization's structure and its processes are explored and documented in the PL Vision. The product manager and the senior developers then determine an overall plan for the scoping phase.

2) Pre-Scoping

This stage, performed by the senior manager, product manager, and senior developers of the scoping team, consists of three sub-stages:

Planning: The iteration plan is elicited based on the overall plan.

Identifying Goals: Business and organizational goals are recorded in the PL Vision.

Analyzing the Market: The PL Vision is completed by studying the markets related to the candidate domains (as to their characteristics and success factors).

3) Domain Selection

The scoping team determines the target domains of the PL in two sub-stages, which are typically performed in tandem:

Studying Relevant Domains: The relevant domains are explored by the team members.

Selecting Domains: Domains are analyzed based on certain parameters that verify the potential of each domain for inclusion in the PL; domains are then selected based on this analysis and the parameters important to the organization.

4) Selecting Requirements and Products

The scoping team selects the PL products and requirements; sub-stages are as follows:

Defining Domains Requirements: The requirements of the selected domains are elicited. Requirements are then reviewed in order to resolve redundancies and ambiguities.

Selecting Products: Candidate products are defined for each domain based on domain requirements. Candidate products are then prioritized based on the parameters defined in the instantiated methodology, and PL products are selected.

Building PL Scope: The PL Scope is completed by relating products with requirements. Then, the customers review and validate the PL scope.

Prioritizing PL Scope: Reusable parts that will be implemented in the CAD phase are identified. We recommend two methods for this purpose: 1) The method used in [7] and [19], in which the goals are operationalized with the aim of defining certain metrics (the GQM method is typically used); prioritization is then conducted based on the derived metrics; and 2) The method used in [14] and [16], in which each stakeholder prioritizes the products and their requirements; stakeholders then discuss the priorities, reach a consensus, and select the core asset requirements.

b) Core Assets Development (CAD)

Reusable core assets are developed based on the results of scoping. Constituent stages include the following:

1) Initializing

This stage sets the stage for building the core assets. Sub-stages are as follows:

Forming CAD Team(s): Each CAD team is led by a senior developer, and is made up of several experienced developers. Developers are selected based on the knowledge, skills, and experience levels required.

Planning: Requirements prioritization is first conducted with the help of the product manager. Next, the overall plan is elicited and a subset of the requirements is selected for the next release. Also, a date for the next release and a duration for CAD iterations are determined.

2) Pre-Construction

The requirements of the next release are defined in a more detailed fashion, and the PL architecture is designed. Sub-stages are as follows:

Acquiring Knowledge (Optional): If the team requires more information on the requirements, knowledge acquisition is performed with the help of the product manager.

Modeling the Requirements: Requirements are modeled by specifying their commonalities and variabilities; requirements can be modeled in several formats: use-cases [20], acceptance tests [11], feature diagrams [21][22], features (as in the FDD methodology) [4][5], and a textual feature-based format [12]. The dependencies among the requirements are also identified, which can affect the selection of the requirements [22] and their implementation sequence.

Preparing for the Build: The architecture is designed, and architecture-level variabilities are specified; the architecture is then evaluated [4]. A list of implementation units is then produced, which can be based on the requirements [3], components [4][6], or any other relevant concept.

3) Pre-Iteration

An iteration plan is developed in the following sub-stages:

Planning: Prioritization is applied to the implementation units. Iteration planning is then performed, and a number of units are selected for the current iteration.

Assigning: If more than one team is involved, assigning to teams is performed. Assigning to developers is then conducted inside each team; this can be done in two ways: 1) the senior developer in each team assigns the units to the developers [4]; or 2) the developers choose what they intend to implement (common in self-organizing teams [23][24]).

4) Implementation

Detailed design and implementation is performed on the iteration's implementation units, in the following sub-stages:

Designing: Documents are studied and domain experts are interviewed in order to enrich the team's knowledge of the implementation units; these tasks are executed in tandem with other tasks of this stage, and may result in changes to the requirements model. Detailed design is then conducted, resulting in the design model. Finally, model notes [4] are added to document the design alternatives, and the reasons behind the design decisions.

Building: Test design is first conducted to produce test-cases for the current iteration's implementation units. Coding and refactoring are then performed [6]. Testing is performed continuously throughout this stage. Code inspection is the final task, which can be done in two ways: 1) the senior developer of each team inspects the code [4], or 2) the developers inspect one another's code [6].

5) Post-Iteration

The activities required for concluding the iteration are performed. Sub-stages are as follows:

Reviewing: Testing is performed with the cooperation of AE team members, and acceptance tests are run on the implemented units. A review meeting is then held to conduct regular review activities. The requirements model, implementation units list, and architecture (and if necessary, the PL scope document) are updated. The team and the product manager then discuss the AE team's requests for extending the PL scope (implementing product-specific parts as core assets); if they decide to implement certain parts as core assets, the PL models are changed as required.

Addition to Repository: Core assets are added to the repository (as directed by the core assets manager) for the implemented units and their corresponding requirements and tests.

2) Application Engineering (AE) Sub-process

This sub-process's goal is to build the target products by reusing the core assets built in the CAD phase. An important undertaking in this sub-process is to send requests to the CAD team for extending the PL scope. Three approaches are recommended for this purpose: 1) *Request-In-Advance*: requests are sent prior to starting the development of the product [15] (before forming the implementation units list, as the result may affect this list), and also at the beginning of each iteration (due to possible changes in requirements); the tasks corresponding to this approach reside in the *Pre-Implementation* and *Planning* sub-stages; 2) *Request-During-Implementation*: requests are sent when product development is underway in the *Building* sub-stage [10]; and 3) *Request-In-Retrospect*: requests are sent at the end of each iteration (for the units implemented in the iteration); this approach is implemented in the *Reviewing and Revising* sub-stage. AE phases are explained throughout the rest of this subsection.

a) Pre-Construction

The activities required for launching a new product development project are performed. The only stage of this phase is explained below.

1) Preparation for Build

This stage mainly focuses on analysis activities. Sub-stages are as follows:

Founding: AE teams are formed, with the same structure as in CAD.

Defining Requirements: The AE team elicits the requirements and builds the product's Requirements Model. Two methods are recommended for this task: 1) the requirements available in the core assets repository are provided to the customer, who then selects a subset of them according to his/her requirements [13] (we recommend interviewing the customer for eliciting the requirements that are not present in the core assets); and 2) the customer expresses his/her requirements from scratch [3], and the team matches these requirements with the core assets requirements. The product manager and the AE teams' senior developers then compare the product's requirements to the PL scope to decide whether this product is an instance of the PL; if it is, the product's information is added to the PL scope, and the AE team and the core assets manager extract the core assets related to the product.

Feasibility Analysis: This stage is only performed if the project requires certain resources that are not needed for other PL instances, or if certain risks or constraints are involved. The senior manager and the AE teams' senior developers cooperate in this stage. Analyzing the risks and constraints is first performed, followed by estimating the required resources (based on the amount of core assets that can be used in developing the product); the results of both tasks are recorded in the Project Vision. Finally, feasibility study is performed.

Overall Planning: The overall project plan is produced; again, the amount of core assets usable in developing the product is a crucial factor.

Pre-Implementation: Extension of the PL is requested if the "Request-In-Advance" approach is selected; if the DE team approves the implementation of product-specific requirements as core assets, it develops new core assets. The next task is designing the product architecture: if a PL architecture is available, it is instantiated; if not, a product-specific architecture is developed. Finally, a list of implementation units is produced.

b) Construction

This phase is executed in an iterative-incremental manner. The constituent stages are explained below.

1) Pre-Iteration

This stage is the starting point for development iterations. Sub-stages are as follows:

Planning: The first task, requesting for PL extension, will be performed if "Request-In-Advance" has been chosen. After prioritizing the implementation units, iteration planning is conducted. If any bug-fixes or new requirements are received from the Support Team, they are checked; if they are related to AE, they are added to the iteration plan; if not, they are relegated to the CAD team.

Assigning: Implementation units are assigned to developers (as in CAD).

2) Implementation

AE teams build the product by reusing the core assets. Sub-stages are as follows:

Designing: If the team needs to complete its knowledge of the requirements, customer interviews are conducted. This task is performed in tandem with detailed design, which is performed by instantiating the Domain Design Model (if available) and adding the product-specific parts.

Building: Test design is performed, and the tests in the core assets base are reused. If suitable core assets are available, a partial configuration of the product [10] is produced by assembling them. Product-specific parts are then built, either by adding the product-specific parts to the partial product configuration, or by building the product from scratch; if "Request-During-Implementation" is selected, requests for extending the PL Scope are sent to the CAD team during this task: if the product-specific parts are to be built as core assets, the CAD team designs their interfaces, based on which the AE team develops the product in parallel with the actual implementation of the assets by the CAD team [10]. Code refactoring is then applied [6]. Testing is performed continuously, and can be augmented with code inspection.

3) Post-Iteration

The AE team conducts review activities for finishing the iteration. Sub-stages are as follows:

Reviewing and Revising: Testing is conducted and acceptance tests are run on the implemented units (customer involvement is crucial). The next task is holding a review meeting, in which feedback on the usage of the assets is also recorded and conveyed to the CAD team [15]. The requirements, architecture, PL scope document, and implementation units are then updated. For new or changed requirements, relevant core assets are elicited with the help of the core assets manager. PL extension is requested if "Request-In-Retrospect" is selected. Finally, if there is a product-specific requirement that has recently been implemented as a core asset (as the result of a request for PL extension), the product is re-instantiated so that it includes this requirement as a core asset. The core assets manager ensures that the re-instantiation is done completely.

Transitioning: After the support team is trained, it prepares the training documents. The software product is deployed into the user environment, and conversion is applied. System testing is then conducted, and users are trained.

3) Maintenance Sub-Process

This sub-process spans maintenance and post-mortem activities in the phases explained below.

a) Support

Bug-fixes and new requirements are sent to the AE team. The AE team sends the requests related to the core assets to the CAD team: after applying the changes, the products that include the changed assets are tested and re-instantiated so that the changes are committed. Maintenance is performed via repeating the development iterations.

b) Death

This phase is carried out when a system is not maintainable anymore. Post-project activities are performed: the support team and the senior manager perform the legal, financial, and social activities related to closing the project. Post-mortem activities are then conducted, and the lessons learnt from the project are recorded for use in future projects.

V. EVALUATION

GMAP has been evaluated through two different approaches, as explained in the following subsections.

A. Criteria-based Evaluation

As mentioned before, we have used the criteria introduced in [2] as a basis for developing GMAP; in other words, these criteria have helped us identify the deficiencies and the strengths of previous APLE methodologies, which were then used for constructing GMAP. These criteria can also be used for evaluating GMAP to show that it does indeed address the deficiencies of previous methodologies. The results of evaluation based on criteria related to PLE characteristics are presented in Table III, the results of evaluation based on a set of general methodology-evaluation criteria are illustrated in Table IV, and the results of evaluation based on criteria related to agility characteristics are given in Table V. In all these tables, results are presented for a set of existing methodologies as well as GMAP, so that the results can be compared. In order to produce the results, we searched each methodology for mechanisms that satisfied each criterion. It should be noted that due to lack of space, we have only included the major criteria introduced in [2]. In these tables, "N/A" denotes "Not relevant to the context or properties of the methodology".

B. Evaluation by Instantiating the Proposed Method

To show that GMAP has the capability to be instantiated into a concrete and practicable APLE methodology, we have built a concrete method by instantiating GMAP. The concrete methodology was developed through a PLE project at a major Iranian utilities company. The Customer Management (CM) system used by this company, specializing in purification and distribution of water throughout the country, was the target of this project. The first author worked for three months at this company to help in performing the activities of the concrete methodology, and also in producing its work products. The project served as an effective testbed for improving and validating the methodology in the field.

The company's CM system (operated in most Iranian cities) has certain features common to all the cities. In addition, each city demands its own specific features. This system has long been deemed suitable for development as a product line; however, it has not yet been implemented as such. The main problem is that the commonalities and variabilities among the systems of different cities have not been managed systematically; instead, a common system encompassing the features needed in all the cities has been developed. This has spawned other problems as well: 1) many unusable parts exist for each city; developers try to fix this problem at the code level, but this solution itself has resulted in unreadable code; and 2) a nontrivial modification in the system propagates throughout the whole system. These problems have motivated the company's CM system supervisor to consider the systematic development of a software product line. Since the PL and its instances need to be developed rapidly, it was concluded that an APLE approach would work best for the company. At the beginning of this project, the first version of the concrete methodology was developed by instantiating GMAP based on the project's initial requirements. The concrete methodology was then used at the company, and was gradually configured to better fit the company's needs. At the end of the project, the CM system's manager reported that the concrete methodology had indeed been capable of addressing their problems.

VI. CONCLUSION AND FUTURE WORK

APLE is a new paradigm that has emerged as the result of the need for managing changes in requirements, reducing time-to-market, promoting product quality, and decreasing development costs in software organizations. This approach can be applied to real projects only if adequate guidelines are provided on the activities, people, and work-products involved in the project. A software development methodology can satisfy this need; thus, several attempts have been made to propose practical APLE methodologies. After studying and analyzing these methodologies, we have sensed the need for an APLE methodology that possesses the strengths of existing APLE methodologies while addressing their weaknesses. To this aim, we have defined GMAP, a generic APLE methodology that spans the activities defined in all the studied APLE methodologies and also possesses the desirable features of PLE and agility. This methodology is abstract enough to be instantiated to produce a concrete bespoke methodology. Although adequately abstract, it is detailed to the task level, and provides suggestions as to ways for applying the tasks. The results of criteria-based evaluation of GMAP show that it satisfies the targeted APLE requirements and is indeed superior to existing APLE methodologies.

We aim to continue this work by reporting on the GMAP instance (concrete methodology) that was mentioned in Section V, and also by exploring the potentials of GMAP in addressing diverse APLE requirements. The research can be furthered by applying GMAP to a variety of project situations with different characteristics.

TABLE III. RESULTS OF EVALUATION BASED ON CRITERIA RELATED TO PLE CHARACTERISTICS

Criterion	Possible Values	CDD [4]	de Souza & Vilain [6]	RiPLE-SC [7]	Díaz et al. [3]	A-Pro-PD [10]	Ghanam & Maurer 2008 [11]	Ghanam & Maurer 2009 [13]	Ghanam et al. [12]	da Silva [14]	Carbon et al. [15]	Noor et al. [16]	GMAP
Presence of PL-Specific Activities													
Coverage of DE Activities	"S": Scoping; "A": Reference architecture; "CA": Core assets development.	A-CA	A-CA	S	A-CA	N/A	A-CA	N/A	A-CA	S	N/A	S	S- A-CA
Coverage of AE Activities	"R": Matching product requirements & core requirements; "A": Reference architecture instantiation; "CA": Core assets selection; "V": Binding of variation points to variants; "P": product-specific parts development.	N/A	R-CA	N/A	A-CA-V	CA-P	R-CA	R-CA- P	N/A	N/A	R-A-CA-V-P	N/A	R-A-CA-V-P
Product Line Characteristics													
Extensibility of PL Scope	Yes/No	N/A	Y	Y	Y	Y	Y	Y	Y	Y	Y	Y	Y
Production and Adherence to Reference Architecture	1: Not produced; 2: Produced, but not adhered to; 3: Produced, and adhered to.	2	2	N/A	3	1	1	1	3	N/A	3	N/A	3
Techniques for Performing PL-Specific Activities													
Prescription of Specific Method for Identifying Core Assets & Commonalities/Variabilities (C/V)	Yes/No	N	N	Y	N	N/A	Y	N/A	Y	Y	N/A	Y	Y
Prescription of Specific Method for Documenting C/V	Yes/No	Y	Y	Y	Y	N/A	Y	N/A	Y	Y	N/A	N	Y

TABLE IV. RESULTS OF EVALUATION BASED ON GENERAL CRITERIA FOR EVALUATING METHODOLOGIES

Criterion		Possible Values	CDD [4]	de Souza & Vilain [6]	RiPLE-SC [7]	Díaz et al. [3]	A-Pro-PD [10]	Ghanam & Maurer 2008 [11]	Ghanam & Maurer 2009 [13]	Ghanam et al. [12]	da Silva [14]	Carbon et al. [15]	Noor et al. [16]	GMAP
Lifecycle														
Coverage of Generic Lifecycle Phases		"D": Definition; "C": Construction; "M": Maintenance	D-C	D-C	D	D-C	D-C	D-C	D-C	D-C	D	C	D	D-C-M
Coverage of Design Activities		Yes/No	Y	Y	N/A	Y	N	N	N	N	N/A	Y	N/A	Y
People														
Definition of Roles and Their Responsibilities		1: No; 2: Roles yes, responsibilities no; 3: Roles and responsibilities defined.	3	1	3	1	1	1	1	1	1	1	3	3
Usability														
Well-definedness	Completeness of Methodology Definition	"L": Lifecycle; "A": Activities; "R": Roles; "P": Products; "RL": Rules; "TP": Techniques/Practices; "U": Umbrella Activities; "ML": Modeling Language.	L-A-TP-R-P-U-RL-ML	L-A (Partial)-PT-P-U (Partial)-RL	L-A-PT-R-P-U (Partial)-RL	L-A-P-U (Partial)	L-A-PT-U (Partial)-P	L-A-PT-P	L-A-PT-P	L-A-PT-P	L-A-PT-U (Partial)-P	L-A-PT-U (Partial)-P	L-A-PT-R-U (Partial)-P	L--TP-R-P-U-RL
Well-definedness	Management of Definition Complexity	Yes/No	Y	Y	Y	N	N	N	N	N	N	N	N	Y
Well-definedness	Attention to Detail in Definitions of Phases/Tasks	Details provided for: 1: none; 2: some of the phases/tasks; 3: all the phases/tasks	3	2	3	1	1	2	3	3	2	2	3	3
Process Manipulation	Configurability of Process (at the start of the project)	1: No; 2: Possible, but not addressed explicitly; 3: Explicitly addressed	2	2	1	1	2	1	1	1	1	2	2	3
Process Manipulation	Flexibility of Process (while running the project)	1: No; 2: Possible, but not addressed explicitly; 3: Explicitly addressed	2	2	1	1	1	1	1	1	1	1	2	3

TABLE V. RESULTS OF EVALUATION BASED ON CRITERIA RELATED TO AGILITY CHARACTERISTICS

	Criterion	Possible Values	CDD [4]	de Souza & Vilain [6]	RiPLE-SC [7]	Díaz et al. [3]	A-Pro-PD [10]	Ghanam & Maurer 2008 [11]	Ghanam & Maurer 2009 [13]	Ghanam et al. [12]	da Silva [14]	Carbon et al. [15]	Noor et al. [16]	GMAP
Attention to Customer														
	Support for Active User Involvement	Yes/No	Y	N	Y	Y	Y	N	Y	Y	Y	Y	Y	Y
	Support for Continuous Customer Feedback	Yes/No	N	N	Y	Y	Y	N	Y	Y	N	Y	N	Y
Teams														
	Support for Self-Organizing Teams	1: Not discussed; 2: No; 3: Yes.	2	3	1	1	1	1	1	1	1	1	3	3
	Support for Face-to-Face Conversation	Yes/No	N	Y	Y	Y	N	Y	N	N	Y	Y	Y	Y
Product														
	Support for Continuous Integration	Yes/No	Y	Y	N/A	N	Y	N	Y	Y	N/A	Y	N/A	Y
Process														
	Support for Iterative-Incremental Development	Yes/No	Y	Y	Y	Y	Y	Y	Y	Y	Y	Y	Y	Y
	Prescription of Common Agile Practices	Yes/No	Y	Y	N	N	Y	Y	Y	Y	Y	Y	Y	Y
Degree of Agility	Support for Rapid Development of Products	1: No; 2: To some extent; 3: Yes.	2	3	2	3	3	2	3	3	2	2	2	3
	Support for Leanness Factors	Yes/No	Y	Y	N	Y	N	N	N	Y	N	N	Y	Y
	Support for Learning (from previous iterations/projects)	1: No; 2: Yes, implicitly; 3: Yes, explicitly.	2	3	1	1	1	1	1	1	2	2	1	Y
	Support for Responsiveness (provision of process feedback)	Yes/No	Y	Y	Y	Y	Y	N	N	Y	Y	Y	Y	Y

REFERENCES

[1] G. K. Hanssen and T. E. Fægri, "Process fusion: An industrial case study on agile software product line engineering," Journal of Systems and Software, vol. 81, no. 6, pp. 843–854, 2008.

[2] F. Farmahini Farahani and R. Ramsin, "Methodologies for Agile Product Line Engineering: A Survey and Evaluation," Proc. International Conference on Intelligent Software Methodologies, Tools, and Techniques, 2014, pp. 545–564.

[3] J. Díaz Fernández, J. Pérez Benedí, A. Yagüe Panadero, and J. Garbajosa Sopeña, "Tailoring the Scrum Development Process to Address Agile Product Line Engineering," Proc. Jornadas de Ingeniería del Software y base de Datos, 2011.

[4] X. Wang, "Towards an Agile Method for Building Software Product Lines," M.Sc. Thesis, University of York, UK, 2005.

[5] R. Ramsin and R. F. Paige, "Process-centered Review of Object Oriented Software Development Methodologies," ACM Computing Surveys, vol. 40, no. 1, p. 3:1–89, 2008.

[6] D. S. de Souza and P. Vilain, "Selecting Agile Practices for Developing Software Product Lines," Proc. International Conference on Software Engineering & Knowledge Engineering, 2013, pp. 220–225.

[7] M. Balbino, E. S. de Almeida, and S. R. de Lemos Meira, "An Agile Scoping Process for Software Product Lines," Proc. International Conference on Software Engineering & Knowledge Engineering, 2011, pp. 717–722.

[8] A. Abouzekry and R. Hassan, "Software Product Line Agility," Proc. International Conference on Software Engineering Advances, 2011, pp. 1–7.

[9] "The Agile Unified Process (AUP)." [Online]. Available: http://www.ambysoft.com/unifiedprocess/agileUP.html. [Retrieved: August-2017].

[10] P. O'Leary, F. McCaffery, S. Thiel, and I. Richardson, "An agile process model for product derivation in software product line engineering," Journal of Software: Evolution and Process, vol. 24, no. 5, pp. 561–571, 2012.

[11] Y. Ghanam and F. Maurer, "An Iterative Model for Agile Product Line Engineering," Proc. International Software Product Line Conference, 2008, pp. 377–384.

[12] Y. Ghanam, D. Andreychuk, and F. Maurer, "Reactive Variability Management in Agile Software Development," Proc. Agile Conference, 2010, pp. 27–34.

[13] Y. Ghanam and F. Maurer, "Extreme product line engineering: Managing variability and traceability via executable specifications," Proc. Agile Conference, 2009, pp. 41–48.

[14] I. F. da Silva, "An agile approach for software product lines scoping," Proc. International Software Product Line Conference, 2012, pp. 225–228.

[15] R. Carbon, M. Lindvall, D. Muthig, and P. Costa, "Integrating product line engineering and agile methods: Flexible design up-front vs. incremental design," Proc. International Workshop on Agile Product Line Engineering, 2006, pp. 1–8.

[16] M. A. Noor, R. Rabiser, and P. Grünbacher, "Agile product line planning: A collaborative approach and a case study," Journal of Systems and Software, vol. 81, no. 6, pp. 868–882, 2008.

[17] T. Vale et al., "SPLICE: A Lightweight Software Product Line Development Process for Small and Medium Size Projects," Proc. Brazilian Symposium on Software Components, Architectures and Reuse, 2014, pp. 42–52.

[18] F. van der Linden, K. Schmid, and E. Rommes, Software Product Lines in Action - The Best Industrial Practice in Product Line Engineering. Springer, 2007.

[19] J. M. DeBaud and K. Schmid, "A systematic approach to derive the scope of software product lines," Proc. International Conference on Software Engineering, 1999, pp. 34–43.

[20] H. Gomaa, Designing software product lines with UML: From use cases to pattern-based software architecture. Addison-Wesley, 2005.

[21] K. C. Kang, S. G. Cohen, J. A. Hess, W. E. Novak, and A. S. Peterson, "Feature-Oriented Domain Analysis (FODA) Feasibility Study," Carnegie Mellon University, 1990.

[22] K. C. Kang, J. Lee, and P. Donohoe, "Feature-oriented product line engineering," IEEE Software, vol. 19, no. 4, pp. 58–65, 2002.

[23] K. Schwaber and M. Beedle, Agile Software Development with Scrum. Prentice Hall, 2001.

[24] K. Beck and C. Andres, Extreme Programming Explained: Embrace Change, 2nd edition. Addison-Wesley, 2004.

A Benchmarking Criteria for the Evaluation of OLAP Tools

Fiaz Majeed
Department of Information Technology, University of Gujrat,
Gujrat, Pakistan.
Email: fiaz.majeed@uog.edu.pk

Abstract— **Generating queries on Online Analytical Processing (OLAP) tools for complex analysis is a difficult assignment for the novice users. To compose accurate OLAP queries for fulfilling demand, technical knowledge about schema and the data is required. This deficiency can be covered by providing an easy design for OLAP tool for the purpose of querying. In this paper, a scheme is proposed for comparison of the OLAP tools to identify easy and standardized aspects. For this purpose, seven parameters have been used which are interface, query, drill-down options, roll-up options, aggregation function support, data access and performance. For experimental analysis, two tools SQL Server and MicroStrategy Express have been evaluated based on the proposed parameters. The benefits and drawbacks of the standardization of tools for non-technical users have been identified.**

Keywords-OLAP tool; evaluation criteria; parameters; benchmark; standardize.

I. Introduction

The Online Analytical Processing (OLAP) comprises a relational or multidimensional database intended to deliver fast retrieval of multidimensional analysis and pre-summarized data. The OLAP contains three fundamental operations for results presentation including drill-down, slicing & dicing, and roll-up. The drill-down operation provides navigation towards details (upper to lower levels). For example, the user may be interested to view the detail of region's sale in the form of individual products. By contrast, roll-up operation consolidates the results (lower to upper levels). For instance, individual products can be roll-up to region's sale. Further, slice and dice operation is used to select data from the OLAP cube. The OLAP tools provide these and many other functionalities. Most popular tools include MicroStrategy Express, SQL Server, SAP business object, Oracle, QlickView and Pentaho Business Intelligence (BI).

To explore information by diverse angles, OLAP tools are utilized extensively and vendors related to them claim excellent performance. A number of tools are available which have distinct characteristics. All tools have a different way of responsiveness, the design of the interface, input query and performance. To the best of our knowledge, there is no benchmark to design an OLAP tool available. The users face a problem in the selection of an appropriate tool due to lacking standard. They cannot easily understand which OLAP tool is suitable for their requirement. In other words, a standard OLAP tool is needed to support novice users.

In this paper, a method has been formulated to identify standardized aspects for the comparison of the OLAP tools. For this purpose, seven parameters have been proposed which are the interface, query, drill-down, roll-up, aggregation function support, data access and performance. This is the list of parameters available in all of the existing tools. We have performed a comparative analysis of two OLAP tools: SQL Server and MicroStrategy Express. The experiments have been performed using the dataset AdventureWorksDW. The comparison exhibits basically the opportunities for non-technical users.

The paper is arranged as follows: detailed literature survey is furnished in Section II. The assessment parameters are introduced in Section III, while an experimental evaluation has been incorporated in Section IV. Finally, conclusions and future directions are given in Section V.

II. Related Work

The OLAP supports for multi-dimensional complex analysis on data warehouses for decision making [1]. To compare OLAP tools, several features should be considered. The features to evaluate the usefulness of OLAP are ease of use, user-friendly, easy learning and easy to get information. Seven features are used to measure the OLAP tool, which is: visualizations, summarization, Navigation, query function, Sophisticated analysis, Dimensionality, and performance [2]. An important feature that makes the design of OLAP tool user friendly and easy to use is the interface. Visualization is an important aspect of interface design.

A. *Interface*

Visualizations of statistical data need to present relationship among data. Existing tools show isolated graphs and do not provide support for the relationship in different reports. A visual language named as CoDe is used to present relationship among data in tabular form. The visualization is performed in four phases: CoDe Modeling, OLAP operation pattern definition, OLAP Operation and Report Visualization [3]. Thus, graphs are an integral part of the interface so big process graph refers to process-related partly unstructured execution and heterogeneous data of large hybrid collections. A set of methods and a framework are given for initiating OLAP analytics which is called P-OLAP. The P-OLAP introduces analytics over process execution data based on the scalable graph. It is the extension of traditional OLAP analytics [4].

Key Performance Indicators (KPI) are manually integrated into scorecards and dashboards used by the decision makers. Due to this, KPIs are not related to their business objectives and strategy. To make the KPIs dynamic, the modeling language Object Constraint Language (OCL) is used to represent OLAP actions, which are then translated to Multi-Dimensional eXpressions (MDX) query to be executed on OLAP engine [5]. As OLAP tools visualize results in the form of aggregations, drill-down up to maximum detail is also the important feature of the interface. Thus, the user may drill-down data to the maximum level where maximum measures are to be returned. In such a case, pivot table may not visualize data with full precision [6].

B. *Aggregations*

The aggregation operations are key to OLAP BI tools. The OLAP tools perform several operations including roll-up, drill-down slice and dice, ranking, selection and computed attributes [1]. The OLAP operation "shrink" balances data precision with the size of data cube via pivot table. It combines similar data in a single slice (f-slice) for the purpose of shrinking [6]. An aggregation operator has been built for the text embedded in the tweets content based on the Formal Concept Analysis (FCA) theory [7].

C. *Performance*

The selection of an appropriate server type plays a role in the performance of query processing. The OLAP servers generate aggregations for efficient query processing based on dimensions. The servers are categorized as ROLAP, MOLAP and Hybrid of ROLAP and MOLAP [1]. MOLAP presents data in multi-dimensional arrays format while ROLAP provides query processing on Relational databases [2]. Near real-time BI reduces the time of acquisition of data in operational sources and analyses on that data. Event processing on streaming data is an application of near real-time BI. Additionally, MapReduce paradigm can search in schema-less input files in comparison to parallel database approach. For enhanced BI performance, private clouds provide more security. Currently, BI is being switched to mobile devices as such devices are pervasive [8].

There are several advanced OLAP domains, which have emerged recently. The Skalla system has been built, which translates GMDJ operator into local site level plans. The Packet header, flow level traffic statistics, and router statistics can be analyzed effectively using OLAP. Heavy traffic cannot be loaded into a central data warehouse, thus local data warehouses on each site should be implemented to avoid loss of data and for efficient execution of OLAP queries. The Skalla performs optimization to minimize synchronization traffic and local level executions [9]. The tweet streams available in unstructured form are organized in an OLAP cube for analytics using Time-Aware Fuzzy Formal Concept Analysis theory. The microblog summarization algorithm is introduced and it provides the subset of the tweet that best represents the OLAP cube data for the analytic purpose. The definition of the multi-dimensional data model for the storage of tweet data streams for enabling OLAP analysis is performed [7]. The AOLAP maintains data stream's aggregations by providing OLAP queries in the form of approximate answers and maintains them in smaller space on the primary memory. In the OLAP cube, data summaries are stored related to each materialized node which is performed by the proposed Piece-wise Linear Approximation (PLA). To minimize overall querying error, lattice nodes based optimization technique is proposed [10].

Based on the literature, it is clear that there is no benchmark available to compare the existing tools. There is a need to develop such a benchmark to standardize the design and working of each tool to facilitate non-technical users.

III. ASSESSMENT PARAMETERS OF OLAP TOOLS

The evaluation criteria for OLAP tools contain seven parameters which include interface, query, drill-down options, roll-up options, aggregation function support, data access and performance. The parameters are depicted in Figure 1.

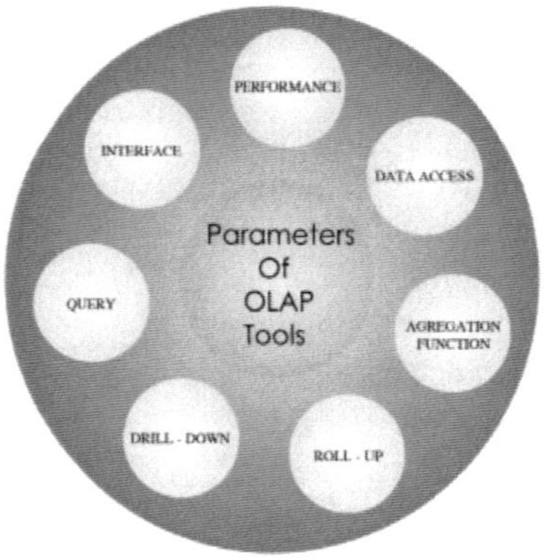

Figure 1. Evaluation criteria for the OLAP tools

For instance, User A wants to analyze his company's revenue with the revenue of his competitive companies. He wants to choose a BI tool for this purpose, which can provide him with a point and click environment to fulfill his demand. He selects SQL Server to input a query, but it requires training. Here the problem is that there should be a standard available based on which each tool can be designed. Each tool should provide similar easy query input mechanism for novice users.

The OLAP tools can be compared based on following seven parameters:

A. *Interface*

The interface is a fundamental source of communication between the user and the system. If interface design is adequate, the user can effortlessly interact with the system. The interface is evaluated based on following features:

Design: The aspects of design that are necessary to be considered are user understandability, first look impact of front page, the size of everything which is shown, colors effect, formal things to be used in designing, formatting of text and objects, number of formats to display the results, support of graphical results, and user understandability about results.

User-friendly: The user-friendly feature of the interface can be compared based on the sequence of steps understandable by the user, user understanding, how the response is shown at any step, and support with help and documentation. Understandability at each step during any task, make no confusion for the user, and user understandability at first look.

Type: The interface is graphical or query based. The graphical user interface is easy to use for novice users whereas a query based interface is preferable for expert users. Hybrid approach (a mixture of graphical and query based) provide an advantage to both types of the users.

User type: There are commonly two types of users for OLAP tools are available 1) novice user and 2) expert user. Interface comparison of different tools can be performed according to the facilities provided for each type of users such as the use of interface at first time and support available for the new user.

Visualizations: The interfaces are divided into three categories which are text-based, visualization-based and voice-based. The visualization-based interfaces provide analysis in the form of plots, trees, and charts. The comparison can be made based on easy to interpretable results, understanding at first glance, a large volume of data summarized in simple graphs.

Interactive: By this feature, user interaction at the front end of the tool is measured. At how many levels, the user can perform the task in an interactive way. The user finds a correct answer of the query and he may correct query on the basis of feedback provided by the system.

Complexity: The interface should have the capability to take input complex query in its simplest form. It should visualize complex OLAP analytics results in easy formats which may be the mixture of text, visualizations and voice. Many OLAP tools display simplified results on dashboards.

B. Query

The query is evaluated based on following features:

Format: It defines the format of query writing. There are four common formats of query input that are Command-based, Menu-based, Natural language-based, and Wizard-based. The easiest formats for query input considered for novice users are Menu-based, Natural language-based, and Wizard-based.

Procedure: It is categorized as query input procedure and results display procedure. The steps of query input are simple and natural as commonly input on web or other parallel interfaces. It should be according to previous familiar interfaces. The display of results is converged to the ease of understanding of results. The results must be focused for the less technical users.

Drill-down options: The comparison can be made based on summarization level of drill-down e.g. detailed level. How drill-down facility is provided either point and clicking way or another indirect way. If a user reaches to the detailed level of drill-down, how much a tool provides backtracking to roll-up levels?

Expertise required: This feature defines the type of users utilizing the tool. How much time is required for a particular user to achieve expertise of using the tool? For instance, the novice user may get expertise after 10 sessions span one-hour long.

Training required: Did any type of training requirements to use the tool? Further, if training is required then what level of training is demanded to learn and use the tool proficiently. Which training options are available? Few tools provide a manual for training while a professional training is necessary to utilize other tools.

C. Drill-down options

Support: According to support feature, the tools are compared based on whether drill-down support is available to navigate the results. Most of the tools provide this feature available in their interface whereas few of the tools do not provide drill-down options.

Options: How much depth and breadth level of navigation are provided? The tool provides drill-down support in one of the visualizations such as graphs, charts, tables or a mixture of them. Does drill-down performed on pre-built aggregations or run-time aggregations may be generated upon requirement?

Point and click: How drill-down facility is provided both point and clicking way or another indirect way? Does the tool expand a summarized value in the tree format or show detailed data in another format? If the user reaches to the detailed level of drill-down, how much a tool provides backtracking to roll-up levels?

Grouping different way: Is the grouping of data provided at run-time? How many attributes can be added in a group? Which grouping functions are supported by the tool?

Complexity: How drill-down results are presented to the user? Whether complex results are presented in simplest graphical formats? Does track of drill-down is given in some tree-like format to memorize the forward and backward tracking and switching to any other level of hierarchy?

D. Roll-up options

Support: In this feature, the tools are compared based on whether roll-up support is available to navigate the results. Most of the tools provide this feature available in their interface whereas few of the tools do not provide roll-up options.

Options: How much depth and breadth level of navigation are provided? The tool provides roll-up support in one of the visualizations such as graphs, charts and tables or the mixture of them. Does roll-up performed on pre-built aggregations or run-time aggregations may be generated upon requirement.

Point and click: How roll-up facility is provided either point and clicking way or another indirect way? Does the tool collapse a detailed value in the tree format or show summarized data in another format? If a user reaches the upper level of roll-up, how much a tool provides backtracking to drill-down levels?

Grouping different way: Does grouping of data is provided at run-time? How many attributes can be added in a group? Which grouping functions are supported by the tool?

Dimensions selection: How many dimensions can be selected at a time for grouping the data? How many dimensions can be used by default?

E. *Aggregation function support*

The OLAP servers use Materialized Views (MVs). If a particular MV is not found, then minimal MVs are further roll-up to generate required summarization level. The OLAP servers maintain data aggregated with several aggregation functions. At query processing time, the system selects desired MVs, aggregated data computed with the use of particular aggregation function. Furthermore, user query specifies the aggregation level with grouping attributes. These maintain aggregated data in specific structures to efficiently retrieve the results. The structures are relational and multi-dimensional etc. The tools can be compared based on aggregation functions supported by these tools.

F. *Data access*

In this, tools are analyzed by data type supported by them. The support of a number of fact tables, dimensions and measures are also verified.

G. *Performance*

The performance is measured by analyzing the response time by input queries on the tools.

IV. Experimental Evaluation

For experimental analysis, two OLAP tools SQL Server and MicroStrategy Express have been taken. These tools are evaluated with respect to interface, query, drill-down options, roll-up options, aggregation function support, data access and performance.

SQL Server helps to build secure, reliable and scalable enterprise applications for the organizations. It also supports to deploy and maintain the applications. It provides analytical services to build data warehouses and the OLAP applications. It supports relational, multi-dimensional and hybrid data manipulations and provides facilities for complex analysis. The OLAP analytics has been successfully provided to the organizations using the SQL Server.

MicroStrategy Express facilitates secure and twenty times faster access to business data. There is no expert help needed, no data modeling, and no SQL scripts required. Get business insights quickly with interactive dashboards, pixel-perfect documents, and data visualizations.

A. *Comparison of Tools*

We analyzed these tools with respect to an interface, query writing, drill-down options, roll-up options, aggregation function support, data access and performance point of view. A survey has been conducted for the evaluation of both tools from 150 users. We are able to get different ideas of users about query-ability, performance, and interface point of view based on the questionnaire. The survey is comprised of three types of users which are categorized based on their level of expertise:

- Novice user
- Average user
- Professional user

Different type of user gave response according to their understanding. The professional user analyzes the tools according to their own needs. Average users analyze the tools according to their views and novice user analyzes the tools according to their understanding. The results gained for interface parameter are given in Table 1. The score is calculated in the range between 0 and 1. The response of each user is taken and the score is normalized within the specified range for each feature.

Table 1. Results for the interface parameter

Ser. #	Features	SQL Server	Micro Strategy Express
01	Design	Good(0.64)	Very Good(0.81)
02	User-friendly	Yes(0.63)	Yes(0.83)
03	Type	GUI (Desktop)(0.9)	GUI (Web)(0.7)
04	User type	Known User(0.50)	Novice(0.77)
05	Graph support	Yes(0.5)	Yes(0.83)
06	Understanding	Yes(0.64)	Yes(0.82)
07	Interactive	Yes(0.73)	Yes(0.88)
08	Complexity	Yes(0.83)	No(0.63)
09	Ease of query input	Yes(0.73)	Yes(0.73)
10	Format of result	Grid(0.8)	Multiple format(0.9)

Similarly, the survey results have been calculated for each parameter. Based on the average score for both OLAP tools, the comparative analysis is depicted in Figure 2. It presents the comparative analysis of both tools based on seven parameters. According to this, both tools show following results:

Interface design: There are better features in MicroStrategy Express with respect to the interface. The design is more understandable, user friendly and simple of the MicroStrategy Express. Further, it is easy for novice users and having availability of additional options for visualizations.

Query: According to query parameter, SQL Server outperforms but requires training and expertise to use it. Whereas, from the structural point of view MicroStrategy Express is easier in query input.

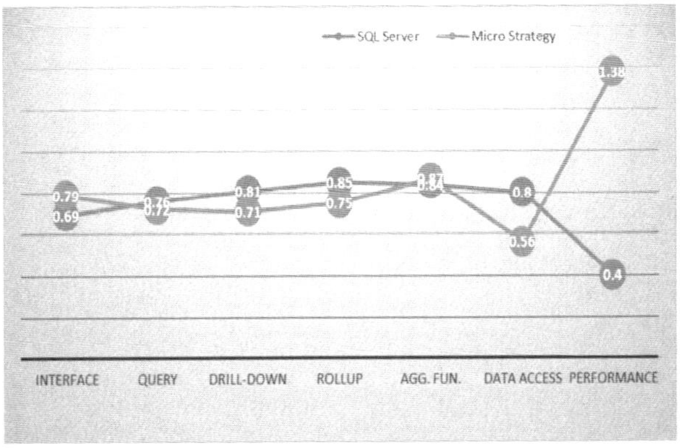

Figure 2. Comparison results of SQL Server and MicroStrategy Express

Drill-Down: SQL Server performs well for drill-down parameter and provides better options in comparison to the MicroStrategy Express. The SQL Server has point and click environment having descriptions in detailed level while MicroStrategy Express gives initial level drill-down options.
Roll-up: SQL Server provides additional roll-up options. For further aggregations, it delivers complete choices. Overall, SQL Server is best with respect to the roll-up options.
Aggregation function support: The average score of the MicroStrategy Express is 0.87 which is 0.03 better than the SQL Server. It replies quickly in the calculation of the aggregation functions.
Data access: From all point of views, this parameter is considered best in SQL Server. SQL Server supports the additional quantity of measures, data volume and dimensions. One of the deficiencies of the MicroStrategy Express is that it supports only excel-based datasets.
Performance: Performance is calculated based on response time in seconds. The MicroStrategy Express outperforms in comparison to the SQL Server.

V. CONCLUSIONS AND FUTURE WORK

In this paper, criteria for the evaluation of tools have been proposed. Seven parameters include an interface, query writing, drill-down options, roll-up options, aggregation function support, data access and performance. For experimental evaluation, comparative analysis of two tools i.e., MicroStrategy Express and SQL Server has been performed. The results show that MicroStrategy Express outperforms in interface and aggregation method whereas input query is easy in comparison to the SQL Server. The SQL Server is more attractive along drill-down options, roll-up options and data access. The MicroStrategy Express only supports to excel-based datasets and does not compatible with the large databases. Similarly, any tool can be assessed based on seven parameters and variation in them can be eliminated for standardization purpose. As future work, it is required to implement a standardized tool for non-technical users for training purpose. After getting training of such a tool, the user will be able to use any OLAP tool.

REFERENCES

[1] S. Chaudhuri and U. Dayal, "An Overview of Data Warehouse and OLAP Technology," *Sigmod Rec.*, vol. 26, no. 1, pp. 65–74, 1997.

[2] N. Gorla, "Features to consider in a data warehousing system," *Communications of the ACM*, vol. 46, no. 11, pp. 111–115, 2003.

[3] M. Risi, M. I. Sessa, M. Tucci, and G. Tortora, "CoDe modeling of graph composition for data warehouse report visualization," *IEEE Trans. Knowl. Data Eng.*, vol. 26, no. 3, pp. 563–576, 2014.

[4] S. B. B. Benatallah and H. R. Motahari-nezhad, "Scalable graph-based OLAP analytics over process," *Distributed and Parallel Databases*, pp. 379–423, 2014.

[5] A. Maté, J. Trujillo, and J. Mylopoulos, "Specification and derivation of key performance indicators for business analytics: A semantic approach," Data Knowl. Eng., pp. 30–49, 2016.

[6] M. Golfarelli, S. Graziani, and S. Rizzi, "Data & Knowledge Engineering Shrink : An OLAP operation for balancing precision and size of pivot tables," *DATAK*, vol. 93, pp. 19–41, 2014.

[7] A. Cuzzocrea, C. De Maio, and G. Fenza, "OLAP Analysis of Multidimensional Tweet Streams for Supporting Advanced Analytics," pp. 992–999, 2016.

[8] S. Chaudhuri, U. Dayal, and V. Narasayya, "An overview of business intelligence technology," *Commun. ACM*, vol. 54, no. 8, p. 88-98, 2011.

[9] M. Akinde and T. Johnson, "Efficient OLAP Query Processing in Distributed Data Warehouses Michael B ¨," *Data Eng.*, vol. 32, no. 4, pp. 6382–6382, 2002.

[10] S. A. S. B and H. Kitagawa, "Approximate OLAP on Sustained Data Streams," vol. 1, pp. 102–118, 2017.

A Precondition Calculus for Correct-by-Construction Graph Transformations

Amani Makhlouf, Christian Percebois, Hanh Nhi Tran

IRIT, University of Toulouse
Toulouse, France
Email: {Amani.Makhlouf | Christian.Percebois | Hanh-Nhi.Tran}@irit.fr

***Abstract*—We aim at assisting developers to write, in a Hoare style, provably correct graph transformations expressed in the $\mathcal{ALCQ}$ Description Logic. Given a postcondition and a transformation rule, we compute the weakest precondition for developers. However, the size and quality of this formula may be complex and hard to grasp. We seek to reduce the weakest precondition's complexness by a static analysis based on an alias calculus. The refined precondition is presented to the developer in terms of alternative formulae, each one specifying a potential matching of the source graph. The developer chooses then the formulae that correspond to his intention to obtain finally a correct-by-construction Hoare triple.**

***Keywords*–Graph transformation; Description Logics; weakest precondition calculus; static analysis; alias calculus.**

I. INTRODUCTION

All approaches applying production rules to a graph require to implement a binary relation between a source graph and a target graph. In the theory of algebraic graph transformations, Habel and Pennemann [1] defined nested graph conditions as a graphical and logical formalism to specify graph constraints by explicitly making use of graphs and graph morphisms. Nested conditions have the same expressive power as Courcelle's first-order graph logic [1][2][3]. However, they need to be derived into specific inference rules in order to be proved in a specific theorem-prover that suits them [4][5]. Moreover, this transformation requires the proof of a sound and complete proof system for reasoning in the proposed logic.

Another way to express and reason about graph properties is to directly encode graphs in terms of some existing logic [6]. This solution leads to consider connections between graph constraints and first-order graph formulae. Adopting this approach, we define graphs axiomatically by $\mathcal{ALCQ}$ Description Logic (DL) predicates [7] and manipulate them with specific statements. In this way, we designed a non-standard imperative programming language named Small-t$\mathcal{ALC}$ dedicated to transform labeled directed graphs. Note that $\mathcal{ALC}$ is prototypical for DLs.

Despite the above differences from algebraic graph transformations, we point out the common idea to use satisfiability solvers to prove rules'correctness. This technique requires to assign a predicate transformer to a rule in order to compute the rule's weakest precondition. The setup is rather traditional: given a Hoare triple $\{P\}S\{Q\}$, we compute the weakest (liberal) precondition $wp(S, Q)$ of the rule transformation statements S with respect to the postcondition Q, and then verify the implication $P \Rightarrow wp(S, Q)$. The correctness of the rule is proved by a dedicated tableau reasoning, which is sound, complete and which results in a counter-example when a failure occurs.

Since writing complete and correct specifications may not be easy for novice developers, we aim to assist them in achieving provably correct transformations [8]. In this context, we propose a static analysis of the weakest precondition based on an alias calculus in order to suggest precondition formulae that are easier to understand but still ensuring the correctness of the Hoare-triple. The result is presented to developers in a disjunctive normal form. Each conjunction of positive and negative literals specifies a potential matching of the source graph. By letting developers choose a conjunction as a premise that reflects the rule's intention, our approach can filter and reduce some combinatorial issues.

In this paper, Section II first defines logic-based formulae to annotate pre- and postconditions of a transformation rule. This choice yields manageable proof obligations in a Hoare's style for rules'correctness. Then, we introduce in Section III Small-t$\mathcal{ALC}$ atomic statements that manipulate graph structures. Each statement is characterized by a weakest precondition with respect to a given postcondition. On the basis of an alias calculus that is presented in Section IV, we show in Section V how to reduce some combinatorial issues while ensuring the program correctness by finely analyzing the weakest precondition. An illustrative example is presented in Section VI. We finally give some discussions on related work in Section VII and wrap up the paper with a conclusion and possible improvements in Section VIII.

II. LOGIC-BASED CONDITIONS

Slightly diverged from the standard approach, we choose a set-theoretic approach for our transformation system [9]. The basic idea is to specify sets of nodes and edges of a subgraph using a fragment of first-order logic. It turns out that replacing graph patterns by graph formulae yields manageable proof obligations for rules'correctness in a Hoare style $\{P\}S\{Q\}$ [6]. A precondition formula P designates a subgraph matching a substructure that should exist in the source graph. The postcondition Q requires the existence of the subgraph represented by Q in the target graph. For instance, consider a rule requiring that: (1) x must be a node (individual) not connected by the relation (role) R to a node y; (2) y is of class (concept) C; (3) x is linked to at most three successors (qualified number of restrictions) of class C via

R. This precondition can be expressed by the logic formula $x \neg R\ y\ \wedge\ y : C \wedge\ x : (\leq\ 3\ R\ C)$.

At this point, readers familiar with Description Logics (DLs) may recognize a DL formula. Labeled directed graphs can be directly modeled by entities of DLs, a family of logics for modeling and reasoning about relationships in a domain of interest [10]. Most DLs are decidable fragments of first-order logic. They are organized around three kinds of entities: individuals, roles and concepts. Individuals are constants in the domain, roles are binary relations between individuals and concepts are sets of individuals. Applied to our graphs, individuals are nodes labeled with concepts and roles are edges. Accordingly, pre- and post-assertions are interpreted as graphs by using unary predicates for nodes and binary predicates for edges. The correctness of a graph transformation rule is checked by assigning to each of its statements a predicate transformer in order to compute the corresponding weakest precondition.

To design our own experimental graph transformation language, we chose the $\mathcal{ALCQ}$ logic, an extension of the standard DL Attributive Language with Complements ($\mathcal{ALC}$) [11], which allows qualifying number restrictions on concepts ($\mathcal{Q}$). $\mathcal{ALCQ}$ is based on a three-tier framework: concepts, facts and formulae. The concept level enables to determine classes of individuals ($\emptyset, C, \neg C, C1 \cup C2$ and $C1 \cap C2$). The fact level makes assertions about individuals owned by a concept ($i : C, i : \neg C, i : (\leq\ n\ R\ C)$ and $i : (\geq\ n\ R\ C)$), or involved in a role ($i\ R\ j$ and $i \neg R\ j$). The third level is about formulae defined by a Boolean combination of $\mathcal{ALCQ}$ facts ($f, \neg f, f1 \wedge f2$ and $f1 \vee f2$).

Figure 1 depicts a model (graph) satisfying the previous precondition $x \neg R\ y\ \wedge\ y : C \wedge\ x : (\leq\ 3\ R\ C)$. In this graph, the white circles designate the nodes variables x and y manipulated by the formula. Nodes variables refer (by a dotted edge) to real nodes represented by black circles. The «◉» node outlines a concept labeled with C. Note that the subgraph having two anonymous nodes each one outfitted with an incoming edge from x and an outgoing edge to the concept C is a model which checks the fact $x : (\leq\ 3\ R\ C)$.

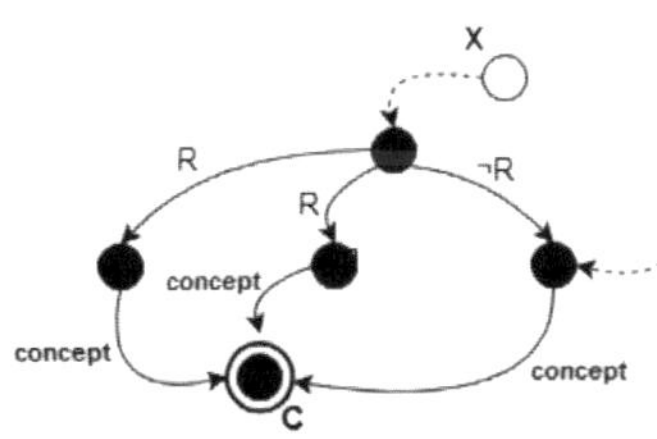

Figure 1. Model satisfying the precondition $x \neg R\ y\ \wedge\ y : C \wedge\ x : (\leq\ 3\ R\ C)$

Our formulae contain free variables that assign references to nodes in a graph. Equality and inequality assertions can be used to define constraints on the value of these variables. If x and y are node variables, $x = y$ means that x and y refer to the same node and $x \neq y$ means that x and y are distinct. The inequality relationship enforces injective graph morphisms.

III. THE SMALL-T$\mathcal{ALC}$ LANGUAGE

The $\mathcal{ALCQ}$ formulae presented in the previous section have been plugged into our Small-t$\mathcal{ALC}$ imperative language and used in atomic transformation actions on nodes (individuals) and edges (roles), as well as in traditional control-flow constructs as loops ($while$) and conditions ($if...then...else...$). In the transformation code, statements manipulate node variables which are bound to the host graph's nodes during the transformation's execution.

We have defined five atomic Small-t$\mathcal{ALC}$ statements according to the following grammar where i and j are node variables, C is a concept name, R is a role name, F is an $\mathcal{ALCQ}$ formula and v is a list of node variables:

atomic_statement ::=

$add(i : C)$	(node labeling)
$\mid\ delete(i : C)$	(node unlabeling)
$\mid\ add(i\ R\ j)$	(edge labeling)
$\mid\ delete(i\ R\ j)$	(edge unlabeling)
$\mid\ select\ v\ with\ F$	(assignment)

The first four statements modify the graph structure by changing the labeling of nodes and edges. Note that since we consider a set-theoretic approach, the statements $add(i : C)$ and $add(i\ R\ j)$ have no effects if i belongs to the set C and (i, j) to R respectively. Hence, no parallel edges with the same label are allowed. An original construct is the $select$ statement that non-deterministically binds node variables to nodes in the subgraph that satisfies a logic formula. This assignment is used to handle the selection of specific nodes where the transformations are requested to occur. For instance, $select\ i\ with\ i : C$ selects a node labeled with C. If the selection is satisfied the execution continues normally with the value of the node variable i. Otherwise, the execution meets an error situation.

A Small-t$\mathcal{ALC}$ program consists of a sequence of transformation rules. A rule is structured into three parts: a precondition, the transformation code (a sequence of statements) and a postcondition. We illustrate in Figure 2 an example of a transformation rule written in Small-t$\mathcal{ALC}$. The rule first selects a node n of concept A that is R-linked to a. Then, it deletes this link and removes a from the concept A.

```
pre: (a : A) ∧ a : (≥ 3 R A);
select n with (a R n) ∧ (n : A)
delete(a R n);
delete(a : A);
post: (a : ¬A) ∧ a : (≥ 2 R A);
```

Figure 2. Example of a Small-t$\mathcal{ALC}$ rule

We aim at using a Hoare-like calculus to prove that Small-t$\mathcal{ALC}$ graph programs are correct. This verification process is based on a weakest (liberal) precondition (wp) calculus [12]. Each Small-t$\mathcal{ALC}$ statement S is assigned to a predicate transformer yielding an $\mathcal{ALCQ}$ formula $wp(S, Q)$ assuming the postcondition Q. The correctness of a program prg with respect to Q is established by proving that the given precondition P implies the weakest precondition: every model that satisfies P also satisfies $wp(prg, Q)$. Weakest preconditions of Small-t$\mathcal{ALC}$ statements are given in Figure 3.

The weakest precondition calculus computes predicates which are not closed under substitutions with respect to

$wp(add\ (i : C), Q) = Q[C + i/C]$
$wp(delete\ (i : C), Q) = Q[C - i/C]$
$wp(add\ (i\ R\ j), Q) = Q[R + (i, j)/R]$
$wp(delete\ (i\ R\ j), Q) = Q[R - (i, j)/R]$
$wp(select\ v\ with\ F, Q) = \forall v(F \Rightarrow Q)$

Figure 3. Small-t$\mathcal{ALC}$ weakest preconditions

$\mathcal{ALCQ}$. To resolve this situation, substitutions are considered as constructors and should be eliminated. For instance, $wp(add(i : C), x : C) = x : C\ [C + i/C] = x : (C + i) = x : C \lor x = i$.

The conventional precondition calculus presented above does not take into account particular situations of a transformation program and thus may result in a complex precondition. In the following sections, we look at how the precondition's formula can be improved to be more specific and simple on the basis of an alias calculus.

IV. Alias calculus

The principle of alias calculus was proposed by Bertrand Meyer in order to decide whether two reference expressions appearing in a program might, during some execution, have the same value, meaning that the associated references are attached to the same object [13].

Since our rewriting system allows non-injective morphisms, two or more node variables may reference to the same node in a graph. On the other hand, a node variable can be assigned to a random node of the graph. This is one reason why a Small-t$\mathcal{ALC}$ formula can be represented by several graph patterns. For example, Figure 4 shows two potential models satisfying the formula $x : C \land i\ R\ j$. In Figure 4a, i and j refer to the same node. In 4b, i and j are different but i and x are combined.

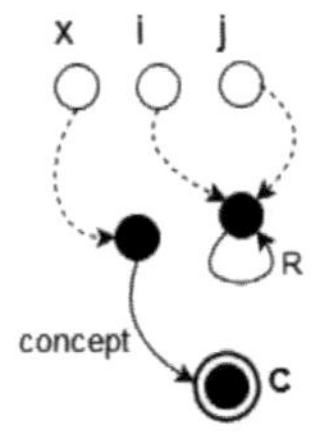

(a) $i = j, i \neq x$

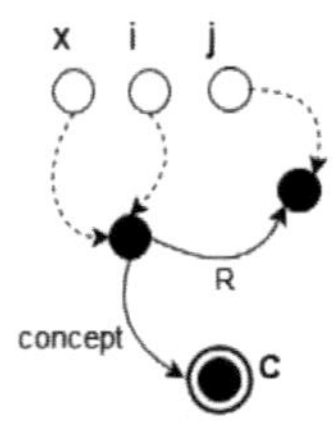

(b) $i \neq j, i = x$

Figure 4. Example of models satisfying the formula $x : C \land i\ R\ j$

In this regard, for a transformation program, we apply an alias calculus to determine the node variables that can never refer to the same node. Discerning such specific circumstances helps to discard later unsatisfied subformulae of the weakest precondition. Thus, our method consists in assigning to each node variable *x*, a set of other node variables that may reference to the same node in the graph as *x*. We identify four atomic conditions in which two individuals *x* and *y* can never refer to the same node in the graph:

- $x \neq y$
- $\exists C\ /x : C \land y : \neg C$
- $\exists R.\exists z\ /x\ R\ z \land y\ \neg R\ z$
- $\exists R.\exists z\ /z\ R\ x \land z\ \neg R\ y$

The first case ($x \neq y$) states that *x* and *y* are naturally distinct so they can never be assigned to the same node. The second one asserts that *x* and *y* belong to two complement subsets C and $\neg C$. The same applies to the last two cases where the nodes connected by R and $\neg R$ refer to two disjoint subsets R and $\neg R$.

For each of the above four conditions, *x* and *y* are said to be *non-possibly equivalent* nodes. We note this relation by $x \not\simeq y$. As a result we assert that $x \not\simeq y \Rightarrow x \neq y$. However, no conclusion can be drawn from the *possibly equivalent* relation $x \simeq y$.

Consider, as a simple example, the following formula that is presented in the disjunctive normal form: $(x = y \land x\ R\ y) \lor (x : C \land x\ \neg R\ y)$, and suppose that a static analysis deduces from the code that *x* and *y* are non-possibly equivalent, which means that $x \neq y$. As a result, the initial formula can be reduced to $x : C \land x\ \neg R\ y$ because the first conjunction $x = y \land x\ R\ y$ can never be true in this case. In the section that follows, we show how this calculus helps in reducing the complexness of the weakest precondition.

V. Precondition extraction

To formally verify the correctness of a Small-t$\mathcal{ALC}$ graph transformation, besides the code, the program's pre- and post-conditions must be properly specified. This task may not be easy for novice developers, so a suggestion of a valid precondition that corresponds to a given code and a postcondition would be useful to them.

Since the computed weakest precondition is often very complex and hard to comprehend, we propose a finer static analysis on the basis of the alias calculus of the program to achieve a simpler precondition. The resulting precondition P is presented in a disjunctive normal form (DNF) where each conjunction of P can be considered as a valid precondition on its own. The analysis consists first in converting the postcondition Q to DNF i.e., $Q = \lor Q_i$ where $Q_i = \land q_j$ is a conjunction of facts, then calculating for each statement and for each conjunction Q_i the weakest precondition. This process maintains correctness because $wp(S, Q_1) \lor wp(S, Q_2) \Rightarrow wp(S, Q_1 \lor Q_2)$. In each and every step, the formula of the $wp(S, Q_i)$ may be filtered by discarding subformulae according to the identified non-possibly equivalent node variables. A precondition P is obtained such that $P \Rightarrow wp(prg, Q)$, which makes the transformation program prg correct. This process is applied to *add* and *delete* statements as detailed in Section V-1. Regarding the *select* statement, *wp* is reduced differently as presented later in Section V-2.

1) add *and* delete *statements:*
Let us consider first the *add(i : C)* statement. Its weakest precondition with respect to the postcondition *x : C* is $x : C \lor x = i$, which means that either the node x was already of concept C before adding i to C, or x and i are equal. Knowing that *x* and *i* are non-possibly equivalent, it can be stated that $x \neq i$, and so the weakest precondition can be reduced to the first subformula *x : C* of the disjunction.

A more glaring example is reducing the weakest precondition of the *add(i R j)* statement with respect to the postcondition $Q = x : (\leq\ n\ R\ C)$ which indicates that there are at most n edges labeled R outgoing from the node x to nodes of concept C. Adding an R-edge between i and

TABLE I. WEAKEST PRECONDITION'S FILTERING FOR THE $add(i : C)$ STATEMENT

Statement	Identified fact	wp	Condition	Precondition
$add(i : C)$	$x : C$	$x : C \vee x = i$	$x \not\simeq i$	$x : C$
	$x : \neg C$	$x : \neg C \wedge x \neq i$	$x \not\simeq i$	$x : \neg C$
	$x : (\leq n\ R\ C)$	$(x\ R\ i \wedge i : \neg C \wedge x : (\leq (n-1)\ R\ C))$ $\vee (x \neg R\ i \wedge x : (\leq n\ R\ C))$ $\vee (i : C \wedge x : (\leq n\ R\ C))$ $\vee (x : (\leq (n-1)\ R\ C))$	$x \neg R\ i$	$x : (\leq n\ R\ C)$

TABLE II. WEAKEST PRECONDITION'S FILTERING FOR THE $add(i\ R\ j)$ STATEMENT

Statement	Identified fact	wp	Condition	Precondition
$add(i\ R\ j)$	$x\ R\ y$	$(x = i \wedge y = j) \vee x\ R\ y$	$x \not\simeq i \vee y \not\simeq j$	$x\ R\ y$
	$x \neg R\ y$	$(x \neq i \vee y \neq j) \wedge (x \neg R\ y)$	$x \not\simeq i \vee y \not\simeq j$	$x \neg R\ y$
	$x : (\leq n\ R\ C)$	$(x = i \wedge j : C \wedge i \neg R\ j \wedge x : (\leq (n-1)\ R\ C))$ $\vee (x \neq i \wedge x : (\leq n\ R\ C))$ $\vee (j : \neg C \wedge x : (\leq n\ R\ C))$ $\vee (i\ R\ j \wedge x : (\leq n\ R\ C))$ $\vee (x : (\leq (n-1)\ R\ C))$	$x \not\simeq i \vee j : \neg C$	$x : (\leq n\ R\ C)$

j may have a direct impact on Q regarding the concept of j, the existence of a relation between i and j and the equality between i and x. Hence, $wp(add(i\ R\ j), x : (\leq n\ R\ C)) =$

$$(x = i \wedge j : C \wedge i \neg R\ j \wedge x : (\leq (n-1)\ R\ C))$$
$$\vee (x \neq i \wedge x : (\leq n\ R\ C))$$
$$\vee (j : \neg C \wedge x : (\leq n\ R\ C))$$
$$\vee (i\ R\ j \wedge x : (\leq n\ R\ C))$$
$$\vee (x : (\leq (n-1)\ R\ C))$$

Knowing that $x \not\simeq i$ or $j : \neg C$, the first conjunction $x = i \wedge j : C \wedge i \neg R\ j \wedge x : (\leq (n-1)\ R\ C)$ can be discarded as it will never be satisfied in this case. Furthermore, the whole formula of the wp can be reduced to $x : (\leq n\ R\ C)$ according to the second and third conjunction which indicates that the number of restrictions remains unchanged in case one of these two conditions is satisfied.

We illustrated how to reduce the *wp* with respect to a postcondition composed of a single fact. In case of a postcondition consisting of a conjunction of facts, only the facts that manipulate the same concepts and roles given in the statement parameters are identified as a first step. For example, adding an instance to a concept $(add(i : \underline{C})$ results in considering in the given postcondition only the facts that manipulate this concept $(x : \underline{C}, x : \neg\underline{C}, x : (\leq n\ R\ \underline{C}))$.

Tables I and II represent the preconditions calculated by our static analyzer for the statement $add(i : C)$ and $add(i\ R\ j)$ respectively. For each statement s, we show in the second column the facts that should be identified in the postcondition to derive a precondition. The third column shows the standard weakest precondition $wp(s, f)$ of the statement s with respect to an identified fact f. To simplify this formula, we present in the fourth column the conditions that allow to discard some conjunctive clauses of the wp. The resulting formula is presented in the last column.

Consider the first row of the Table II. If a fact $x\ R\ y$ is identified within the postcondition during calculation, we look for simplifying $wp(add(i\ R\ j), x\ R\ y) = (x = i \wedge y = j) \vee x\ R\ y$. If the alias calculus asserts that at least one of the conditions $x \not\simeq i$ or $y \not\simeq j$ is true, wp is reduced to $x\ R\ y$.

As observed in Tables I and II, many complex disjunctions in the *wp* can be reduced to only one conjunction on the basis of a condition calculated by the alias calculus or a condition given explicitly in the postcondition. Note that the results of the *delete(i : C)* and *delete(i R j)* statements are similar to the *add* statements.

2) The select *statement:*
So far, the static analysis transforms the predicate Q into a new predicate P regarding statements already presented. However, it operates differently when it comes to the *select* statement where $wp(select\ v\ with\ F, Q) = \forall v\ (F \Rightarrow Q)$. The weakest precondition here involves two formulae that may be complex: F given by the *select*, and the postcondition Q. Consequently, the implication $F \Rightarrow Q$ makes the wp more obscure for the developer. In this case, the static analyzer simplifies the wp by eliminating this implication as further detailed below.

For each conjunction Qi of the postcondition Q, the static analysis isolates first the facts that manipulate the node variables v of the *select* statement. Let Qi_v be the conjunctive formula of these identified facts, and $Qi_{v'}$ the conjunctive formula of the others facts, so that $Qi = Qi_v \wedge Qi_{v'}$. For example, given a formula $Q_1 = x\ R\ y \wedge y : C$ and the statement $select\ x\ with\ x : C$, we have $Q_{1v} = x\ R\ y$ and $Q_{1v'} = y : C$.

Then, the static analysis checks, via our logic formula evaluator, if the implication $\forall v\ (F \Rightarrow Qi_v)$ holds. If so, the precondition $wp(select\ v\ with\ F, Qi) = \forall v\ (F \Rightarrow Qi)$ is reduced to Qi without affecting the validity of the Hoare triple as $Qi \Rightarrow wp(select\ v\ with\ F, Qi)$. Conversely, the non-validity of the implication $\forall v\ (F \Rightarrow Qi_v)$ results in transforming Qi to the predicate $false$ $(\perp)$ so that nothing can be concluded about the transformation correctness. This situation is meant to warn the developer that there are inconsistencies in his transformation between the *select* statement and the predicate formula Q. The two presented cases are given in Table III.

TABLE III. REDUCING THE WP OF THE *select* STATEMENT

Statement	Postcondition	wp	Condition	Precondition
$select\ v\ with\ F$	Qi	$\forall v\ (F \Rightarrow Qi)$	$\forall v\ (F \Rightarrow Qi_v)$	Qi
			$\forall v\ (F \not\Rightarrow Qi_v)$	$\perp$

We presented how the static analyzer filters the weakest precondition of a statement with respect to each conjunction $Q_i = \wedge q_j$ of Q where $Q = \vee Q_i$. Hence, the final result of the precondition will be presented as a DNF formula too that expresses different possible alternatives. Each alternative represents a conjunction of facts, constituting a graph that matches a subgraph of the source graph on which the transformation rule is applied.

We filter the weakest precondition by discarding conjunctive clauses that are invalid. This reduction leads to a precondition P stronger than the weakest precondition $wp(S, Q)$. In particular, when two node variables are non-possibly equivalent, a deductive reasoning is carried out by applying equivalence and implication connectives between P and $wp(S, Q)$. We adopt a similar deduction for a node variable belonging to a concept complement and for a role complement. Using these deductions and the well-behaved wp properties, such as distributivity of conjunction and disjunction, we construct the formula P, which satisfies the implication $P \Rightarrow wp(S, Q)$ so that the triple $\{P\}S\{Q\}$ is always correct-by-construction.

VI. EXAMPLE

Using the static analyzer to suggest a precondition formula in the disjunctive normal form, the developer can select the conjunctions that reflect his intention. He can then update his transformation code or refine his specification by injecting into them the facts of the chosen conjunctions.

Consider as an example the transformation code and the postcondition given in Figure 5. The first statement adds a node y to the concept C. The second one adds an R-edge between nodes x and y. The postcondition asserts that x has at most three R-successors to nodes of concept C, and that y belongs to C.

```
add(y : C);
add(x R y);
post: x : (≤ 3 R C) ∧ (y : C);
```

Figure 5. Example of an initial code and postcondition

To achieve the given postcondition, a precondition calculus is done in two stages: the first to extract a precondition P with respect to the statement $add(x\ R\ y)$ and the given postcondition, the second to extract a precondition with respect to the statement $add(y : C)$ and P, as $wp(s1; s2, Q) = wp(s1, wp(s2, Q))$. Consequently, the static analyzer extracts seven possible conjunctions as a precondition:

$$x : (\leq 1\ R\ C) \quad (1)$$

$$y : C \wedge x : (\leq 2\ R\ C) \quad (2)$$

$$x\ R\ y \wedge x : (\leq 2\ R\ C) \quad (3)$$

$$x\ \neg R\ y \wedge x : (\leq 2\ R\ C) \quad (4)$$

$$x\ \neg R\ y \wedge y : C \wedge x : (\leq 2\ R\ C) \quad (5)$$

$$x\ R\ y \wedge y : \neg C \wedge x : (\leq 2\ R\ C) \quad (6)$$

$$x\ R\ y \wedge y : C \wedge x : (\leq 3\ R\ C) \quad (7)$$

Each of these conjunctions is a potential precondition that yields a correct Hoare triple. The first formula is the weakest one. It does not take into account neither the concept of y nor the existence of an R-edge between x and y. On the contrary, the other conjunctions are stronger formulae specifying the mentioned properties of x and y. For example, the formula (7) indicates that there exists an R-edge between x and y and that y is of concept C. In this case, both of the two statements of the code have no effects, and so the number of restrictions remains 3 in the fact $x : (\leq 3\ R\ C)$. The various levels of formulae's strength gives the choice to the developer to specify the constraints of rule's applicability in the precondition as much as he wishes to.

Suppose that the developer focuses on the non-existence of an R-edge between x and y before the transformation as it is indicated in the formulae (4) and (5). Thus, he decides to inject the fact $x\ \neg R\ y$ into the transformation by adding the statement $select\ y\ with\ x\ \neg R\ y$ at the beginning of his code. By relaunching the static analyzer, the number of conjunctions extracted decreases from seven to one conjunction which is $x : (\leq\ 2\ R\ C)$. At this point, the developer can choose to put the resulting formula as a precondition as shown in Figure 6.

```
pre: x : (≤ 2 R C);
select y with x ¬R y;
add(y : C);
add(x R y);
post: x : (≤ 3 R C) ∧ (y : C);
```

Figure 6. The final correct-by-construction triple

In this sense, we help developers to update and annotate their code with specifications based on their intention to achieve finally a correct-by-construction triple.

As described below, our framework guides developers to achieve correct transformation programs. Moreover, it verifies the resulting triple formally using the Small-t$\mathcal{ALC}$ prover. The latter is a formal verification tool that verifies a transformation program with respect to its pre- and postconditions by translating it into Isabelle/HOL logic and generating verification conditions. In case of failure, the prover displays a counter-example which is a model of the precondition that does not satisfy the postcondition when applying the transformation.

VII. RELATED WORK

Most of the logic-based approaches for graph transformations focus on the verification question. Thus, they attempt to encode graph conditions in an appropriate logic that is both expressive and decidable. Like us, Selim et al. [14] proposed a direct verification framework for their transformation language DSLTrans so that no intermediate representation for a specific proving framework is required. They used symbolic execution to build a finite set of path conditions representing all transformation executions through a formal abstraction relation and thus allow formal properties to be exhaustively proved. Their property language based on graph patterns and propositional logic proposes a limited expressiveness and the property-proving algorithm was presented as a proof-of-concept.

The works in [15] and [16] share with ours some ideas with respect to the assistance in producing a Hoare triple. Given a modeling language with well-formedness constraints and a refactoring specification, Becker et al. [15] uses an invariant checker to detect and report constraint violations via counter-examples and lets developers modify their refactoring iteratively. Similarly to us, Clariso et al. [16] used backward reasoning to automatically synthesize application conditions for model transformation rules. Application conditions are derived from the OCL expression representing the rules's postconditions and the atomic rewriting actions performed by the rule. However, OCL expressions are not really suitable for exploring the graph properties of the underlying model structures. It is thus rather cumbersome when used for verifying complex model transformations.

VIII. Conclusion and Future Work

The distinctive feature of Small-t$\mathcal{ALC}$ is that it uses the same logic $\mathcal{ALCQ}$ to represent graphs, to code a transformation and to reason about graph transformations in a Hoare style. In order to assist users in developing correct transformations, we propose a fine analysis of the weakest precondition to take into account special situations of a program on the basis of an alias calculus. Our approach allows developers to select a precondition to annotate their code according to their intention.

It would be interesting in our framework to automatically infer and test invariant candidates for loop constructs gathered from their corresponding postcondition as proposed in [17]. This attempt is based on the fact that a Small-t$\mathcal{ALC}$ loop often iterates on individuals selected from a logic formula in order to achieve the same property for the transformed elements.

As a complement to a Hoare triple verification, we expect to focus on effects of rules execution in terms of DL reasoning services at the specification rule level. A Small-t$\mathcal{ALC}$ rule execution updates a knowledge base founded upon a finite set of $\mathcal{ALCQ}$ concept inclusions (TBox) and a finite set of $\mathcal{ALCQ}$ concept and role assertions (ABox). This leads to a reasoning problem about a knowledge base consistency embodied by a graph in Small-t$\mathcal{ALC}$ [18].

Acknowledgment

Part of this research has been supported by the *Climt* (Categorical and Logical Methods in Model Transformation) project (ANR-11-BS02-016).

References

[1] A. Habel and K.-H. Pennemann, "Correctness of high-level transformation systems relative to nested conditions," Mathematical. Structures in Comp. Sci., vol. 19, no. 2, Apr. 2009, pp. 245–296.

[2] A. Rensink, "Representing first-order logic using graphs," in Graph Transformations: Second International Conference ICGT,. Berlin, Heidelberg: Springer Berlin Heidelberg, 2004, pp. 319–335.

[3] B. Courcelle, "Handbook of theoretical computer science (vol. b)." Cambridge, MA, USA: MIT Press, 1990, ch. Graph Rewriting: An Algebraic and Logic Approach, pp. 193–242.

[4] K.-H. Pennemann, "Resolution-like theorem proving for high-level conditions," in Graph Transformations: 4th International Conference, ICGT. Berlin, Heidelberg: Springer Berlin Heidelberg, 2008, pp. 289–304.

[5] F. Orejas, H. Ehrig, and U. Prange, "A logic of graph constraints," in Fundamental Approaches to Software Engineering: 11th International Conference, FASE. Berlin, Heidelberg: Springer Berlin Heidelberg, 2008, pp. 179–198.

[6] M. Strecker, "Modeling and verifying graph transformations in proof assistants," Electron. Notes Theor. Comput. Sci., vol. 203, no. 1, Mar. 2008, pp. 135–148.

[7] N. Baklanova, J. H. Brenas, R. Echahed, A. Makhlouf, C. Percebois, M. Strecker, and H. N. Tran, "Coding, executing and verifying graph transformations with small-t$\mathcal{ALCQ}$e," in 7th Int. Workshop on Graph Computation Models (GCM), 2016, URL: http://gcm2016.inf.uni-due.de/ [accessed: 2017-09-25].

[8] A. Makhlouf, H. N. Tran, C. Percebois, and M. Strecker, "Combining dynamic and static analysis to help develop correct graph transformations," in Tests and Proofs: 10th International Conference, TAP. Switzerland: Springer International Publishing, 2016, pp. 183–190.

[9] M. Nagl, "Set theoretic approaches to graph grammars," in Proceedings of the 3rd International Workshop on Graph-Grammars and Their Application to Computer Science. London, UK, UK: Springer-Verlag, 1987, pp. 41–54.

[10] M. Krötzsch, F. Simancik, and I. Horrocks, "A description logic primer," arXiv preprint arXiv:1201.4089, 2012, URL: http://arxiv.org/abs/1201.4089 [accessed: 2017-09-25].

[11] M. Schmidt-Schauß and G. Smolka, "Attributive concept descriptions with complements," Artif. Intell., vol. 48, no. 1, Feb. 1991, pp. 1–26.

[12] E. W. Dijkstra and C. S. Scholten, Predicate Calculus and Program Semantics. New York, NY, USA: Springer-Verlag New York, Inc., 1990.

[13] B. Meyer, "Steps towards a theory and calculus of aliasing," Int. J. Software and Informatics, vol. 5, no. 1-2, 2011, pp. 77–115.

[14] G. M. Selim, L. Lúcio, J. R. Cordy, J. Dingel, and B. J. Oakes, "Specification and verification of graph-based model transformation properties," in International Conference on Graph Transformation. Springer, 2014, pp. 113–129.

[15] B. Becker, L. Lambers, J. Dyck, S. Birth, and H. Giese, "Iterative development of consistency-preserving rule-based refactorings," in Theory and Practice of Model Transformations: 4th International Conference, ICMT. Berlin, Heidelberg: Springer Berlin Heidelberg, 2011, pp. 123–137.

[16] R. Clarisó, J. Cabot, E. Guerra, and J. de Lara, "Backwards reasoning for model transformations," J. Syst. Softw., vol. 116, no. C, Jun. 2016, pp. 113–132.

[17] J. Zhai, H. Wang, and J. Zhao, "Post-condition-directed invariant inference for loops over data structures," in Proceedings of the 2014 IEEE Eighth International Conference on Software Security and Reliability-Companion, ser. SERE-C '14. Washington, DC, USA: IEEE Computer Society, 2014, pp. 204–212.

[18] U. Sattler, "Reasoning in description logics: Basics, extensions, and relatives," in Reasoning Web: Third International Summer School. Berlin, Heidelberg: Springer Berlin Heidelberg, 2007, pp. 154–182.

FANTASIA: A Tool for Automatically Identifying Inconsistency in AngularJS MVC Applications

Md Rakib Hossain Misu
Institute of Information Technology
University of Dhaka
Dhaka, Bangladesh
email: bsse0516@iit.du.ac.bd

Kazi Sakib
Institute of Information Technology
University of Dhaka
Dhaka, Bangladesh
email: sakib@iit.du.ac.bd

***Abstract*—AngularJS is prone to inconsistency issues because of the abstract interactions between Document Object Model (DOM) and JavaScript. It creates hidden bugs, and leads the application to failure. It becomes acute when developers use custom AngularJS directives for increasing code reusability and maintainability. To resolve the inconsistency issues, a static code analysis based approach FANTASIA is proposed. FANTASIA first extracts Abstract Syntax Tree (AST) and DOM from the AngularJS application's MVC modules including its custom directives. By traversing AST and DOM, next it finds the defined identifiers along with the associated data types of those identifiers. Finally, the extracted identifiers and data types are mapped and compared using a string matching algorithm to determine the consistency across the application. To evaluate FANTASIA, 25 open source AngularJS applications are used where 15 applications contain only MVC modules and rest of the applications contain both MVC modules and custom directives. The experimental result shows that FANTASIA produces overall 97.63% recall and 100% precision to correctly detect inconsistency in those 15 applications similar to existing approach AUREBESH. Interestingly, when custom directives are present, FANTASIA outperforms with a significant increase of overall 96.66% recall and 100% precision comparing to 76.97% recall and 100% precision of AUREBESH.**

Keywords-JavaScript; MVC; Inconsistency; Static Analysis.

I. Introduction

AngularJS is a JavaScript-based MVC framework used for developing loosely coupled web applications, which are known as Single Page Applications (SPA) [1]. It provides developers the flexibility to separate business logic in several reusable modules and components, such as model, view, controller, directive, service, etc. However, AngularJS is still prone to inconsistency issues because of wrong interaction between DOM and JavaScript [2]. This wrong interaction occurs, as AngularJS facilitates the application development by abstracting the DOM API method call between the JavaScript and HTML code.

AngularJS depends on the use of identifiers to represent *model variable*(s) (*mv*) and *controller function*(s) (*cf*). To represent the functionality, the identifiers of *mv* and *cf* should be consistent in the view. Besides, in AngularJS, views consist of various built-in directives, such as *ng-if*, *ng-count* [3]. To use built-in directives, developers have to assign *mv* and *cf* to these directives with a defined form, such as *ng-if="{mv}"*, along with specific data types. For example, *ng-if* directive takes boolean type of *mv* and *cf*. So, *mv* and *cf* are used in *ng-if* directive should be boolean type. Since JavaScript is loosely typed dynamic programming language, the developers have to keep in mind that, values assigned to *mv* and returned by *cf*, should be consistent to their expected types. Inconsistencies among these identifiers and the types, can potentially incur significant loss in the functionality and performance. The reason is that, the major functionalities of an application rely on *mv* and *cf*.

AngularJS also supports the Do not Repeat Yourself (DRY) feature [4]. It allows developers to create one directive and reuse it anywhere within the entire application. Despite having a lot of built-in directives, it also encourages the developers to create custom directives to enhance the re-usability of the code. Every custom directive has some specific properties that define its own view, model and controller. Sometimes, it is also used inside a view under a specific controller by following a parent child relationship. While using custom directives, inconsistency may arise not only within its own model, view and controller, but also between its parent view and controller. Unfortunately, developers do not get exceptions and warnings when inconsistency issue occurs [5]. It becomes the worst to find inconsistencies when an application contains multiple models, views and controllers.

Since the usages of AngularJS MVC framework for client-end application development are fairly new, there are few papers addressing the inconsistency issues. Two state-of the art works, TypeDevil [6] and AUREBESH [7] are proposed to detect inconsistencies in JavaScript applications. TypeDevil is capable of detecting inconsistency only within the JavaScript source codes. It performs dynamic source code analysis to detect data type inconsistency. On the contrary, AUREBESH is also able to detect inconsistencies in JavaScript MVC applications by performing static code analysis on both the JavaScript and HTML code. However, these approaches are not able to accurately identify inconsistencies in AngularJS MVC applications. The reason is that TypeDevil only dynamically analyzes the JavaScript source code instead of analyzing both JavaScript and HTML source code. AUREBESH only performs static source code analysis in MVC modules and never analyzes the presence of custom directives in AngularJS applications.

To resolve the inconsistency issues in AngularJS MVC applications, a static code analysis based approach FANTASIA is proposed. It first extracts Abstract Syntax Tree (AST) and DOM by performing static code analysis among the modules, such as model, view, controller and custom directive including its associated files. Then using AST and DOM, it searches for the identifiers that are used to represent *mv* and *cf*. The data types of *mv* and return types of *cf* are also drawn by exploring the AST nodes and DOM elements. Finally, to determine the inconsistencies across application, identifiers and data types, extracted from model and controllers are compared to those identifiers and data types extracted from views.

In order to evaluate FANTASIA, 25 open source AngularJS applications are used. Among these 25 applications, 15 applications contain MVC modules and rest of the 10 applications contain both MVC modules and custom directives. From experimental result analysis, it is observed that FANTASIA performs accurate with overall 97.63% recall and 100% precision to find inconsistencies in 15 applications with MVC modules, comparing to the existing approach AUREBESH [7]. When custom directives are present, FANTASIA achieves a significant overall 96.66% recall and 100% precision to identify inconsistencies in 10 AngularJS MVC applications that contain inconsistencies within both the MVC modules and custom directives.

The remainder of this paper is structured as follows. Section II describes the proposed approach for inconsistency detection with a concise description of each step. Implementation, evaluation and result analysis are discussed in Section III. Section IV deals with the existing techniques for fault and inconsistency detection in JavaScript applications. Finally, Section V concludes the paper by summarizing the contribution and possible future direction of this work.

II. Proposed Approach

To resolve the inconsistency issues, a static code analysis based approach FANTASIA is proposed. An overview of the proposed approach is depicted in Figure 1 as a block diagram. From the block diagram, it is seen that there are 9 modules, such as *MVC Components and Directive Identifier (MCDI)*, *DOMExtractor (DMEx)*, *DirectiveExtractor (DEx)*, *ASTExtractor (AEx)*, *ViewExtractor (VEx)*, *ModelExtractor (MEx)*, *ControllerExtractor (CEx)*, *MVC Group Builder (MGB)* and *Inconsistency Detector (InD)* that work collaboratively in several phases. TABLE I also represents the terms used for describing the proposed approach. The modules are depended on each other for taking input, providing output and giving feedback. A brief description of each of the modules is discussed in the following subsections.

A. MVC Components and Directive Identifier (MCDI)

MCDI module identifies and filters the MVC component source files (except library files) based on the file names and module types. It is assumed that every module is written in a single source file and the file name should be self descriptive to figure which and what type of AngularJS module it is. After filtering, the module makes a list of directive definition files and extracts the application configuration file which is responsible for defining the routes and the correspondent views and controllers related to that routes. It provides the view and controller file names that are related and responsible for each route of the application. Using this information, a *Primary MVC Group (PMG)* is made that contains a list of HTML code for view file and JavaScript code for controller file in a form of tuple <view HTML code, controller JavaScript code>. Further, this group is used by the *DMEx* and *AEx* module and the list of directive files is used by the *DEx* module.

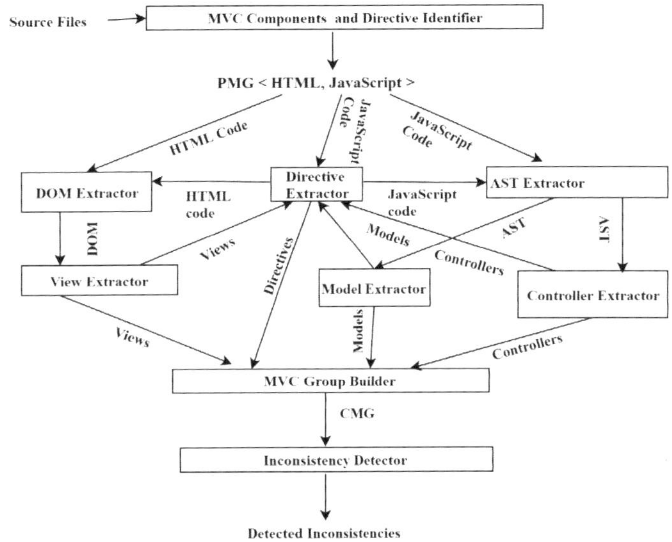

Figure 1. Block diagram of proposed approach.

B. DOM Extractor (DMEx)

DMEx module uses HTML code as input from *PMG* that is provided by *MCDI* module. It also gets HTML source code from the *DEx* module (shown in Figure 1). It is responsible for transforming the HTML code into its DOM representations, which is used for analyzing the HTML elements and attributes. This module provides the extracted DOM to the *VEx* module for further extracting the AngularJS built-in directives and elements.

C. AST Extractor (AEx)

Similar to *DEx*, *AEx* module gets the input from *PMG*. It also gets JavaScript code from *DEx* module. The responsibility of *AEx* is to transform the JavaScript code into its AST representation. It provides the AST to the *ME* and *CEx* module. Those modules analyze the AST for further extracting *mv* and *cf*.

D. View Extractor (VEx)

VEx module analyzes the DOM and produces a set of *View (V)* objects. It extracts all the identifiers of *mv* and *cf* that are

TABLE I. LIST OF TERMS USED IN PROPOSED APPROACH

Term	Descriptions	Term	Descriptions
MCDI	MVC Components and Directive Identifier	*DMEx*	DOM Extractor
AEx	AST Extractor	*VEx*	View Extractor
MEx	Model Extractor	*CEx*	Controller Extractor
DEx	Directive Extractor	*MGB*	MVC Group Builder
InD	Inconsistency Detector	*M*	Model Object
V	View Object	*C*	Controller Object
CD-M	Model Object for Custom Directives	*CD-V*	View Object for Custom Directives
CD-C	Controller Object for Custom Directives	*PMG*	Primary MVC Group
UMG	Updated MVC Group	*CMG*	Complete MVC Group

used in the view. Generally, *mv* and *cf* are appeared as DOM elements or attribute value of AngularJS built-in directives. The attributes of AngularJS built-in directives accept a specific type of value. So, the accepted type of these built-in directives are also analyzed. Besides, *VEx* finds the presence of custom directives that are used in the DOM and makes a list of custom directives.

E. Model Extractor (MEx)

MEx takes AST as input from *AEx* module. It analyzes the AST of controller files and produces a set of *Model (M)* objects. It finds all the *mv* that are defined in the controller. The *mv* which are used in the view are binded with a view model variable (generally it is represented by *$scope* or *vm*). To find the identifiers of *mv*, *MEx* looks for the left hand side of the assignment expression. So, the identifiers are found as the properties of view model variable. For getting the type of *mv*, *MEx* considers the right hand side of the assignment expression and infers the assigned type based on the AST node (e.g., if the right hand side is StringLiteral node than the inferred type is String). If the right hand expression is too complex, the assigned type cannot be inferred. In this case, the type is considered as *complex* for that identifier.

F. Controller Extractor (CEx)

Similar to *MEx*, *CEx* also receives AST from *AEx* module and analyzes the AST of controller files and generates a set of *Controller (C)* objects. It extracts the *cf* identifiers following the same way described in *MEx*. However, to get the assigned types for *cf* identifiers, the return type of each *cf* is considered. Finally, the modules *VEx*, *MEx* and *CEx* generates the sets of *Models (M)*, *Views (V)* and *Controllers (C)* objects. Each element of the set of *M*, *V* and *C* is considered as a tuple of *UMG* in a form of <M,V,C> that is used by *MGB* module.

G. Directive Extractor (DEx)

DEx module gets a list of custom directive definition files from *MCDI* module. Using the definition files, it extracts directive type, related view and controller files that are responsible for representing the functionality of that directive. The view files are fed to the *DMEx* module to generate DOM. After that, DOM is similarly extracted by the *VEx* module to create a View object for that custom directive that is represented by *CD-V*. It contains a list of *mv* and *cf* identifiers and types used in the custom directive view. The controller file of that custom directive is fed to the *AEx* module that also generates AST. Next, this AST is extracted by the *MEx* module to produce a Model object for that custom directive represented by *CD-M*. The *MEx* extracts identifier and type of the *mv*. Similarly, *CEx* generates a Controller object *CD-C* for that custom directive. It extracts the identifier and return type of *cf*. Finally, *DEx* module builds a list of *Directive* objects that contains the related model, view and controller for each directive.

H. MVC Group Builder (MGB)

The module *MGB* receives *UMG* and gets a list of *Directive* objects from the module *DEx*. It is responsible for building *CMG* by adding some new tuple with *UMG*. For every element of *UMG*, each directive is analyzed from the list of *Directive* objects based on its type. At first, for each directive, an empty tuple of Model *M*, View *V* and Controller *C* object is initialized and the View object of the directive *CD-V* is assigned to it. The reason is that the directive has its own view and it cannot be inherited from the parent view. Next, for each directive the type of the directive is checked. The type of a directive is determined by its scope property. If the scope is false, it refers that this directive does not manipulate the *cf* and *mv* of its parent controller. It directly uses the *cf* and *mv* properties from its parent controller to its view. So, the *CD-M* and *CD-C* of that directive are directly assigned to the empty M and C. If the scope is true, it means that this directive can prototypically inherit and manipulate the *cf* and *mv* of its parent controller. So, the collection of *mv* and *cf* used in both directive and its parent controller are assigned to the M and C, respectively. When the scope is isolated, it means that the *mv* and *cf* of this directive are isolated from its parent controller. For such, the directive's *CD-M* and *CD-C* are assigned to the empty M and and C, respectively. Finally, new tuple of <M,V,C> are added to the *UMG* to form the *CMG*.

I. Inconsistency Detector (InD)

The module *InD* gets *CMG* from *MGB* and provides a list of inconsistency. It mainly compares all the *mv* and *cf* among the Model, Controller and View object of each tuple of *CMG*. It is performed to identify the potential inconsistencies that exist within each tuple. At first, it searches the inconsistencies related to *mv* by iterating every *mv* that is used in the view and controller. For all such *mvs* that are defined in the controller, their identifiers are checked to see whether these also exists and are defined to the corresponding view. The checking is done based on string comparison. If it does not exist it means either these *mv* are not used in the view or their identifiers are inconsistent. So, there exists an identifier inconsistency and it is included in the inconsistency list. However, if *mv* exists, next the data type of the *mv* is checked into the view and controller. If the data type of the *mv* is dissimilar, corresponding to the view and controller, it means that a type inconsistency is present that is also included in the inconsistency list. Following the same process, inconsistencies in the *cf* are identified. It is assumed that *mv* and *cf* with unknown and complex types are matched with all types.

III. Evaluation

This section deals with the evaluation of proposed approach. A brief description of each aspect of evaluation is described in the following subsection.

A. Implementation

Since Command Line Interface (CLI) tools are getting popular for client-end application development, FANTASIA [8] is implemented in the form of a CLI using JavaScript programming language on top of *Node.js* framework. It is available as an open source *Node.js* package that can easily be installed using *Node.js* package manager (*nmp*). For identifying inconsistencies, developers have to run a command called *find-incons* in the application's base directory using the command prompt. For each identified inconsistency, an error message is shown containing the inconsistency type, file name and the location of the code where the inconsistencies are occurred. Tool demonstration of FANTASIA is available in [8].

B. Experimental Dataset

In total, 25 AngularJS MVC applications are used. These are chosen from a list of MVC applications mentioned in AngularJS Git-Hub page [9]. The applications that were chosen here were also used to evaluate the existing approach AUREBESH. Based on the presence of inconsistencies in the custom directives, these applications are categorized into two classes. Among the 25 applications, 15 applications containing MVC modules are categorized as Class A and rest of the 10 applications containing both MVC modules along with custom directives are categorized as Class B.

C. Fault Injection Study

Similar to AUREBESH [7], the efficiency of FANTASIA was measured by performing a fault injection study on the experimental dataset. The injection was performed by initializing mutations in the applications. The mutations were initialized in a way so that these could create inconsistencies in those applications. Inconsistencies within the applications depend on consistency properties. According to Frolin et al. [7], JavaScript MVC applications are inconsistent if the applications do not satisfy one of the following four consistency properties.

1) The controller and view can only use *mv* that are defined in the model.
2) The view only uses *cf* that are defined in the controller.
3) The expected types of corresponding *mv* in the view match the assigned types in the model or controller.
4) The expected and returned types of corresponding *cf* match in the view and controller.

Based on the consistency properties, Frolin et al. introduced 10 types of mutations [7]. The description of each mutation type is represented in TABLE III. Among these types, every mutation type corresponds to a violation of the above 4 consistency properties. In this experiment, these 10 types of mutations (mentioned in TABLE III) were also used. At first, the mutations were injected into the source code of those applications. After that, FANTASIA was run on the mutated version of the applications and analyzed whether FANTASIA could identify the inconsistencies initialized by the mutations. If the inconsistencies were identified, the result of the injection was noted as successful, otherwise failed. Finally, the numbers of successful and failed detections were counted for measuring precision and recall. For comparative analysis, AUREBESH was also run on the mutated applications and counted the number of successful and failed detections.

The results of identifying mutation type represent how well FANTASIA can detect the violation of corresponding consistency properties. For this study, at least 4 injections were performed per mutation type that amounts 30 to 40 injections in each application. It was noted that some mutation types were not applicable for all applications. For example, it is not mandatory that all controllers use the model variables. For these types of specific case, some mutation types were not considered. As a result, there were less than 40 injections injected in some applications. The location of the mutated code was chosen arbitrarily only if that line of code was applicable for current mutation type.

D. Result

After running both FANTASIA and AURBESH on the mutated version of Class A dataset, recall and precision are calculated based on successful and failed detection. TABLE II shows the fault injection study results over the Class A dataset where TI refers to total injection, SD refers to successful detection and FD refers to failed detection. As TABLE II shows, FANTASIA is very accurate yielding to an overall recall of 97.63% with 100% precision and gets perfect recall in 11 out of 15 applications. From TABLE II, it is also observed that existing approach AUREBESH also performs accurately with an overall recall of 97.20% with 100% precision and gets perfect recall in 11 out of 15 applications. So, both FANTASIA and AUREBESH perform similarly for identifying inconsistencies in those applications which contain inconsistencies only in MVC modules and not in custom directives.

Again FANTASIA and AUREBESH both were run on mutated version of Class B dataset to calculate the recall and precision. TABLE IV shows the fault injection study results over the Class B dataset. Here, FANTASIA also performs accurately with an overall recall of 96.66% with 100% precision and gets perfect recall in 5 out of 10 applications. However, AUREBESH does not perform well with an overall recall of 76.97% and 100% precision with no perfect recall. The reason for AUREBESH's poor performances is that it never analyzes the presence of custom directives in those applications. So, it was unable to identify those inconsistencies which were occurred within the custom directives. On the other hand, FANTASIA analyzes the presence of custom directives and

TABLE II. COMPARATIVE RESULT BETWEEN FANTASIA AND AUREBESH ON CLASS A DATASET

Applications	**Application Category**	**Size (LOC)**	**TI**	**FANTASIA**				**AUREBESH**			
				SD	**FD**	**Recall(%)**	**Precision(%)**	**SD**	**FD**	**Recall(%)**	**Precision(%)**
Angular Tunes	Music Player	185	35	35	0	100.00	100.00	35	0	100.00	100.00
Balance Projector	Finance Tracker	511	40	34	6	85.00	100.00	33	7	82.05	100.00
Cafe Townsend	Employee Tracker	452	40	40	0	100.00	100.00	40	0	100.00	100.00
Cryptography	Encoder	523	40	40	0	100.00	100.00	40	0	100.00	100.00
Dematerializer	Blogging	379	40	36	4	90.00	100.00	37	3	92.05	100.00
Dustr	Template Compiler	493	40	40	0	100.00	100.00	40	0	100.00	100.00
ETuneBook	Music Manager	5042	40	40	0	100.00	100.00	40	0	100.00	100.00
Flat Todo	Todo Organizer	255	40	40	0	100.00	100.00	40	0	100.00	100.00
GQB	Graph Traversal	1170	40	38	2	95.00	100.00	37	3	92.05	100.00
Hackynote	Slide Maker	236	40	40	0	100.00	100.00	40	0	100.00	100.00
Kodigon	Encoder	948	40	40	0	100.00	100.00	40	0	100.00	100.00
Memory Games	Puzzle	181	37	35	2	94.59	100.00	34	3	91.89	100.00
Shortkeys	Shortcut Maker	407	40	40	0	100.00	100.00	40	0	100.00	100.00
Sliding Puzzle	Puzzle	608	34	34	0	100.00	100.00	34	0	100.00	100.00
TwitterSearch	Search	357	40	40	0	100.00	100.00	40	0	100.00	100.00
Overall		**11747**	**626**	**612**	**14**	**97.63**	**100.00**	**610**	**16**	**97.20**	**100.00**

TABLE III. TYPES OF INJECTED FAULTS

No	Description	Property
1	Change the name of a *mv* used in line N of a view	1
2	Change the name of a *mv* used in line N of a controller	1
3	For a particular *mv* used in line N of a view, remove the declaration of that *mv* in a corresponding model	1
4	For a particular *mv* used in line N of a controller, remove the declaration of that *mv* in a corresponding model	1
5	Change the name of a *cf* used in line N of a view	2
6	For a particular *cf* used in line N of a view, remove the declaration of that *cf* in a corresponding controller	2
7	For a particular *mv* used in the view that expects a certain type T1, change the declaration of that *mv* in line N of a corresponding model so that the type is changed to T2	3
8	For a particular *mv* used in the view that expects a certain type T1 and declared in line N of a corresponding model, change the expected type to T2 by mutating the *ng* attribute name	3
9	For a particular *cf* used in the view that expects a certain type T1, change the return value of that *cf* in line N of the controller to a value of type T2	4
10	For a particular *cf* used in the view that expects a certain type T1 and returns a value in line N of a corresponding controller, change the expected type to T2 by mutating the *ng* attribute name	4

able to identify the inconsistencies that are occurred within the custom directives.

From TABLE II and TABLE IV, it is observed that both FANTASIA and AURBESH attain 100% precision. The reason is that there is no occurrence of getting false positive results for successful and failed inconsistency identification. As, it is the assumption that all applications are developed by following proper coding convention, it prevents both approaches from getting false positive results.

IV. RELATED WORK

Inconsistency occurs in JavaScript applications because of wrong interaction between DOM and JavaScript code. As a result, DOM-related faults and errors are partially responsible for inconsistency issues. However, AngularJS has gradually been developed over the last couple of years. Therefore, it is considered to be a new area of research. A few works have been found that directly discusses inconsistency issues in AngularJS MVC applications. Among those works, several studies [2][5][10][11] rigorously discuss DOM-related faults and errors that occur in JavaScript applications. Moreover, two recent studies [6][7] have addressed the inconsistency issues in JavaScript application development. So, considering all of those works, the knowledge domain is classified in two categories, such as *DOM Related Fault in JavaScript* and *Inconsistency in JavaScript*. A brief description of each category is mentioned in the following subsections.

A. DOM Related Fault in JavaScript

Since AngularJS MVC framework contains both HTML DOM and JavaScripts, DOM related errors and faults are directly responsible for inconsistency issues. Several studies have been conducted to analyze the behavior of DOM in JavaScript applications, such as Forlin et al. performed an empirical study [10] for identifying numerous errors and faults in JavaScript based web applications. Both static and dynamic source code analysis are performed in this study that has identified different characteristics of JavaScripts faults. Further, these characteristics of JavaScript faults are used by Ocaizer et al. [11] to identify errors and faults during JavaScript application development. They proposed an automatic fault localization approach AUTOFLOX by analyzing the JavaScript fault characteristics. By performing dynamic backward program slicing, AUTOFLOX can localize faults within the JavaScript based web applications. Besides, the evaluation result of AUTOFLOX shows that about 79% of reported JavaScript errors and faults are DOM related [11].

On the other hand, based on those results, Forlin et al. [2] observed that almost 65% of JavaScript faults are DOM related faults that occur because of the wrong interaction of JavaScript code and DOM element using incorrect identifier. However, in development phase, these located faults are needed to be resolved. In order to resolve these faults, an automatic fault repairing technique VEJOVIS was proposed by Forlin et al. [5]. This technique includes the combination of both static and dynamic code analysis with backward program slicing. The outcome of this technique is the categorization of some

TABLE IV. COMPARATIVE RESULT BETWEEN FANTASIA AND AUREBESH ON CLASS B DATASET

Applications	Application Category	Size (LOC)	TI	FANTASIA				AUREBESH			
				SD	FD	Recall(%)	Precision(%)	SD	FD	Recall(%)	Precision(%)
Angular Qize	Quiz Maker	523	36	36	0	100.00	100.00	30	6	83.33	100.00
Angular Table	Component	327	35	35	0	100.00	100.00	30	5	85.71	100.00
Angular Ui-Grid	Component	243	35	35	0	100.00	100.00	26	9	74.78	100.00
C3-Chart	Librery	763	35	35	0	100.00	100.00	27	8	77.14	100.00
Color Chooser	Component	134	30	30	0	100.00	100.00	23	7	76.66	100.00
Date Picker	Component	278	40	37	3	92.20	100.00	30	10	75.00	100.00
Directives Lab	Directive Example	412	40	39	1	97.50	100.00	31	9	77.50	100.00
GemStore2	Game	453	40	38	2	95.00	100.00	28	12	70.00	100.00
Responsive Slider	UI Design	359	37	33	4	89.18	100.00	25	12	67.56	100.00
Text Editor	Editor	192	40	37	3	92.50	100.00	33	7	82.50	100.00
Overall		**3684**	**368**	**355**	**13**	**96.66**	**100.00**	**283**	**85**	**76.97**	**100.00**

common types of faults. However, FANTASIA completely differs from these works, as in these works non-MVC applications and frameworks are considered. These applications have various architectural patterns compared to AngularJS MVC framework. So, these works are not compatible to resolve inconsistency issues in AngularJS MVC applications.

B. *Inconsistency in JavaScript*

Since, JavaScript is a dynamic programming language, it does not provide compile-time warning if a program contains identifier or data type inconsistencies [11]. Both of these inconsistencies are responsible of creating hidden bugs and failures. However, in a survey study, it is found that among 460 developers, 39% of those consider that silent failures caused by identifier or type inconsistencies, are real problems during application development [12]. For identifying type inconsistencies, Michael et al. proposed an approach called TypeDevil [6] that can detect type inconsistencies by performing dynamic analysis on JavaScript code. To evaluate the approach, TypeDevil [6] was applied on JavaScript code collected from various applications. The evaluation shows that it can detect type consistency within the JavaScript files.

In order to detect inconsistency, an approach AUREBESH [7] was proposed that can detect both the type and identifier consistencies by performing static code analysis in JavaScript MVC applications. To evaluate AUREBESH, a fault injection study was conducted on 20 open source AngularJS applications considering to be representative of MVC applications. The result of this study shows that AUREBESH can detect inconsistencies and some real world bugs in those applications.

However, TypeDevil [6] cannot find inconsistency in AngularJS MVC applications since to find type and identifier inconsistencies in MVC applications, both the controller JavaScript and view HTML code should be analyzed. TypeDevil [6] does not analyze the inconsistencies between the HTML and JavaScript code rather it only analyzes the JavaScript code. FANTASIA resolves this problem by performing static analysis on both HTML and JavaScript code instead of performing dynamic analysis only within JavaScript code. On the other hand, while using custom directives in AngularJS applications, AUREBESH [7] cannot detect inconsistencies because it does not analyze the presence of custom directives. FANTASIA also differs from AUREBESH as it considers the presence of custom directives across the applications and identifies those inconsistencies that occur within the custom directives and MVC modules.

V. Conclusion and Future Work

The presence of inconsistencies (e.g., identifier and type inconsistency) in AngularJS applications produces hidden bugs, which reduce the maintainability and readability of code. During development, it is hard to identify inconsistencies since JavaScript does not provide compile time warn if any inconsistency occurs. Detecting inconsistency becomes more difficult when developers use custom directives with MVC modules. However, existing approach can only identify inconsistencies that occur in MVC modules omitting the presence of custom directives. To resolve this issue, FANTASIA is proposed that performs static code analysis across the application and analyzed the presence of custom directives to detect inconsistencies.

According to the result analysis, FANTASIA achieves an overall 97.63% recall and 100% precision similar to existing approach AUREBESH, to detect inconsistency in 15 applications that contain inconsistency in MVC modules. Comparing to AUREBESH, it outperforms with an overall 96.66% recall and 100% precision to detect inconsistency in 10 applications containing inconsistency both in MVC modules and custom directives. The reason for FANTASIA's significant increase of recall is analysis the presence of custom directives.

Incorporating FANTASIA with the existing tool AUREBESH, to detect inconsistency in other JavaScript MVC frameworks (e.g., *Ember.js*), can be a future research scope. As FANTASIA is only applicable to the primary version of AngularJS framework, the future work is to make FANTASIA compatible to the latest versions of AngularJS. Future scope also includes to make FANTASIA compatible for TypeScript or CoffeScript based MVC applications. Currently, the scope of this proposed technique is to identify inconsistency only in AngularJS MVC applications developed in JavaScript. However, in future this approach can be further used to automatically remove and fix inconsistency in MVC applications.

References

[1] V. Balasubramanee, C. Wimalasena, R. Singh, and M. Pierce, "Twitter bootstrap and angularjs: Frontend frameworks to expedite science gateway development," in *2013 IEEE International Conference on Cluster Computing (CLUSTER)*. IEEE, 2013, pp. 1–1.

[2] F. Ocariza, K. Bajaj, K. Pattabiraman, and A. Mesbah, "An empirical study of client-side javascript bugs," in *2013 ACM/IEEE International Symposium on Empirical Software Engineering and Measurement*. IEEE, 2013, pp. 55–64.

[3] Angular, "Ng-if directive," https://docs.angularjs.org/api/ng/directive/ngIf, 2017, [Online], [Accessed 2017-06-15].

[4] AngularJS, "AngularJS.org," https://angularjs.org/, 2017, [Online], [Accessed 2017-06-15].

[5] F. S. Ocariza Jr, K. Pattabiraman, and A. Mesbah, "Vejovis: suggesting fixes for javascript faults," in *Proceedings of the 36th International Conference on Software Engineering*. ACM, 2014, pp. 837–847.

[6] M. Pradel, P. Schuh, and K. Sen, "Typedevil: Dynamic type inconsistency analysis for javascript," in *2015 IEEE/ACM 37th IEEE International Conference on Software Engineering*, vol. 1. IEEE, 2015, pp. 314–324.

[7] F. S. Ocariza Jr, K. Pattabiraman, and A. Mesbah, "Detecting inconsistencies in javascript mvc applications," in *Proceedings of the 37th International Conference on Software Engineering-Volume 1*. IEEE Press, 2015, pp. 325–335.

[8] FANTASIA, "FANTASIA," https://www.npmjs.com/package/fantasia-inconsistency-detector, 2017, [Online], [Accessed 2017-06-15].

[9] GitHub, "GitHub/AngularJS," https://github.com/angular/angular.js, 2017, [Online], [Accessed 2017-06-15].

[10] F. S. Ocariza Jr, K. Pattabiraman, and B. Zorn, "Javascript errors in the wild: An empirical study," in *Software Reliability Engineering (ISSRE), 2011 IEEE 22nd International Symposium on*. IEEE, 2011, pp. 100–109.

[11] F. S. Ocariza Jr, K. Pattabiraman, and A. Mesbah, "Autoflox: An automatic fault localizer for client-side javascript," in *2012 IEEE Fifth International Conference on Software Testing, Verification and Validation*. IEEE, 2012, pp. 31–40.

[12] M. Ramos, M. T. Valente, R. Terra, and G. Santos, "Angularjs in the wild: a survey with 460 developers," *arXiv preprint arXiv:1608.02012*, 2016.

Scope Management on Software Projects

An updated approach to maturity levels and services in the Gaia Scope Framework

Darlan Dalsasso
Departamento de Computação, Universidade Estadual de Londrina - UEL
Londrina, Brazil
darlan_dalsasso@hotmail.com

Rodolfo Miranda de Barros
Departamento de Computação, Universidade Estadual de Londrina - UEL
Londrina, Brazil
rodolfomdebarros@gmail.com

Abstract— **Software development is a complex activity and one of the most important activities to be developed in working with the requirements of each software project. This work addresses the development of the Gaia Scope Framework [3], as a tool and as a methodology to be followed by engineering and product scope management in software projects. The structure of the framework is composed of services. These services are the activities to be developed and are divided into different levels of maturity, where the goal is to get the company to reach the optimized level. Allied to that, the main work is the diagnostic evaluation questionnaire and the implementation process of the framework. This article presents an update of the maturity levels and services that had been initially defined, due to the need to make the framework easier to understand and take care of. The main objective of this study is the development of the Gaia Scope Framework, and that it guides and assists system and software engineers in the production of complete, correct and unequivocal requirements that meet the needs of users.**

Keywords - quality; software; framework; requirements; project management.

I. INTRODUCTION

Software development is an activity that is constantly evolving. The search for new techniques that will help and improve the way to build software with higher quality and that mainly meets the needs of its users motivated the development of the Gaia Scope Framework.

Studies are carried out and applied in the corporate and academic environment with the objective of developing better techniques and tools that assist in the development of software; the Gaia Scope Framework focuses on the scope of products in software projects because it has its focus on what 'needs' to be developed in software.

Many of the difficulties that are encountered are often due to not knowing which activity needs to be developed first and what sequence of steps is needed later. There is also the situation of knowing what is the ultimate goal to be achieved, but not knowing how to achieve this goal.

In this study, we are proposing the development of a framework for managing the product scope in software projects, known as the Gaia Scope Framework.

The framework has undergone an update the levels of maturity. In the first version they were known as: undefined, known, managed, quantitatively managed, optimized. In the current version, the levels have been updated to: undefined, known, defined, managed, and optimized. In the same way, the services of the first version were: establishing the strategy, planning the scope management, collecting the requirements, defining the scope, creating the project analytical framework (EAP), validating the scope, controlling the scope, costs, the time, stakeholders, and the last service was in continuous improvement. In the current version, services are known as: establishing strategy, requirements and scope research and analysis, requirements / scope specification and negotiation, requirements / scope validation, requirements / scope management, maintenance and requirements / improvement (involves all areas and scope management services). This update was necessary due to the in-depth study and the need to make the framework more coherent and functional in relation to the purpose of the framework, which is to facilitate working with the elicitation, specification, approval, management and control of the product scope in the known projects as requirements.

This framework can be treated as a tool to be used or a methodology to be followed because it expresses through services the activities that need to be developed and how they can be carried out to reach the final objective.

The services are divided into levels of maturity so that the implementation of the framework is gradual and incremental. An example would be the following: in order for the company/institution to achieve the defined level of the framework, it must be able to develop the services that comprise this level, which are: requirements specification or scope negotiation and the requirements validation service. When reaching the objectives of each of the two services, it is understood that the defined level has been successfully achieved, which enables the company/institution to seek to develop the services of the above level that is managed.

One of the ideas that surround the framework is that users can develop the activities necessary to successfully reach the services that make up each level of maturity in a gradual way, until reaching all services of the highest level, which is optimized, where it is possible to affirm that all services of the levels have been successfully achieved [3].

The structure is different from other works like [1][7], [8][12] because it not only suggests what needs to be developed but also the goal to be delivered. In the case of the

Gaia Scope Framework, the services are responsible for presenting the information that needs to be elaborated.

An example is that each service presents some templates that can be used by analysts to develop their work. Services are key items within the framework, as they facilitate the conduct of analysts in the work required to achieve the expected goal.

The Gaia Scope Framework is formed by different services, which are the activities to be performed, which have a structure composed of different information, such as service description, document templates, questions related to the diagnostic questionnaire, among other information.

Referring to the Gaia Scope Framework, the level of maturity refers to knowing how adequate, apt and matured the company is to carry out or develop the implementation of the necessary services for the management of the scope of software products. The maturity level also facilitates the institutionalization and application of services in a gradual way.

The Gaia Scope framework includes the diagnostic assessment questionnaire and the framework implementation process. One of the main ideas is to make services simple and objective, easy to understand. The main idea for the development of this framework was the fact that we know that one of the main causes of the failure in software projects is the existence of difficult-to-interpret requirements, poorly defined, or sometimes due to poor management of requirements, among other factors. These difficulties can compromise all the work that will be developed in relation to activities related to software requirements.

In the software industry is also known that activities related to engineering and requirements management need special attention, since it is a complex and fundamental activity that justifies the development of this framework; if the work related to the requirements is performed correctly, complete and unambiguous, the chance to develop and deliver software that meets the needs of end users is bigger.

This article is divided as follows: in Section 2, the concepts of requirements engineering will be discussed. Section 3 refers to project scope management. Section 4 discusses Information Technology (IT) services concepts and the idea of maturity levels. Section 5 presents a comparative study of engineering and requirements management. Section 6 will address the Gaia Scope Framework and their advantages. Subsection A of Section 6 presents the maturity levels of the Framework Gaia Scope. Subsection B of Section 6 introduces the integration of maturity levels with their respective services. Section 7 presents the conclusions and future works about the study.

II. Requirements Engineering

As we approach the software development context, we need to keep in mind what we are going to build for, and to whom we are going to build it for. We can simply understand that a requirement can be a need that has to be satisfied or even a property of a product that already exists [11].

This reflects in the discovery of the minimum details of the product that will be implemented and in the understanding of all the stakeholders involved. In general way, it is called requirements or requirements engineering.

The task of obtaining the knowledge and understanding the requirements is a problem to be solved and presents itself one of the most complex challenges faced by analysts and software engineers [7]. This is due to the fact that often the customers themselves are in doubt of what they really expect the software to do.

The requirements are the descriptions or specifications of the application to be developed, its operating restrictions, and the services they will offer [8]. These specifications serve as the basis for all the work that is going to be done ahead and are critical to the correct understanding of what is needed to be developed.

The vast amount of tasks and techniques that make analysts aware of what is needed to be developed is called software engineering [7].

Requirements engineering can also be understood as a process that is used to identify, analyze, develop the documentation and verify the resources that the application must offer and the constraints that need to be considered in the development of the solution [8].

Analyzing the concepts presented above, it is possible to be aware of the complexity that such activity has in the software development process.

Obviously, the greater the competence in performing the activity of identifying and documenting the requirements in a simple, clear and objective way, thus maintaining a good management of these activities, can cause the produced work product to have a greater chance and probability of success.

So, the Gaia Scope Framework aims to assist analysts and software engineers in performing their daily work tasks in a standardized, simple and controllable way.

III. Project Management and Project Scope Management

We can identify the existence of projects in practically everything around us. To find a new job, to open a company, to carry out a university, to write a scientific article, among others, involves understanding the needs that we intend to develop in order to reach the main objective, and also, its management in an efficient way to know where we are in the project.

In company/institution, the idea of design becomes more practiced, according to the large number of projects that happen in the world at the same time. Many of these projects are about the development of software to meet the most varied demands of the market.

A survey conducted by the Project Management Institute shows that company/institution, seeking to achieve a high degree of performance in their projects implement twice the number of strategic initiatives that are successfully carried out (76%) from the comparison to low performance company/institution, (38%) [10].

To understand how is possible to be able to evolve in our project, we need to seek continuous improvement, adopting strategies that make it possible to get the most out of the performance and quality of the product generated.

In addition to that, high-performance company/institution lose twelve times less money when compared to non-high performing company/institution,, leaving $ 20 million lost to high-performing companies and $ 230 million lost to company/institution, that were non-high-performing. This amount is considered for each U $$ 1 billion spent in project expenditures [10].

So that, it is known the difference between company/institution, that are high performance and the ones that are not.

The amount of losses is so bulky that makes us wonder how many projects could be developed with the resources that are lost.

The development of software projects fits well in this need, which leads us to seek to develop them, thinking carefully about the format of projects, and consequently, giving emphasis to the area of project scope management, which is the basis of all work.

A project is an enterprise that does not repeat itself, and which has a clear and logical sequence of events or activities to be developed which seeks to achieve a clear and specific objective, that is accomplished and led by people, considering parameters of time, cost, resources involved and quality [10].

By understanding that each project is unique and theoretically has an established beginning and end, we need to seek to develop the right requirements, primarily by lowering the time for survey and validation of requirements.

According to the Project Management Institute (PMI), a project is a temporary effort, with the aim of creating a product or service considered unique. It is ended when the project objectives are: met, have not been successfully achieved, can not be achieved or the need for the project is over. It can still be ended if it is the client's will or sponsor [9].

Project quality can also be understood as the source of customer satisfaction and project success. When clients are satisfied, we can measure the project success [6].

Project scope management encompasses the activities necessary to ensure that the project includes only what is necessary for its development, nothing else [9].

It means that when we develop projects, we need to think only about what is necessary to be done and delivered, not worrying about activities and artifacts that are not part of the scope.

The Gaia Scope Framework will serve as a tool to be used or a methodology to be followed that will address the key activities that need to be created to ensure that the development and management of the product scope is performed in a correct, complete, clear, modifiable, prioritized, verifiable and traceable.

It will contribute to generating the effective, efficient, reliable and quality product that reach the needs of the product scope management area, but mainly, achieving the needs of the users.

IV. IT Services and Levels of Maturity

The Gaia Scope Framework is developed in the service format as discussed below, in section VI. These services are the activities to be built up or can be understood as the objectives to be achieved.

The purpose of a service is to offer something value to customers, enabling them to accomplish their expected results in a measurable way [3].Obviously, each of these services aims some value for the project in a unitary way, and all of these services add high value and success in the activities of engineering and requirements management in a general way.

The services strategy refers to IT skills in the generation of service assets [4]. Services are classified as intangible assets, not presenting physical characteristics, but can generate economic benefits for company/institution, [4].

The value consists of two main components that are utility and assurance, where utility is about what the customer receives, and it turns the guarantee on how this value is provided to customers [2].

Another characteristic of the services is due to the fact that clients do not have to bear certain costs and risks [2].

Finally, service management is a set of specialized organizational skills aimed at providing value to all of its customers in the form of services.

The Gaia Scope Framework is developed using maturity levels, as discussed below, in section VI.

Maturity levels are a combination of processes or activities and process empowerment [5].

It is possible to understand that maturity levels are composed of a set of processes that need to be satisfactorily achieved or contemplated, achieving the minimum expected favorable results to ensure that such process is considered satisfactory or unsatisfactory.

Process capability refers to the set of skills to meet business objectives, both current and future, meeting what is required in each process [1].

Each process has its value within the maturity level. It is worth emphasizing that each process has a significant value, which, together with the other processes that make up the level, cause the level of maturity to be reached.

The level of maturity of an company/institution, makes it possible to gain a better understanding of its future performance. This is due to the fact that by the logic, after the company/institution, reaches a certain level, it means that it has the minimum of excellence in the processes that develops from that level, being able to work to implement the processes of the upper levels, that is, trying always to reach improvement in their processes.

It is worth mentioning that once an reaches a level of maturity, it has to work to maintain it, because if it does not, it may not go through an eventual revaluation of the level in the future.

V. Comparative Study on Engineering and Requirements Management

In the opportunity to develop this research, and as a way to better understand the main initiatives regarding requirements engineering, a comparative study was developed between the main references of this area.

In order to develop this study, the works of Ian Sommerville, Roger S. Pressmam, MPS-BR, CMMI, in their most current versions were analyzed.

Through the analysis of the literature, it was possible to better understand the activities proposed by each author regarding requirements engineering, and an important asset was developed for the development of the Gaia Scope Framework, which is about updating services as also update the maturity levels that will make up the framework.

This study made it possible to change the version of the services being proposed, as we are going to see later.

A comparative study is presented. See Table I.

TABLE I. MAPPING AND RELATIONSHIP OF ENGINEERING ACTIVITIES AND REQUIREMENTS MANAGEMENT

Mapping and relationship of engineering activities and requirements management	
Ian Sommerville [8]	Viability Study
	Elicitation and Requirements Analysis
	Requirements Specification
	Requirements Validation
	Requirements Management
	Software Reuse: Does not specifically address the process
Roger S. Pressman [7]	Conception
	Survey
	Elaboration
	Negotiation
	Specification
	Validation
	Management
	Reuse of Software: It is approached within the construction of the analysis model
	Historical database: Mentioned within the requirement survey activity and within the construction of the analysis model
MPS-BR [1]	The understanding of the requirements is obtained from the suppliers of requirements
	The requirements are evaluated on the basis of objective criteria and a commitment of the technical team to these requirements is obtained
	Bi-directional traceability between requirements and work products is established and maintained
	Revisions to project work plans and products are conducted to identify and correct inconsistencies with requirements
	Requirements changes are managed throughout the project
	Organizational Culture: It is mentioned in the process attribute that refers to whether project execution is managed.
	Historical database: Does not deal specifically with these terms but can be seen the use of historical data in the activity "Changes in requirements are managed throughout the project"
	Lessons learned: It does not deal specifically with these terms but you can see the use of historical data in the activitye "Changes in requirements are managed throughout the project," which can generate lessons learned.
CMMI [12]	1 - Develop customer requirements (Formed by the activities of eliciting needs and transforming the needs of those involved in customer requirements.)
	2 - Develop product requirements (Formed by the activities of establishing product and product component requirements, allocating product component requirements and identifying interface requirements.)
	3 - Analyze and validate requirements (Formed by the activities of establishing operational concepts and scenarios, establishing a definition of required functionality and quality attributes, analyzing the requirements and analyzing the requirements to achieve balance and validate requirements.)
	REQUIREMENT MANAGEMENT (Formed by the activities of understanding requirements, obtaining requirements commitment, managing requirements changes, maintaining bidirectional traceability of requirements, ensuring alignment between project work and requirements)
	Reuse of Software: Addresses the idea of reuse of software in the area of requirements development
	In requirements management, the needs passed by the organization are considered. This gives an idea of the consideration of organizational culture.
	Historical database: Addresses requirements database and history of requirements changes. This refers in some way to the historical database.
	Lessons learned: Does not directly mention lessons learned, but does mention the use of history of requirements changes.
Gaia Scope Framework	Establish strategy
	Requirements / scope survey and analysis
	Requirements specification / scope and negotiation
	Validation of requirements / scope
	Requirements / Scope Management (- Involves control of requirements / scope; - Involves control and change management; - Involves requirements / scope traceability)
	Maintenance and requirements / scope history (Involves reuse of requirements - Involves historical database - Involves lessons learned - Involves company/institution culture and company/institution process assets)
	Continuous improvement (Involves all areas and services of scope management)

From this comparative study, we were able to extract the best practices applied in each of the references, where it was possible to design the services that will compose the Gaia Scope Framework.

Soon we were able to create a framework that serves to manage product scope in software projects of any size.

VI. Gaia Scope Framework

The Gaia Scope Framework is a tool to be used or a methodology to be followed to assist the engineering and management of the product scope in software projects.

From this proposal, leaders and requirements engineers will have a greater ease to surveying, specifying, validating, and managing the product scope of their software projects, thus ensuring greater management, ensuring ease of handling during the work that must be developed and achieving greater assurance and integrity of information.

The composition of the framework will be through services that will be divided into different levels of maturity, as will be analyzed next.

The idea of working with services is due to the fact that we focus on delivering value to users, who will be clients of the framework.

Each service consists of the following elements; service description, document templates, questions related to the diagnostic questionnaire, vocabulary, tools and techniques, performance indicators and workflow.

The service description will provide an objective and direct context about the service. Document templates are basic standards that can be used.

The questions related to the diagnostic questionnaire refer to verifying through this questionnaire whether the service in question is answered or not.

The vocabulary refers to the terms used in the service. The tools and techniques represent what can be used to develop the service. The performance indicators are the parameters that are used to measure the progress and service. And finally, the workflow is the process of each service.

Another point is that the implementation through maturity levels facilitates the deployment process, since it will happen gradually as the company/institution, is able to achieve the objectives of each service.

The framework will also be composed of an implementation process that is adherent to the software development processes in general, and a diagnostic evaluation questionnaire that will be used to identify, in the first moment, which level of maturity the company/institution is, and also in future revaluations, to know if the level will be maintained, lowered or raised.

The image below, presents the process of gaia scope implementation, which is initiated by the application of the diagnostic evaluation questionnaire, to understand in which level of maturity the company/institution, is.

Then, from the understanding of the maturity level, services are reviewed and optimized so that one can start working to reach the highest levels of the framework, or to maintain the level in which one is.

From the moment the company/institution, understands that it is able to seek the next level of the framework or the time comes for a reassessment of the company/institution, at the level it is in, the diagnostic assessment questionnaire is applied again to identify the company/institution, situation in the activities that are part of the services of the desired level.

In the sequence, the performance indicators in the historical database are registered and the maturity level is redefined, and in the sequence it is checked to see if it meets all the requirements of the level.

In the event of a reassessment, if the requirements are met, the level is maintained, or it is passed to a higher level in case of evaluation for level change.

The specified process is presented below, according to [4]. See Figure 1.

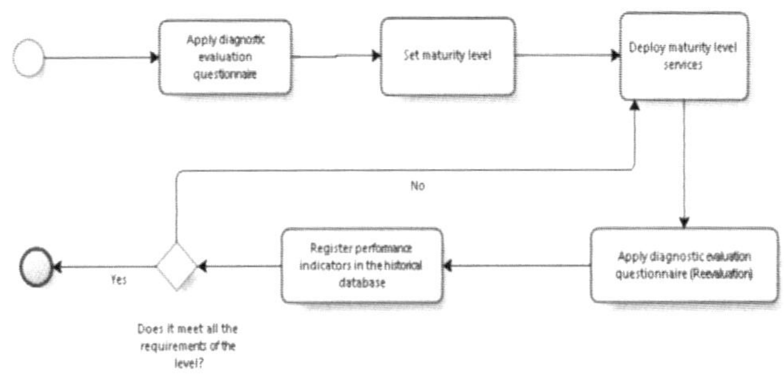

Figure 1. Implantation process of Gaia Scope Framework

A. *Gaia Scope Framework Maturity Levels*

The Gaia Scope Framework has been updated to become more adherent to its functional objective, which is product scope management in software projects.

The levels that had been initially defined were: undefined, known, managed, quantitatively managed, and optimized [3].

The services that were initially planned were: establishing strategy, planning scope management, collecting requirements, defining scope, creating EAP, validating scope, controlling scope (integration, risks, costs, time, stakeholders) and improvement to be continued.

However, as mentioned, there was a need of updating both the maturity levels and the services to compose the framework, and the comparative study between the different references was important for the more fruitful clarification of the ideas and the main objective of the Framework. Currently the maturity levels are as follows:

- Undefined;
- Known;
- Defined;
- Managed;
- Optimized;

The maturity levels presented are those that are institutionalized in the Gaia Scope Framework currently.

B. *Integration of maturity levels with their respective upgraded services.*

The maturity levels presented are those that are institutionalized in the Gaia Scope Framework currently.

- Undefined
  - The company/institution, does not have defined and institutionalized processes and artifacts.
- Known
  - Establish strategy
  - Requirements and scope survey and analysis
- Defined
  - Requirements specification / scope and negotiation
  - Validation of requirements / scope
- Managed
  - Requirements / Scope Management
    - Involves control of requirements / scope
    - Involves change control and management
    - Involves requirements / scope traceability
  - Maintenance and requirements / scope history
    - Involves requirements reuse
    - Involves historical database
    - It involves lessons learned
    - Involves company/institution, culture and company/institution process assets
- Optimized
  - Continuous improvement (Involves all areas and services of scope management)

At the indefinite level, company/institution, do not have the knowledge about their scope of requirements, nor about their strategy. At the known level the company/institution, will establish a strategy and know the requirements analytically.

At the defined level, the company/institution, already have important information about the scope, carrying out the specification, negotiation and validation of the scope of requirements. At the managed level, as its name implies, there is management of the requirements scope through requirements management activities, and maintenance of requirements and a historical database.

The highest level is optimized, which suggests a continuous improvement of all the services that are implemented.

This is the current model of the structure of maturity levels and services of the Gaia Scope Framework. To analyze the hierarchy of maturity levels, see Figure 2.

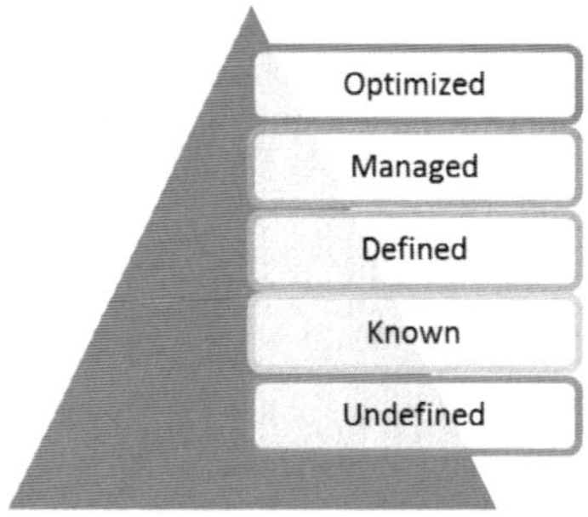

Figure 2. Hierarchy of maturity levels

The Gaia Scope Framework has different advantages, where we can mention the following: A) Possibility of being used by any institution or company/institution, that develops software; B) It is a tool or methodology that does not have acquisition costs; C) Ease of application because it is divided into maturity levels and not bureaucratic; D) Designed to be constantly updated; E) It adds ideas of important references of the area like Roger Pressmam, Ian Sommerville, Mps-Br, CMMI, among other bibliographies; F) Simple and objective; G) The requirements for the development of software that supports the Gaia Scope framework are already being analyzed.

VII. Conclusions and Future Work

The development of the Gaia Scope Framework is an initiative that comes to assist any agent that is directly or indirectly involved in the area of engineering and requirements management.

The development of this tool, which can also be understood as a methodology, meets the need of many company/institution,, which is to identify and manage their requirements in the best possible way.

Allied to the simplicity that the framework values, it is still possible to emphasize that it is free, which facilitates even more the use by them.

It is important to clarify that the research work, as well as the necessary adjustments continue to guarantee continuous improvement in the framework, but the basis of the whole study is already structured by defining and updating the levels of maturity and services that the framework will Contemplated, which were presented in this article

It is expected that, with the development of this framework, it will be possible to better identify and manage the requirements in software projects, aiming at a work that is carried out with ever more quality, guaranteeing the identification, analysis, development, documentation and requirements, which will be the basis for the development of all project needs.

The work that will be carried out in the future deals with the detailed specification of each service and its elements, the development of the diagnostic evaluation questionnaire, the implementation of the framework in the Gaia company, the analysis of the results after the application in at least two projects, and if necessary, making the necessary adjustments, until the institutionalization of the final version of the framework.

And then, the finalization of the software requirements specification to be developed that will support what the framework values.

ACKNOWLEDGMENT

I would like to thank Dr. Rodolfo Miranda de Barros for his help, advice and guidance for the development of this work.

REFERENCES

[1] Association for the Promotion of Excellence in Brazilian Software. General Software Guide. Brasilia: SOFTEX. January, 2016.

[2] Bon, Jan Van., 2012. ITIL [recurso eletrônico] : guia de referência, edição 2011, Elsevier. Rio de Janeiro.

[3] Dalsasso, Darlan., Barros, Rodolfo Miranda de, GAIA scope: Framework for the project scope management in software development proccess. In, *11th Iberian Conference on Information Systems and Technologies (CISTI)*, 2016, Gran Canaria, v.1. p. 1-6, 2016.

[4] Freitas, Marcos André dos Santos., 2013. Fundamentals of IT service management, Brasport. Rio de Janeiro, 2nd edition.

[5] Koscianski, André., Soares, Michel dos Santos., 2007. Software quality: learn the most modern methodologies and techniques for software development, Novatec Editora. São Paulo, 2nd edition.

[6] K. L. Madhuri and V. Suma, Influence of domain and technology upon scope creep in software projetcs. In. *International Conference on Advances in Electronics, Computers and Communications*, ICAECC 2014, pp. 1-6, 2014.

[7] Pressman, Roger S., 2011. Software Engineering A Professional Approach, AMGH. Porto Alegre, 7nd edition.

[8] Sommerville, Ian., 2011. Software Engineering, Pearson Prentice Hall. São Paulo, 9th edition.

[9] A project management knowledge guide (PMBOK guide) / (text and translation) Project Management Institute. - 5 ed. - São Paulo: Saraiva, 2014.

[10] Viana, Ricardo Vargas., 2014. Practical handbook of the project plan: using the PMBOK Guide, Brasport. Rio de Janeiro, 5th edition.

[11] Vazquez, Carlos Eduardo. Simões, Guilherme Siqueira, 2016. Requirements engineering: software oriented to business, Brasport. Rio de Janeiro.

[12] Software Engineering Institute. (2010). CMMI for Development, Version 1.3. *Carnegie Mellon University*, (November), 482. http://doi.org/CMU/SEI-2010-TR-033 ESC-TR-2010-033.

IoT Caching in Information Centric Networks

A Systematic Mapping

[1] Higgor Leimig da Silva Valença, [2] Felipe Silva Ferraz, and [3] Francisco Icaro do Nascimento Ribeiro
CESAR – Recife Center for Advanced Studies and Systems
Brazil, Recife
E-mail: {[1]hlsv, [2]fsf, [3]finr}@cesar.org.br

Abstract—**The Internet of Things will connect billions of devices to the Internet. However, our current Internet infrastructure does not support this amount of connected devices and cannot process the amount of data generated by them. In order to improve our Internet, a novel architecture has being proposed, Information Centric Networks. This work has the objective of identify and analyze the current state of the art solutions for Caching Schemes in Information Centric Networks. To achieve that, a mapping of these solutions was conducted. This mapping resulted in the finding of 127 works, of which 20 were identified as primary studies. This mapping shows what is being researched and which directions have been considered for improving Caching in Information Centric Networks.**

Keywords-Information Centric Networks; Caching; In-network Cache; Internet of Things; Systematic Mapping.

I. INTRODUCTION

Everyday, different types of objects are being connected to the Internet. Objects like an irrigation monitor and control systems, thermostats, refrigerators, and door lockers that were not previously connected are now part of a network of things with the purpose of providing data and/or acting on its environment. This trend is called Internet of Things (IoT), and it is a concept that has the potential to change our day to day lives.

The IoT is enabling business models that rely on data from a variety of different physical objects, like health systems that monitor pacemakers. Current forecasts estimate that 28-34 billion devices will be connected by the year 2020, from which 17.5-24 billion will have IoT as their primary purpose [1]–[3]. They also estimated that, by 2020, nearly 6 trillion dollars will be invested in IoT solutions focusing on lowering costs, increasing productivity, expanding business to new markets, and developing new products [2].

This amount of connected devices provides us with a unique opportunity to create solutions capable of interacting with different areas of human knowledge to improve our lives, like Urban Infrastructure, Agriculture, and Manufacturing. Among the currently targeted areas, Health Care is considered as the most promising of those [4]. Digitally delivered services like disease prevention, diagnose, monitoring, and treatment are expected to create a global growth in economy by 2025 of $1.1-2.5 trillion [4].

Even though the predictions for the IoT reveal a promising area, it is not yet a reality. Challenges like interoperability, security and privacy, scalability, performance, availability, and device mobility [5][6] are still being researched before we are able to connect the amount of devices the IoT requires or to process the amount of data that will be produced by these devices.

In order to solve these issues, researchers and companies are working on multiple fronts. For example, the interoperability and scalability issues are being tackled by, among other things, the development of IoT platforms. These platforms enable the connection and communication of devices under a single protocol, like KNoT [7], Xively [8], and Amazon IoT [9]. Regarding the performance issue in IoT, a novel solution has emerged. It is called Information Centric Networks (ICN).

ICN is a novel network architecture that aims to replace TCP/IP as the default protocol of the Internet. The ICN architecture proposes a shift in paradigm, from a host-centric network to a data-centric network. In ICN, the focus is on the data the user is trying to retrieve instead of from where the data is coming. Focusing on the data means that the data the user is looking for can come from anywhere in the network. That encourages the use of in-network caching [10][11], allowing popular data to be stored near the users that request them the most.

In this paper we will map the state of the art of Caching approaches in ICN. We will use a process defined by [12] in order to minimize any possible bias during the analysis of papers. This work aims to be a concise overview of the research being made in this field.

This paper is organized as follow: Section II briefly explains ICN's protocol, how it works and what is still being researched. Section III will describe the methods, processes, and protocols that were used in this mapping. In Section IV, we will present the analysis made in the primary studies found during the process described in Section III. Finally, in Section V, we will depict the results found in our mapping.

II. INFORMATION CENTRIC NETWORKS

ICN is a novel approach to network architecture that changes the paradigm from a host-centric Internet to a data-centric Internet. In order to achieve that, content is promoted to a first class citizen in ICN. That means that instead of requesting data to an Internet Service Provider (ISP) through TCP/IP and URL, in ICN the user requests the data through an Unified Content Name. This approach decouples data from its host and allows it to be stored anywhere in the network [10].

In ICN, users do not connect directly with a host in order to access their data. Instead, they send an Interest Packet to all nodes in its Forwarding Information Base (FIB). Upon receiving an Interest Packet, the node looks for the data in its Content Store. If it is present, then the node consumes the Interest Packet and answers the message with the desired Data Packet [13]. In case the data is not present, the Interest Packet is queued in the Pending Interest Table (PIT) and the node forwards the Interest Packet to all nodes in its FIB. Once the Packet reaches a node that has the desired data – be it an ISP or another node in the network – it answers the message with a Data Packet. The Data Packet then follows the trail of breadcrumb left by the Interest Packet in the PIT of each node in the network until it reaches the original requester [13]. While following the breadcrumb, the Data Packet meets nodes that implement and nodes that do not implement cache policies. The ones that implement cache policies will evaluate the Data Packet to decide if it is worth caching or not, depending on the criteria configured for that node. This characteristic of ICN allows Data Packets to be spread in the network, making it easier to be accessed.

Because of the protocol described in the previous paragraph, cache has gained primary importance in ICN. Through in-network caching, data can be retrieved from neighbor nodes in the network, instead of the ISP, decreasing the delay of data retrieval.

The default implementation of the caching protocol in ICN is called Cache All [13]. However, this protocol imposes a high storage cost to all nodes in the network. Moreover, duplicating all data in all nodes can lead to duplication where the data is not necessary. In order to make ICN viable for day to day use, ICN's Caching Scheme needs to be improved. Several research are being made with this goal in mind. This work will map some of these research.

III. Applied Protocol

The objective of this mapping is to identify the state of the art solutions for Caching in ICN. In order to identify the studies related to this topic, the following question was thought:

- How the Internet of Things will affect the performance of the Internet?

From this question, secondary questions were developed in order to help the comprehension of the solutions:

- How is Information Centric Networks handling information cache?
- In what ways can we use cache to improve the data availability in the Information Centric Networks?
- What are the main challenges in using cache in Information Centric Networks?

The protocol used in this study is based on the protocol used in [12], which is based on the guidelines of Kitchenham [14] and the analysis of [15]. This review process is composed of the following five stages: (1) identification of inclusion and exclusion criteria, (2) search for relevant studies, (3) critical assessment, (4) extraction of data, and (5) synthesis. Each of these stages is elaborated in the next sections.

A. *Inclusion and Exclusion Criteria*

For this review, we focused on studies that present novel caching solutions for ICN. These solutions ranged from novel forwarding algorithms to monetized caching policies. Since the focus was to analyze the state of the art considering Caching for ICN, the studies were excluded in case they did not fit at least one of the following criteria:

- Published after 2015.
- Published in English.
- Studies that were not available online.
- Call for works, prefaces, conference annals, handouts, summaries, panels, interviews, and news report.

B. *Search Strategies*

The studies gathered for this review were found in the databases below:

- IEEE Xplore.
- ACM Digital Library.
- SpringerLink.

Keywords were identified and combinations of those were used to make sure relevant content were not missed. The queries below were the result of these combinations:

- ICN AND cache
- ICN AND caching
- "information centric network" AND cache
- "information centric network" AND caching

These queries were combined into one query and used in order to search the databases. The searches were performed in March 2017. The results of each search were grouped and were later examined in order to remove duplications. Table I shows the amount of studies found on each database.

TABLE I. AMOUNT OF STUDIES FOUND ON EACH DATABASE

Database	*Number of Studies*
IEEE Xplore	24
ACM Digital Library	47
SpringerLink	57

C. *Studies Selection Process*

This section describes the Selection Process from search in the databases engines all the way through the identification of the primary studies.

In the first stage, the studies gathered in the databases through the queries were grouped in a spreadsheet for further analysis. This search returned 127 non-duplicated studies.

The second stage consists of the analysis of the titles of all the resulting studies to determine its relevance for this mapping. At this point, many works that were not related to caching in ICN were discarded. From the original 127 works, 40 remained after selecting them by titles. Among the works left, some were put aside to be analyzed in the next stage due to ambiguous titles.

After analyzing the titles, the abstracts of the remaining studies were analyzed in the third stage. In this stage several other studies were discarded since many did not match our expectations of presenting solutions for caching in ICN. After this stage another 18 works were discarded, leaving 22 to be analyzed.

Table II summarizes the amount of studies left after each stage of the Selection Process.

TABLE II. AMOUNT OF STUDIES LEFT AFTER EACH STAGE OF THE SELECTION PROCESS

Phase of Selection Process	*Number of Studies*
1. Database Search	127
2. Title Analysis	40
3. Abstract Analysis	22

D. *Quality Assessment*

In this stage, the remaining works went through a careful analysis. This analysis took into account not only the title and abstracts, but the whole content of the study. During this analysis, 2 (two) studies were considered uninteresting for this mapping so they were discarded.

In this analysis, relevance grades were used to classify each of the studies according to five questions. These questions helped in the identification of studies related to our mapping of caching solutions in ICN. From these five questions, the first two were crucial to the process of assessing the study contribution for this mapping. The remaining questions were used to assess the quality of the studies. The questions were:

- Does the study propose a solution to improve the performance of Information Centric Networks?
- Does the study adequately describe the proposed solution?
- Was the solution adequately tested? e.g., did it use an ICN Simulator?
- Were the conditions of the test adequately described?
- Were the results adequately compared with other solutions?

Of the remaining 22 works, 20 were selected as primary studies. These studies then went to the Data Extraction and Synthesis stage. The quality assessment process will be explained in more details in the Results section, along with an assessment of the 20 studies.

IV. RESULTS

As stated before, 20 works were selected as primary studies [15]–[35] after the Selection Process. These studies approached the caching issue in ICN in a variety of ways. Some proposed novel Replication and Content Eviction algorithms [17][18]. Some proposed Collaborative Caching polices among routers [23]. And some worked on the possibility of using monetization to incentive popular content caching throughout the network [27][28].

The following sections will dive deeper into the qualitative and quantitative analysis of the selected studies.

A. *Quantitative Analysis*

This section brings a quantitative analysis of the selected studies. This analysis intends to show who is studying Caching in ICN, where they are, and which keywords to use in order to find these studies.

The 20 selected studies were written by 66 authors affiliated to institutions in 12 countries. These studies were published between January 2015 and March 2017. In total, the studies used 63 different keywords.

The most common keywords used in these studies were: information centric network (13), caching (6), ICN (6), ccn (3), content centric networking (3), in-network caching (3), cache (2), content delivery networks (ccn) (2), game theory (2), named data networking (2), and network pricing (2). All the other keywords appeared only once. It is worth noticing that the first seven keywords are directly related to the theme of this mapping.

An analysis of these keywords can show how the primary studies are subdivided. The most frequent keywords represent the common theme among the studies, keywords like caching, networking, and information centric are present in all studies. Moving past these keywords, we can see keywords that state some of the concerns of these studies, like performance and bandwidth. One step further revels keywords that represent the strategies used by the researchers, like forwarding, replication, and popularity based algorithms. At last, the least common keywords are the names of the proposed solutions. Fast-Start [24], CLCE [17], LFRU [17], and RB-CCC [32] are a few of them.

Regarding the country of origin, China had the most published studies (4.07). United States came in second place with 4 publications, Japan in third with 3 studies, India and France with 1.66 each. Brazil, Canada, Greece, United Kingdom, and South Korea came in fifth place, all with 1 publication, Germany in sixth with 0.33, and Sweden in seventh with 0.25.

B. *Qualitative Analysis*

As described before, each of the selected primary studies have been assessed according to five quality criteria related to their relevance. When considered, these five criteria can provide a clear view of how much each of the primary studies is relevant to this work. Each study has been classified for each of the criteria using a positive or negative answer.

Table III presents the result of this analysis. Each row represents a study and the columns 'Q1' to 'Q2' represent each of the defined quality criteria: Solution Proposal and Description, Validation, and Comparison with other solutions. For each criteria, '1' is used to represent a positive answer and '0' is used to represent a negative one.

All but [19][27][28] had positive answers for 'Q1' and 'Q2'. As stated before, these questions were used as a way of measuring the contribution each study could have to this mapping. However, even though these studies did not proposed any novel approaches to ICN caching, they were included in the study since they either evaluated [19] an approach that was not present in the database search or proposed improvements in an already existing approach [27][28]. Including these studies allows us to have a bigger picture of the research in ICN caching.

TABLE III. QUALITY ANALYSIS OF PRIMARY STUDIES

Study	*Q1*	*Q2*	*Q3*	*Q4*	*Q1*	*Total*
[17]	1	1	1	1	1	5
[18]	1	1	1	1	1	5
[19]	0	0	1	1	1	3
[20]	1	1	1	1	1	5
[21]	1	1	1	1	1	5
[22]	1	1	1	1	1	5
[23]	1	1	1	1	1	5
[24]	1	1	1	1	1	5
[25]	1	1	1	1	1	5
[26]	1	1	1	1	1	5
[27]	0	0	0	1	0	1
[28]	0	0	0	1	0	1
[29]	1	1	1	1	1	5
[30]	1	1	1	1	1	5
[31]	1	1	1	1	1	5
[32]	1	1	1	1	1	5
[33]	1	1	1	1	1	5
[34]	1	1	1	1	1	5
[35]	1	1	0	0	0	2
Total	17	17	17	19	17	

Other than the studies discussed above, [35] was the only other study that did not met all the expected criteria. It does describe a new approach to ICN caching, but the validation is not properly described nor it is compared to other approaches.

V. DISCUSSION

After the analysis and data extraction phases, it was possible to notice some aspects of the research that have been made regarding ICN caching. Firstly, almost all of the studies analyzed proposed a novel approach to ICN caching. This shows that there is currently no agreement on which solution should be considered standard. Secondly, a great variety of solutions have been proposed. From simply replacing the Storage [17] or Forwarding [20] algorithms, to solutions involving monetization in order to incentive other routers to cache data relevant to the payer router [27][28]. Finally, although most of the research have been made for caching in applications of general use, some research have also been made for niche-specific applications, like video streaming [24].

The next sections will discuss the questions that guided this mapping, and a important aspect of the performance evaluations made in the studies.

A. How is Information Centric Networks handling information cache?

The analysis of the primary studies reviewed several different approaches to in-network caching. The first (and most common) approach was to replace the algorithms used in the Content Store. According to [17], the Content Storage of a network is composed by two elements – the Replication Algorithm and the Eviction Algorithm. The Replication Algorithm defines the policy used to spread the content throughout the network. Examples of Replication Algorithms are Leave Copy Everywhere (LCE) [13][37] and Leave Copy Down (LCD) [38][39]. The Eviction Algorithm defines the rules used to decide whether an arriving content should replace an existing one. An example of Eviction Algorithm is the LRU (Least Recently Used) [40].

Here are a few examples of the proposed algorithms:

- Conditional Leave Copy Everywhere (CLCE) and Least Frequent Recently Use (LFRU), by [17].
- Progressive and Fast Progressive, by [31].
- Object-Oriented Packet Caching, by [29].

These algorithms were built using different assumptions and techniques. Some do popularity-based decisions [31], others use assumptions regarding user behavior as input for its algorithm [35], and some try to fix issues in previously proposed approaches [17].

One of the studies leverages the use of monetization in order to incentive nodes of the network to store data in their caches. The studies [27][28] try to improve the original approach by improving the algorithm used to determine the price. Another study proposes a fixed network layout in order to achieve optimal result with video streaming [24]. At last, one study proposes a change in the Routing Algorithm [20] to improve the changes of finding the data that the user is looking for in neighbor nodes, different than the usual Routing Algorithm that creates a tree-like structure.

This variety of approaches shows that there are many aspects that can be tackled when improving Cache in ICN, not only the most common one: improving the heuristic behind the Eviction and Replication algorithms.

B. In what ways can we use cache to improve the data availability in the Information Centric Networks?

An analysis of the primary studies shows that, although, most of the proposed solutions are not domain specific, some have very specific niches. At one hand, general-application solutions have the advantage of being able to deal with a broader set of situations. These solutions can handle applications like web searching, file downloads, and so forth. On the other hand, however, these solutions have the disadvantage of not being fully optimized for demanding niches, like video streaming.

According to a forecast by Cisco [36], by 2020 82% of Internet traffic will be video stream; against 70% in 2015. This shows a significant growth in video consumption.

In order to minimize network traffic, ICN can be used as a way to cache video content near the consumers. Requiring less hops to find the desired content and creating less overhead in the network nodes. However, it can also be used to store other types of streaming, like music, for example, as well as for general web applications like news feed and data access when the main ISP is offline.

ICN's distributed cache nature allows us to improve the Quality of Service in several different application domains, as well as decrease the load in data centers and Internet Providers, by increasing data availability.

C. *What are the main challenges in using cache in Information Centric Networks?*

Even though caching can be used to improve the performance of many different application domains, not all domains have the same requirements and not all protocols work the same way. Because of this, caching schemes that deliver great performance for video streaming may not work so well when caching data in for autonomous vehicles. Moreover, these protocols are not always compatible among each other.

In order to ICN to become commercially viable, the authors identified three requirements:

- The network nodes should be able to cache relevant amount of data. Consider as "relevant amount of data", data quantities appropriate to the context. Hub nodes should be able to store more data than the local nodes the users will have at his/hers home.
- These nodes should be widely spread in order to ICN to truly show its potential.
- The caching scheme should either be universal, i.e. caching regardless to the protocol, or multiple protocols that are compatible and can work together to complement each other. However, it is necessary to point out that caching protocols should be fast in order to deliver the requested packets as fast as possible. And that this limitation should be in mind when designing a caching scheme for ICN.

D. *Performance evaluation*

As shown in Section IV, most of the primary studies evaluated their solutions and compared to others. After analyzing the experiments performed, some trends were noticed.

Firstly, the majority of studies used a Zipf distribution [41] to generate the randomness in the network traffic. It is based on the the fact that many types of studied data have a similar distribution. This uniformity in input ensures the comparisons are unbiased, distribution-wise.

In order to implement and test the proposed solutions, most of the primary studies used network simulators. Here are a few simulators related to ICN:

- NS-3 network simulator [42]
- ccnSIM [43]
- ndnSIM [44]
- Icarus [45]

These aspects should be followed in order to lessen the bias and create a more uniform approach to evaluate the performance of ICN caching schemes.

VI. CONCLUSION

The objective of this mapping was to identify and analyze studies that contributed to the state of the art of Caching Schemes in ICN. In the search phase, 127 works were found. From which 20 were considered as primary studies, after the phase of quality assessment. These studies were then classified regarding the aspects of the solution proposed.

The analysis of these studies showed that there is the need of a standardization of the Caching Scheme in ICN. Several different approaches were mapped, but none have been particularly successful in establishing itself as a standard. Most of the proposed approaches were only compared to simpler solutions, other than the most sophisticated ones. Leaving a gap of how these solutions compare to each, performance-wise.

This mapping shows how ICN can improve the Quality of Service in many areas. It also lists the approaches used by the studies to try and improve the Caching performance in ICN. And which techniques are being used in order to validate new Caching solutions.

Regarding future works, we propose a comparison between the mapped solutions in order to point the direction to be followed by future researchers of ICN.

ACKNOWLEDGMENT

This work was developed under the Professional Master of Software Engineer's program of the Educational branch of CESAR, a Brazilian innovation center.

REFERENCES

[1] T. Barros, "What is missing to the Internet of Things?" https://medium. com/cesar-reports/o-que-falta-na-internet-para-as-coisas-f6f7cdf05aa6, retrieved: August, 2017.

[2] J. Greenough, "How the 'internet of things' will impact consumers, businesses, and governments in 2016 and beyond," http://www.businessinsider.com/how-the-internet-of-things-market-will-grow-2014-10, retrieved: August, 2017.

[3] Nordrum, "Popular internet of things forecast of 50 billion devices by 2020 is outdated," http://spectrum.ieee.org/tech-talk/telecom/internet/popular-internet-of-things-forecast-of-50-billion-devices-by-2020-is-outdated, retrieved: August, 2017.

[4] J. Manyika et al., Disruptive technologies: Advances that will transform life, business, and the global economy. McKinsey Global Institute San Francisco, CA, 2013, vol. 180.

[5] V. Gazis et al., "Short paper: Iot: Challenges, projects, architectures," in 2015 18th International Conference on Intelligence in Next Generation Networks, Feb 2015, pp. 145–147.

[6] S. H. Shah and I. Yaqoob, "A survey: Internet of things (iot) technologies, applications and challenges," in 2016 IEEE Smart Energy Grid Engineering (SEGE), Aug 2016, pp. 381–385.

[7] "Knot: the open source meta platform for iot," https://www.knot.cesar. org.br/, retrieved: August, 2017.

[8] "Xively," https://www.xively.com/, retrieved: August, 2017.

[9] "Amazon iot," https://aws.amazon.com/iot, retrieved: August, 2017.

[10] G. Zhang, Y. Li, and T. Lin, "Caching in information centric networking: A survey," Comput. Netw., vol. 57, no. 16, Nov. 2013, pp. 3128–3141. [Online]. Available: http://dx.doi.org/10.1016/j.comnet. 2013.07.007

[11] B. Ahlgren, C. Dannewitz, C. Imbrenda, D. Kutscher, and B. Ohlman, "A survey of information-centric networking," IEEE Communications Magazine, vol. 50, no. 7, July 2012, pp. 26–36.

[12] F. I. N. Ribeiro, F. S. Ferraz, M. C. T. Silva, and G. H. S. Alexandre, "Big data solutions for urban environments a systematic review," 2015, pp. 22–28.

[13] V. Jacobson et al., "Networking named content," in Proceedings of the 5th international conference on Emerging networking experiments and technologies. ACM, 2009, pp. 1–12.

[14] B. Kitchenham and S. Charters, "Guidelines for performing systematic literature reviews in software engineering," *Inf. Softw. Technol.* 52, 8 (August 2010), 2007, pp. 792-805.

[15] T. Dyb and T. Dingsyr, "Empirical studies of agile software development: A systematic review," Information and Software Technology, vol. 50, no. 910, 2008, pp. 833 – 859. [Online]. Available: http://www.sciencedirect.com/science/article/pii/S0950584908000256

[16] F. Lai, F. Qiu, W. Bian, Y. Cui, and E. Yeh, "Scaled VIP Algorithms for Joint Dynamic Forwarding and Caching in Named Data Networks," in Proceedings of the 3rd ACM Conference on Information-Centric Networking, ser. ACM-ICN '16. New York, NY, USA: ACM, 2016, pp. 160–165. [Online]. Available: http://doi.acm.org/10.1145/ 2984356.2984377

[17] M. Bilal and S. G. Kang, "A Cache Management Scheme for Efficient Content Eviction and Replication in Cache Networks," in IEEE Access, vol. 5, 2017, pp. 1692-1701.

[18] X. Sun and Z. Wang, "An Optimized Cache Replacement Algorithm for Information-centric Networks," 2015 IEEE International Conference on Smart City/SocialCom/SustainCom (SmartCity), Chengdu, 2015, pp. 683-688.

[19] G. Carofiglio, L. Mekinda, and L. Muscariello, "Analysis of Latency-Aware Caching Strategies in Information-Centric Networking," In Proceedings of the 1st Workshop on Content Caching and Delivery in Wireless Networks (CCDWN '16). ACM, New York, NY, USA, no. 5, 2015, pp. 1-7.

[20] K. Sato, T. Kamimoto, R. Shinohara, and H. Shigeno, "Cache Management with Extended Interest for Information-centric Networking," In Adjunct Proceedings of the 13th International Conference on Mobile and Ubiquitous Systems: Computing Networking and Services (MOBIQUITOUS 2016). ACM, New York, NY, USA, 245-250.

[21] P. Sena, A. Ishimori, I. Carvalho, and A. Abele´m, "Cache-Aware Interest Routing : Impact Analysis on Cache Decision Strategies in Content-Centric Networking," In Proceedings of the 9th Latin America Networking Conference (LANC '16). ACM, New York, NY, USA, 39-45.

[22] Z. Li and G. Simon, "Cooperative Caching in a Content Centric Network for Video Stream Delivery," Journal of Network and Systems Management, vol. 23, no. 3, 2015, pp. 445–473.

[23] S. Wang, J. Bi, J. Wu and A. V. Vasilakos, "CPHR: In-Network Caching for Information-Centric Networking With Partitioning and Hash-Routing," in IEEE/ACM Transactions on Networking, vol. 24, no. 5, pp. 2742-2755, October 2016.

[24] Z. Liu et al., "Fast-Start Video Delivery in Future Internet Architectures with Intra-domain Caching," Mob. Netw. Appl. 22, 1 (February 2017), 98-112.

[25] Ravi, P. Ramanathan, and K. M. Sivalingam, "Integrated network coding and caching in information-centric networks: revisiting pervasive caching in the ICN framework," Photonic Network Communications, 2015.

[26] W. Quan, Y. Liu, X. Jiang, and J. Guan, "Intelligent popularity-aware content caching and retrieving in highway vehicular networks," EURASIP Journal on Wireless Communications and Networking, 2016. [Online]. Available: http://dx.doi.org/10.1186/s13638-016-0688-z

[27] M. Hajimirsadeghi, N. B. Mandayam and A. Reznik, "Joint Caching and Pricing Strategies for Information Centric Networks," 2015 IEEE Global Communications Conference (GLOBECOM), San Diego, CA, 2015, pp. 1-6.

[28] M. Hajimirsadeghi, S. Member, and N. B. Mandayam, "Joint Caching and Pricing Strategies for Popular Content in Information Centric Networks," vol. 8716, no. c, 2017.

[29] Y. Thomas, C. Tsilopoulos, G. Xylomenos, and G. C. Polyzos, "Object-oriented Packet Caching for ICN," In Proceedings of the 2nd ACM Conference on Information-Centric Networking (ACM-ICN '15). ACM, New York, NY, USA, 2015, pp. 89-98

[30] G. Zheng and V. Friderikos, "Optimal proactive cache management in mobile networks," 2016 IEEE International Conference on Communications (ICC), Kuala Lumpur, 2016, pp. 1-6.

[31] N. Abani, G. Farhadi, A. Ito and M. Gerla, "Popularity-based partial caching for Information Centric Networks," 2016 Mediterranean Ad Hoc Networking Workshop (Med-Hoc-Net), Vilanova i la Geltru, 2016, pp. 1-8.

[32] J. Li, H. Wu, B. Liu, and Z. Fang, "RBC-CC : RBC-Based Cascade Caching Scheme for Content-Centric Networking," Journal of Network and Systems Management, 2016.

[33] W. Li, S. M. A. Oteafy, and H. S. Hassanein, "StreamCache : Popularity-based Caching for Adaptive Streaming over Information-Centric Net-works," 2016.

[34] B. Panigrahi, S. Shailendra, H. K. Rath, A. Simha, and T. C. Services, "Universal Caching Model and Markov-based Cache Analysis for Information Centric Networks," 2014, pp. 1–6.

[35] Z. Liu, Y. Ji, X. Jiang, and Y. Tanaka, "User-behavior Driven Video Caching in Content Centric Network," In Proceedings of the 3rd ACM Conference on Information-Centric Networking (ACM-ICN '16). ACM, New York, NY, USA, 2016, pp. 197-198.

[36] V. Cisco, "Forecast and methodology, 2015-2020."

[37] G. Carofiglio, V. Gehlen, and D. Perino, "Experimental evaluation of memory management in content-centric networking," in Communications (ICC), 2011 IEEE International Conference on. IEEE, 2011, pp. 1–6.

[38] Psaras, W. K. Chai, and G. Pavlou, "Probabilistic in-network caching for information-centric networks," in Proceedings of the second edition of the ICN workshop on Information-centric networking. ACM, 2012, pp. 55–60.

[39] N. Laoutaris, H. Che, and I. Stavrakakis, "The lcd interconnection of lru caches and its analysis," Performance Evaluation, vol. 63, no. 7, 2006, pp. 609–634.

[40] C. Fricker, P. Robert, J. Roberts, and N. Sbihi, "Impact of traffic mix on caching performance in a content-centric network," in Computer Communications Workshops (INFOCOM WKSHPS), 2012 IEEE Conference on. IEEE, 2012, pp. 310–315.

[41] D. M. Powers, "Applications and explanations of zipf's law," in Proceedings of the joint conferences on new methods in language processing and computational natural language learning. Association for Computational Linguistics, 1998, pp. 151–160.

[42] T. R. Henderson, M. Lacage, G. F. Riley, C. Dowell, and J. Kopena, "Network simulations with the ns-3 simulator," SIGCOMM demonstration, vol. 14, 2008.

[43] R. Chiocchetti, D. Rossi, and G. Rossini, "ccnsim: An highly scalable ccn simulator," in Communications (ICC), 2013 IEEE International Conference on. IEEE, 2013, pp. 2309–2314.

[44] S. Mastorakis, A. Afanasyev, I. Moiseenko, and L. Zhang, "ndnsim 2.0: A new version of the ndn simulator for ns-3," NDN, Technical Report NDN-0028, 2015.

[45] L. Saino, I. Psaras, and G. Pavlou, "Icarus: a caching simulator for information centric networking (icn)," in Proceedings of the 7th International ICST Conference on Simulation Tools and Techniques. ICST (Institute for Computer Sciences, Social-Informatics and Telecommunications Engineering), 2014, pp. 66–75.

Survey on Microservice Architecture - Security, Privacy and Standardization on Cloud Computing Environment

Washington Henrique Carvalho Almeida, Luciano de Aguiar Monteiro, Raphael Rodrigues Hazin, Anderson Cavalcanti de Lima and Felipe Silva Ferraz
Center of Advanced Studies and Systems of Recife
Recife, Brazil
E-mail: {washington.hc.almeida, lucianoaguiarthe, raphaelhazin, andclima}@gmail.com
E-mail: {fsf}@cesar.org.br

Abstract — **Microservices have been adopted as a natural solution for the replacement of monolithic systems. Some technologies and standards have been adopted for the development of microservices in the cloud environment; API and REST have been adopted on a large scale for their implementation. The purpose of the present work is to carry out a bibliographic survey on the microservice architecture focusing mainly on security, privacy and standardization aspects on cloud computing environments. This paper presents a bundle of elements that must be considered for the construction of solutions based on microservices.**

Keywords-Microservice; Cloud; Architecture; API; REST

I. INTRODUCTION

Migration of the monolithic architecture to the cloud has been a major problem. In this paper a research was carried out on the topic of microservices that have been adopted as a natural solution in the replacement of monolithic systems. The main question lies in how its architecture has been used and issues of security and privacy keys in a cloud computing environment. The motivation for this collection was the fact that more and more microservices have been found as a solution for applications in the cloud. Cloud computing provides a centralized pool of configurable computing resources and computing outsourcing mechanisms that enable different computing services to different people in a way similar to utility-based systems, such as electricity, water, and sewage.

For the recent advances of cloud computing technologies, the use of microservices on applications has been more widely addressed due to the rich set of features in such architecture. These applications can be deployed on clouds that make users use it at low cost, threshold, and risk. Therefore, their practical use in business can be expected as a trend for the next generation of business applications [1].

Scaling monolithic applications is a challenge because they commonly offer a lot of services. Some of them are more popular than others. If popular services need to be scaled because they are highly demanded, the whole set of services will also be scaled at the same time, which implies that unpopular services will consume a large amount of server resources even when they are not going to be used [2].

The architecture based on microservices has emerged to simplify this reality and are a natural evolution to application models.

Microservices are a software oriented entity, which have the following features [3]:

Isolation from other microservices, as well as from the execution environment based on a virtualized container;

Autonomy – microservices can be deployed, destroyed, moved or duplicated independently. Thus, microservices cannot be bound to any local resource because microservice environment can create more than one instance of the same microservice;

Open and standardized interface that describes all specific goals with effectiveness, efficiency and available communication methods (either API or GUI);

Microservice is fine-grained – each microservice should handle its own task.

The microservice architecture is a cloud application design pattern that implies that the application is divided into a number of small independent services, each of which is responsible for implementing a certain feature, as noted in Figure 1.

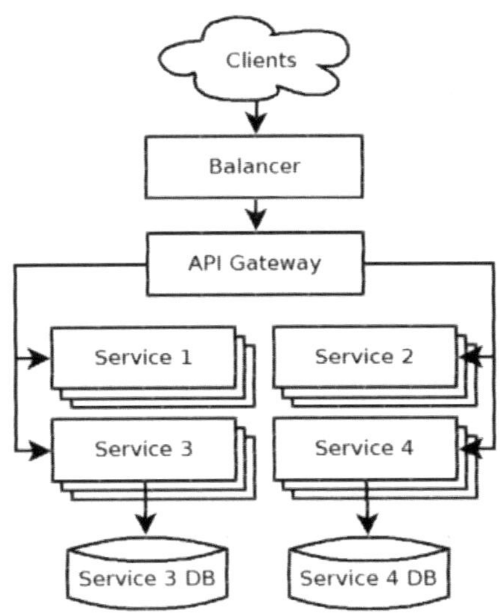

Figure 1. Microservice system architecture[3].

Microservices can be considered meta-processes in a Meta operating system (OS); they are independent, they can communicate with each other using messages and they can be duplicated, suspended or moved to any computational resource and so on [3].

The remainder of this article is structured as follows: Section II introduces the architecture of implemented microservices. Section III presents security in the cloud computing environment and Section IV shows the privacy model adopted in the cloud applications for microservices. In Section V, we present the standards of cloud environment and then conclude and summarize all the results of that exercise in Section VI.

II. MICROSERVICE ARCHITECTURE

The microservice architecture has become a dominant architectural style choice in the service oriented software industry. Microservice is a style of architecture that puts the emphasis on dividing the system into small and lightweight services that are purposely built to perform a very cohesive business function, and is an evolution of the traditional service oriented architecture style [4].

The idea of splitting an application into a set of smaller and interconnected services (microservice) is currently getting many interests from application developers and service providers (e.g., Amazon [5][6], Netflix [7][8], eBay [9][10]).

A Microservice based architecture has a pattern for development of distributed applications, where the application is composed of a number of smaller "independent" components; these components are small applications in themselves [11].

A microservice normally comprises three layers as a typical 3-tiered application [12], consisting of an interface layer [13], a business logic layer [9] and a data persistence layer, but within a much smaller bounded context. This sets a broad scope of the technical capabilities that a microservice could possess. However, not every microservice provides all capabilities. This would vary depending on how the function provided is meant to be consumed. For example, a microservice used primarily by providers of API's would have a communications interface layer, business logic and data persistence layers but not necessarily have user interfaces [11].

We are considering a reference architecture model of microservices, demonstrating the main components and elements of this standard [11]. Table 1 presents a comparison between monolithic architecture and microservice architecture

TABLE I. COMPARING MONOLITHIC AND MICROSERVICE ARCHITECTURE [14]

Category	Monolithic Architecture	Microservice Architecture
Code	A single code base for the entire application.	Multiple code bases. Each microservice has its own code base.
Understandability	Often confusing and hard to maintain.	Much better readability and much easier to maintain.
Deployment	Complex deployments with maintenance windows and schedules downtimes.	Simple deployment as each microservice can be deployed individually, with minimal if not zero downtime.
Language	Typically, entirely developed in one programing language.	Each microservice can be developed in a different programing language.
Scaling	Requires you to scale the entire application even though bottlenecks are localized.	Enables you to scale bottle-necked services without scaling the entire application.

In this paper, we will cover the following main elements:

A. *API Proxy*

To "de-couple" the microservice from its consumers, this proxy pattern is applied at the microservice interface level, regardless of the "API proxy" component. Organizations will provide API's to different consumers, some of whom are within and others outside the enterprise. These microservices would differ in service level agreements (SLA), security requirements, access levels, etc [11].

B. *Enterprise API Registry*

The "discovery" requirements of the microservices are met through the use of the API registry service. Its purpose is to make the interfaces exposed by the microservice visible to consumers of the services both within and outside the enterprise. An "Enterprise API registry" is a shared component across the enterprise, whose location must be well known and accessible. Its information content is published in a standard format, information should be in consistent and human readable format, and must have controlled access. It must have search and retrieval capabilities to allow users to look up details on available API specifications at design time [11].

C. *Enterprise Microservice Repository*

The "enterprise microservice repository" would be a shared repository for storing information about microservices. It provides information such as microservice lifecycle status, versions, business and development ownership, detailed information like its purpose, how it achieves the purpose, tools, technologies, architecture, the service it provides, any API's it consumes, data persisted and queried and any specific non-functional requirements. In the absence of well-defined repository standards, the enterprise must define its own standard specification artefacts for microservices [5].

These elements are fundamental to the organized implementation of microservices and have been considered in this survey.

III. SECURITY ON CLOUD COMPUTING

Switching from a monolithic or centralized architecture to a decentralized architecture requires some care. In the past, security was focused on a single point [15], responsible for receiving all service requests. In the microservice-based architecture, the resources are offered through several points of access that interconnect each other, forming a unique solution.

Monolithic security services are relatively easier to implement than microservices. Monolithic services have a clear boundary and encapsulate their intercommunications. This will obscure security vulnerabilities [16][17] within the inner layers of the system. A microservice also encapsulates its communications. Both microservices and services are based upon clear requirements.

In a microservice-based system a simple routine completion requires the microservices to communicate with each other over network, for example. This will expose more data and information (endpoints) about the system and thus it expands the attack surface [8]. Some care must be taken in the communication between other services in the same network, and this is one of the major challenges [13][15][18] in this approach.

The organization of teams for the development of a system based on microservices are generally subdivided into teams and services, and these teams are generally responsible for the implementation and delivery of services. For this type of implementation, the teams have to be aligned in the purposes of the microservices and the interconnection between them, thus also synchronizing the protocol [19] used to carry out the communication, thus respecting a standard for access protection or improper interception. Defining the way services are interconnected and interacting is the key point of security [20].

The security challenge brought by such network complexity is the ever-increasing difficulty in debugging, monitoring, auditing and forensic analysis of the entire application [21]. Since microservices are often deployed in a cloud that the application owners do not control, it is difficult for them to construct a global view of the entire application [10].

In microservice architecture, an application is essentially a collection of workflows. These workflows can compose many levels of services, each processing and modifying the data before its final destination. What we need is a way to certify the metadata related to a data stream and manage its validity during time and re-elaboration [22].

Security is a major challenge that must be carefully thought of in microservices architecture. Services communicate with each other in various ways creating a trust relationship. For some systems, it is vital that a user is identified in all the chains of a service communication happening between microservices. OAuth and OAuth2 are well-known solutions that are employed by designers to handle security challenges [4].

Although the microservices are independent and do not cause dependencies among the modules, the biggest challenge nowadays is to guarantee availability [23]. The DevOps movement (set of practices to integrate the software development to IT operations) is currently collaborating with cloud environments and microservice architecture, providing continuous integration from the code compilation to the availability of the test and production environment, making it a facilitator for systems implementation utilizing microservices.

Ensuring the availability of services is presented as a security requirement facilitated by the use of the microservice architecture. This approach usually works by fragmenting the entire solution in smaller pieces [24]. Considering that these fragments are parts of the code with specific functions (microservices), in the event of a fragment failure, it would not result in the unavailability of all system resources. Availability has some critical points as they are bound to be observed such as: implementing software versions, software crash recovery, invasions, unavailability of infra features beyond points.

In a microservice architecture, it is typical for many instances of a particular service to be running at any one time and for these instances to stop and start over time [25]. The problem of service discovery is to enable service consumers to locate service providers in real time to facilitate communication [26]. Docker Containers have been gaining a lot of hard work because of their agility and ease of making new services available [23]. The containers allow the microservices to be packaged [27] and available next to their dependencies in a single image, thus facilitating the availability of the service in a timely manner, minimizing downtime. This mode is called code portability [28]. In the context of microservices, the use of docker containers for service delivery has resulted in benefits under various aspects, such as: automation, independence, portability and security, especially when considering ease of management, creation and continuous integration of environments systems offered by the docker platform. In Docker, each container consists of only the application and the dependencies that the application needs to run, ideally no more and no less [28].

IV. PRIVACY MODEL

Privacy has been a barrier to adoption of cloud computing [24][29]. The migration to microservices has helped overcome this obstacle due to the scale gains proposed in this architecture.

In general, privacy refers the condition or state of hiding the presence or view [30]. There is a need to attain this state in the places where confidential things are used such as data and files. In cloud data storage privacy is needed to attain the data, user identity and controls [31]

The exchange of sensitive data is intense in large-scale scenarios of cloud computing, with several federations, where multiple Identity Providers (IdP) and Service Providers (SP) work together to provide services. Therefore, identity management should provide models and privacy mechanisms in order to manage the sensitive data of its users [15].

Cloud service provides various options to the business customers to choose the level of protection needed for their data. The most common of these approaches is encryption. The customer chooses the type of encryption that they prefer and store the encryption key in a safe place under their control [19].

To ensure privacy, a well referenced model is used. This model is presented in Figure 2.

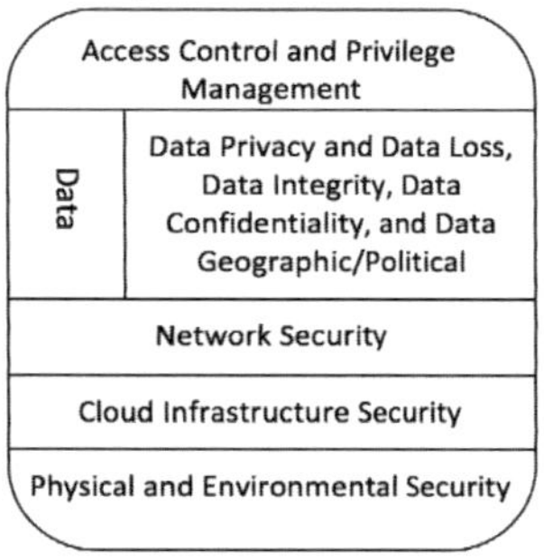

Figure 2. Cloud security and privacy model [29].

According to the proposed model in [29], a secure and private cloud model is divided into five layers: Physical and Environmental Security, Cloud Infrastructure Security, Network Security, Data and Access Control and Privilege Management.

1. *Physical and Environmental Security*
   Layer of policies adopted with the objective of protecting physical access to the cloud provider [5].
2. *Cloud Infrastructure Security*
   Addresses issues with cloud infrastructure security, but specifically with the virtualization environment [32].
3. *Network Security*
   Specifies the medium to which the end user connects to the cloud, comprising browsers and their connection [9].
4. *Data*
   Layer covers data privacy, integrity, confidentiality, and geographic location [22].
5. *Access Control and Privilege Management*
   Policies and processes used by cloud services provider to ensure that only the users granted appropriate privileges can use or modify data. It includes identification, authentication [33] and authorization issues [29].

V. MICROSERVICE STANDARDS AND SOLUTIONS

In the centralized structure, the standardization becomes almost a natural way, but in the implementation of microservices this philosophy changes.

Teams building microservices prefer a different approach to standards too. Rather than using a set of defined standards, written down somewhere on paper, they prefer the idea of producing useful tools that other developers can use to solve similar problems to the ones they are facing. These tools are usually harvested from implementations and shared with a wider group, sometimes, but not exclusively, using a git and github has become the de facto version control system of choice. Open source practices are becoming more and more common in-house [34].

A microservice is an application on its own to perform the functions required. It evolves independently and can choose its own architecture, technology, platform, and can be managed, deployed and scaled independently with its own release lifecycle and development methodology. This approach takes away the construct of the SOA and ESB and the accompanying challenges by making "smart endpoints" and treating the intermediate layers as network resources whose function is that of data transfer [11].

The applications that expose interfaces that can be used by other applications to interact with are defined as "application programming interfaces" (API) [5]. Microservice API's which are built using internet communication protocols like HTTP, adhere to open standards like REST [35][36] and SOAP [2] and use data exchange technologies like XML [18] and JSON [5].

Applications developed in a monolithic architecture perform multiple functions such as providing address validation, product catalogue, customer credit check, etc. When using the microservice based architecture pattern, applications are created for specific functions, such as address validation, customer credit check and online ordering; these applications are cobbled together to provide the entire capability for the proposed service. The approach to application development based on microservice architecture addresses the challenges of "monolithic" application and services [11].

In the research undertaken in this paper, the microservices are implemented and documented as follows:

A. *Architectural views/diagrams* [4]
   - UML
   - Standard modeling languages, e.g. RAML and YAML.
   - Specifically designed modeling languages, e.g. CAMLE.
   - Standard specification languages, e.g. Javascript (Node.js), JSON and Ruby.
   - Specifically designed specification languages, e.g. Jolie.
   - Pseudocode for algorithms.

B. *REST*
   REpresentational State Transfer (REST) consisting of a set of architectural principles that, when followed, allows a well-defined interface design to be created. Applications that use REST principles are called RESTFul. REST [10][18][36][37] is often applied to provide services to other services (web services) and to the same full use of messages. To better understand the architectural style, it is

important to highlight three important concepts: (i) feature; (ii) operations and (iii) representations. Resource is any information that is made available to customers through a unique identifier (URI). We can also define resource as being the source of representations. The representations are a set of data that explains the state of the requested resource. URIs must have a notation pattern, be descriptive, and have a previously defined hierarchy. The same resource can be identified by one or more URIs, but a URI [38] [39] identifies only one resource.

C. *API*

Application Program Interface (API) are (a) basic authentication, including API user registration with strong password protection, (b) modern security mechanisms such as message level security, web signature and web encryption, and (c) security mechanism within API and its backend services as a third security factor such as token based API for backend authentication, public key infrastructure and transport layer handshake protocol [13].

REST APIs [7] are developed in many technologies and microservices developed using different types of programing languages (Java, .NET, PHP, Ruby, Phyton, Scala, NodeJs,etc.) and persistent technologies (SQL, No-SQL, etc.) [2][28]. They can be managed and exposed to web clients, who can then access the microservices and receive their responses through a "livequery" mechanism whereby updates to database data are instantly communicated to subscribing clients [18]. Figure 3 best presents categories of practices for designing REST-based web services.

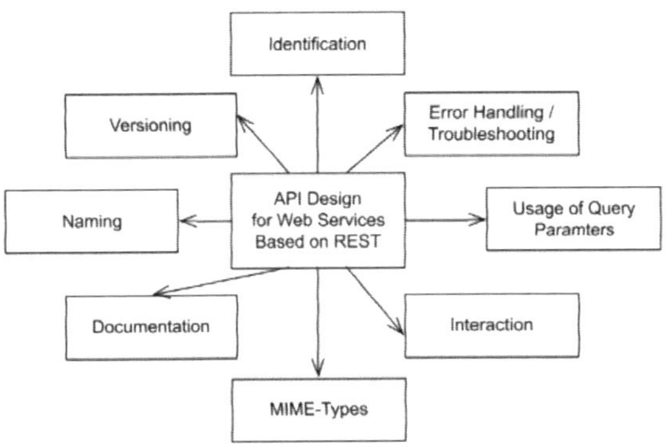

Figure 3. Categories of best practices for designing REST-based web services [40].

NoSQL database are used in these implementations [18][41][42][43]. The NoSQL nature of the database is essential for providing the scaling, sharding and replication functionality expected from modern architectures, as well as to better support hierarchical data required for collaborative document editing [18].

The popularity of the architecture based on microservices is evident from the report by the popular jobs portal *indeed.com,* in which the number of job openings on microservices-related technologies, such as JSON [10][20][39] and REST [2][18][36] has grown more than 100 times in the last six years, whereas jobs in similar technology areas like SOAP and XML have remained nearly identical [10].

Solutions for microservices seek to implement simple algorithms that meet specific needs with the elements presented in this section.

VI. Conclusions and Future Work

Microservice-based architecture has been a growing choice as an architectural style for software development. In this architectural style, the services provided by software solutions are divided into smaller parts and focused on the specific service of some functionalities. The approach of developing microservices with the construction of smaller software components has a number of advantages over the traditional monolithic architecture, such as increasing the resilience of the software implemented as a microservice and the ease of scaling the solution implemented through the microservices.

The development of software using the microservice-based architecture comprises important aspects that must be observed in order to obtain good results. The objective of this article is to present the elements that should be considered for the development of solutions based on microservices, describing how the architecture based on microservices is defined, identifying the elements related to their implementation in the cloud computing environment, explaining the privacy model applicable and relating the elements that integrate the standards and solutions linked to the architecture based on microservices.

Future work can be developed to present case studies demonstrating the implementation of the microservice architecture in a cloud computing environment with the use of docker containers for its construction.

References

[1] J. Lin, L. Chaoyu, and S. Huang, "Migrating Web Applications to Clouds with Microservices Architectures," *Int. Conf. Appl. Syst. Innov.*, pp. 1–4, 2016.

[2] M. Villamizar and et al, "Evaluating the Monolithic and the Microservice Architecture Pattern to Deploy Web Applications in the Cloud Evaluando el Patrón de Arquitectura Monolítica y de Micro Servicios Para Desplegar Aplicaciones en la Nube," *10th Comput. Colomb. Conf.*, pp. 583–590, 2015.

[3] D. I. Savchenko, G. I. Radchenko, and O. Taipale, "Microservices validation: Mjolnirr platform case study," *2015 38th Int. Conv. Inf. Commun. Technol. Electron. Microelectron. MIPRO 2015 - Proc.*, no. May, pp. 235–240, 2015.

[4] N. Alshuqayran, N. Ali, and R. Evans, "A systematic mapping study in microservice architecture," *Proc. - 2016 IEEE 9th Int. Conf. Serv. Comput. Appl. SOCA 2016*, pp. 44–51, 2016.

[5] A. Krylovskiy, M. Jahn, and E. Patti, "Designing a Smart City Internet of Things Platform with Microservice Architecture," *Proc. - 2015 Int. Conf. Futur. Internet Things Cloud, FiCloud 2015 2015 Int. Conf. Open Big Data, OBD 2015*, pp. 25–30, 2015.

[6] H. Khazaei, C. Barna, N. Beigi-Mohammadi, and M. Litoiu, "Efficiency analysis of provisioning microservices," *Proc. Int. Conf. Cloud Comput. Technol. Sci. CloudCom*, pp. 261–268, 2017.

[7] R. Heinrich *et al.*, "Performance Engineering for Microservices: Research Challenges and Directions," *Proc. 8th ACM/SPEC Int. Conf. Perform. Eng. Companion*, pp. 223–226, 2017.

[8] M. Ahmadvand and A. Ibrahim, "Requirements reconciliation for scalable and secure microservice (de)composition," *Proc. - 2016 IEEE 24th Int. Requir. Eng. Conf. Work. REW 2016*, pp. 68–73, 2017.

[9] T. Q. Thanh, S. Covaci, T. Magedanz, P. Gouvas, and A. Zafeiropoulos, "Embedding security and privacy into the development and operation of cloud applications and services," *2016 17th Int. Telecommun. Netw. Strateg. Plan. Symp.*, pp. 31–36, 2016.

[10] Y. Sun, S. Nanda, and T. Jaeger, "Security-as-a-service for microservices-based cloud applications," *Proc. - IEEE 7th Int. Conf. Cloud Comput. Technol. Sci. CloudCom 2015*, pp. 50–57, 2016.

[11] Yale Yu, H. Silveira, and M. Sundaram, "A microservice based reference architecture model in the context of enterprise architecture," *2016 IEEE Adv. Inf. Manag. Commun. Electron. Autom. Control Conf.*, pp. 1856–1860, 2016.

[12] J. Rufino, M. Alam, J. Ferreira, A. Rehman, and K. F. Tsang, "Orchestration of Containerized Microservices for IIoT using Docker," pp. 1532–1536, 2017.

[13] M. B. Mollah, M. A. K. Azad, and A. Vasilakos, "Security and privacy challenges in mobile cloud computing: Survey and way ahead," *J. Netw. Comput. Appl.*, vol. 84, pp. 38–54, 2017.

[14] K. Bakshi, "Microservices-based software architecture and approaches," *IEEE Aerosp. Conf. Proc.*, 2017.

[15] J. Werner, C. M. Westphall, and C. B. Westphall, "Cloud identity management: A survey on privacy strategies," *Comput. Networks*, vol. 122, pp. 29–42, 2017.

[16] I. Khalil, A. Khreishah, and M. Azeem, "Cloud Computing Security: A Survey," *Computers*, vol. 3, no. 1, pp. 1–35, 2014.

[17] C. Saravanakumar and C. Arun, "Survey on interoperability, security, trust, privacy standardization of cloud computing," *Proc. 2014 Int. Conf. Contemp. Comput. Informatics, IC3I 2014*, pp. 977–982, 2014.

[18] C. Gadea, M. Trifan, D. Ionescu, and B. Ionescu, "A reference architecture for real-time microservice API consumption," *Proc. 3rd Work. CrossCloud Infrastructures Platforms - CrossCloud '16*, pp. 1–6, 2016.

[19] S. Srinivasan, "Data privacy concerns involving cloud," *2016 11th Int. Conf. Internet Technol. Secur. Trans. ICITST 2016*, pp. 53–56, 2017.

[20] A. Ciuffoletti, "Automated Deployment of a Microservice-based Monitoring Infrastructure," *Procedia Comput. Sci.*, vol. 68, pp. 163–172, 2015.

[21] M. Fazio, A. Celesti, R. Ranjan, C. Liu, L. Chen, and M. Villari, "Open Issues in Scheduling Microservices in the Cloud," *IEEE Cloud Comput.*, vol. 3, no. 5, pp. 81–88, 2016.

[22] F. Callegati, S. Giallorenzo, A. Melis, and M. Prandini, "Data security issues in MaaS-enabling platforms," *2016 IEEE 2nd Int. Forum Res. Technol. Soc. Ind. Leveraging a Better Tomorrow, RTSI 2016*, pp. 0–4, 2016.

[23] H. Kang, M. Le, and S. Tao, "Container and microservice driven design for cloud infrastructure DevOps," *Proc. - 2016 IEEE Int. Conf. Cloud Eng. IC2E 2016 Co-located with 1st IEEE Int. Conf. Internet-of-Things Des. Implementation, IoTDI 2016*, pp. 202–211, 2016.

[24] K. Bao, I. Mauser, S. Kochanneck, H. Xu, and H. Schmeck, "A Microservice Architecture for the Intranet of Things and Energy in Smart Buildings," *Proc. 1st Int. Work. Mashups Things APIs - MOTA '16*, pp. 1–6, 2016.

[25] D. Escobar *et al.*, "Towards the understanding and evolution of monolithic applications as microservices," *Proc. 2016 42nd Lat. Am. Comput. Conf. CLEI 2016*, 2017.

[26] J. Stubbs, W. Moreira, and R. Dooley, "Distributed Systems of Microservices Using Docker and Serfnode," *Proc. - 7th Int. Work. Sci. Gateways, IWSG 2015*, pp. 34–39, 2015.

[27] R. Roostaei and Z. Movahedi, "Mobility and Context-Aware Offloading in Mobile Cloud Computing," *Proc. - 13th IEEE Int. Conf. Ubiquitous Intell. Comput. 13th IEEE Int. Conf. Adv. Trust. Comput. 16th IEEE Int. Conf. Scalable Comput. Commun. IEEE Int.*, pp. 1144–1148, 2017.

[28] D. Jaramillo, D. V. Nguyen, and R. Smart, "Leveraging microservices architecture by using Docker technology," *Conf. Proc. - IEEE SOUTHEASTCON*, vol. 2016–July, pp. 0–4, 2016.

[29] K. El Makkaoui, A. Ezzati, A. Beni-Hssane, and C. Motamed, "Data confidentiality in the world of cloud," *J. Theor. Appl. Inf. Technol.*, vol. 84, no. 3, pp. 305–314, 2016.

[30] C. Perra and S. Member, "A Framework for the Development of Sustainable Urban Mobility Applications," 2016.

[31] M. Thangavel, P. Varalakshmi, and S. Sridhar, "An analysis of privacy preservation schemes in cloud computing," *Proc. 2nd IEEE Int. Conf. Eng. Technol. ICETECH 2016*, no. March, pp. 146–151, 2016.

[32] H. Gebre-amlak, S. Lee, A. M. A. Jabbari, Y. Chen, and B. Choi, "MIST : Mobility-Inspired SofTware-Defined Fog System," 2017.

[33] R. H. Steinegger, D. Deckers, P. Giessler, and S. Abeck, "Risk-based authenticator for web applications," *Proc. 21st Eur. Conf. Pattern Lang. Programs - Eur. '16*, no. February 2017, pp. 1–11, 2016.

[34] J. Fowler, Marthin; Lewis, "Microservices: a definition of this new architectural term," *Microservices:a definition of this new architectural term*, 2014. [Online]. Available: https://martinfowler.com/articles/microservices.ml. [Accessed: 07-May-2017].

[35] S. Yamamoto, S. Matsumoto, and M. Nakamura, "Using cloud technologies for large-scale house data in smart city," *CloudCom 2012 - Proc. 2012 4th IEEE Int. Conf. Cloud Comput. Technol. Sci.*, pp. 141–148, 2012.

[36] J. Bogner and A. Zimmermann, "Towards Integrating Microservices with Adaptable Enterprise Architecture," *Proc. - IEEE Int. Enterp. Distrib. Object Comput. Work. EDOCW*, vol. 2016–Septe, pp. 158–163, 2016.

[37] D. Guo, W. Wang, G. Zeng, and Z. Wei, "Microservices architecture based cloudware deployment platform for service computing," *Proc. - 2016 IEEE Symp. Serv. Syst. Eng. SOSE 2016*, pp. 358–364, 2016.

[38] P. Marchetta, E. Natale, A. Pescape, A. Salvi, and S. Santini, "A map-based platform for smart mobility services," *Proc. - IEEE Symp. Comput. Commun.*, vol. 2016–Febru, pp. 19–24, 2016.

[39] A. de Camargo, I. Salvadori, R. dos S. Mello, and F. Siqueira, "An architecture to automate performance tests on microservices," *Proc. 18th Int. Conf. Inf. Integr. Web-based Appl. Serv. - iiWAS '16*, pp. 422–429, 2016.

[40] P. Giessler, R. Steinegger, S. Abeck, and M. Gebhart, "Checklist for the API Design of Web Services based on REST," vol. 9, no. 3, pp. 41–51, 2016.

[41] A. Gueidi, H. Gharsellaoui, and S. Ben Ahmed, "A NoSQL-based Approach for Real-Time Managing of Embedded Data Bases," *Proc. - 2016 World Symp. Comput. Appl. Res. WSCAR 2016*, pp. 110–115, 2016.

[42] T. I. Damaiyanti, A. Imawan, and J. Kwon, "Extracting trends of traffic congestion using a NoSQL database," *Proc. - 4th IEEE Int. Conf. Big Data Cloud Comput. BDCloud 2014 with 7th IEEE Int. Conf. Soc. Comput. Networking, Soc. 2014 4th Int. Conf.*

Sustain. Comput. C, pp. 209–213, 2015.

[43] R. Simmonds, P. Watson, and J. Halliday, "Antares: A Scalable, Real-Time, Fault Tolerant Data Store for Spatial Analysis," *Proc. - 2015 IEEE World Congr. Serv. Serv. 2015*, pp. 105–112, 2015.

Function-as-a-Service X Platform-as-a-Service: Towards a Comparative Study on FaaS and PaaS

Lucas F. Albuquerque Jr.[1,2], Felipe Silva Ferraz[3], Rodrigo F. A. P. Oliveira[1], and Sergio M. L. Galdino[1]

[1]Polytechnic School of Pernambuco, University of Pernambuco, Recife, Brazil
Email: {lfaj,rfapo}@ecomp.poli.br, sergio.galdino@ieee.org
[2]IFPE - Federal Institute of Technology, Palmares, Brazil
Email: lucasjr@palmares.ifpe.edu.br
[3]Recife Center for Advanced Studies and Systems (CESAR), Recife, Brazil
Email: fsf@cesar.org.br

Abstract—**The adoption of cloud computing for service delivery is a market trend and attracts customers seeking elastic, scalable, and cost-effective infrastructures. Instance-based models, such as Platform-as-a-Service (PaaS), are being used to support mobile applications. Despite the management facilities, the PaaS receives criticism for the inefficient use of resources. Studies point to a new model, known as Function-as-a-Service (FaaS), as an alternative that would offer a more efficient use of resources and lower costs. The present work has proposed to perform a comparative evaluation between FaaS and PaaS service delivery models regarding performance, scalability and costs issues in support of mobile applications based on microservices. The conclusions obtained showed that FaaS presented an equivalent performance, a more efficient scalability and the costs influenced by workload type.**

Keywords–Cloud Computing; FaaS; PaaS; Serverless; Mobile; Microservices

I. Introduction

The term virtualization is associated with the abstraction of computational resources for the purpose of optimizing their use, allowing users and applications to transparently share resources [1]. Thus, with virtualization of the infrastructure, servers become a mere abstraction of resources, being more easily managed [2]. Virtualization technologies form the basis of what we now know as cloud computing, which is the provision of information or computing resources as a service accessible through the network [3]. Cloud models, such as Infrastructure-as-a-Service(IaaS) and Platform-as-a-Service (PaaS) use the concept of instance to define the amount of computational resources allocated to carry out their tasks.

In parallel to the advances related to cloud computing, the dissemination of mobile devices led to the emergence of the Mobile Cloud Computing (MCC) [4] concept, which is the use of cloud computing by mobile devices for service delivery anytime, anywhere, managing a large volume of data from a variety of device platforms. To meet performance and scalability requirements in mobile applications, microservice architectures have emerged to enable the development of decoupled applications in separate, scalable and portable modules that communicate through common protocols [5].

Considering mobile application support, PaaS model has been used as the cloud computing alternative for many microservices applications [6]. One of the advantages of PaaS would be its independence from operational issues, allowing the customer to focus on code development. However, the PaaS model is criticized for being a instance-based model, requiring pre-allocating resources, increasing costs for certain types of workloads [7]. In this context, the Function-as-a-Service (FaaS) model, commercially known as Serverless Computing, has been cited as an alternative model for meeting the requirements of mobile applications in microservices [8], offering a scalable, on-demand infrastructure that operates in response to events, adopting a granular demand-based billing model.

FaaS has been cited in several studies as a computational model with potential to meet many of the challenges of mobile computing, as an alternative to the PaaS model. Works such as [9]–[13] point out that due to platform variability, data volume and temporal data characteristics of MCCs, event-based models like FaaS, would be an alternative model in support of mobile devices, Internet of Things (IoT), real-time processing, artificial intelligence, among others. However, as a newly proposed model, many questions remain open about the benefits of using and applying FaaS model.

Considering the several open questions related to the FaaS models, this paper presents a comparative analysis between the PaaS and FaaS models in the mobile application support, as well as a performance and scalability evaluation between these two models. Finally, the paper also proposes to present a cost comparison between the PaaS and FaaS models from a case study based on a geolocation microservices-based application.

This paper is structured as follows. In Section 2, we introduce the basic idea behind FaaS (Function-as-a-Service) and present a comparative analysis to PaaS. In Section 3, we discuss the experiment setup and test plan performed. In Section 4, we discuss the findings, analyzing the performance, scalability results (Section 4.1) and costs (Section 4.2). Section 5 discusses related research, and finally Section 6 concludes the paper with lessons learned and an outlook on future work.

II. Function-as-a-Service

Serverless computing was initially associated with two scenarios:

- Applications that depend on external services for their operation, having their business rules concentrated on the client side. This development model was initially called Backend-as-a-Service (BaaS) and included the

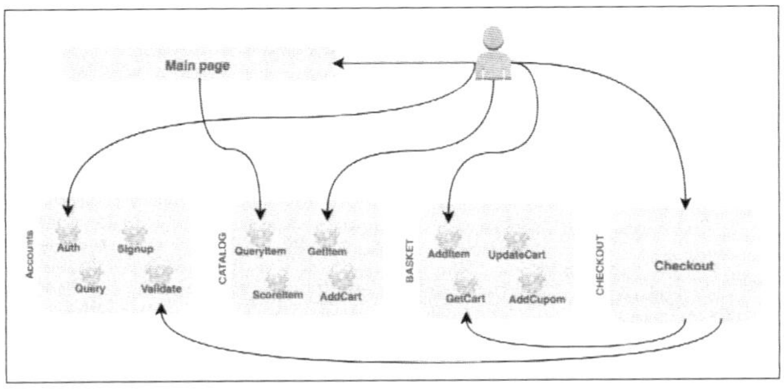

Figure 1. A Faasified application where each service is decomposed into functions that can be performed or escalated independently.

use of external services as databases, authentication services, messaging services, among others [14].

- Applications whose business rules are located in the cloud, running on demand only, in response to events and in an ephemeral way (no relation between events). This approach is more recent and usually referred as FaaS (Function-as-a-Service) or Event-Driven Computing [?].

The BaaS model was an important driver for both cloud computing and popularization of mobile devices, but it did carry with it some complications. Business rules on the client side were making it difficult to update and deploy new features as well as reverse engineering risks. In FaaS, business rules can be server-centric or divided between the server and the client, and the application is decomposed into small, specific, well-defined tasks, called functions. Each executed function is treated as an ephemeral event (independent and stateless) and its lifetime is the same as the task being executed. The client has an environment that responds to events, rather than dedicated full-time infrastructure [8].

FaaS enables the decomposition of service in micro-functions, which can be performed and scaled independently, introducing the concept of nanoservices [15]. Another concept introduced by FaaS is related to the transformation process of monolithic or microservice applications to functions (Figure 1), process known as FaaSification [16] [17].

Studies that have already been carried out, place FaaS as a variant of the PaaS model, or a type of specialized PaaS [6], but do not present in a consolidated form the characteristics of each of the models. From Table I it is possible to observe the main differences that can be pointed out in relation to the PaaS and FaaS models considering several aspects.

III. Experimentation

The purpose of this section is to present the environment used to perform the experiments (Subsection III-A) and the results obtained (Subsection III-B). At the end of the Section, performance, scalability and cost analyzes will also be presented for the scenarios evaluated (Subsections III-C and III-D, respectively).

A. *Experiment Setup*

For the experiments, we developed an application using the architecture based on microservices (Figure 2) composed

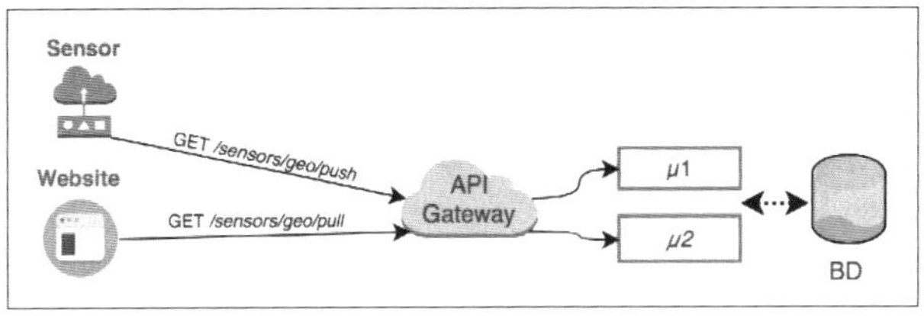

Figure 2. Diagram of the microservice application for storage and availability of Geolocation data

of two services (µ1 e µ2), responsible for receiving and making available geolocation information collected from mobile devices. The µ1 was responsible for receiving and storing data received through HTTP (Hypertext Transfer Protocol) REST (Representational State Transfer) requests, while µ2 receives requests and returns the results in JSON ((JavaScript Object Notation) format (Figure 2).

To perform the experiments, we use Amazon Web Services (AWS) Elastic Beanstalk as the PaaS environment and AWS Lambda as FaaS solution for running an application developed in Node.JS with MongoDB database as persistence layer. For the tests, the following operations were performed, in three rounds, with an interval of one hour between them:

- **Write** - Write operations targeting µ1 for both environments.
- **Read** - Read operations targeting µ2 for both environments.
- **Write/Read** - Write and read operations for µ1 and µ1 simultaneously, for both environments.

Beyond the one hour interval, upon completion of each round, both environments were destroyed and re-implemented, to ensure that results from previous rounds did not interfere in the results of subsequent rounds.

In order to carry out the performance tests, we use JMeter 3.1 [18] configured in an EC2 *c4.large* instance connected to the same Virtual Private Cloud (VPC) as the environments to be evaluated. The performance tests were executed with the objective of identifying the maximum number of requests supported by each scenario and the scalability efficiency. The tests simulated concurrent requests (threads) that were gradually increased to the limit of 100 users. Tests started with 10 threads and started another 10 every 10 seconds (with ramp-up of 2 Seconds). After reaching 100 requests, the test remained active for 120s, finally being finalized in a controlled way, at a rate of 5 req/sec (Figure 3).

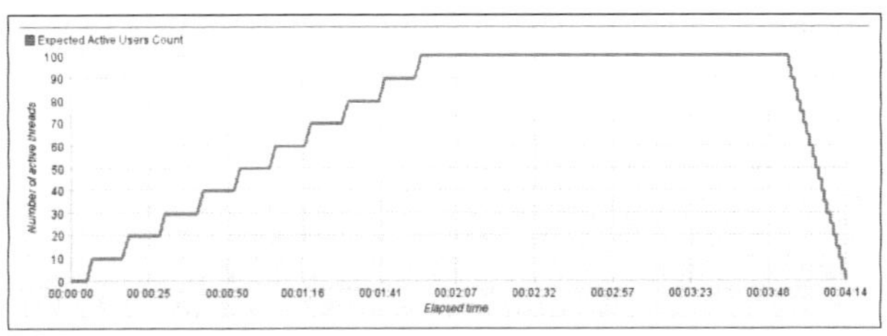

Figure 3. JMeter test plan used during experiments

In test plan, it was defined that the tests would be interrupted if any of the conditions listed below were met:

TABLE I. COMPARATIVE ANALYSIS BETWEEN PAAS AND FAAS MODELS CONSIDERING DIFFERENT ASPECTS.

Aspects	PaaS	FaaS
Coding and Delivery	Focused on services, with development teams being responsible for one or more parts of the application. Service-based delivery.	Focused on tasks (functions) with development teams being responsible for a set of functions. Function-based delivery.
Sizing	Based on the number of instances and resources required by the services. Risks of overestimating or underestimating workloads.	Based on the amount of resources for the execution of each event.
Environment	Fully operated by the provider with possibility of customization by the client.	Fully operated by the provider with no possibility of customization by the client.
Application Maintenance	Interventions in the code need to take into account the entire service.	Interventions in the code need to take into account a specific function. Less code.
Resources Allocation	Pre-allocation of resources with the possibility of allocating additional instances on demand.	No pre-allocated resources. Transparent and on-demand allocation.
Execution	Permanent waiting state, no restrictions on the duration of events.	No waiting state. The function is executed when required. Restriction of maximum duration per event.
Billing	By instantiated resources, whether used or not.	Per event executed. Without commitment.

1) If the latency for any of the requests destined for μ1 and μ2 reaches the Maximum Latency Accepted (MLA) for the test scenario being performed;
2) If any of the tested requests return errored responses to the requests made;
3) If the time planned for the tests is completed, considering the test plan defined on JMeter for μ1 and μ2;

B. Results

The results obtained during the tests will be presented in tables throughout the section. In each table, the rounds in bold with $^{(1)}$ indicate that the test round did not return positive results, representing 100% errors in the samples. The rounds in bold with $^{(2)}$, however, indicate successful samples, but errors were observed during execution that forced premature interruption of threads, as indicated in Section III-A. And, finally, rounds without indication mean that the round was completed successfully, with no observed errors.

For Lambda(A) scenario (Table II), the application executed in the FaaS environment presented errors in 100% of the samples tested, the round being closed due to the requests having exceeded the MLA limit. The Cloudwatch logs showed that the initial requests made to the Application Programming Interface (API) Gateway reached a latency of 14.50 seconds, which extrapolated the MLA for the scenario (5000 ms). This latency observed in the execution of the FaaS functions was an issue already cited in other works, being known as *Cold Start* [19] [20], this behavior is observed in FaaS implementations, and affects functions of eventual use or that present long temporary lapses between the requisitions, causing the deallocation of resources. In order to try to overcome *cold start*, for the Lambda(B) scenario the MLA was increased to 10000ms, but some rounds still showed errors, returning 100% of failures.

For the Lambda(C) scenario (Table III), the MLA was increased to 15000ms, which allowed the *cold start* to be overcome and the samples returned successfully. But despite overcoming *cold start*, the samples presented errors during execution. When analyzing the Lambda logs, it was observed that the errors occurred because the Lambda was taking a lot of time to process the requests, exceeding the default maximum duration for Lambda environment (3 secs), causing timeout errors. In the Lambda (D) scenario, with the memory increased to 256MB, the FaaS environment started to complete the rounds successfully. The results confirmed the existence of a direct proportionality between the allocated memory and CPU resources.

TABLE II. RESULTS FOR THE SCENARIOS (A) AND (B) FOR LAMBDA ENVIRONMENT, SETTING WITH MLA of 5000MS AND 10000MS, RESPECTIVELY.

Operation		Lambda (A)				Lambda (B)			
		128MB			Average Latency (ms)	128MB			Average Latency (ms)
Write	Round	**#1**$^{(1)}$	**#2**$^{(1)}$	**#3**$^{(1)}$	10854	**#1**$^{(1)}$	**#2**$^{(2)}$	**#3**$^{(1)}$	9821
	Suceeded Requests	0	0	0		0$^{(1)}$	202	0$^{(1)}$	
	Latency (ms)	11210	10020	11332		11425	4057	13981	
Read	Round	**#1**$^{(1)}$	**#2**$^{(1)}$	**#3**$^{(1)}$	11915	**#1**$^{(2)}$	**#2**$^{(1)}$	**#3**$^{(1)}$	9501
	Suceeded Requests	0	0	0		162	0	0	
	Latency (ms)	13642	12901	9201		4322	10939	13241	
		Timeout: 5000ms				Timeout: 10000ms			

TABLE III. RESULTS FOR THE SCENARIOS (C) AND (D) FOR LAMBDA ENVIRONMENT, SETTING MEMORY TO 128MB AND 256MB RESPECTIVELY, AND 15000MS OF MLA

Operation		Lambda (C)				Lambda (D)			
		128MB			Average Latency (ms)	256MB			Average Latency (ms)
Write	Round	**#1**$^{(2)}$	**#2**$^{(2)}$	**#3**$^{(2)}$	4134	#1	#2	#3	129
	Suceeded Requests	152	189	177		>10000	>10000	>10000	
	Latency (ms)	4232	4057	4112		139	127	121	
Read	Round	**#1**$^{(2)}$	**#2**$^{(2)}$	**#3**$^{(2)}$	4338	#1	#2	#3	585
	Suceeded Requests	150	150	141		>10000	>10000	>10000	
	Latency (ms)	4322	4292	4401		571	604	580	
		Timeout: 15000ms				Timeout: 15000ms			

In the case of the Beanstalk(A) scenario (Table IV), the same issues observed in Lambda(C) were also observed for this scenario. During the execution of the tests, the PaaS environment started to return errors, caused by the resource saturation of the instance used (*t1.micro*). For the Beanstalk (B) scenario, the multi-instance feature was enabled, allocating more instances on demand, allowing the successful completion of the test rounds.

Considering that the Lambda(D) and Beanstalk(B) scenarios completed the tests successfully, other scenarios were analyzed, adding extra features to the tested environments in order to evaluate the existence of a direct relation between resources and performance considering the proposed application. For the FaaS environment, the scenarios included the increase of memory per function performed and the use of SSD disks. For

TABLE IV. RESULTS FOR THE SCENARIOS (A) AND (B) FOR BEANSTALK ENVIRONMENT, USING SINGLE-INSTANCE AND MULTI-INSTANCE, AND 15000MS OF MLA

Operation		Beanstalk (A)				Beanstalk (B)			
		Single Instance (t1.micro)			Average Latency (ms)	Multi Instance (t1.micro)			Average Latency (ms)
Write	Round	#1[2]	#2[2]	#3[2]	114	#1	#2	#3	162
	Suceeded Requests	>10000	>10000	>10000		>10000	>10000	>10000	
	Latency (ms)	111	96	136		158	183	144	
Read	Round	#1[2]	#2[2]	#3[2]	179	#1	#2	#3	523
	Suceeded Requests	>10000	>10000	>10000		>10000	>10000	>10000	
	Latency (ms)	203	157	177		458	579	531	
		Timeout: 5000ms				Timeout: 15000ms			

the PaaS environment, tests were performed using instances with more resources (2x) and Solid State Disks (SSD) also. The results (Table V) show that, for the tested scenarios, based on the Lambda(D) and Beanstalk(B), latency reduction did not show a proportionality between the addition of resources and performance, depending also on the type of operation (writing or reading).

TABLE V. COMPARISON BETWEEN SEVERAL LAMBDA AND BEANSTALK SCENARIOS SHOWING THE REDUCTION IN LATENCY OBTAINED IN DIFFERENT SCENARIOS

L - 256 - HDD	WRITE	L - 512 - HDD %	L - 256 - SSD %	L - 512 - SSD %
		-69,51	-57,62	-78,30
	READ	L - 512 - HDD %	L - 256 - SSD %	L - 512 - SSD %
		2,74	-48,83	-54,76

L-256-HDD = Lambda - 256MB - HDD
L-512-HDD = Lambda - 512MB - HDD
L-256-SSD = Lambda - 256MB - SSD
L-512-SSD = Lambda - 256MB - SSD

B - T1 - HDD	WRITE	B - T2 - HDD %	B-T1-SSD %	B-T2-SSD %
		-43,51	-25,98	-45,98
	READ	B - T2 - HDD %	B-T1-SSD %	B-T2-SSD %
		64,73	-50,57	-50,89

B-T1 Micro-HDD = Beanstalk - 256MB - HDD
B-T2 Small-HDD = Beanstalk - 512MB - HDD
B-T1 Micro-SSD = Beanstalk - 256MB - SSD
B-T2 Small-SSD = Beanstalk - 256MB - SSD

C. *Performance and Scalability Analysis*

Considering the results for the scenarios tested, some considerations:

- The results showed that the *cold start* observed in FaaS environments affected the performance of applications executed in FaaS environments. This behavior is observed in applications of occasional use or that present long temporary lapses between the requisitions, causing the deallocation of resources and is common to all serverless implementations evaluated.
- The results showed that the allocation of more resources to the tested environments had a positive impact on overall performance. For FaaS environments, there was a direct relationship between the amount of memory and the processing resources allocated by function. However, at the application level, the allocation of more resources was not proportional to the performance gains;
- The results showed that the scalability mechanisms adopted by the PaaS and FaaS environments were efficient in all scenarios evaluated. The scalability of the PaaS environment was based on instance and occured in resource jumps, being less granular. In FaaS environments scalability was linear, occurring based on volume of events.

D. *Cost Analysis*

Some types of applications tend not to benefit from the characteristics of PaaS, especially those that present variations in workload. For these types of applications, which can range from zero requests to thousands in a few seconds, the permanent instantiation of resources is not advantageous, considering that the instances are kept alive and are charged regardless of usage. For applications that present variations in workloads, the FaaS model presents itself as more adequate, considering the dynamic allocation of resources. The economic benefits of serverless computing heavily depend on the execution behavior and volumes of the application workloads.

Considering the scenarios tested, it was possible to extract a cost basis in order to compare infrastructure costs. For comparison purposes, the monthly quantity of requests were used as a metric, since a direct cost comparison was not possible. In order to obtain the number of monthly requests supported by a Beanstalk instance, the number of 10,000 requests per minute was used as a reference, based on the maximum number of requests supported per minute by one instance during the tests performed. In order to obtain the maximum number of requisitions per month, the maximum number of requisitions supported (10,000) was multiplied by 43,200, which is the number of minutes per month, totaling 432,000,000 monthly requisitions.

For the costing of the FaaS environment, the durations of 100ms and 300ms were considered for writing and reading operations, respectively, so that cost simulations were based on 50/50 (50% write/50% read), 70/30 (70% write/30% read) and 90/10 (90% write/10% read). The proposed durations were based on the mean reading and writing values obtained from the median latencies during the tests performed. Table VI presents the results of the comparison for the three proposed scenarios, as well as the monthly cost of an instance *t1.micro*. As can be seen in the results, for the 50/50 scenario the monthly cost was US$44.65, while for the 70/30 scenario the monthly cost was US$ 37.45, both scenarios presented a higher monthly cost than the AWS Beanstalk, which was US$ 33.86. However, for the third scenario (90/10), the monthly cost was US$ 30.25, falling below the monthly value for Beanstalk.

TABLE VI. COMPARISON OF COSTS BETWEEN AWS LAMBDA AND AWS BEANSTALK CONSIDERING A TOTAL OF 43,200,000 MONTH REQUESTS IN THREE DIFFERENT SCENARIOS

	50/50		70/30		90/10	
	21.600.000	21.600.000	30.240.00	12.960.000	38.880.000	4.320.000
	100ms	300ms	100ms	300ms	100ms	300ms
Operation	**Write**	**Read**	**Write**	**Read**	**Write**	**Read**
AWS Lambda 256MB	US$ 13.32	US$ 31.33	US$ 18.65	US$ 18.80	US$ 23.98	US$ 6.27
Montlly Cost	**US$ 44.65**		**US$ 37.45**		**US$ 30.25**	

AWS Beanstalk (*t1.micro*)	744 hours/month	**US$ 33.86**

From the costs shown in Table VI, the following conclusions were obtained regarding the costs related to the case study in question:

- FaaS and PaaS environments presented cost variations considering the different scenarios presented (50/50, 70/30 and 90/10), depending on the type of predominant operation. The cost of the FaaS environments was higher in the first two scenarios due to the duration observed during the writing operations;

- For FaaS, the longer the duration of the functions, the higher the cost. Investing in the use of more performative database instances and caching features could reduce the duration of read operations, enabling a reduction in cost per read event;
- Different FaaS providers may offer lower costs per event (Table VII). Providers seeking to build a portfolio of clients or seek to consolidate their product on the market can offer attractive prices;

TABLE VII. COMPARISON OF COSTS BETWEEN FAAS PROVIDERS CONSIDERING A TOTAL OF 43,200,000 MONTH REQUESTS FOR THE 90/10 SCENARIO

	90/10		
	38.880.000	4.320.000	
	100ms	300ms	
Provider	**Read**	**Write**	**Montly Cost**
AWS Lambda	US$ 23.98	US$ 6.27	**US$ 30.25**
Azure Functions	US$ 23.33	US$ 6.05	**US$ 29.38**
Google Functions	US$ 33.53	US$ 7.72	**US$ 41.25**
IBM OpenWhisk	US$ 16.52	US$ 5.51	**US$ 22.03**

- The commercial policies adopted by the PaaS and FaaS providers follow a similar model to their respective scalability characteristics. For the PaaS environment, the costs increase based on the allocated instances (in jumps) (Figure 4). In the case of FaaS environments, the cost increases due to the number of requests received and executed.

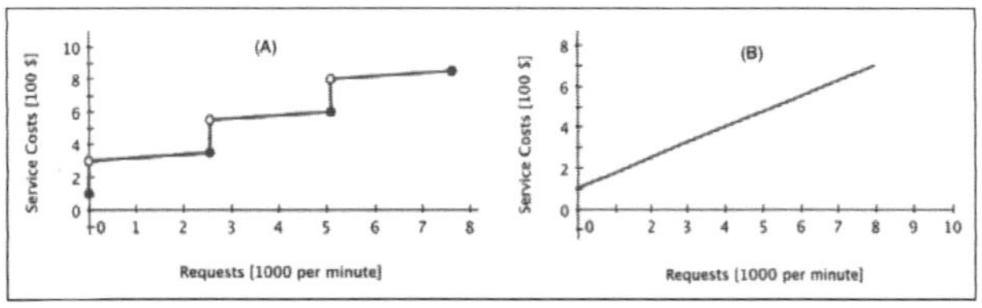

Figure 4. Graphs showing the evolution of costs in the Paas (A) and FaaS (B) environment in relation to the number of requisitions [21]

This section was dedicated to present and discuss the results obtained during the performed experiments regarding to performance and costs for the proposed scenarios. In the next section will be presented the works that served as reference or are related with the present work.

IV. Related Work

As a newly proposed model, scientific work related to FaaS is still scarce, and most use the term Serverless to refer to the model. Works such as [11] and [19] propose Serverless implementations as proof of concept and experimental, to be used for research purposes and for evaluation of applications in event-based environments, addressing conceptual issues regarding scalability and performance. Some papers are dedicated to proposing Serverless implementations and present results of experiments performed, such as [22], which addresses the inefficiency of instance-based models, and [23] that analyzes scalability issues, *cold start* and execution in FaaS environments.

Some papers focus on cost issues in Serverless environments, such as [24] that addresses performance, scalability, and cost issues in FaaS environments. In [25] and [26], the authors present results comparing a single application implemented as monolithic, an instance-based microservices and an event-based microservices (Lambda), and presenting significant cost reductions with the adoption of the FaaS model. As in [21], the authors present CostHat, a graphical model for evaluating costs for instance and event-based microservices, which simulates the impact of changes in applications.

In [16], the authors addressed FaaSification, which is a process of migrating applications to nanoservices, or event-based architectures that, although functional, still requires more in-depth research. Works related to the use of Serverless computing in several applications, such as for rejuvenation of environments [27], support for weareables [28], cognitive services [20], among others.

Considering previous works, the present paper has the purpose to contribute with a comparison between the FaaS and PaaS model with a focus on performance, scalability and cost on support of microservices applications. The work seeks to cover the characteristics of both the models, intrinsical aspects of FaaS and its pitfalls, such as cold start and execution limitations in different workload scenarios, points not covered by other published papers.

V. Conclusion

The growth of cloud computing has been boosting and enabling the emergence of parallel research areas, which use computational clouds to support various applications, such as mobile devices support. Variations in the volume of requests, the use of heterogeneous platforms and the availability requirements are peculiar characteristics of mobile computing environments that, in association with the use of microservice architectures, allow scale gains, independence and the availability required to support modern applications.

Although the PaaS is a consolidated model and recognized as efficient in supporting applications in microservices, the FaaS model has been identified as an alternative model for meeting mobile computing scenarios, providing more efficient use of resources and lower costs. This paper proposed to perform a comparative evaluation between FaaS and PaaS cloud service delivery models regarding performance issues, scalability and costs in the use of mobile applications based on microservices.

Based on the experiments carried out, the comparative analyzes and the case study, it was possible to reach the following conclusions:

- The FaaS application performance during the experiments was shown to be equivalent to the PaaS for most of the scenarios tested. And the addition of resources did not represent proportional gains in performance.
- *Cold Start* issues observed in FaaS environments must be taken into account prior to the adoption of the model and can significantly impact the performance of the application, despite the existence of techniques to reduce these latencies;
- In terms of scalability, FaaS has proven to be most interesting for services whose workloads are variable

or unpredictable, while PaaS best applies to constant or predictable workloads;

- In terms of costs, FaaS presented a better cost benefit in the treatment of requests that require short and predictable execution times, while PaaS was better suited for requests that require longer execution times or variable duration;
- In order to keep costs low using FaaS, in addition to the concern with the execution time of the requests, the results showed that the dependence on the use of external services, such as database, authentication services, among others, can interfere considerably with the expenses . In these cases, it is worth investing in better-performing external services, to reduce the time to perform functions while reducing costs.

In order to reduce the cold start impacts, some preliminar techniques can be applied. (1) in applications that have a higher latency tolerance, adjust the response threshold times, as performed during the performed experiments; (2) maintain an external routine (heartbeat) to keep resources permanently active through requisitions at regular times; (3) associate microservices of frequent and occasional use under the same API endpoint, so that access to the most used microservices guarantees the instantiation of resources to those of less access.

The results showed that the use of FaaS can help reduce costs depending on the workload. As FaaS market implementations take a charge per event taking into account the execution time of the function, the longer the time required to process a request, the higher the cost of the operation. In addition, applications whose execution times are short and predictable tend to benefit from the use of FaaS, which, together with the infinite scalability of the model, can aid in the support of seasonal workloads. The results obtained can help solution architects in the decision making regarding the use of FaaS to support their applications.

A. *Future Research Directions*

The presented work requires future work in three directions:

- To deepen the cost studies in FaaS environments from a service provider's point of view, in order to evaluate if, in comparison with other models, FaaS enables a more efficient use of resources, thus reducing costs reduction with infrastructure.
- Evaluation of techniques to reduce cold start in FaaS environments in order to reduce latency in occasional applications;
- Evaluate FaaSification techniques for the portability of microservice applications for FaaS environments.

Acknowledgment

This research has been supported by an AWS in Education Research Grant which helped us to run our experiments on AWS Lambda as representative public commercial FaaS.

References

[1] J. Sahoo, S. Mohapatra, and R. Lath, "Virtualization: A survey on concepts, taxonomy and associated security issues," in 2010 Second International Conference on Computer and Network Technology, April 2010, pp. 222–226.

[2] M. Portnoy, Virtualization Essentials. Sybex, 2012.

[3] Y. Tsuruoka, "Cloud computing - current status and future directions," vol. 24, no. 2. Information Processing Society of Japan, 2016, pp. 183–194.

[4] Y. Wang, I.-R. Chen, and D.-C. Wang, "A survey of mobile cloud computing applications: Perspectives and challenges," Wireless Personal Communications, vol. 80, no. 4, Feb 2015, pp. 1607–1623.

[5] M. Fazio et al., "Open Issues in Scheduling Microservices in the Cloud," in IEEE Cloud Computing, vol. 3, no. 5, sep 2016, pp. 81–88.

[6] C. Pahl and P. Jamshidi, "Microservices: A systematic mapping study," in Proceedings of the 6th International Conference on Cloud Computing and Services Science - Volume 1, INSTICC. ScitePress, 2016, pp. 137–146.

[7] T. Reeder, "What is serverless computing and why is it important — iron.io," https://goo.gl/0oDIcT, Jul 2016, (Accessed on 06/16/2017).

[8] M. Roberts, "Serverless architectures," http://martinfowler.com/articles/serverless.html, 2016, (Accessed on 06/16/2017).

[9] F. Renna, J. Doyle, V. Giotsas, and Y. Andreopoulos, "Query Processing For The Internet-of-Things: Coupling Of Device Energy Consumption And Cloud Infrastructure Billing," ArXiv e-prints, Feb. 2016.

[10] M. Diaz, C. Martin, and B. Rubio, "State-of-the-art, challenges, and open issues in the integration of internet of things and cloud computing," in Academic Press Ltd., vol. 67, no. C. Academic Press Ltd., May 2016, pp. 99–117.

[11] I. Nakagawa, M. Hiji, and H. Esaki, "Dripcast - Server-less java programming framework for billions of IoT devices," Proceedings - IEEE 38th Annual International Computers, Software and Applications Conference Workshops, COMPSACW 2014, vol. 23, no. 4, 2014.

[12] S. Nastic, S. Sehic, D.-H. Le, H.-L. Truong, and S. Dustdar, "Provisioning software-defined iot cloud systems," in Proceedings of the 2014 International Conference on Future Internet of Things and Cloud, ser. FICLOUD '14. IEEE Computer Society, 2014, pp. 288–295.

[13] Y. Jararweh et al., "Sdiot: a software defined based internet of things framework," Journal of Ambient Intelligence and Humanized Computing, vol. 6, no. 4, 2015.

[14] K. Lane, Overview of the backend as a service (BaaS) space. API Evangelist, 2015.

[15] E. Wolff, Microservices: Flexible Software Architecture. Pearson Education, 2016.

[16] J. Spillner and S. Dorodko, "Java Code Analysis and Transformation into AWS Lambda Functions," ArXiv e-prints, Feb. 2017.

[17] J. Spillner, "Transformation of Python Applications into Function-as-a-Service Deployments," ArXiv e-prints, May 2017.

[18] D. Rahmel, "Advanced joomla!" in Apress. Apress, 2013, ch. 8, pp. 211–247.

[19] S. Hendrickson et al., "Serverless computation with openlambda," in Proceedings of the 8th USENIX Conference on Hot Topics in Cloud Computing, ser. HotCloud'16. USENIX Association, 2016, pp. 33–39.

[20] M. Yan, P. Castro, P. Cheng, and V. Ishakian, "Building a chatbot with serverless computing," in Proceedings of the 1st International Workshop on Mashups of Things and APIs, ser. MOTA '16. New York, NY, USA: ACM, 2016, pp. 5:1–5:4.

[21] P. Leitner, J. Cito, and E. Stckli, "Modelling and managing deployment costs of microservice-based cloud applications," in 2016 IEEE/ACM 9th International Conference on Utility and Cloud Computing (UCC), Dec 2016, pp. 165–174.

[22] J. Spillner, "Snafu: Function-as-a-Service (FaaS) Runtime Design and Implementation," ArXiv e-prints, Mar. 2017.

[23] E. Jonas, S. Venkataraman, I. Stoica, and B. Recht, "Occupy the Cloud: Distributed Computing for the 99%," ArXiv e-prints, Feb. 2017.

[24] T. Hoff, "The serverless start-up - down withservers!" http://highscalability.com/blog/2015/12/7/the-serverless-start-up-down-with-servers.html, Dec 2015, (Accessed on 06/16/2017).

[25] M. Villamizar et al., "Infrastructure cost comparison of running web applications in the cloud using aws lambda and monolithic and microservice architectures," in 2016 16th IEEE/ACM International Symposium on Cluster, Cloud and Grid Computing (CCGrid), May 2016, pp. 179–182.

[26] M. Villamizar, O. Garcs, H. Castro, and M. Verano, "Evaluating the monolithic and the microservice architecture pattern to deploy web applications in the cloud," in 2015 10th Computing Colombian Conference (10CCC), Sept 2015, pp. 583–590.

[27] B. Wagner and A. Sood, "Economics of resilient cloud services," in 2016 IEEE International Conference on Software Quality, Reliability and Security Companion (QRS-C), Aug 2016, pp. 368–374.

[28] I. Baldini et al., "Cloud-native , event-based programming for mobile applications," 2016 IEEE/ACM International Conference on Mobile Software Engineering and Systems, 2016, pp. 287–288.

Architectural Programming with MontiArcAutomaton

Arvid Butting, Oliver Kautz, Bernhard Rumpe, Andreas Wortmann

Software Engineering
RWTH Aachen University
Aachen, Germany
Email: {lastname}@se-rwth.de

Abstract—**Modeling software architectures usually requires programming the behavior of components interfacing general programming language (GPL) libraries. This raises a gap between modeling activities and programming activities that entails switching between both activities, which requires considerable effort. Current research on architecture description languages (ADLs) focuses on employing state-based component behavior modeling techniques or integrating handcrafted GPL artifacts into skeletons generated from architecture models. The former is rarely feasible to interface with GPL libraries, the latter opens the aforementioned gap. We integrate GPLs, reified as modeling languages, into the MontiArcAutomaton ADL to enable defining component behavior on model level without considering the idiosyncrasies of generated artifacts. To this effect, we apply results from software language engineering to enable a configurable embedding of GPLs as behavior languages into ADLs. This ultimately enables architecture modelers to focus on modeling activities only and, hence, reduces the effort of switching between modeling and programming activities.**

Keywords–Model-Driven Engineering, Architecture Description Languages, Architectural Programming.

I. Introduction

Component-based software engineering pursues the vision of constructing software from reusable, off-the-shelf building blocks that hide their implementation details behind stable interfaces to facilitate their composition. The behavior of such software components requires implementation with general-purpose programming languages (GPLs), which creates a conceptual gap between the problem domains and the solution domains of discourse and ultimately gives raise to the accidental complexities of programming [1]. Model-driven engineering aims at reducing this gap. To this end, it lifts models to primary development artifacts. These models are better suited to analysis, communication, documentation, and transformation. Consequently, the notion of software components has been lifted to component models that conform to architecture description languages (ADLs) of which research and industry have produced over 120 [2]. However, most of these languages focus on structural architecture aspects only. Where component behavior is considered, it is either in form of state-based modeling techniques or requires integration of handcrafted GPL artifacts. The former usually is insufficient to describe the behavior of components interfacing GPL libraries or frameworks. The latter requires architecture modelers to switch between modeling and programming activities, which require different mindsets and different tooling. Both approaches ultimately complicate development, especially considering the fact that developers switch between various activities 47 times per hour on average already [3].

We present a notion of *architectural programming* that lifts programming to modeling by reifying GPL (parts) as behavior languages and embedding these into ADL components. This enables reusing libraries and frameworks from within component models. Ultimately, this prevents architecture modelers from facing the idiosyncrasies of generated GPL artifacts and from the elaborate patterns [4] to integrate handcrafted code. Achieving this requires:

- **R1** The GPL of choice is integrated into the ADL such that a single model contains ADL parts and GPL parts.
- **R2** The relevant modeling elements of the ADL are accessible from the GPL.
- **R3** The integration of GPL elements is configurable to prevent introducing unnecessary accidental complexities into the ADL.
- **R4** The integrated artifacts consisting of ADL and GPL parts are translatable into various target languages.

In the following, Section II presents preliminaries, before Section III motivates our approach by example. Section IV presents the language embedding mechanism and its application. Afterwards, Section V presents a case study with the MontiArcAutomaton ADL. Section VI debates related work and Section VII discusses our approach. Section VIII concludes.

II. Preliminaries

To prevent architecture modelers from switching between modeling and programming, we apply the language composition mechanisms of the MontiCore [5] language workbench to the MontiArcAutomaton ADL [6] and embed the Java/P [7] modeling language into its components. This section introduces all three.

A. *MontiCore*

MontiCore [5] is a workbench for compositional modeling languages. It supports the integrated definition of concrete syntax (words) and abstract syntax (structure) via extended context-free grammars. From these, it generates Java parsers and abstract syntax classes for each production as depicted in Figure 1. Each generated class yields members to capture the production's right-hand sides. Underspecified *interface productions* are translated to Java interfaces. MontiCore uses the generated parsers and abstract syntax classes to translate

```
grammar MontiArcAutomaton {     concrete                MCG
  Component = "cmp" Name "{"    syntax only
    Port* (Subcomponent* Connector* | Behavior?)
  "}";
  interface Behavior;    iteration disjunction optionality
  // ... other productions ...
}
```

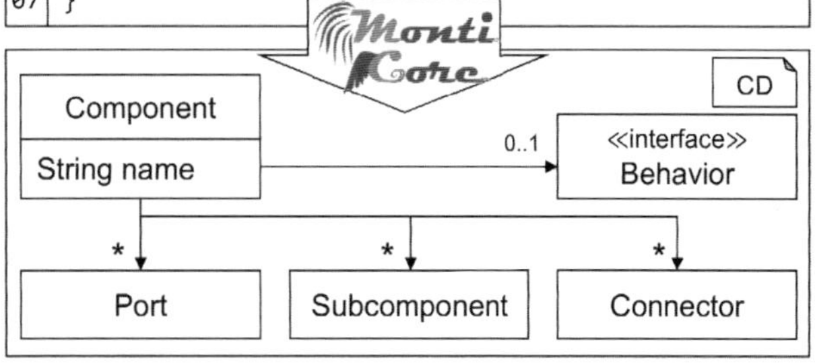

Figure 1. MontiArcAutomaton grammar describing hierarchical components with ports and connectors and the resulting abstract syntax classes.

textual models into abstract syntax trees (ASTs) on which model analyses and transformations are performed. Its visitor framework enables registering Java rules that process the ASTs to ensure the models' static semantics (well-formedness). Template-based code generators realize the languages' dynamic semantics (behavior) by translating ASTs into target language artifacts. MontiCore supports language inheritance, language embedding, and language aggregation to integrate modeling languages [8]. Inheriting languages can arbitrarily reuse productions of their parent languages (*e.g.,* to create specialized language variants). Embedding languages integrates parts of embedded languages into their underspecified *interface productions* (*e.g.,* Java embedding SQL to realize database queries). Language aggregations loosely couple languages via references (*e.g.,* state machines referencing members of the class diagram types they operate in). The language integration mechanisms rest on grammar combination (inheritance, embedding) and symbolic integration (all). For the symbolic integration of behavior languages with MontiArcAutomaton, *e.g.,* to check the validity of assignments to ports, the AST types of relevant language elements are adapted to their MontiArcAutomaton counterparts (*e.g.,* variables to ports).

B. MontiArcAutomaton

MontiArcAutomaton [6] is an architecture modeling infrastructure that comprises an extensible component & connector (C&C) ADL, various model transformations, and a modular, template-based code generation framework. Its ADL is realized with MontiCore and the infrastructure employs MontiCore's language integration mechanism to enable plug-and-play embedding of modeling languages to describe component behavior, including concrete syntax, abstract syntax, static semantics, and dynamic semantics. Core concepts of its ADL are sketched in Figure 1. It has been configured with various state-based behavior modeling languages and successfully deployed to service robotics applications [9].

C. Java/P

Java/P [7] is a MontiCore language resembling Java 1.7. It is used as action language in the UML/P [7] language family and supports the complete concrete and abstract syntax of Java 1.7 as well as its well-formedness rules. Figure 2 displays

```
grammar JavaP {                                          MCG
  JavaClass = "class" Name "{" (Method | ... )* "}";
  Method = ReturnType Name "{" MethodBody* "}";
  MethodBody = (Assignment | ReturnStatement | ... )*;
  // ... other productions ...
}                                       further alternatives
```

Figure 2. Simplified excerpt of the Java/P grammar.

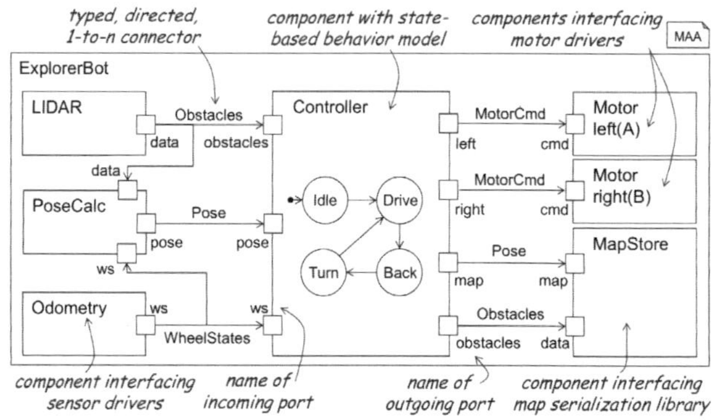

Figure 3. Software architecture for a mobile exploration robot.

an excerpt of its grammar. Its models are translated into Java artifacts using MontiCore's code generation framework. Reifying a GPL as a modeling language enables to easily extend it with new constructs (*e.g.,* notions of components as in ArchJava [10]), well-formedness rules (such as preventing assignment of `null` values), and shortcuts (for instance, automatically generating getters and setters for members). Reifying Java with MontiCore furthermore yields a parser capable of processing Java 1.7 classes, which allows to *model* Java programs interacting with libraries and frameworks.

III. Example

Consider modeling the software architecture of a mobile service robot that should explore and map uncharted territories. Such a robot must be able to perceive its environment, calculate actions based on these perceptions, and perform these actions to manipulate the environment. Perception and manipulation require interfacing sensors and actuators, respectively. Usually, these are accessed using GPL libraries providing high-level functionalities based on their mechatronic realization and software drivers. To interface these libraries, model-driven approaches must either lift GPL-like imperative programming mechanisms to model level or postpone integration to the level of generated code. For the latter, various patterns have been developed [4], all of which require by nature comprehending the idiosyncrasies of the GPL code generated from the models. The C&C software architecture for such a system is depicted in Figure 3. It perceives the environment via components interfacing a LIDAR scanner and the robot's odometry, decides on the next action via its fully modeled controller, and passes the results to its two motors and the map storage. The sensors and motors interface GPL code ultimately controlling the respective drivers. The components `PoseCalc` and `MapStore` interface GPL libraries for mathematical operations and serialization respectively.

Without lifting sufficient expressive GPL-like programming to model level, the architecture modeler must describe the

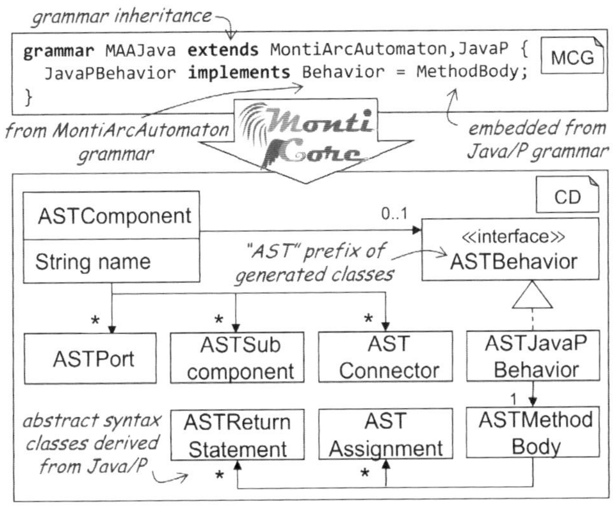

Figure 4. Grammar integrating Java/P into MontiArcAutomaton.

behavior of each of these components in the same GPL than code generated from the architecture elements. This might entail coping with various accidental complexities not directly related to computing behavior based on incoming port values, such as networking, exception handling, type casting, *etc.* Most of this can be abstracted away on model level. Additionally, the pattern selected for integrating handcrafted component behavior with generated code might give rise to further accidental complexities also not arising on model level. Selecting, for instance, the popular generation gap [4] pattern exposes the architecture modeler to all implementation details of the technical component concerns via subclassing. This exposure is another source of errors. Delegation, partial classes, protected regions, *etc.*, all yield similar complexities due to operating on GPL level. Reifying and integrating (parts of) GPLs, such as Java/P can reduce these. Finally, generation to multiple target GPLs requires re-implementing the behavior of each component type for each GPL, whereas using behavior models requires a corresponding code generator only.

IV. EMBEDDING JAVA/P INTO MONTIARCAUTOMATON

Embedding a modeling language into another requires combining their concrete syntaxes, abstract syntaxes, static semantics, and dynamic semantics [11]. Embedding Java/P into MontiArcAutomaton consequently rests on combining the related MontiCore artifacts accordingly. For concrete syntax and abstract syntax, this entails binding the production `MethodBody` of the Java/P grammar (Figure 2) to the interface production `Behavior` of the MontiArcAutomaton grammar (Figure 1). With MontiCore, this is achieved by leveraging its language inheritance mechanism as depicted in Figure 4. Through language inheritance, integrating the related concrete syntax and abstract syntax into MontiArcAutomaton requires to provide a corresponding implementation of its `Behavior` interface only. This enables parsing integrated artifacts into combined ASTs (**R1**).

To ensure the integrated models are well-formed with respect to both MontiArcAutomaton and Java/P, we provide an extensible well-formedness checking visitor that applies the MontiArcAutomaton well-formedness rules by default and can be extended with additional rules. As the well-formedness rules of MontiCore languages are Java classes responsible for processing a specific abstract syntax class, they can be reused without modification through registration with the MontiArcAutomaton visitor.

The integration of behavior languages into components aims at describing their input-output behavior. Hence, models of these languages must be related to the inputs and outputs of components (*i.e.*, their ports). To this effect, the names used in embedded Java/P assignments must be interpreted as symbolic references to the surrounding component's ports. For Java/P, these names usually reference to variables, hence, with MontiCore, this requires registering a corresponding adapter acting as a variable of Java/P that delegates to a port of MontiArcAutomaton [8]. In contrast to Java/P variables, ports of MontiArcAutomaton cannot be used bidirectionally: incoming ports are read-only and outgoing ports are write-only. As the Java/P well-formedness rules must be unaware of such a restriction, embedding Java/P requires integrating new well-formedness rules ensuring this. Figure 5 (top) illustrates the adaptation between MontiArcAutomaton's `Port` and Java/P's `Variable`, which takes place between the *symbols* created for each named relevant AST element. These symbols act as intermediate layer for language integration and support resolving and caching named entities from the same and other models. This adaptation enables reusing all Java/P well-formedness rules in the context of ports (**R2**). Details on symbols, their creation, and processing are available [8]. Figure 5 (bottom) also shows a new well-formedness rule to ensure incoming ports cannot be assigned values. To this effect, its `check()` method (ll. 4-12) is called by MontiArcAutomaton's visitor framework for each assignment found in an integrated model. It resolves the symbol of the assignment's target (l. 5) and, in case this actually adapts to MontiArcAutomaton's port (l. 6), checks that the ports have the correct direction (l. 8) or reports an error (l. 9). Ultimately, symbolic adaptation facilitates integration of static semantics and enables integration of new well-formedness rules easily. Eliminating and adding new well-formedness rules can also be used to tailor the language to application-specific requirements. To this effect, MontiArcAutomaton features a well-formedness rule to check for prohibited AST classes. The rule can be parametrized with a set of abstract syntax classes and iterates over all embedded abstract syntax instances to ensure none of the passed classes is used. This restriction mechanism enables excluding language elements from integration (such as `ASTReturnStatement`, which does not make sense in our integration context) as well as tailoring the embedded language to application-specific requirements (**R3**).

As MontiCore languages typically realize their dynamic semantics via code generation, integrating the dynamics of Java/P into MontiArcAutomaton requires composing their code generators. To this end, the code generator integrated for Java/P must agree on the same run-time system (RTS) as the MontiArcAutomaton code generator. A RTS is a collection of interfaces and classes enabling execution of generated models and entails, for instance, the interfaces implemented by generated component behavior realizations [6]. The interface for behavior implementation artifacts imposed by the MontiArcAutomaton RTS entails input-output semantics, *i.e.*, generated behavior realizations must provide a specific method receiving and

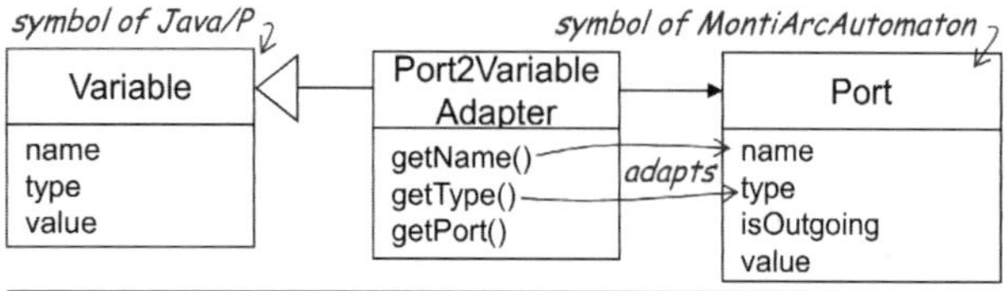


```
class AssignOutgoingPortsOnly extends                         Java
  ContextCondition<ASTVariable> {
                                                              
  public void check(ASTAssignment a) {
    Variable v = a.getSymbol().getTarget();
    if (v instanceof Port2VariableAdapter) {
      Port p = ((Port2VariableAdapter)v).getPort();
      if (!p.isOutgoing)
        reportError("Writing to incoming port: " + p);
    }
  }
}
```

symbol resolving — *abstract syntax element of Java/P*

Figure 5. Symbolic integration between ports and variables and a well-formedness rule using it.

returning a set of named values. The artifacts generated from components delegate behavior computation to this method by passing the current values on incoming ports and assigning the returned name-value pairs to outgoing ports accordingly. Details on this generator composition mechanism are available [6]. The integration of Java/P into MontiArcAutomaton consequently requires a code generator agreeing on the same RTS that produces classes receiving input values, performing computations according to the method body's statements, and returning the results. Creating a generator wrapping the code generated for instances of `ASTMethodBody` (*cf.* Figure 2) requires little effort.

For MontiArcAutomaton and Java/P, code generation is template-based using the FreeMarker [12] template engine. With this, generator integration requires the single template depicted in Figure 6. This constructs a method called `compute` (l. 1) with a signature expecting all incoming ports of the component type it is generated for (ll. 2-4). Afterwards, the method creates local variables from each outgoing port (ll. 6-8) and calls the Java/P generator template responsible for translating method bodies (l. 9). Code generated from the latter operates on method parameters and local variables created for the ports and, hence, is correct by construction. This is ensured by restricting references in embedded method bodies to ports or local Java/P variables. Finally, the resulting values are collected and returned (ll. 10-14). The code generated for structural component aspects receives the resulting map and assigns the values to corresponding ports. Through enforcing type-compatibility on model level already, this assignment is straightforward.

All of this is configured by a specific internal domain-specific language (DSL) for language embedding into MontiArcAutomaton. Its models can be configured with the behavior language's grammar production to be embedded, its well-formedness rules to be reused, and its code generator to be integrated [13]. Figure 7 presents a model of this DSL responsible for embedding Java/P. Internal DSLs usually are realized via fluent GPL APIs [14] in which the methods yield names corresponding to language keywords. This enables interacting with libraries of the host GPL easily, but restricts

```
01 public Map<String,Object> compute(                          FM
02 <list incomingPorts as p>
03   ${p.getType()} ${p.getName()}<if_has_next>,</if>
04 </list>
05 ) {
06 <list outgoingPorts as p>
07   ${p.getType()} ${p.getName()};
08 </list>
09   ${op.call(MethodBodyTemplate)}
10   Map<String,Object> results = new HashMap<>();
11 <list outgoingPorts as p>
12   results.put(${p.getName()},${p.getValue()});
13 </list>
14   return results;
15 }
```

static text — *accessing ASTPort members* — *FreeMarker built-in conditional* — *calling template from original Java/P generator* — *FreeMarker built-in iteration*

Figure 6. FreeMarker template wrapping code generator parts of Java/P for usage with MontiArcAutomaton.

qualified name of the grammar production to be embedded — *well-formedness rules to reuse* — *code generator to integrate*

```
01 name "javap"                                                 BCL
02 behavior "javap.JavaP.MethodBody"
03 cocos javap.cocos.CoCoCreator().create()
04 generator new javap.generators.JavaPTimeSync()
05 coco new montiarcjava.cocos.AssignOutgoingPortsOnly()
```

integration-specific well-formedness rule

Figure 7. Model integrating Java/P into MontiArcAutomaton.

language extension. Various modern GPLs enable omitting syntactic elements if their context is unambiguous, such as the parentheses of method calls with single arguments. This further enables designing fluent APIs to resemble DSLs. The behavior configuration language model depicted in Figure 7 is realized on top of a Groovy fluent API. It consists of five concatenated method calls that configure the integration of Java/P into MontiArcAutomaton: The first line defines the unique name of the embedded behavior language. Afterwards, it references the grammar production to be embedded (l. 2) from which the integration framework synthesizes a grammar similar to `MontiArcJava` depicted in Figure 2. Subsequently, it collects the well-formedness rules of the embedded language (l. 3) and the code generator to be integrated (l. 4). Finally, it also adds the new well-formedness rule `AssignOutgoingPortsOnly` (*cf.* Figure 5) to the resulting language composition (l. 5).

V. Case Study

Reconsider the exploration robot's software architecture (Figure 3). Without lifting reifying and integrating a GPL into the ADL, implementing the behavior of its `Motor` component requires switching between modeling and programming activities, comprehending patterns for integrating handcrafted with generated implementations, and exposes the architecture modeler to the accidental complexities of the generated code.

Figure 8 describes the integrated model for component `Motor`: after declaring its type and parameters (l. 1), it yields an incoming port `cmd` of data type `MotorCommand` (l. 2) and contains an embedded behavior description (ll. 4-12). Everything between the opening bracket (l. 4) and the closing bracket (l. 12) is an embedded Java/P model. The embedded `MethodBody` (*cf.* Figure 2, l. 4) instance declares a local integer variable `speed` (l. 5), checks the value of port `cmd` and

```
01 component Motor(lejos.nxt.Motor m) {
02   port in MotorCommand cmd;
03
04   behavior {
05     int speed = 0.1; // cannot convert from double to int
06     if (cmd == MotorCommand.FORWARD)
07       speed = 720;
08     else if (cmd == MotorCommand.BACKWARD)
09       speed = -720;
10     m.setSpeed(speed)
11     return speed; // prohibited modeling element
12   }
13 }
```

MAA

embedded Java/P

error raised by reused Java/P well-formedness rule

error raised by integration-specific well-formedness rule

Figure 8. Textual `Motor` component with embedded Java/P behavior (ll. 5-10).

sets the value of `speed` accordingly (ll. 6-9), sets the speed of the leJOS API [15] motor instance `m` passed to the component (*cf.* l. 1), and returns the value of `speed`. Assigning a float value to an integer variable is prohibited by one of the reused Java/P well-formedness rules and consequently an error is raised (l. 5). Additionally, a prohibited instance of Java/P's return statement is found and reported also (l. 11). Overall, this syntactic and semantic integration of Java/P prevents the architecture modeler from facing generated code, supports developing with artifacts integration component structure and behavior as depicted in Figure 8. It also reduces the effort of continuously evolving and aligning two separate artifacts.

VI. Related Work

Most ADLs focus on structural concerns. Where describing component behavior is considered, many languages support state-based behavior modeling only. More complex behavior usually requires linking component models to GPL artifacts.

DiaSpec [16] is an ADL for pervasive computing systems that supports integrating behavior via the generation gap pattern [4]. Koala [17] is an ADL for the development of embedded software. Its code generator produces `C` interfaces (header files) from components and developers provide component behavior via handcrafted interface implementations. ArchFace [18] uses program points and their implementations to separate structure and behavior. Program points in component interfaces are coordinated with implementations in different GPLs. Component behavior in DAOP-ADL [19] is divided into an interface definition in form of a pointcut and its implementation potentially defined in a different artifact and language. Specifying component behavior in C2SADEL [20] requires integrating handcrafted code also.

Other ADLs feature embedded state-based behavior descriptions. In AADL [21], state-based behavior can be modeled following its behavior annex. Palladio [22] enables modeling behavior via service effect specifications, a variant of activity diagrams that describe the quality-of-service properties of components, that describe component behavior. The xADL [23] supports mapping components, connectors, and types to Java classes [23]. An extension on modeling component behavior with state machines [24] enables integrated development of structural and behavioral aspects.

Only few ADLs support other behavior descriptions. For example, in Æmilia [25], behavior is structured in blocks containing EMPA_{gr} terms [26], which are then translated into state machines. ArchJava [10] embeds ADL concepts into Java, hence it can use Java to describe component behavior. However, it does not support tailoring the language to specific requirements and is bound to Java. The π-ADL [27] also supports producing GPL code: Its behavior description mechanism supports dynamically composing, decomposing, and replicating (parts of) architectures, conditional statements, and directives for sending or receiving values via component interfaces. PiLar [28] is a reflective ADL for evolving software system structures. It provides various constructs for integrated behavior and structural modeling, such as directives for dynamically modifying architectures, conditionals, loops, and commands for exchanging message. Neither π-ADL, nor PiLar support tailoring the behavior description mechanism.

VII. Discussion

Our approach to architectural programming requires reifying the GPL of choice as a modeling language. While being of similar complexity than developing and integrating state-based behavior languages (*cf.* [29]), the lower effort in code generator development (essentially pretty printing the GPL model parts) for contexts where only a single target GPL is relevant compensates for this. Where multiple target languages are required, transforming the concepts of embedded GPL parts into another GPL is feasible as long as these concepts are generally supported or can be worked around. However, the inclusion of libraries is feasible only, if they are available for both target GPLs. Moreover, including libraries might require considering complexities that may be excluded from the embedded GPL parts (*e.g.*, exception handling is used in a library, but not included in the embedded part of the GPL). Another challenge arises from the integration of code generators through wrapping and reuse, which requires that relevant parts of the embedded GPL's code generator are accessible for wrapping. Where this is not fulfilled, generator reuse might not be possible.

VIII. Conclusion

We presented a method for pervasive architecture modeling by reifying programming languages as action languages and embedding these into the C&C ADL MontiArcAutomaton. Embedding relies on grammar interfaces, symbol adaptation, and code generator composition, all of which focus on minimizing the integration effort. The integration method supports tailoring the embedded action languages in the process by embedding what is required only and prohibiting undesired action language concepts. Modeling component behavior with integrated action languages reduces the need for switching between modeling and programming activities and, hence, ultimately reduces the effort in modeling architectures.

References

[1] R. France and B. Rumpe, "Model-driven Development of Complex Software: A Research Roadmap," Future of Software Engineering (FOSE '07), 2007.

[2] I. Malavolta, P. Lago, H. Muccini, P. Pelliccione, and A. Tang, "What Industry Needs from Architectural Languages: A Survey," Software Engineering, IEEE Transactions on, 2013.

[3] A. N. Meyer, T. Fritz, G. C. Murphy, and T. Zimmermann, "Software developers' perceptions of productivity," in Proceedings of the 22nd ACM SIGSOFT International Symposium on Foundations of Software Engineering, 2014.

[4] T. Greifenberg, K. Hoelldobler, C. Kolassa, M. Look, P. Mir Seyed Nazari, K. Mueller, A. Navarro Perez, D. Plotnikov, D. Reiss, A. Roth, B. Rumpe, M. Schindler, and A. Wortmann, "A Comparison of Mechanisms for Integrating Handwritten and Generated Code for Object-Oriented Programming Languages," in Proceedings of the 3rd International Conference on Model-Driven Engineering and Software Development, 2015.

[5] H. Krahn, B. Rumpe, and S. Völkel, "MontiCore: a Framework for Compositional Development of Domain Specific Languages," International Journal on Software Tools for Technology Transfer (STTT), 2010.

[6] J. O. Ringert, A. Roth, B. Rumpe, and A. Wortmann, "Language and Code Generator Composition for Model-Driven Engineering of Robotics Component & Connector Systems," Journal of Software Engineering for Robotics, 2015.

[7] B. Rumpe, Modeling with UML: Language, Concepts, Methods. Springer International, 2016.

[8] A. Haber, M. Look, and P. e. a. Mir Seyed Nazari, "Integration of Heterogeneous Modeling Languages via Extensible and Composable Language Components," in Proceedings of the 3rd International Conference on Model-Driven Engineering and Software Development, 2015.

[9] R. Heim, P. M. S. Nazari, J. O. Ringert, B. Rumpe, and A. Wortmann, "Modeling Robot and World Interfaces for Reusable Tasks," in 2015 IEEE/RSJ International Conference on Intelligent Robots and Systems (IROS), 2015.

[10] J. Aldrich, C. Chambers, and D. Notkin, "ArchJava: connecting software architecture to implementation." in International Conference on Software Engineering (ICSE) 2002, 2002.

[11] T. Clark, M. v. d. Brand, B. Combemale, and B. Rumpe, "Conceptual Model of the Globalization for Domain-Specific Languages," in Globalizing Domain-Specific Languages, 2015.

[12] L. A. Tedd, J. Radjenovic, B. Milosavljevic, and D. Surla, "Modelling and implementation of catalogue cards using FreeMarker," Program, vol. 43, no. 1, 2009, pp. 62–76.

[13] A. Butting, , B. Rumpe, and A. Wortmann, "Modeling Embedding of Component Behavior DSLs into the MontiArcAutomaton ADL," in Proceedings of the 4th Workshop on the Globalization of Modeling Languages (GEMOC), 2016.

[14] M. Fowler, Domain-Specific Languages. Addison-Wesley Professional, 2010.

[15] "leJOS API Website," (accessed: 2017-02-21). [Online]. Available: http://www.lejos.org/

[16] D. Cassou, J. Bruneau, C. Consel, and E. Balland, "Toward a Tool-Based Development Methodology for Pervasive Computing Applications," IEEE Transactions on Software Engineering, 2012.

[17] R. van Ommering, F. van der Linden, J. Kramer, and J. Magee, "The Koala Component Model for Consumer Electronics Software," Computer, 2000.

[18] N. Ubayashi, J. Nomura, and T. Tamai, "Archface: a contract place where architectural design and code meet together," in Proceedings of the 32nd ACM/IEEE International Conference on Software Engineering-Volume 1, 2010.

[19] M. Pinto, L. Fuentes, and J. M. Troya, "A dynamic component and aspect-oriented platform," The Computer Journal, 2005.

[20] N. Medvidovic, D. S. Rosenblum, and R. N. Taylor, "A language and environment for architecture-based software development and evolution," in Software Engineering, 1999. Proceedings of the 1999 International Conference on, 1999.

[21] R. B. Franca, J.-P. Bodeveix, M. Filali, J.-F. Rolland, D. Chemouil, and D. Thomas, "The AADL behaviour annex–experiments and roadmap," in Proceedings of the 12th IEEE International Conference on Engineering Complex Computer Systems. Washington, DC: IEEE Computer Society, 2007.

[22] R. Reussner, S. Becker, and E. e. a. Burger, The Palladio Component Model. Karlsruhe, 2011.

[23] E. M. Dashofy, A. van der Hoek, and R. N. Taylor, "An Infrastructure for the Rapid Development of XML-based Architecture Description Languages," in Proceedings of the 24th International Conference on Software Engineering, 2002.

[24] L. Naslavsky, L. Xu, M. Dias, H. Ziv, and D. J. Richardson, "Extending xADL with Statechart Behavioral Specification," in In Third Workshop on Architecting Dependable Systems (WADS'04), Edinburgh, Scotland, 2004.

[25] S. Balsamo, M. Bernardo, and M. Simeoni, "Combining stochastic process algebras and queueing networks for software architecture analysis," in Proceedings of the 3rd International Workshop on Software and Performance, 2002.

[26] M. Bravetti and M. Bernardo, "Compositional asymmetric cooperations for process algebras with probabilities, priorities, and time," Electronic Notes in Theoretical Computer Science, 2000.

[27] F. Oquendo, "π-ADL: An Architecture Description Language Based on the Higher-order Typed π-calculus for Specifying Dynamic and Mobile Software Architectures," SIGSOFT Softwware Engineering Notes, 2004.

[28] C. E. Cuesta, P. de la Fuente, M. Barrio-Solórzano, and M. E. G. Beato, "An "abstract process" approach to algebraic dynamic architecture description," The Journal of Logic and Algebraic Programming, 2005.

[29] L. Naslavsky, H. Z. Dias, H. Ziv, and D. Richardson, "Extending xADL with Statechart Behavioral Specification," in Third Workshop on Architecting Dependable Systems (WADS), Edinburgh, Scotland, 2004.

Which API Lifecycle Model is the Best for API Removal Management?

Dung-Feng Yu, Cheng-Ying Chang

Institute of Computer and
Communication Engineering,
National Cheng Kung University,
Tainan, Taiwan
Email:{dfyu, zhengying}@nature.ee.ncku.edu.tw

Hewijin Christine Jiau, Kuo-Feng Ssu

Department of Electrical
Engineering,
National Cheng Kung University,
Tainan, Taiwan
Email:{jiauhjc, ssu}@mail.ncku.edu.tw

***Abstract*—Frameworks and libraries are reused through application programming interfaces (APIs). Normally, APIs are assumed to be stable and serve as contracts between frameworks/libraries and client applications. However, in reality, APIs change over time. When these changes happen, API users must spend additional effort in migrating client applications. If the effort is too much to afford, the frameworks/libraries that API developers have built will lose market share. In order to reduce migration effort, API developers should manage API changes through API lifecycle. Before construction of API lifecycle, investigation of the following question is required: Which API lifecycle model is the best for API removal management? To answer this question, we first construct three API lifecycle models based on the observation of current practices, and then devise a set of metrics to assess those models using case studies. Assessment results conclude the best model is deprecation involved model which benefits API developers and users most with the least costs. Such model becomes the base for API developers to build API lifecycle which enables API developers to manage API changes, and reduces migration effort.**

Keywords–API lifecycle; API lifecycle model; API change; API removal management; software migration.

I. Introduction

Software reuse offers many benefits, such as acceleration of software development and reduction of the overall development cost [1]. Reusable software provides common functionalities through application programming interfaces (APIs). Normally, APIs are assumed to be stable and serve as contracts between reusable software and client software. But, in fact, as reusable software evolves to meet changing requirements and solve emerging bugs over time, APIs will inevitably and frequently change [2]. These changes will cause client software to fail and increase maintenance cost [3]. Therefore, API changes must be managed.

API developers manage API changes to web service using tools, such as *API Manager* [4], *Lifecycle Manager* [5], and *Oracle API Management* [6]. Each tool contains API lifecycle, which is represented as a set of specific stages and the transitions between them. Different tools contain different API lifecycles. As a result, API developers need to choose the tool that contains the most suitable API lifecycle. After API lifecycle is chosen, API of the web service must follow the lifecycle from its birth (i.e., API addition) to its death (i.e., API removal). Throughout API lifecycle, API developers can control API addition, removal, and other changes.

Unlike API changes to web service, API changes to frameworks and libraries are not well managed [3][7][8]. From previous study, API changes happen frequently across different versions of a frameworks/libraries and commonly across different frameworks/libraries [9]. These API changes often cause a large amount of effort in migrating client application [10]-[12]. As a result, API users will complain through communication channels, such as online forums or mailing lists. If API developers do not handle those specific complaints, the framework or library that they have built will lose market share because API users will choose other frameworks or libraries instead.

To reduce migration effort, we first investigate the origin of API changes and then propose an effective way to manage them. According to previous research [3][9][10], most API changes occur when API developers *directly make them* in the design improvement tasks, without considering the affected client applications. As a result, the most effective way to manage API changes of frameworks and libraries is to *plan them* based on API lifecycle. API lifecycle can enable API developers to make API changes according to predefined stage and transitions. It also guarantees that API developers consider the affected client applications when making API changes. However, there is no one-size-fits-all API lifecycle for all API developers. Hence, we investigate the best API lifecycle model, instead of the best API lifecycle.

In this work, API lifecycle model is an abstraction of API lifecycles, and is represented as a set of general stages and transitions between them. To choose the best API lifecycle model, we first construct three API lifecycle models according to the observation on current practices, and then analyze those models from the perspective of API removal management. This perspective is chosen because API removal management enables API developers to prevent unintentional API removals and therefore avoid causing client applications to fail. We assess the impact of API lifecycle models on API developers and API users through three case studies. The best model is determined by the assessment results.

Main contributions of this work are as follows: 1) We are the first to provide API developers with a solution to manage API changes. 2) The best model is the base for API developers to build a suitable API lifecycle. Such API lifecycle enables API developers to manage API changes and therefore avoid causing client applications to fail. As a result, migration effort will be reduced. 3) We devise a metric set that enables API developers to assess the impact of their API lifecycle on both API developers and API users.

A preliminary analysis is performed in Section II to introduce API lifecycle models and assess the impact on both API developers and API users. Case studies of models are conducted in Section III, and then results are presented in Section IV. The best model is determined according to the results. Related work is discussed in Section V. Finally, conclusion and future work are provided in Section VI.

II. Preliminary Analysis

The goal of this preliminary analysis is to approximately assess the impact of API lifecycle models on API developers and API users from the perspective of API removal management. Therefore, three generic API lifecycle models are introduced, which are shown in Figure 1. The support for API removal management is discussed, and the positive and negative impacts are further analyzed in detail. Finally, the analysis result is summarized to provide an overview of API lifecycle models.

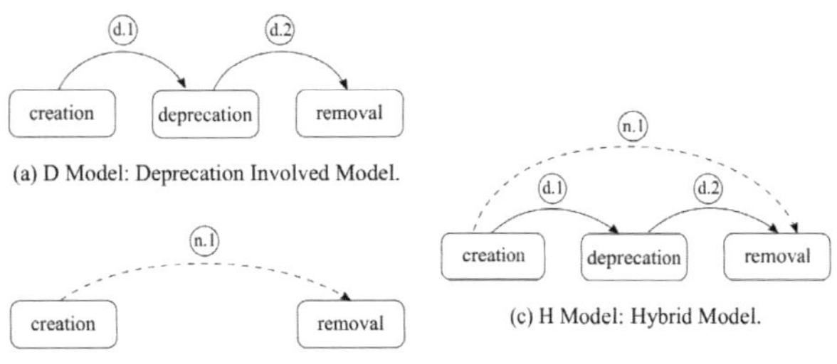

(a) D Model: Deprecation Involved Model.

(b) ND Model: Non-Deprecation Involved Model.

(c) H Model: Hybrid Model.

Figure 1. Three API Lifecycle Models.

A. D Model: Deprecation Involved Model

As shown in Figure 1(a), *Deprecation Involved Model* (*D Model*) contains three stages, including creation stage, deprecation stage, and removal stage. In D Model, API (e.g., A_D) enters creation stage when it is designed to provide functionality and exposed to API users. Through extensive usage, A_D might be found buggy or insufficient. Hence, API developers decide that A_D should be scheduled for removal because it is no longer recommended to use. To notify API users of the decision, API developers often label A_D 'deprecated' and provide the corresponding migration information (e.g., using other API instead) in API documents. After the notification, A_D enters deprecation stage from creation stage, and becomes a deprecated API. Meanwhile, API developers plan the future removal of the deprecated API. Once A_D is removed, it enters removal stage and ends its lifecycle.

D Model provides API developers full support for API removal management through the following ways. First, all API removals are planned before they occur. Therefore, API developers are able to control the timing of API removals. Second, migration problems caused by API removals (e.g., compilation errors occur when API users compile client applications and new version of frameworks/libraries) are mitigated through the provision of migration information. As a result, API developers have control over the impact of API removals on API users.

Although D Model provides full support for API removal management, it still has one negative impact on API developers. When maintaining deprecated APIs, API developers have to keep implementation of deprecated APIs in each new version of frameworks/libraries, and thus encounter the problem of code bloat. On the other hand, D Model has three positive impacts on API users. First, migration information enables API users to adapt client applications to API removals. Second, API users are informed of API removal schedules in advance through API documents, and thus they have sufficient time to adapt client applications. Third, the probability that API users have to adapt client applications is low because API developers often remove APIs only when necessary. This reduces the effort in migrating client applications.

B. ND Model: Non-Deprecation Involved Model

Figure 1(b) shows *Non-Deprecation Involved Model* (*ND Model*). ND Model contains creation and removal stages, but deprecation stage is excluded. As a result, the API following ND Model is always a non-deprecated API, and will never become a deprecated API. In ND Model, API (e.g., A_{ND}) enters creation stage when it is designed and exposed to API users. After A_{ND} is used, it might be found buggy or insufficient. Hence, the non-deprecated API, A_{ND}, will be directly removed in the new version of frameworks/libraries without planning. Such API is called *NR API* in this work, where *NR* stands for *Non-deprecated* and *Removed*. After A_{ND} is removed, it enters removal stage from creation stage. Such stage transition is denoted by the dotted arc in Figure 1(b).

ND model does not provide API developers with any support for API removal management. The reasons are listed as follows. First, all API removals occur without any planning. As a result, API developers are not able to control the timing of API removals. Second, migration problems will occur because of lacking of migration information in API document. API users need to find the alternative APIs by themselves to replace the removed APIs. Therefore, API developers do not have control over the impact of API removals on API users.

ND Model not only lacks the support for API removal management, but also has three negative impacts on API users. First, API users have difficulties in adapting client applications to API removals because no migration information is provided in API documents. Second, API users do not have sufficient time to adapt client applications because they are aware of API removals only after those API removals occur. Third, the probability that API users have to adapt client applications to API removals is high because such API removals occur without planning. Despite those negative impacts, ND Model has one positive impact on API developers: there is no deprecated API in ND Model, and thus API developers will not encounter the problem of code bloat.

C. H Model: Hybrid Model

As illustrated in Figure 1(c), *Hybrid Model* (*H Model*) is a hybrid of D Model and ND Model. In H Model, API in creation stage has two possible paths to removal stage. Path 1 includes two solid arcs in Figure 1(c), which is the same as D Model. Path 2 includes one dotted arc in Figure 1(c), which is the same as ND Model. The API which follows Path 1 becomes a deprecated API, and its removal is planned. The API which follows Path 2 becomes an NR API, and its removal is unplanned.

H Model provides partial support for API removal management. In H Model, both deprecated APIs and NR APIs exist. For deprecated APIs, API developers have control over the timing and impact of their removal. But, for NR APIs, API developers do not have any control. H Model has both

TABLE I. SUMMARY OF THE PRELIMINARY ANALYSIS RESULT.

Model	API removal management	Negative impacts	Positive impacts
D Model	Full support	1. Deprecated APIs cause API developers the problem of code bloat. (*cBloat*)	1. Migration information of deprecated APIs enables API users to adapt client applications to planned API removals. (*mInfo*) 2. Prior notification of planned API removals enables API users to have sufficient time to adapt client applications. (*aTime*) 3. The probability that API users have to adapt client applications to planned API removals is low. (*aPro*)
ND Model	No support	1. No migration information of NR APIs hinders API users from adapting client applications to unplanned API removals. (*mInfo*) 2. API users do not have sufficient time to adapt client applications due to the lack of prior notification of unplanned API removals. (*aTime*) 3. The probability that API users have to adapt client applications to NR APIs is high. (*aPro*)	1. NR APIs do not cause API developers the problem of code bloat. (*cBloat*)
H Model	Partial support	1. No migration information of NR APIs hinders API users from adapting client applications to API removals. (*mInfo*) 2. For unplanned API removals, the lack of their prior notification causes API users the problem of not having sufficient time to adapt client applications. (*aTime*) 3. For unplanned API removals, the probability that API users have to adapt client applications is high. (*aPro*) 4. Deprecated APIs cause API developers the problem of code bloat. (*cBloat*)	1. Migration information of deprecated APIs enables API users to adapt client applications to planned API removals. (*mInfo*) 2. For planned API removals, their prior notification enables API users to have sufficient time to adapt client applications. (*aTime*) 3. For planned API removals, the probability that API users have to adapt client applications is low. (*aPro*) 4. NR APIs do not cause API developers the problem of code bloat. (*cBloat*)

Note 1: The words in the parentheses are the abbreviations of impacts.
Note 2: The negative and positive impacts of H Model which are inherited from D Model are highlighted with the gray background, while those which are inherited from ND Model are shown with the white background.
Note 3: Planned API removals are the removals of deprecated APIs, while unplanned API removals are the removals of NR APIs.

positive and negative impacts. Some of them are inherited from D Model, and the others are inherited from ND Model. The whole list of those impacts is provided in Table I, which is introduced in the next section.

D. Summary

To have an overview of those API models, we summarize the analysis result in Table I. The analysis result reveals the following three types of information on the models: 1) degree of support for API removal management, 2) negative impacts, and 3) positive impacts. Furthermore, the impact categories, which are shown as index words in Table I, are described as follows:

1) *Code bloat (cBloat)*. It includes the impacts related to the problem of code bloat.
2) *Migration information (mInfo)*. It includes the impacts related to the provision of migration information.
3) *Adaptation time (aTime)*. It includes the impacts related to the time which API users have for software adaptation.
4) *Adaptation probability (aPro)*. It includes the impacts related to the probability that API users have to adapt client applications to planned or unplanned API removals.

III. CASE STUDIES

The goal of the case studies is to assess the positive and negative impacts of the models in four impact categories. Through the assessment, the best model will be concluded if it outperforms the others in the most impact categories.

A. Research Questions

To conclude the best model, we have to answer the following research questions:

1) RQ1: Regarding the impact category of code bloat, which model performs the best?
2) RQ2: Regarding the impact category of migration information, which model performs the best?
3) RQ3: Regarding the impact category of adaptation time, which model performs the best?
4) RQ4: Regarding the impact category of adaptation probability, which model performs the best?

To answer these research questions, we assess impacts of the models in four impact categories through a set of metrics. As shown in Table II, those metrics are organized according to targeted impact categories, and definitions are also provided. With these metrics, we can assess the impacts and answer the research questions.

B. Data Collection

Three subjects are chosen for data collection, and each one is the representative of a specific API lifecycle model. Those subjects are all medium-scaled open source projects with hundreds of Java classes. The duration of data collection for each subject is approximately three years. The subjects and the collected data are introduced as follows.

Subject for D Model: JFace with versions from 3.6 to 4.3. JFace is a popular user interface framework on Eclipse platform. The duration of the data collection is from June 2010 to June 2013. The collected data includes API documents and source code. From API documents, the deprecated APIs are extracted to measure the values of $PC_{d/all}$ and T_d. Besides, migration information for the deprecated APIs is investigated to enable the measurement of $PC_{dMI/d}$. The value of PB_p is measured through extracting APIs from API documents, detecting planned API removals, and confirming the occurrence of those planned API removals in the source code.

Subject for ND Model: JFreeChart with versions from 0.9.4 to 1.0.0. JFreeChart is a mature and widely used chart library. According to download statistics, it has been downloaded for more than three million times since its registration in SourceForge. The duration of the data collection is from October 2002 to December 2005. During data collection,

TABLE II. DEFINITION OF METRICS.

Targeted impact category	Metric	Definition
Code bloat	$PC_{d/all}$	In all APIs, the percentage of deprecated APIs.
	$PC_{nr/all}$	In all APIs, the percentage of NR APIs.
Migration information	$PC_{dMI/d}$	In all deprecated APIs, the percentage of deprecated APIs with migration information.
	$PC_{nrMI/nr}$	In all NR APIs, the percentage of NR APIs with migration information.
Adaptation time	T_d	The average time, measured in months, of a deprecated API from being announced to-be-removed to being removed. (i.e., the average time of a deprecated API staying in the deprecation stage)
	T_{nr}	The average time, measured in months, of an NR API from being announced to-be-removed to being removed.
Adaptation probability	PB_p	The probability of the occurrence of planned API removals.
	PB_u	The probability of the occurrence of unplanned API removals.

TABLE III. ASSESSMENT RESULTS FOR THE CODE BLOAT CATEGORY.

Model	$PC_{d/all}$, the metric for assessing negative impacts				$PC_{nr/all}$, the metric for assessing positive impacts			
	package	class	method	field	package	class	method	field
D	0.00%	4.01%	1.43%	2.69%	–	–	–	–
ND	–	–	–	–	6.81%	12.28%	13.19%	14.57%
H	0.00%	2.60%	1.81%	1.84%	0.00%	0.00%	0.02%	0.00%

Note 1: The label "–" means that the value of the metric is not available because the negative or positive impact of the corresponding model does not exist.
Note 2: The model which performs the best is highlighted with the gray background.

API documents are not provided. As a result, the collected data includes the source code, online forum, and jfreechart-commit mailing list, but no API documents. From the source code, packages, classes, methods, and fields with public or protected access modifiers are extracted as APIs. NR APIs and their removals are then detected to measure the values of $PC_{nr/all}$ and PB_u. In the online forum, migration information is identified to measure the value of $PC_{nrMI/nr}$. In jfreechart-commit mailing list, notification of the removals of NR APIs is also identified to measure the value of T_{nr}.

Subject for H Model: JFreeChart with versions from 1.0.2 to 1.0.13. The duration of the data collection is from August 2006 to April 2009. API documents are provided during data collection. Therefore, the collected data includes API documents, source code, online forum, and jfreechart-commit mailing list. In API documents, the deprecated APIs and their migration information are investigated to measure the values of $PC_{d/all}$, T_d, and $PC_{dMI/d}$. From API documents and source code, NR APIs, planned API removals, and unplanned API removals are detected to measure the values of $PC_{nr/all}$, PB_p, and PB_u. In the online forum, migration information of NR APIs is identified to measure the value of $PC_{nrMI/nr}$. In jfreechart-commit mailing list, notification of the removals of NR APIs is identified to measure the value of T_{nr}.

IV. RESULTS OF CASE STUDIES

In Section IV-A, results of case studies are presented to answer the four research questions. In Section IV-B, answers to those research questions are summarized to conclude the best model. Then, the cost-effectiveness of the best model is also discussed.

A. Answers to Research Questions

RQ1: Assessment of Impacts in the Code Bloat Category. The assessment results are summarized in Table III. The values of $PC_{d/all}$ show that little of APIs are deprecated APIs. Thus, the problem of code bloat caused by deprecated APIs in D Model is insignificant. On the other hand, NR APIs in ND Model not only avoid the problem of code bloat for API developers, but also reduce API developers' effort in maintaining API implementation by 6.81% to 14.57%. Regard to H Model, the values of $PC_{d/all}$ are between two models, but the values of $PC_{nr/all}$ are very low. So, the negative impact is medium but the positive is insignificant. In summary, ND Model is the best model because of the following two reasons. First, it only has the positive impact in the code bloat category. Second, it has the largest $PC_{nr/all}$ values, which means its positive impact is the most significant. As a result, ND Model performs the best regarding the code bloat category.

TABLE IV. ASSESSMENT RESULTS FOR THE MIGRATION INFORMATION CATEGORY.

Model	$PC_{nrMI/nr}$, the metric for assessing negative impacts				$PC_{dMI/d}$, the metric for assessing positive impacts			
	package	class	method	field	package	class	method	field
D	–	–	–	–	*	87.10%	86.39%	58.97%
ND	0.00%	0.52%	0.04%	0.00%	–	–	–	–
H	*	*	0.00%	*	*	88.48%	92.87%	71.56%

Note 1: The label "–" means that the value of the metric is not available because the negative or positive impact of the corresponding model does not exist.
Note 2: The label "*" means that the value of the metric is not available because of division by zero.
Note 3: The model which performs the best is highlighted with the gray background.

RQ2: Assessment of Impacts in the Migration Information Category. Table IV summarizes the assessment results. Both D Model and H Model have significant positive impacts with large $PC_{dMI/d}$ values. But, D Model is better than H Model because D Model has only positive impact. Unlike D Model, H Model has not only positive impact but also negative impact. Regarding the positive one, H Model has slightly larger positive impact than D Model. Regarding the negative one, the $PC_{nrMI/all}$ value of H Model reveals that none of NR APIs in the method level are provided with migration information. Unfortunately, lack of migration information hinders API users from migrating client applications. Two discussion topics in the online forum of JFreeChart have been found as the evidence. The first one is "Arrrgh! Lots of API changes again", in which API users state that "*..., these API changes really are not funny! It takes a lot of time, researching, looking in the new JFreeChart source code because there is no migration description.*" [13]. The second one is "API changes: undocumented (again)", in which API users state that "*Could documentation be improved and more information be provided to ease migration?*" [14]. With this evidence, it is concluded that the negative impact of H Model is significant enough to offset the positive impact of H Model. In summary, answer to RQ2 is that D Model performs the best regarding the migration information category.

RQ3: Assessment of Impacts in the Adaptation Time

TABLE V. ASSESSMENT RESULTS FOR THE ADAPTATION TIME CATEGORY.

Model	T_{nr}, the metric for assessing negative impacts	T_d, the metric for assessing positive impacts
D	–	24.01
ND	0.40	–
H	1.75	14.19

Note 1: The label "–" means that the value of the metric is not available because the negative or positive impact of the corresponding model does not exist.
Note 2: The model which performs the best is highlighted with the gray background.

TABLE VI. ASSESSMENT RESULTS FOR THE ADAPTATION PROBABILITY CATEGORY.

Model	PB_u, the metric for assessing negative impacts				PB_p, the metric for assessing positive impacts			
	package	class	method	field	package	class	method	field
D	–	–	–	–	0.00	0.00	0.00	0.00
ND	0.39	0.94	1.00	0.83	–	–	–	–
H	0.00	0.00	0.64	0.00	0.00	0.00	0.00	0.00

Note 1: The label "–" means that the value of the metric is not available because the negative or positive impact of the corresponding model does not exist.
Note 2: The model which performs the best is highlighted with the gray background.

Category. The positive and negative impact are assessed by T_d and T_{nr}. However, the subjects for D Model and H model do not contain the deprecated APIs which are removed. To measure the values, we assume that deprecated APIs in the subjects are finally removed in the last version. Because of the assumption, actual T_d values must larger than the measured T_d values. The assessment results are summarized in Table V. Compared with T_d values, values of T_{nr} are very small. It means that API users have only a short time to adapt client applications to unplanned API removals. Hence, the negative impact of ND Model and H Model is significant in those cases. Based on the assessment results, D Model is the best model because it has the most significant positive impact with the largest T_d value. Besides, D Model does not have negative impact. As a result, the answer to RQ3 is that D Model performs the best regarding the adaptation time category.

RQ4: Assessment of Impacts in the Adaptation Probability Category. Table VI summarizes the assessment results. Because deprecated APIs are not removed in our subjects, values of PB_p are all zero. It means the positive impact on API users is significant for D Model and H Model. On the other hand, the high values of PB_u for ND Model indicate that API users must adapt client applications to unplanned API removals. So, the negative impact of ND Model is significant. As a result, D Model is the best model because it has only positive impact and such positive impact is significant. Although H Model has positive impact with the same significance, it has some of negative impact assessed by PB_u. Hence, D Model is still better than H Model. In summary, the answer to RQ4 is that D Model performs the best regarding the adaptation probability category.

B. The Best Model

The answer to RQ1 is ND Model, while the answers to RQ2, RQ3, and RQ4 are D Model. As a result, ND Model outperforms the others only in the code bloat category, while D Model performs the best in the migration information, adaptation time, and adaptation probability categories. According to the summary, D Model is the best model because it outperforms the others in the most of categories.

The advantages of D Model are presented in Section II-A. According to four impact categories, the following discussion is to demonstrate that the cost of getting the advantage is low.

Code bloat category. The cost of maintaining deprecated APIs is low. As discussed the answer of RQ1 in Section IV-A, very few APIs in D Model are deprecated APIs. Hence, the cost of maintaining deprecated APIs is low.

Migration information category. The cost of providing migration information is low. Migration information is naturally derived because deprecated APIs are often planned to be replaced with new APIs. Besides, adding migration information to API documents requires little cost. As a result, the cost of providing migration information is low.

Adaptation time category. The cost of prior notification is low. The notification of API removals is often performed through 1) labelling an API 'deprecated' in API documents and 2) publishing updated API documents to API users. Because both of such costs are low, the cost of prior notification is low.

Adaptation probability category. The cost of planning API changes is low. Planning API removals requires designing new APIs and scheduling API removals. The former is the integral part of API design, which does not cause any additional cost. The latter needs little cost because API developers have to consider API removals for software release. Hence, the total cost of planning API changes is low.

V. RELATED WORK

Support for API removal adaptation. Chow and Notkin [15] proposed an approach for semi-automatic adaptation to API removals in libraries. Their approach required library developers to annotate API changes with a specific language, and the annotation was used by API users for API removal adaptation. The drawback of this approach was that library developers had to learn a new language. Perkins [16] developed a technique to replace calls to deprecated API methods with their method bodies. The assumption of the technique was that the method bodies contained appropriate replacement code. Many approaches [17][18] were developed to support API removal adaptation by recording and replaying refactorings with refactoring engines. In those approaches, API developers and API users were required to utilize the same refactoring engines so that recorded refactorings could be replayed by API users. An alternative solution to API removal adaptation was to develop matching techniques [2][19]-[21] for discovering replacement APIs, by which deprecated or removed APIs were replaced. Some of the techniques directly performed replacement without API users involvement, and thus the appropriateness of discovered replacement APIs was not guaranteed. On the contrary, the others provided a set of replacement API candidates from which API users could choose. But, API users had to spend additional effort in guaranteeing the appropriateness.

Although many approaches and techniques are developed to help API users with API removal adaptation, they all have limitations. Recently, API deprecation is a promising solution for adapting API changes. An empirical study of Hora et al. [10] indicate that the deprecation mechanism should be adopted. The study shows that API deprecation reaction is faster and larger compared with NR API reaction. Besides, the study of McDonnel et al. [22] indicate that client applications need a longer adaptation time when APIs are evolving fast. Such adaptation time can be preserved through deprecation because it signals API users that which API ought to be avoided [23]. In addition, Brito et al. [24] argue that replacement messages with deprecated APIs facilitate API users to adapt APIs. This argument complies with the study of Ko et al. [25], which empirically indicates that migration information promotes the reaction to API evolution. However, all these previous studies focus on why API developers should adopt deprecation. How to apply deprecation has not been investigated. Therefore, we discover the best model embedded with deprecation to present how deprecation can be applied to API removal management. In the best model, API removals are planned in advance and early announced to API users. Moreover, API developers provide migration information, which contains replacement APIs. As a result, the appropriateness of replacement APIs is guaranteed because of the credible information source. In summary, the best model ensures the support for API removal adaptation.

VI. Conclusion and Future Work

The best model for API removal management is presented in this work. The characteristics of the best model include 1) planning of API removals, which prevents unintentional API removals and makes APIs stable, 2) provision of migration information, which reduces migration effort, and 3) prior notification of planned API removals, which preserves sufficient time to adapt client applications. The goal behind the best model is to benefit both API developers and API users, who are the major stakeholders in the ecosystem formed by frameworks/libraries and client applications. As a result, following the best model will make API developers design more stable APIs with planning, and API users will spend less effort in constructing and maintaining client applications.

While we conclude D Model is the best in two popular, mature, and open source systems of Eclipse, the selected subjects might not be representative in other domains, such as web framework. Web framework is widely adopted in different ways to build kinds of web apps, and is changing at an extremely rapid pace right now. For the purpose of preserving market share, web framework developers are forced to evolve the framework in time to catch up with the trend. API removals will happen more frequently compared with those observed subjects in this study. Therefore, to investigate the best API lifecycle model further within such context will be our future work.

References

[1] I. Sommerville, *Software Engineering*. Pearson Education Limited, 2010, vol. Ninth Edition ed.

[2] Z. Xing and E. Stroulia, "API-Evolution Support with Diff-CatchUp," *Journal of IEEE Transactions on Software Engineering*, vol. 33, no. 12, Dec. 2007, pp. 818–836.

[3] D. Dig and R. Johnson, "The Role of Refactorings in API Evolution," in *Proceedings of the 21st IEEE International Conference on Software Maintenance (ICSM), 26–29 Sept. 2005, Budapest, Hungary*, 2005.

[4] "About API Manager," 2017, URL: https://docs.wso2.com/display/AM110/About+API+Manager [accessed: 2017-08-22].

[5] "Lifecycle Manager for APIs," 2015, URL: https://www.roguewave.com/products-services/akana/lifecycle-manager [accessed: 2017-08-22].

[6] "Oracle API Management," 2015, URL: http://www.oracle.com/us/products/middleware/soa/api-management/overview/index.html [accessed: 2017-08-22].

[7] D. Dig and R. Johnson, "How do APIs Evolve? A Story of Refactoring," *Journal of Software Maintenance and Evolution: Research and Practice*, vol. 18, no. 2, Mar. 2006, pp. 83–107.

[8] Z. Xing and E. Stroulia, "Differencing Logical UML Models," *Journal of Automated Software Engineering*, vol. 14, June 2007, pp. 215–259.

[9] L. Xavier, A. Brito, A. Hora, and M. T. Valente, "Historical and Impact Analysis of API Breaking Changes: A Large-scale Study," in *Proceedings of the IEEE 24th International Conference on Software Analysis, Evolution, and Reengineering (SANER), 20–24 Feb. 2017, Klagenfurt, Austria*, 2017, pp. 138–147.

[10] A. Hora et al., "How Do Developers React to API Evolution? A Large-scale Empirical Study," *Journal of Software Quality Journal*, 2016, pp. 1–31.

[11] W. Wu, F. Khomh, B. Adams, Y. G. Guhneuc, and G. Antoniol, "An Exploratory Study of API Changes and Usages based on Apache and Eclipse Ecosystems," *Journal of Empirical Software Engineering*, vol. 21, no. 6, Dec. 2016, pp. 2366–2412.

[12] G. Bavota et al., "The Impact of API Change and Fault-Proneness on The User Ratings of Android Apps," *Journal of IEEE Transactions on Software Engineering*, vol. 41, no. 4, Apr. 2015, pp. 384–407.

[13] "Arrrgh! Lots of API changes again!" 2003, URL: http://www.jfree.org/forum/viewtopic.php?f=3&t=5093 [accessed: 2017-08-22].

[14] "API changes: undocumented (again)," 2004, URL: http://www.jfree.org/forum/viewtopic.php?f=3&t=9265 [accessed: 2017-08-22].

[15] K. Chow and D. Notkin, "Semi-automatic Update of Applications in Response to Library Changes," in *Proceedings of the IEEE International Conference on Software Maintenance (ICSM), 4–8 Nov. 1996, Monterey, CA, USA*, 1996, pp. 359–368.

[16] J. H. Perkins, "Automatically Generating Refactorings to Support API Evolution," in *Proceedings of the 6th ACM SIGPLAN-SIGSOFT workshop on Program analysis for software tools and engineering (PASTE), 5–6 Sept. 2005, Lisbon, Portugal*, 2005, pp. 111–114.

[17] J. Henkel and A. Diwan, "CatchUp! Capturing and Replaying Refactorings to Support API Evolution," in *Proceedings of 27th International Conference on Software Engineering (ICSE), 15–21 May 2005, St. Louis, MO, USA*, 2005, pp. 274–283.

[18] D. Dig, S. Negara, V. Mohindra, and R. Johnson, "ReBA: Refactoring-aware Binary Adaptation of Evolving Libraries," in *Proceedings of 30th International Conference on Software Engineering (ICSE), 10–18 May 2008, Leipzig, Germany*, 2008, pp. 441–450.

[19] M. Kim, D. Notkin, and D. Grossman, "Automatic Inference of Structural Changes for Matching across Program Versions," in *Proceedings of the 29th international conference on Software Engineering (ICSE), 20–26 May 2007, Minneapolis, MN, USA*, 2007, pp. 333–343.

[20] W. Wu, Y.-G. Gueheneuc, G. Antoniol, and M. Kim, "AURA: A Hybrid Approach to Identify Framework Evolution," in *Proceedings of 32nd ACM/IEEE International Conference on Software Engineering (ICSE), 1–8 May 2010, Cape Town, South Africa*, 2010, pp. 325–334.

[21] Z. Xing and E. Stroulia, "Identifying and Summarizing Systematic Code Changes via Rule Inference," *Journal of IEEE Transactions on Software Engineering*, vol. 39, no. 1, Jan. 2013, pp. 45–62.

[22] T. McDonnell, B. Ray, and M. Kim, "An Empirical Study of API Stability and Adoption in the Android Ecosystem," in *Proceedings of 29th IEEE International Conference on Software Maintenance (ICSM), 22–28 Sept. 2013, Eindhoven, Netherlands*, 2013, pp. 70–79.

[23] J. Zhou and R. J. Walker, "API Deprecation: a Retrospective Analysis and Detection Method for Code Examples on the Web," in *Proceedings of 24th ACM SIGSOFT International Symposium on Foundations of Software Engineering, 13–18 Nov., 2016, Seattle, WA, USA*, 2016, pp. 266–277.

[24] G. Brito, A. Hora, M. T. Valente, and R. Robbes, "Do Developers Deprecate APIs with Replacement Messages? A Large-Scale Analysis on Java Systems," in *Proceedings of the IEEE 23rd International Conference on Software Analysis, Evolution, and Reengineering (SANER), 14–18 Mar. 2016, Suita, Japan*, 2016, pp. 360–369.

[25] D. Ko et al., "API Document Quality for Resolving Deprecated APIs," in *Proceedings of 21st IEEE Asia-Pacific Software Engineering Conference (APSEC), 1–4 Dec., 2014, Jeju, South Korea*, 2014, pp. 27–30.

Evaluating an Application Ontology for Recommending Technically Qualified Distributed Development Teams

Larissa Barbosa, Gledson Elias
Informatics Center
Federal University of Paraíba
João Pessoa, Brazil
e-mail: larissa@compose.ufpb.br, gledson@ci.ufpb.br

Abstract—**As a reflection of globalization, Distributed Software Development (DSD) has become a mainstream approach, in which the cooperation among globally distributed software development teams has the potential to reduce cost and development time. However, in order to make such promises a reality, it is important to find teams with specific technical background, required for implementing software modules that constitute the software product under development. Thus, it is a key aspect to contrast technical background of development teams against specified technical requirements for implementing the software project, making possible to select the most skilled teams to develop each software module. In such a context, this paper presents the evaluation of an application ontology that supports selection processes of distributed development teams, which are technically skilled to implement software modules in distributed software projects. Experimental results show that the evaluated ontology represents and formalizes an extremely complex problem in a systematic and structured way, allowing its direct or customized adoption in selection processes of globally distributed development teams.**

Keywords-ontology; distributed software development; selection process.

I. INTRODUCTION

In software engineering, a great body of knowledge has been accumulated over the last decades regarding methods, techniques, processes and tools, improving productivity and software quality. As such, several software development approaches have been proposed by academia and industry. Nowadays, as a mainstream approach, Distributed Software Development (DSD) promotes the cooperation among globally distributed teams for implementing different software product modules, reducing the development cost and time, favored by the hiring of cheaper staff in different locations, the fast formation of development teams and the adoption of the follow-the-sun development strategy [1][2]. Besides, DSD also enables to find qualified workforces and domain experts in worldwide outsourced teams or even teams in global coverage companies [3][4][5].

In order to make DSD promises a reality, it is a key task to identify development teams with specific skills and technical knowledge required to develop software modules that compose the software product under development. In such a context, it is important to compare the skills and technical knowledge of the candidate development teams against the technical requirements specified to implement each software module, making possible to identify those that are more qualified to implement each one.

However, in DSD projects, geographic dispersion may cause difficulties for the project manager to assess the skills and technical knowledge of the candidate teams. In most cases, the project manager does not develop face-to-face activities with remote teams, having neither direct personal contact nor drinking fountain talks [6]. Hence, it is therefore hard to get precise and up-to-date information about members of such remote teams, given that the formal communication mechanisms based on documents or data repositories do not react as quickly as informal ones. Besides, even when the project manager has a bit of information about candidate teams, in large software projects, the task of selecting teams may still be quite complex and prone to evaluation errors, since different teams may adopt ambiguous vocabulary and incompatible methods to identify and evaluate their skills and technical knowledge.

As a consequence, we have proposed a layered recommendation framework [7] as a mean to help project managers in the selection and allocation of development teams in DSD projects. The framework is composed of three recommendation phases: *recommending software modules* – intends to cluster components into software modules, reducing dependencies among modules and hence, minimizing communication requirements; *recommending qualified teams* – aims to identify technically qualified teams to implement each software module; and *recommending teams allocation* – intends to suggest possible allocations of software modules to qualified development teams, concerning their non-technical attributes as a mean to reduce inter-team communication requirements.

In the context of the framework, this paper presents the experimental evaluation of an application ontology, called *OntoDSD* [8], whose main goal is to support the selection of distributed development teams that are technically skilled to implement software modules in DSD projects. Note that *OntoDSD* is part of the second phase of the recommendation framework which, as mentioned, is called *recommending qualified teams*. As the main contribution, experimental results show that *OntoDSD* represents and formalizes an extremely complex problem in a systematic and structured way, allowing its direct or customized adoption in selection processes of globally distributed development teams.

The rest of this paper is organized as follows. Section II introduces the main concepts and components related to an ontology. Section III presents an overview of the *OntoDSD* ontology, explaining its main concepts and relationships associated to the selection of technically qualified distributed teams. In order to observe the usability and applicability of the proposed ontology, Section IV presents the experimental evaluation. Next, Section V presents final remarks, identifies limitations and indicates future work.

II. FUNDAMENTS

The literature contains many definitions of an ontology. For the purposes of this paper, as defined in [9], an ontology is a formal explicit description of concepts in a given domain of discourse, properties of each concept describing its features and attributes, and restrictions on such properties.

In general, the concepts in the modeled domain are represented by elements called *classes*, which can adopt inheritance abstraction to formulate a class hierarchy, in which each class inherits properties from one or more superclasses. Classes can have *instances*, which correspond to individual objects in the modeled domain. A class has several characteristics, attributes and restrictions that are represented by elements called *properties*.

Each property has a *domain* and a *range*, which can belong to a specific type and can have a set of allowed values, ranging from simple types to instances of classes. Properties can be divided into *object properties* and *datatype properties*. Object properties associate instances of one or two classes. Datatype properties create a relationship between a class instance and values of a certain simple type, such as strings and numbers. Each instance can have concrete values for the properties of its respective class.

In relation to development methodologies, there are several proposals in the literature to systematize the construction and evolution of ontologies [10]. However, despite the valuable contributions, none of them can be considered the correct one. Indeed, none of them has enough maturity, and therefore, there is no consensus on the best, most complete or most appropriate methodology that can be widely applicable in varied domains and application needs.

As a result, due to its simplicity of documentation, ease of application, extensive tooling support and focus on the construction of ontologies, we opted for the methodology *Ontology Development 101* [9], which defines a very simple guide based on an iterative approach that assists ontology designers, even non-experts, in the creation of ontologies using a support tool, such as Protégé [11].

In the *OntoDSD* development, we decided to adopt a *top-down* approach because it favors better control of the level of details, avoiding excessive details present in a *bottom-up* approach, which may lead to greater rework, effort and inconsistencies, and moreover, may hinder the identification of relationships and similarities among concepts [12].

It is important to highlight that the development of the ontology was specified using the Protégé tool [11], which provides support for the constructors of the Web Ontology Language (OWL) [13], recommended by the World Wide Web Consortium (W3C).

III. ONTODSD

OntoDSD is an application ontology, which has the main goal of supporting the selection of distributed development teams, technically skilled to implement software modules in DSD projects. Thus, the modeled domain is *DSD projects*, and, in a more specific way, the scope is the *selection of technically qualified teams to implement software modules*. Figure 1 presents the *OntoDSD* conceptual map.

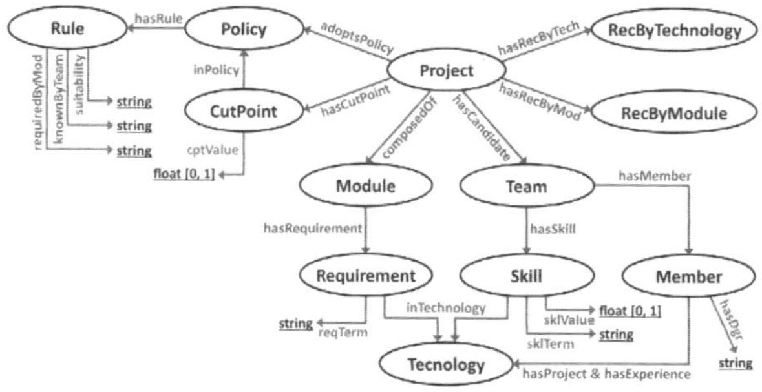

Figure 1. OntoDSD conceptual map.

In *OntoDSD*, a DSD project (*Project*) is composed of a set of software modules (*Module*) that can be developed by a set of globally distributed development teams (*Team*). In Figure 1, the object property *composedOf* represents the relationship between a project and its constituting software modules. The object property *hasCandidate* represents the relationship between a project and distributed development teams, which are candidates to implement software modules.

A software project (*Project*) adopts selection policies (*Policy*) for recommending development teams to implement software modules based on different criteria (*Rule*) and cut points (*CutPoint*), which establish a minimum suitability level for considering a team adequate to implement software modules. In Figure 1, the object property *adoptsPolicy* represents the relationship among a project and possible selection policies, according to specific project needs. The object property *hasCutPoint* represents the relationship between a project and defined cut points, each on related to each possible policy using the object property *inPolicy*.

OntoDSD provides two types of recommendations. The first, called *RecByTechnology*, represents the suitability level of candidate teams in relation to each technology required by software modules. The second, called *RecByModule*, represents the suitability level of candidate teams for implementing each software module. In Figure 1, the object properties *hasRecByTech* and *hasRecByMod* represent the relationships between a project and their recommendations.

A. Representing Software Modules

Considering a given software module (*Module*), it is important to characterize the knowledge requirements (*Requirement*) imposed in relation to technologies (*Technology*) adopted to implement the module. In *OntoDSD*, the knowledge requirement indicates the knowledge level required in each technology.

As illustrated in Figure 1, the object property *hasRequirement* associates a specific software module with a knowledge requirement, and through its datatype property *reqTerm*, flags the required knowledge level, whose initially proposed levels are *low*, *medium* and *high*. It is important to note that the number and the value of the terms used to label the knowledge level may be redefined by the project manager. Now, regarding a given knowledge requirement, the object property *inTechnology* associates the knowledge requirement with a specific technology. Hence, together, these classes and properties represent the fact that a given module has a certain knowledge requirement in relation to a particular technology, demanding a given specified knowledge level.

B. *Representing Development Teams*

In *OntoDSD*, a development team (*Team*) is composed of a set of members (*Member*). In Figure 1, the object property *hasMember* represents the relationship between a team and its constituting members. Regarding a given development team, it is vital to gather information about each member in relation to technologies (*Technology*) required by software modules. To do that, for each required technology, three pieces of data must be gathered: *years of experience*, *number of developed projects* and *number of degrees*. As can be seen in [14][15][16], in general, such information can indicate whether an individual is an expert in a specific technology.

In *OntoDSD*, via the datatype property *hasDgr* and the object properties *hasExperience* and *hasProject*, each member (*Member*) is associated to a specific technology (*Technology*). Note in Figure 2 that properties *hasExperience* and *hasProject* have sub-properties for representing respectively, the years of experience a given member has in a specific technology, as well as the number of projects developed by the member in such a technology. Hence, together, such classes and properties represent that a given team has members with degrees, projects and experiences in many technologies.

Figure 2. Sub-properties for years of experience and number of projects.

Now, such gathered information about members of a given team (*Team*) allows to infer the skill and technical knowledge (*Skill*) possessed by the whole team in relation to each technology (*Technology*). In Figure 1, the object property *hasSkill* associates a given team to one or more skills, which in turn are associated to their respective technologies using the object property *inTechnology*. For each skill, the datatype properties *sklValue* and *sklTerm* signalize the real numeric value within the interval [0, 1] and the correspondent textual term, such as *none*, *low*, *medium* and *high*, representing the skill level of the team. Hence, together, such classes, object and datatype properties represent that a given team has a specified technical skill level in a certain technology. Again, the number and the value of the terms used to label the skill level may be redefined by the project manager.

C. *Representing Selection Policies*

In order to evaluate the technical suitability of candidate teams, it is necessary to define a selection policy. According to the needs of the software project, different policies may be adopted, changing the way the teams can be selected. A selection policy is a table of rules (Table I), stated by *if-then* expressions, which correlate terms in rows and columns, defining rules that generate desired results, represented by cells in their intersections. We can realize the rule rationale with an example: *IF Skill Level is "none" AND Knowledge Level is "medium" THEN Suitability Level is "low"*.

TABLE I. SELECTION POLICY

			Technical Requirements		
			Knowledge Level		
			low	**medium**	**high**
Teams	Skill Level	**none**	*medium*	*low*	*none*
		low	*high*	*medium*	*low*
		medium	*medium*	*high*	*medium*
		high	*low*	*medium*	*high*

OntoDSD represents policies as individuals of the classes *Policy* and *Rule*, which are related by the object property *hasRule*, as shown in Figure 1. Observe that a certain policy must be associated with a set of rules, modeling each cell of the selection policy table. In turn, rules are modeled using the datatype properties *requiredByMod*, *knownByTeam* and *suitability*, representing, respectively: the knowledge level required in a given technology, the technical skill possessed by a certain team in that technology and accordingly, the suitability level owned by that team in that technology.

D. *Representing Technically Skilled Teams*

Now, it is time to apply the selection policy in order to discover the technical suitability owned by each team to implement each software module. *OntoDSD* represents the technical suitability possessed by teams as recommendations. As discussed before, there can be two kinds of recommendations, *RecByTechnology* and *RecByModule*, which are characterized in the conceptual map in Figure 3.

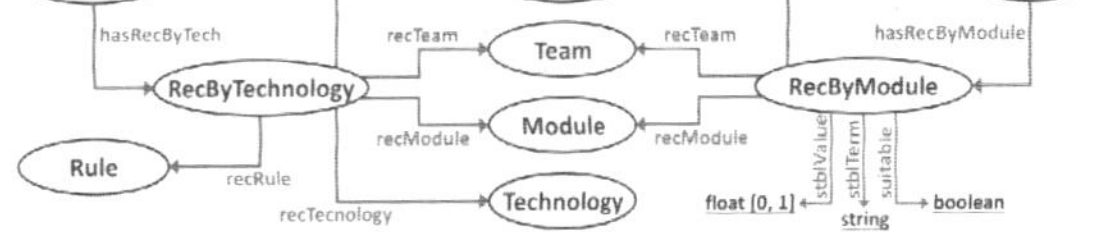

Figure 3. Recommendations in OntoDSD.

1) *Recommendation of Teams to Required Technologies*

A recommendation *RecByTechnology* represents the suitability level possessed by a certain team (*Team*) in relation to a particular technology (*Technology*) required by a specific module (*Module*) according an adopted policy (*Policy*). Indeed, the suitability level is signalized by an instance of the rule (*Rule*) trigged by the adopted selection policy, in which the datatype property *suitability* (Figure 1) indicates the textual term representing the suitability level.

As can be seen in Figure 3, the relationship between such concepts is represented using a set of object properties:

recPolicy, *recTeam*, *recModule*, *recTechnology* and *recRule*. It should be noted that such object properties can be derived through inference from information already stored in the ontology. In order to infer such properties, *OntoDSD* has a set of specified axioms, which are not discussed herein for simplicity, but interested readers can found details in [8].

2) Recommendation of Teams to Software Modules

Based on the suitability level possessed by a given team for each required technology, it is possible to estimate the suitability level owned by that team in each software module, which in *OntoDSD* is represented by the recommendation *RecByModule*. To do that, the project manager ought to adopt an empirical or mathematical method, like the one proposed in [14].

A recommendation *RecByModule* represents the suitability level possessed by a given team (*Team*) in relation to a particular module (*Module*) according an adopted policy (*Policy*). Indeed, the suitability level is signalized by the datatype properties *stblValue* and *stblTerm* associated to the respective recommendation (Figure 3), which indicate its numerical value and textual term, respectively.

As shown in Figure 3, the relationship between such concepts is represented via the object properties *recPolicy*, *recTeam* and *recModule*. Note that such object properties can also be derived by inference from information already present in the ontology. However, for simplicity, the set of related axioms are not discussed herein, but detailed in [8].

3) Application of the Cut Point

With the goal of filtering out the teams that might have a low suitability level, a cut point defined by the project manager must be used. This step consists simply in eliminating those teams that do not reach the cut point. As depicted in Figure 1, the object property *hasCutPoint* associates a project (*Project*) to a specific cut point (*CutPoint*), which through its datatype property *cptValue* stores a real numeric value in the interval [0, 1], stipulated by the project manager to determine the suitability possessed by a given team in relation to a certain software module.

To do that, we must update the instances of the recommendation *RecByModule*, setting the value of its datatype property *suitable*, illustrated in Figure 3. It is important to point out that the update of the property *suitable* is also inferred automatically through an ontology axiom.

IV. CASE STUDY

In order to evaluate the usability and applicability of the *OntoDSD* ontology, we developed three use cases based on the project of two different software product lines. The two first cases were developed using a hypothetical software product line in the e-commerce area, documented in [17]. These two first use cases were organized in two development iterations, contemplating the phases of domain engineering and application engineering of the product line. Next, another use case was developed based on a real project of a middleware product line for mobile devices called *Multi-MOM* [18], whose instantiation will be illustrated next in this section.

When conducting the use cases, first the *OntoDSD* ontology was completely specified and validated in the Protégé tool [11], which supports the OWL specification language [13]. Using Protégé, it was possible to create and model classes, object and datatype properties, restrictions and axioms. Next, each use case was also instantiated and validated in Protégé, including individuals of the several *OntoDSD* ontological elements. Besides, Protégé allows for queries and visualization of the results that are automatically generated by several *OntoDSD* axioms.

A. *Representing Software Modules*

Multi-MOM [18] is a middleware product line for mobile computing. As shown in Figure 4, its component-based architecture has five software modules, indicated in the small rectangles labeled from *M0* to *M4*, according to the first phase of the proposed framework [7], explained in Section I.

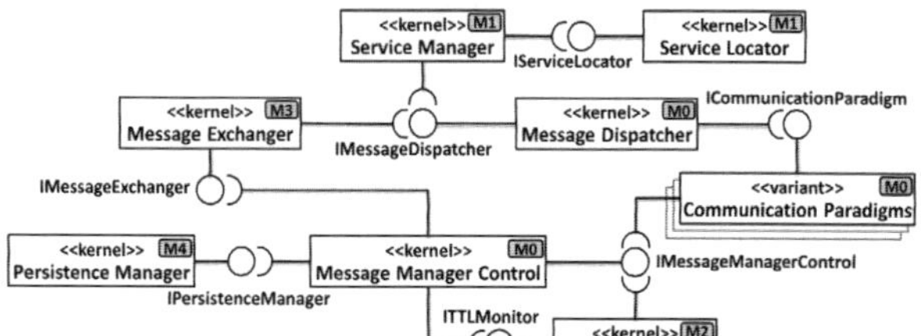

Figure 4. Multi-MOM architecture.

The characterization of the technologies required by those modules was performed by the software architecture that created and designed *Multi-MOM*. As an example, Figure 5 illustrates the *OntoDSD* instantiation to characterize the technologies required to implement module *MD0*. As illustrated in Figure 5, module *M0* requires technologies *Communication Paradigms*, *Reflexive Programming*, *Android* and *Java* with *"high"* knowledge level. Besides, it requires *"medium"* knowledge level on *SQL*.

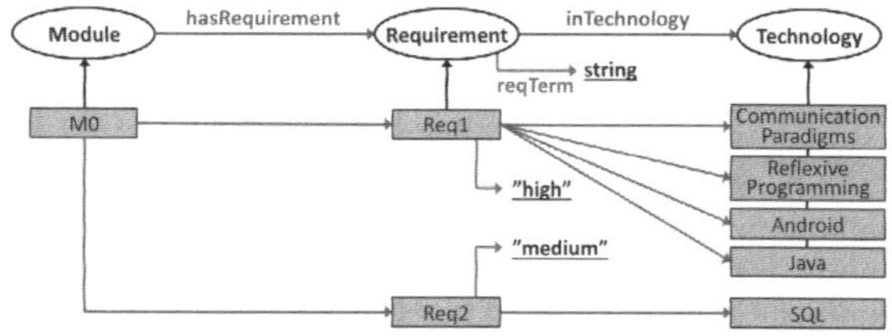

Figure 5. Characterization of module M0.

B. *Representing Development Teams*

Considering the difficulty of finding real development teams for use cases, the development team definition was performed based on the local market and computer science students, resulting in a set of 179 participant developers, which answered online forms covering all technologies required by modules of the use cases. The adopted forms and the respective answers can be found in [14].

Next, based on the answered forms, the skills and technical knowledge of the 179 developers were characterized in each technology required by modules.

Figure 6 shows an example instantiation for characterizing the skills and technical knowledge in *Android* possessed by member *MB1* that belongs to team *T20*. As can be seen, *MB1* has between three and five years of experience in *Android* and has participated in up to five projects that adopt *Android*.

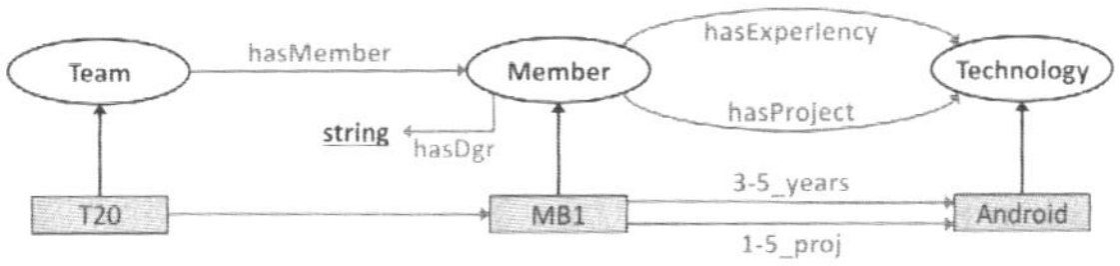

Figure 6. Characterization of member MB1 in Android Technology.

Regarding 179 developers, we created 22 teams with different sizes, varying from 2 to 18, dividing the members randomly until complete all teams. The final composition of the teams was: 1 team with 2 members, 3 teams with 3 members, 5 teams with 5 members, 4 teams with 8 members, 2 teams with 9 members, 3 teams with 10 members, 3 teams with 15 members, and 1 team with 18 members.

Next, based on the skills and technical knowledge of each developer, it is possible to characterize the skills and technical knowledge of the respective teams for each technology required by modules. Figure 7 shows the instantiation for characterizing team *T20* in *Android* technology. As can be seen, considering the skills and technical knowledge of its developers, team *T20* has a technical skill level with value *0,88* in *Android* technology, which, according to the ranges of levels adopted, characterizes a "*high*" skill.

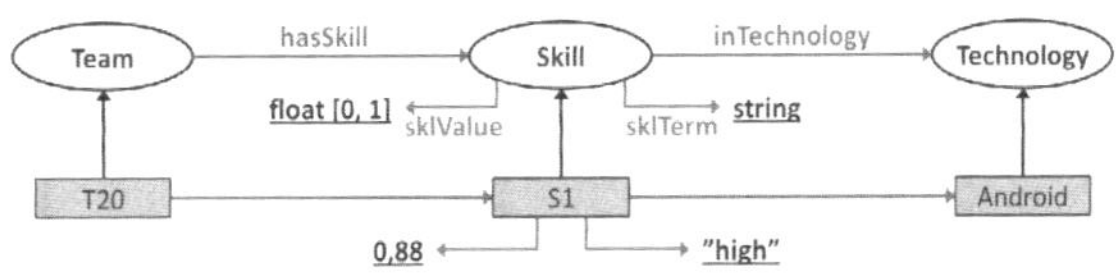

Figure 7. Characterization of team T20 in Android technology.

It is important to stress that each candidate team can consist of colocalized members only. Thus, if one needs to consider a candidate team consisting of members from different locations, it is suggested to model different teams for each location. Besides, *OntoDSD* does not represent non-technical aspects related to DSD projects in geographical, temporal, cultural and economic dimensions. Such a design decision is a consequence of the layered architecture of the proposed framework [7], introduced in Section I, which deals with such non-technical aspects in its third phase called *recommending teams allocation*.

C. Characterization of Selection Policies

In the *OntoDSD* instantiation, we initially specified four different selection policies, created based on the observations and analysis presented in other related proposals in the literature [19][20][21][22]. The four proposed policies are:

a) **Equivalent qualification:** selects teams with technical skills close to knowledge level required by modules.

b) **Most skilled teams:** selects teams that have the highest technical skills, independently of the knowledge level required by modules.

c) **Minimum qualification:** selects teams that possess minimum technical skills required by modules.

d) **Training provision:** selects teams that have technical skills bellow the required by modules.

For instance, considering equivalent qualification policy, defined in Table I, the rule instantiation represented by the intersection of the fourth row with the third column, here called *R12*, is presented in Figure 8. The instantiated rule is interpreted as follows: *IF Skill Level is "high" AND Knowledge Level is "high" THEN Suitability Level is "high"*. It is important to point out that the 12 rules in Table I were numbered from *R1* to *R12*, going from the left to the right and the top to the bottom.

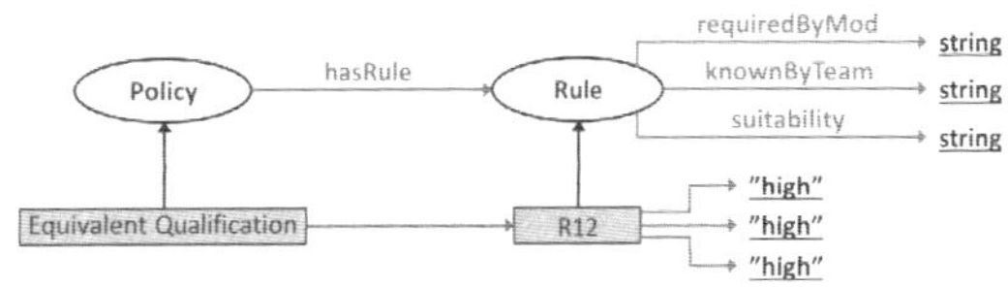

Figure 8. Characterization of rule R12 in selection policy.

Table II shows that different cut points were used for each selection policy. Based on the use cases, it was perceived that the suitability values for the teams varied in relation to adopted selection policies, reinforcing that different policies assign different suitability to teams. Nevertheless, in an experiment analysis where each use case was evaluated according to each selection policy, we saw a trend of the training provision policy to present suitability values higher than all other ones. On the other hand, the minimum qualification policy tends to present higher values than the equivalent qualification and more skilled team policies. Finally, we also realized that the equivalent qualification policy tends to generate higher values than the more skilled team policy. Given this empirical evidence, we decided to use different cut points for each selection policy.

TABLE II. ADOPTED CUT POINTS

Selection Policiy	Cut Point
Equivalent Qualification	0,60
Most skilled teams	0,55
Minimum Qualification	0,70
Training Provision	0,75

Figure 9 exemplifies the instantiation of the cut points in *OntoDSD*, showing the representation of the cut point of value *0,60* adopted in the selection policy *Equivalent Qualification* used in the *Multi-MOM* project.

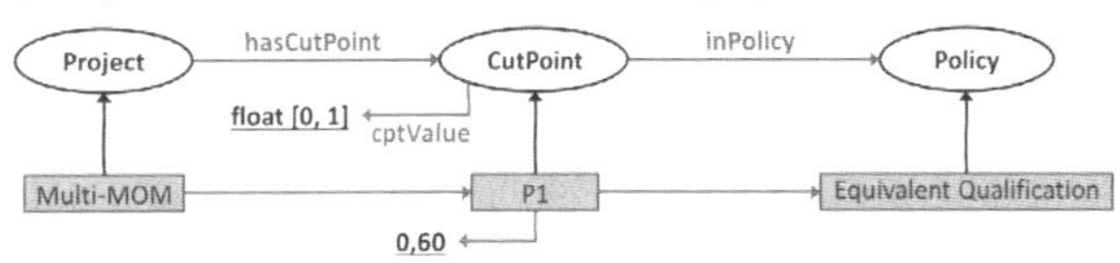

Figure 9. Cut point for policy Equivalent Qualification.

D. Evaluation of Team Suitability

At this point, considering technologies required by modules, the team technical skills in each technology and the selection policy adopted in the project, we can infer the technical suitability for each team in each technology required by each module, according to the selection policy. Figure 10 shows the technical suitability inference for team *T20* in *Android*, which is required by module *M0*, according to the selection policy *Equivalent Qualification*.

As we can see in Figure 10, the referred suitability is defined by the application of rule *R12*, whose instantiation in *OntoDSD* was shown in Figure 8.

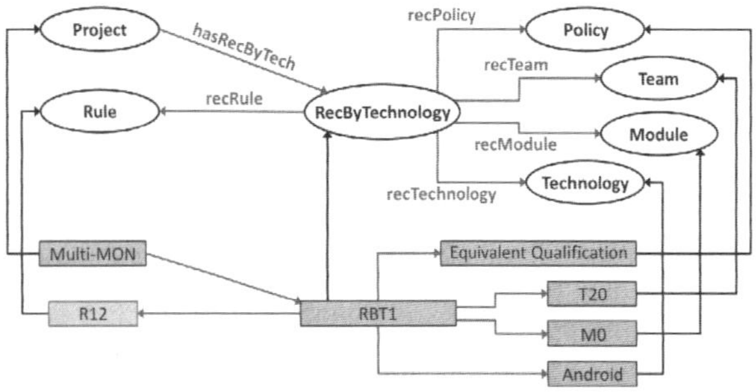

Figure 10. Technical suitability of team T20 to Android in module M0.

It is relevant to point out that the adopted rule *R12* is inferred by an *OntoDSD* axiom, illustrated in Figure 11, as specified in Protégé. As already indicated, *OntoDSD* has six axioms for inferring six ontological elements: selection rules, suitability terms and technically suitable teams. Herein, figures show ontological elements inferred by axioms in orange color. However, for simplicity, the other axioms are not presented, but interested readers can found them in [8].

RecByTechnology(?re), hasRecByTech(?pr, ?re), recPolicy(?re, ?po), recTeam(?re, ?e), recModule(?re, ?m), recTechnology(?re, ?t), knownByTeam(?r, ?vh), requiredByModule(?r, ?vreq) -> recRule(?re, ?r)

Figure 11. Axiom for recommending a selection rule.

At this point, it is possible to measure empirically or mathematically the suitability of the teams to the software modules. For that, in these use cases, we adopted the mathematical approach proposed by Santos [14] to derive suitability level possessed by teams in software modules, based on suitability possessed by those teams in each technology required by software modules. In this mathematical approach, based on forms filled by each developer about years of experience, number of degrees and projects in each technology, the answers are weighted in a set of equations that derive the knowledge level owned by each developer in each technology. Next, based on the skill level owned by each member of each team in a specific technology, we can derive mathematically the knowledge level of the whole team in that technology.

Figure 12 shows an example of the final recommendation of team *T20* to module *M0*, whose numeric suitability value is *0,71*. Note that, applying *OntoDSD* axioms, it is possible to infer the textual terms that represent the suitability. In Figure 12, the suitability textual term is *"medium"*.

Finally, based on *OntoDSD* axioms, we can infer the technically suitable teams for each software module from the evaluation of the cut point defined in the software project to the selection policy at hand, defining hence the possible candidate teams for the implementation of software modules. Please note that in the datatype property *suitable*, Figure 12 already includes the result of the suitability inference of team *T20* to module *M0* in policy *Equivalent Qualification*.

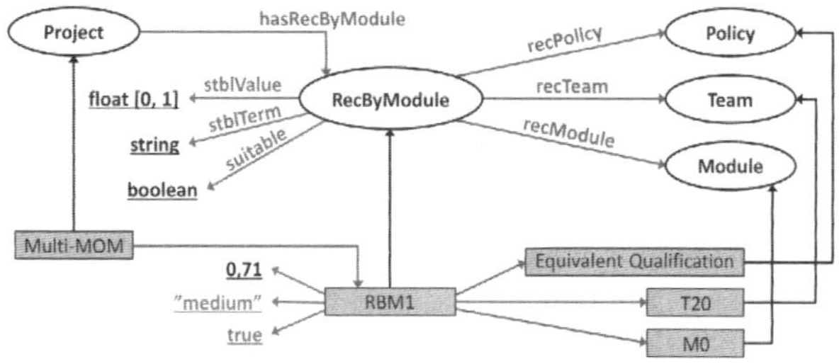

Figure 12. Recommendation of team T20 to module M0.

In the *Multi-MOM* use case, after applying the cut point, among the 22 candidate teams, *OntoDSD* recommended 5, 11, 12, 21 and 19 teams to implement modules *M0, M1, M2, M3* and *M4*, respectively. For instance, analyzing the recommendation for module *M0*, in sequence, teams *T20, T11, T16, T18* and *T19* are recommended as suitable considering the *Equivalent Qualification* policy.

Considering the high to medium knowledge levels required by module *M0* in all related technologies (Figure 5), an inspection by hand, in relation to skill levels possessed by all teams in such technologies, reveals that the recommended teams are better suited because their technical skills are closer to knowledge levels required by module *M0* in such technologies. Following such a rationale, it is possible to conclude that recommended teams are the most appropriate with respect to all adopted policies, but due space limitation, it is not possible to present and discuss in detail such manual inspection and assessment rationale.

In summary, regarding four selection policies defined and three use cases developed to evaluate the usability and applicability of the *OntoDSD* ontology, each use case resulted in four recommendations of suitability of the teams to the modules, generating one recommendation for each selection policy. Hence, considering all use cases, we generated 12 different set of recommendations.

V. CONCLUSION AND FUTURE WORK

In this paper, we presented the evaluation of an application ontology, called *OntoDSD*, which supports the selection of technically qualified distributed teams for the implementation of software modules in DSD projects. As the main contribution, adopting the strategy divide and conquer, *OntoDSD* represents and formalizes an extremely complex problem in a systematic and structured way, allowing its direct or customized adoption in selection processes of globally distributed development teams.

The general structure of *OntoDSD* is shown in the conceptual map in Figure 1, where the whole problem is modeled using only 12 classes, related by 23 object properties and 11 datatype properties, which, when instantiated, can systematize the decision-making process of the project manager, especially when observed through the viewpoint of the high complexity of the problem, which is clear when this problem is handled in ad-hoc ways. Besides, *OntoDSD* facilitates the communication between the project manager and team members, establishing a common vocabulary between all stakeholders in the selection process.

The *OntoDSD* instantiation may require a considerable effort for creating instances and their object and datatype properties, and consequently is prone to error and may cause a waste of time. For instance, considering *Multi-MOM*, which includes 5 software modules, 7 technologies, 22 teams, and 4 selection policies, the number of class instances (3.267), object properties (19.150) and datatype properties (1.982) is staggering, requiring a remarkable effort to manipulate them in Protégé. In such a case, it was required around 500 man-hours to represent gathered information as instances and properties in Protégé.

Nevertheless, *OntoDSD* offers as an additional facility a set of axioms, allowing the automatic inference of object and datatype properties. In *Multi-MOM*, such axioms infer 2.376 object properties and 880 datatype properties, representing a coverage around 12.5% and 44.4%, in relation to object and datatype properties, respectively.

OntoDSD has potential to be reused in many different scenarios. For instance, once a given software project is instantiated, with its software modules, required technologies, candidate teams and adopted selection policy, the evaluation of another selection policy may easily reuse all instances and object/datatype properties related to software modules, required technologies and candidate teams. In a most significant way, if we devise a data base of previous software projects, including most technologies usually required to implement software modules, a large number of candidate teams and the main adopted selection policies, the evaluation of a new software project may also reuse all instances and object/datatype properties related to technologies, teams and selection policies.

Even considering the reuse potential of the *OntoDSD* ontology, it is still required a considerable effort during the manual instantiation to identify and manipulate the instances and their object and datatype properties that may be reused and those that need to be created. In order to decrease this effort, as a future work, its instantiation could be performed programmatically, exploring the Protégé API, avoiding errors and saving time. Just as an illustration to the extremely positive impact of the programmatic approach, consider an application where the user signalizes in a specific set of tables: software modules, required technologies, candidate teams and their members. In such an application, it could almost all be created in an automatic and transparent way, including all instances and object/datatype properties.

REFERENCES

[1] R. Martignoni, "Global Sourcing of Software Development: A Review of Tools and Services", 4th IEEE International Conference on Global Software Engineering (ICGSE 2009), IEEE, 2009, pp. 303-308.

[2] E. Carmel, Y. Dubinsky, and A. Espinosa, "Follow the Sun Software Development: New Perspectives, Conceptual Foundation, and Exploratory Field Study", 42nd Hawaii International Conference on System Sciences (HICSS'09), IEEE, 2009, pp. 1-9.

[3] J. Herbsleb and D. Moitra, "Global Software Development", IEEE Software, issue 2, pp. 16-20, 2001.

[4] P. Ovaska, M. Rossi, and P. Marttiin, "Architecture as a Coordination Tool in Multi-site Software Development", Software Process: Improvement and Practice, vol. 8, issue 4, pp. 233-247, 2003.

[5] R. Prikladnicki, J. L. N. Audy, and R. Evaristo, "Global Software Development in Practice: Lessons Learned", Software Process: Improvement and Practice, vol. 8, issue 4, pp. 267-281, 2003.

[6] A. Mockus and J. Herbsleb, "Challenges of Global Software Development", 7th International Symposium on Software Metrics (METRICS 2001), IEEE, 2001, pp. 182-184.

[7] T. A. B. Pereira, V. S. Santos, B. L. Ribeiro, and G. Elias, "A Recommendation Framework for Allocating Global Software Teams in Software Product Line Projects", 2nd International Workshop on Recommendation Systems for Software Engineering (RSSE'10), ACM, 2010, pp. 36-40.

[8] L. Barbosa, "An Ontological Approach for Recommending Technically Qualified Teams in Distributed Software Projects", Master Dissertation, UFPB, Brazil, 2013.

[9] N. F. Noy and D. L. McGuinness, "Ontology Development 101: A Guide to Creating Your First Ontology", Stanford Knowledge Systems Laboratory Technical Report KSL-01-05, 2001.

[10] M. Cristani and R. Cuel, "A Survey on Ontology Creation Methodologies", International Journal on Semantic Web and Information Systems, vol. 1, no. 2, pp. 48-68, 2005.

[11] Protégé. Available in: http://protege.stanford.edu 2017.08.16.

[12] M. Uschold and M. Gruninger, "Ontologies: Principles, Methods and Applications", The Knowledge Engineering Review, vol. 11, issue 2, pp. 93-136, 1996.

[13] OWL Web Ontology Language Guide. Available in: http://www.w3.org/TR/owl-guide 2017.08.16.

[14] V. S. Santos, "An Approach for Selecting Technically Qualified Teams in Software Projects", Master Dissertation, UFPB, Brazil, 2014.

[15] J. Shanteau, D. J. Weiss, R. P. Thomas, and J. C. Pounds, "Performance-Based Assessment of Expertise: How to Decide if Someone is an Expert or not", European Journal of Operational Research, vol. 136, issue 2, pp. 253-263, 2002.

[16] D. J. Weiss, J. Shanteau, and P. Harries, "People Who Judge People", Journal of Behavioral Decision Making, vol. 19, issue 5, pp. 441-454, 2006.

[17] H. Gomaa, "Designing Software Product Lines with UML: From Use Cases to Pattern-Based Software Architectures", Addison-Wesley, 2004.

[18] Y. M. Bezerra, "Multi-MOM: A Multi-Paradigm, Extensible and Message-Oriented Mobile Middleware", Master Dissertation, UFPB, Brazil, 2010.

[19] A. S. Barreto, "Staffing a Software Project: A Constraint Satisfaction Based Approach", Master Dissertation, Federal University of Rio de Janeiro, Brazil, 2005.

[20] M. A. Silva, "WebAPSEE-Planner: Supporting People Instantiation in Software Projects through Policies, Master Dissertation, Federal University of Pará, Brazil, 2007.

[21] D. A. Callegari, L. Foliatti, and R. M. Bastos, "MRES: A Tool for Resource Selection in Software Projects through a Fuzzy, Multi-Criteria Approach, Brazilian Symposium on Software Engineering (SBES 2009), Tools Session, 2009, pp. 61-66.

[22] J. Collofello, D. Houston, I. Rus, A. Chauhan, D. M. Sycamore, and D. S. Daniels, "A System Dynamics Software Process Simulator for Staffing Policies Decision Support", 31st Annual Hawaii International Conference on System Sciences (HICSS'98), IEEE, 1998, vol. 6, pp. 103-111.

Validation of Specification Models Based on Petri Nets

Radek Kočí and Vladimír Janoušek

Brno University of Technology, Faculty of Information Technology,
IT4Innovations Centre of Excellence
Bozetechova 2, 612 66 Brno, Czech Republic
{koci,janousek}@fit.vutbr.cz

Abstract—**Each validation process of the software system requirements should include an analysis of all possible scenarios. Whereas only some of them are valid, some scenarios are redundant, and some scenarios cause unsafe behavior of the system. An important factor for successful checking of all possible scenarios is the appropriate support of searching and evaluation of scenarios. In this area, there is a gap between what formal approaches can offer and how they are actually used. It comes from the belief that formal approaches are difficult for understanding and using, and that they are not suitable for validation because they have no executable form. Nevertheless, systematic formal description techniques allow to specify the system properties and the detailed form of the solution during the design process and to analyze system specification, including user interactions, and implement architectural design decisions. This work focuses on the use of Petri nets for specifying requirements and generating and analysis scenarios to validate this specification.**

Keywords–Object Oriented Petri Nets; Use Cases; Sequence Diagrams; requirements specification; requirements validation.

I. Introduction

This work builds on the paper [1] and describes possible validation procedures for the specification models. It is part of the *Simulation Driven Development* (SDD) approach [2], which combines basic models of the most used modeling language Unified Modeling Language (UML) [3][4] and the formalism of Object-Oriented Petri Nets (OOPN) [5].

One of the fundamental problems associated with software development is the specification and validation of the system requirements [6]. The use case diagram from UML is often used for requirements specification, which is then developed by other UML diagrams [7]. The disadvantage of such an approach is an inability to validate the specification models and it is usually necessary to develop a prototype, which is no longer used after fulfilling its purpose. Utilization of OOPN formalism enables the simulation (i.e., to execute models), which allows to generate and analyze scenarios from specification models. All changes enforced during the validation process are entered directly in the specification model, which means that it is not necessary to implement or transform models.

There are methods of working with modified UML models that can be transformed to the executable form automatically. Some examples are the MDA methodology [8], Executable UML (xUML) [4] language, or Foundational Subset for xUML [9]. These approaches are faced with a problem of model transformations. It is hard to transfer back to model all changes that result from validation process and the model becomes useless. Further similar work based on ideas of model-driven development deals with gaps between different development stages and focuses on the usage of conceptual models during the simulation model development process [10]. This approach is called *model continuity*. While it works with simulation models during design stages, the approach proposed in this paper focuses on *live models* that can be used in the deployed system.

The paper is organized as follows. Section II summarizes concepts of the design method with using use cases and Petri nets. It also introduces the simple case study. Section III demonstrates possibilities of recording scenarios based on Petri nets. Section IV deals with scenarios exploration including generating scenarios and sequence diagrams. The summary and future work is described in Section V.

II. Design Method

In this section we will briefly introduce basic concepts of the design method [11] and will demonstrate these concepts on a simple case study.

A. Case Study in Basic Diagrams

The basis of design method is to identify use cases and roles that interact with individual use cases; the use case diagrams from the UML language are used. The behavior of use cases and roles are described by special variant of Petri nets, Object-Oriented Petri Nets (OOPN). Use cases and roles correspond to classes of OOPN. One use case invocation corresponds to creating an instance, i.e., an object of the class. The basic behavior of each element is described by one object net that represents independent autonomous behavior of the object. Because the life of object and its object net is closely related, we can use the notion *object* and *net* in the same meaning. The object net, i.e., the basic behavior, can be supplemented with method nets. Nets describing behavior of roles are called *role nets*, nets describing behavior of use cases are called *activity nets*.

The case study consists of simplified robotic system. For our purposes, we will consider only one robot whose motion is controlled by a predefined algorithm. So that the model consists of one role of *Robot* and one use case *Algorithm1*. The actor *Robot* represents a role of the real robot in the system.

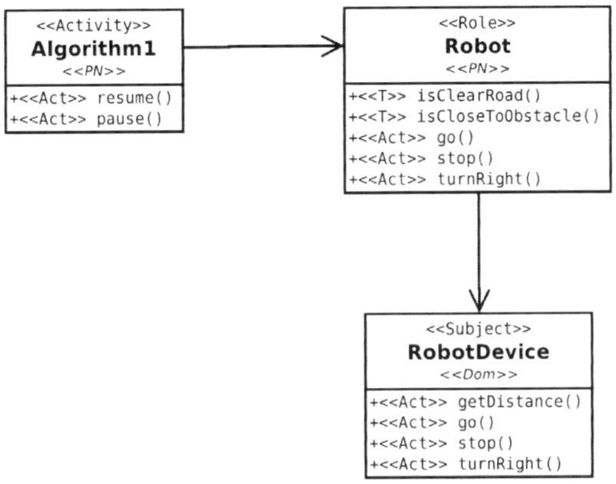

Figure 1. The basic class diagram.

The real actor, i.e., robot, has to have own representation is the system too. For terminological reasons we denote a real actor by the term *subject*. The actor *Robot* has its subject called *RobotDevice*. The classes of role, activity, and subject nets are shown in Figure 1. A more detailed description of the model can be found in the paper [1].

B. Behavioral modeling

Each object net, i.e., use case or role specification, describes a set of scenarios of the same type. From the Petri nets definition, the common behavior is defined as an oriented graph consisting of two kinds of nodes, transitions and places. Transitions representing actions or commands and places representing partial states of the scenario. Only nodes from different kinds can be connected by arcs.

The system state is represented by places of the nets. System is in a particular state if an appropriate place contains a *token*. Actions that can be performed in a particular state are modeled as part of the transition whose execution is conditioned by a presence of tokens in that state. The transition is modeled as an element that moves tokens between places, i.e., particular states. Except the input places, the transition firing can be conditioned by a *guard*. The guard contains expressions resulting in boolean value. The expression may also be a synchronous port call. Synchronous port is a special variant of transition, i.e., it may have input places, output places, and a guard. Synchronous port cannot be fired independently but has to be called from another transition or sycnhronous port. These ports serve for synchronous communication between nets, i.e., calling transition and called port have to be fired simultaneously.

The transition can be fired only if the guard is evaluated as true. It means that every boolean expression gets true and every called synchronous port gets fireable. If the transition fires, it executes all called synchronous ports that can have a side effect, i.e., the executed synchronous port can change a state of the called net.

C. Activity Net Algorithm1

The activity net *Algorithm1* of the use case *Algorithm1* (see Figure 2) consists of states *testing*, *walking*, *stopped*, *turnRight*, and *turnRound* that are represented by appropriate places. States *turnRight* and *turnRound* are only temporal and the activity goes through these states to the one of stable states *walking* or *stopped*. This net describes the following algorithm. The robot goes straight and if it encounters an obstacle, it turns to the right and tries to go straight. If it can not go straight, it turns around. If it can not go straight, it stops.

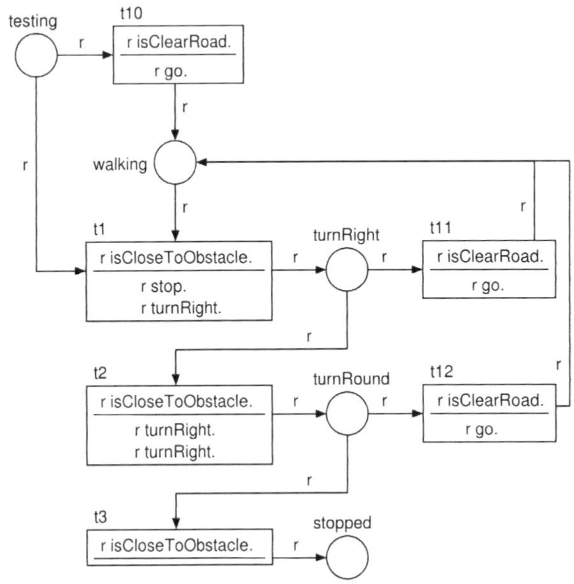

Figure 2. Model of the use case *Algoritm1*.

Control flow is modeled as the sequence of transitions. Each transition execution is conditioned by events representing the state of the robot. Let us take one example for all, the state *testing* and linked transitions *t10* and *t1*. The transition *t1* is fireable, if the condition *isCloseToObstacle* is met. This condition is modeled by calling the synchronous port in the guard. When firing the transition, actions *stop* and *turnRight* the robot are performed and the system moves to the state *turnRight*. The transition *t10* is fireable, if the condition (modeled by the synchronous port) *isClearRoad* is met. When firing the transition, the action *go* (the robot goes straight) is performed and the system moves into the state *walking*.

Both testing condition and message passing represent the interaction between the system (especially the activity net *Algorithm1*) and the role of robot (the role net *Robot*). The object of the robot role serves as token moving through the control flow. Presence of this token in places represents particular states and allows the activity net to communicate with the robot at the same time.

D. Role Net Robot

As already mentioned, actor represents a *role* of the user or device (i.e., a real actor), which the actor can hold in the system. One real actor may hold multiple roles, so that it can be modeled by various actors.

A role is modeled as a use case and its behavior by Petri nets. Interactions between use cases and actors are synchronized through *synchronous ports* that test conditions, convey

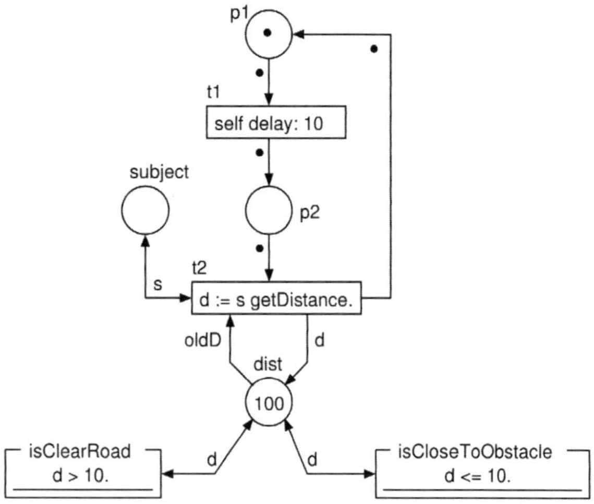

Figure 3. Model of the role net *Robot*.

the necessary data and can initiate an alternative scenario on both sides. For instance, the robot state is tested by a pair of synchronous ports *isClearRoad* and *isCloseToObstacle*.

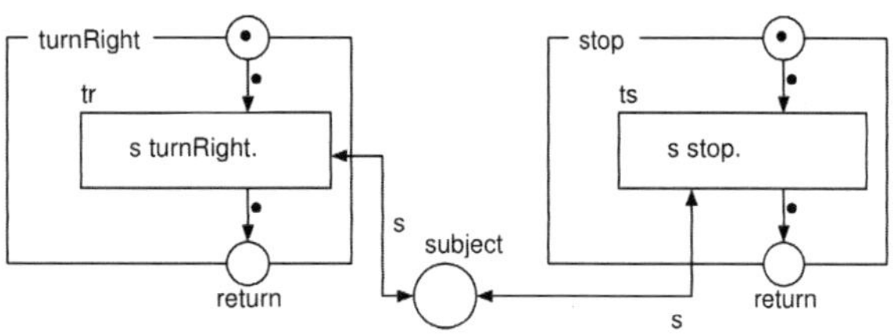

Figure 4. Methods of the role net *Robot*.

The net can send or receive instructions through messages too. In our example, the role *Robot* checks the distance from an obstacle each 10 time unit by sending the message *getDistance* to the robot subject. Methods *turnRight*, *go*, and *stop* that control the robot moving are delegated to the subject. They are shown in Figure 4.

III. Modeling of Scenarios

Petri nets models describe possible scenarios of one type of behavior, i.e., a behavior of a use case or an actor. For testing purposes it is necessary to investigate specific scenarios for individual situations. This section demonstrates possibilities of recording individual scenarios based on Petri nets models.

A. Scenario records

To record one scenario, we use the notation common to the Petri nets, the sequence of fired transitions. The basic notation of the record is $<\mathrm{tName1}, \mathrm{tName2}, \ldots>$. For instance, the record $<\mathrm{t10}, \mathrm{t1}, \mathrm{t11}>$ means that the robot will go straight, after a while it encounters an obstacle, turns right, and continuous walking. The record may be complemented with data including place markings and constraints. The previous example may be complemented with place markings after the scenario ends. At this moment, all places are empty except the place $\mathrm{walking}$, which contains object of the class Robot as the control token. The sequence is $<\mathrm{t10}, \mathrm{t1}, \mathrm{t11}, \ldots, \mathrm{t3}\{\mathrm{stopped}(\trianglelefteq\mathrm{Robot})\}>$, where the notation $\trianglelefteq\mathrm{Robot}$ means *an instance of the class Robot*. If it is needed to name the instance, we will write $\mathrm{name}\trianglelefteq\mathrm{Robot}$.

B. Subject Model

To have the model complete, we will simulate the subject representing the real robot and the environment the robot is moving in. We come out of the labyrinth model, which is shown in Figure 5. The subject *RobotDevice* is modeled by the Petri net, which is captured in Figure 6.

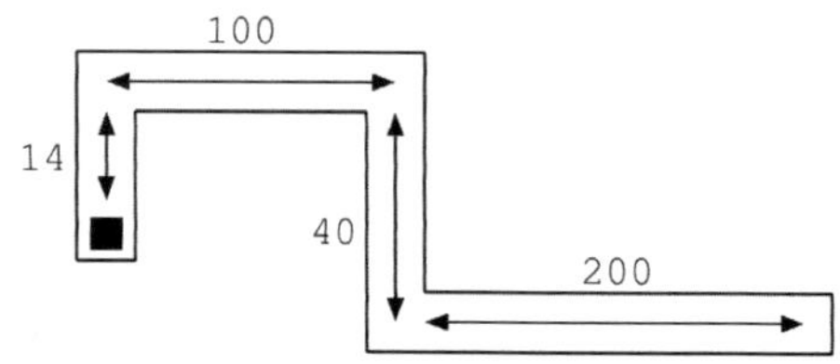

Figure 5. Labyrinth scheme.

The model has two places representing stable states of the net—state (the symbol in this place indicates whether the robot walks or not) and $\mathrm{distance}$ (the pair of numbers represents the position in labyrinth and the distance from an obstacle). If the net is in the state *to go* (symbol $\#g$ is placed in the state state), the distance from the obstacle is reduced by two length units each time unit. If the robot reaches the obstacle, the distance does not change anymore. The shape of labyrinth is modeled by pairs of values in the place $\mathrm{listDistances}$. The first value denotes the position, i.e., the corridor the robot should walk in, and the second value denotes the length of this corridor. The position changes by calling method $\mathrm{turnRight}$.

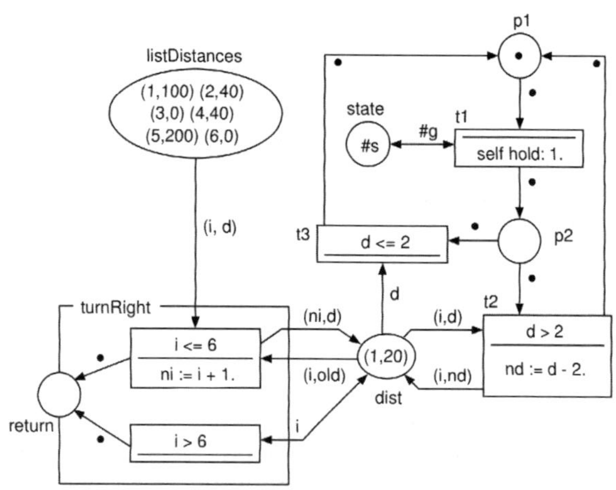

Figure 6. Model of the subject *RobotDevice* simulating the real device.

The formalism of OOPN allows working with time using a special method *delay* that is called from transitions. When transition containing a *delay* message is invoked, this transition is delayed for the specified time. It has the same meaning as the timed transition in Timed Petri Nets. The simulator can interpret the time in two ways. Either it works with model time that simulates real time during simulation run or directly real time.

C. Sequence of events

The transition sequence of the net *Algorithm1* representing the particular scenario, which corresponds to the labyrinth model, is shown in Figure 7. Such listings are well machine-readable, but are less readable for humans. It is possible to graphically record the sequence of the performed transitions, which can include additional information about the selected states or time.

$$\langle t10, t1, t11, t1, t11, t1, t2, t12, t1, t2, t3 \rangle$$

Figure 7. The transition sequence of the *Algorithm1* net.

An example of the graphical notation of the record is shown in Figure 8. The record is a sequence of fired transition with no conditions and branches. The information about chosen places are displayed above arcs before and after the transition fires. For our purposes, we have chosen the place Robot.dist (first line, e.g., (100)) and the place RobotDevice.dist (second line, e.g., (1, 20)). Each record of fired transitions can be supplemented by an information about model time (e.g., t = 0).

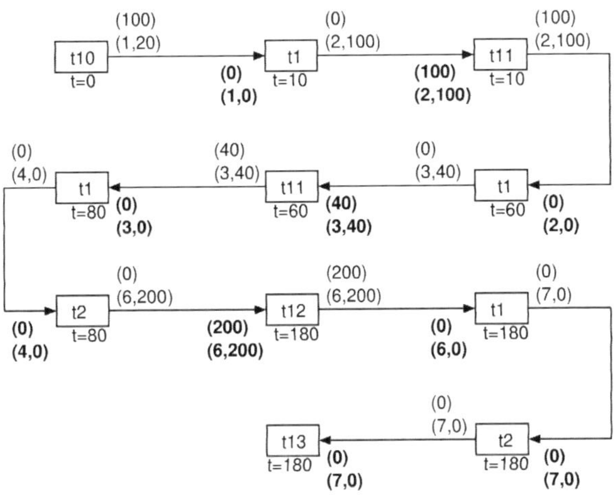

Figure 8. Graphic record of the expected scenario.

The transition sequence can be recorded manually or automatically. The first approach serves as a test case, which is compared to the sequence obtained by model simulation. In the case of manual recording, it is not advisable to declare states and model time for all transitions, but only for significant points in the sequence of transitions. In our example, there are important locations before performing transitions t11, t12, and t13. Figure 9 shows the initial part of the declared sequence (show at the top) and the obtained (real) sequence (shown at the bottom). By comparison, we can find out that the real sequence differs from expected sequence in the third step (transition).

IV. Exploration of Sequences

In this section, we will explore the difference between expected and obtained sequences. Since the model simulation is not limited to one net, we have to take into account the behavior of other interconnected networks. Therefore, we will analyze transitions over time across all participating nets.

A. Records of sequence

To save space, we will not display sequences of events graphically, but describe them in a table. The table record includes model time t, fired transitions trans, states of chosen places Alg1.walking (p1), Alg1.turnRight (p2), Alg1.turnRound (p3), Robot.dist (Rdist), RobotDevice.dist (Ddist), and RobotDevice.state (Dstate).

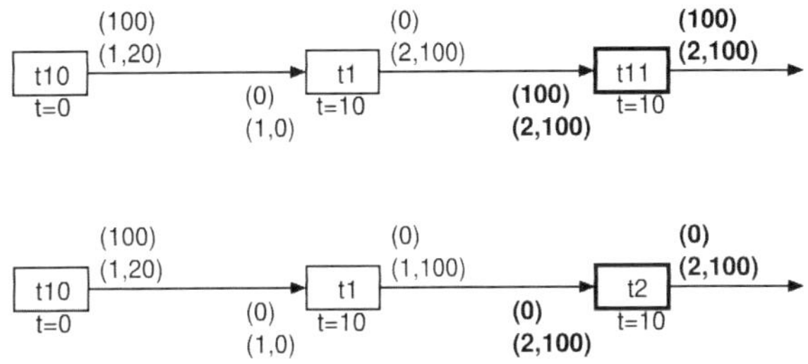

Figure 9. Graphic record of the declared and obtained scenarios.

TABLE I. SEQUENCE OF EVENTS OF THE BASIC SCENARIO.

t	trans	p_1	p_2	p_3	Rdist	Ddist	Dstate
0	Alg1.t10	r			100	(1, 20)	#g
	Robot.t1	r			100	(1, 20)	#g
	RDev.t1	r			100	(1, 20)	#g
1	RDev.t2	r			100	(1, 18)	#g
	RDev.t1	r			100	(1, 18)	#g
2	RDev.t2	r			100	(1, 16)	#g
...	...	...	...	...	...	...	...
9	RDev.t2	r			100	(1, 2)	#g
	RDev.t1	r			100	(1, 2)	#g
10	RDev.t2	r			100	(1, 0)	#g
	Robot.t2	r			0	(1, 0)	#g
	<S>Alg.t1				0	(1, 0)	#g
	Robot...t				0	(1, 0)	#g
	RDev...t				0	(1, 0)	#s
	Robot...t				0	(1, 0)	#s
	RDev...t				0	(2, 100)	#s
	<F>Alg.t1		r		0	(2, 100)	#s
	<S>Alg.t2				0	(2, 100)	#s
	Robot...t				0	(2, 100)	#s
	RDev...t				0	(3, 40)	#s
	Robot...t				0	(3, 40)	#s
	RDev...t				0	(4, 0)	#s
	<F>Alg.t2			r	0	(4, 0)	#s
	Alg.t3				0	(4, 0)	#s

Table I shows the sequence of transitions from the beginning of the simulation, i.e., from the Alg1.t10 transition. We find out that the transitions of nets Robot and RDev are performed between the transitions Alg1.t10 and Alg1.t1 of the base sequence. Sequence of these transitions simulates the robot movement and updates the distance information. Transition Alg.t1 is activated when information of the distance is updated to value of 0. This activation corresponds to the line with <S>Alg.t1 symbol. When this transition fires, the transitions of Robot.stop and RDev.turnRight nets are performed. After completing the Alg1.t1 transition, the system is in a state that is captured on the line with <F>Alg.t1 symbol. The next step is an activation of the Alg1.t2 transition even though the declared sequence of events expects an activation of Alg1.t11. There is a problem because the Alg.t1 transition did not change the condition guarding transitions Alg.t2 and Alg.t11.

TABLE II. SEQUENCE OF EVENTS OF THE CORRECTED SCENARIO.

t	trans	p_1	p_2	p_3	Rdist	Ddist	Dstate
0	Alg1.t10	r			100	(1, 20)	#g
	Robot.t1	r			100	(1, 20)	#g
	RDev.t1	r			100	(1, 20)	#g
1	RDev.t2	r			100	(1, 18)	#g
	RDev.t1	r			100	(1, 18)	#g
	Robot.t2	r			18	(1, 18)	#g
	Robot.t1	r			18	(1, 18)	#g
2	RDev.t2	r			18	(1, 16)	#g
...	...	...	...	...	...	...	...
5	RDev.t2	r			12	(1, 10)	#g
	RDev.t1	r			12	(1, 10)	#g
	Robot.t2	r			10	(1, 10)	#g
	Robot.t1	r			10	(1, 10)	#g
	<S>Alg.t1				10	(1, 10)	#g
	Robot...t				10	(1, 10)	#g
	RDev...t				10	(1, 10)	#s
	Robot...t				10	(1, 10)	#s
	RDev...t				10	(2, 100)	#s
	<F>Alg.t1		r		10	(2, 100)	#s
	<S>Alg.t2				10	(2, 100)	#s
...	...	...	...	...	...	...	...

According to the state analysis, it can be deduced that the information in the *Robot* net about distance to the obstacle has not been updated. In addition, there is a long delay in passing the current information from the subject *RobotDevice* to the role *Robot*. If we focus on this problem, the solution is relatively simple. We need to change the interval in which the information is obtained so that the response is faster. We change the action of Robot.t1 transition to the self hold: 1 statement. The resulting sequence is shown in Table II. The information is being updated but the previous issue is not addressed—the actual scenario is still different from the expected one. We will analyze this situation in next subsections.

B. Sequence Diagrams

It is not easy to get an overview of the communication between objects in large models. One scenario corresponds to a sequence of interactions between system objects. Interactions are usually described by diagrams. The activity diagram and the sequence diagram of the UML language being widely used in this area. The activity diagram is suitable for modeling the behavior of the use case, i.e., modeling all possible scenarios in general way. The sequence diagram models one particular scenario and makes it possible to better represent the external view of the system dynamic, i.e., the messaging sequence. We will present the possibilities of using sequence diagrams in conjunction with Petri nets.

The Petri net model is conceived as a sequence of internal and external events. Internal events may represent message sending to another objects, external events may arise in response to incoming events. Having a classical concept into account, it is necessary to map the external events to methods. Nevertheless, it makes the model less readable and understandable. When using Petri nets, the scenario is clearly defined as a sequence of events. One can then monitor system dynamics directly in the base model without event mapping. On the other hand, the sequence diagram makes it possible to better represent the external view of the system dynamic, i.e., the sequence of messages.

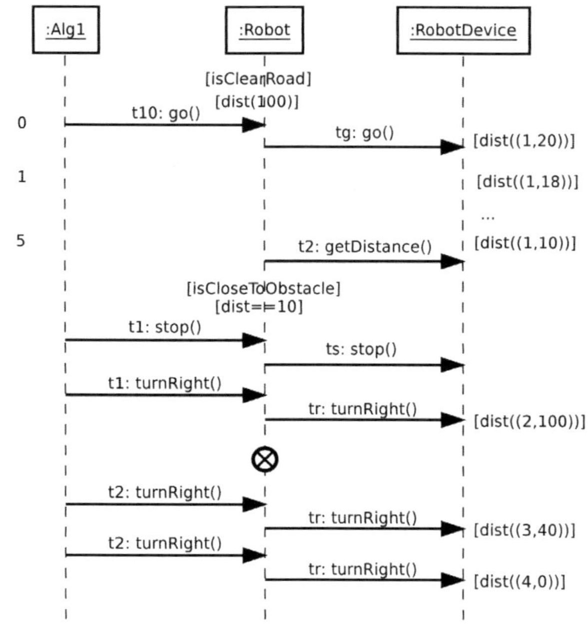

Figure 10. Sequence diagram modeling the scenario.

In addition to statistical data, the information needed to generate the sequence diagram can be collected during the simulation. It is therefore possible to generate individual scenarios in the form of sequence diagrams. The message linked to the event is generated to the sequence diagram as the message between sender and receiver. The synchronous port connected to an event is captured in the sequence diagram as the state of the object on which the port has been executed.

$$\langle \mathrm{Alg1.t10}, \mathrm{Robot.isClearRoad}, \mathrm{Robot.go.t1}, \mathrm{RobotDevice.go.t1} \rangle$$

Figure 11. Part of the complete transition sequence.

Let us get back to our example. Since we know that the problem occurs before executing the transition Algorithm1.t2, it is sufficient to generate a sequence diagram from the first event Algorithm1.t10 to the event Algorithm1.t2. The resulting sequence diagram is shown in Figure 10. For instance, at time 0, the object $o_1 \trianglelefteq \mathrm{Alg1}$ sends a message go to the object $o_2 \trianglelefteq \mathrm{Robot}$ from the transition Alg1.t10. This execution is conditioned by synchronous port isClearRoad and the initial marking of the place Robot.dist is 100. The object o_2 responds by forwarding the message to $o_3 \trianglelefteq \mathrm{RobotDevice}$ object. This sequence corresponds to the initial part of the scenario shown in Table II, the formal notation is captured in

Figure 11.

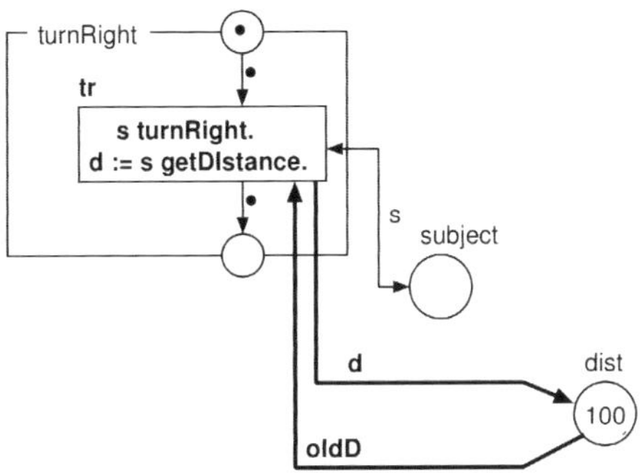

Figure 12. Fixed method of the role net *Robot*.

In Figure 10, there is a special symbol ⊗ marking the position in the sequence where is a difference between expected and obtained scenario. We knew there is a problem of transmitting information about robot's distance. In the sequence diagram, we can find out that the message of getting distance is not called after turning the robot. We fix this by calling the message getDistance inside the transition Robot.tr as shown in Figure 12.

C. *Interface to real robot*

In the next step, we will analyze the behavior of model connected to the real robot. From the model point of view, only the subject stored in the place Robot.subject changes. Because we work with a real component, we run the simulation in real time rather than model time. The first steps of the simulation are shown in Table III.

TABLE III. SEQUENCE OF EVENTS OF THE OBTAINED SCENARIO.

t	trans	p_1	p_2	p_3	Rdist
0.00	Alg1.t10	r			100
	Robot.t1	r			100
1.03	Robot.t2	r			18
...	...	...	...	...	...
5.10	Robot.t2	r			9
5.10	Robot.t1	r			9
5.10	<S>Alg.t1				9
5.11	Robot...ts				9
5.11	Robot...tr				0
5.11	<F>Alg.t1		r		0
5.12	<S>Alg.t2				0
...	...	...	...	...	...

We have got the same situation—the robot stops prematurely. Looking at the sequence of events, we find out that the robot turns too early and stands in front of the wall of corridor that it came. It is necessary to adjust the role behavior so that it can slow down and gradually stop just before the obstacle.

V. CONCLUSION

The paper dealt with the concept of modeling software system requirements using the formalism of OOPN. This concept allows to model and validate specifications through the scenarios exploration in simulated or real surroundings with no need to transform models. We presented basic concepts based on declaration, generation, and comparison of individual scenarios. The concept is supported by mapping Petri net model to sequence diagrams helping display the sequence of messages. During the process of model analysis, we discovered several inaccuracies in the description of role behaviors, but own algorithm, i.e., the basic work-flow of the system, was not modified. This approach of creating the requirements specification combines an abstract view of the system with implementation details, all of which are implemented by the same formalisms.

At present, we have developed the tool supporting requirements modeling using use cases and the formalism of OOPN. In the future, we will focus on the tool completion, a possibility to interconnect model to others languages, and feasibility study for different kinds of usage.

ACKNOWLEDGMENT

This work has been supported by the internal BUT project FIT-S-17-4014 and The Ministry of Education, Youth and Sports of the Czech Republic from the National Programme of Sustainability (NPU II); project IT4Innovations excellence in science - LQ1602.

REFERENCES

[1] R. Kočí and V. Janoušek, "Modeling System Requirements Using Use Cases and Petri Nets," in ThinkMind ICSEA 2016, The Eleventh International Conference on Software Engineering Advances. Xpert Publishing Services, 2016, pp. 160–165.

[2] R. Kočí and V. Janoušek, "Modeling and Simulation-Based Design Using Object-Oriented Petri Nets: A Case Study," in Proceeding of the International Workshop on Petri Nets and Software Engineering 2012, vol. 851. CEUR, 2012, pp. 253–266.

[3] J. Rumbaugh, I. Jacobson, and G. Booch, The Unified Modeling Language Reference Manual. Addison-Wesley, 1999.

[4] C. Raistrick, P. Francis, J. Wright, C. Carter, and I. Wilkie, Model Driven Architecture with Executable UML. Cambridge University Press, 2004.

[5] M. Češka, V. Janoušek, and T. Vojnar, "Modelling, Prototyping, and Verifying Concurrent and Distributed Applications Using Object-Oriented Petri Nets," Kybernetes: The International Journal of Systems and Cybernetics, vol. 2002, no. 9, 2002.

[6] K. Wiegers and J. Beatty, Software Requirements. Microsoft Press, 2014.

[7] N. Daoust, Requirements Modeling for Bussiness Analysts. Technics Publications, LLC, 2012.

[8] R. France and B. Rumpe, "Model-driven development of complex software: A research roadmap," in International Conference on Software Engineering, ICSE, 2010.

[9] S. Mijatov, P. Langer, T. Mayerhofer, and G. Kappel, "A framework for testing uml activities based on fuml," in Proc. of 10th Int. Workshop on Model Driven Engineering, Verification, and Validation, vol. 1069, 2013.

[10] D. Cetinkaya, A. V. Dai, and M. D. Seck, "Model continuity in discrete event simulation: A framework for model-driven development of simulation models," ACM Transactions on Modeling and Computer Simulation, vol. 25, no. 3, 2015.

[11] R. Kočí and V. Janoušek, "Formal Models in Software Development and Deployment: A Case Study," International Journal on Advances in Software, vol. 7, no. 1, 2014, pp. 266–276.

An OO and Functional Framework for Versatile Semantics of Logic-Labelled Finite State Machines

Callum McColl   Vladimir Estivill-Castro   René Hexel

School of Information and Communication Technology
Griffith University, Nathan QLD 4111, Australia
callum.mccoll@griffithuni.edu.au
v.estivill-castro@griffith.edu.au
r.hexel@griffith.edu.au

***Abstract*—Logic-Labeled Finite State Machines (`LLFSMs`) offer model-driven software development (MDSD) while enabling correctness at a high level due to their transparent semantics that enables testing as well as formal verification. This combination of the three elements (MDSD, validation, and verification) results in more reliable behaviour of software components, but semantics is constrained to specific scheduling. We offer a framework that allows to obtain significant variations that suit specific domains while maintaining the capability to generate Kripke structures for formal verification or to execute corresponding monitor or testing `LLFSMs` for validation in a test-driven development framework. The framework is Object-Oriented so new software patterns for scheduling can be derived to suit a particular embedded, robotic, or cyber-physical system, while at the same time enabling functional programming constructs.**

Keywords–Logic-labelled finite-state machines; Model-Driven Engineering; Real-Time Systems; Verification; Validation.

I. INTRODUCTION

By following a transparent semantics that includes a synchronous model, Logic-Labelled Finite State Machines (`LLFSMs`) enable the design of software that can achieve high levels of complexity and sophistication while guaranteeing deterministic execution and facilitating formal verification [1].

The semantics specify precisely when variables affected by sensors outside the system are inspected as well as the particular points in the execution of the software where snapshots of the environment variables are taken [2]. However, this constrains the execution to just one specific semantics, and in particular, to one specific frequency and pace, which may not be suitable in another robotic or embedded system. It should be possible to configure rapidly and efficiently the semantics and constructs of `LLFSMs` providing developers the freedom to adapt or tailor the system semantics to particular cases. This paper enables such versatility. We provide the capacity to instantiate new scheduling semantics with incarnations of template methods and classes while still providing the capacity to generate the corresponding Kripke structure for formal verification with standard tools, such as NuSMV.

Therefore, this new framework removes the need to adhere to the strict semantics currently implemented in tools such as `clfsm`. Importantly, we maintain the ability to perform formal verification. We illustrate two areas where we create abstractions to the semantics of `LLFSMs` and show how instantiation of these abstractions into concrete derivations maintain the ability to perform formal verification. We introduce `swiftfsm` [3], a framework for `LLFSMs` written in `Swift`, which enables formal verification, but allows developers more freedom to design, adapt and create new `LLFSM` models that are particular to application-specific use cases.

II. LOGIC-LABELLED FINITE STATE MACHINES

Finite state machines are ubiquitous models of system behaviour. Variants of finite-state machines appear in many system modelling languages, most prominently SysML [4] and UML [5], [6]. Despite their widespread use and penetration in model-driven software development, the semantics of SysML [4] and UML [7] are ambiguous [8] and restricted versions are offered to create executable models [9], real-time systems [10] or enable formal verification [11]. Moreover, languages such as SysML and UML have historically adopted the event-driven form of finite-state machines inspired by Harel's STATEMATE. Unfortunately, event-driven systems cannot offer a simple semantics, as it becomes cumbersome to manage event queues and the concurrent arrival of events while handling the current event. The issue is intrinsic to these types of machines, where a system is modelled as being in a finite set S of states, and where transitions 'immediately' fire upon arrival of an event (more complexity usually results as executing a transition can itself fire a series of other events).

Complementary to this, `LLFSMs` model a system as being in a finite set S of states. As before, each state ($s \in S$) represents a possible situation that the system may find itself in. But here it is more explicit that while in that state, the `LLFSM` will execute some actions. The system also moves from state to state by means of transitions. However, in sharp contrast with the event-driven approach, each transition is predicated by a logical expression. States are executable states. A state machine is not waiting for events to happen and reacting to them. It is executing its current state s_c, and at a precise point in the execution, the expressions labelling the associated transitions are evaluated. If one of these expressions evaluates to true, the system moves to the target state of the transition, updating the current state. Each `LLFSM` has a state designated as the initial state ($s_0 \in S$), representing the state at the point when execution commences.

Each state contains a set of executable actions. These actions are executed at specific times and under certain conditions. For example Wagner *et al.* define four distinct types of actions [12]:

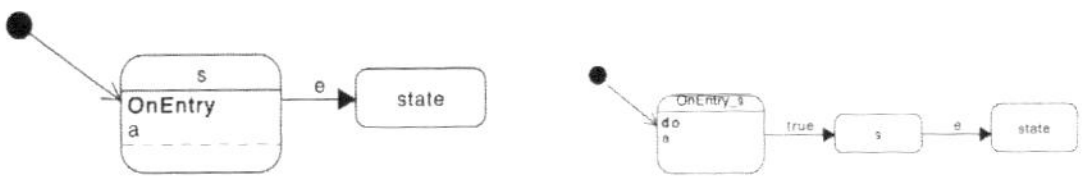

(a) Diagram for **Entry Actions**.

(b) Diagram providing semantics for **Entry Actions**.

Figure 1. Equivalence Wagner et al. [12] **Entry Actions** in terms of states without sections and transitions.

1) **Entry Actions**: Executed when the system first enters a state.
2) **Exit Actions**: Executed when the system leaves the state.
3) **Transition Actions**: Executed when the system is transitioning between states.
4) **Input Actions**: Executed when an input satisfies a particular condition. These actions can be independent of the state.

We use Wagner *et al.* to illustrate the first point of why a general framework is of interest. We suggest that the fundamental execution cycle is the very simple notion of two states between a transition: a source state s_s and target state s_t. The distinction of an Entry Action a is merely semantic sugar for the removal of an extra state. We illustrate this in Figure 1. Wagner *et al.*'s **Entry Actions** [12] are essentially a pre-state to the state s. Figure 1a is the construct that actually has the semantics of Figure 1b. This is important, because if the expression e in Figure 1 is also `true`, it becomes very transparent that the action a will be performed at least once even if execution exits state s immediately (we note that ambiguities of this type were already identified in standards like `SCXML`).

The proper specification of semantics becomes even more important when the actions in a state access a set of variables that affect subsequent actions and transitions. That is, the attached Boolean expressions (usually named *guards*) involve variables. The first issue is the scope of the variables and the second issue is the potential race conditions that could be generated upon such variables if they are shared in some way. Common cases of variables that are shared are the variables where sensors record a status of the environment. Thus, while the software is executing, the value of a sensor variable may change. Similarly, control variables for effectors are shared. The software modelled by `LLFSMs` may set a control variable and the driver of the effector reads such a variable to act. The prototype `clfsm` [2] for `LLFSMs` provides three levels of scope for variables.

1) **External Variables**: Variables external to the system from the perspective of the software, usually corresponding to the sensors and effectors. They may change at any point in time.
2) **FSM Local Variables**: These are variables that are shared between all states within a single `LLFSM`.
3) **State Local Variables**: These are variables that are local to a state.

Naturally, one can specify more variants. For example, why not have variables that are shared between all the `LLFSMs` of a system, but not sensors and effectors? Why not have variables whose scope is even more local than that of a state, e.g., only local to the **OnEntry** section? These examples illustrate the need for a flexible approach to extending the possibilities of `LLFSM` constructs and form the proposed framework of this paper.

III. Protocol Oriented Design

Protocols (akin to interfaces in `Java`) are a common mechanism to establish the contract a module (or set of classes under a main class) is to adhere to in order to participate and implement some functionality. he protocol itself defines the signatures (names and parameters) of the methods (and if appropriate return values with types) in order for objects to cooperate. In some cases the protocol also specifies invariants and exceptions.

Our `swiftfsm` framework uses protocols extensively to stipulate the required functionality. However, typically, the protocols themselves contain no implementation (although it is possible in `Swift` to have a default implementation), thus a type (class) that conforms to a protocol provides its specific implementation for the functionality that the protocol encapsulates. We use protocol-oriented design to model the semantics of a model, and thus, we focus on describing a set of protocols. When a software engineer wants to develop an implementation of the semantics; these shall conform to a specific set of protocols and implement the required functionality. This therefore enables a developer to design how different parts of the system interact and function, without the need to create a global implementation of behaviour or a new implementation to generate Kripke structures for verification. Moreover, the framework allows the developer to create different implementations for specific, convenient modelling of constructs that conform to the same semantics modelled by these protocols.

IV. Modelling States and Transitions

We are now ready to present our first abstraction: the type for transitions. To introduce the idea, consider the following scenario where allowing developers to create custom semantics leads to more robust designs. Let's focus on a state A (Fig. 2). The `clfsm` semantics [1] explicitly specifies that the *onEntry* action will execute once and only once for each state, after which the sequence of transitions will be evaluated in the order α, then β. If the associated expression (not shown) evaluates to `true`, the corresponding transition will fire and the state will execute its *onExit* action. If none of the transitions fire, the *Internal* action will be run. In either case, the execution token passes to the next `LLFSM` in the arrangement.

Importantly, this way it is not possible to implement an *atLeastOnce* semantics for the *Internal* action without adding another state. If transitions α or β cause a state transition, (in the `clfsm` semantics [1]), then the *Internal* action will never execute. If this functionality is required, a pattern similar to Figure 3 needs to be implemented. Note that this involves creating two states and copying (duplicating) implementation, obstructing factorisation and creating the danger of introducing failures. Both $a1$ and $a3$ need to be copied into the new state $A0$ in order to implement the *atLeastOnce* semantics. State $A1$ is almost the same as the original state A. This becomes arduous to maintain and modify as the developer must keep the $A0$ actions in sync with the $A1$ actions.

With `swiftfsm`, we overcome this problem by allowing developers to define custom state types. The result is shown in Figure 4. Because of the wide breadth of state models, `swiftfsm` only assumes that a state has a unique name.

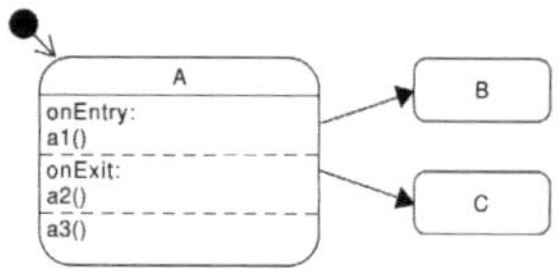

Figure 2. A simple scenario

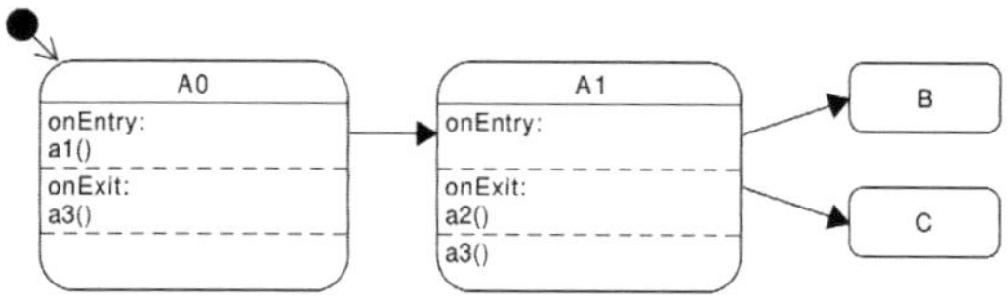

Figure 3. Implementing "atLeastOnce" semantics in `clfsm`

Therefore `swiftfsm` defines a `StateType` protocol only containing that name. The developer has complete freedom to define any number of phase-actions that make up a state.

The `swiftfsm` framework does not even assume that a state can transition. This is a separate requirement, modelled as a separate protocol. The `Transitionable` protocol adds a sequence of transitions to conforming states. All transitions contain

1) a predicate function that, when it evaluates to `true`, represents a situation where the `LLFSM` will transition; and
2) a *target* state the `LLFSM` will transition to.

The type of the transition predicate function is defined as:

$$StateContext \rightarrow Boolean$$

This abstracts a state context type that encapsulates all (and only) the necessary variables that influence the evaluation of the predicate function. In this way, a transition function can access the necessary variables through its source state. This is an important concept when generating the corresponding Kripke structure of an executable model in order to perform formal verification. The generation of the Kripke structure depends on referential transparency, i.e., transitions will be evaluated with any possible combination of state context variations passed in with no further dependencies or side-effects.

This allows for an important optimisation. Typically, an `LLFSM` state corresponds to several Kripke states, because of

- state sections (e.g., **onEntry**, **onExit**, **Internal**, **atLeastOnce**, etc.), and
- the potential semantics of snapshotting external variables between these state sections.

However, our semantics recognises that external variables that are not involved in a transition will not need to create a new transition evaluation context. Therefore, the above transition type is side-effect free and removes the need to consider all possible combinations of external variables outside those appearing in the transaction.

The traditional conceptualisation of the class of transitions is that transitions have a source and a target state. Such a conceptualisation complicates the optimisation we just mentioned, as the transition is in a static relationship with its source

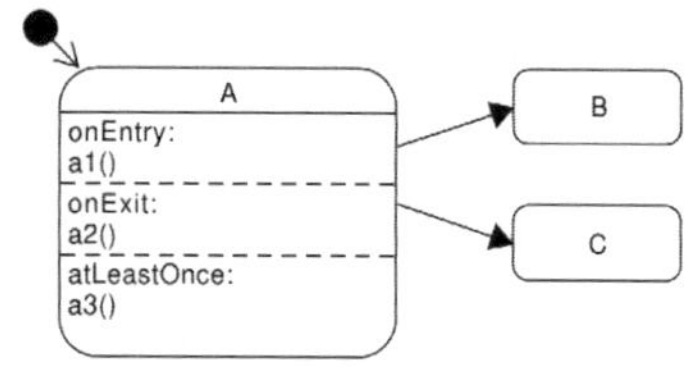

Figure 4. Implementing "atLeastOnce" semantics in `swiftfsm`

state (typically implemented as a reference). Our approach does not need to change the source state of a transition in an `LLFSM` to create the Kripke states for sections. Our framework only updates the possible changes to the external variables of relevance, and submits the State with this new context for evaluation to the transition (which is a pure function). Importantly, this means that the evaluation of any transition is referentially transparent as it is a pure function with explicit inputs and outputs. The Kripke structure generated in this way is guaranteed to obtain the effect of evaluation of the transition without possible side effects influencing the transition as all the variables are in the context attached to the state.

V. SCHEDULING

Here, we introduce a new abstraction over the original concept of an `LLFSM` ringlet [1]. A ringlet defines how the sections within a state are executed, and more specifically, how and in what order each action is executed. We propose to view ringlets as pure functions that take a state and return the next state to execute. Therefore we have them as objects of the following type.

$$State \rightarrow State.$$

If a new state is returned, then the `LLFSM` has transitioned. By modelling a ringlet in this fashion, we enable developers to create custom ringlets which determine how their states are executed. As an illustration of the adaptability of this approach, it is also possible to create different ringlets that execute the same states in different ways. Importantly, the execution of the state becomes orthogonal to the definition of the state.

However, in practice it is common that a ringlet may require to modify state information. To this end, the `swiftfsm` framework provides the `Ringlet` protocol which defines an `execute` function. If we look at previous semantics for `LLFSMs`, and in particular to the semantics offered by the `clfsm` compiler, we can see that the ringlet only executes the *onEntry* section when the previously executed state does not equal the current state being executed (in particular, if a state has a transition to itself, this is a legal construct, but if the transaction executes, in `clfsm` this does not re-run the *onEntry* section). If a developers wished to extend the semantics that all arriving transitions (including self-transitions) cause the *onEntry* section to execute, our framework here allows the creation of a `CLFSMRinglet` that contains a `previousState` member variable that the `execute` function refers to and manages when executing the current state. That is we are using the `Method` pattern, and the developer supplies the method that defines the specific ringlet to sequence sections of a state.

Because `LLFSM` are not event-driven, they are scheduled using a round robin scheduler. We provide such scheduling as the default in the framework `swiftfsm`. Therefore, a single ringlet, for the current state of each LLFSM, is executed in a sequential fashion. This creates concurrent execution in a predictable manner reducing state explosion for formal verification. The sequential execution avoids thread management and avoids complexities associated with parallel execution, (there are essentially no critical sections or mutual exclusion challenges). Because of the sequential scheduling, we have a deterministic execution of an arrangement of the LLFSMs, thus when the Kripke structure is created for the entire arrangement, we have a smaller Kripke model (a smaller NuSMV input file) that with unconstrained concurrency of event-driven systems. By preventing side-effects (as shown in the previous Section), we further reduce the size of the Kripke structure enhancing the feasibility of performing model checking.

Furthermore, swiftfsm uses a stricter snapshot semantics when executing the ringlets. A snapshot is taken of the external variables before the ringlet is executed. The state then uses the snapshot when executing actions and evaluating transitions (recall our execution context). Only once the ringlet has finished executing, any modifications made made visible externally (e.g., to the environment). This defines the granularity at which the system is reactive to changes observable by sensors in the environment and does not need to make a dangerous assumption of well-behaved environments and that the software always runs faster than any external part of the system. Compare this with many formal verification approaches that only work with ideal event-driven systems, that do not exist in practice. For example, approaches where extended finite-state machines handling of external variables is simply assumed to be irrelevant. "During a macrostep, the values of the inputs do not change and no new external events may arrive; in other words, the system is assumed to be infinitely faster than the environment" [13, p. 172]. Alternatively, the environment is assumed to be well-behaved, so that it sends the input the software requires at the right time, forming "a closed model corresponding to the complete mathematical simulation of the pair formed by the software controller and the environment" [14, p. 89]. Finally, a simplistic approach where any external stimulus (change of external variables) will not happen until all internal changes take place "giving priority to internal actions over external actions" [15].

We argue that the specification of when a snapshot is taken defines the level of atomicity of the sections within the state run by the ringlet with respect to the external variables. This becomes particularly important when performing formal verification.

VI. Formal Verification

If one strictly follows the derivation of Kripke structures from the artefact of sequential program constructs [16], the corresponding Kripke states would not only be the boundaries of sections of LLFSM states, but every assignment and operation in those sections correspond to extended FSMs, containing programming language statements (e.g., in Swift). The sequential execution of LLFSMs and its default snapshot semantics enables more succinct Kripke structures, where the delicate point is the handling of the external variables [17], [18]. Nevertheless, as we mentioned, such a default semantics requires recording all of the variables influencing the execution before and after every state section in order to generate the Kripke structure [17]. For consistency, we configured a version of swiftfsm that followed such an approach [3].

These earlier approaches relied on the ringlet itself to record variables, influencing the execution of a state. However, a more succinct approach can be used and a further optimisation can be made. Since the swiftfsm framework not only uses a sequential scheduling similar to clfsm, but a ringlet's execution is atomic with respect to the external variables, ringlet execution can now be treated as a black box.

Consequently, a snapshot should only be taken of the variables before and after the entire ringlet for a state is executed. This variation also prevents statements being executed that make modification to variables that are not reflected in the final context for the next Kripke state. For example, a state may make changes to an external variable during an **onEntry** section that is cancelled by a further modification in the **onExit** section. Since no effect of this will occur during the state's execution, as we now identify a Kripke state *before* and *after* an entire ringlet execution, interim changes are not reflected in the resulting Kripke structure.

Importantly, we argue that this is a benefit, not a problem! In swiftfsm, the statements within sections of the state operate within a context derived from a snapshot of the external variables, which gets taken precisely when the state is scheduled. There is absolutely no way that any modification could (nor should) affect the environment until the snapshot is saved. External variables are updated precisely once when the ringlet has finished executing. Similarly, since swiftfsm uses sequential scheduling, there is no way for the modification of non-external variables to have side-effects and influence the execution of other machines, because the semantics is equivalent to a single thread. The only important record for the construction of the Kripke states (to be part of the Kripke structure or verification) is the context (of the variables) before and after each ringlet is executed.

VII. Case Study

We present a case study where we simplify the model of a microwave oven, a ubiquitous example in the software engineering literature of behaviour modelling through states and transitions [19]. This model has been extensively studied in formal verification [20, p. 39], as the safety feature of *disable cooking when the door is open* is analogous to the requirement that a radiation machine should have a halt-sensor [21, p. 2]. Software models for microwave behaviour are widely discussed [22], [23], [24], [25], [26], [27]). Figure 5 shows the standard executable model with LLFSMs. While this model is transparent and formal verification establishes requirements, the full machinery of Kripke states for each of the three state-sections is not required (note that all **Internal** sections are empty and the only **onExit** section that is used is in the timer LLFSM, in state 3 to ADD_60. Moreover, the model would also be simplified if the timeLeft variable were to be removed by making it equivalent to the condition 0<currentTime. With respect to the requirements specified in Myers and Dromey [27, p. 27, Table 1] or in Shlaer and Mellor [23, p. 36] the behaviour of such a simplification is irrelevant. But, for model checking, removing the Boolean variable timeLeft alone would half the number of Kripke states (and the corresponding size of the NuSMV file where formal verification is conducted is thus halved). By removing the state sections, the number of Kripke states would be halved again. Thus, it would be advantageous to derive LLFSMs, where states have no **onExit** nor **Internal** actions.

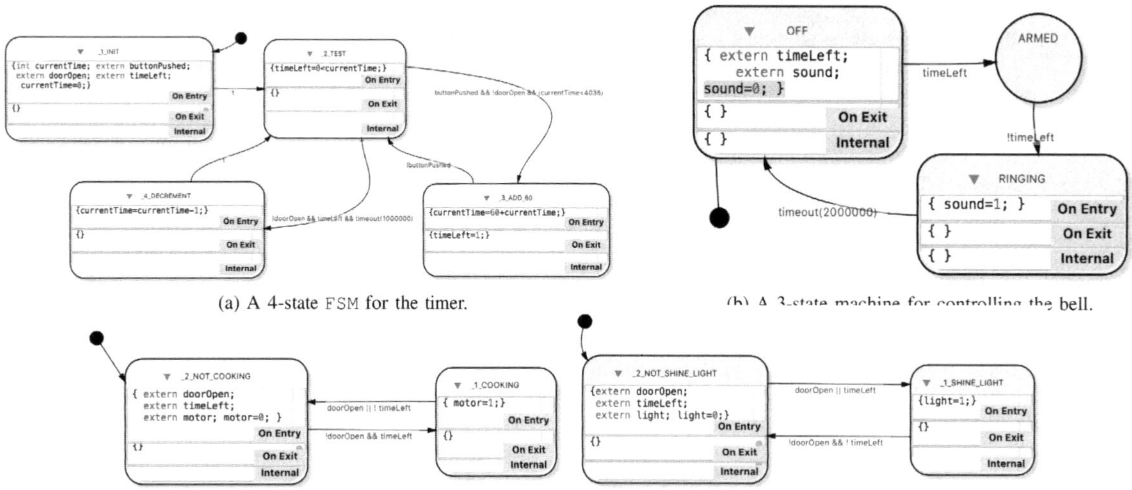

(a) A 4-state FSM for the timer.

(b) A 3-state machine for controlling the bell.

(c) A 2-state machine for controlling the cooking engine.

(d) A 2-state machine for the light.

Figure 5. Complete model of one-minute microwave.

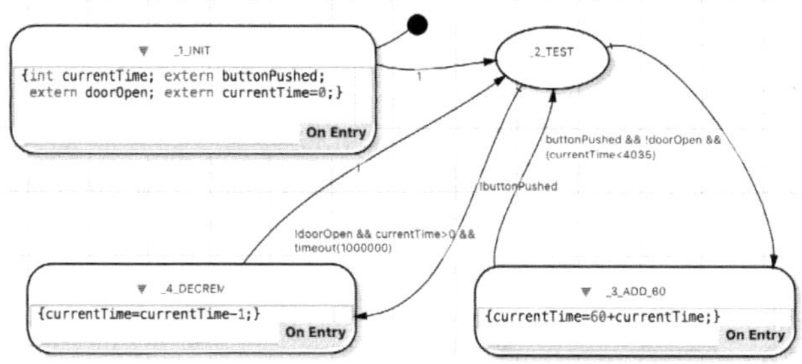

Figure 6. Simplified timer with **onEntry** sections only.

The new model would globally replace `timeLeft` by `0<currentTime`. All declarations of `extern timeLeft` disappear from all `LLFSMs`. Thus, the timer machine changes to Figure 6. We point out the slight change of behaviour. With the executable model of Figure 5, when the button is pressed for the first time and not released, nothing would happen. With the changes suggested, when the button is pressed for the first time and not released, if the door is closed, cooking will commence and the light will go on. As long as the button is pressed and not released such cooking with the light on will continue and the timer will not be decremented. This behaviour does exist in a slightly similar form in Figure 5, but only happens from the second time onwards. That is, the user must press the button; upon releasing the button, cooking starts and the light turns on. If the user presses and holds the button now that cooking has started, it also blocks timing counting down. Again, we do not consider this subtle difference in behaviour relevant as it is never identified in the requirement. However, the variation simplifies the Kripke structure radically for more efficient formal verification of the requirements. With our framework, the designers can easily alternate between the two executable models, and conduct model checking on both.

A further optimisation can be made when considering how `swiftfsm` currently handles the snapshots of external variables. Recall that a snapshot is taken before the ringlet executes, and then saved back to the environment once the ringlet has finished executing. By changing these semantics to a per-schedule cycle, as opposed to a per-ringlet cycle, we can further minimise the number of Kripke States that are generated. Taking the microwave as an example, instead of taking a snapshot of the external variables before executing each state, we instead take a single snapshot of the environment before executing the ringlet for the current state within each `LLFSM`. Each `LLFSM` would therefore share the same snapshot and any modifications made to the snapshot will only be saved once each `LLFSM` has executed its current state.

This has a drastic impact to the number of Kripke States that are generated for the Kripke Structure. Consider all possible combinations of a snapshot of the external variables. The microwave uses three Boolean variables, therefore this results in $2^3 = 8$ possible combinations. There are normally four snapshots taken per schedule cycle as there are four `LLFSMs` executing and a snapshot is taken when a ringlet in each `LLFSM` is executed. Therefore, there are $2^{3^4} = 4096$ possible combinations of snapshots per schedule cycle. When taking a single snapshot at the start of the schedule cycle, the result is $2^{3^1} = 8$ possible combinations of snapshots. Removing the `timeLeft` variable further reduces this to

$2^{2^1} = 4$ combinations of snapshots per schedule cycle, a reduction by three orders of magnitude.

VIII. CONCLUSION

In this paper, we have introduced a flexible semantic model for logic-labelled finite-state machines. Compared to traditional event-driven state machines and `LLFSMs`, our approach allows a more direct mapping of UML semantics [5], [6], allowing high-level, executable models, which are less error-prone and eliminate duplication. Moreover, we have shown these semantics can be modelled in a referentially transparent way that creates simpler Kripke structures, allowing formal verification of our executable models, that is orders of magnitudes faster for the same model than previous approaches.

In software engineering, there is a prevalence for modelling using UML state charts (which is a derivation of Harel's State Charts [28]) and which are event-driven. Moreover, Sommerville [29], states that "state models are often used to describe real-time systems" [29, p. 544], citing UML. We note that Sommerville also uses a microwave to illustrate how `FSMs` model the behaviour of systems [29, p. 136]. Because of these associations among systems that respond to stimuli, we thank the reviewers for suggesting to clarify the terminology regarding what constitutes an event-driven system, a reactive system and more importantly, a real-time system.

We refer to an event-driven system as one typically based on a software architecture built around stimuli-driven call-backs, a subscribe mechanism and listeners that enact such call-backs (very much as GUIs are composed for desktops today). Reacting to stimuli in this way implies uncontrolled concurrency (e.g. using separate threads or event queues). The counterpart to event-driven systems are time-triggered systems. Lamport [30] provided fundamental proofs of the limitations of event-driven systems. Reactive-systems are responsive systems without much processing, as opposed to deliberative systems (which reason, plan, learn). Real-time systems are required to meet time-deadlines in response to stimuli. Therefore, although closely related, these terms are not the same, and in this paper, we argue (supported by the work of Lamport [30]) that there are many solid reasons why real-time systems may be better served by time-triggered systems and pre-determined schedules, rather than the unbounded delays that may occur in event-driven systems.

The work presented in this paper illustrates how `LLFSMs` can be used as executable models. Moreover, we argue that their deterministic execution and verifiability is more suitable for real-time systems than systems where threads proliferate.

REFERENCES

[1] V. Estivill-Castro and R. Hexel, "Arrangements of finite-state machines - semantics, simulation, and model checking," in MODELSWARD, S. Hammoudi, L. F. Pires, J. Filipe, and R. C. das Neves, Eds. SciTePress, 2013, pp. 182–189.

[2] V. Estivill-Castro, R. Hexel, and C. Lusty, "High performance relaying of c++11 objects across processes and logic-labeled finite-state machines." Springer Int. 2014, pp. 182–194.

[3] C. McColl, "swiftfsm - A Finite State Machines Scheduler," Honours Thesis, Griffith University, Nathan QLD, 4111, Australia, 2016.

[4] S. Friedenthal, A. Moore, and R. Steiner, A Practical Guide to SysML: The systems Modeling Language. San Mateo, CA: Morgan Kaufmann, 2009.

[5] M. Samek, Practical UML Statecharts in C/C++, Second Edition: Event-Driven Programming for Embedded Systems. Newton, MA, USA: Newnes, 2008.

[6] D. Pilone and N. Pitman, UML 2.0 in a Nutshell. O'Reilly Media, 2005.

[7] M. Fowler, UML Distilled: A Brief Guide to the Standard Object Modeling Language, 3rd ed. Boston, MA, USA: Addison-Wesley Longman, 2003.

[8] R. Rumpe, "Executable modeling with UML – a vision or a nightmare? –," in Issues and Trends of Information Technology Management in Contemporary Associations Volume 1, M. Khosrowpour, Ed. Idea Group, 2002, pp. 697–701.

[9] S. J. Mellor and M. Balcer, Executable UML: A foundation for model-driven architecture. Reading, MA: Addison-Wesley, 2002.

[10] B. P. Douglass, Real Time UML: Advances in the UML for Real-Time Systems (3rd Edition). Redwood City, CA, USA: Addison Wesley Longman, 2004.

[11] A. Krupp, O. Lundkvist, T. Schattkowsky, and C. Snook, "The adaptive cruise controller case study — visualisation, validation, and temporal verification," in UML-B Specification for Proven Embedded Systems Design, J. Mermet, Ed. Springer US, 2004, pp. 199–210.

[12] F. Wagner, R. Schmuki, T. Wagner, and P. Wolstenholme, Modeling Software with Finite State Machines: A Practical Approach. CRC Press, Boca Raton, FL 2006.

[13] W. Chan, R. J. Anderson, P. Beame, D. Notkin, D. H. Jones, and W. E. Warner, "Optimizing symbolic model checking for statecharts," IEEE Trans. Softw. Eng., vol. 27, no. 2, Feb. 2001, pp. 170–190.

[14] J.-R. Abrial, Modeling in Event-B - System and Software Engineering. Cambridge Uni., 2010.

[15] L. Grunske, K. Winter, N. Yatapanage, S. Zafar, and P. A. Lindsay, "Experience with fault injection experiments for FMEA," Software, Practice and Experience, vol. 41, no. 11, 2011, pp. 1233–1258.

[16] E. M. Clarke, O. Grumberg, and D. Peled, Model checking. MIT Press, 2001.

[17] V. Estivill-Castro and D. A. Rosenblueth, Model Checking of Transition-Labeled Finite-State Machines. Berlin, Heidelberg: Springer Berlin Heidelberg, 2011, pp. 61–73.

[18] V. Estivill-Castro, R. Hexel, and D. A. Rosenblueth, "Efficient modelling of embedded software systems and their formal verification," 19th Asia-Pacific Software Engineering Conf., vol. 1, 2012, pp. 428–433.

[19] I. Sommerville, Software engineering (9th ed.). Boston, MA, USA: Addison-Wesley Longman, 2010.

[20] E. M. Clarke, O. Grumberg, and D. Peled, Model checking. MIT Press, 2001.

[21] C. Baier and J.-P. Katoen, Principles of model checking. MIT Press, 2008.

[22] S. J. Mellor, "Embedded systems in UML," OMG White paper, 2007, www.omg.org/news/whitepapers/ label: "We can generate Systems Today" Retrieved: April 2017.

[23] S. Shlaer and S. J. Mellor, Object lifecycles : modeling the world in states. Englewood Cliffs, N.J.: Yourdon Press, 1992.

[24] F. Wagner, R. Schmuki, T. Wagner, and P. Wolstenholme, Modeling Software with Finite State Machines: A Practical Approach. NY: CRC Press, 2006.

[25] L. Wen and R. G. Dromey, "From requirements change to design change: A formal path," 2nd Int. Conf. Software Engineering and Formal Methods (SEFM 2004). Beijing, China: IEEE Computer Soc., 2004, pp. 104–113.

[26] R. G. Dromey and D. Powell, "Early requirements defect detection," TickIT Journal, vol. 4Q05, 2005, pp. 3–13.

[27] T. Myers and R. G. Dromey, "From requirements to embedded software - formalising the key steps," 20th Australian Software Engineering Conf. Gold Cost, Australia: IEEE Computer Soc., 2009, pp. 23–33.

[28] D. Harel and M. Politi, Modeling Reactive Systems with Statecharts: The Statemate Approach. New York, NY, USA: McGraw-Hill, 1998.

[29] I. Sommerville, Software Engineering, 9th ed. USA: Addison-Wesley, 2010.

[30] L. Lamport, "Using time instead of timeout for fault-tolerant distributed systems," ACM Transactions on Programming Languages and Systems, vol. 6, 1984, pp. 254–280.

A Reusable Adaptation Component Design for Learning-Based Self-Adaptive Systems

Kishan Kumar Ganguly, Kazi Sakib
Institute of Information Technology
University of Dhaka, Dhaka, Bangladesh
Emails: bsse0505@iit.du.ac.bd, sakib@iit.du.ac.bd

***Abstract*—In self-adaptive systems, according to the separation of concern principle, the adaptation logic and the business logic components should be kept apart for reusability. However, this promotes reuse of the whole adaptation component while reuse of its subcomponents and their classes can also be helpful. Existing techniques do not consider this. Moreover, existing approaches also do not consider application and environment factors together for a more accurate adaptation. In this paper, a learning-based adaptation component design has been proposed which supports these. Machine learning is used to express metrics that measure system goals, as a combination of application and environment attributes. These are used to select application components to turn on or off by solving an optimization problem, aimed at maximizing system goal conformance. Components are turned on or off using a customizable effector component. Design patterns are utilized for increasing the reusability of the adaptation subcomponents. The proposed method was validated using the popular Znn.com problem. The reusability and learning accuracy metrics used indicate that it performs well for both. The system was also put under high load for observing adaptation of response time. It was seen that adaptation occurred as soon as the response time was over a provided threshold.**

Keywords–Reusable Adaptation Component; Environment Feature; Application Feature; Design Pattern.

I. Introduction

For self-adaptive systems, developing the business logic and then, augmenting it with the adaptation logic are easier due to the adaptation component complexity. Apart from this component-level reuse, subcomponent-level reuse (i.e., reuse of adaptation subcomponents and their classes) can further reduce development time. For this, the adaptation component needs to be customizable to easily add or remove any classes. Moreover, adaptation effectiveness should be ensured for maximum goal conformance (e.g., performance, cost, etc.) [1].

In self-adaptive systems, goals are generally non-functional requirements. These requirements are expressed using metrics (e.g., response time, throughput, etc.), which help to detect goal violation by checking metric thresholds. Goal violation leads to adaptation which triggers reconfiguration to toggle (turn on or off) components. These components, also called *features*, are variation points of the system [2]. For example, modules for turning on and off a server can be called separate features. Generally, adaptation logic is a mathematical model that provides a *feature selection* to toggle. In the proposed methodology, these features, which can be toggled are called *application features*. However, *environment features* may exist that have impact on adaptation (e.g., service time, bandwidth, etc.) but cannot be toggled. The challenge is to incorporate these two types of features for effective adaptation and structuring the adaptation logic modularly for reusability.

A number of design techniques for self-adaptive systems have been proposed where a few seem to have considered reusability. Garlan et al. proposed the Rainbow framework where adaptation condition-action rules were hardwired into the system which hampered reuse [1]. Esfahani et al. proposed the FUSION framework, which used learning to derive equations for predicting metrics and used these to construct an optimization problem. This was solved to get a feature selection. However, incorporating environment features in the optimization problem leads to a feature selection that provides specific numerical values for the environment features. This is not useful because environment features cannot be controlled or selected, rather these depend on the underlying system environment. So, environment features cannot be directly used with the FUSION framework. Ramirez et al. discussed twelve design patterns for self-adaptive systems [3]. However, breaking these down to lower level patterns can facilitate reuse [4].

The contributions of this work are: 1) A generic design for the adaptation component that supports both component and subcomponent-level reuse. 2) A learning-based adaptation technique that considers environment features and generates training data automatically. The proposed approach applies machine learning to derive feature-metric equations to predict metric values from application feature statuses (on or off) and environment feature values. These more accurate metric equations are combined with the user provided metric thresholds to construct utility functions. These are used to devise an integer linear optimization problem similar to FUSION in case of goal violations. However, unlike FUSION, the environment features are also considered. The feature selection given by solving the optimization problem is applied to the system using components called *customizable effectors*. The proposed methodology also introduces a technique to automatically derive the data for learning. All these make the adaptation logic generic, which helps to reuse the component as a whole. For subcomponent-level reuse, design patterns are utilized to structure the adaptation component modularly.

The proposed technique was applied to the Znn.com model problem [1]. This system was deployed in five servers with a load balancer. Reusability was assessed using renowned metrics (e.g., Afferent Coupling, Rate of Component Observability, etc.). Effectiveness was validated by observing whether the response time stays under an empirically derived threshold in a high load environment. The reusability metric values indicate higher reusability in both component and subcomponent-level. The proposed technique also performs better in the high load as it brings down the response time once it rises. Moreover, learning accuracy metrics (e.g., Adjusted R^2, Correlation Coefficient, etc.) were used to show that considering environment feature produces more accurate metric equations.

The rest of the paper is structured as follows. In Section II, the proposed reusable adaptation component design is presented. In Section III, a case study is provided along with

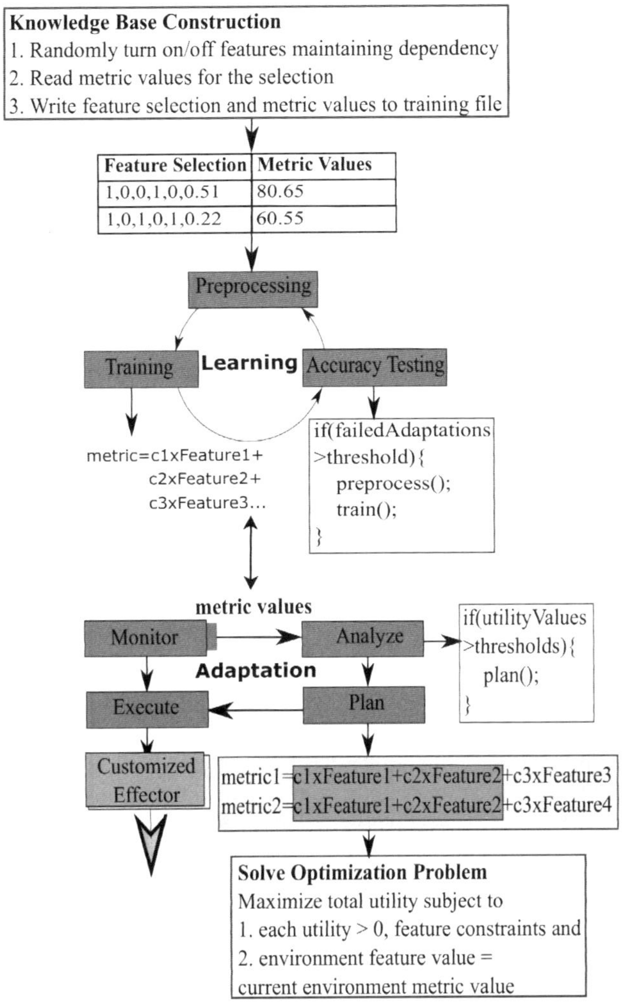

Figure 1. The Logical View of the Proposed Methodology.

an evaluation of reusability and effectiveness of the proposed approach. Section IV contains the related works. Section V holds the conclusion and future research directions in this area.

II. Reusable Adaptation Component Design

Here, a generic adaptation logic has been designed based on learning. Although this ensures reusability of the whole adaptation component, reusability of the subcomponents (for example, learning, preprocessing algorithm, etc.) is not guaranteed. For this, the subcomponents are structured with design patterns. These two perspectives are discussed below.

A. Logical View

The adaptation logic consists of three processes - Knowledge Base Construction (KBC), Learning and Adaptation. These three processes and the required system specific inputs are depicted in Figure 1 and discussed below.

1) Input: Information about application and environment feature, feature dependency, metric, utility and initial feature selection are required where application feature information consists of feature name only.

For feature dependency, the dependent features and their types are needed. The proposed method uses the dependency

TABLE I. Constraints for Feature Relationships

Feature Constraint	Feature Relation
$\sum_{\forall f_n \in \text{zero-or-one-of-group}} f_n \leq 1$	zero-or-one-of-group
$\sum_{\forall f_n \in \text{exactly-one-of-group}} f_n = 1$	exactly-one-of-group
$\sum_{\forall f_n \in \text{at-least-one-of-group}} f_n \geq 1$	at-least-one-of-group
$\sum_{\forall f_n \in \text{zero-or-all-of-group}} f_n \bmod n = 0$	zero-or-all-of-group
$\forall$child $\in$ Conflicting Feature Set$f_{parent} - f_{child} \geq 0$	parent child relation

types mentioned by Esfahani et al. [2] (Table I) because these cover common feature relationships and can be represented mathematically for the optimization problem. Here, *zero-or-one-of-group* means more than one feature cannot be enabled. *Exactly-one-of-group* means exactly one feature can be enabled at a time. *At-least-one-of-group* means at least one of the features must be enabled. *Zero-or-all-of-group* indicates either all or none of the features can be turned on. *Parent child relation* means enabling a specific (parent) feature requires all other features of the group to be enabled.

The existing system needs to expose an API for metric calculation. The metric information contains metric names, types, thresholds and API location (e.g., URL, class file path etc.). Two types of metrics are used representing maximization and minimization goals. For maximization goals, the metric values must be greater than the thresholds and the opposite for minimization goals. Metric types are used to form the utility equations using (1).

$$u_n = \begin{cases} m_n - th_n & \text{if } Type_n = Maximization \\ th_n - m_n & \text{otherwise} \end{cases} \quad (1)$$

Where u_n and m_n represent the utility and metric values respectively. th_n is the threshold value for the nth metric.

The initial feature selection is the feature selection for the first run. This is used in KBC. The environment features are also given. These features must have corresponding metrics provided in the aforementioned metric information. The metrics calculate current values for these environment features. In the optimization problem, these current values are considered for better accuracy of the solution.

2) KBC: This component generates training data for the learning process. As seen from Figure 1, training data consists of feature combination and metric values. Environment features generally have numeric values. So, the number of possible feature combination is infinite and cannot be generated. So, the application is put under a simulated or real environment and application features are toggled randomly (Figure 1). The environment feature values and metric values are read from the Monitor process and all the feature-metric values are written as training data. For example, in Figure 1, the random application feature selection is 1, 0, 0, 1, 0 for the first row and 0.51 is the environment feature value. Here, 1 and 0 indicates application feature status (enabled or disabled). This feature selection results in metric value 80.65. All these are written as the training data.

Features in each of the feature dependency groups are randomly toggled maintaining the dependency. For example, in case of at-least-one-of group, when one feature is randomly selected to turn on, all the other features are turned off. For parent-child relation, a number between 0 and 1 is chosen to

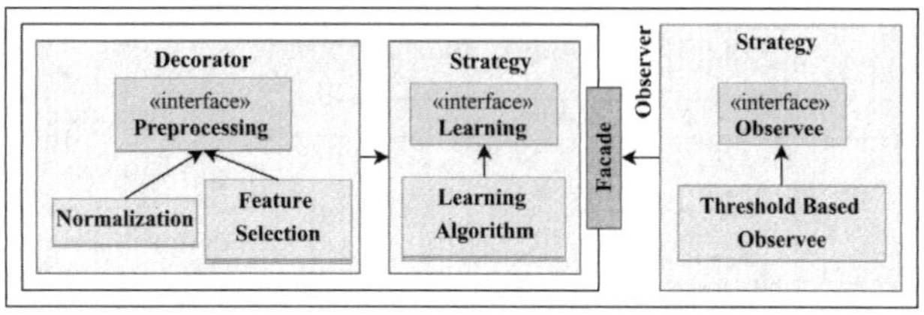

Figure 2. The Structural View of the Learning Component.

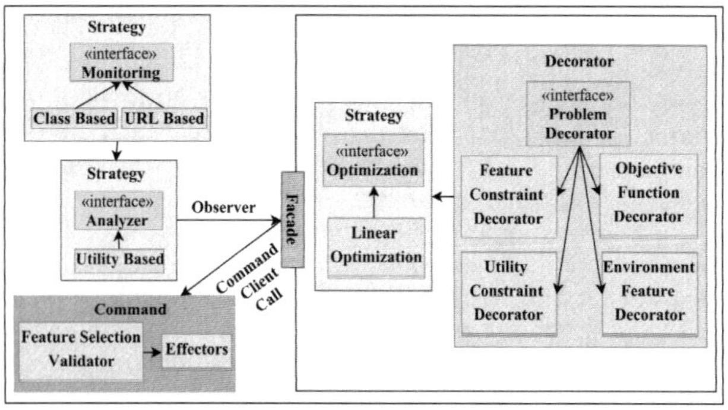

Figure 3. The Structural View of the Adaptation Component.

toggle the parent feature and all the child features are turned off or on accordingly. This random sampling with dependency groups ensures that feature dependency is maintained and the generated training data represents the population of training data appropriately.

3) Learning: Learning process aims to generate equations that predict metric values from feature selection. These equations are used in the Plan process. The generated training data from KBC is preprocessed to be properly used in the learning algorithm. For example, training data can be normalized for scaling. Preprocessing methods depend on the training data and the learning algorithm. So, it needs to be customizable. Strategy pattern is used for this purpose (Section II-B).

The next step is training where the preprocessed data is passed to a learning algorithm to derive metric equations. These equations help to predict metric values provided application and environment feature values. Training can be done using a regression algorithm. For example, in Figure 1, the metric equation from training is a linear regression equation.

As adaptation process will show, the training data is gradually updated with monitored metric values and feature selection. However, as the adaptation decision is taken using metric equations derived from previous training data, this can lead to failed adaptation when new patterns of data arrive. In this case, training is rerun when the number of failed adaptations exceed an empirically defined threshold (Figure 1).

4) Adaptation: Adaptation process consists of Monitor, Analyze, Plan and Execute components following the MAPE-K approach [5]. This process detects violated goals using the utility equations and solves an optimization problem to find a feature selection with maximum total utility function value. Although this technique closely resembles FUSION [2], the environment features are incorporated for better adaptation, which is one of the contributions of this work. The four components of Adaptation are discussed below.

a) Monitor: This collects metric values from the system using the metric API. These are stored in the knowledge base along with the current feature selection as training data.

b) Analyze: The metric values from Monitor are used in the utility equations for goal violation detection. From Equation (1), goal violations lead to $u_n < 1$. This is used to detect goal violations in this technique.

c) Plan: Detection of goal violation invokes Plan component. The metric equations from the learning process are used to find conflicting goals. The conflicting goal detection mechanism has been shown in Figure 1. The violated goal metric equation is matched with other metric equations to find overlapping features (shaded area in Figure 1). If overlapping features are present, these metrics are conflicting to the violated metric and these need to be considered together for optimization. Then, an optimization problem is formed.

$$F_{selection} = maximize(\sum_{i=1}^{n_c} U_i(M_i(F)))$$

Subject To

$$\forall i \leq n_c \,.\, U_i(M_i(F)) > 0$$
$$\wedge \forall f \in F \,.\, F_d(f)$$
$$\wedge \forall f_e \in F_e \,.\, f_e = c$$

Where

$$\forall i \leq n_c, M_i(F) = \sum c \times f \qquad (2)$$

Here, $F_{selection}$ is the feature selection after solving the optimization problem. This feature selection contains all the feature values (0 or 1) to toggle. The optimization problem states that the total utility for n_c conflicting goals needs to be maximized. The constraints show that all utility functions in the maximization function must be greater than zero because individual goals must not be violated. Besides, feature dependencies must be maintained (i.e., F_d must be true). All the environment features f_e from the environment feature set F_e will have corresponding environment metric values. All The metrics $M_i(F)$ in the utility equation will be replaced by metric equations from the learning process.

d) Execute: Execute component helps to toggle selected features in the existing system. This component consists of some effectors which are used to toggle each of the features. These effectors are specific to the system and so, and abstractions are provided for later customization.

B. Structural View of The Model

In the structural view, the subcomponents of Learning and Adaptation have been organized with Gang of Four (GoF) design patterns [6] for reusability and customization. These were chosen by comparing the functionality of the subcomponents with the applicability of the design patterns [6].

Figure 2 and 3 show the design patterns for the Learning and the Adaptation components. *Decorator pattern* is used to provide additional functionality at runtime. In preprocessing, the training data is dynamically filtered with algorithms such as normalization, feature selection, etc., using this pattern (Figure 2). In optimization problem construction, decorators that add the feature, utility and environment feature constraints, and the objective function, build a complete optimization problem (Figure 3). *Strategy pattern* helps to support interchangeable algorithms. So, it has been used to support different learning algorithm and failed adaptation testing strategies in Learning.

TABLE II. DEFINITIONS AND THRESHOLDS FOR REUSABILITY METRICS

Metric Name	Level	Definition	Range/ Value
RCO	Component	Rate of Component Observability	[0.17, 0.42]
RCC	Component	Rate of Component Customizability	[0.17, 0.34]
SCCr	Component	Self-Completeness of Components Return Value	[0.61, 1.0]
SCCp	Component	Self-Completeness of Components Parameter	[0.42, 0.77]
LCOM4	Class	Lack of Cohesion of Methods 4	1
DIT	Class	Depth of Inheritance Tree	2
AC	Class	Afferent Coupling	[0,1]
WMC	Class	Weighted Methods per Class	[0,24]

In Adaptation, it has been used to support different algorithms for monitoring, analyzing goal violation and optimization.

Observer pattern helps to notify all the dependent objects. This has been used to notify the learning process to restart when a new pattern arrives. In the Adaptation component, Analyze component notifies the Plan component about goal violations using this pattern. *Facade pattern* provides a set of interfaces to a group of components. This is used to provide interfaces for the Preprocessing and Training, and the Plan component. *Command pattern* helps to decouple the caller and receiver of a request. It has been used to validate the feature selection from the Plan facade and pass to the effectors. This helps to separate the effectors and the Plan component.

The logical view indicates effective adaptation and separation of the adaptation logic from the business logic. The structural view enables reuse of the whole subcomponents and their classes. So, the proposed methodology supports effective adaptation with component and subcomponent-level reuse.

III. CASE STUDY: ZNN.COM

Znn.com is a model problem used in numerous papers [7]. It is a news serving application where a load balancer is connected to a server group. Its business goal is to serve with a minimum content fidelity and within the budget while maintaining a minimum performance. These interrelated goals demand a self-adaptive mechanism to operate optimally.

In Znn.com, every server is an application feature as these need to be added or removed at runtime. Content fidelity types (high, low and text) are application features as these can be toggled. Server and content fidelity features belong to *at-least-one-of* and *exactly-one-of* dependency types respectively. Performance, content fidelity and cost can be calculated by response time, content size and number of active servers respectively. Service time and request arrival rates can be considered as environment features.

A. Experimental Setup

Znn.com was deployed on five virtual machines running Apache2 web server, which were connected to a load balancer. Two more virtual machines were used to collect metric values and to simulate user requests respectively. An adaptation component was developed in Java following the proposed approach and incorporated with Znn.com.

Prior to the experiment, the inputs mentioned previously were provided. Moreover, in a simulated environment, Queueing Theory was used to calculate response time where the M/M/c queue model was utilized to represent a system with c servers. Reusability was evaluated using metrics mentioned in Table II. To assess effectiveness, an experiment similar to [8] was performed with a higher load, which is, 1) 15 seconds of load with 30 visits/min 2) 2.5 minutes of ramping up to 3000

TABLE III. CLASS-LEVEL REUSABILITY METRIC VALUES

Metric	Components	Mean	Max	Min	%-Acceptable Classes
LCOM4	Monitor	1	1	1	100
	Analyze	1	1	1	100
	Plan	1	4	1	87.5
	Execute	1	2	1	75
	Learning	1	2	1	80
	KBC	1	2	1	85.7
DIT	Monitor	1.33	2	1	100
	Analyze	1	1	1	100
	Plan	1.35	2	1	100
	Execute	1.25	2	1	100
	Learning	1.2	2	1	100
	KBC	1	1	1	100
AC	Monitor	1.14	2	1	87.5
	Analyze	1	1	1	100
	Plan	1.37	5	1	84.21
	Execute	1.33	3	1	83.33
	Learning	1.13	2	1	87.5
	KBC	1	1	1	100
WMC	Monitor	2.67	8	1	100
	Analyze	2	3	1	100
	Plan	4.6	18	1	100
	Execute	5.5	15	1	100
	Learning	2.92	9	1	100
	KBC	2.83	9	1	100

TABLE IV. COMPONENT-LEVEL REUSABILITY METRICS VALUES

Metric	Monitor	Analyze	Plan	Execute	Learning	KBC
RCO	0.17	0.33	0.29	0.33	0.25	0.2
RCC	0.33	0.33	0.29	0.33	0.5	0.6
SCCr	1	1	1	1	0.67	1
SCCp	1	0.67	0.67	1	0.67	0.75

visits/min 3) 4.5 minutes of fixed load to 3000 visits/min 4) 9 minutes of ramping down to 60 visits/min.

This experiment was performed five times starting from a single server and high fidelity feature selection as this results in the worst performance. The load was increased by 120 visits/min on every run and the system reached its maximum memory limit after five runs. Following the literature, the main objective (response time) was compared in two situations, namely adaptation and without adaptation [2][7][9].

B. Metrics

Table II shows the metrics used to assess reusability of Monitor, Analyze, Plan, Execute, Learning and KBC components. Reusability was evaluated for the whole component as well as for its classes. Four popular reusability metrics by Washizaki et al. were used to evaluate component-level reusability [10] (Table II). Reusability of the classes was evaluated by Lack of Cohesion of Methods 4 (LCOM4) and Afferent Coupling (AC) as these are well-known and valid reusability metrics [11][12]. Depth of Inheritance Tree (DIT) and Weighted Methods per Class (WMC) were also used as these are well-understood and well-validated [13]. The thresholds for LCOM4, WMC, DIT and AC are provided in [11], [14] and [15]. It is notable that multiple metrics have been used as no single metric can represent the overall reusability of the system [12].

1) Reusability of Adaptation: Table III summarizes the reusability metric values for classes from each aforementioned component. It shows the minimum, maximum and average of the metric values for the classes and the percentage of acceptable classes according to the metric thresholds. From the table, the mean LCOM4 values are close to the ideal value (i.e.,1). Here, Execute component has the lowest acceptable classes as it contains system-dependent customizable effectors. For DIT and WMC, all the classes are acceptable as per their

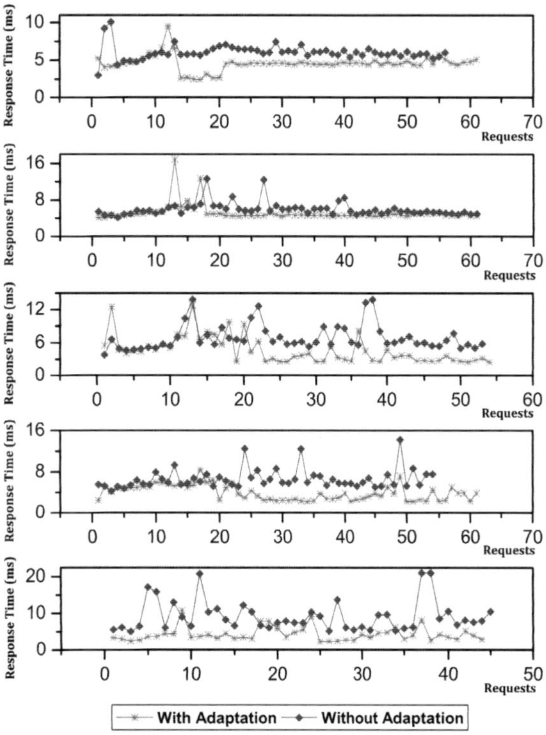

Figure 4. Comparison of Performance: Adaptation vs Without Adaptation.

thresholds. However, the average WMC values are much lower than the threshold because using design patterns have resulted in smaller methods. For AC, 87.5, 100, 84.21, 83.33, 87.5 and 100 percent classes are acceptable. Here, Execute has the lowest AC value for the aforementioned reason.

The component-level reusability metric values are shown in Table IV. Here, all the Rate of Component Observability (RCO) and Self-Completeness of Components Return Value (SCCr) values are within the threshold. The RCC values are also within the acceptable range except for Learning. This is because Learning component is highly customizable as all the preprocessing, learning algorithms etc. can be easily substituted. For Self-Completeness of Components Parameter (SCCp), only Monitor and Execute have out of range values as these depend on the metric API and system-specific effectors respectively.

2) Effectiveness of Adaptation: Figure 4 shows the five runs of the experiment. By analyzing the system average performance, the response time threshold was chosen to be 6.2 ms. In the first run, response time gradually decreases after about 12 requests and rises after about 20 requests. Then, the response time is almost constant due to the constant load scenario (Section III-A). With adaptation, the response time gradually decreases under 6.2 ms and remains as such. However, without adaptation, response time remains more frequently over 6.2 ms. Second run shows a similar pattern.

In the third run, for with adaptation scenario, the response time gradually drops down the threshold after about 22 requests and remains stable up to about 36th request when a sudden performance goal violation occurs. However, adaptation quickly reduces the response time under the threshold. The fourth run shows a similar structure. The fifth run

TABLE V. COMPARISON OF REGRESSION MODEL ACCURACY WITH AND WITHOUT ENVIRONMENT FEATURES

Runs	With Environment Features			Without Environment Features		
	RMSE	Adjusted R^2	Correlation Coefficient	RMSE	Adjusted R^2	Correlation Coefficient
1	0.7428	0.6637	0.7093	0.9373	0.278	0.4553
2	0.8626	0.7804	0.8683	1.6502	0.12322	0.3184
3	0.862	0.787	0.869	1.6444	0.16069	0.3439
4	0.7944	0.8114	0.888	1.4944	0.28563	0.5043
5	0.7884	0.8126	0.8946	1.6054	0.19748	0.4165

represents the highest load run of all. In this case, the system becomes unstable and response time varies a lot. However, the mechanism without adaptation produces response time above the threshold where the system with adaptation crosses the threshold only about five times, but runs down within threshold instantly.

Table V shows the accuracy of the regression model regarding environment features. In this case, three metrics, namely Root Mean Squared Error (RMSE), Adjusted R^2 and Correlation Coefficient are used. Among these, RMSE is smaller by 0.6563 on average considering environment features. Adjusted R^2 and Correlation Coefficient are higher by 0.562 and 0.4382 on average respectively. These indicate that considering environment features results in more accurate metric prediction, and so, better adaptation decision.

C. Discussion

The following observations can be made from the results.

- The class reusability metrics indicate overall high reusability of the component classes on average. The 100 percent accepted classes for DIT and WMC, and low mean WMC values indicate that using design patterns have resulted in classes with smaller methods and lower inheritance depth. This makes the behavior of the classes more predictable. Besides, LCOM4 and Afferent coupling indicate that an overall higher cohesion and lower coupling is achieved, leading to higher reusability.
- The component reusability metrics indicate that all the components have higher reusability. However, Learning has the highest customizability and, Monitor and Execute have external dependencies.
- Figure 4 and Table V indicate that adaptation improves the performance of the system gradually. As knowledge base is gradually enriched, this justifies the effectiveness of this process. Moreover, the accuracy measures for the first run from Table infers that knowledge base generation provides useful training data. The high accuracy scores also indicate that adaptation decisions are effective.
- Table V infers that accuracy largely suffers when environment features are not considered. This validates the use of environment features in the proposed approach.

IV. RELATED WORK

In the literature, most of the learning-based self-adaptive systems aim to achieve effectiveness. Kim et al. proposed a Q-learning-based approach where learning derived Q-values and adaptation actions with maximum Q-values were chosen [9]. Han et al. proposed a reinforcement learning-based approach where learning discovered the model of the environment in context in order to pick adaptation policies [16]. None of [9] and [16] considered application factors and reusability. Elkhodary et al. proposed supervised learning-based FUSION technique, which applied learning to derive relationships between application features and metrics, and used these to optimally select features [2]. However, environment features were not considered. FUSION tool also could not be effectively reused as it needed to be changed from system to system [2]. It also could not be applied when training data was not available.

A few techniques that address reusability have been proposed. Garlan et al. proposed the Rainbow framework [1] for adaptation with infrastructural reusability. Rainbow captured commonalities using architectural styles where systems with same architectural style could reuse elements such as rules, parameters etc. However, reuse among different architectural styles was limited. Component Model-based approaches such as the K-Component Framework [17] and the Fractal component model-based approach [18] relied on structuring the system with a specific component model for reusability. However, a specific component model made reuse between different component models costly because the full code base needs to be refactored. Ramirez et al. produced a list of twelve design patterns for self-adaptive systems and applied these in Rainbow [1]. However, it would be better if these patterns could be mapped into more well-known GoF patterns [4].

None of the proposed techniques consider application and environment features together for more effectiveness. Besides, the learning-based approaches do not consider increasing reusability. Learning-based approaches like FUSION also fails if training data is absent. The proposed approach overcomes all these by considering application and environment features, applying design patterns for reusability and providing a training data generation mechanism.

V. Conclusion and Future Work

This paper introduces an adaptation component design considering reusability and effectiveness. A knowledge base constructor is presented that randomly toggle features and considers corresponding metric values to derive training data. This data is used to produce equations to predict metrics from application and environment features using Machine Learning. These equations and the feature dependencies help to derive an optimization problem. Solving this, a feature selection with maximum total utility function value is obtained, which can be executed through customizable effectors. This overall generic logic supports component-level reuse. Design patterns are used to enable reuse of the subcomponents. The reusability metric values for each subcomponent are within the acceptable threshold, indicating high reusability. Adaptation effectiveness is also achieved as the system gradually decreases the response time under a provided threshold when goal violation occurs. The learning accuracy regarding environment features also validates adaptation effectiveness and utilization of these features.

In future, the technique will be enhanced to take adaptation decision by foreseeing future effects of the decision on the system. It will also be extended to automate threshold selection for metrics and failed adaptations.

References

[1] D. Garlan, S.-W. Cheng, A.-C. Huang, B. Schmerl, and P. Steenkiste, "Rainbow: Architecture-based self-adaptation with reusable infrastructure," *IEEE Computer*, vol. 37, no. 10, pp. 46–54, 2004.

[2] N. Esfahani, A. Elkhodary, and S. Malek, "A learning-based framework for engineering feature-oriented self-adaptive software systems," *Software Engineering, IEEE Transactions on*, vol. 39, no. 11, pp. 1467–1493, 2013.

[3] A. J. Ramirez and B. H. Cheng, "Design patterns for developing dynamically adaptive systems," in *Proceedings of the 2010 ICSE Workshop on Software Engineering for Adaptive and Self-Managing Systems*. ACM, 2010, pp. 49–58.

[4] M. L. Berkane, L. Seinturier, and M. Boufaida, "Using variability modelling and design patterns for self-adaptive system engineering: application to smart-home," *International Journal of Web Engineering and Technology*, vol. 10, no. 1, pp. 65–93, 2015.

[5] IBM Corporation, "An architectural blueprint for autonomic computing," *IBM White Paper*, 2006.

[6] E. Gamma, *Design patterns: elements of reusable object-oriented software*. Pearson Education India, 1995.

[7] S.-W. Cheng, D. Garlan, and B. Schmerl, "Architecture-based self-adaptation in the presence of multiple objectives," in *Proceedings of the 2006 international workshop on Self-adaptation and self-managing systems*. ACM, 2006, pp. 2–8.

[8] S.-W. Cheng, *Rainbow: cost-effective software architecture-based self-adaptation*. ProQuest, 2008.

[9] D. Kim and S. Park, "Reinforcement learning-based dynamic adaptation planning method for architecture-based self-managed software," in *Software Engineering for Adaptive and Self-Managing Systems, 2009. SEAMS'09. ICSE Workshop on*. IEEE, 2009, pp. 76–85.

[10] H. Washizaki, H. Yamamoto, and Y. Fukazawa, "A metrics suite for measuring reusability of software components," in *Software Metrics Symposium, 2003. Proceedings. Ninth International*. IEEE, 2003, pp. 211–223.

[11] M. Hitz and B. Montazeri, "Measuring coupling and cohesion in object-oriented systems," in *Proceedings of International Symposium on Applied Corporate Computing*, 1995, pp. 25–27.

[12] N. Fenton and J. Bieman, *Software metrics: a rigorous and practical approach*. CRC Press, 2014.

[13] S. R. Chidamber and C. F. Kemerer, "A metrics suite for object oriented design," *IEEE Transactions on software engineering*, vol. 20, no. 6, pp. 476–493, 1994.

[14] R. Shatnawi, W. Li, J. Swain, and T. Newman, "Finding software metrics threshold values using roc curves," *Journal of software maintenance and evolution: Research and practice*, vol. 22, no. 1, pp. 1–16, 2010.

[15] K. A. Ferreira, M. A. Bigonha, R. S. Bigonha, L. F. Mendes, and H. C. Almeida, "Identifying thresholds for object-oriented software metrics," *Journal of Systems and Software*, vol. 85, no. 2, pp. 244–257, 2012.

[16] H. N. Ho and E. Lee, "Model-based reinforcement learning approach for planning in self-adaptive software system," in *Proceedings of the 9th International Conference on Ubiquitous Information Management and Communication*. ACM, 2015, p. 103.

[17] J. Dowling and V. Cahill, "The k-component architecture meta-model for self-adaptive software," in *International Conference on Metalevel Architectures and Reflection*. Springer, 2001, pp. 81–88.

[18] P.-C. David and T. Ledoux, "Towards a framework for self-adaptive component-based applications," in *Distributed Applications and Interoperable Systems*. Springer, 2003, pp. 1–14.

Immersive Coding: A Virtual and Mixed Reality Environment for Programmers

Roy Oberhauser
Computer Science Dept.
Aalen University
Aalen, Germany
email: roy.oberhauser@hs-aalen.de

***Abstract*—While virtual reality (VR) has been applied to various domains to provide new visualization capabilities, the leveraging of VR capabilities for programmers doing software development or maintenance has not been sufficiently explored. In this paper, we present a VR environment for programmers called MR-FTC (mixed-reality FlyThruCode) providing software code structure visualization in multiple metaphors with integrated real keyboard/mouse viewing and interaction in mixed reality (MR) to enable basic programming task support without leaving the VR environment. A prototype implementation is described, with a case study demonstrating its feasibility and initial empirical evaluation results showing its potential. This MR solution concept enables programmers to benefit from VR visualization while supporting their more natural keyboard interaction for basic code-centric tasks. This can support programmers in exploring, understanding, and directly interacting with and maintaining program code while leveraging new VR paradigms and capabilities.**

Keywords—mixed reality; virtual reality; programming; software engineering; software visualization.

I. INTRODUCTION

As digitalization progresses, the volume of program source code created and maintained worldwide is increasing steadily. For instance, Google is said to have at least 2bn lines of code (LOC) accessed by over 25K developers [1], and GitHub has over 61m repositories and 22m developers [2]. Worldwide it has been estimated that well over a trillion LOC exist with 33bn added annually [3]. This is exacerbated by a limited supply of programmers and high employee turnover rates for software companies, e.g., 1.1 years at Google [4].

A challenge faced by programmers who are now more frequently facing unfamiliar preexisting codebases is how to familiarize and understand its structure in a short time. Code structures and their dependencies can be difficult to visualize. According to F. P. Brooks Jr., the invisibility of software is an essential difficulty of software construction because the reality of software is not embedded in space [5]. While common display forms used in the comprehension of source code include text and the two-dimensional Unified Modeling Language (UML), there may be a place for leveraging the opportunities afforded by a virtual reality (VR) for software visualization to make it seem less abstract and a more immersive experience for programmers. For instance, it could enhance the ability to comprehend and navigate software structures in a different reality without relying on the typical abstractions they are given, such as hierarchical file structures.

In our prior work, we developed VR-FlyThruCode (VR-FTC) [6][7], an immersive VR software visualization environment supporting flythrough navigation and virtual tablet and virtual keyboard interaction within dynamically-switchable metaphors but which lacked any support for keyboard usage. Programmers typically are keyboard and mouse/trackpad centric when interacting with code, which would typically require removing the VR headset and leaving the VR environment. Virtual keyboards which require selecting one key at a time using the VR controllers are an inefficient means for code input for experienced programmers.

This paper contributes a solution concept enabling mixed reality FTC (MR-FTC) keyboard and mouse viewing and interaction and provides an initial empirical evaluation. Our mixed reality (MR) solution concept enables real keyboard and mouse/trackpad integration while remaining in an immersive visualization and navigation experience through the code structures, allowing the user to view logical modularization and dependencies while enabling code object creation/deletion and source code modification with real keyboard access in the VR environment.

The paper is organized as follows: the next section discusses related work; Section III then describes the solution concept. Section IV provides details about our prototype implementation of the solution concept. In Section V, the evaluation, based on a case study, is described, which is followed by a conclusion.

II. RELATED WORK

As to non-VR software visualization, Teyseyre and Campo [8] give an overview and survey of 3D software visualization tools across the various software engineering areas. Software Galaxies [9] provides a web-based visualization of dependencies among popular package managers and supports flying, whereby every star represents dependency-clustered packages. CodeCity [10] is a 3D software visualization approach based on a city metaphor and implemented in SmallTalk on the Moose reengineering framework [11]. Rilling and Mudur [12] use a metaball metaphor (organic-like n-dimensional objects) combined with dynamic analysis of program execution. X3D-UML [13] provides 3D support with UML in planes such that classes are grouped in planes based on the package or hierarchical state machine diagrams.

Work on VR-based software visualization includes Imsovision [14] which visualizes object-oriented software in

VR using electromagnetic sensors attached to shutter glasses and a wand for interaction. ExplorViz [15] is a Javascript-based web application that uses WebVR to support VR exploration of 3D software cities using Oculus Rift together with Microsoft Kinect for gesture recognition.

With regard to MR and augmented reality support for programming tasks, [16] describe an approach for authoring tangible augmented reality applications with regard to scenes and object behaviors within the AR application being built, so that the development and testing of the application can be done concurrently and intuitively throughout the development process. Billinghurst and Kato [17] show possible concepts for collaboration in VR, but do not depict a keyboard or show how programming task support would work.

In contrast to the above work, the MR-FTC approach combines VR and game engines for software visualization and direct code access, support multiple metaphors, supporting basic programming tasks by integrating real keyboard and mouse views and interaction in the VR environment. To the best of our knowledge, no other software visualization in VR includes real hardware and mouse support.

III. SOLUTION

Our MR-FTC concept uses VR flythrough for visualizing program code structure or architecture, such as software architecture recovery, which can be useful in software maintenance tasks. Our inherent 3D application domain view visualization [8] arranges customizable symbols in 3D space to enable users to navigate through an alternative perspective on these often hidden structures. Certain metadata not readily accessible is visualized, such as the relative size of classes (not typically visible until multiple files are opened or a UML class diagram is created), the relative size of packages to one another, and the number of dependencies between classes and packages. To support programming within the VR environment, our solution concept utilizes MR for integrating keyboard and mouse access to permit coding.

A. Principles

Our previous work [7] details the solution principles which we summarize here: multiple customizable 3D visual metaphors (dynamically switchable between universe and terrestrial), flythrough navigation, a grouping metaphor (solar systems and glass bubbles), a connection metaphor (colored light beams), and a virtual tablet to provide information and interaction capabilities on tagging, metrics, UML, filtering, source code, and project configuration. Figure 1 shows VR system interaction (without the keyboard).

A further solution principle specific to this paper is *MR keyboard/trackpad/mouse integration*. A live camera view is integrated into the VR landscape. This allows the user to determine where their hands and fingers are relative to the actual hardware. Assuming the subject is seated, for instance, tilting their head down can be interpreted as a gesture to activate a live webcam on the VR headset, activating MR, similar to the natural head movement made at a desktop PC to look at the keyboard.

Figure 1. System setup with a subject wearing a Vive HTC headset, the controller visible in a universe metaphor scene selecting a planet (a class)).

B. Process

The process used by the solution approach consists of interaction and round-trip support for change propagation, whereby any changes to code outside of VR is reflected in VR, and any changes made to code in VR is reflected both with the VR visualization and to the actual code.

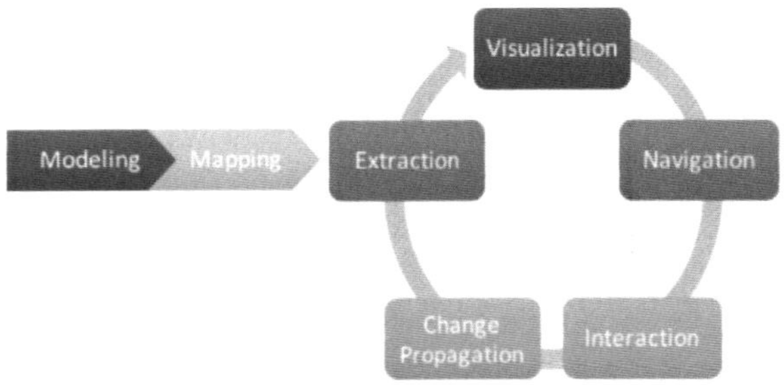

Figure 2. MR-FlyThruCode process steps.

The steps shown in Figure 2 are as follows:

1) Modeling: the modeling of generic program code structures, metrics, and artifacts as well as visual objects.

2) Mapping: the mapping of a program code artifact model to a visual object metaphor, such as universe or terrestrial objects.

3) Extraction: extracting a given project's metadata, structure (via source code import and parsing), and metrics.

4) Visualization: visualizing a given model instance within a metaphor.

5) Navigation: supporting navigation through the model instance (via camera movement based on user interaction), to provide a flythrough experience.

6) Interaction: providing interaction via hardware, such as the VR controller and keyboard or trackpad/mouse, or virtual objects, such as a virtual tablet and the visual equivalent of code artifacts that can be created, deleted, displayed (including metrics or metadata), or modified using a virtual tablet, virtual keyboard, and virtual controllers.

7) Change Propagation: for any interactions that incur changes (create/delete/modify), a background process is triggered that restarts step 3 and step 4 updates the visualization. For instance, if methods were added or removed, then the height of the buildings or the size of the planet would be affected.

IV. IMPLEMENTATION

We utilized the Unity game engine for 3D visualization due to its multi-platform support, VR integration, and popularity, and for VR hardware both HTC Vive, a room scale VR set with a head-mounted display with an integrated camera and two wireless handheld controllers tracked using two 'Lighthouse' base stations.

We integrated a live camera view into the VR landscape via a virtual plane object. This allows the user to determine where their hands and fingers are relative to the actual keyboard. When the VR user tilts their head down, it is interpreted as a gesture to activate the live webcam on the VR headset and blend this into the virtual plane object. When the head is tilted starkly up, MR is deactivated.

Our MR-FTC architecture is shown in Figure 3.

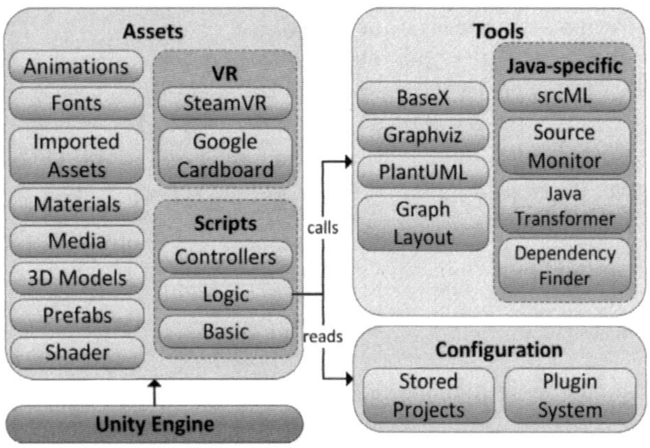

Figure 3. MR-FlyThruCode software architecture.

Assets are used by the Unity engine and consist of Animations, Fonts, Imported Assets (like a ComboBox), Materials (like colors and reflective textures), Media (like textures), 3D Models, Prefabs (prefabricated), Shaders (for shading of text in 3D), VR SDKs, and Scripts. Scripts consist of Basic Scripts like user interface (UI) helpers, Logic Scripts that import, parse, and load project data structures, and Controllers that react to user interaction. Logic Scripts read Configuration data about Stored Projects and the Plugin System (input in XML about how to parse source code and invocation commands). Logic Scripts can then call Tools consisting of General and Language-specific Tools. General Tools currently consist of BaseX, Graphviz, PlantUML, and Graph Layout - our own version of the KK layout algorithm [18] for positioning objects. Java-specific tools are srcML, Campwood SourceMonitor, Java Transformer (invokes Groovy scripts), and Dependency Finder. Our Plugin system enables additional tools and applications to be easily integrated.

A. Code Information Extraction

srcML [19] is used to extract existing code structure information into our model. The source code is converted into XML and stored in the BaseX XML database. Campwood SourceMonitor and DependencyFinder are used to extract code metrics and dependency data, and plugins with Groovy scripts and a configuration are used to integrate the various tools.

B. Project Structure Model

A software project contains the following files, which are used to access the data mapped to the VR objects:

- *metrics_{date}.xml*: metrics obtained from SourceMonitor and DependencyFinder are grouped by project, packages, and classes.
- *source_{date}.xml*: holds all classes in XML
- *structure_{date}.xml*: contains the project structure and dependencies utilizing the DependencyFinder.
- *swexplorer-annotations.xml*: contains user-based annotations (tags) with color, flag, and text including both manual and automatic (pattern matching) tags.
- *swexplorer-metrics-config.xml*: contains thresholds for metrics.
- *swexplorer-records.xml*: contains a record of each import of the same project done at different times with a reference to the various XML files, such as source and structure for that import. This permits changing the model to different timepoints as a project evolves.

V. EVALUATION

The evaluation consists of a case study with usage by master computer science students currently involved in the prototype implementation and familiar with VR.

A. Visualization and Navigation

Two metaphors were used for visualization: Figure 4 shows the universe or space metaphor, where planets represent classes which are grouped in solar systems. Figure 5 shows the terrestrial or city metaphor, where buildings represent classes with a label at the top and the number of stories represents the number of methods in that class, classes being grouped by glass bubbles. For the connection metaphor, in both metaphors colored light beams were are to show directional dependencies between classes or packages (see Figure 6 with extra cones placed around the light beams). To assist the user in remembering objects or characteristics, tagging is supported, which allows any label to be placed on an object (e.g., the Important Tag in Figure 4).

To realize flythrough navigation, the camera position is moved with the touchpad on the left controller of the HTC Vive controlling altitude (up, down) and the one on the right hand controlling direction (left, right, forward, backward). The controllers are shown in the scenery when they are within the view field. A virtual laser pointer was created for selecting objects, as was a virtual keyboard (in case no real keyboard is accessible or desired) to support text input for searching, filtering, and tagging. Menus and screens showing source code, code metrics, UML, tags, filtering, and project data are placed on the screen of the virtual tablet. To highlight a selected object, we utilized a 3D pointer in the form of a rotating upside-down pyramid (see Figure 4 and Figure 5). This was needed because, once an object is selected, after navigating away one may lose track of where the object was, especially if the object was small relative to its surrounding objects.

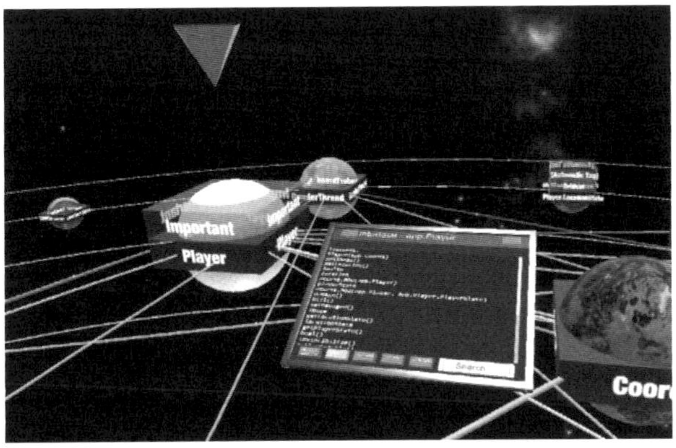

Figure 4. Universe metaphor: selected planet (class) has inverted pyramid as arrow, tags evident, and tablet is visible and shows the class interface.

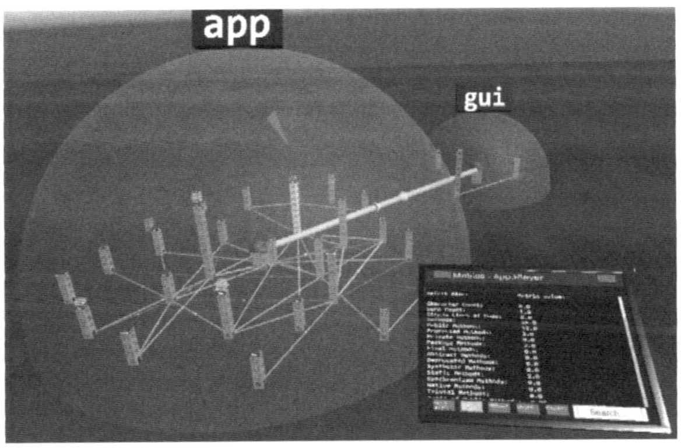

Figure 5. Terrestrial metaphor with bubbled cities (packages) and oracle with metrics for selected object (pyramid pointer).

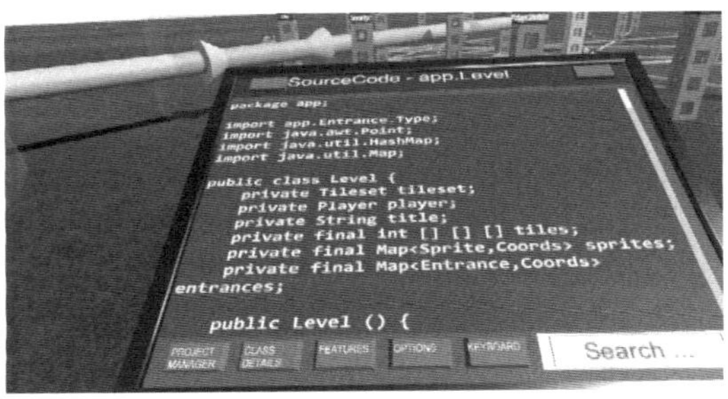

Figure 6. The virtual tablet interface showing source code. A bidirectional (dependency) pipe is visible in the background.

B. Mixed Reality Interaction

To achieve MR and access the video stream of the front camera, the standard Unity Plane asset was used and a small Script added to this game object. From the SteamVR TrackedCamera script, the method VideoStreamTexture is invoked, which returns a Texture that is set to the material of the Plane (see Figure 7 and Figure 8).

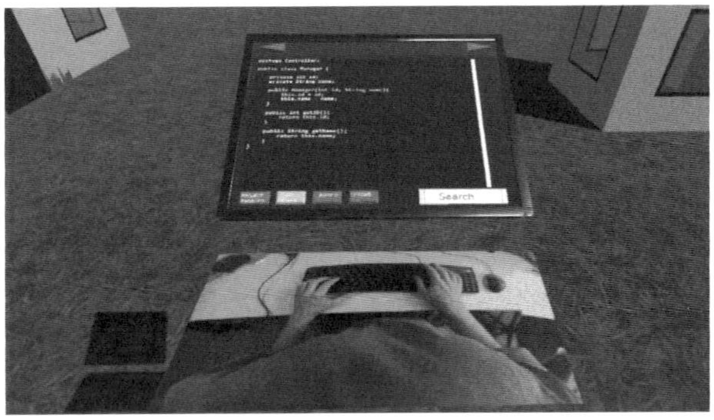

Figure 7. Coding with MR view of keyboard and mouse blended in and scroll bar shown on the virtual tablet.

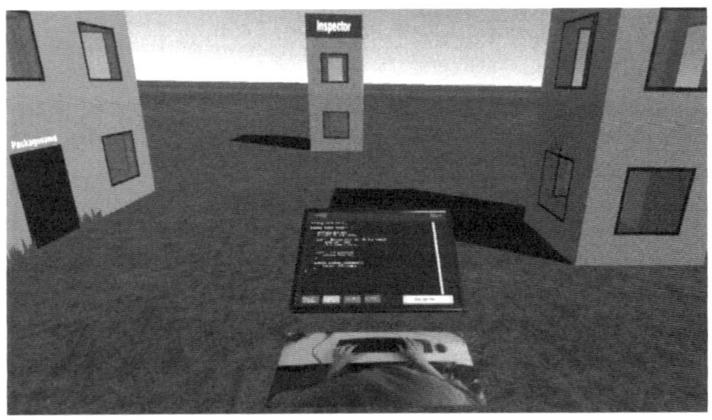

Figure 8. Far view in MR of keyboard with VR object visible.

The Vive camera must be activated (manually) in the SteamVR settings. We chose to automatically activate and show MR when the user's tilts the goggles low enough, as one would if one were to wish to see the keyboard when using it, and turn MR off again if one tilts the head up far enough again. Keyboard and mouse inputs are accessible at any time, not just when MR is activated.

For an initial empirical evaluation of the MR keyboard capability, we utilized a convenience sample of Computer Science students.

For evaluating typing speed in particular for comments which are full words without special characters, five subjects were required to write two unique pangrams consisting of 18 words using a text editor (Notepad++), the MR keyboard, and the VR only keyboard. We varied the starting configuration order among the subjects to minimize training effects. As shown in Table I, the text editor was the most efficient with 50 seconds duration and 22.5 words per minute (wpm) with an average error rate of 3.3%. With MR 75 seconds were required (16.0 wpm) with an error rate of 3.3%. With the VR keyboard 110 seconds were required

(10.1 wpm) with an error rate of 4.4%. Thus the MR keyboard was faster than the VR keyboard and did not exhibit a higher error rate. However, the subjects needed 11 seconds on average between laying down the VR controllers and pressing the first letter on the keyboard.

TABLE I. TEXT EDITOR, MR, AND VR PANGRAM MEASUREMENTS (AVERAGE)

	Text Editor	MR	VR
Duration (seconds)	50	75	110
Words per minute	22.5	16.0	10.1
Error rate	3.3%	3.3%	4.4%

For evaluating programming, four subjects were required to view a certain class and then create a class and were given certain specified modifications thereafter (creating some object and setting some variable to some value) using either a text editor or the MR keyboard. As seen in Table II, using a text editor (Notepad++), they needed on average 50 seconds to analyze a similar class, 30 seconds to create a new class, and 144 seconds to do the programming. Using the MR keyboard, they needed 84 seconds to analyze a similar class, 77 seconds to create a class, and 245 seconds to complete the programming.

TABLE II. TEXT EDITOR AND MR MEASUREMENTS (AVERAGE IN SECONDS)

	Analysis	Class Creation	Programming
Text editor	50	30	144
MR	84	77	245

While a text editor remains more efficient, usage of the MR keyboard was faster than a purely VR keyboard and, once familiar with a certain keyboard, we expect the overhead of MR to be reduced to an acceptable level given sufficient practice. The overhead of switching between VR controllers to keyboard and back again can be seen as analogous to the overhead of keyboard use on a PC and moving the hand to the mouse and back again and may thus be considered acceptable for certain users. We will investigate this further in future work.

We were pleased that none of the subjects reported motion sickness despite the inclusion of MR and the average response to how they felt afterwards was 4.75 (on a scale of 1 to 5 with 5 best).

Although the keyboard was a German layout keyboard, we noted that some subjects already had used that specific keyboard model before (Logitech K280e) while others had not and thus needed more time to search for certain specific keys. In searching they needed to get close with the VR goggles to see the key label, so we will consider providing a zoom or magnification option in the interface in the future.

C. *Coding Support Interaction and Change Propagation*

To provide basic programming support, package and class creation are supported via a VR controller wrist-based selection capability in both metaphors (see Figure 9 and Figure 10). Thereafter a screen appears on the VR tablet for naming the object (Figure 11 and Figure 12), which can be done with a real or virtual keyboard and the change is then propagated. For deletion, an object must first be selected, then a deletion option appears as an "X" (not shown) on the left VR controller, and if this "X" is targeted by the right controller, the object and underlying source code file (or directory in case of a package) is then removed from the file system via change propagation. File editing can be performed by pointing the VR controller or mouse at a character on the virtual tablet when it is showing source code and then typing with the physical (or virtual) keyboard. A blinking cursor is then shown and editing via insertion/deletion can be performed (selection not yet supported). The code state is transmitted and change propagation triggered when the virtual tablet is switched to a different view, updating the visualization.

Figure 9.VR controller wrist-based palette selection for package (bubble) or class (building) creation in the terrestrial metaphor.

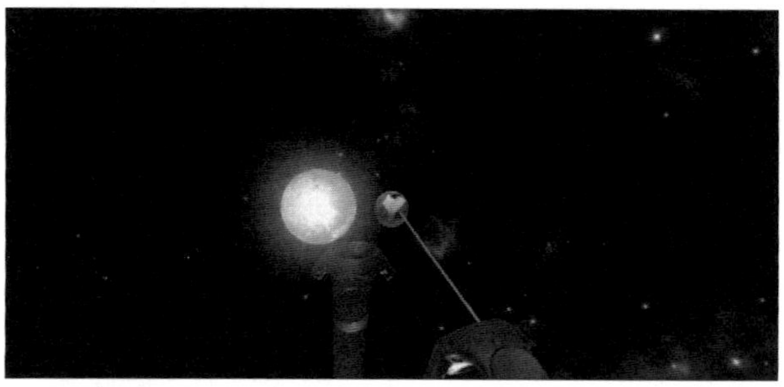

Figure 10. VR controller wrist-based palette selection for package or class creation in the universe metaphor.

Figure 11. Package creation (glass bubble) input screen.

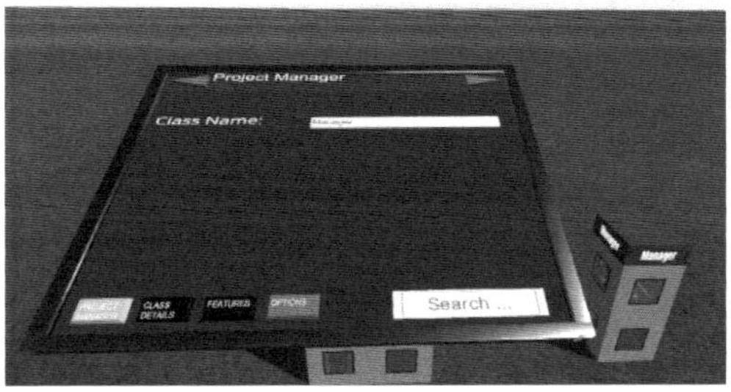

Figure 12. Class creation (building) input screen.

Our case study subjects found the ability to interact and make changes to the software structure to be an improvement over pure visualization, and the use of VR controller wheel and pointer selection to be a natural in VR mode for creating and removing object. The accessibility of a real keyboard instead of a virtual keyboard via MR integration was also found to be more natural and efficient versus virtual keyboard usage for code editing.

Our prototype demonstrated that the MR solution concept is feasible and can be a viable alternative to a virtual keyboard. This enables touch typing and the use of the mouse for screen interaction where appropriate, enabling programmers to interact more naturally for their code-centric programming tasks in the VR environment, without having to interrupt their VR experience to take of the goggles and do programming changes, and then put the VR gear on again. In future work we will investigate empirical usage of our MR-FTC concept prototype including programmers who are not familiar with VR.

VI. CONCLUSION

As VR devices become ubiquitous, it is only a matter of time before programmers wish to utilize VR capabilities as well. Visualization of code structures in various metaphors permits VR users to view code structures in new ways. However, current interaction mechanisms are hampered due to a lack of keyboard and mouse access for programmers working directly with code, which can frustrate programmers or require them to remove the VR headset and work with a PC directly, and then return to VR mode.

This paper described our solution concept MR-FTC, which provides a direct integration via mixed reality of the keyboard and mouse into the VR landscape when the user looks down, allowing them to orient their hands and fingers after laying down the VR controllers. The prototype demonstrated the feasibility of our solution concept, and the case study with its empirical evaluation showed the potential of MR using keyboards for supporting programming in VR environments.

Future work includes a comprehensive empirical study and the inclusion of additional features specific to the programming interface such as syntax highlighting.

ACKNOWLEDGMENT

The author thanks Carsten Lecon, Dominik Bergen, Alexandre Matic, Lisa Philipp, and Camil Pogolski for their assistance with various aspects of the design, implementation, and evaluation.

REFERENCES

[1] C. Metz, *Google Is 2 Billion Lines of Code—And It's All in One Place.* http://www.wired.com/2015/09/google-2-billion-lines-codeand-one-place/ [retrieved 2017.08.31]

[2] GitHub. https://github.com [retrieved 2017.08.31]

[3] G. Booch, "The complexity of programming models," Keynote talk at AOSD 2005, Chicago, IL, Mar. 14-18, 2005.

[4] PayScale, Full List of Most and Least Loyal Employees. http://www.payscale.com/data-packages/employee-loyalty/full-list [retrieved 2017.08.31]

[5] F. P. Brooks, Jr., The Mythical Man-Month. Boston, MA: Addison-Wesley Longman Publ. Co., Inc., 1995.

[6] R. Oberhauser and C. Lecon, "Virtual Reality Flythrough of Program Code Structures," Proc. of the 19th ACM Virtual Reality International Conference (VRIC 2017). ACM, 2017.

[7] R. Oberhauser and C. Lecon, "Immersed in Software Structures: A Virtual Reality Approach," Proc. of the Tenth International Conference on Advances in Computer-Human Interactions (ACHI 2017). IARIA, 2017, pp. 181-186, ISBN 978-1-61208-538-8.

[8] A. R. Teyseyre and M. R. Campo, "An overview of 3D software visualization," Visualization and Computer Graphics, IEEE Trans. on, vol. 15, no. 1, 2009, pp. 87-105.

[9] A. Kashcha. *Software Galaxies.* http://github.com/anvaka/pm/ [retrieved 2017.08.31]

[10] R. Wettel and M. Lanza, "Program comprehension through software habitability," in Proc. 15th IEEE Int'l Conf. on Program Comprehension, IEEE CS, 2007, pp. 231–240.

[11] R. Wettel, M. Lanza, and R. Robbes, "Software systems as cities: A controlled experiment," in Proc. of the 33rd Int'l Conf. on Software Engineering, ACM, 2011, pp. 551-560.

[12] J. Rilling and S. P. Mudur, "On the use of metaballs to visually map source code structures and analysis results onto 3d space," in Proc.. 9th Work. Conf. on Reverse Engineering, IEEE, 2002, pp. 299-308.

[13] P. M. McIntosh, "X3D-UML: user-centred design, implementation and evaluation of 3D UML using X3D," Ph.D. dissertation, RMIT University, 2009.

[14] J. I. Maletic, J. Leigh, and A. Marcus, "Visualizing software in an immersive virtual reality environment," 23rd Intl. Conf. on Softw. Eng. (ICSE 2001) Vol. 1, IEEE, 2001, pp. 12-13.

[15] F. Fittkau, A. Krause, and W. Hasselbring, "Exploring software cities in virtual reality," IEEE 3rd Working Conference on Software Visualization (VISSOFT), IEEE, 2015, pp. 130-134.

[16] G.A. Lee, D. Nelles, M. Billinghurst, and G.J.Kim, "Immersive authoring of tangible augmented reality applications," Proc. of the 3rd IEEE/ACM international Symposium on Mixed and Augmented Reality, IEEE Computer Society, 2004, pp. 172-181.

[17] M. Billinghurst and H. Kato, "Collaborative mixed reality," Proc. First International Symposium on Mixed Reality (ISMR '99), Springer Verlag, 1999, pp. 261-284.

[18] T. Kamada and S. Kawai, "An algorithm for drawing general undirected graphs," Information processing letters, 31(1), 1989, pp. 7-15.

[19] J. Maletic, M. Collard, and A. Marcus, "Source code files as structured documents," in Proc. 10th Int. Workshop on Program Comprehension, IEEE, 2002, pp. 289-292.

International Academy, Research,
and Industry Association (IARIA)
412 Derby Way
Wilmington, DE 19810

ISBN 978-1-5108-5142-9

CURRAN ASSOCIATES INC.
proceedings.com